D1314727

The DK Handbook

ANNE FRANCES WYSOCKI
University of Wisconsin, Milwaukee

DENNIS A. LYNCH
University of Wisconsin, Milwaukee

PEARSON
Longman

New York   San Francisco   Boston
London   Toronto   Sydney   Tokyo   Singapore   Madrid
Mexico City   Munich   Paris   Cape Town   Hong Kong   Montreal

Text design, page layout,
and cover design:
Dorling Kindersley

Pearson Longman
Publisher: Joseph Opiela
Executive Editor: Lynn M. Huddon
Development Editor: Michael Greer
Senior Supplements Editor: Donna Campion
Senior Marketing Manager: Windley Morley
Director, Market Research and Development: Laura Coaty
Production Manager: Bob Ginsberg
Project Coordination: Elm Street Publishing Services
Cover Design Manager: Wendy Ann Fredericks
Cover Photos: (*clockwise from top left*) Thomas Northcut/Getty Images/
    Photodisc; Apple/Splash News/News.com; C. Squared Studios/Getty
    Images/Photodisc; Howard Shooter/© Dorling Kindersley; and Siede Preis/
    Getty Images/Photodisc
Photo Researcher: Dorling Kindersley; additional photo research by Linda Sykes
Senior Manufacturing Buyer: Alfred C. Dorsey
Printer and Binder: RR Donnelley & Sons Company/Crawfordsville
Cover Printer: Coral Graphic Services, Inc.

For permission to use copyrighted material, grateful acknowledgment is made to the copyright holders on pp. 624–625, which are hereby made part of this copyright page.

Library of Congress Cataloging-in-Publication Data

Wysocki, Anne Frances
  The DK handbook / Anne Wysocki.
    p. cm.
  Includes bibliographical references and index.
  ISBN-13: 978-0-321-42053-4 (alk. paper)
  ISBN-10: 0-321-42053-5 (alk. paper)
  1. English language--Rhetoric--Handbooks, manuals, etc. 2. Report writing--Handbooks, manuals, etc.
  3. English language--Grammar--Handbooks, manuals, etc. I. Title.
  PE1408.W97 2008
  808'.042--dc22

                                                                                    2007044386

Copyright © 2009 by Pearson Education, Inc.

Visit us at **www.pearsonhighered.com**

ISBN-13: 978-0-321-42053-4 (comb bound)   ISBN-13: 978-0-205-62908-4 (spiral bound)
ISBN-10:   0-321-42053-5 (comb bound)   ISBN-10:   0-205-62908-3 (spiral bound)

  2 3 4 5 6 7 8 9 10—DOC—11 10 09 08   1 2 3 4 5 6 7 8 9 10—DOC—11 10 09 08

WHY WE WROTE THIS HANDBOOK

We wrote this handbook to be useful. We wrote the previous sentence knowing it can be read in two ways, both of which we intend: **We** want to be useful and we want **the handbook** to be useful.

We want to be useful to a community that matters to us, the community of writing learners and writing teachers. We offer this book—shaped out of the particular strengths we each bring to teaching and writing—in small return for this community's generosity in sharing knowledge and optimism.

We want **the handbook** to be useful to the many students we have watched try to find their ways through the dense and complex details that characterize any comprehensive handbook. We hope that our particular approaches—making visible the patterns of composition, keeping details visibly discrete, emphasizing the rhetorical nature of all aspects of writing—support learners in easily comprehending the details (and the pleasures) of writing...

...for, finally, we also wrote this handbook to be pleasurable in its use and application. We both know the delights of writing when we are confident and engaged with our words, when we can play with a range of possibilities and know that we can choose among them appropriately. We want those who use this book to use it with confidence and even delight so that they can then write with confidence and take delight and satisfaction in the shape and effectiveness of their words.

HOW WE WROTE THIS HANDBOOK

Because we wanted this handbook to be useful, we commissioned a usability test for it early in the development process. Participants in the user testing were first-year writing students in both community college and research university classrooms. In considering the results of this test—which included over 27 hours of videotaped student feedback and an extensive summary report—we learned what worked and what frustrated students in early drafts of our sections on evaluating sources, using commas, and MLA documentation. By watching students work with these drafts, we learned how and why they got stuck at certain points in the tasks assigned them—and we applied what we learned to help us shape and refine some of the core principles of the handbook's design.

We describe these principles to the right.

1 Pages can be designed to support the conceptual work of learning. Learning to compose requires learning the communication genres, conventions, and processes around us. Once we are familiar with them we can use them inventively to meet our needs; becoming familiar with them means (as in any learning) moving from their general shapes to their specific applications.

Our handbook's **layered structure** helps learners move from the general to the specific. Each new topic begins with a two-page spread that is a **topic overview**; each overview helps students grasp quickly and visually the key steps of processes and concepts.

Students needing more information can turn to the **detail pages** following each overview. The detail pages expand on one step or concept at a time, helping learners **zoom in** on strategies or ideas.

Finally, **application pages** (again, made up of two-page spreads) present illustrated examples demonstrating how to apply processes.

The following principles follow from this first one.

2 Consistent and uncluttered layout helps learners find what they need. Each topic fits on its two-page spread, making information and ideas readily graspable visually and so conceptually. The topic of every two-page spread appears dependably at its top left corner. Because finding and seeing information is made easy, students can focus on what they need to learn instead of on finding it.

3 **Students search for visual and verbal patterns that match the problems they wish to solve.**
Our user testing reminded us just how much students—unfamiliar with rhetorical or grammatical terminology—navigate handbooks by flipping pages, looking for what matches a current composing need. Two aspects of this handbook's design support such learning:

- **Pattern pages** provide learners with straightforward visual explanations of compositional processes or grammatical structures. If students can see a pattern, they can hold it in their minds for later application.

- The pattern pages are visually differentiated from other pages in the book so that students can find them quickly.

4 **Students look for examples first.**
In the user testing, students turned through the handbook looking for sample sentences or other examples that matched their needs; only after finding the examples did they read accompanying explanatory text.

Our handbook's design puts **examples front and center**. We've included as many examples—of sentences, student writing, or source evaluation—as we could and we built explanations inductively from the examples. We want students to find easily what will help them solve their writing and editing concerns—and then (as above) we want them to remember the pattern of what they learn so they can apply it later.

5 **The processes of research and documentation process can be presented visually.**
Many of our reviewers told us how frustrated students are by the details of documentation. We worked **to make visible the patterns of documentation**, so that students won't feel as though each citation requires starting anew. We have provided as many citation examples from different media as possible.

From our user testing, we also learned that students often don't know the kinds of sources they are using: How do they tell a personal homepage from a nonprofit website or a corporate author from an individual author? In addition, students—like many of us—can be vexed by the complexities of database searches. We designed our research coverage to provide as much visual support as possible for such needs. You will find many **visual samples of different print and online sources** and detailed step-by-step **visual explanations of how to use databases of journals**.

Our hope is that these approaches help students make informed and critical judgments about the media and information that now fill their—and our—lives.

SUPPLEMENTS

MyCompLab is a Web application that offers comprehensive and integrated resources for every writer. With MyCompLab, students can access a dynamic eBook version of *The DK Handbook*; learn from interactive tutorials and instruction; practice and develop their skills with grammar, writing, and research exercises; share their writing and collaborate with peers; and receive comments on their writing from instructors and tutors. Go to http://www.mycomplab.com to register for these premiere resources and much more.

A booklet of **Exercises to accompany The DK Handbook** provides assignments and activities that allow students to practice the writing and grammar lessons in the handbook. Instructors can assign the exercises according to their own teaching styles and their students' needs. The variety of short answer and open-ended questions also allows instructors to use the exercises as both an assessment and a diagnostic tool. A separate **Answer Key** is available to instructors for this *Exercises* booklet.

An **Instructor's Resource Manual,** developed by Anne Wysocki, Dennis Lynch, and Kristi Apostel, offers guidance to new and experienced teachers for teaching composition with *The DK Handbook* and using its media resources.

VangoNotes are audio chapter reviews and practice tests students can download to any mp3 player. Visit vangonotes.com for details.

ACKNOWLEDGMENTS

Although composing this handbook took longer than we imagined and than our editors hoped, the process has been deeply pleasurable. We have learned much and have valued the time we have gotten to spend with others— either in person or through their work.

Lynn Huddon got us started on this project, kept her humor and patience, and contributed finer features. Michael Greer's intelligence, thoughtfulness, humor, and energy are present on every page, and his evenness and encouragement are also a reason this book is now in your hands. Joe Opiela gently kept us focused and determined. Stuart Jackman kept us colorful and delighted us with each new page. Christine Holten provided valuable insight and contributed much to our sections for multilingual writers. Megan Galvin-Fak has creatively and energetically thought about how to get this book into people's hands and infectiously kept us excited. In working with our advisory board and focus groups, Laura Coaty kept us thinking about this work's real applications. Bob Ginsberg and Kim Nichols managed the production process with grace and style. And Tharon Howard carried out the smart and detailed user testing— with live students—that helped us understand how others really do use handbooks.

We thank (and will continue to thank for a long time) all the above for the extraordinary efforts they have made on behalf of this book—but nonetheless our most emphatic thanks go to our reviewers (listed below), whose generosity with their time and care for student learning has contributed to and strengthened every bit of this book.

John Bennett, Lake Land College; Paula Berggren, Baruch College; Lori M. Butler, Rogers State University; Arnold Bradford, Northern Virginia Community College; Joel R. Brouwer, Montcalm Community College; Shanti Bruce, Nova Southeastern University; Ron Christiansen, Salt Lake Community College; Joseph Colavito, Northwestern State University; Dean R. Cooledge, University of Maryland Eastern Shore; Philip Kevin Coots, Ashland Community and Technical College; MaryAnn K. Crawford, Central Michigan University; Joe Davis, North Iowa Area Community College; Darren DeFrain, Wichita State University; Erika Deiters, Moraine Valley Community College; Ronda Leathers Dively, Southern Illinois University–Carbondale; Scott Douglass, Chattanooga State Technical Community College; Kerith Dutkiewicz, Davenport University Online; Jacqueline Gray, St. Charles Community College; Ann E. Green, Saint Joseph's University; Dianne Gregory, Kaplan University; Max Guggenheimer, Lynchburg College; Monica Fortune Hatch, Southwestern Illinois College; Gail Odette Henderson, Baton Rouge Community College; Joel B. Henderson, Chattanooga State Technical Community College; Charlotte Hogg, Texas Christian University; Ned Huston, Eastern Illinois University;

PART 1
A PROCESS FOR COMPOSING

CONTENTS

WHAT IS COMPOSING?

Composing a paper, you arrange words into sentences into paragraphs, hoping that the arrangement will engage your readers. Composing a poster, you arrange words, photographs, and colors, so that viewers will want to look at the poster and will heed its purposes. Composing a podcast, you arrange voices and other sounds so that others will want to listen.

The New London Group—British and American teachers who research how we learn to communicate—argues that composing requires three steps:

1 No matter the medium—written, visual, oral, or some mix—we always compose with elements and arrangements already familiar to others. These existing elements and arrangements are called **Available Designs** by the New London Group.

2 As we compose our texts out of available designs, we are **Designing**, trying out new shapes and combinations of what is available.

3 When we finish composing, we have made the **Redesigned**, something new out of past possibilities. The redesigned, in turn, becomes new available designs for our, or others', future composing.

This process shapes what we propose in this handbook. If you are to be an effective and satisfied composer, you need to learn the designs that are available to you—the conventions, grammars, and expectations—so you can make what audiences can understand but also so that you can design for your own purposes.

WHAT IS RHETORIC?

Rhetoric is a method for understanding how communication happens.

Rhetoric developed in the western Mediterranean area over 2,000 years ago as political systems became democratic and as legal institutions came into being. People saw that audiences were moved by some speeches and writings more than by others, and that some speeches and writings not only failed but achieved the exact opposite of what their composers had hoped.

Some people—*rhetoricians*—started systematically studying what underlay effective speeches and writing.

The result of the rhetoricians' studies was rhetoric.

AUDIENCE

Rhetoric begins with the understanding that writers (and composers of any text) address audiences. Audiences are not mindless and automatically under a composer's sway; instead, audiences come to texts with beliefs, values, and ideas. Using rhetoric, composers consider the relationships they can build with audiences so that audiences will want to listen and engage with the composer around the issue at hand.

PURPOSE

The earliest rhetoricians realized that composers need to have purposes. This might seem so obvious as to be useless, but if composers cannot articulate their purposes in detail, then they cannot decide how to proceed in composing. (As when one young woman went to court to appeal a ticket for driving through a red light, it was only after her appeal was denied that she realized her purpose was not to tell the judge how the traffic light was hidden by a truck, but rather how she did not know there even was a traffic light where she should have stopped.)

CONTEXT

Where and when do composer and audience meet? Is it face to face or through an essay? Late Saturday night or early Monday? How will recent events influence an audience's attitude? Rhetoricians recognize that composers need to consider the contexts of communication because the contexts shape how audiences respond.

STRATEGIES

Once composers have a sense of audience, purpose, and context, they can begin making all the particular decisions—big and small—that shape a composition. Composers need to consider how a choice of a particular word, just as much as a choice of what comes first in a text, are likely to affect an audience's attitude toward a purpose.

RHETORICAL SITUATIONS

The combination of audience, purpose, and context make up what rhetoricians (starting in the twentieth century) call *the rhetorical situation*. This term helps us keep in mind that communication is not a simple transfer of information but is rather an interaction of real, complicated people within the real, complex events of lives and cultures.

Even classrooms are rhetorical situations, where writing an essay involves people with different cultural and educational backgrounds: students and teachers. How do you use the audiences, purposes, and contexts of classrooms—and the strategies available to you—to learn to communicate as you hope?

■ ■ ■

THIS HANDBOOK

This book is about helping you discover as much as you can about your audiences, purposes, and contexts so that you can use the available strategies of writing (and also, to a lesser extent, of visual and oral communication) to construct the connections you want to build with your audiences.

WHAT IS RHETORIC?
AUDIENCE

WHO WILL BE READING, VIEWING, OR HEARING WHAT YOU COMPOSE? WHAT ASPECTS OF YOUR AUDIENCE MATTER TO WHAT YOU HOPE TO ACHIEVE?

That a text you are composing has to be shaped for other people is the central concern of rhetoric.

Perhaps the need to think about your audience when you compose seems obvious to you, but the understanding that we write and compose texts for others takes a while to develop.

Before entering college, most writing education focuses on grammar, research, and the logical structures of writing. Before college, most people move in fairly small circles of friends and family, and so their communications are informal and relaxed: Most often, people in high school know well the people to whom they are writing and speaking. After high school, when we go to college, start working to support ourselves, and start taking more active roles in our communities, we have to learn how to communicate with people we may not know so directly.

We need, in other words, to build upon what we learned about writing in high school: We need to start thinking about the people who read, view, or hear what we compose, and how those people are likely to respond to the many choices we make while composing.

AUDIENCES ARE NEVER FULL, REAL PEOPLE

Even when you are talking with your mother or best friend, you are addressing only some part of that person. Your mother is your mother, after all, and so you speak to her as **mother**; she may also be a boss, an employee, a sister, a daughter—but, when **you** talk with her, you are addressing only that part of her that is **mother**.

Likewise, when you write work memos, they go to your boss and co-workers insofar as they have the role of **boss** and **co-worker**; you do not address the sides of them that are **parent**, **churchgoer**, or **novel reader**.

People have rich emotional and intellectual lives and different cultural backgrounds. When you compose texts for others, you focus on a particular topic and hope your audience will pay attention to your concerns. What emotions play around your topic—and how can you compose to arouse or to dampen those emotions? What possible opinions and values might your audiences hold on your topic—and how can you compose to focus their attention on some particular aspect they might not have considered before or are likely to dismiss?

Audiences, in other words, are always a bit imaginary, in that you ask them to step into the roles and beliefs that the purposes and contexts of your composing require. You call audiences into being from where they really are.

→ Because the consideration of audience is so important, a whole part of this book is focused on shaping writing for audiences. See pages 149–184.

WHAT IS RHETORIC?
PURPOSE

WHAT DO YOU WANT TO HAPPEN AS A RESULT OF YOUR COMPOSING EFFORTS?

What do you hope your audience will think, feel, believe, or do after engaging with you through your text? What do you want to learn through engaging with your audiences?

PURPOSE IS NOT THE SAME AS THESIS

A thesis is the idea—usually with reasons—you hope readers will take away from a piece of argumentative writing. But when you compose such writing, you hope readers will do something with that idea: Do you hope they will write to their national or state political representatives, buy energy-saving light bulbs, or think a little differently about religion or women's lives?

Purposes take into account the emotions and possible actions of readers as well as their thoughts.

PURPOSES ARE NEVER SIMPLE

Here are some purposes for composing:

"I hope that my paper will encourage readers to feel angry enough about teacher salaries in this district that they will join the demonstration to be held at the state capitol next month."

"Because of my poster, I'd like my audience to look more carefully at how others treat pets, knowing there is a relation between pet and child abuse."

"I want my readers to be happy that women's rights have advanced so much in the last century, and to understand why it's important to protect those rights. I want them to see the connection between what happened in the last century and the improved lives of their mothers, sisters, daughters, and themselves."

By thinking about purpose, you start thinking about what your writing and composing need to do, and you start thinking concretely about how to do it.

IMAGINING PURPOSE

As with audience, you need to imagine your purpose as closely as you can: If you picture for yourself exactly the response you hope the text you are composing brings about, you will be more likely to compose texts that appeal in concrete and engaging ways to audiences.

What emotions should your composing arouse or dampen in your audience?

Are you working to build connections with individuals by themselves or to bring people together?

Are you hoping people will take specific action, or quietly consider an issue in more depth?

→ Considerations of purpose weave throughout the rest of this book, but if you want specific help with purpose, see pages 14–15, 23, and 160–165.

WHAT IS RHETORIC?
CONTEXT

WHERE ARE YOUR READERS AT THE MOMENT THEY ENGAGE WITH THE TEXT YOU ARE COMPOSING?

WHAT IS GOING ON AROUND THEM? HOW ARE THE PLACE AND TIME LIKELY TO AFFECT HOW THEY READ?

How can you take those circumstances into account while composing so that the text fits its context and reaches its readers?

LOCAL AND IMMEDIATE CONTEXTS

When you write an essay for a class, the teacher has to respond to your essay as well as to the essays of everyone else in your class, usually at night or on the weekend, at home. How is this likely to shape how your teacher reads?

When you write a memo at work, your boss or co-workers will receive the memo amid a pile of other paperwork, in the middle of distracting days. How is this likely to shape how they read?

When you design a flyer for a campus event, it goes up on walls or telephone poles alongside hundreds of others; it has to attract the attention of people who are hurrying by, ten feet away.

When you design a website for a non-profit organization, readers will probably read it alone, at their computers.

Each of these circumstances, describing the particulars of how audiences come to texts, can help you consider composing. What do you need to do to show a tired, weary-eyed teacher that you've done what an assignment asked? How can you compose a memo so that your busy boss and co-workers will understand exactly what you want? What photographs and words—and what sizes, and how many—can help you attract the eyes of a passing poster audience? What words, colors, and photographs can help you take advantage of the intimacy of a computer screen reader?

The more you can imagine the time and place in which someone will read your text, the more you can shape the text to fit when and where the text will be read.

LARGER CONTEXTS

What are the values and concerns of your time and place? What has happened recently—in your town or country or in the world—that might affect how someone responds to a text?

For example, after September 11, 2001, no one could write an editorial about travel or world events without taking September 11 into account. It was a long time before people felt it was appropriate to tell jokes and be humorous about politics or world events.

But also imagine that your town is struggling over whether to allow Wal-Mart to build a megastore or over how to find funding to keep the hospital open or the factory from shutting down. If you were to write a letter to the editor about school funding, for example, or about the need for a new stoplight on your corner, taking into account those larger community concerns shows readers that you understand the consequences of what you argue—and so readers are more likely to listen.

Composing texts while mindful of the larger contexts in which your readers move can help you figure out what tone of voice to use, the beliefs and values that shape how readers read, and the mood your readers are likely to be in. Considering all these details helps you understand how and why readers might respond. It helps you build bridges to readers, and thus helps you shape a text that readers are more likely to read, understand, and want to engage.

WHAT IS RHETORIC?
STRATEGIES

WHAT ARE THE CHOICES YOU CAN MAKE AS YOU COMPOSE A TEXT?

What words, or tone of voice, or colors will you choose, or what should come first? What examples will you use? Will you use photographs or charts? Which typefaces?

Every choice is a strategy affecting how your audience responds. Your choices depend on your purpose, context, and audience.

IN TERMS OF STRATEGIES,

becoming an effective composer of texts involves:

1 Your ability to identify the widest possible range of choices—of strategies—available to you in your rhetorical situation.

2 Your ability to shape choices to address your audience, given your purpose and context.

Regarding the first ability: When you first start considering a text you have to compose (or even when you are partly into composing it), if you list every choice you could make, you'll see how much room there is for you to experiment with possibilities; you're more likely therefore to achieve your purposes. (You'll also probably realize the impossibility of listing every possible strategy—but it's useful to try.)

Regarding the second ability: If you want your audience to write to their congressional representatives to support a bill funding more space exploration, don't begin with a discussion of where the money should come from: That starts your readers thinking about why space exploration might be bad. Start instead with a discussion of the wonders of space, and then describe the medical and industrial advances resulting from space exploration; your audience will approach your request with a positive point of view.

You can consider every possible strategy in light of how your readers are likely to respond, and how your choice will shape their attention and thus their receptiveness to your purpose.

THE STRATEGY OF ARRANGEMENT

In the example of space exploration, the strategy we discussed is arrangement. Arrangement is about what comes first in a composition, and what follows.

For some rhetorical situations, audiences expect certain arrangements. When you write a business letter, the letter starts with a date and a greeting, and then discusses the matter at hand, with (often) a final paragraph suggesting what the next actions should be. Scientific papers are usually arranged with an abstract first, then a description of experimental method, then a description of the results of the experiments, then a discussion of the results, and finally a list of other papers consulted during the research.

→ Because arrangement is such a crucial strategy in composing, a whole part of this book is devoted to it; see pages 185–236.

THE STRATEGY OF MEDIUM

Sometimes you enter a composing situation with all choices open to you, including that of the medium. If, for example, you have been asked to help a nonprofit organization improve its outreach to teenagers, would you recommend composing webpages or brochures, organizing a fair or school visits, or handing out printed T-shirts at the mall? Each of these media engages with the audience in different ways, and so can help you achieve your purpose in different—and differently effective—ways.

RHETORIC AND A PROCESS FOR COMPOSING A RESEARCH PAPER

People who study writers and writing have learned that all effective writers have processes they follow to develop writing. These processes differ in their particulars from writer to writer, but generally—when it comes to composing a research paper—the processes contain the steps shown on the next page.

(Keep in mind that, although the process looks linear, writers often move back and forth through the steps, especially between revising and getting feedback, as they produce several drafts of the work.)

With each step, you become more certain about audience, purpose, context, and—eventually—strategies, until it is time to declare a project finished.

We include the chart on the right at the beginning of each part of this book to help you stay oriented in a project. When we do this, we won't show the rhetorical concerns, because they will be spelled out in each part.

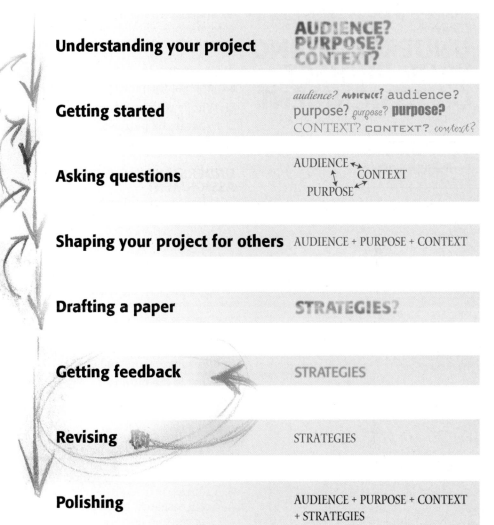

Understanding your project

AUDIENCE?
PURPOSE?
CONTEXT?

Getting started

audience? AUDIENCE? audience?
purpose? purpose? **purpose?**
CONTEXT? CONTEXT? context?

Asking questions

AUDIENCE
CONTEXT
PURPOSE

Shaping your project for others   AUDIENCE + PURPOSE + CONTEXT

Drafting a paper

STRATEGIES?

Getting feedback

STRATEGIES

Revising

STRATEGIES

Polishing

AUDIENCE + PURPOSE + CONTEXT
+ STRATEGIES

UNDERSTANDING YOUR PROJECT OR ASSIGNMENT

To understand any new project or assignment—whether you are in school, at work, or anyplace else where you need to develop communication—you need to understand the rhetorical situation of the project or assignment:

❑ **Who is your audience?**

❑ **What is the purpose?**

❑ **What is the context?**

UNDERSTANDING A CLASS ASSIGNMENT

❑ **Who is your audience?**

In a writing class, you will often hear that the audience is your classmates—but probably your teacher will give you a grade on how well you address the concerns and beliefs of your classmates, so the teacher is also a very important part of your audience. (Sometimes teachers ask you to write for other audiences besides the class; you will have to ask how you are to learn about those audiences.)

❑ **What is the purpose?**

There are three levels of purpose within a class writing assignment, all of which you probably hope to satisfy:

• There are the teacher's purposes. You might be asked to demonstrate that you know how to produce polished prose; can carry out research, integrate it into a paper, and document it; and can develop and produce a persuasive argument. Look at each new assignment for explicit statements of what the teacher hopes you will learn; if they are not there, ask.

- You can have your own purposes related to your own learning: If there are skills on which you need to focus (such as some particular aspect of grammar, or transitions, or writing complex paragraphs), how can you work them in?

- There is your particular purpose within the paper you write and its audience, such as *I want to persuade the people in class that replacing the light bulbs in their houses with compact fluorescent bulbs is a useful thing to do* or *I would like to persuade people to write to their representatives about [xxx].*

When you are trying to understand what a teacher is hoping you will achieve, look for the following key terms in an assignment:

summarize: to describe as concisely as possible the main points of writing

define: to explain a term or concept

inform: to tell others about an issue, with supporting examples and data

analyze: to break a process or object into its conceptual parts while showing how the parts relate to make a whole

persuade: to present your opinions on a topic using evidence, so that others might come to agreement with you

❑ What is the context?

The classroom is the immediate context, of course—but so is your campus and its values and recent events. The values of the community around the school, current national and international events—how are these likely to shape how your audience will read?

Once you have done some thinking about these questions, you will help yourself tremendously if you reflect on the assignment in writing, asking any questions that come up, as the person who wrote the following did:

The assignment says that I am to write an argumentative research paper on a topic of my choosing, providing lots of evidence, with the class as my audience. I've written research papers before, but I don't know what "argumentative" means regarding research, so I have to ask what that means. But that sounds like the overall purpose for the teacher, to show that I know how to make research be an argument. (I'm also not sure what counts as evidence; I'll have to ask about that, too.) And I don't really know the people in class yet, but they seem to be just like everyone else I know on this campus, so I can ask my friends to help me think about this paper. The context? Well, it's this writing class—so I guess that means I also have to be careful about how I write. But we also just had that big sports scandal here, so maybe that's something to write about.

UNDERSTANDING OTHER PROJECTS

Here are questions to help you start your initial thinking about new communication projects. Later parts of this book will help you continue to develop your understanding of your rhetorical situation, as your questions and concerns become more focused with further work.

❑ **Who is your audience?**

What particular people will read, see, or hear the communication I am building? What are my relationships with those people? What values and beliefs do they hold concerning the topic of the communication? Why should this communication matter to them? What will be most important to them in this communication? Is there an immediate audience and then a secondary audience (as, for example, when someone writes a report for a boss, who will then pass the report on to the next boss)?

→ Part 4 of this book goes into detail about audiences; see pages 150–159.

❑ **What is the purpose?**

Why am I doing this? What am I hoping to achieve? What should my audience think, feel, or do when they are finished reading? What relationships am I hoping to build with my audience?

→ Part 4 of this book goes into detail about purposes; see pages 160–165.

❑ **What is the context?**

Where and when will my audience receive the communication from me? How does that context shape them to respond? Are there any recent events that might affect how they respond?

PART 2
FINDING IDEAS

CONTENTS

WHERE ARE WE IN THE PROCESS FOR COMPOSING?

Understanding your project

Getting started
Finding a topic
Narrowing the topic
Developing research questions
Finding sources
Keeping track of sources

Asking questions

Shaping your project for others

Drafting a paper

Getting feedback

Revising

Polishing

COMPOSING TO LEARN & COMPOSING TO COMMUNICATE

PART 2 OF THIS BOOK IS ABOUT COMPOSING TO LEARN

At the earliest stage of the composing process, you need to let yourself wander through the possible opinions and perspectives on a topic, finding as wide a range as you can. By letting yourself wander, you are more likely to come upon ideas that resonate for you and your audience. That is why this part of the book—Part 2—is set up to help you identify and narrow a topic and then find a wide range of sources on your topic.

Part 3, Analyzing Arguments and Evaluating Sources, will help you consider the ideas, opinions, and perspectives you discover in relation to your audience.

WHY DO YOU NEED TO KNOW ABOUT THIS DISTINCTION?

Effective and successful writers understand that sometimes they need to lose themselves in their own words in order to figure out what ideas matter to them; they also recognize that sometimes they need to look at their ideas from a little distance in order to think about how to shape words for readers.

If you can recognize when you are composing to learn versus when you are composing to communicate, or if you can recognize that sometimes you need to back off from shaping your ideas for readers in order to figure out your own ideas, your composing process will be quicker and easier and will yield stronger results.

COMPOSING TO LEARN

If you are writing, sketching, or reading to figure out what **you** think, believe, or feel, then you are composing to learn. You have no one else in mind as you work: You are simply working things out for yourself. In this stage, you think about possible audiences as little as possible.

Composing to learn can take place on scraps of paper, in journals, on white boards, on dinner napkins and tablecloths, in dreams.

COMPOSING TO LEARN SUPPORTS...

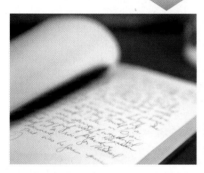

JOURNALS, DIARIES, AND MEMORIES

This is writing meant to be read only by you.

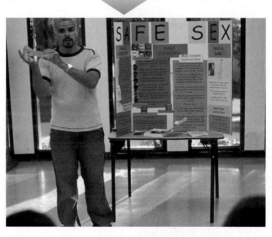

COMPOSING TO COMMUNICATE

When you alertly shape your ideas so that others can understand them, you are composing to communicate. You make clear reasons for and connections between ideas. You think about how others might respond, and you shape all aspects of a text so that others can understand what you do.

Composing to communicate requires composing to learn. Until you have a pretty good idea of what matters to you, you can't know what it is you want others to hear or see.

A RESEARCH PROCESS

Successful writers articulate for themselves exactly what they know at each step of their composing process. This helps them see what they know—and what they still need to learn. This also helps them see when they can really be confident that they have an argument to put on the page (or screen) for others.

What moves writers from step to step of the composing process is research that becomes more focused.

Almost all writers—all composers in almost any medium—start with a general idea or general interest in a topic. By doing initial and broad research into their area of interest, they learn what aspects of the topic might be of concern to their audiences.

Once writers have a narrowed topic, they can generate questions about the topic. These questions help writers learn what further research—now very focused research—they need to do.

All this time, writers are moving toward a thesis statement, which is a statement of the logical aspects of a focused argument, one that is appropriately narrowed for the audience.

Once they have a thesis statement, writers can then build a statement of purpose, which uses a thesis statement and a writer's knowledge about an audience to describe the various compositional strategies that will help the writer reach the audience.

With all that research behind them, writers are well prepared to draft an effective and strong composition.

GENERAL TOPIC

RESEARCH

the economy
politics   technology   file sharing
                                    health
the draft   war   video games
global warming   immigration   music
         globalization   education

NARROWED TOPIC

RESEARCH

electronic voting machines
file sharing
the success of new bands
global warming
the distribution of tree species
charter schools and public schools

QUESTIONS TO GUIDE RESEARCH

RESEARCH

What is electronic voting? Why do people suggest we use electronic voting? What makes electronic voting machines better (or worse) than other voting methods? Who oversees electronic voting machines? Who makes electronic voting machines? Who recommends electronic voting machines? Who says we shouldn't use electronic voting machines?

THESIS STATEMENT

RESEARCH

Government-developed and owned electronic voting machines that print receipts for voters will help voting be faster and fairer.

STATEMENT OF PURPOSE

RESEARCH

Because I am writing to people in class, many of whom will not even yet have voted, I need to explain about different kinds of voting machines—and how each one causes troubles in tracking and counting votes. I also need to show how electronic voting machines—given how they are now developed—seem more vulnerable to tampering and fraud than other existing kinds of voting.

FINISHED WRITING

COMPOSING TO LEARN

COMPOSING TO COMMUNICATE

TIP: THE RESEARCH PROCESS IS NOT LINEAR

This graphic makes the research process look fast and streamlined. It isn't. You will probably repeat steps as you come across sources that lead your thinking in new directions or as you think more about your own position.

A RESEARCH PROCESS, CONTINUED

GENERAL TOPIC

RESEARCH

NARROWED TOPIC

RESEARCH

QUESTIONS TO GUIDE RESEARCH

RESEARCH

THESIS STATEMENT

RESEARCH

STATEMENT OF PURPOSE

RESEARCH

FINISHED WRITING

RESEARCH BROADLY, THEN DEEPLY

During the early stages of research, *general and popular sources* can help you research broadly to get a general sense of what matters to people. Online sources like Google and Wikipedia and popular magazines like *Time* and *Newsweek* can provide help with this broader, preliminary inquiry.

During the later stages of research, *academic journals and other specialized sources* can help you deepen your research and develop your thesis. In academic and other kinds of formal writing, audiences also expect you to provide multiple sources to support your main points.

See pages 38–59 for more on kinds of sources and the expectations audiences have about them.

A SKETCH OF ONE WRITER'S PROCESS

GENERAL TOPIC
file sharing

NARROWED TOPIC
file sharing and the careers of new bands

QUESTIONS TO GUIDE RESEARCH
Developing a set of guiding questions can help you gain a better sense of what is at stake, for whom, and why.
Who shares files? How many files are shared in a year? What is file sharing? What are different ways to file-share? What kinds of files are shared? Are there competing interpretations of what counts as file sharing? Who assigns different interpretations? Who decides whether file sharing is good or bad? What criteria do they use? Some people think file sharing is always theft; are there conditions under which it is beneficial? Who benefits from file sharing? Who doesn't? When does file sharing help a band? Do the effects of file sharing differ when different kinds of files are shared? What aspects of file sharing ought to be protected? When should file sharing be prohibited?

THESIS STATEMENT
A thesis statement is about logic: It offers reasons for your position that will be persuasive to your intended audience.
Musicians who make their music freely available online for sharing sell more of their music than those who do not, because they attract new audiences.

→ See pages 102–103 for more on thesis statements.

STATEMENT OF PURPOSE
Writers use statements of purpose to shape a thesis statement for a particular audience. A statement of purpose helps a writer think through the details (such as tone of voice, arrangement, or kinds of examples) of how to present a thesis to an intended audience.

→ Because a statement of purpose is usually several paragraphs long, we cannot give an example here; see pages 161–163 for examples.

In this part of the book, we help you work on developing a narrow topic and questions to guide your research into that topic. Part 3 helps you develop a thesis statement. Part 4 helps you develop a statement of purpose.

GETTING STARTED WITH RESEARCH

ONE PERSON'S PROCESS

Here is how Jessica Rankin, a Senior Technical Writer for a large corporation, describes her research—including how she gets started—when she has to write manuals about a new software product:

I begin by researching and reading the feature specification documents that an engineer writes for the product. These contain descriptions of the feature and what types of things the feature should be used for. After reading through these documents, I usually have a general idea of what the feature is supposed to do, the main parts that would need to be clarified for a user, and where it has been integrated into the software. From there, I go to the software and start playing with the feature to see if it correlates to the feature specification that was written for it. At this point, I have identified odd behaviors and areas that are not intuitive to the general user. These become my starting points for what I document and discuss with the engineer. I act as his first usability tester and I can see the areas that I feel need further development in terms of documentation. Plus, the dialogue that is established between the two of us allows for greater flow of information when changes come up in the feature after development has gotten further along. I know this iterative process has come to a close when the feature no longer changes and I have no further questions about the feature. The real test comes when an outside peer who isn't familiar with the feature reviews my research and documentation. The outside peer is my gauge: Have I conveyed enough information to give the most basic user a good understanding of what they're using?

SETTING UP A SCHEDULE

Unless they are projects you start out of general interest, research projects almost always have due dates—so part of getting started with a research project is figuring out how to schedule your work to be done on time. Making a schedule is also a useful way to remind yourself of just how much work goes into a research paper that is worthy of your efforts and is a learning opportunity. Start with the due date, and work backward. Here is one student's schedule (you may have less time):

Research Paper

DUE DATE	12/15
date assigned	11/1
STEPS	DATE TO COMPLETE STEP
Analyze project (p. 14)	11/2
Find & narrow a topic (pp. 26–33)	11/6
Develop questions for guiding my research (pp. 34–37)	
and figure out the kinds of research I need to do (pp. 38–43)	11/7
[Will I need to do any interviews, surveys, or	
observations? (pp. 78–79)]	
[Do I need to do archival research? (pp. 76–77)]	
Carry out my research (pp. 60–79)	
and start keeping running list of sources (pp. 82–83)	11/14
Develop working thesis (pp. 102–103)	11/16
Do further research required by my thesis (pp. 104–113)	11/23
Evaluate sources, deciding what to include (pp. 130–143)	11/24
Develop statement of purpose (pp. 160–165)	11/25
Develop Works Cited list (pp. 328–350)	11/30
First draft due	12/1
Receive draft back with comments	12/8
If more research is necessary...	12/10
Revise first draft	12/13
Edit first draft	12/14
Get Dad to proofread it for me	12/14
FINAL DRAFT DUE	12/15

FINDING A TOPIC

WHAT A TOPIC IS

A topic is a general area of interest. It's often just a name or a word or two, or two ideas together:

- computer game violence
- children's education
- automobiles
- racism
- women's rights
- sports and advertising
- health and aging
- microloans
- viruses

A topic is a place to start, but it is too broad for a paper; you have to narrow it by doing research that helps you shape your topic for a particular audience in a particular context.

IF AN ASSIGNMENT GIVES A GENERAL TOPIC

You may be given broad guidelines within which to choose a topic. For example, in a history class you might be asked to *Write a short biography of a person who lived through World War I* or *Find two articles that take different positions on an event we've discussed and compare the two articles.* Start by identifying an area—a topic—within the parameters of the assignment, an area in which you want to do further research. If an idea does not immediately spring to mind, use the recommendations on the opposite page to help you choose.

IF YOUR ASSIGNMENT ASKS YOU TO CHOOSE A TOPIC

In writing classes, you are often asked to write a research paper on a topic you choose. Sometimes a topic comes immediately to mind; if not, try:

- **Asking yourself some questions.** What current issues matter to you—or are affecting a friend or someone in your family? What current events or issues do you not understand?

- **Talking to others.** Ask friends and family members what matters to them these days, and why.

- **Going online.** Some library and writing center websites provide lists of current topics that are rich with possibilities for research.

  Old Dominion University Libraries' Idea Generator <http://www.lib.odu.edu/libassist/idea/index.php>

  University of Illinois at Urbana–Champaign Library's Topic Ideas <http://www.library.uiuc.edu/ugl/howdoi/topic.html#ideas>

  Harvard University's Research Matter's Topics <http://www.researchmatters.harvard.edu/topic_list.php>

Once you have a list of possible topics, try these strategies to determine which you want to develop further:

- **Write a little bit on each possible topic.** Use these questions to help:

  Audience questions: Why might my audience care about this topic? What might they already know about it?

  Purpose questions: How does this topic help me address the assignment's purposes? Will this topic expand my learning? How can I shape this topic into a purpose that will interest my audience?

  Context questions: Does this topic seem rich enough to help me write a paper of the length asked by the assignment? Does it seem complex enough for the assignment? What is happening locally/nationally/ internationally around this topic?

  → See pages 2–9 to review the concepts of audience, purpose, and context.

- **Do a Google search on the topic.** Does it look like there's lots of interest in the topic? What are people's different positions on the topic? Do the webpages you visit suggest other, related topics, or other directions for research?

TIP: GET STARTED EARLY

Given the time constraints of school—and of producing a solid research paper—you usually need to decide quickly on a research topic. If you start working early enough, you'll have time to explore possibilities and find a topic that engages you.

Keep in mind, too, that a research paper takes shape in many stages, and you will (if you start early) have time to modify your topic and the research question that grows out of it as you deepen your understanding of your topic. Leaving this work until the night before doesn't necessarily doom you to failure—just to fear, nerves, and the temptation to let someone else do the work for you.

NARROWING A TOPIC

A TOPIC HAS TO BE NARROWED DOWN BEFORE IT CAN HELP YOU SHAPE RESEARCH AND WRITING

Imagine you want to write about the 1960s, and you tell this to one of your slightly more obnoxious friends, who responds, "Groovy! Are you going to tell us about the Vietnam War and the draft and hippies and the free speech movement and the civil rights movement and the Black Panthers and Women's Rights and the deaths of Jimi Hendrix and Janis Joplin and then there's Woodstock and the Young Republicans...? And do you want to talk about the 1960s in Africa, Asia, and Europe?"

You probably already had some idea of where within that long list you wanted to focus, but **until you can make your focus clear and specific to others, simply being able to name your topic sets you up to be unfocused**—and if you are unfocused, your writing will also be unfocused and you will find it hard to plan and organize your paper.

STARTING TO NARROW A TOPIC THROUGH INITIAL, BROAD RESEARCH

One way to find possibilities for narrowing a topic is to start researching the topic using general and popular research sources, as in this example where a Google search on the topic, talking with friends about the topic, and reading the paper and watching television give this writer a sense of how to focus the topic:

TOPIC:
microloans

GOOGLE SEARCH:
Microloans are small loans (usually under $100) made to people without credit, usually in developing countries; they support self-employment and are often made to women because then the whole family benefits; one example is the Grameen bank in Bangladesh, whose founder won the Nobel Peace Prize in 2005.

READING THE PAPER:
The *New York Times* has an editorial by Nicholas Kristof on how anyone in the U.S. can loan even a little bit of money to individuals in other countries, through websites like kiva.org.

TALKING TO OTHERS:
A friend's mother has made loans to women in other countries (through online organizations) so that the women can buy sewing machines and start businesses; all the loans she's made have been repaid.

TELEVISION SHOW:
Small Treasures: Microcredit and the Future of Poverty on PBS says that many microloans are to small businesses that make products out of what others have thrown away, like a woman who makes shopping bags out of discarded cement bags.

After such initial research, this writer could narrow the possibilities to these:
• Microloans and the role of women in developing countries
• Small business options for people living in poverty
• Ways of using your money to help others
• Alternative approaches to traditional economic development

HOW DO YOU KNOW WHEN YOU HAVE A NARROWED TOPIC?

A NARROWED TOPIC IS LINKED TO AN ISSUE OR CONTROVERSY THAT WILL BE OF INTEREST TO YOUR AUDIENCE

Using what you know about your audience, use your initial, broad research (as described on the previous page) to find possible areas that might be useful, surprising, or provocative to your audience.

For example, if you are writing about the 1960s for a class research paper, you probably already have some sense of how others in class think about what happened in the 1960s. If everyone else thinks of the 1960s in terms of free love and music, then imagine how you will catch their attention if you can narrow your topic to *The liberatory social movements in the United States in the 1960s and the conservative political responses of the 1980s and 1990s.*

TIP: KEEP YOUR MIND OPEN

While doing initial informal research, cast a wide net and keep as open a mind as possible. The wider you look for information on a topic, the more likely you are to be surprised by what you find—and being surprised can help you be more interested and engaged and thus write more strongly.

Also, don't look only for sources that support your initial thoughts on a topic. Seek a range of positions so that you have the widest sense of how people are thinking. (In Part 3 of this book we help you evaluate the sources you find through your research so that you can decide what is most useful for your project.)

NARROWED TOPICS

Notice how narrowed topics usually relate a general topic to specific places, times, actions, or groups of people. A narrowed topic can focus on one aspect of a general topic (as in the examples below about the Internet or religion), and relate that aspect to a place, time, action, or group.

GENERAL TOPIC	NARROWED TOPIC
women in the workforce →	the number of women in politics in the United States the last fifty years
advertising →	advertising and democratic participation in the United States
water as a resource →	water management in the Middle East
the Internet →	how corporations shape Internet social networking sites
poetry →	poetry written by people rooted in two cultures
racial profiling →	racial profiling and law-enforcement policies
global warming →	global warming education in elementary schools
sports →	college sports training and men's body images
religion →	the tax-exempt status of churches and their role in political races
technology →	the development of the compass, gunpowder, and papermaking in China
the civil rights movement →	organizational strategies of the civil rights movement

TIP: USE GOOGLE TO TEST YOUR TOPIC

There are two ways Google can tell you if your topic is narrow enough:

- If the first websites that Google suggests come from academic sources or respected organizations, your topic is narrow enough to be worth further research. (Pages 140–143 can help you determine if the sources are academic.)
- If Google responds with hundreds of millions of possible links, your topic is not yet focused enough.

OTHER STRATEGIES FOR NARROWING A TOPIC

BRAINSTORMING

Brainstorming is letting your brain run loose to jump from one idea to the next. Coming up with ideas that will engage an audience can sometimes happen when you think hard and with focus; other times you need simply to let your brain's associative abilities do what they will.

You can brainstorm alone or with others; with others, you have the advantage of playing off each other's ideas. In either case, work in the same way:

- Set aside five or ten minutes.

- For that five or ten minutes, say your topic out loud, and then say out loud—but also write down—every single thought that comes to mind in response.

- Do not stop to judge. If an idea seems too absurd to record, record it nonetheless: It might lead to something you can use. (And let yourself laugh: The energy of laughter is part of what makes brainstorming work.)

- If you hit a dead end, go back to an earlier term and see what other associations you have with it. (Try thinking of synonyms or opposites to spur your thinking—or come up with as absurd an association as you can.)

- At the end, read your ideas out loud to see if anything else comes up. If one or two ideas seem useful or potentially fruitful now, hold on to them. Otherwise, put the list aside and look at it the next day.

FREEWRITING

Freewriting is a little like extended brainstorming. Give yourself five minutes, and just write on your topic. As with brainstorming, just record whatever ideas come up: Let one idea lead into the next without stopping.

Freewriting becomes easier the more you do it; it's a good way to help your mind run more easily, and it's a practice of many successful writers.

At the end of your time limit, read over what you have written to see if any ideas stand out for development. If not, put the writing aside and go back to it later.

CLUSTERING

Like brainstorming and freewriting, clustering is a strategy for making your ideas visible to yourself—but instead of writing, you draw. Clustering helps you see relations among ideas, which can help you see potential arrangements you can use later when you start writing your paper.

To cluster, write your topic in the center of a page. Around the topic, write down as many related ideas as you can. Turn to each of those related ideas, and see what other ideas relate to them. If one idea suggests a chain of related ideas, follow it.

Below is the cluster Shelly made in thinking about body image, which led her to think about how the media shape our sense of our bodies and how our body image affects our health; by doing this clustering, and thinking about how pro-ani sites work, she came up with this narrowed topic: *body images in the media produced for you by others, and body images in the media that you produce about yourself.*

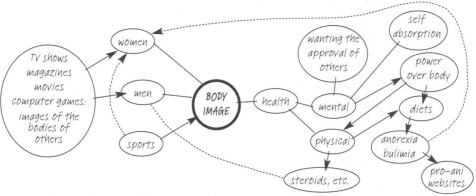

TIP: USE IDEA MAPPING TOOLS

There are free online applications that can help you cluster ideas (in information design and management, clustering is called **mapping**): try FreeMind <http://freemind.sourceforge.net/wiki/index.php/Main_Page> or CMapTools <http://cmap.ihmc.us/>.

QUESTIONS TO GUIDE RESEARCH

Once you have a narrowed topic, you can go online or to the library to start doing more focused research. But if you take time to carry out one more step—generating questions to help guide your research—you will have a better sense of what you need to find to write a solid paper, and where to look for that information.

On the next page, we show you one way to generate questions on your topic. Doing this can help you see

- areas of research you might not have considered otherwise.
- possible ways for shaping your purpose.
- questions your audience might have that you need to address.
- the specific research directions you need to take.

You may not need to address all the questions you develop, but you won't know for sure until you start using them to dig into sources with focus.

THE ORIGINS OF THESE QUESTIONS

Courtroom observations helped rhetoricians see that most questions fit into a set of categories. Rhetoricians called the categories *stases*, the plural of *stasis*, the Greek word for *place*. Stasis questions—like the ones to the right—help communicators determine what is at stake in any argument and the complexity of what is at stake.

KINDS OF QUESTIONS TO GUIDE RESEARCH

These categories can help you not only invent questions to ask but also determine which questions are likely to lead to rich research, as we show on the next pages.

QUESTIONS OF FACT

- What happened?
- Who was involved?
- Where did it happen?
- When did it happen?

QUESTIONS OF DEFINITION

- What is the thing or issue under discussion? What is it made of?
- What is the expected way (in the particular context) of using the thing, word, title, or expression?

QUESTIONS OF INTERPRETATION

- How do we understand and make sense of what happened?
- How are we to incorporate facts and definitions into a story that makes sense to us?

QUESTIONS OF CONSEQUENCE

- What caused what happened? What changes—to which persons, processes, or objects—led to the issue at hand?
- What are the effects of what happened? What changes might result from what happened?

QUESTIONS OF VALUE

- Is what is at stake good, useful, worthy of praise, or worthy of blame?
- What audiences will value the matter at hand? What do people say about the issue?
- Which of our (or our audience's) values are called upon as we make judgments about what happened?

QUESTIONS OF POLICY

- Given the circumstances, what should we do?
- Given the circumstances, what rules should we make or enforce?
- Given the circumstances, what laws should we write?

USING RESEARCH QUESTIONS TO DEVELOP A TOPIC

USING THE QUESTIONS

Use the research questions to generate as many other questions on your narrowed topic as you can, as the examples to the right suggest.

Doing this work will help you gain a sense of questions your audience might have, questions your research and composing will need to answer.

Generating questions will also help you see what research you need to do to gain authority on your topic.

Finally, generating questions will help you see whether your initial opinion on your topic is sufficiently informed. You will learn whether your opinions really are the ones you want to hold.

■ ■ ■

When you use the research questions to help you generate more questions, just let the questions come: Don't judge them, but let one question lead to another. The more questions you can generate, the more you will have a sense of what further research you need to do.

→ See pages 42–43 for using the questions to help you determine the kinds of research to do.

TIP: TRY TO ANSWER ALL THE QUESTIONS YOU GENERATE

Even though (as you will see in coming pages) you will eventually further narrow your research to focus on one or two questions, using your research to find answers to all the questions you generate will help you.

1 Learn the broad information you will need to give your readers at the beginning of your writing so that they understand why the topic matters.

2 Develop the most thorough and complete answers in your writing.

USING THE RESEARCH QUESTIONS, EXAMPLE 1

Kwan chose the topic of stem-cell research for an argumentative research paper, and has narrowed his topic to the possibilities of stem-cell treatments for paralysis. Using the research questions, he brainstorms the following questions:

QUESTIONS OF FACT
What are researchers able to do now with stem cells to help paralysis? How far away do viable stem-cell treatments seem?

QUESTIONS OF DEFINITION
What are stem cells? What is stem-cell research? What is paralysis?

QUESTIONS OF INTERPRETATION
Do stem-cell treatments cure paralysis? Should paralysis always be treated?

QUESTIONS OF CONSEQUENCE
What happens to people who have stem-cell treatments for paralysis? How do stem-cell therapies work in treating paralysis?

QUESTIONS OF VALUE
Who thinks stem-cell research is worthwhile, and who doesn't? Why? What values are called upon as people make judgments about stem-cell research? What values *aren't* called upon? Are the bad results of stem-cell research offset by the good results?

QUESTIONS OF POLICY
What are the different policies we could have toward stem-cell research and paralysis? What are the policies of other countries on stem-cell research?

USING THE RESEARCH QUESTIONS, EXAMPLE 2

Eva has chosen the topic of road building, and has narrowed her topic to the effects of road building on rural communities. Using the research questions, she brainstorms the following questions:

QUESTIONS OF FACT
Who decides where and when roads are built? How expensive is a new road? What affects the cost of a new road? Who pays for roads in rural areas?

QUESTIONS OF DEFINITION
What counts as a new road? What, really, is a road?

QUESTIONS OF INTERPRETATION
What do new roads bring to a rural community? What do existing roads bring to a rural community?

QUESTIONS OF CONSEQUENCE
What happens when a new road is built in a rural community—or not? Who or what is affected when a new road is built, and how?

QUESTIONS OF VALUE
Are the consequences of new roads good—or bad—for a community? For whom or what are new roads good or bad (including nonhumans)? What values are at stake in making judgments about whether roads are good or bad? What values underlie the different laws that exist about road building?

QUESTIONS OF POLICY
What laws already exist about the development of roads? How have laws and policies changed over the years?

KINDS OF SOURCES, KINDS OF RESEARCH

You have a narrowed topic and a series of questions that can help you learn more about your topic, in a focused and organized manner.

Now you need to determine where to look to find answers to your questions. In these pages we cover

- **KINDS OF SOURCES** for research
- **KINDS OF RESEARCH**
- **USING YOUR GUIDING RESEARCH QUESTIONS** to determine what kinds of sources and kinds of research to carry out
- **WHERE TO FIND THE SOURCES** for the research that will help you answer your questions

UNDERSTANDING DIFFERENT KINDS OF SOURCES

Sources are the texts—written, filmed, videotaped, recorded, photographed—from which you learn about your topic. Sometimes sources provide evidence and examples to use in your writing or other composing.

PRIMARY AND SECONDARY SOURCES

To determine whether a source is primary or secondary, ask yourself if you are reading someone's original words or reading **about** the person. In a paper about Ida B. Wells, for example, speeches and books by Wells are primary sources; commentary about Wells by other writers is a secondary source.

Examples of primary sources:

- Novels, poems, autobiographies, speeches, letters, diaries, blogs, e-mails.
- Eyewitness accounts of events, including written, filmed, and photographed accounts.
- Field research (surveys, observations, and interviews) that **you** conduct.

Examples of secondary sources:

- Biographies.
- Encyclopedias.
- News articles about events.
- Reviews of novels, poems, autobiographies, speeches, letters, diaries, e-mails, blogs.

Knowing the distinction between primary and secondary sources helps you seek out both kinds, and cover all the bases in your research.

SCHOLARLY AND POPULAR SOURCES

This distinction depends on the authority and reliability of the information in the sources.

In scholarly sources:

- Authors have academic credentials: they have studied the topic in depth and know how to weigh and present different sides of the topic.
- The sources used by the writer are listed so readers can check that the sources have been used fairly.
- Topics are examined at length.
- Their purpose is to spread knowledge: These sources are usually found in libraries; they contain little or no advertising.

In popular sources:

- Authors are journalists or reporters, usually without academic study in the topic.
- The sources are not listed.
- Topics are addressed briefly.
- Their purpose is to be quickly informative or entertaining: You find these sources at newsstands and stores, and they contain advertising.

Starting research with a range of popular sources can help you quickly get an overview of available perspectives on a topic. But the expectation for an authoritative research paper is that most of its sources are academic.

KINDS OF RESEARCH

Most research projects require you to do different kinds of research, seeking sources in different places and seeking different kinds of sources. Here are general categories of the kinds of research you can carry out, in recommended order:

ONLINE RESEARCH

Not everything is online—nor does Google link to all that is online.

Unspecialized search engines—like Google and Yahoo!—are useful for the following, usually early in research:

- Developing a sense of popular opinion on topics.
- Finding popular sources on topics, in both popular magazines and in blogs.
- *Finding person-on-the-street* quotations.
- Finding links or references to academic sources.

Specialized search engines provide access to material to which popular search engines often don't have access.

→ See pages 72–73 for descriptions of some specialized search engines.

TIP: USE VISUAL AND AUDIO SOURCES

With any of the research sites we mention here you can do *visual research* and *aural research*. Almost all the kinds of research we mention access not only print sources but also photographs, videos, historic printed matter such as brochures and posters, and speeches. If any visual or aural sources can support your research, search for them online and ask librarians about them.

LIBRARY RESEARCH

There are two ways to use most libraries these days: in person and online.

We encourage you to get to know, in person, a reference librarian at your library: Being able to have a conversation with a librarian about a topic can help you open up new approaches you might not have thought of on your own. A reference librarian can help you with both in-library and online uses of the library's resources.

In-library resources include the obvious books, journals, and reference materials. But some libraries also house historical or art archives, as well as map and government repositories. If you do not know how to find these—or even what materials are available—see if your library gives tours or workshops; knowing what is in your library can help you find creative possibilities for research.

Online library resources can include catalogs of the library's holdings and databases of newspapers and journals from across disciplines. (Later we discuss how to use such databases.)

Finally, libraries usually give you access to interlibrary loans: If your library does not have a book or journal you need, they can order it for you from another library.

RESEARCH IN ARCHIVES AND SPECIAL LIBRARY COLLECTIONS

Physical archives include local history associations or museums that have collections of old manuscripts, furniture, clothing, or other items. Such archives are usually private or provide limited access in order to protect their collections; they have different access policies that you can learn by contacting the archive. To find archives that might be close to you, do an online search using *archive* or *museum* as a keyword along with the kind of information you are trying to find, look in the phone book under *museum*, or ask a librarian.

Virtual archives are online collections of digitized materials such as letters, posters, photographs, or speeches.

Many libraries also have special collections of paintings and prints, films and video, and sound recordings—often not digitized. If you are writing on a topic that has a historical dimension, or are just curious, such special collections can be fascinating.

→ For more information on finding and using both physical and virtual archives and special collections, see pages 76–77.

FIELD RESEARCH

Interviews, observations, and surveys are all forms of research. To carry them out, you have to go out *into the field*— which could be a suburban strip mall, urban nonprofit organization, classroom, or rural farm.

→ For more on carrying out interviews, observations, and surveys, see pages 78–79.

KINDS OF SOURCES, KINDS OF RESEARCH

DETERMINING WHERE TO RESEARCH

Using the research categories to develop questions around your topic can help you with two aspects of research:

1 Developing search terms to use for online and database searches.

2 Knowing the kinds of sources and research that will be useful.

DEVELOPING SEARCH TERMS FOR ONLINE AND DATABASE SEARCHES

From your questions, pick out words and phrases directly related to your topic, and use them in search engines.

Here are terms coming from all the questions Kwan generated:

stem cell, stem-cell research, viable stem-cell treatments, stem-cell treatments, stem-cell controversy, stem-cell controversies, stem-cell results, paralysis, stem-cell therapies, consequences of stem-cell research, results of stem-cell research, stem-cell policy, stem-cell research in Europe, stem-cell research in Asia.

→ Page 73 shows how to combine several terms to do a very focused search.

WHAT SOURCES AND RESEARCH WILL HELP?

From all your questions, choose those most tied to your purpose, context, and audience. Almost all research writing starts by grounding its readers in definitions and facts on the topic; then the writing often focuses on interpretation of the issue to show a problem (which could be a consequence of an event) or to argue for certain policies. Once you have a set of focused questions, use the chart at right to choose kinds of sources and research.

Once you have a limited set of questions, use this chart to find the kinds of sources and research that will help you find answers to your questions.

	primary source	secondary source	academic source	popular source	online research	library research	archival research	field research
QUESTIONS OF FACT								
encyclopedias, atlases, and other reference works		✓	✓	✓	✓	✓		
statistics	✓			✓	✓	✓		
government or organizational documents	✓				✓	✓	✓	
firsthand accounts (interviews, autobiographies)	✓			✓	✓		✓	✓
photographs of events	✓			✓	✓		✓	
trial transcripts	✓				✓	✓	✓	
surveys and polls	✓			✓	✓	✓		✓
QUESTIONS OF DEFINITION								
dictionaries (for general audiences as well as specialized)	✓	✓	✓	✓	✓	✓		
academic journal articles		✓	✓		✓	✓		
QUESTIONS OF INTERPRETATION								
editorials and opinion pieces	✓			✓	✓	✓		
partisan news sources	✓			✓	✓	✓		
people's stories	✓			✓	✓			✓
artwork (movies, novels, short stories, documentary photography)	✓				✓	✓	✓	
position statements	✓				✓			
biographies	✓	✓			✓	✓		
academic journal articles			✓		✓	✓		
QUESTIONS OF CONSEQUENCE								
statistics	✓	✓			✓	✓		
historical accounts	✓	✓		✓	✓	✓		
photographs of the aftermaths of events				✓	✓		✓	
academic journal articles			✓		✓	✓		
the items listed under INTERPRETATION								
QUESTIONS OF VALUE								
organizational mission statements	✓				✓			✓
voting results	✓			✓	✓	✓	✓	
surveys and polls	✓			✓	✓	✓		✓
position statements	✓				✓		✓	✓
academic journal articles			✓		✓	✓		
the items listed under INTERPRETATION								
QUESTIONS OF POLICY								
government decisions	✓				✓	✓	✓	
organizational policy statements and decisions	✓				✓	✓	✓	✓
business records	✓				✓		✓	✓
trial decisions	✓				✓	✓	✓	
academic journal articles			✓		✓			

KINDS OF SOURCES, KINDS OF RESEARCH
CHOOSING SOURCES THAT HELP YOUR RESEARCH AND SUPPORT YOUR ARGUMENTS

Compositions that audiences take seriously offer as much support as possible from a range of supporting sources. The kinds of sources appropriate for your argument depend on the argument you are making, the audience to whom you are making the argument, and your context.

TIPS: CHOOSING WISELY

• MOST IMPORTANT: Teachers want you to compare and make judgments about a range of positions on your topic. Such thinking helps you contribute to community and civic decision making. When you do any research, seek out the widest range of others' positions.

• Sometimes teachers will give you guidelines for how many sources to use. If you have not been given guidelines and you want to indicate that you have looked carefully at a range of ideas in a 7- to 10-page research paper, a minimum of 10 sources is reasonable.

• Not just any 10 or more sources will do. Generally, use only one or two popular sources—perhaps to present the voices and opinions of others to show how and why an issue is a problem. The rest of your sources should be academic, from journal articles and books.

• Avoid using only one kind of source. Having all your citations come from one reference work (whether that work is in print or online, such as Wikipedia) indicates you have not done your research.

CHARACTERISTICS THAT DISTINGUISH SOURCES

On the next pages, we describe different often-used sources so you can judge their appropriateness for your purposes. We use the following criteria:

- **Audience**
  If a source is aimed at a general audience, the information it offers will generally be broad but shallow.

  Sources for academic or other specialized audiences will usually be more developed and better supported.

- **Writers**
  When writers are paid by the company or organization for which they write, they might offer opinions and information that is in line only with the goals of the company or organization.

- **Appearance**
  A professional appearance is a reflection of an overall ethic of care and attention to detail.

- **Format**
  If information is presented alongside advertisements, it can mean that the advertiser has some say in what information is presented.

- **Language**
  Sources using informal language are for general audiences; although they are easier to read, such sources are considered less authoritative than sources that use the language and vocabulary of specialized disciplines.

- **Review**
  If a source's information is reviewed by people who are unpaid and have no connection with the publisher, readers will grant it more authority.

- **Bibliography**
  Your readers will consider as most authoritative those sources that provide information that allows them to check the sources—such as a Works Cited list or other kind of bibliography.

- **When to use**
  We make general suggestions for using sources in ways readers will trust—but keep in mind that you always need to consider your readers, your purposes, and your context in making choices about what kinds of sources to use and how to use them. If you have any questions about using a source, ask several people from your intended audience how they would respond to your use of the source.

OTHER KINDS OF SOURCES

Almost any composition can be a source: You can cite song lyrics to show how hip-hop artists interpret current events differently than mainstream media; you can use a computer game screenshot to discuss representations of women; you can interview a neighbor about the history of local development.

We cannot possibly list all the sources you might use because what you use is limited only by what will engage your audience, given your purpose. The characteristics we consider on these pages can help you decide whether and how to use sources we have not listed.

CHOOSING SOURCES—**BOOKS**

Nonfiction Books

Such books may have more than one author but be written with a single voice throughout.

WRITERS: Publishing companies solicit writers or accept proposals from writers and choose which ones to publish.

REVIEW: Publishers approve the writing and can arrange for fact-checking.

BIBLIOGRAPHY: References are usually mentioned.

WHEN TO USE: Because publishers usually publish books only after carefully determining writers' qualifications, books tend to have authority for readers.

Reference Books

These books provide factual information such as definitions or statistics.

WRITERS: Authorities on a topic usually write entries in reference books.

REVIEW: Publishers approve the writing and check facts.

BIBLIOGRAPHY: References may be given.

WHEN TO USE: To provide definitions of words unknown to an audience or to support factual claims. Conventionally, use reference books sparingly in academic writing.

Edited Collections

An edited collection is a series of essays written by multiple authors with shared concerns, bound into one book.

WRITERS: Publishing companies solicit writers or accept proposals from writers and choose which to publish.

REVIEW: Publishers approve the writing and can arrange for fact-checking.

BIBLIOGRAPHY: References are usually mentioned.

WHEN TO USE: Because publishers usually publish books only after carefully determining writers' qualifications, collections tend to have authority for readers.

Corporate Author

Companies publish annual reports on their finances and accomplishments; they might publish books or pamphlets relevant to their products or services.

WRITERS: Written by an employee of the company or by a writer (a free-lancer) hired for the purpose at hand

REVIEW: A company might set up a review.

BIBLIOGRAPHY: References might be mentioned.

WHEN TO USE: The company's reputation on the topic about which you are writing will shape how readers respond to your use of such sources.

Government Author

The U.S. government publishes a wide range of books, pamphlets, guides, and reports on health, agriculture, economics, statistics, education, and other issues.

WRITERS: Writers can be government employees or people hired because of their expertise.

REVIEW: The writing can be reviewed by other writers in the same or other government agency.

BIBLIOGRAPHY: References may or may not be given.

WHEN TO USE: When your readers will accept the authority of the government on a topic.

KINDS OF SOURCES, KINDS OF RESEARCH
CHOOSING SOURCES— **PERIODICALS**

Periodicals are so named because they are published periodically: daily, weekly, monthly, quarterly.

Daily Newspapers

AUDIENCE: General public

WRITERS: Newspaper employees (***staff writers***) or freelance journalists who are paid; writers who work for news services; a writer's credentials often are not given.

FORMAT: Articles might be accompanied by illustrations or photographs, and newspapers contain advertising.

LANGUAGE: Nontechnical, informal

REVIEW: Articles are assigned to writers and reviewed by editors working for the newspapers.

BIBLIOGRAPHY: References might be mentioned in the text, but there are usually few ways given for readers to check a writer's sources.

WHEN TO USE: When you are writing to a general audience, examples and supporting evidence drawn from newspapers can be appropriate; introductions for more specialized audiences can be enlivened with examples from newspapers.

Popular Journals

AUDIENCE: General public

WRITERS: Employees of the journal (***staff writers***) or freelance journalists who are paid; a writer's credentials often are not given.

FORMAT: Articles are usually accompanied by color illustrations or photographs, and the journals contain advertising.

LANGUAGE: Nontechnical, informal

Popular Journals
continued

REVIEW: Articles are selected and reviewed by editors working for the journal.

BIBLIOGRAPHY: References might be mentioned in the text, but there are usually few ways given for readers to check a writer's sources.

WHEN TO USE: When you are writing to a general audience, examples and supporting evidence drawn from popular journals can be appropriate; introductions for more specialized audiences can be enlivened with examples from popular journals.

Academic Journals

AUDIENCE: Researchers, scholars, specialists

WRITERS: Experts or specialists in a field or discipline, whose credentials are often provided and who are usually not paid for writing.

FORMAT: If articles contain illustrations, charts, tables, or maps, it is usually because they directly support the articles' arguments.

LANGUAGE: Uses the specialized language of a field or discipline

REVIEW: Reviewers who are recognized experts in the field review the articles, for no pay.

BIBLIOGRAPHY: Articles end with a list of works cited (and/or contain footnotes) to document the research performed by the writer so that readers can check the sources.

WHEN TO USE: When you want to show readers that your arguments are as well informed as possible, draw on the research in academic journals.

KINDS OF SOURCES, KINDS OF RESEARCH
CHOOSING SOURCES— **WEBPAGES**

Just as there are many kinds of books, there many kinds of webpages.

Because there are so many kinds of webpages, and because webpages can be published by anyone with design abilities and access to hardware and a server, it is often hard to judge webpages' potential to support your research. On these next pages, we provide strategies for recognizing kinds of webpages as well as considering what kind of webpage might be appropriate to support the arguments you are making.

As always, keep in mind that—as with any source—the appropriateness of a webpage for supporting your argument depends on the argument you are making, the audience to whom you are making the argument, and your context. The most important question you can ask yourself in considering whether to use a source is **"Will the audience to whom I am writing see the makers of this website as authoritative on the issues with which I am concerned?"** (Keep in mind, though, that sometimes you will use sources to show how the opinions and ideas of some writers are not well argued or well supported.)

→ For ideas on judging the relevance and credibility of websites, see pages 130–143.

Personal Websites and Blogs

These present the very personal opinions of individuals who may or may not have credentials to write on a particular topic.

AUDIENCE: General public or people interested in the particular topic addressed by the website or blog

WRITERS: Such websites can be produced by anyone with at least minimal technical understanding and access to a computer and the appropriate software.

APPEARANCE: Such websites can look amateurish or completely professional; they may or may not have ads. Look at the URL to see if the website is sponsored by a company or organization.

LANGUAGE: Nontechnical, informal

REVIEW: No one reviews this information except the writer.

BIBLIOGRAPHY: Writings can be accompanied by listings of sources or links to supporting webpages.

WHEN TO USE: If the writer is an authority on the topic you are researching and your audience is likely to have heard of the person, you can use the writings to support claims you make—but you will probably also want to offer other support. If the writer is unknown to you, it is probably a good idea to use the person's opinions only as illustration of opinions people might hold on your topic.

Group Blogs

Several people who care about similar issues can agree to work on a blog together; each contributes individual entries.

AUDIENCE: Because group blogs are usually on a shared set of interests, the audience is people interested in those issues.

WRITERS: Because these writers want to be read, they are usually careful to choose each other on the quality of their knowledge and writing.

APPEARANCE: Group blogs tend to be carefully presented so that their appearance encourages others to take the blog seriously. Advertising on the blog can indicate that the blog is taken seriously enough that others want to advertise there, or it can mean the writers are trying to make money. Academic group blogs rarely have advertising.

LANGUAGE: The writing indicates the audience the blog wants to attract: Is it academic, or conversational, or…?

REVIEW: Because writers for these blogs want to be read and care about the reputation of the blog, they often discuss with each other the quality of the writing.

BIBLIOGRAPHY: Writings can be accompanied by listings of sources or links to supporting webpages.

WHEN TO USE: If the writers are well respected in their fields or disciplines, citing their opinions can support your writing—but keep in mind that when you are writing an academic paper, citing a blog will not have as much authority as citing an article published in a journal.

---

boingboing
A DIRECTORY OF WONDERFUL THINGS

suggest a link | defeat censorware | rss | archives
podcast feed | mark | cory | david | xeni | john

Search Boin

WEDNESDAY, MARCH 28, 2007

Stasi chief was an Orwell fan, bent reality to get room 101

Erich Mielke, the head of the East German secret police, was a great Orwell's novel 1984, and desperately wanted his office to be in the location of the torture chamber in the novel). His office was on floor. So he renamed the first floor the mezzanine.

"I'd long been fascinated by George Orwell's work, but I re reading 1984 until I finished the manuscript for Stasiland devoured it, and I couldn't believe Orwell's prescience. W into Mielke's office, I saw it had the number 101, which number of the torture chamber. 1984 was banned in th course, Mielke and Honecker had access to banned m told me that Mielke wanted this number so much tha office was on the 2nd floor, he had the entire first fl Mezzanine so that he could call his room 101."

--Anna Funder, author of Stasiland

Link
posted by Cory Doctorow at 05:23:11 PM permalink | blogs' comm

White House subpoena evaders put nationa

OUT OF THE
CROOKED TIMBER
OF HUMANITY, NO STRAIGHT THING WAS EVER MADE.

« Gnomewatch | Main | Bookstores again »

The White Tyger
Posted by Henry

I blogged a while back about Paul Park's "A Princess of Roum which was the first in a series of four fantasy novels. I recentl finished the third in the series, The White Tyger (Powells, A which is just as wonderful. The novels are profoundly chara in a way that few genre novels are; they deliberately and sp refuse to conform to a conventional quest narrative. None characters know exactly what they're supposed to do; all to a greater or lesser extent, making it up as they go alor main protagonists (and some of the minor ones) are in s another *doubled*; their selves are split in two so that th difficulty in explaining their motivations to themselve: less a conventional fantasy story in which the story is characters, determining who they are and what they working through of the ways that individuals make fantasies, spinning out *ex post* narratives to explain themselves and others. The main protagonists don

This is most fully drawn out in the character of th Ceaucescu, who sees herself as the heroine of an

---

we?
tram ∞
bérubé ∞
righouse ∞
Davies ∞
Farrell ∞
a Farrell ∞
er Hargittai ∞
ran Healy ∞
in Holbo ∞
cott McLemee ∞
on Mandle ∞
Montagu Norman ∞
John Quiggin ∞
Ingrid Robeyns ∞
Belle Waring ∞
Brian Weatherson ∞

Guest Bloggers ∞
Click on the ∞ symbol next to a name for a list of all of that author"s posts.

Corporate Websites and Blogs

These present information about and opinions provided by companies. The companies can be large or very, very small.

AUDIENCE: General public, consumers, people interested in the particular topic addressed by the website or blog

WRITERS: Employees of the company or freelancers

APPEARANCE: Such websites can look amateurish or completely professional, depending on the ethos the company wishes to present and the resources they wish to put toward development. Well-established companies will have their name in their URL. The company name and contact information should be somewhere on the main page.

LANGUAGE: The language will reflect the company's purposes: It might be friendly and informal, to appeal to potential clients or customers; it might be formal, to show the company's solidity and authority.

REVIEW: Corporate webpages might be reviewed by lawyers to protect the company from lawsuits; otherwise, the content is provided and approved only by the company itself.

BIBLIOGRAPHY: Writings can be accompanied by listings of sources or links to supporting webpages.

WHEN TO USE: Because such websites are usually promotional, the information you find on them will rarely be useful for supporting arguments, unless you are writing about the company itself or using the company's website as an example of how companies operate.

Nonprofit Websites

According to the Internal Revenue Service, an organization is nonprofit if its income does not go to stockholders, directors, or anyone else connected with the organization; instead, its income supports only the work the organization does. A nonprofit's URL usually ends in **.org***.*

AUDIENCE: Anyone interested in the work done by the organization, perhaps to donate or to learn more about the organization.

WRITERS: The website might be composed by an employee of the organization or by someone hired to represent the organization.

APPEARANCE: Organizations try to present themselves as competent and dependable in order to gain support from those who see the site.

LANGUAGE: Generally, nontechnical, informal language for general audiences

REVIEW: The organization approves what is on the website.

BIBLIOGRAPHY: Writings can be accompanied by listings of sources or links to supporting webpages.

WHEN TO USE: Generally, the facts and statistics you find on the websites of nonprofit organizations are reliable—although remember that organizations want to present information that supports their purposes. It is always useful to find additional supporting information. (You can always use an organization's description of itself in your writing when you want readers to know about an organization.)

Government Websites

*U.S. government website URLs usually end in **.gov**. State websites end with the two-letter abbreviation for the state followed by **.gov**.*

AUDIENCE: General public as well as specialists looking for information the government compiles

WRITERS: The website might be composed by a government employee or by someone hired as a freelancer.

APPEARANCE: The look of government websites will tell you whether the site has been designed for general-audience or specialist use.

LANGUAGE: The language of government websites can range from friendly and informal to highly technical, depending on the intended audience.

REVIEW: Governmental websites are supposed to adhere to accessibility, writing, and navigational policies established within agencies as well as across some agencies.

BIBLIOGRAPHY: Writings can be accompanied by listings of sources or links to supporting webpages.

WHEN TO USE: Use government websites when you want to give statistics or the wording of policies. Because claims made about science or social research can be shaped for political ends, use such claims in your writing only if you can back them up with support from disinterested parties whom your readers will trust.

Online Periodicals

Distinguish among online periodicals just as you would among print periodicals, as on pages 48–49.

AUDIENCE: Depending on the periodical, the audience can be general or highly specialized, academic or popular.

WRITERS: If the periodical is an online version of a print periodical, then the writers for both versions are usually the same people. Online-only journals can have paid writers or volunteer writers.

APPEARANCE: Such websites can look amateurish or completely professional, depending on the organization behind them and their purpose.

LANGUAGE: The language will depend on the audience and purpose.

REVIEW: Online versions of print periodicals tend to have the same review policies as the print version. Academic periodicals will generally have some sort of review policy for articles; look on the website to find out. For other periodicals, the website might include such policies.

BIBLIOGRAPHY: Academic periodicals will provide sources and ways to find those sources; other periodicals may or may not provide sources.

WHEN TO USE: Use each kind of periodical as you would use its print counterpart, as described on pages 48–49.

Databases of Journals

Through your school library, you probably have access to these databases, which are like search engines into collections of periodicals: You enter terms for topics of interest to you, and the database returns to you listings of articles in which those terms appear. Databases are usually specialized. Each database provides access to a particular subject, such as medicine, law, literature and the arts, newspapers, or engineering.

AUTHORITY: Unless you are writing about databases, you are not going to be citing databases; you will instead be using them to find periodical articles that help you think about your writing or that support your points.

Because of this, the authority of databases is not an issue to consider in your use of them.

WHEN TO USE: Any time you want to find a generally credible range of articles to help you think about your topic or to support your claims, use online databases of journals.

→ See pages 64–71 for more information on using databases.

Image published with permission of ProQuest LLC. Further reproduction is prohibited without permission.

Online Reference Works

These can be online versions of print reference works or reference works created only to be online.

AUTHORITY: The information and thus authority of these sites is the same as that of print reference sources.

WHEN TO USE: Generally, make only limited use of reference works: They are best used for giving a quick fact or an authoritative definition of a term. Readers of academic research papers expect you to use a range of sources, but they especially expect you to use specialized sources primarily.

Online Reference Works—Wikipedia

Wikipedia is a particular kind of online reference, developed by volunteers who write on topics of interest to them and who edit each other's entries. Teachers consider Wikipedia use to be controversial because the entries can be shaped by nonspecialists; because there are no easy ways to check the authority and accuracy of any particular entry; and because the ease of using Wikipedia sometimes encourages writers not to seek further support for their arguments.

WHEN TO USE: Wikipedia is useful in the early stages of research, when you are looking for quick and preliminary information to help you learn how others think about a topic—just as you can use Google or any general encyclopedia. In addition, your audience (including your teacher) will probably not object if you use Wikipedia as the source for the definition of a term in your writing.

When you are ready to research a topic in depth, Wikipedia can help you go deeper because many entries include good listings of further resources—but citing Wikipedia in a Works Cited listing shows readers that you have probably done only quick and dirty research.

FINDING SOURCES

SEARCHING

You've determined that a scholarly journal article, oral history, or some census statistics ought to help you learn enough to turn your narrowed topic into a statement of purpose. Finding the sources you need means that you have to understand the way sources are cataloged, no matter the kind of source.

Prior to the Internet, libraries had card catalogs for their materials. For every book, journal, map, or governmental record kept in a library there was a small card that listed the object's title, author, date, and place of publication; a few keywords about the object's topic; and a general subject area into which the object's contents fit.

Now, instead of those cards, library objects have associated online records in databases, which carry the information that used to be on the cards. The library computer system provides a webpage into which you type search terms; the database compares your search terms to all the terms listed in the database records and then shows you any matches.

Online search engines that give you access to sources outside of libraries **look** at webpages of all kinds and develop their own database records for those pages, based on what words are on the page or in its code. When you use a search engine, it compares your search terms to its database and shows you the matches.

Both processes are similar, and both require that you know how to generate search terms that will help you find useful sources.

BE SPECIFIC

Having a narrowed topic will help you find sources that specifically address your questions.

It is useless to enter one word into a search engine. Try two words and then three: *cars fuel* or *cars ethanol*—and then *cars alternate fuels*.

In library catalogs and databases, you can enter the key terms from your narrowed topic; you can also enter any synonyms for those terms.

In search engines like Google, you can enter the key terms from your narrowed topic—but you can also enter a question such as "Does ethanol provide better mileage than a hybrid car?" and receive the most focused information possible from the websites to which Google has access. Use the research questions you generated for such searches.

→ See page 73 to help you with this.

TRY ALTERNATE TERMS

If you cannot readily think up synonyms for the key terms of your narrowed topic, use a thesaurus, or ask someone else what other terms come to mind for your topic. The more terms you can use, the more likely you are to find helpful sources.

ASK FOR HELP

Teachers, librarians, and people in your class who seem to be good at searching are usually happy to help.

CHECK THE SEARCH ENGINE'S HELP TIPS

All search engines—the library's online catalog, a library database, or a general search engine—have a link to help or usage tips. Read this information so that you can take advantage of the particular features of a search engine.

USE A FAMILIAR SEARCH ENGINE TO FIND SOURCES YOU CAN THEN CHECK IN A MORE SPECIALIZED SEARCH ENGINE

Library joural databases can have confusing interfaces; many people, including faculty, use Google to find a source and then check to see if it's in their library. For example, you might find through Google an academic article exactly on your topic. You can then enter into your library's journal database the journal name, author, and date to have access to a full-text version of the journal. (Similarly, some researchers use Amazon.com to find books because they can usually read some of the book and check reviews. If the book looks useful, they will then see if their library has it. This is useful only for recently published books.)

PERSIST

The more creative you are with your terms and the longer you search during this stage, the more information you will find that pushes you to weigh differing opinions. This sort of thinking leads to writing others want to read.

LIBRARY RESEARCH

USING LIBRARY INDEXES

If you think information you need will be in a print source that was published before the rise of networked computers (or, roughly, before the early 1990s), then you are likely to be successful with the print indexes in your library for journal articles, newspapers, and books in several subject areas. A reference librarian can help you find the appropriate index.

TIP: GET TO KNOW A REFERENCE LIBRARIAN

Reference librarians know a tremendous amount about different kinds of sources and how to find them, in print and online. Whenever you have research questions, ask your librarian.

You can help your librarian help you if you have specific questions. "I need some statistics about how many manufacturing jobs have been lost in the U.S. in the past 10 years. What are the best places you can suggest for finding that information?" will help the librarian find you useful and specific information. "I want to learn something about job loss in the U.S." is less likely to do so.

USING LIBRARY CATALOGS

Most library catalogs have similar features to the one below. The features may show up in different places on-screen or in checkboxes instead of pop-up menus—but they will work in the same way. To prepare to use such a catalog, be sure you have a focused set of search terms, as we describe on page 61.

Pop-up menus

These pop-up menus allow you to choose how you want to search for a source. You can search using just a word or phrase or just the subject, or you can combine searches, looking for a periodical title and a word or phrase together.

Search selection

If your campus is part of a system of schools or has multiple libraries, this option allows you to search within just one of the available libraries.

Choose a language

If you are searching for a source in a specific language, this option allows you to choose from a range of available languages.

Choose your source

With this option you can choose to search specifically for a book, magazine, map, poster, or for any other type of source the library has.

Select the location of your search

This library has different archives and collections; the *location* option allows you to search within one specific location or across all of them.

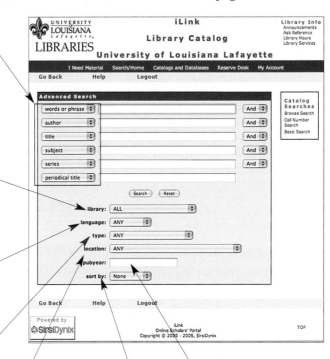

Sort the search results

This option allows you to see the search results sorted by year, author name, or title.

Select the time period of your search

If you are searching for sources from a specific year or range of years, enter that information here.

USING LIBRARY JOURNAL DATABASES

Most scholarly journals and popular periodicals are now online—and most are not accessible through Google. Different companies provide online access to these publications through subscription services; your college library subscribes to some of these services. Different subscription services give access to databases in different disciplinary areas. For example, some services provide access only to engineering or only to humanities databases.

These databases often provide only basic bibliographic information for a source—the article title, author's name(s), date and place of publication, and journal or periodical name—and an abstract giving a brief description of the source. Once you find this information, you have to find out if your library has a subscription to the journal or periodical so that you can see the full article.

More frequently, however, these databases are providing full-text versions of journal articles and periodicals that you can read online.

STEPS IN USING DATABASES

1 Find the database search page on your library website.

2 Choose a database to search.

3 Use the database's search features to find references to relevant articles.

4 Choose the references that seem the most relevant.

5 Once you decide on the most relevant references, get hold of the articles.

1 FINDING THE DATABASE SEARCH PAGE ON YOUR LIBRARY WEBSITE

On the main page of your school library's webpage will be some sort of link to the databases. There may be an option labeled **Resources for research**, **Indexes and Databases**, or **E-Resources**.

Clicking such a link will take you to a screen where you can choose the database to search, as on page 66.

WHAT IS A DATABASE?

When you have lots of data—journal articles, patient records, sports statistics, census numbers—you need to organize it so that you can find what you need. On computers, databases do this. The data are stored in particular arrangements (for example, journal articles will be stored in records that indicate the title, author, keywords, and so on); the database software can then use your search terms to find records that match. The database is the collection of data; a database management system is the software that organizes the data and shapes your search. In day-to-day conversation, however, people use *database* to mean both the collection of the data and the software used to access it.

2 CHOOSING A DATABASE TO SEARCH, PART 1

First, it helps to know about some of the more popular databases that (for the most part) give you access to general information. Here are such databases, with short descriptions, to help you decide which might be useful to your research purposes:

ABI/INFORM
(information from 1971 to the present)
This database covers U.S. and international business and management topics, with information on 60,000 companies.

AH SEARCH
(information from 1984 to the present)
This is an index to more than 1,150 arts and humanities journals and over 7,000 science and social sciences journals.

ALTERNATIVE PRESS INDEX ARCHIVES
(information from 1969 to 1990)
This is the archives for the AH Search database, and includes book, film, and television reviews, obituaries, and bibliographic information as well as articles.

CSA ILLUMINA
This is a database of other databases, giving you access to more than 100 full-text and bibliographic databases in the arts and humanities, natural sciences, social sciences, and technology.

EXPANDED ACADEMIC ASAP
(information from 1980 to the present)
This database covers subject areas in the humanities, technology, social sciences, and sciences, with full-text articles available. The database includes scholarly journals, news magazines, and newspapers.

FIRSTSEARCH
This database searches a wide variety of other databases, giving you access to educational, literary, medical, and religious topics; Latin American journals; government publications; conference proceedings; and the *World Almanac*.

JSTOR
JSTOR gives access to academic journals (dating back to 1665 in one case) in the areas of arts and sciences; health, biology, and general science; and business. (Your library may not subscribe to all the areas JSTOR covers.)

LEXISNEXIS ACADEMIC
This database provides full-text access to news, business, legal, and reference information.

PSYCFIRST
(information from 2002 to the present)
This database gives you access to citations and abstracts about worldwide research in psychology and related fields.

TIP: WHEN TO USE THESE DATABASES IN YOUR RESEARCH
The scholarly sources to which these databases can give you access are focused, detailed, and scholarly. These sources carry considerable authority for readers, but they also require effort on your part to find and to read. These sources will therefore be most useful to you when you have a solid, narrowed topic or statement of purpose to shape your searching.

⟶ See Part 3 on statements of purpose.

CHOOSING A DATABASE TO SEARCH, PART 2

Because there are hundreds of databases, your first step in working with the databases to which your library subscribes will probably involve a webpage that looks like the one below, which helps you choose among available databases. (The screen below comes from Michigan Technological University's Van Pelt Library website.)

Your college library's page for searching databases may not have all the features of the page shown below, but it will be similar.

Such a screen gives you many options for finding databases useful to you, as the callouts below indicate.

If you know the name of the database you want

Type its name in the *Search for Databases* box, or use the alphabetic search option to access it.

If you are new to using databases, or are searching in a new subject area, start here

These pop-up menus (which might be checkboxes on other webpages) give you access to lists of databases chosen because of their relevance to specific subject areas. Look at the list of subjects, and choose the one (or two) in which your topic best fits. (On the next pages, we show you what to do next.)

If you have some familiarity with popular databases

These are links to some of the most used databases. (Some of these are described on page 65.)

Search for Databases

☑ Title ☑ Description (Go!)

Databases A-Z

New   All | A B C D E F G H I J K L M N O P Q R S T U V W X Y Z

Database Quick Links

- ABI/Inform
- CSA Illumina
- Compendex
- ENGnetBASE
- FirstSearch
- IEEE *Xplore*
- JSTOR
- LexisNexis
- Thomson Gale
- Web of Science
- WorldCat

Search by Subject Headings | Browse All Subject Headings

1st Subject (Agriculture, Forestry & Environmental Science ⬍)
AND
2nd Subject (* (use only first subject) ⬍) (Go!)
(To narrow your search select a 2nd subject heading)

Search by Providers | Browse All Providers

(American Chemical Society (ACS) ⬍) (Go!)

CHOOSING A DATABASE TO SEARCH, PART 3

If you are researching a geographic topic, for example, you may find that the **Database Quick Links** databases listed in the dialogue box to the left don't get you what you need; in such a case, choose **Geography** from the **Search by Subject Heading** option on the screen shown to the left.

Below is the result of such a choice. This is a list of the databases to which this library subscribes that will most likely help you find geographic information.

How do you choose which databases to search?

Read the descriptions of the databases' scope

Look for descriptions that seem most focused in your area of interest. Below, the descriptions of scope suggest that GEOBASE, ScienceDirect, and Web of Science might be the best places to start.

Which databases give you full-text access?

Full text means that you will see the article online and not just its bibliographic information. If articles do not have full-text access, use the bibliographic information to see if your library has the journal you need; you might need to order it through interlibrary loan.

	Full Text Available Show All	Access Restrictions
Academic OneFile Coverage: 1995 - Present	F	M
Scope: premier source for peer-reviewed, full-text articles from the world's leading journals and reference sources. With extensive coverage of the physical sciences, technology, medicine, social sciences, the arts, theology, literature and other subjects.		
Article1st Coverage: 1990 - Present		M
Scope: contains bibliographic citations for items listed on the table of contents pages of over 12,600 journals in all subject areas.		
GEOBASE Coverage: 1980 - Present		M
Scope: contains citations with abstracts covering worldwide literature in geography, geology, and ecology.		
Google Scholar Coverage: 1900 - Present	F	M
Scope: web search engine designed specifically to locate scholarly literature, including peer-reviewed papers, theses, books, preprints, abstracts and technical reports across broad areas of research. **Access Note:** click here for additional information about Google Scholar. Also if you are coming from off campus you will be asked for your ISO Login and Password. This will grant you full text access to those full text resources that the JRVP library has secured.		
ScienceDirect Coverage: 2003 - Present	F	M
Scope: extensive and unique full-text collection covers authoritative titles from the core scientific literature. ScienceDirect is designed as a basic electronic version of Elsevier Science print allowing you to access full-text articles published since 2003.		
Social Sciences Abstracts Coverage: 1983 - Present		M
Scope: covers periodicals in anthropology, economics, geography, law and criminology, political science, social work, sociology, and international relations.		
Web of Science Coverage: 1973 - Present		M
Scope: offers Web of Science access to ISI Citation Indexes (Science Citation Index Expanded, Social Sciences Citation Index and Arts and Humanities Citation Index), which contains multidisciplinary, high quality research information from the world's leading science, social science and art and humanities journals. **We now have unlimited access to WoS.**		

TIP: **THE EARLY STAGES OF RESEARCH**

Keep in mind that you need to search more than one database when you are in the early stages of research looking for broad background information.

3 USING A DATABASE

Once you have chosen a database to search, you will see on your screen the search tools particular to that database; every database company presents this information somewhat differently.

WHAT DATABASE SEARCH SCREENS USUALLY HAVE IN COMMON
Here is the initial search screen for the LexisNexis database.

Start by entering your search terms

With most database searches, you will probably start by entering your search terms into the text entry box and then clicking *Search*.

Using the database tips

As you become more comfortable with database searches, you can become more fluent by checking out how the database creators recommend you use their search features.

Explore the features of the database

Database search screens can be somewhat visually daunting, in part because they offer researchers so many possible ways to research. As you become more at ease with these sorts of searches, you will make your work and research richer if you take time to explore the features of the databases that most tie to your interests.

Searching databases that give you access to other databases

Sometimes, when you choose a database following the advice we've given in step 2, you will come to a screen like the one below; this screen shows that you have chosen a database that gives you access to still other databases. These other databases tend to be focused and specialized.

To use a screen like this, look over the databases that are listed just as you would in step 2. Choose those databases that look most relevant to your topic. When you click **Continue to Search**, you will come to a screen similar to the one shown at left, where you can enter your search terms.

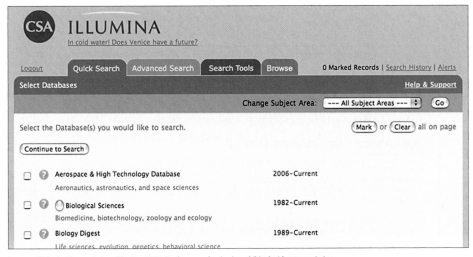

Image published with permission of ProQuest LLC. Further reproduction is prohibited without permission.

TIP: FINE-TUNING DATABASE SEARCHES

Just about every database search screen will give you a choice between a **Quick Search** and an **Advanced Search**. In **Quick Search**, you simply enter your search terms. In **Advanced Search**, you will have some set of options: You might be able to specify that the database search for articles only from within the last five years or from twenty years ago; you might be able to specify very specific subject areas for the search, or that you want only full-text searches or searches in a specific language.

Such fine-tuning can help reduce your search time if you know you need such specific information.

4 CHOOSING THE REFERENCES THAT SEEM MOST RELEVANT

After you have entered your search terms into a database search screen and clicked **Search**, you will see a screen like the one below (each database will look slightly different). This is the list of articles in the database that match your search terms.

Understanding the search results

This search was made by someone looking into recent cultural notions of beauty and the ways they affect how women think about themselves. This information shows that this researcher used the search terms **beauty** and **culture**, and was looking for articles published between 1995 and 2007. (Note that there were 4,017 matches—an indication that this search could be narrowed even more.)

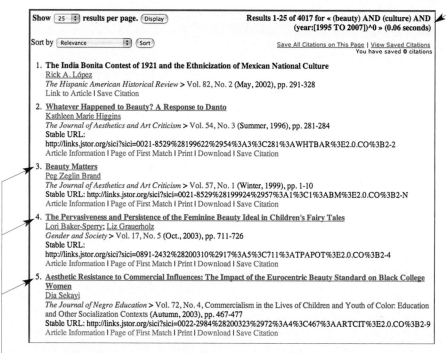

Show 25 results per page. (Display)

Results 1-25 of 4017 for « (beauty) AND (culture) AND (year:[1995 TO 2007])^0 » (0.06 seconds)

Sort by Relevance (Sort)

Save All Citations on This Page I View Saved Citations
You have saved **0** citations

1. **The India Bonita Contest of 1921 and the Ethnicization of Mexican National Culture**
   Rick A. López
   The Hispanic American Historical Review > Vol. 82, No. 2 (May, 2002), pp. 291-328
   Link to Article I Save Citation

2. **Whatever Happened to Beauty? A Response to Danto**
   Kathleen Marie Higgins
   The Journal of Aesthetics and Art Criticism > Vol. 54, No. 3 (Summer, 1996), pp. 281-284
   Stable URL:
   http://links.jstor.org/sici?sici=0021-8529%28199622%2954%3A3%3C281%3AWHTBAR%3E2.0.CO%3B2-2
   Article Information I Page of First Match I Print I Download I Save Citation

3. **Beauty Matters**
   Peg Zeglin Brand
   The Journal of Aesthetics and Art Criticism > Vol. 57, No. 1 (Winter, 1999), pp. 1-10
   Stable URL: http://links.jstor.org/sici?sici=0021-8529%28199924%2957%3A1%3C1%3ABM%3E2.0.CO%3B2-N
   Article Information I Page of First Match I Print I Download I Save Citation

4. **The Pervasiveness and Persistence of the Feminine Beauty Ideal in Children's Fairy Tales**
   Lori Baker-Sperry; Liz Grauerholz
   Gender and Society > Vol. 17, No. 5 (Oct., 2003), pp. 711-726
   Stable URL:
   http://links.jstor.org/sici?sici=0891-2432%28200310%2917%3A5%3C711%3ATPAPOT%3E2.0.CO%3B2-4
   Article Information I Page of First Match I Print I Download I Save Citation

5. **Aesthetic Resistance to Commercial Influences: The Impact of the Eurocentric Beauty Standard on Black College Women**
   Dia Sekayi
   The Journal of Negro Education > Vol. 72, No. 4, Commercialism in the Lives of Children and Youth of Color: Education and Other Socialization Contexts (Autumn, 2003), pp. 467-477
   Stable URL: http://links.jstor.org/sici?sici=0022-2984%28200323%2972%3A4%3C467%3AARTCIT%3E2.0.CO%3B2-9
   Article Information I Page of First Match I Print I Download I Save Citation

Three promising articles

Given this researcher's purposes, these three articles look promising. He won't know for sure until he looks at the full articles, but the titles of these three suggest that they will address his concerns. (Number 2 looks as though it was written specifically in response to another article, and so won't be useful.) Note that these are not the first articles in the list; note also that there are 4,012 more articles to consider. How would you narrow this search?

5 GETTING THE ARTICLE, ONCE YOU FIND A RELEVANT REFERENCE

- The database listing to the left is from a full-text database; clicking any of the links will take you to the listed article, which you can then read.
- Sometimes, however, you will get a listing like the one below, which has no link to access a full-text version.

A listing with no link to a full text version

In such cases, look for links like these, which allow you to see if your library carries the journal from which this article comes and, in case your library doesn't, to see other libraries that have the journal. (If your library does not carry the journal, you will need to use your library's interlibrary loan service; ask a librarian for help with this if you've never used this before.)

Availability:	**Check the catalogs in your library.** • <u>Libraries worldwide that own item</u>: 347 • 📖 <u>Search the catalog at J Robert Van Pelt</u>
Author(s):	<u>Charles, S</u> **Reprint Address:** Charles, S; Univ Sherbrooke, Sherbrooke, PQ J1K 2R1, Canada **Research Address:** Univ Sherbrooke, Sherbrooke, PQ J1K 2R1, Canada
Title:	**The meaning of beauty. From its origins to modern culture**
Source:	*DIALOGUE-CANADIAN PHILOSOPHICAL REVIEW* 40, no. 2 (SPR 2001): 416-419 **Additional Info:** CANADIAN PHILOSOPHICAL ASSOC: MORISSET HALL #375, UNIV OTTAWA, OTTAWA, ONTARIO K1N 6N5, CANADA
Standard No:	**ISSN:** 0012-2173
Language:	French
Reviewed Item:	**Author:** Ferry, L **Publication:** 1998 **Language:** French
References:	**Number:** 1
	SUBJECT(S)
Journal Subject:	PHILOSOPHY -- H UA
Cited Reference:	FURRY, L, 1998, SENS BEAU ORIGINES C
Article Type:	Book Review
Accession No:	000169393900022
Database:	AHSearch

TIPS: **WORKING WITH DATABASES**

- As with all research, database work takes time. You will need to try more than one database, performing variations on your basic search in each. Have patience, and look for the sources that expand your thinking on your topic.
- When you use an article from a database in your writing, you cite it differently from articles you find in a journal on the library shelf.

➡ See pages 346–347.

FINDING SOURCES
ONLINE RESEARCH

SEARCH ENGINES AND SEARCH DIRECTORIES

Search engines work because they access large databases of websites, which have been collected by automated programs called **spiders** or **robots**. The websites are indexed: The words and phrases they contain are compiled into lists that are structured for easy computer searching.

When you enter your search terms, the search engine compares your terms to its indexes, and returns to you a list of websites containing your terms.

Search directories are similar to search engines because each compiles databases of websites—but a directory lists or searches through only the sites that have been inspected for their relevance.

Because each search engine or directory has been designed to search the Web differently, and to index its terms differently, different search tools can return differing results for the same search terms—so you are more likely to find helpful information by using more than one search tool.

RESOURCES FOR KEEPING TRACK OF YOUR ONLINE RESEARCH
—and for taking advantage of other people's searches
If you do lots of online searches and have not yet learned about furl *<http://www.furl.com>* or del.icio.us *<http://del.icio.us>*, check them out. Each site works a little differently, but each gives you ways to save and organize links that matter to you.

In addition, each site gives you ways to search other people's collections of website links on topics related to yours; by looking at how others have labeled—or **tagged**—their finds, you can also learn new terms to use for further searching.

You are probably familiar with Google and Yahoo!, which are generalized search tools, but also check these tools, designed to aid academic searches:

INFOMINE: SCHOLARLY INTERNET RESOURCE COLLECTIONS
<http://infomine.ucr.edu/>
Infomine is constructed by college and university librarians to be a library of resources specifically for college and university students and faculty. Infomine links you to databases, electronic books and journals, and other useful resources.

ACADEMIC INDEX
<http://www.academicindex.net/>
A librarian developed this search tool, which searches through databases of information on topics of academic interest and quality, compiled or recommended by librarians, teachers, and researchers.

LIBRARIANS' INTERNET INDEX
<http://www.lii.org/>
This is a publicly funded directory, which also sends out a free weekly newsletter of websites; the online directory and newsletter websites are chosen and organized by librarians.

TIPS: USING ONLINE SEARCH TOOLS

- *Use more than one search engine.* Because each search engine is designed to search the Web differently than others, different search engines give different results for the same search terms—so you are more likely to find helpful information by searching in different engines.

- Most search engines have both *a simple search*—where you enter a few search terms—and *an advanced search*, where you can specify date ranges, the kind of file you want (html, pdf, or doc), or that the search results be only webpages containing noncopyrighted information. When you have a narrowed topic or know you need information from 1995, for example, using these features saves time. Explore these features in your favorite search engine so that—when you have a very focused search to carry out—you know what is possible.

- Many search engines will allow you to carry out what is called a *boolean search*. George Boole, a nineteenth-century mathematician, developed ways for thinking logically about how terms interact. His system has been taken up in computer searches, in which you can use the words AND, OR, NOT, and XOR (always in capital letters) to help narrow your search.

  If you are researching the Buddhist concept of Nirvana, you could enter these terms so as not to be deluged with returns about music: *Nirvana AND Buddhism NOT Cobain*

  To search once with synonyms instead of doing two searches: *women AND workplace OR office*

  Be sure to check the advanced search features of the search engine you are using for its particular approach to boolean searches.

ONLINE REFERENCES

There is a wide range of online reference materials on all subjects. Your library will probably have an online listing of all kinds of reference materials, longer than what we can include here. Here are links to some widely used sources:

BARTLEBY.COM
<http://www.bartleby.com/>
Bartleby.com gives you searchable access to dictionaries, quotations, thesauruses, usage and style references, and literature and poetry.

THE INTERNET MOVIE DATABASE
<http://us.imdb.com/>
If you are discussing a movie, this database provides you with information about the actors, directors, and writers and gives you links to reviews.

ONELOOK
<http://www.onelook.com/>
This website gives you access to over 900 dictionaries.

PERRY-CASTAÑEDA MAP COLLECTION
<http://www.lib.utexas.edu/maps/ map_sites/map_sites.html>
The library of the University of Texas at Austin has produced this long list of links to all kinds of maps.

STATISTICAL RESOURCES ON THE WEB
<http://www.lib.umich.edu/govdocs/ stats.html>
The library of the University of Michigan maintains this very valuable website of links to sites that track statistics about the environment, housing, the cost of living, and education, among many other topics.

WIKIPEDIA
<http://en.wikipedia.org/wiki/Main_Page>
Wikipedia is an online encyclopedia written and edited by users who wish to contribute their knowledge. This is a controversial website for teachers precisely because anyone can edit and contribute. Wikipedia is a good place to start research, when you are composing to learn: It can be a quite accurate source that gives you deeper openings into a topic. You should always check with your teacher to learn his or her position on this source. In general, however, know that using Wikipedia as a source in an academic paper will not give your paper the authority you probably want it to have—and using Wikipedia as your only source is a sure way to show readers that you have not done appropriate research.

ONLINE NEWSPAPERS

ONLINENEWSPAPERS.COM
<http://www.onlinenewspapers.com/>
This website, out of Australia, gives you access to hundreds of newspapers around the world (many in English).

ONLINE ARCHIVES
→ See pages 76–77.

GOVERNMENT SOURCES

Every government agency has a website, so if you are looking for educational or agricultural information, for example, check the websites of the Department of Education or the Department of Agriculture. Keep in mind that some of the information is shaped by the political ends of the current administration.

THE U.S. CENSUS BUREAU
<http://www.census.gov/>
The Census Bureau compiles a wide range of statistics on the U.S. population and economic systems.

MEDLINE PLUS
<http://www.nlm.nih.gov/medlineplus/>
The U.S. National Library of Medicine and the National Institutes of Health provide this nonspecialist information on health and medical issues. The site also provides a medical dictionary and encyclopedia.

THOMAS
<http://thomas.loc.gov/>
This website helps you search for U.S. government legislative information such as what is happening in Congress and its bills and resolutions.

THE WORLD FACTBOOK
<https://www.cia.gov/library/publications/ the-world-factbook/index.html>
The U.S. Central Intelligence Agency regularly updates this website of information about every country in the world. You can learn about a country's population, geography, government, and so on.

PHOTOGRAPHIC AND OTHER VISUAL RESOURCES

Many museums have collections of photographs; many U.S. government agencies also have collections of photographs. For example, check the NASA Image Exchange *<http://nix.nasa.gov/>* or the National Oceanic and Atmospheric Administration's Photo Library *<http://www.photolib.noaa.gov/>*.

NYPL DIGITAL
<http://www.nypl.org/digital/>
The New York Public Library offers this resource of "520,000 images... including illuminated manuscripts, historical maps, vintage posters, rare prints, photographs, illustrated books, and printed ephemera."

PRINTS AND PHOTOGRAPHS ONLINE
<http://www.loc.gov/rr/print/catalog.html>
This website is part of the U.S. Library of Congress. Many of the visual materials available here—posters, photographs, maps, magazines—are copyright free, but you need to check.

WIKIPEDIA: PUBLIC DOMAIN IMAGE RESOURCES
<http://en.wikipedia.org/wiki/ Wikipedia:Public_domain_image_resources>
This webpage contains a long, categorized list of online photographs and other visual text.

→ To cite photographs and other visual texts in your writing, see pages 398–402.

ARCHIVAL AND SPECIAL LIBRARY COLLECTION SOURCES

SPECIAL LIBRARY COLLECTIONS

Duke University has special collections related to women's history and culture, to African and African American Documentation, and to the history of sales, advertising, and marketing. Haverford College has special collections of materials related to the Quakers. The University of Idaho and the University of Utah have special collections on the history of their states.

Check your library's website to see what special collections it holds.

PHYSICAL ARCHIVES

Archives store documents of historic interest such as letters, diaries, newspapers, sermons, and postcards. Archives can store the documents of a town or county, a church or synagogue, or a person or family; they can be about labor history or African American music.

Many small museums, historical organizations, and libraries have archives of local materials. Some archives collect materials related to the life of a political or literary figure who was from or lived in the area.

To find archives in your area, look in the phone book under **Historical Organizations** and **Museums**.

To learn about archives at your university, check the library website, which will list the library's collections.

Archival research can be captivating: Holding a pioneer woman's diary from the 1860s will give you an exciting sense of differences in lives then and now—and using the diary's words in your writing will give your writing life and authority.

VIRTUAL ARCHIVES

Many physical archives have digitized their materials and made them available online. (If you use a virtual archive, keep in mind that digitization is time-consuming and costly; an archive may have only a small portion of its collection online, so you may still want to try to visit the physical archive if possible.) Each archive will have its own system for searching its collection. Individual archives might also tell you how they would like to be cited if you use their materials in your work.

Some rich virtual archives are

THE INTERNET ARCHIVE
<http://www.archive.org/index.php>
This is an archive of video, music, sound, and texts.

THE LIBRARY OF CONGRESS'S AMERICAN MEMORY PROJECT
<http://memory.loc.gov/ammem/index.html>
This collection gives you access to "written and spoken words, sound recordings, still and moving images, prints, maps, and sheet music that document the American experience."

THE NATIONAL ARCHIVES OF THE UNITED STATES
<http://www.archives.gov/research/arc/education/>
The Archives have a tremendous collection of materials (primarily government related) about this country. You have to go to the archive to look at most materials, but some are available digitally. If you are carrying out research in genealogical, social, political, or economic areas, check out the archives that have been put in searchable databases: *<http://aad.archives.gov/aad/>*

TIP: FINDING ARCHIVES OUTSIDE YOUR AREA
Go online if historical materials will answer your research questions and there are no useful local archives.

Using your search terms, do at least three searches:
your topic + **archive**
your topic + **special collection**
your topic + **museum**
Try out variations on your topic, too, because you cannot know how websites describe themselves and are cataloged by a search engine.

For example, if you were researching organizational strategies used in the Civil Rights movement, you could do a Google search with the terms **civil rights movement** and **archive**. Among other useful links, this search turns up a link to the "Voices of Freedom" website at Virginia Commonwealth University, where you can listen to a recording of Dr. Joyce E. Glaise speaking about the church's role in organizing.

Keep in mind that such searches may not turn up materials you can access digitally, but may suggest books you can order through your library's interlibrary loan service.

THE UNIVERSITY MUSEUMS AND COLLECTIONS
<http://publicus.culture.hu-berlin.de/umac/>
This is an international database giving access to 150 museums.

→ To cite materials from an archive, see page 375.

FIELD RESEARCH SOURCES

Field research can be performed in more depth than we can describe here. Your teacher or a librarian can help you find further information.

→ See page 110 on evaluating field research.

TIP: GETTING PERMISSION FOR FIELD RESEARCH

Almost all colleges and universities have an Institutional Review Board (IRB), a committee that ensures the proper treatment of those who participate in research studies. Such boards were started to oversee medical and other kinds of technological research, but their responsibility has spread to cover research in the humanities and social sciences.

Every campus's Institutional Review Board will have different policies for field research carried out in writing classes. If you will use the results of your field research only in a classroom paper, it is possible you do not need IRB permission—but the only way to know is to ask your teacher. (If a teacher requires you to do field research, the teacher might have gotten approval for the whole class, or will help you through the process.)

If you think you might do field research on your own, ask your teacher what permissions you need.

INTERVIEWS

You can interview experts on the topic you are researching, people who have lived through an event central to your research, or those who have opinions about your topic.

Here is a sample e-mail for requesting an interview:

Dear Professor/Ms./Mr./Dr. [Name],
For my writing class, I am doing research into [your topic] and would like to interview you, informally, on this topic.

If you are willing, I would need only 30 minutes of your time. I would like to use a tape recorder during the interview.

If an interview is amenable to you, here are several times in the next two weeks when I could come to your office: [list times here].

Sincerely, [your name]

PREPARE FOR AN INTERVIEW
- What would you like to learn from this person? Write down questions that can draw that information out of the person. (You can use the guiding questions for research you developed.)

AT THE INTERVIEW
- Start by thanking the person.
- Explain your research.
- Ask your questions, and don't hesitate to ask other questions that come to you as you listen.
- End with a "Thank you!" Ask if you can contact her or him for clarifications.

AFTERWARD
- Send a thank you e-mail or note.
- Call or e-mail for clarifications.

OBSERVATIONS

If you are researching the effects of video games on social relations among men, you could observe a group of friends playing a game together and then observe a group playing softball, to see if there are differences in how the friends interact. If you are writing about cell phone use among teenagers and adults, you could go the mall and count the percentage of teenagers and the percentage of adults using cell phones.

PREPARE FOR AN OBSERVATION

- Consider where you can observe without others being very aware of you so that they don't change their behavior because of your presence.
- Determine what kinds of actions or behaviors you want to observe and record.
- Determine how you will record what you see. (If you are doing multiple observations, set the same time limit for each one.)

WHILE OBSERVING

- Start your records with the time and date of your observation.

AFTERWARD

- If you have not learned what you thought you would, have you learned something else? Do you need to change your overall purpose, or do you need to do another observation, one set up slightly differently?
- Think about how you will justify your observations to your readers; you will need to include this in your writing.

SURVEYS

Small, focused surveys (the kind you are probably prepared to carry out, instead of state or national surveys) help you learn others' opinions about events or policies.

Small surveys can take two forms (which you can mix):

YES-OR-NO QUESTION SURVEYS

For example: *Do you think there should be a traffic light at the intersection of Bridge and Montezuma Streets?*

- Solicit quick decision making with no room for gray areas.
- Allow for tabulation to make arguments; for example, *Ninety percent of the respondents favor a traffic light.*
- Tend to get more responses because they are quick and easy to take.

OPEN-ENDED QUESTION SURVEYS

For example: *What additional school programs do you think would better prepare elementary school students to use developing technologies?*

- Solicit more thoughtful responses.
- Require interpretation. Sometimes answers group together and sometimes you get a range of very different responses. You will need to present the answers you get with explanations of what you learned.

Before you give your survey, test your questions on a few people to be sure respondents understand the questions and can answer them easily.

Also, consider how many people you need to survey so that your readers will accept that your results are well supported.

WHAT IF YOU CAN'T FIND ANYTHING ON YOUR NARROWED TOPIC?

If you are not finding information on your narrowed topic, there are several possible reasons:

- You have a creative and original topic.
- Your topic might not yet be narrow enough.
- You haven't yet found the right search terms or combination of search terms.
- You haven't yet found the right places to search.
- You have not yet learned how to use search tools comfortably.
- You are not putting in enough time.

IF YOU HAVE A CREATIVE AND ORIGINAL TOPIC

You have a decision to make: find a new topic, or continue searching?

Making effective arguments around creative and original topics is challenging, and can teach you much. You still need to find supporting evidence for the points you want to make, so you have to get creative with finding sources that inform you about the positions of others; you also have to be creative and careful with weaving those sources together into supporting evidence for the position you ultimately take. The following suggestions for generating search terms can still help you.

IT'S POSSIBLE YOUR TOPIC IS NOT YET NARROW ENOUGH

If Google or another search engine returns millions of responses on your topic—none of which seems to address what matters to you—go back to pages 28–33 to work on further narrowing your topic.

IF YOU HAVEN'T YET FOUND THE RIGHT SEARCH TERMS

- Be open to what you find: Remember that, at this stage of producing a research paper, you are trying to gather as much information as you can on a topic. You might need to shift the focus of your topic as you learn what information is available.

- Develop lists of synonyms for your terms. For example, if you are searching the topic of childhood obesity and its relationship to food advertising using cartoon characters, you are going to want to search with different combinations of the following:

  childhood, youth, young
  obesity, overweight, weight
  food, junk, diet, cereal, candy
  advertising, commercials
  cartoons, animation

  To find other words for searching, look for terms people use in the articles and websites you do find; ask others—teachers, librarians, and anyone you know who is good with words or reads a lot—what terms come to mind when you describe your topic.

- Keep track of other terms that come up as you search. In any article or webpage that seems at all close to your concerns, note what terms the authors use to describe your topic, and use those for further searches.

- Try a different search tool. Because each search tool works differently, different search tools will give you different results.

KNOWING IF YOU HAVE FOUND THE RIGHT PLACES TO SEARCH

If you have tried only one search engine or database, you need to try others. If you have tried multiple databases without luck, talk to your teacher or a librarian: They can help you determine other databases that might be fruitful.

But perhaps you are searching online when you need to be interviewing others or looking in an archive. Again, talking to a teacher or librarian about your narrowed topic—and about what you are hoping to learn—can help you find out where to look.

IT'S POSSIBLE YOU ARE NOT USING SEARCH TOOLS COMFORTABLY ENOUGH

If every time you do your research you get frustrated or confused, it is definitely time to make an appointment with your teacher, a librarian, or someone from your campus's Writing (or Learning) Center. Be specific about the help you need: First, describe your narrowed topic and what you are hoping to learn, and then describe the research you have carried out so far. Finally, ask for someone to sit by you while you search, to guide you and give advice.

IT'S POSSIBLE YOU ARE NOT GIVING YOUR RESEARCH ENOUGH TIME

If you expect research to take fifteen minutes or even an hour one night, you are wrong. Effective research requires patience, spread out over hours and days: It takes time to find the information that will help you be smart.

KEEPING TRACK OF SOURCES: Starting a running source list

As you find sources that are useful to you or that contain phrases or sentences that will attract your readers' attention, keep track of both the sources and the quotations. You can do this on paper or online.

Keep all this information in order to produce writing that meets current academic expectations. In the academic world, writers acknowledge the sources from which they draw their ideas and they make it easy for readers to check their sources. There are standard forms for showing this information in a research paper.

→ For information on the forms for documenting sources, see Part 8, pages 307–462.

When you find a source you might use, enter it in a running list, recording the information you need for that kind of source:

→ For a book or part of a book, see pages 328–331 and pages 332–335 for the information you will need.

→ For a newspaper, magazine, or journal article, see pages 336–341.

→ For an article you find in a database, see pages 346–347.

→ For a webpage or website, see pages 342–345.

→ For other kinds of texts, see pages 348–349.

If you think you might quote words from any source, record the words and the pages on which they appear.

→ See pages 316–321 for how to do this with a print source.

→ See pages 342–345 for how to do this with an online source.

HELPING YOURSELF AVOID PLAGIARISM

Because respecting the work of others and therefore acknowledging when you use their work is so important in academic writing, find strategies to keep track of when you copy the words of others. Whenever you copy words off a website into your notes or into a paper, color-code or otherwise mark those words.

→ See pages 144–145 and 308–311 to learn more about plagiarism.

EXAMPLE OF A RUNNING SOURCE LIST

March 22, 2008

"Africa Debt Cancellation -- FAQ." January 2007. American Friends Service Committee. <http://www.afsc.org/africa-debt/learn-about-debt/debt-faq.htm>

"Debt: The Illegitimate Legacy of Continent's Dictators." January 25, 2007. Africa News. LexisNexis. Van Pelt Lib., Houghton, MI <http://library.lib.mtu.edu:2082/universe/document?_m=62be476dbc43903fc53cef9fb438 32d5&wchp=dGLbVzW-zSkVA&_md5= a9cda7d0ad24dda40259c9c16d4ddad1>

Meredith, Martin. The Fate of Africa: A History of Fifty Years of Independence. New York: PublicAffairs, 2006.

TIP: KEEP A PAPER TRAIL

If you have the slightest feeling that you might use a source—to paraphrase or quote—keep track of it. It is awful to finish a paper only to realize you have a quotation whose source you don't remember: Either you have to remove the source from your writing or you have to find it.

TIP: CITE VISUAL SOURCES

If you use visual material made by others—such as charts, graphs, posters, photographs, and so on— you need to document the source.

→ See pages 348–349 for information on citing visual materials.

TIP: ORGANIZE YOUR LINKS

If you don't already know about them, take a look at websites like <www.furl.com> and <del.icio.us> for tracking your online sources. These websites can also help you see the research other people have carried out on your topic.

STARTING A PAPER

The night before she received an assignment to write a research paper, Riley was talking with a friend's mother and learned that, through an online organization, the mother makes small loans to women in other countries to help the women start or develop small businesses. The mother explained that this process of making small loans is called *microcredit* or *microloans* and is often set up to help women who might not otherwise have access to loans.

General topic

When she received her assignment, Riley decided to learn more about microcredit, and started her research.

Some of her initial research work is shown on page 29.

This initial research taught her that microcredit or microloans can also be called *microfinance*, and so she searched with this term as well as the two others. She learned how these small loans were started in Bangladesh in the 1980s and have since spread all over the world—and that such small loans are overwhelmingly made to women.

Narrowing the topic

Riley is curious about why microcredit focuses on women, so she decides to research *women and microcredit in developing countries*.

Questions for research

Based on what she had learned from her initial research, Riley brainstormed questions to guide her further research; the bold questions are those that, at this stage of her research, matter most to her:

QUESTIONS OF FACT
- How and where did microcredit get started?
- How large is a typical loan?
- How do the people who borrow the money pay it back?

QUESTIONS OF CONSEQUENCE
- Why is microcredit necessary?
- Who benefits from microcredit?
- What are negative results of microcredit?
- **How do microloans change women's lives?**

QUESTIONS OF VALUE
- Why are so many people praising microcredit now?
- Why are so many governments encouraging microcredit organizations in their countries?

QUESTIONS OF DEFINITION
- What is microcredit?
- How is it different from other kinds of loans?

QUESTIONS OF INTERPRETATION
- Why did microcredit get started?
- **Why are loans made mostly to women?**

QUESTIONS OF POLICY
- Who decides who will receive microcredit loans?
- What laws or other policies have been enacted to support microcredit?
- What kinds of organizations support microcredit?
- What organizations oppose it?

Choosing sources

From her initial work, Riley realized that her first Google searches were helping her answer questions of fact and definition but not other types of questions.

Because the questions that matter most to her are questions of interpretation and consequence, she used the chart on page 43 to help her determine where to look.

1 She knew that stories of women who had received microloans would help her, but because she couldn't interview women in developing countries, she used Google to find websites of microcredit organizations, hoping they would have women's stories. She also looked for the organizations' mission statements, to see if they discussed why they focused on women.

2 Her library's online resources helped her search databases on current economic topics, as well as women's issues and newspaper editorials. (The ProQuest database suggested additional search terms, such as **women AND poverty AND microcredit OR microfinance**.)

3 The databases also helped her find organizational and governmental reports with statistics that might show how women's lives were changed because of small loans.

→ Riley didn't find any one source that answered all her questions, but she found many that helped her develop a thesis for her own argument—as you can see in Part 3, on pages 146–147.

HINTS & TIPS FOR FINDING IDEAS

HOW DO YOU KNOW IF YOU HAVE FOUND ENOUGH SOURCES?

In the earliest stages of research, you won't know, exactly, if you have all the sources that will help you develop an argument that will satisfy readers.

But you are researching broadly enough—finding enough sources—if you can answer most of the research questions you've generated.

HOW DO YOU KNOW IF YOU ARE KEEPING AN OPEN MIND?

You might think that you should have definitive answers to all your research questions. But—*especially for questions of consequence, interpretation, value, and policy*—if your research makes you hesitate over deciding between two or three possible responses, then you are keeping an open mind. If you can offer good reasons for several differing possibilities, then you are researching as you should.

Academic writing is rarely about offering final solutions to anything; there are few situations in life where the evidence obviously supports one final conclusion. Instead, you need to acknowledge the differing possibilities and offer the best evidence and arguments you can for the position you believe to be best.

HOW CAN YOU KEEP A TOPIC FRESH AND INTERESTING?

If you get bored with your topic, you won't enjoy the writing, your writing will reflect your emotion, and your readers will pick up on it.

Because there are different ways to get bored with a topic, there are different approaches for becoming unbored:

- Perhaps you've chosen a topic that isn't controversial or challenging enough to keep you engaged. Talk with a teacher or someone who knows about the topic to determine if you can make the topic more challenging or if you need a new topic.

- Sometimes topics become boring when you've done a lot of research and feel that you know all there is to know. If this happens, remember that not everyone knows what you do: If you talk to someone else and lay out why the topic should matter, you might see how writing about your topic can help others learn important information.

ANALYZING ARGUMENTS & EVALUATING SOURCES

CONTENTS

WHERE ARE WE IN THE PROCESS FOR COMPOSING?

Understanding your project

Getting started

Asking questions
Critical thinking and questioning
Evaluating sources
Developing a thesis statement

Shaping your project for others

Drafting a paper

Getting feedback

Revising

Polishing

WHAT IS ANALYSIS?

Analysis is about breaking something into its pieces to learn how the pieces fit together into a whole.

To learn about and prevent diseases, doctors analyze bodies, looking at organs and bodily functions: They analyze the skeletal and muscular systems, the organs of digestion and sight, and the cellular processes of those different systems and organs. Once doctors understand how these different parts fit together, they can start questioning how a change in one part affects other parts, how (for example) a disease of the liver affects stomach functioning.

Similarly, social scientists analyze crises that are the result of human action (such as wars and economic depressions) and crises that result from a mixture of human and natural causes (deaths from heat waves or hurricanes). They try first to understand the political, social, economic, and techological structures of towns, cities, countries, and regions so that they can ask how actions and events affect those different structures. They hope in this way to learn what went wrong and how a similar crisis might be avoided in the future.

Similarly, communication specialists analyze the texts we give each other. Some specialize in analyzing political speeches, some in television advertising, some in film, some in literature, some in digital communication. These specialists bring different analytic tools to their work. In this book, we use the analytic tools of rhetoric.

In the upcoming pages, we follow the scheme for analysis shown below, to help you move from analyzing to understand to analyzing to ask questions of a text.

ANALYSIS

By breaking a text down into its parts, we can:

understand

If we can describe the parts of a text and how they fit together into a whole, then we can say we understand the text, and what its composer's purpose might have been in producing it.

ask questions

Once we understand a text, we can question it:

Does the text achieve the composer's purpose?

- Do the strategies used in the text fit with its purpose?
- Is the intended audience likely to be persuaded by the strategies used?

What do I think about that purpose and the strategies used to achieve it?

- Can I support the purpose?
- Are the strategies used valid?
- Do I accept those strategies, or think they are ethical?
- Do I think the text's composer respects the text's audience?

UNDERSTANDING AND ANALYZING TEXTS

In this book, we use the analytic tools of rhetoric to understand what the parts of a communication are and how those parts fit together to make a whole—and how the parts work to make a communicator's purposes clear to the intended audience in a particular context.

BEGINNING RHETORICAL ANALYSIS

Almost any rhetorical analysis begins with these two steps:

1 Determining the choices composers make in developing a text.

2 Considering how those choices help composers achieve their purposes with their particular audience in the context at hand.

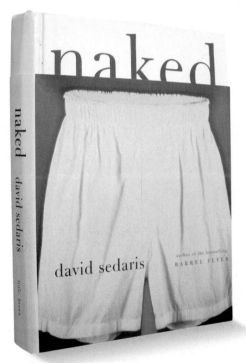

BEGINNING A RHETORICAL ANALYSIS OF A BOOK COVER

This example for starting a rhetorical analysis looks at the book cover to the left.

1 Determining the choices composers make in developing a text.

To do this, we list as many choices as we see, in any order:

- the book's title
- the book's size
- the typefaces used, and their size
- the placement of the elements, such as the title relative to the photograph
- any information about the book in addition to its title
- the book cover is different from what we usually see: The paper cover doesn't cover the whole, just part of it—so there must be something hidden under it
- the use of a photograph
- the colors used
- the overall feeling: humorous

2 Considering how those choices help composers achieve their purposes with their particular audience in the context at hand.

It's tempting to say that the cover's purpose (like any book cover) is to sell the book—and that is certainly part of the purpose. But if a cover helps persuade someone to buy the book, the cover must interest the buyer. If the buyer knows the author's writing, maybe the cover design doesn't matter; if, however, someone doesn't know the author, then the cover's purpose has to be about giving someone a strong, particular sense of what is inside **this** book. What do the strategies above suggest about *naked*?

The title and photograph are important choices because they are emphasized. The photograph is of boxer shorts, which for some reason in American culture are objects of some silliness. Their presence tells us this book is about fairly recent topics and not about people living long ago.

Naked is a word we apply to humans, not animals, and though it can imply serious things, the word can also imply awkwardness, like losing your clothes while swimming—or being caught in public in your underwear. Because the title is printed without a capital letter—which implies informality—and is combined with the photograph, we get the sense that this book is not about heavy topics. The cover also has only the one photograph, telling us that what is in the book is probably not complicated: This is, probably, not a book of detailed history. It is about people, possibly their awkward behaviors.

THERE ARE CATEGORIES FOR ANALYZING THE STRATEGIES USED IN COMPOSING…

as we discuss on the next pages. Also, analyzing a composition is easier when we compare it to another composition, as we do with this book cover on the next pages.

UNDERSTANDING AND
ANALYZING TEXTS

DEVELOPING A SENSE OF THE AUTHOR

WE MAKE ASSUMPTIONS ABOUT THE COMPOSERS OF TEXTS

Whenever you use a text, you develop a sense of the person who made it.

Listening to the radio, you probably develop—without thinking—a sense of any speaker's gender and age, and probably also a sense that the person is serious, funny, or well-informed. You could be wrong in all your assumptions—but that doesn't stop you from making such assumptions.

We make the same assumptions when we read and even when we look at photographs, posters, or video games: We develop, consciously or not, a sense of who made the text and whether the person is trustworthy, authoritative, knowledgeable, intelligent, and so on.

WE NEVER KNOW A REAL PERSON THROUGH THE ASSUMPTIONS WE MAKE

Text producers choose how they want to appear in their texts: Writers choose tone of voice, the evidence they use, and how they describe others. Because the evidence is limited—and sometimes carefully crafted—the sense we develop of composers is always limited and partial; we never get to know a real person through a text.

Composers can use any strategy available to them to shape how audiences understand who the composers are. In traditional rhetorical terminology, the sense that audiences develop about composers is called

ETHOS.

ETHOS IN BOOK COVERS

The context of book cover design says something about ethos. Rarely do writers design their own book covers; instead, a book's publisher chooses a designer. The designer works alone, or with an art director or photographer, but the work has to be approved by the publisher and (usually) by the author.

The ethos we associate with a cover is therefore not necessarily the ethos of the books—but the two should be close if the cover is to achieve its purpose of suggesting what the book is about. Notice that ethos can, therefore, be the result not of one person's decisions but of several people's.

The cover for *naked* looks professional, composed by someone who knows about using words, typefaces, and photographs together. Its humor suggests not only that the book will be funny but also that the person who made the cover has a sense of humor.

The cover for *The Little Friend* was composed by the same designer, and it too looks professional and has similar elements: one photograph, the title of the book, the author's name, and information about another of the author's books. Even though the strategies are similar, however, the second cover is a bit creepy: The extreme close-up on the face of a doll looking sideways suggests someone trying to see what's going on behind her, an undoll-like emotion.

Both covers show us someone who is able to suggest that objects have more life than we usually expect.

All these facets of this ethos—the professionalism, the humor, the attention to objects—suggest that these books are connected with makers who are clever and able to get readers to look below surfaces.

UNDERSTANDING AND
ANALYZING TEXTS
UNDERSTANDING APPEALS TO EMOTIONS

PEOPLE COMPOSE TEXTS TO MOVE OTHERS

Every text is composed for a purpose—
and for that purpose to be achieved, the
audience has to shift. The shifting can
be as simple as the audience's attention
being shifted from one object to
another—but most often it is larger: a
shift from passivity to engagement,
from not knowing or caring about a
topic to knowing and caring, from
feeling hopeless to wanting to act.

In all of this, there is a shifting in the
audience's emotion.

What emotions does a composer
consider the audience to hold on a
topic before they read, see, or hear a
text—and what emotions does the
composer hope the audience will hold
afterward?

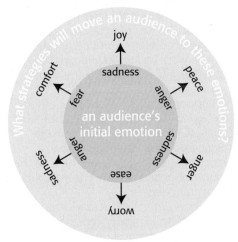

In rhetoric, a composer's use of strategies
to shift an audience's emotions is called

PATHOS.

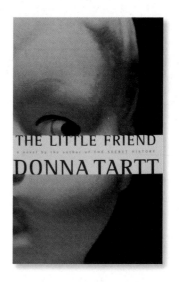

PATHOS IN BOOK COVERS

Earlier, we talked about how *naked*'s cover is about engaging with an audience's sense of humor: The title of the book and the photograph of boxer shorts are simple and funny. Perhaps we can say, then, that the cover's main pathos appeal is that of humor.

But there is another strategy we mentioned that we have not discussed: the part of the cover that comes off.

The boxer shorts are printed on a paper jacket that covers only part of the book. The jacket overlaps *naked*; the paper does not—as we expect with most book covers—cover the whole book; we are led to wonder what is under the cover, under the boxers.

In addition to its humor, the cover therefore also offers some interaction and provocation. It asks the audience to expect something under the cover … and under the cover is an x-ray, a body

more naked than we might have expected. Our emotions are called into play as we realize that we were (perhaps) hoping to see something else but instead are given a very exposed naked body. We are teased by this cover—perhaps made to laugh, perhaps made to question why we were expecting to see something else.

The second book's title, *The Little Friend,* suggests childhood—but the photograph plays emotionally with the associations we probably have with childhood. A close-up photograph of a face engages us with the face's emotion. A close-up of a face turning its eyes toward shadows behind it suggests worry, concern, fear of something about to happen. When the face is a doll's, we have entered the realm of fairy tales and fantasy. The emotions encouraged by this cover are in your face, and unsettling.

UNDERSTANDING AND
ANALYZING TEXTS

UNDERSTANDING ARRANGEMENT
(including logic)

EVERY TEXT UNFOLDS IN TIME

Even in posters and book covers, we see some elements first and some second because some elements are big or at the top. We have to look longer to see the arrangements of novels, essays, films, and video games. We may read a book's conclusion first, but in the Table of Contents we see that the composer put the chapters into a particular order. On a website we can look at individual pages in any order, but we see that the designers have designated one page as the home page—and we still have to look at each page starting at the top.

To move audiences, composers make choices about the order in which (they hope) audiences experience their work.

Choices about order can concern the

- **Large scale of a text.** What introduces someone to the text and what concludes it, or what does someone see first, then second, and so on?

- **Middle scale.** How are intermediate parts of a text given shape, such as sections or paragraphs in writing, the arrangements of one photograph in an advertisement that contains ten photographs, and so on?

- **Small scale.** In writing, the order of words in a sentence shapes how readers read; in sound recordings, background music or ambient sounds play behind main sounds, but still shape a listener's overall experience.

In rhetoric, a text's arrangements (including its logical arguments) are referred to as the strategy of

LOGOS.

THE BREADTH OF LOGOS

Logos may make you think of logic, and that is appropriate: Both words developed from the same Ancient Greek word.

Logos, as a name for a strategy that looks at the arrangement of a text, includes logic. Logic is about how ideas are structured—arranged—to have a very specific kind of effect.

So when you hear the word **logos**, it is fine to think about all kinds of arrangements that are used to structure texts, including the particular set of arrangements we call **logic**.

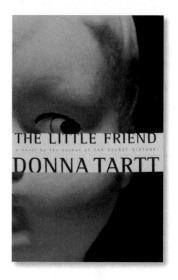

LOGOS IN A BOOK COVER

When readers first encounter *naked*, they probably notice the photograph first, because of its size, and then the title. The author's name is smaller than the title, and tied into the photograph.

When an author is well known, sometimes the person's name is larger than the title, but in this case we can see that the composers believed the suggestive title would probably attract more readers than the author's name— even though this author is now quite well known. Even smaller than the author's name, however, are two short lines of text that inform readers that this author has written another (best-selling) book; the cover's composers decided that this informa-tion is important enough to include, but not important enough to make bigger than any of the other elements.

A final element of arrangement—of logos—is the strategy of having another photograph hidden under the first.

Whereas the arrangements of *naked* encourage eyes to move over the cover, putting together (and taking apart) the pieces, the arrangements of the cover of *The Little Friend* keep a viewer's eyes held close to the middle. The placement of the doll's eye right on top of the title—which is lined up closely with the author's name and information about another of the author's books—puts the points of visual interest of this cover close together. There is really nothing else to look at, so the arrangements support the pathos of this cover: We are aware of the darkness to the side, but we do not know what is there. This arrangement asks us to identify with the doll, to wonder what might be over there.

UNDERSTANDING AND ANALYZING TEXTS
A SAMPLE ANALYSIS ESSAY

As we wrote earlier, the first step of doing analysis is to analyze for understanding. Can you describe what you think the purpose of the text is, and for whom it was intended? Can you find evidence from the text—quotations, your observations about how ethos, pathos, and logos are used—that supports your understanding? If you can do that, then you understand a text.

Your understanding may differ from others' analysis of the same text, but as long as you can use as evidence the strategies you've noted, then you have built your own understanding. Listen to how others analyze, and notice how they use the evidence of the text.

On the opposite page is a written rhetorical analysis of one of the book covers we examined on the previous pages, as an example of how you can write such an analysis for understanding.

■ ■ ■

You'll notice that the writing uses some of the descriptions from the preceding pages; this is one way to develop an analysis: Write down your observations, and then use them to build a more formal analysis (such as one required by a class assignment).

The introduction

The introduction of the essay tells readers something of what the essay is arguing—but only enough to give readers direction and (the writer hopes) curiosity.

The subject of the essay

The writer of this short essay is careful to explain to readers what the explicit subject of the essay is.

The strategy of the essay

Here the writer lists pertinent strategies used by the composer of the text being analyzed.

The conclusion

In the conclusion to the essay, the writer argues for the main strategy used by the composer of the text being analyzed, and (in the last sentences) shows how that strategy connects to the purpose of the text.

I would have thought a book cover made of a single photograph and a few words would give a reader only a bare, literal sense of the book, telling a reader, for example, that "this book is about boxer shorts." The book cover I analyze—designed by Chip Kidd for the book *naked* by David Sedaris —contains such limited elements, and yet it engages potential readers in puzzling out odd emotional relationships and so gets them engaged with the book even before they turn to page 1.

The cover of *naked* is composed, at first glance, of a simple photograph of bright white boxer shorts on a shaded blue background. The word "naked"—all in lower-case letters in a straightforward serifed typeface—is at the top, on a white background, partially covered by the photograph. The author's name is in the same typeface on top of the boxer shorts, along with a few words about another book he's published. This combination of elements is informal, straightforward, and balanced, with everything symmetric and centered. Based on such a description, this cover suggests a book that could be mundane and perhaps even boring. But boxer shorts are rarely on book covers, especially so large in proportion to everything else, and to put them together with "naked" presented so informally encourages a reader to wonder where the person is who wore the shorts: Is that person running around naked somewhere?

But there is more to the cover. Kidd has readers wondering about who was wearing those shorts, but his design also suggests an answer might be available. The boxer shorts are printed on a paper jacket that covers about three-quarters of the book. The jacket partially overlaps "naked"; the overlapping, combined with how the paper does not—unlike most book covers—cover the whole book, leads readers to wonder what is under the cover, under the boxers.

In addition to its humor, the cover therefore also offers some interaction and provocation. It asks the audience to expect something under the cover…but what is under the cover is probably unexpected.

Under the cover is an x-ray of a lower torso, a body more naked than we might have expected. Readers are teased by this cover—perhaps made to laugh and perhaps made to question why they were expecting to see something else.

Most book covers show people or objects that give readers a literal sense of what is in the book: A book cover with a dog on a leash is about dog training; a book with a palm tree is about the South Pacific. Kidd has instead used the rhetorical strategy of pathos as his primary strategy: While the arrangement of elements (including the order of seeing the boxer shorts before seeing the bony torso) encourages readers to see the informal relationship between the elements, it is the humor and surprising interaction and discovery that give readers a sense of this book. A reader who looked at this cover and in response thought that this book was a funny but edgy intimate look at a man's life would not be far off. It is possible readers would buy this book—the general purpose of the cover—because they have gotten involved emotionally with that man's life only by picking up the book to look closer.

ANALYZING ARGUMENTS

Once you understand a text, you can make judgments about it.

- Do you agree with the arguments the text is making?

- Is there enough evidence to persuade you to agree? Does the evidence offered truly support the arguments being made?

- What are consequences of the arguments being made?

Experienced researchers and scholars do not respond only to isolated chunks of a text but instead try to be fair to the whole text, to how its various strategies build to a whole.

On the next pages we show steps for taking apart arguments to see whether enough evidence is offered (and thus also discuss kinds of evidence and how to judge different kinds). We suggest questions you can ask of texts to support your analysis of them.

JUDGING EVIDENCE, JUDGING SOURCES

In the next few pages on analysis, we help you judge the evidence offered in a text: Such judgments help you decide whether you accept the evidence and thus the arguments built on the evidence. Later in Part 3, we offer strategies for judging the relevance and credibility of sources you are considering using in your writing.

Judging the evidence of a text for yourself will help you decide later if your readers will see the text as a credible source that supports the arguments you are building.

Here is an editorial from the *San Francisco Chronicle*, from March 2007:

Food ad blitz

IT CAN'T be healthy for a 9-year-old—or any child—to be bombarded with an average of 21 food ads on television each day.

That's especially the case when most of the products being peddled don't come close to meeting the ordinary definition of the word "food."

According to the most exhaustive study yet done on advertising to children by the Kaiser Family Foundation in Menlo Park, one-third of all "food" ads are for candy and snacks. Just under a third are for cereals (almost all of them loaded with sweeteners). Ten percent are for fast foods.

Of the 8,854 ads reviewed, none was for fruits or vegetables.

All those commercials add up. So-called "tweens"—kids between the ages of 8 and 12—see some 7,600 food ads each year. On average, teenagers see slightly fewer—6,000 a year, or 17 a day, while 2-to-7-year-olds see 4,400, or 12 ads a day.

To view these ads as an inevitable, and even normal, part of childhood in America is not acceptable. As an authoritative report last year by the Institute of Medicine concluded, food ads have a direct impact on children's health. "Television advertising influences the food preferences, purchase requests and diets, at least of children under 12, and is associated with the increased rates of obesity among children and youth," the report found.

What's more, food ads swamp public-service advertising that promote fitness and nutrition. Children between ages 2 and 12 see a pitiful 164 such messages each year, or one every two or three days. Teenagers see one such PSA, on average, once a week.

Marketers of food products can, and must, do better. Last year, 10 of the top 10 food companies formed the "Children's Food and Beverage Advertising Initiative," and promised to devote at least half of their ads to healthier food messages that encourage fitness and nutrition.

This must be a serious effort on the part of the food industry—and must embrace more than just the major food companies. Given the high stakes—the health of future generations of Americans—it would not be premature for Congress to begin to exercise more oversight over the glut of food advertising intruding into the lives of children.

On the next pages, we offer strategies for questioning the arguments offered in this editorial. The strategies will help you:

- **Make judgments about sources you are considering using in support of your own composing.** If you question a source and find its arguments to be poorly made, you do not want to base your arguments on that source.

- **Make judgments about the validity and strengths of your own composing.** You can use the strategies we offer to be sure your arguments are well supported and are therefore more likely to be taken seriously by others.

ANALYZING ARGUMENTS
THESIS STATEMENTS

WHY CAN'T A PAPER BE A THESIS STATEMENT?

Sometimes student writers ask why, instead of having to write a whole paper, they can't just present a thesis statement—or a thesis statement and its warrants and evidence. Isn't that persuasive enough?

If human beings were completely and only logical beings, this might work.

But human beings are swayed by different kinds of logic as well as by emotional appeals and the character of others. Thesis statements, warrants, and evidence are only one part of logos, and they do very little to appeal to the fullness of other humans. That is why they are only part of writing.

Many writers develop thesis statements to help them prepare to write—as we will be helping you do later in this part of the book.

→ See pages 146–147.

People who study how arguments work have studied the logic of thesis statements. They have learned that thesis statements with certain logical structures help writers make decisions about how to turn a thesis statement into a full paper; when thesis statements are thought about in terms of specific audiences, they can help writers make decisions about how to arrange the parts of a paper and what sorts of evidence to include.

The ideas here about thesis statements come from the work of mid-twentieth-century philosopher Stephen Toulmin. Through his studies into the structure of argument, Toulmin developed an understanding of an argument's **claims**, **reasons**, **warrants**, and **evidence**.

When you compose an argumentative paper, you can use a thesis statement (and its claim, reasons, warrants, and evidence) to help shape the paper—but when you read an argument written by someone else, you can decompose the writing: You can analyze the writing to pull out a thesis statement, along with its claims, reasons, warrants, and evidence, as we will do in a few pages.

The next page shows one way of conceiving a thesis statement for the editorial on page 101. The work of pulling out one possible thesis helps you see just what underlies the argument—and so helps you decide if enough (or the right) evidence is being offered.

DO YOU THINK THE EDITORIAL ON PAGE 101 OFFERS GOOD EVIDENCE TO SUPPORT ITS CLAIM THAT CONGRESS SHOULD REGULATE TELEVISION ADS FOR CHILDREN?

Congress should have oversight of food advertising on TV because food advertising is affecting the future health of young people.

A THESIS STATEMENT is composed of...

Congress should have oversight of food advertising on TV.

a CLAIM, which is a statement about a condition, policy, or event that a writer believes should come to pass. Notice how the claim is made up of two parts: *Congress should have oversight...* and *food advertising*.

Food advertising is affecting the future health of young people.

a REASON, which states one reason the claim should come to pass. Notice how the reason is made up of two parts: *Food advertising* and *affecting the future health....*

Congress should have oversight of what affects the future health of young people.

A WARRANT is an idea or value that a writer believes the audience is likely to accept; the whole argument hangs on this. Notice how the claim and reason each repeat a similar phrase; the warrant links the claim and the reason logically—by linking the parts that aren't repeated.

A study by the Kaiser Family Foundation in Menlo Park reviewed 8,854 ads; none was for fruits or vegetables and the majority were for foods heavy in sugars. Another report, by the Institute of Medicine, says that food ads affect children's eating habits and thus their health, and are "associated with the increased rates of obesity among children and youth." Children see almost no ads that encourage healthy eating practices.

EVIDENCE justifies the reason.

WHAT COUNTS AS EVIDENCE

Evidence is what you offer audiences to persuade them that your position on a topic is worth considering.

There are many kinds of evidence composers can use to support their warrants; on these pages we consider:

1 EXPERT TESTIMONY
2 PERSONAL EXPERIENCE
3 ANALOGIES
4 FACTS (AND STATISTICS)
5 FIELD RESEARCH
6 SHARED VALUES
7 EXAMPLES

EXPERT TESTIMONY

An expert has special and thorough knowledge on a particular topic because of education, profession, study, or experience. Experts can be individuals or groups. Because of their knowledge, we believe we can rely on experts' judgments in the areas in which they know more than the average person.

Text composers can use the words of experts—their testimony—as authoritative backing on the topics about which the expert is knowledgeable.

In the editorial on page 101, for example, the Kaiser Family Foundation and the Institute of Medicine are both cited as experts; excerpts from reports they have published are offered as evidence in support of the editorial's arguments.

EVALUATING EXPERT TESTIMONY

If you are wondering whether to accept expert testimony:

• Do an online search on the person or organization. Does the person have credentials—education and experience—for offering the evidence? Does the organization specialize in the topic? Does the person or organization have an affiliation indicating potential bias?

• Ask others what they know about the person or organization.

When you compose your own texts:

• Ask people from your audience if they know and trust the experts you are citing.

• If your audience might not know an expert you are citing, include descriptions of the expert, saying why the expert has authority for you.

PERSONAL EXPERIENCE

Personal experience is what we know through living. Each of us has experiences with families, schools, jobs, and romance; we've paid taxes, driven cars, eaten, shopped, and seen changes in our communities. Every experience—and especially repeated experiences—shapes our sense of how the world works.

Personal experience is limited evidence precisely because it is personal. Without considerable research, you cannot know how many other people share your experiences; you cannot know if they draw the same knowledge from their experiences as you do.

Because personal experience is limited, it ought to play only a small part in formal writing. It can serve as a single example in support of a point. An introductory anecdote about your experiences working in a fast-food restaurant can draw readers emotionally into an argument about the moral satisfactions of low-paying jobs, but you would need much more evidence to show that others found the same moral satisfaction.

The same holds true for using others' experiences as evidence. A friend who has been to Burundi on a missionary trip might have interesting observations about how donations are spent in that country, but those observations have no place in your writing unless your friend is also an expert on the economics of donations or the observations are backed up by other evidence.

Personal experience can become facts or statistics when it is joined with and examined alongside the experiences of others through field research.

EVALUATING PERSONAL EXPERIENCE

When you see others using personal experience—whether their own or of others—as examples in their writing, ask these questions:

• Is the experience used as logical evidence in support of the composer's ability to discuss this topic (ethos), or as an emotional appeal (pathos)?

• If the experience is used as logical evidence, does the writer acknowledge that the experience is necessarily limited? Is other evidence also given as support?

• If the experience is used to show that the composer has relevant experience for taking on the topic at hand, is the experience sufficient? Does the experience indicate that the composer has any bias on the topic?

• If the experience is used as an emotional appeal, does the emotion draw the audience away from what is at issue or does it help show why the issue might be worth the audience's attention?

When you compose your own texts, keep in mind the following:

• Be wary of generalizing from your own experiences. Always try to find out if your audience has shared the same experiences—and drawn similar conclusions.

• When you use the experiences, observations, anecdotes, or opinions of others, use them only to illustrate examples and to offer other evidence of the kinds we describe on these pages.

ANALOGIES

Analogies are quasi-logical structures: When you use an analogy, you compare—usually at length—two objects, events, or processes so that the more familiar can explain the less familiar. For example, a long description of how the brain is like a computer would be an analogy in which the composer relies upon the audience's knowledge of computers to explain how the brain works.

Similarly, to call the Internet the **Information Superhighway** is to use an analogy in which one is to understand the abstract Internet networked system as being like a highway. Most people in the United States have experienced highways, and so can think of the Internet as a series of roads and interchanges with information traveling between locations in little packets just like cars.

But analogies work more than descriptively. They carry a whole set of assumptions from the more familiar object being named to the less familiar object being named to the less familiar. For example, the **Information Superhighway** analogy implies that the Internet should be a public resource as highways are, and regulated, supported, and repaired with public funds just as highways are.

Analogies can be used in focused ways, or can shape the argument of a whole book: The writer Malcolm Gladwell, for example, one of whose short essays we examine later, has used a whole book to consider how *ideas can be contagious in exactly the same way that a virus is.*

The following analogy is a blog entry; the writer describes a day in which he and others from his company discussed leadership and teamwork:

I mentioned something I recently read on migratory birds in flight. This study found that a flock of birds in a V-formation can fly at least 70% farther than a bird on its own. Birds at the back of the V work much less because they can take advantage of the draft created by the birds at front. When a bird at the front tires, it drops out of the lead and goes to the back to rest. The V-formation also improves visual contact and communication.

I like to tell this story to show how natural teamwork should be. This story also highlights the importance of individual excellence and leadership. Every bird in the V-formation at some point assumes the leadership role at the front. Similarly, each member of my leadership team has a key responsibility to drive the priorities and vision for their area in the company, while at the same time being able to understand how that fits into the overall vision of our company.

The comments appearing after the blog entry develop the shortcomings of the analogy: If you carry out the analogy, as one person commented, it would be appropriate for the company's *top managers to drop out of the lead positions and for some others to either die or recover;* another points out that the V-formation *is a pattern learned over the millions of years of evolution* and so not easy for humans to learn or apply.

Visual analogies also exist. The example above comes from early in World War II, when—with so many men in battle—industries encouraged women to work in factories producing weaponry and machinery needed for the war effort. The poster above uses analogies between the work to which women were already accustomed— sewing and cooking—and industrial production. The visual analogies between the two kinds of work are offered as evidence that, if women can do the familiar work, they can also do the unfamiliar work.

EVALUATING ANALOGIES

In reading and developing analogies, consider:

- Analogies are an odd sort of evidence because they prove nothing. They do not guarantee that situations will play out as an analogy suggests.

  Instead, composers use analogies to shape an audience's attitudes. A compelling analogy can persuade audiences to consider an object or process in a positive light, which is a large part of any successful argument. A compelling analogy is therefore both a pathos appeal and a form of logos.

- When it is compelling, an analogy can so focus your perceptions that you cannot think outside the analogy. When you see an analogy being used as evidence in an argument, or want to use one yourself, try carrying out the implications of the analogy, as those commenting on the bird–human leadership example did.

  You can also explore how an analogy shapes thinking by coming up with alternative analogies. For example, consider how the **Internet as a Superhighway** analogy asks us to think of the Internet as roads and exchanges—and implies that the Internet should be built and supported with public funds. To consider an alternative analogy, ask what implications accompany thinking of the Internet as a marketplace or huge library.

FACTS

A fact is a statement about an event or condition that exists or has happened. Facts are true or false; there is no gray area to a fact. Facts are verifiable: They can be checked. If someone claims, for example, that it is a fact that cold climate turtles hibernate, we ought to be able to go see such hibernating turtles for ourselves.

Facts can be presented in words and through numbers, firsthand experience, illustrations, charts, and graphs.

Facts can be about historical events—

In the late 18th century, Haiti's nearly half million slaves revolted under Toussaint L'Ouverture. After a prolonged struggle, Haiti became the first black republic to declare its independence in 1804.

—more recent events—

He graduated from the University of Hawaii in 2008.

—or natural objects and events:

Jupiter is the largest planet.

The maximum age of a snapping turtle recorded in nature is 24 years.

Facts can be presented in diagrams, as in this explanation of swimmer's itch:

This diagram brings together small facts about a parasitic flatworm's life cycle to build a larger fact about how swimmers get infected with the worm.

TIP: **USE FACTS, NOT OPINIONS**

Zbigniew Boniek is the greatest male soccer player of all time.

The sentence above is an opinion: People can argue about who is the greatest soccer (or baseball or football) player of all time.

In 2006, Sharma Wing of Daniel Webster College scored the most points per game in Division III soccer.

The sentence above gives a fact: It can be verified by checking data collected about college soccer in 2006.

STATISTICS—A KIND OF FACT

Statistics result from manipulations of sets of numbers.

They can appear in charts or graphs—

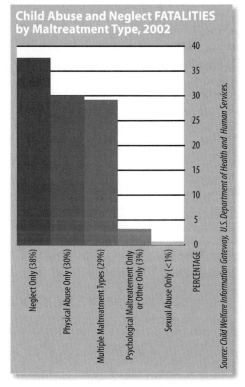

Child Abuse and Neglect FATALITIES by Maltreatment Type, 2002

Neglect Only (38%) / Physical Abuse Only (30%) / Multiple Maltreatment Types (29%) / Psychological Maltreatment Only or Other Only (3%) / Sexual Abuse Only (<1%)

PERCENTAGE

Source: Child Welfare Information Gateway, U.S. Department of Health and Human Services.

—be written—

In 2002, more than one-third (38 percent) of child maltreatment fatalities were associated with neglect alone. Physical abuse alone was cited in more than one-quarter (30 percent) of reported fatalities. Another 29 percent of fatalities were the result of multiple maltreatment types.

—or presented in tables:

Table 1: DOCTORATE AWARDS
by selected characteristics of recipients, 1995 and 2004

	1995	2004
All doctorates	41,750	42,155
Male	61%	55%
Female	39%	45%

Source: National Science Foundation/Divisions of Science Resources Statistics, Survey of Earned Doctorates, 2004.

Charts, graphs, and tables allow viewers to make comparisons.

EVALUATING FACTS & STATISTICS

To evaluate these, ask the following:

• Are sources given for the facts and statistics? If so, are they authoritative? If not, do you trust the author enough to accept the facts?

• Do the facts and statistics support the conclusions that are based on them?

• Can you find other facts that contradict those you are questioning?

When you are using facts and statistics in your own compositions, consider:

• Will your audience accept the authority of the sources from which you've drawn the facts or statistics?

• Have you made clear how the facts support the points you are making?

• If you are working with a source that offers a wide range of facts or statistics—census data, for example— are you using the facts responsibly, using them fully, and not choosing only those that support your points?

FIELD RESEARCH

If researchers are fair and open-minded in their research, honestly looking for what others think, then their interviews, observations, and surveys will create facts. When researchers compile information, they can demonstrate what a group of people think or believe in a particular place and time. They can, for example, provide statistics about how many people desire a particular policy or show, through interviewing older people in an area, what Sunday activities were popular a few decades ago.

You can use the following questions both to evaluate field research carried out by others and to help you shape field research you might perform.

EVALUATING INTERVIEWS

- Did the interviewer ask open-ended questions, allowing the person or people being interviewed to provide their opinions and beliefs?

- Did the interviewer present the interview fairly, showing where the words of the person interviewed were cut or edited?

- What sort of relationship does the interviewer appear to have had with the person being interviewed? Does the interviewer seem hostile, or overly friendly?

EVALUATING OBSERVATIONS

- Does the researcher describe the goals and methods of the observation?

- Does the researcher appear to have approached the observation seeking particular results—or been open to whatever happened?

- Does the researcher appear to have observed well, or with too much focus?

- Are the researcher's results only positive, in support of the researcher's goals, or does the researcher note any observations that went against expectations?

EVALUATING SURVEYS

- Did the survey ask open-ended questions, allowing the person or people being interviewed to provide their opinions and beliefs?

- Was the number of people surveyed sufficient for providing support for any assertions a researcher is making based on the research? (To learn how many people need to be surveyed depending on what a researcher is trying to find out, see the article "How Many People are Enough?" <http://survey.pearsonncs.com/planning/people.htm>.)

- Did the researcher seek information from an appropriately wide group of people, or only from those likely to give responses the researcher wanted?

SHARED VALUES

The editorial on page 101 relies on the warrant that *Congress should have oversight of what affects the future health of young people* (as shown on page 103). This statement presumes that its readers will be concerned about anything affecting young people's future health. Whoever wrote the editorial does not have to argue for this value or offer further evidence to support this; it can simply be assumed.

Composing an argument that does not rely on readers' values is impossible.

One could argue whether such values are evidence, but many arguments depend on such assumptions. Simple arguments such as *Don't do that—you'll get hurt!* can work only if the person at whom they are directed believes that getting hurt is a bad thing. The person who makes the statement doesn't have to explain the assumption.

Longer and more complex arguments about going to war or about health care, for example, will appeal to shared values about patriotism, nationalism, the right of people to a doctor's care, or the right not to suffer.

Because the composers of texts rely on such shared values to encourage readers to accept their arguments, these values work to support arguments just as other kinds of evidence do.

EVALUATING SHARED VALUES

When you are questioning shared values or making use of them in your own work, keep in mind:

- Using shared values to support arguments depends on what the audience believes—so you must pull assumed shared values from arguments and ask if audiences truly do believe the assumptions. Under what conditions will an audience accept those assumptions?

- People can hold contradictory values or accept some values only under certain conditions, as when some people are against violence except in response to aggression. When you are considering the shared values underlying an argument, ask if the assumptions hold in all cases or only in some.

- When you are composing your own texts, be aware of the values you are assuming your readers share with you. If you do not make those values explicit to yourself, you will not be able to use them alertly in your writing—and so you may be surprised when your audience responds negatively.

EXAMPLES

Examples can make general or abstract arguments specific and concrete for audiences. Detailed examples can help audiences visualize what might otherwise be only conceptual.

Examples can be in a sentence—

Classes at our college emphasize personal attention, especially in the first year, when all classes are limited to fifteen students.

—or a paragraph:

What always amazed me about my father was how multifaceted he was. He was an intellectually curious physician living in a small town who had traveled the world, read at least a book a week up until he died, could continually kick my ass in Scrabble even though he didn't learn English until he was 23, and knew practically everything there was to know about classical music, Spanish wines, and French cinema. All I wanted to be when I grew up was as smart as my dad.

In each example above, a general statement comes first—*Classes at our college emphasize personal attention* and *What always amazed me about my father was how multifaceted he was*—followed by examples to show concretely what **personal attention** and **multifaceted** mean to the writers.

Like analogies, examples do not prove anything. Rather, they help audiences better understand a point or concept, and so can enhance an audience's engagement with your work. Like analogies, they are logos and pathos appeals.

USING VISUAL EXAMPLES

Notice how the following selection uses both written and visual examples to clarify what it is arguing:

By immersing players in political or economic structures, the makers of *serious games* hope to encourage critical thinking and even activism. For example, in *Bacteria Salad* from Persuasive Games, players learn about agribusiness because they have to (in the words of the Persuasive Games website) "Harvest mass amounts of cheap produce and sell it for as much profit as possible. But watch out for floods and animal waste, or your greens might turn, uh—brown—and your customers will get E. Coli." As you can tell from the description, the game is humorous and, as the screenshot below shows, has lighthearted graphics, all to seduce players to engage critically with serious issues. I wonder, however, if the playfulness encourages or distracts from that purpose.

Screenshot of Bacteria Salad *from* Persuasive Games *website.*

EVALUATING EXAMPLES

Whether you are analyzing others' examples or considering how to use them in your own work, consider:

- Do the examples make clear the general or abstract point they are meant to explain? Do they distract from the point, or will audiences easily understand why the examples are there?

- How do the examples support the general or abstract points being made? Are the examples too specific, causing the general points to get lost?

- If more than one example is used to clarify a general or abstract point, are all the examples appropriate? Are the examples ordered to move from least complex to most, or from most known to least known?

In addition, for **visual examples**, consider the following:

- Are the examples used only to support and explain general points, or do they distract from the purpose?

- Are the examples labeled, both to give proper attribution and to help readers understand their relationship to the words?

TIP: SHARED VALUES

Shared values underlie every argument you make, so we have not mentioned them on the right. Nonetheless, because they underlie all arguments, working to identify them is central to analysis.

TIP: CHOOSING KINDS OF EVIDENCE FOR YOUR COMPOSITIONS

On pages 34–37 in Part 2 we encouraged you to develop questions to guide research; on pages 42–43, we showed how those questions guide choosing research sources. Also use those questions to choose useful kinds of evidence. Decide which questions most guide your research; use the information below to help you develop evidence or find it in sources. Also use what we've written in Part 3 to evaluate your evidence.

QUESTIONS OF FACT: Facts!

QUESTIONS OF DEFINITION: Expert testimony (from a person or authoritative text) can help.

QUESTIONS OF INTERPRETATION: Expert testimony, analogies, personal experience, and field research can help persuade audiences to consider the interpretation you offer.

QUESTIONS OF CONSEQUENCE: Expert testimony, analogies, facts about what has already happened, and field research can be persuasive about what might result from a proposed action.

QUESTIONS OF VALUE: Expert testimony, personal experience joined with field research, and facts about people's behaviors help identify values.

QUESTIONS OF POLICY: Use expert testimony and facts.

FURTHER QUESTIONS TO GUIDE CRITICAL READING

In the previous pages, we have been focusing on paying critical attention to logical elements of texts. Here, we offer you questions to help you consider an even broader range of choices composers make in their texts.

Once you have done preliminary analysis to be sure you understand a text, ask these questions to help you decide if you want to be persuaded by a text:

QUESTIONS ABOUT AUDIENCE

• Whom is the composer including in the audience? Who is excluded from the audience—and why?

• To what is the composer drawing the audience's attention? What might the composer be able to overlook by focusing the audience's attention in this way?

• What does the composer assume the audience knows or believes?

QUESTIONS ABOUT PURPOSE

• Why does this purpose matter at this time and in this place?

• Are there secondary purposes as well as a main purpose?

• Is the purpose clearly stated or easy to determine? If not, why might the composer have decided not to make the purpose obvious?

QUESTIONS ABOUT CONTEXT

• Where does the audience encounter the text? How might this shape their responses?

• When is an audience likely to encounter the text? How might this shape their responses?

• What events at the time of the text's production are likely to shape an audience's expectations about the topic?

TIP: USING STYLE TO SUPPORT ANALYSIS

When you are analyzing writing, use Part 7 of this book, on style, to help you identify a writer's choices. Part 7 will help you name the strategies a writer uses for emphasizing parts of an essay and thus will help you figure out what is emphasized (logos) as well as how to describe the writer's ethos and pathos strategies. Such identifications help you see a writer's purposes more easily.

QUESTIONS ABOUT ETHOS

- Does the composer have the appopriate background or experience for pursuing this purpose?

- Does the composer seem open to multiple perspectives on the task at hand? Is the composer treating those perspectives fairly?

- What cultural backgrounds and expectations shape the composer's positions?

- Is the composer using a tone of voice appropriate to the purpose?

- What role does the composer take toward the audience? Is the composer acting as a teacher, a lecturer, a parent, a peer, a friend? Is this role appropriate for the purpose?

- Is the composer respectful of the audience, treating them as intelligent, thoughtful people?

QUESTIONS ABOUT PATHOS

- What emotion is the intended audience likely to have about the issue before they encounter the text? How does the text acknowledge that emotion, and try to shift it?

- Do the emotional appeals seem reasonable to you—or overblown?

- Are the emotional appeals appropriate to the issue?

QUESTIONS ABOUT LOGOS

- What claims, reasons, and warrants are explicit or implied in the text? (➔ See pages 102–103.)

- What kinds of evidence does the composer use? (➔ See pages 104–113.) Is that evidence relevant, credible, and sufficient? (➔ See pages 104–113.) Do you know of or can you find evidence that points to different conclusions?

- Are the sources cited so that the audience can check them? If so, are the sources relevant and credible? (➔ See pages 130–143.)

- Why might a composer start with particular examples or evidence? To what will these draw the audience's attention? (And from what will these examples distract attention?)

- How does the composition end? How will the end affect how the audience looks back on the rest of the composition?

TIP: GIVING EVIDENCE

If you are using these questions to do the preliminary analysis for writing a paper, include with your responses any evidence in the text that supports your responses. For example, when taking notes about ethos, you might write: *It feels as though the author is yelling at readers: All the sentences are short, emphatic, addressed to "you!" written as though readers know nothing about the topic....*

CRITICAL READING

To the right is a short argumentative essay about zero-tolerance policies in schools.

Read it through once, trying to ignore the questions we've put next to it. Come to your own understanding of the purpose, audience, and context for this text.

Then use the questions from the preceding pages that we've attached to the text to help you shape a critical reading of it.

The beginning: Pathos and an example as evidence

The first sentences give an example and encourage readers to sympathize with for the student before knowing anything else about him. Why might Gladwell start with an introduction dependent on pathos?

Naming

Why might Gladwell tell us the name of the tutor but not the student?

Evidence: A second example

What attitude does Gladwell want readers to have toward Bomar? Toward students now? How has Gladwell prepared his readers to have those attitudes?

Pathos: How readers are addressed

Why do you think Gladwell addresses readers directly here? How might a reader respond to these questions?

TIP: ANNOTATING WHAT YOU READ

The comments we've added to this article suggest how you can mark up readings on your own, to keep track of your own questions and comments. By making such annotations, you'll see patterns in what you read, patterns that can help you determine purpose and other strategies. By making such annotations, you'll also see patterns in your responses—which will help you develop a focused analysis.

No Mercy
Malcolm Gladwell

In 1925, a young American physicist was doing graduate work at Cambridge University, in England. He was depressed. He was fighting with his mother and had just broken up with his girlfriend. His strength was in theoretical physics, but he was being forced to sit in a laboratory making thin films of beryllium. In the fall of that year, he dosed an apple with noxious chemicals from the lab and put it on the desk of his tutor, Patrick Blackett. Blackett, luckily, didn't eat the apple. But school officials found out what had happened, and arrived at a punishment: the student was to be put on probation and ordered to go to London for regular sessions with a psychiatrist.

Probation? These days, we routinely suspend or expel high-school students for doing infinitely less harmful things, like fighting or drinking or taking drugs—that is, for doing the kinds of things that teenagers do. This past summer, Rhett Bomar, the starting quarterback for the University of Oklahoma Sooners, was cut from the team when he was found to have been "overpaid" (receiving wages for more hours than he worked, with the apparent complicity of his boss) at his car dealership. Even in Oklahoma, people seemed to think that kicking someone off a football team for having cut a few corners on his job made perfect sense. This is the age of zero tolerance. Rules are rules. Students have to be held accountable for their actions. Institutions must signal their expectations firmly and unambiguously: every school principal and every college president, these days, reads from exactly the same script. What, then, of a student who gives his teacher a poisoned apple? Surely he ought to be expelled from school and sent before a judge.

Suppose you cared about the student, though, and had some idea of his situation and his potential. Would you feel the same way? You might. Trying to poison your tutor is no small infraction. Then again, you might decide, as the dons at Cambridge clearly did, that what had happened called for a measure of leniency. They knew that the student had never done anything like this before, and that he wasn't well. And they knew that to file charges would almost

Evidence: Examples

How do we know anyone is *incorrigible* or a ***decent kid***? Gladwell seems to believe that these are obvious characteristics of people, but who gets to make these decisions, and based on what evidence?

Evidence: Research

How might readers respond to this move from the made-up stories of Jimmy and Bobby to the *Tennessee study*? Is there enough evidence given in this essay for us to check on the Tennessee study ourselves, to see if we agree with how it was conducted or with Gladwell's characterization of it?

Pathos: How readers are addressed

Gladwell now refers to himself and the audience together as *we*. By assuming we are all in agreement with what he writes, what might he be trying to achieve?

Evidence: Examples

Because of the temporal context surrounding the publication of this essay, Gladwell assumes that his readers know that he is referring in this parenthetical remark to events in Iraq and at Guantanamo; he is also assuming that his readers share his interpretation of the events. Why would he insert such a serious example in parentheses here, when all his preceding examples have involved students?

Evidence: Analogy

Gladwell takes someone else's analogy and turns it around. This analogy involves an event that many take extremely seriously and would not want to see used in a lighthearted way. Do you think Gladwell's overall purpose so far justifies his use of this analogy? What sort of reader, holding what sort of beliefs, would be likely to accept this analogy and find it appropriate? (And why might Gladwell use such a serious analogy here?)

certainly ruin his career. Cambridge wasn't sure that the benefits of enforcing the law, in this case, were greater than the benefits of allowing the offender an unimpeded future.

Schools, historically, have been home to this kind of discretionary justice. You let the principal or the teacher decide what to do about cheating because you know that every case of cheating is different—and, more to the point, that every cheater is different. Jimmy is incorrigible, and needs the shock of expulsion. But Bobby just needs a talking to, because he's a decent kid, and Mary and Jane cheated because the teacher foolishly stepped out of the classroom in the middle of the test and the temptation was just too much. A Tennessee study found that after zero-tolerance programs were adopted by the state's public schools, the frequency of targeted offences soared: the firm and unambiguous punishments weren't deterring bad behavior at all. Is that really a surprise? If you're a teenager, the announcement that an act will be sternly punished doesn't always sink in, and it isn't always obvious when you're doing the thing you aren't supposed to be doing. Why? Because you're a teenager.

Somewhere along the way—perhaps in response to Columbine—we forgot the value of discretion in disciplining the young. "Ultimately, they have to make the right decisions," the Oklahoma football coach, Bob Stoops, said of his players, after jettisoning his quarterback. "When they do not, the consequences are serious." Open and shut: he sounded as if he were talking about a senior executive of Enron, rather than a college sophomore whose primary obligation to Oklahoma was to throw a football in the direction of young men in helmets. You might think that the University of Oklahoma was so touchy about its quarterback being "overpaid" it ought to have kept closer track of his work habits with an on-campus job. But making a fetish of personal accountability conveniently removes the need for institutional accountability. (We court-marshall the grunts who abuse prisoners, not the commanding officers who let the abuse happen.) To acknowledge that the causes of our actions are complex and muddy seems permissive, and permissiveness is the hallmark of an ideology now firmly in disgrace. That conservative patron saint Whittaker Chambers once defined liberalism as Christ without the Crucifixion. But

The end

Why might Gladwell have waited until the end of his essay to mention the name of the student whose actions he described back at the very beginning of the essay? (In case you didn't know, Robert Oppenheimer was one of the people responsible for the atom bomb.)

Context and ethos

What does this essay's being published in the *New Yorker* tell you about Malcolm Gladwell and how others think of his writing? If you know nothing about this magazine, what might that tell you about how Gladwell was viewing his audience while he was writing?

punishment without the possibility of redemption is even worse: it is the Crucifixion without Christ.

As for the student whose career Cambridge saved? He left at the end of the academic year and went to study at the University of Göttingen, where he made important contributions to quantum theory. Later, after a brilliant academic career, he was entrusted with leading one of the most critical and morally charged projects in the history of science. His name was Robert Oppenheimer.

New Yorker, September 4, 2006, pp. 37–38.

Below is one possible way of analyzing Gladwell's claim, reason, warrant, and evidence in the above essay. By separating these elements, you can have a better sense of whether you agree with these elements, whether you think they really do fit together logically, and whether you think the evidence works.

CLAIM: We should apply discretion rather than *zero-tolerance* policies when responding to the bad behavior of youth.

REASON: *Zero-tolerance* policies potentially prevent good people from developing to their full productive potential.

WARRANT: Discretion in response to the bad behavior of youth will help good people develop to their full productive potential.

EVIDENCE: *Facts:* The people who apply zero tolerance apply the policy outside their rightful realm, as the University of Oklahoma case shows. *Shared values:* Zero tolerance does not take into account the differences in people, as the Bobby and Jimmy examples show. Zero tolerance does not take into account the moral development of youth. Zero tolerance removes the need for institutional responsibility. *Appealing to readers' experiences:* Readers are likely to agree, based on their own experiences, that Robert Oppenheimer would perhaps not have gone on to do his important work if *zero tolerance* had been in use in 1925.

A SAMPLE RHETORICAL ANALYSIS

On the opposite page, we show a written rhetorical analysis—a critical analysis—of Malcolm Gladwell's article "No Mercy," which we examined on the previous pages. You should be able to see how this essay grows out of the work of responding to the questions asked of the essay in the previous pages—as well as how this essay cuts to the heart of Gladwell's argument by questioning his warrant.

This rhetorical analysis is one example of how you can write such an analysis.

The beginning: Ethos

This writer gives a quick summary of the Gladwell article, to show that she has done the work of understanding the article. This builds her ethos postively, so her questioning of the article will thus be more persuasive to her readers.

The beginning

Now this writer helps her readers have a sense of what is to come by summarizing—quickly—her main concern about the Gladwell article; she will give evidence for this concern in the paragraphs to follow.

Analyzing ethos

The writer analyzes Gladwell's ethos: He is "confident...but not bullying" and wants to inspire others to think critically.

Logos: Evidence

Here the writer uses direct quotations from the Gladwell article to show that she has read carefully and is responding to specific Gladwell arguments.

→ See pages 316–321 for help with including direct quotations in your writing.

Ethos and pathos: The writer asks questions

After showing her readers the specific parts of Gladwell's writing that concern her, this writer can then raise the questions that motivate her concern.

How would her ethos be different if she had instead phrased these questions as statements? How does asking these questions engage readers (a pathos strategy)?

No Justice, No Mercy?
Responding to Malcolm Gladwell

In his essay "No Mercy," published in the September 4, 2006, issue of the *New Yorker*, Malcolm Gladwell argues implicitly that current "zero-tolerance" policies hurt people more than we realize. For example, Gladwell tells about the brilliant physicist Robert Oppenheimer, who under today's policies probably would have been expelled from college and denied his important career because of dangerous actions he took as a graduate student. With this example Gladwell suggests that current students who are expelled for lesser offenses are losing future careers in which they might contribute to society. While there is much in Gladwell's argument with which I agree, his examples raise for me the question of who is to judge others, and how.

I appreciate the tone of Gladwell's writing. He is a confident writer, but not bullying. There is nothing in his writing to suggest that he thinks anyone who disagrees is somehow stupid or unthoughtful. Instead, Gladwell's writing seems more of a provocation, asking us to think on these matters because they have consequences. I appreciate being drawn into this issue by the range of examples and ideas Gladwell brings into his writing—but those examples lead me to my concerns.

As a possibility for how we might treat the poorly considered actions of the young, Gladwell uses the notion of "discretion," which he describes as being based in an awareness that "every cheater is different" (119). Therefore, Gladwell argues, we need to approach each case with an awareness of who has done the action, and why, in order to decide consequences: "Jimmy is incorrigible, and needs the shock of expulsion," Gladwell writes, but "Bobby just needs a talking to, because he's a decent kid" (119). But how does anyone know these things? What would someone have to do to get to know Jimmy or Bobby well enough to make these decisions with any certainty? And what sort of person would we want to make such decisions that have so much effect on the lives of others? To live together using the discretion that Gladwell asks us to have, we would need to find people who have the time and sensitivity to look carefully into the lives of others, and who have considerable training in understanding the patterns of someone's life so as to make valid decisions.

Ethos: Adding authority by using other sources

After some online searching, this writer found a published report that helps demonstrate that her worry is concrete and real. This source ought to have authority with readers because it is published by a government source—and also because the writer describes the detailed research on which the report is based.

Ethos: Adding authority by quoting the words of others

This writer could have summarized the findings of the report she is citing, but by quoting from it she is able to let the report speak for itself, which tends to be more persuasive to readers.

Concluding

After having given her own evidence in the preceding paragraphs, the writer now summarizes her position so that her readers can leave her writing with a clear idea of her argument. (→ See pages 292–293 on writing conclusions.)

Notice, too, how she shapes her words here: She neither dismisses Gladwell nor insists that she knows it all. How does this shape her ethos? What sort of emotional room does this leave for readers to respond?

Citing sources

→ See Part 8 (pages 307–462) for help with citing sources.

THIS WRITER'S USE OF LOGOS...

To the right is one possible analysis of this writer's use of a claim, a reason, a warrant, and evidence. If you think that this writer has written a persuasive short essay, consider the following:

1 In what order are the claim, reason, and evidence presented in the writing? Why might they be presented in that order?

2 Notice that many other strategies weave into the writing, in support of both the logic of the claim, reason, and evidence, but also to persuade readers to have a sympathetic lean toward the writer's position: Logos matters tremendously, but it cannot stand alone.

Meanwhile, however, many examples exist of discretion that is biased. For one, the United States Department of Justice's Office of Juvenile Justice and Delinquency Prevention published a report in 1995 in which the Office analyzed the available literature on the treatment of minority youth in the juvenile justice system; after analyzing 250 published articles, with 47 being particularly relevant, the report argues that "processing decisions in many State and local juvenile justice systems are not racially neutral" (7).

Whether or not the juvenile justice system is the same now as it was in 1995, what the report shows is that racial bias can enter the system—even from people who are supposed to be professionals in deciding whether a young person committed an offense and how it should be treated. Other kinds of bias—based on class or gender, for example—also seem possible. If we do want discretion as the basis for responding to youth behavior, as Gladwell argues, how do we keep it fair?

I may sound as though I disagree with Gladwell. I do not. I think zero-tolerance policies in high schools harm the futures of people who are still too young to make certain decisions. But until an argument addresses how discretion can be applied knowledgeably and justly, without bias, I will sit uneasily with my beliefs.

Works Cited

Gladwell, Malcolm. "No Mercy." *New Yorker* 4 Sept. 2006: 37–38.
United States. Dept. of Justice. Office of Juvenile Justice and Delinquency Prevention. "Minorities and the Juvenile Justice System: Research Summary." Washington: GPO, 1995.

CLAIM: Discretion is not enough for making decisions about the lives of young people.

REASON: Discretion can be biased.

WARRANT: Young people deserve fair and equal treatment.

EVIDENCE: This writer appeals to the reader's own *experiences* by asking questions about how we make decisions. The writer also uses the *expert testimony* of the U.S. Department of Justice's Office of Juvenile Justice and Delinquency Prevention, and facts supported by that testimony.

QUESTIONS TO GUIDE CRITICAL LOOKING

In the previous pages, we have been focusing primarily on alphabetic texts—but questioning photographs, graphic novels, advertisements, films and videos, and similar texts is equally important.

In our earlier discussions of how to understand what some book covers are doing rhetorically (→ see pages 90–97), we analyzed the covers in terms of the rhetorical choices made by their designers. You can analyze any visual text that way—and then can ask **the same questions on pages 114–115** to help you consider whether you think the text has been designed ethically.

Because visual texts often function differently in society than print texts, you can also ask questions like the following.

QUESTIONS ABOUT AUDIENCE

- Who can see this text? How does the placement of the text (in a museum, on the Internet, in a magazine) shape who can see it? Who won't be able to see it?

- What knowledge is required for an audience to understand the text? Does a viewer have to know something about the history of art, about consumer culture, or about celebrities?

→ The analysis of the book cover on pages 98–99 is one example of critical looking; another example is on pages 128–129.

QUESTIONS ABOUT PURPOSE

• Is the primary purpose of the piece to encourage people to buy or to enjoy? Keep in mind that in either case, you need to say more: If the purpose were simply to sell or to delight for all advertisements or cartoons (for example), then there would be no variety among these texts because they could all achieve their purposes in the same way. If the primary purpose is to encourage people to buy, then there will be secondary purposes such as making people feel they lack something, or that they too can have endless fun, or....

• Why might the text's composers have used a visual text instead of an alphabetic text to achieve their purposes?

QUESTIONS ABOUT CONTEXT

• Are you seeing the text in the context for which it was designed? Where was it designed to be seen?

• How would the text be different if you saw it someplace else? If you are analyzing a painting in a museum, how would it be different in your bedroom? If you are analyzing a comic book, how would the pages be different if you saw them in a formal newspaper like the *New York Times*?

• How would seeing this text change if the number of people around you changed?

QUESTIONS ABOUT ETHOS

• Was this text made by one person or by many? Is it attributed to an organization?

• What knowledge and abilities did the maker(s) of this text need in order to design or produce the text?

QUESTIONS ABOUT PATHOS

• Would you describe this text as simple or complex? Is it cheery or morbid? Active or calm? What features of the text encourage these responses?

• Does this text use pathos as its primary appeal to your attention?

• Where does this piece require you to stand or sit to see it well? Do you need to be close or far away?

• Do you feel that this piece is inviting you to come closer or do you feel as though it is yelling at you to move away? Why?

• How would this piece be different if the colors were different?

QUESTIONS ABOUT LOGOS

• What is made visible in this text? On what people, objects, or processes does this text ask you to focus your eyes?

• What arguments are made by the text?

• What are the parts of this text? Name every element you can visually differentiate.

• What elements of this text do you see first? Which second, which third? Why?

A SAMPLE ANALYSIS OF A VISUAL TEXT

The poster to the right was produced by the Mayor's Office of the City of New York as part of a campaign against domestic violence.

Pathos

This text is simple, composed of one photograph of a woman and a few lines of text. If we were looking at the original poster, the woman would seem almost life-size; as viewers, we are situated as though we were standing close to her, right behind her, as though we could touch her. What emotional relationship might this physical closeness encourage viewers to have with the woman and so the poster?

Pathos

The woman's body is bruised, and she is wearing a hospital gown. How might a viewer's attitude toward the woman and so toward the poster be different if she were wearing a low-cut dress instead?

Logos: Evidence

The poster gives one fact. What evidence is offered in its support? Whose authority is offered in support? Do we know if the fact refers just to high school students in New York City or to those in the entire United States? (Does that matter?) Why might the makers of this poster have chosen to present this fact written on this woman's bruised back instead of on a poster containing only words?

Audience

Who would be interested in this fact about high school students? Notice that the poster's composers have chosen to call attention to "high school students" and not "high school girls." Why might they have made this word choice?

Context

If the audience includes people in high school, then it is likely that the people running the campaign decided to make a poster because schools have many places where posters are easily seen. In addition, the particular visibility of posters says something about why the poster uses pathos as its major strategy: A poster has to catch the eye—quickly—of someone walking by.

Logos: Argument

This poster is encouraging viewers to make phone calls to stop abuse. Does it offer reasons to encourage this action? If so, what are they?

Logos: Arrangement

Why might the words be at the bottom of the poster rather than at the top?

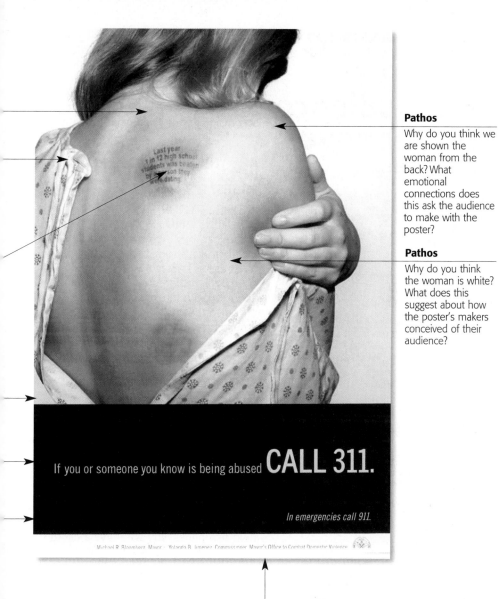

Pathos

Why do you think we are shown the woman from the back? What emotional connections does this ask the audience to make with the poster?

Pathos

Why do you think the woman is white? What does this suggest about how the poster's makers conceived of their audience?

Last year 1 in 12 high school students was beaten by a person they were dating

If you or someone you know is being abused **CALL 311.**

In emergencies call 911.

Michael R. Bloomberg, Mayor · Yolanda B. Jimenez, Commissioner, Mayor's Office to Combat Domestic Violence

Logos: Evidence?

Does the support of the mayor of New York City for this poster serve as expert evidence?

EVALUATING SOURCES
with audience and purpose in mind

The previous pages have asked you to consider your sources carefully to see if you want to be persuaded by them.

Now you can also ask if your sources are appropriate to your composing purposes, given your current understanding of your audience and your purposes.

ARE YOU READY TO APPLY THE INFORMATION IN THE NEXT PAGES?

IF THIS IS YOUR SITUATION, THE ANSWER IS **NO**.

Midnight: Your eyes hurt, and the number of items returned from your database search is 5,652.

Go back to pages 72–73 to learn more about how to narrow down your search terms so that you get fewer but more focused results.

IF THIS IS YOUR SITUATION, THE ANSWER IS **YES**.

You've got a solid research question (although you know you might need to tweak it once you start writing) and you've got a pretty good initial sense of the audience of readers you want to address in your writing. (If you are unsure about your research question, check pages 34–37. If you want to think about your audience a bit more, check pages 150–159.)

If you apply what we present in the next few pages, you will have a list of sources about which you know two important things, as we describe in the next paragraphs.

☐ ONE relevance

☐ TWO credibility

WHAT WILL THIS SECTION HELP YOU ACHIEVE WITH YOUR RESEARCH?

1 **Your sources will be relevant to your audience and purpose.** The sources will supply appropriate support for what you are arguing and will likely be accepted by your audience.

2 **Your sources will be credible to your audience.** Your audience ought to trust the sources, and thus will be more likely to trust any arguments you build based on those sources.

Because you need to know that your sources are both relevant and credible, the process of evaluating sources has two steps—one for evaluating relevance and the other for evaluating credibility.

JUDGING EVIDENCE, JUDGING SOURCES

On pages 104–113, we offered you strategies for judging the evidence offered in others' arguments. Your judgments about those arguments can help you decide if those arguments will be accepted by your readers if you were to use them as evidence in your own writing.

TIP: APPLYING THE CRITERIA IN ORDER

While the criteria of relevance and credibility are equally important, use the steps in order. Determining credibility often takes more effort than determining relevance, so you can save yourself some time by checking relevance first.

FOR RELEVANCE

ask this:
IS THE KIND OF SOURCE
RELEVANT TO YOUR AUDIENCE?

ONE
relevance

TWO
credibility

IF A SOURCE MEETS MOST OF THE CRITERIA TO THE RIGHT, HOLD ON TO IT.

When you are evaluating the relevance of a source, you are evaluating how likely most readers will believe that what is presented in the source is appropriate to your arguments.

Finding sources that meet all the criteria doesn't guarantee that they'll end up in your Works Cited list at the end of your paper—but sources that meet all the criteria are much more likely to help you write a solid, strong, and persuasive argument.

❑ **Given your research question/ purposes, what kinds of sources are likely to be most appealing and persuasive to your particular audience?**

When you are writing an academic research paper, your audience is academic readers, who tend to respect books published by academic presses, academic journal articles, and specialized encyclopedias.

Academic audiences also respect the use of primary sources. (➜ See page 39 on primary sources.)

Depending on your purposes, however, you might need to supplement such sources. For example, if you are writing about the role of women in space exploration, you might want to begin your essay with one woman's personal story about how she got into the U.S. space program; in such a case, you could look in popular periodicals or blogs for such stories—and those sources would be appropriate for your purposes.

then this:
IS A PARTICULAR SOURCE
RELEVANT TO
YOUR ARGUMENT?

☐ **Is the source on topic?**
This might seem too obvious a question to ask, but it isn't. You can save yourself a lot of time if, with each possible source, you ask yourself whether the source really does provide information that is focused on your topic.

☐ **Does the source have a publication date appropriate to your research?**
If you are writing about the current state of a rapidly changing topic—such as AIDS research—you need sources dated close to the moment you are writing; if you are writing about a past event or about past situations that have led to a current event, then you need sources from those time periods as well as from people in the present.

☐ **Does the source bring in perspectives other than those of the sources you've already collected?**
You do not want to collect sources that all take the same position, for two reasons. First, if all you can find are sources that take the same perspective on your topic, then your topic is probably not controversial or interesting enough to be the subject of a paper. Second, your audience is not likely to be persuaded by writing that does not consider multiple perspectives on a topic.

☐ **Does the source provide something interesting?**
Your audience wants to be intellectually engaged with your writing. As you consider a new source, ask yourself if it contains ideas or information that is interesting—funny, provocative, puzzling—and that supports your points. Quoting or citing such ideas or information in your writing helps you write a more engaging paper.

☐ **Does the source bring in data or other information different from the sources you have already collected?**
This criterion is similar to the one preceding, but it asks you to consider how much data or other information is useful for you to collect in order to construct a persuasive position in your writing.

☐ **Does the source suggest other possible directions your research could take?**
We do want you to stay on track in your research as much as you want to stay on track, given that you have a deadline—but we also want you to stay open to the possibilities of reshaping or retouching your research question and purpose as you discover potentially new and exciting approaches.

SAMPLE SOURCES

☑ ONE
relevance

☐ TWO
credibility

To the right are examples showing how
to judge the relevance of a source
based on your research question and
audience.

Pedro's research question is

"What social actions ought the U.S. government be able to take in the face of pandemics?"

He is writing for his classmates and
teacher.

Aaliyah's research question is

"On the Internet, how do ideas spread like viruses?"

She is doing research for a
marketing company whose directors
are considering new online
approaches.

Don't know what "xenotransplantation" means? This is where having a dictionary at hand is helpful—and necessary if your research and knowledge are to grow in sophistication and depth.

Penenberg, Adam L. "Technorati: A New Public Utility." *WIRED News* 14 July 2005. 5 Apr. 2006 <http://www.wired.com/ news/culture/ 0,1284,68204,00.html>.

Fishman, Jay A. "SARS, Xenotransplantation and Bioterrorism: Preventing the Next Epidemic." *American Journal of Transplantation* 3 (2003): 909–12.

This source is **NOT RELEVANT**. Because *Wired News* is generally considered both reputable and hip, and because the story is fairly recent, using this news story could help Pedro make his writing more interesting to his audience. The only connection this story has with Pedro's question, however, is through the analogy between the spread of ideas and the spread of diseases, which will not help Pedro think about how governments ought to counter viral pandemics.

This source is **RELEVANT**. Because this journal article gives recommendations to governments on what they can do—alone and together—to prevent the spread of epidemics, it can help Pedro understand what is planned; he can then research how those plans might affect our rights. The article is important for Pedro's research and is also recently published.

This source is **RELEVANT**. This online news story gives a specific example of how a particular idea spread on the Internet, and compares the spread of the idea to a virus. The story also defines terms that might be useful to Aaliyah because she will have to define terms for her audience.

This source is **RELEVANT**. Because there is much information here about how viruses spread, Aaliyah can use this source to test and develop examples of how viruses and ideas do or do not spread in similar ways. The seriousness of this source—and its timeliness—will also appeal to her audience.

EVALUATING SOURCES

FOR CREDIBILITY: PRINT

IF A SOURCE MEETS MOST OF THE CRITERIA TO THE RIGHT, HOLD ON TO IT.

When you evaluate the credibility of a source, you are evaluating whether most of your readers will accept the facts and arguments you present.

Finding sources that meet all the criteria doesn't guarantee that they'll end up in your Works Cited list at the end of your paper—but sources that meet all the criteria are much more likely to help you write a well-supported and persuasive argument.

A NOTE

Some people are nostalgic for pre-Internet days because the institutions of print publication seem to make evaluating a source's credibility easy. The costs and complexities of print publication and distribution are behind that perception.

The printing of books, magazines, and newspapers is expensive. Those who provide the money want return on their investments, so they want readers to trust what is published. Print publishing therefore developed systems of editors and fact-checkers: Often when you buy a print text its credibility has been checked in different ways. (Libraries contribute to this system, too, because librarians often buy only books recommended to them by trusted sources.)

But, as you know, not all print texts are credible (think supermarket tabloids). Some publishers have political motivations, for example. You cannot therefore count on something you find in print to be absolutely reliable—and you also have to consider what criteria your audience will use for judging credibility.

TIP: HAVE ANY QUESTIONS?
If you have any questions as you apply these criteria to a source, a librarian is a good person to ask.

DETERMINING THE CREDIBILITY OF A PRINT SOURCE

☐ **Who published the source?**
Look at page 44, on Kinds of Sources, to read about the motivations behind different kinds of publishers. A publisher's motivations can help you decide the level of credibility the source will have for your audience.

☐ **Does the author have sufficient qualifications for writing on the topic?**
Most print publications will tell you something about the author so that you can judge; you can also search online to learn about the author.

If you cannot find an author or sponsoring agency, is that because no one wants to take responsibility?

☐ **What evidence is presented?**
Is the evidence of a kind that fits the claims? What kind of evidence would be stronger?

☐ **Does the evidence seem accurate?**

☐ **Do the author's claims seem adequately supported by the offered evidence?**

☐ **Does the source try to cover all the relevant facts and opinions?**
If you are at the beginning of your research, this might be hard to answer, but as you dig deeper into your topic, you'll have a sense of the range of perspectives one can take on your topic, and you'll be able to judge how widely a source engages with the issues at stake.

☐ **What is the genre of the source?**
Is the source an advertisement (or does it contain advertisements)? Advertisers sometimes try to influence what is published near their advertisements to keep their appeal strong.

But it also matters if the source is an opinion piece, a thought-experiment or essay, or a piece of scholarship: Writers and readers have different expectations for different genres regarding how much (unsupported) opinion is appropriate.

☐ **Does the source make its position, perspective, and biases clear?**
When writers do not make their own biases clear, they often do not want readers to think about how those biases affect the writers' arguments.

☐ **Does the source make a point of seeking out different perspectives?**
If so, this is an indication that a writer is trying to understand a topic fully and not just giving a narrow view.

☐ **Does the writing seek to sound reasonable and thoughtful?**
Inflammatory language in a piece of writing is a sign that the writer is trying to move you solely through your emotional responses without engaging your thoughtfulness.

SAMPLE SOURCES

☑ ONE **relevance**

☑ TWO **credibility**

To the right are examples of how to judge the credibility of a print source based on your research question and audience.

Pedro's research question is

"What social actions ought the U.S. government be able to take in the face of pandemics?"

He is writing for his classmates and teacher.

Aaliyah's research question is

"On the Internet, how do ideas spread like viruses?"

She is doing research for a marketing company whose directors are considering new online approaches.

Gorman, Christine. "How Scared Should We Be?" *Time* 17 Oct. 2005: 30–34.

Fishman, Jay A. "SARS. Xenotransplantation and Bioterrorism: Preventing the Next Epidemic." *American Journal of Transplantation* 3 (2003): 909–12.

This source is **NOT CREDIBLE** for this audience and purpose. *Time* is well known but is not a science or policy journal; the author is not a scientist or lawmaker. Though the author quotes credible agencies, she does not give citations for us to check. The article's evidence is patchy because the questions are complex but the space for answering them is small. The language is almost inflammatory, to catch attention, not thoughts. Although this article is relevant to Pedro's question, Pedro and his readers should be skeptical about this article's depth. Pedro could perhaps use anecdotes from this article, but ought not make this a main source.

This source is **CREDIBLE** for this audience and purpose. Pedro's readers will respect the standards of the academic journal: The journal gives the author's scientific credentials (not just those of his sources), the decision to publish the article was made by other scientists (which ensures accuracy of evidence), and there are clear relations between the evidence and claims as well as strong challenges from other perspectives. The writing is exact, key words are defined, and inflammatory language is carefully avoided.

This source could be **CREDIBLE** for this audience and purpose, depending on how Aaliyah uses it. For all the reasons listed above, Aaliyah and her audience ought to be skeptical of this article. Given Aaliyah's purposes, however, the article covers enough different perspectives to be useful for developing the analogy between epidemics and Internet viruses—as long as Aaliyah notes her skepticism about the source.

This source is **CREDIBLE** for this audience and purpose. For all the reasons mentioned above, this source will carry weight with Aaliyah's audience, even if Aaliyah uses this source only to provide examples supporting her descriptions of viruses and how they spread.

EVALUATING SOURCES
FOR CREDIBILITY: ONLINE

✓ ONE relevance

✓ TWO credibility

DETERMINING THE CREDIBILITY OF AN ONLINE SOURCE

Use the criteria for evaluating print sources, with the following additions:

☐ **Who published the source?**

The domain name in the URL can indicate something about a publisher's credibility. (Example domain names are microsoft.com, whitehouse.gov, or lacorps.org.) Look at the last letters in the domain name:

.gov   A website created by an office of the U.S. federal government

.com   A website created for a company that is seeking to publicize itself or sell products

.org   A nonprofit organization—but anyone can register for the .org domain

.edu   Colleges and universities

.mil   U.S. military websites

.me.us A website for one of the fifty U.S. states: The first two letters are the abbreviation of the state name

.de   A website created in a country other than the U.S.—but websites created outside this country can also use .com, .net, and .org

.net   The most generic ending; Internet Service Providers (ISPs) as well as individuals can have websites whose URLs end in .net

What sorts of websites will your audience think are most appropriate and credible, given your purpose?

Does the author have qualifications for writing on the topic?

With some websites you won't be able to answer this because you won't be able to determine who the author is, either because no name is given or a pseudonym is used.

If you cannot find the name of an author or sponsoring agency, perhaps no one wants to take responsibility or someone is worried about the consequences of publishing the information. If you are writing on a controversial topic, you could use information from such a site to describe the controversy and support the fact that there is a controversy—but you couldn't use the site to offer factual support for anything else.

What evidence is offered?

In the most credible print sources, authors list the sources of their evidence; the same holds true for websites. If you cannot find the source of the evidence used, the site is not as credible as a site that does list sources.

Does the source make its position, perspective, and biases clear?

Approach websites just as you approach print pages with this question, except that with websites you can also check where links on the site take you. A website may give the appearance of holding a middle line on a position, but if the websites to which it links support only one position, then question the credibility of the original site.

What is the genre of the source?

Some online genres, such as newspapers and magazines, mimic print genres; approach them with the same questions as you would their print equivalents.

But webpages can easily be made to look like any genre. For example, some websites look like the informational material you pick up in a doctor's office. Just as when you receive such material in a doctor's office, however, you need to look carefully: Is the website actually advertising a company's treatments or products?

Also keep in mind that blogs are a tricky genre to use as sources. There are many well-respected blogs published by experts; if you want to cite such a blog, you will need to give evidence why that particular blog is respected by other experts. On the other hand, if you are citing words from a blog solely to show a range of opinions on a topic, the blog's credibility will not be an issue.

ALSO:

How well designed is the website or webpage?

A site that looks professionally designed, is straightforward to navigate, and loads quickly suggests that its creators put time and resources into all the other aspects of the site; these characteristics could also indicate that the site was published by an organization rather than an individual. Do any of these factors matter for your purpose and audience?

EVALUATING SOURCES FOR CREDIBILITY: ONLINE
SAMPLE SOURCES

ONE relevance

TWO credibility

To the right are examples of how to judge the credibility of an online source based on your research question and audience.

Pedro's research question is

"What social actions ought the U.S. government be able to take in the face of pandemics?"

He is writing for his classmates and teacher.

Aaliyah's research question is

"On the Internet, how do ideas spread like viruses?"

She is doing research for a marketing company whose directors are considering new online approaches.

United States. Dept. of Health and Human Services. *HHS Pandemic Influenza Plan.* 8 Nov. 2005. 4 Apr. 2006 <http://www.hhs.gov/pandemicflu/plan/appendixe.html>.

Wikipedia contributors. "Virus." *Wikipedia, The Free Encyclopedia.* 7 Apr. 2006, 16:10 UTC <http://en.wikipedia.org/wiki/Virus>.

This source is **CREDIBLE** for this audience. It has been published under the authority of the government, which has been charged by its citizenry to provide accurate information on matters of such importance. This source has numerous links to issues Pedro will find useful, each of which includes a long list of sources from which the evidence has been drawn, and which each person can access and check. The perspective of this website is clear: It tries to be open to all the questions people like Pedro are asking and to provide information from all the relevant agencies, institutes, and scientific journals.

This source is (probably) **NOT CREDIBLE** for this audience. Although researchers have shown Wikipedia to be as dependable as *The Encyclopedia Britannica* and that Wikipedia is usually as up-to-date as possible, many audiences do not know this or understand how articles are composed in this online source. If Pedro feels compelled to use this source, he should find out his teacher's view—but even if his teacher approves, Pedro's writing will be more persuasive with backup from multiple sources. (He can use Wikipedia as a link to other sources, taking advantage of the Resources listed at the bottom of the Wikipedia page.)

This source is **CREDIBLE** for Aaliyah's audience because they believe government agencies are public and subject to oversight and that the advice provided is based on the best, most up-to-date evidence available. Because government websites can nonetheless be subject to partisan influence, Aaliyah—like Pedro—will still need to supplement this source with other sources in order to show broad agreement among a range of credible sources.

This source is (probably) **CREDIBLE** for this audience. Aaliyah's purposes are different from Pedro's: She will use the information on the Wikipedia site for defining terms rather than supporting her major arguments, and her overall purpose is speculative, so her audience will read her writing with a different expectation of credibility than will Pedro's audience. If, when she cites it, Aaliyah makes clear how information is compiled in Wikipedia, her audience is likely to accept it as credible.

RESEARCHING ETHICALLY

When others recognize that something legally belongs to you and that you can use it as you see fit, that thing is considered your property.

When we hear **property** we probably think of land or buildings, which, legally, are considered to be *real property*; *personal property*, on the other hand, consists of objects you can move with you. Both real and personal property are things that can be touched.

Intellectual property refers to things you cannot touch: ideas. When someone invents, writes, draws, composes, or performs something, that person's intellectual property isn't in the particular object—the thing invented or the book written—but in the ideas that make the invention or book possible.

There are two kinds of intellectual property: **industrial property**, which is inventions and trademarks like company logos, and **creative property**, which is literary and artistic works. **Creative property** is covered by copyright laws.

Copyright law developed over several hundred years, in a push-pull process between individual authors, singers, and other creators of culture and those who publish and distribute what the creators make. Copyright gives legal protection to creators so that they have control over how what they make gets used by others.

Plagiarism occurs when someone uses another's creative property without the other's consent or knowledge. This can involve using a part of another's work or passing off the whole as one's own. Plagiarism is unethical and can be illegal.

SHARED CULTURE, ACADEMIC RESEARCH, AND FAIR USE

If we had to pay the inventor every time we used certain inventions—such as speech or writing—we would probably have no culture. The same goes for some ideas: If we had to pay someone every time we told a fairy tale, sang an old lullaby, or repeated the story of George Washington chopping down the cherry tree, we would have no shared experiences to bind us as a culture. In recognition of this, it is the law that after a set number of years, creators' copyright control over their productions passes into what is called the **Public Domain**. When a creative production is in the public domain, others can use it freely, as when the Disney Company makes a movie about Pocahantas or the Little Mermaid.

But academic research—in all the disciplines of the sciences, social sciences, and the humanities—cannot wait the length of time it takes for ideas to pass into the public domain. Academic research depends on being able to use and build on the ideas of others *now*, as does artistic development. In recognition of such conditions, there is a doctrine in U.S. copyright law called *fair use*.

TIP: IS IT FAIR USE?

Fair use protects most academic uses of intellectual property—but as soon as you use that property for personal gain or commercial uses, the use is no longer protected.

FAIR USE

Fair use is a doctrine in copyright law that allows certain uses of other's copyrighted material without needing permission. Fair use does not specify exactly how much of another's work one may use; instead, four factors are considered, in legal cases, to help determine if a use is fair:

1 **The purpose and character of the use.** Is the use commercial or for nonprofit and educational purposes—such as criticism, parody, or art? Fair use is meant to support public, not personal, enrichment. If the use transforms the copied work, making something new of it, that is also more likely to be considered fair use.

2 **The nature of the copyrighted work.** Generally, uses of published non-fiction works are considered to benefit the public—and not harm the rights of a copyright holder—more so than uses of unpublished or fiction works.

3 **The amount and substantiality of the portion used in relation to the copyrighted work as a whole.** The less one copies, the more likely the copying is to be considered fair use.

4 **The effect of the use upon the potential market for or value of the copyrighted work.** If the use will not cause the copyright holder to lose income, it is more likely to be considered fair use.

The doctrine of fair use underpins academic uses of the words of others—as in research writing.

DEVELOPING A THESIS STATEMENT— AND PUTTING IT TO WORK

Riley has done initial online and library research into how microcredit changes women's lives in developing countries, as the notes on page 29 describe.

Analyzing the sources

Because Riley asked the research questions she did (page 85), she read her sources looking for why women are the focus of microcredit and how microcredit changes women's lives.

Although most sources spoke glowingly about microcredit, a few pointed out problems—and so Riley looked for more sources to support or refute those claims.

She then found more sources that questioned some of the benefits of microcredit. Through her analysis, she recognized that they tended to come from feminist perspectives—and so she is aware that various audiences will respond to those sources differently.

Because of this continued research, however, Riley believes that pointing out such problems is justified.

First thesis statement

A thesis statement has this basic form, as described on pages 102–103:

CLAIM + REASON

Based on her research, Riley writes:

> Microcredit is not always good for women because it keeps them in poverty and makes them vulnerable to familial violence.

Evaluating the first thesis statement

Effective and engaging papers are most likely to develop from thesis statements that

1 Have a concrete and focused claim.

2 Have a debatable claim.

3 Give a reason (or reasons) that can be supported.

Here's an analysis of Riley's first try:

1 The claim that *microcredit is not always good for women* is vague and broad. What do **good** or **not always** mean here? Is Riley talking about all women everywhere?

2 Because so many sources wrote only positively about microcredit, Riley's claim is certainly debatable.

3 If Riley has found several relevant and credible sources providing evidence for these reasons, then her reasons can work for her—although they still seem a little vague.

Second thesis statement

After evaluating her first try, Riley writes:

> *Microcredit should be offered to women in developing countries only accompanied by discussion support groups and classes in economics, because otherwise the women won't know how to change the community conditions that encourage poverty.*

Evaluating the second thesis statement

1 In her paper, Riley will have to explain more clearly what she means by *discussion support groups and classes in economics*, but this claim is concrete because it makes specific recommendations; it also focuses on a few recommendations rather than many.

2 For the same reasons as before, Riley's claim is debatable.

3 Riley's reasons are now more concrete: They help her understand that she will need to write about conditions that encourage poverty in communities and give evidence that microcredit programs that don't do what she recommends do not result in community change.

The right sources? Enough sources?

By evaluating her thesis statement, Riley can see that she needs to be sure she has enough relevant and credible sources to supply the information described in points 1 and 3 above.

HINTS & TIPS FOR EVALUATING SOURCES

IF YOU ARE UNSURE ABOUT THE RELEVANCE OR CREDIBILITY OF A SOURCE...

Ask someone who might be more familiar with the source, such as your teacher, a librarian, or someone who has researched your topic before.

Knowledge about relevance and credibility of sources increases over time. Those who write repeatedly on similar research topics learn who respected writers and researchers are, and learn (in addition to what we've listed here) lots of subtle signs for what makes a source relevant and credible.

REMEMBER THAT FINDING A SUFFICIENT NUMBER OF SOURCES IS ONLY PART OF WRITING A PERSUASIVE PAPER

Have you ever started to read a letter to the editor or a blog that you had to put aside because the tone of voice was rude or obnoxious? The letter or blog might have had perfectly fine evidence in support of its arguments, but other choices the writer made in constructing the whole argument might have undone the worthiness of the research.

The same can happen to you in writing a research paper. Look on pages 160–179 for help with making choices about the other aspects of a research paper.

HOW DO YOU KNOW YOU HAVE COLLECTED ENOUGH SOURCES?

❏ **Do your sources approach your question from a range of directions?** Readers see it as a sign of careful and thoughtful research when writers consider a range of positions on a topic; you should not consider your research done until you have collected—and can reference—a range of positions.

❏ **Do you have the right range of kinds of sources?** With academic research papers, audiences usually expect sources that are academic. If your writing is for a nonacademic audience, using many kinds of sources can demonstrate that you have done broad and careful research.

❏ **Do you have enough sources to support every step of the argument you are making?**

❏ **Do you have enough sources to help you develop solid and well-supported responses to your research questions?**

❏ **Before you can finally decide if you have enough sources,** however, you need to know if you have the sources that will fully answer your audience's questions on this topic. Look to Part 4—where you turn your thesis statement into a statement of purpose—to help you decide if you really do have all the sources you need for your particular audience.

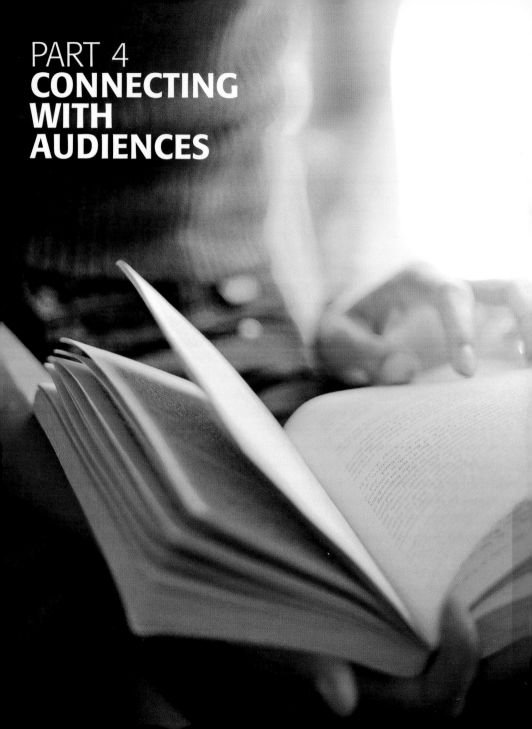

PART 4
**CONNECTING
WITH
AUDIENCES**

CONTENTS

WHERE ARE WE IN THE PROCESS FOR COMPOSING?

Understanding your project

Getting started

Asking questions

Shaping your project for others	Thinking in depth about audience Developing a statement of purpose
Drafting a paper	Writing a rough draft
Getting feedback	Receiving feedback to drafts Developing a revision plan

Revising

Polishing

UNDER-STANDING YOUR AUDIENCE

THE CONCERN

You know what you are writing about. For example, in Parts 2 and 3 we followed Riley's development of ideas for writing about how microcredit loans change women's lives in developing countries. As you saw, Riley put together a thesis statement: *Microcredit should be offered to women in developing countries only accompanied by discussion support groups and classes in economics,* she wrote, *because otherwise the women won't know how to change the community conditions that encourage poverty.* **But who needs to know this? For whom does this argument matter, and why?**

Through her research, Riley has accumulated some supporting evidence for her thesis, but what of that evidence will be most persuasive? Into what order should she put her evidence? What tone of voice should she use in her writing?

Riley can answer these questions only if she has some sense of who will read her writing and why.

Riley can say, *I am writing to people who know about microcredit and think it's always good*—but that level of understanding of audience is vague; it does not help her make the choices posed by the questions above.

How can Riley develop a more discerning and useful sense of her readers so that she can make specific choices about her writing?

WAYS TO ADDRESS THE CONCERN

Experienced writers will tell you that understanding their audiences is the most important step in composing writing that achieves its purposes.

Concrete and persuasive writing grows out of thinking about what your readers believe and why. For example, if Riley is writing to people who think microcredit is good, she needs to ask, *Why do they think microcredit is good? What do they think is good about it? Why haven't they heard about some of the questionable sides of microcredit? Just what do they know about it, at all?*

There is also another important question Riley has to ask, a question that any writer has to ask when addressing an audience that might not know about the topic: *Why should my readers care?*

Those questions suggest further research as well as decisions a writer like Riley has to make about readers. Riley has to research her readers—and their beliefs and opinions—because if she is going to be persuasive about microcredit, she will have to address what matters to her readers about the lives of women in developing countries.

Riley needs to develop a thicker characterization of her audience, so she needs to think about her audience as concretely as possible. If she can think of them as real, living, breathing people with emotions and attitudes toward events, then she can write to them almost as though she would talk with them, taking into consideration their opinions, thoughts, and feelings.

Whether you are writing a business memo, composing a flyer about your band, or producing a research website on the Gilded Age in the United States, taking some steps to help you think about your audiences more concretely will help you produce more effective writing.

Following, we suggest strategies for thinking about your audience in depth. Here are the steps we follow:

general observations about shared characteristics

more specific observations about what audiences know, think, and feel about a topic

narrowing further by thinking about real, specific readers

narrowing further by choosing which audiences you will address (while keeping in mind the complexities of audiences)

developing a statement of purpose

UNDERSTANDING YOUR AUDIENCE
CHARACTERISTICS YOUR AUDIENCE MIGHT SHARE

You can begin thinking about your audience by considering their general characteristics and how those characteristics can affect the attitudes they might have toward your topic.

YOU MIGHT THINK YOU ALREADY KNOW YOUR AUDIENCE…

You are writing a paper for your classmates (which, as you know, also means you are writing for your teacher). Or perhaps you are writing a memo to your boss proposing new procedures.

In each case, you think you know these people. After all, you live and work with them; you spend considerable time in varying degrees of contact.

But do you know their concerns and opinions on your topic? Do you know *why* they hold those concerns and opinions?

If your writing is to catch and hold these readers' attention, you need to give time to what they think about your topic, and why they think those things.

OR MAYBE YOU DON'T KNOW YOUR AUDIENCE

You are writing a letter to the editor of your city's newspaper. You are putting together a grant application for a non-profit organization. You are composing webpages for a new business.

In such cases, you probably don't know your audiences. Newspaper audiences are broad; people from diverse positions make grant decisions; businesses try to reach wide audiences. How do you shape your writing in these cases?

Even when you are writing to audiences with whom you are not in regular contact, you can still make judgments, based on the information you do have, about why the audiences will read what you offer and how their concerns and opinions will shape their reading.

READERS' GENERAL CHARACTERISTICS

No matter how much or how little you know about your readers, use what you do know to help you compose.

Step through the following general characteristics, asking how they might impinge on readers' responses to your thesis:

❑ age ❑ gender

❑ ethnicity ❑ language

❑ level of education ❑ able-bodiness

❑ sexual orientation ❑ class

❑ upbringing ❑ place of living

❑ place of work

❑ other characteristics that might matter

If you know your audience well, you can focus on the characteristics they have in common, such as age or place of living. If your audience is a general audience, or if you do not know your audience, step through these characteristics to consider which matter most.

TIP: USING CARE WITH AUDIENCE CHARACTERISTICS

To define someone just by age, ethnicity, level of education, gender, or class—or even to define based on all the characteristics above—is to miss the complex mix of experiences and culture that shapes each of us. The characteristics above are just a beginning to help you think about how readers *might* respond. You can never know for sure how a person's particular life will affect his or her responses.

FOR EXAMPLE…

For Riley, both the age and gender of her readers might matter. More women are likely to identify with the plights of other women than are men; people who do not have children might not sympathize with women trying to eke out a small living for their families or get an education for their children.

In addition, people who have not traveled much or who have grown up in middle-class neighborhoods might not have experienced the social and economic conditions underlying poverty, which is what Riley wants to discuss.

If Riley is writing to a class of peers—and to her teacher—what do these observations tell her about their concerns? On which of their experiences can Riley draw to increase their interest in what she's writing?

FOR EXAMPLE…

You are writing a letter to the editor of your local paper about a proposed wind power plant that a power company wants to install on land that was once a farm. You live nearby, and are concerned about the potential noise of the plant and an increase in traffic. Are people who do not live as close to the farm going to think your concerns are simply selfish? Are people looking to bring jobs to the area going to think your concerns are only about the niceties of life instead of the essentials, like jobs?

UNDERSTANDING YOUR AUDIENCE

WHAT DO PEOPLE KNOW, THINK, AND FEEL ABOUT THE ISSUE?

The attitudes people have toward an issue can shape how committed they are to their positions.

READERS AS PEOPLE WITH OPINIONS AND ATTITUDES

Move your focus from general characteristics to what people feel about a topic or issue. Talk to potential readers, asking about

❑ what they know of the topic.

❑ their emotional responses to the topic.

❑ how they have learned what they know of the topic.

❑ personal connections they might have to the topic.

❑ values/beliefs/commitments related to the topic.

❑ questions they might have about the topic.

❑ their self-identity as it connects them to the topic. How do they see themselves connected to the topic because of their specific relations to others? That is, does it matter that a reader is a mother, a daughter, unemployed, a Republican or a leftist, rich or not, a boss or a worker, a student or a teacher, ambitious or laid back, or...?

❑ recent events—locally, nationally, or internationally—that might shape their responses to the topic.

If you cannot talk directly with readers, ask yourself the same questions, imagining how people with different backgrounds would respond.

FOR EXAMPLE...

If you were writing to argue that it might be time to build more nuclear power plants in the United States, you might learn that many people are opposed. You might learn that most people learned about the science of nuclear power in high school textbooks; they also learned about nuclear power from reading newspapers and magazines about cancer rates following Chernobyl and how people can no longer live in that community because of radiation. And, silly as it may seem, all the science fiction movies people have seen about mutations do underlie general perception, further adding to the general emotional climate of fear and uncertainty around nuclear power.

In addition, people who have children are perhaps more resistant to nuclear power because they do not want their children to be in danger. On the other hand, businesspeople (or children of businesspeople) might be more concerned about the future costs of power because of how those costs affect their ability to keep their businesses running.

These observations can help writers understand that, for most readers these days, making decisions about nuclear power is not simply a matter of coolly weighing numeric, scientific evidence; it is also about fear of mutations, cancer, and the destruction of communities. This tells writers that they probably should not compose a list of facts but will have to address people's emotional concerns about radiation and its potential long-term effects.

FOR EXAMPLE...

In quick discussions, Riley learns that most of her classmates know nothing about microcredit and the lives of women in developing countries, or they know a little bit from having seen a television show. She learns that many don't think microcredit is something they need to worry about because it happens in other countries and involves people whose lives are very different.

From her research, Riley knows that microcredit organizations are at work in the United States, too, so she thinks that she might be able to make her research interesting because it does apply here—and because she can perhaps shape her writing to help her readers think about the economic conditions of their own lives.

In addition, when Riley talks to men in her class about microcredit, she learns that they at first think it is a women's issue that does not concern them. She also learns, however, that almost all the men care deeply for their mothers and respect the work their mothers do to take care of their families—so Riley realizes that she might be able to help her male readers connect to her writing by encouraging them to keep in mind that the women who receive microcredit loans are often mothers, which she has learned from her research.

MAKING AUDIENCES REAL AND SPECIFIC

Writing a note to friends is different from writing a paper for a group of people you have never met or know only peripherally. When you know the people to whom you are writing, you can imagine their facial expressions and their responses, and you can shape your writing to address them specifically. When you write for people you don't know well, it can feel as though your words float in air.

This is a problem all writers face, and it can cause writers to produce writing that is too abstract and that does not engage its readers.

Companies that design tools or software have the same problem: They need to design objects that real people can use. Companies test their products with real people at all stages of development, but because they can't always have real users around, they also **create** three or four imaginary people who typify the audience they are trying to reach. They name and flesh out these imaginary people as much as they can—and then they design for those *people*.

As a writer, you can do the same thing: **Imagine three to four readers who range across the characteristics that most capture who might be in your real audience.**

Fawn is 29 and owns a small company that builds electro-optic mechanisms for the military. She watches carefully over the bookkeeping for her company, and is very concerned about how the personal and business taxes she pays are used. She also helps support her sister, who is disabled and has two daughters.

Jake is 25 and lives in a large city where he works for a real estate development company. He was raised in a big family. His family worshipped in a denomination that holds as part of its doctrine that women should be obedient to their husbands in all things. Jake continues to attend church and finds much strength from his faith.

Tony is 18, lives in a big city, works at a nonprofit organization part time while he goes to school, and shares a large, old rowhouse with five friends, some of whom grew up outside the United States. He wants to travel after he graduates and perhaps work overseas.

Having thought about a range of readers by doing the work on the preceding pages, Riley can distill her readers into the three imaginary people above. The descriptions above are short because of our space here; Riley can make them longer, and can include specific comments made by people with whom she's spoken. By doing this work, Riley can imagine herself writing to real people, and can keep concretely in mind why her readers might be more or less resistant to microcredit.

Importantly, by thinking of these people, Riley can see that, beyond the features of age, gender, or place of birth, people's different life experiences shape their concerns in many different ways.

If you do this work, you can identify a range of concerns and attitudes that people hold that might help you decide how to shape your writing—as we explore on the next pages.

UNDERSTANDING YOUR AUDIENCE

SOME COMPLEXITIES OF AUDIENCES

By thinking of your readers as real people, you can see how their reasons for caring about a topic vary, and you'll see that sometimes you need to exclude certain kinds of readers; at the same time you might need to address multiple audiences.

(Keep in mind the thesis statement with which Riley is currently working: *Microcredit should be offered to women in developing countries only accompanied by discussion support groups and classes in economics, because otherwise the women won't know how to change the community conditions that encourage poverty.*)

OVERLAPPING AND DIFFERING CONCERNS

By coming up with the imaginary Fawn, Jake, and Tony, Riley can see that people will have varying attitudes toward and concerns about microcredit.

Someone like Fawn will probably be interested in whether microcredit is effective, since many public microcredit institutions (inside and outside the United States) receive some support from U.S. taxes. Because of her experiences with her sister, however, Fawn might also be interested in learning about programs that help women gain economic strengths and abilities.

Jake might resist the whole idea of microloans being made to women because (Riley knows from research) they can encourage women to work outside the house and develop business connections separate from the family.

Tony might be interested because he just generally seems to be curious about global poverty issues—but Riley might also be able to pique his interest by writing about potential job positions with microcredit institutions.

Some of Fawn's and Tony's concerns overlap: They are both interested in the life conditions of other people. Tony might not be at all interested in how taxes get used, but because he might want to work for a microcredit organization, both he and Fawn would be interested in learning about the conditions that make microcredit organizations effective.

Jake's concerns are completely different, based as they are in beliefs about relations between women and men.

WHICH CONCERNS TO ADDRESS?

If Riley wants to write for readers like Jake, she would probably have to change her thesis: She would have to argue about fundamental questions concerning the status of women before she could make any claims about how microcredit is good for women. Such arguments can be very rewarding, because we can learn a tremendous amount about the beliefs of ourselves and others. Often, however, arguments over fundamental beliefs are frustrating because they are arguments over positions with which we have grown up and that most anchor our lives: If one doesn't want to question these beliefs, then argument is not possible.

If Riley doesn't want to change her thesis to address the status of women, she can decide to focus her writing for readers who accept, at the very least, that women ought to be able to make their own economic decisions.

Readers like Fawn and Tony meet that criterion, but Riley needs to decide if she can address all their concerns and interests—taxes, helping women, global poverty, potential jobs—or should focus on one or a few.

In making decisions about audiences, sometimes it is possible to focus narrowly and address only those people who hold very similar beliefs—but this is a rare luxury. Most often, writing situations require us to address audiences who hold overlapping beliefs, people like Fawn and Tony. Writers need to be aware of the overlaps as well as of the differences so that none of those differences are forgotten.

HAVING AN AUDIENCE IN THE BACKGROUND

Many writing situations have multiple audiences, one that's in the foreground and one that's quietly but importantly in the background. Riley, for example, has an assignment that asks her to write to people like her classmates— but she knows that her teacher is in the background. Someone else might be composing an office memo going to a direct supervisor, recommending a particular purchase, but that memo might very well move up to the supervisor's supervisor as the purchasing decision gets made.

In such cases, you do not address that background audience as directly as you do the foreground audience—but your writing decisions need to be alert to the expectations of that background audience. The other people in your class might not care as much about your grammar as your teacher, but your grammar nonetheless has to meet the teacher's expectations. Similarly, you might whip out an informal memo if just your supervisor were reading; more formality is better for the supervisor's supervisor, as is attention to the budgets of the whole company and not just those of the department overseen by your direct supervisor.

STARTING TO WRITE FOR AN AUDIENCE

MOVING FROM A THESIS STATEMENT TO A STATEMENT OF PURPOSE

A thesis statement, as we described in Part 3 of this book, is a short statement summarizing the logic of your argument.

→ See pages 102–103.

Because humans respect logic but are also, well, human, writers also must consider more than just the potential logic of their words. You need to consider how your writing will be emotionally persuasive to a particular audience and how your readers will construct a sense of you—your authority, believability, and general character—based on your words. (→ See pages 92–95 for more on pathos and ethos.) A statement of purpose helps you do this.

A statement of purpose weaves together the logical purpose of a thesis statement with what a writer learns about audience from doing the thinking and research we have described on the preceding pages.

A statement of purpose is not itself a formal piece of writing. Instead, it is thinking-on-paper, a way to help you consider what you really want your readers to think, feel, or do as they read your writing and when they are done reading it.

FOR EXAMPLE...

Here is a thesis statement for a research paper:

> We can build new nuclear power plants in the United States to help take care of our energy needs and reduce reliance on foreign oil because nuclear power plants have become safer and more reliable.

One possible statement of purpose from that thesis statement is this:

> My audience is a general audience, of different ages and backgrounds. They've heard or read about Chernobyl, Three Mile Island, and the government's tests in Utah in the 1950s. They've seen science fiction movies. So they're likely to start reading with some real fears—that nuclear energy, not carefully handled, can result in horrible children's cancers, as in Chernobyl—as well as some fears grounded in speculation, from movies.
>
> Because of those fears, I doubt I can change their minds completely—but I'm hoping to persuade them *just to look again at nuclear power*. I believe recent developments might put them more at ease.
>
> My readers also share concerns that might encourage them to be more open. They are concerned about how current energy sources—oil and coal—affect the environment. They are concerned about the costs of power production and use. So if I can show how nuclear power might just be cleaner and less expensive, they are likely to look at it again.
>
> Should I start by addressing their fears, or should I start by talking about a form of energy that's cleaner and less expensive?

HOW A STATEMENT OF PURPOSE HELPS A WRITER

By writing this statement of purpose, the person writing this paper gets help in making several important decisions:

- **Ethos.** Because this writer is trying to encourage people to be open to something that was feared in the past, he needs to have a careful tone of voice in his writing and admit that he doesn't have all the answers. If he came across as a know-it-all, how do you think his readers would likely respond?

- **Pathos.** This writer will learn that, because he is trying to shift people's thinking about something that has frightened them, he needs to acknowledge the fear and not pretend that it doesn't exist. If he made fun of the fear, or made it sound as though only stupid people are afraid, chances are he'd lose his audience.

- **Examples and evidence that will be useful, given the audience.** This writer will learn that he needs to give many—and very credible—sources to persuade his readers that nuclear power might be cleaner and less expensive than oil or coal.

HOW TO WRITE A STATEMENT OF PURPOSE

To prepare,

- You need to have a thesis statement that you've developed following the guidelines on pages 146–147.

- You need to have thought about your audience in the ways we've described on pages 152–159.

- Set aside some time (thirty minutes to one hour) when you can be relaxed and write without being distracted.

To write a statement of purpose, write in response to the following questions:

- Who, to the best of your ability to describe them, are your readers? What do they know—or not—on your topic?

- Given what you know about your audience, what sort of immediate responses are they likely to have to the claim and reason in your thesis statement?

- When they finish reading your writing, what would you like them to think, feel, or do?

- What sort of shifts—in emotion, in opinion—is your audience going to have to make, to move from their likely initial response to the response you hope they have when finished reading?

This is informal writing, but this is writing that helps you move from writing-to-learn to writing-to-communicate (➔ see pages 18–19). This writing saves you time by helping you make important decisions about your writing before you start it, before you get yourself too tied down to a first draft.

TIP: JUST WHAT CAN YOU ACHIEVE WITH WRITING?

Have you ever had your mind changed **completely** on a topic (especially a very controversial topic like abortion, gun control, gay marriage, or genetic engineering) by reading one article written by someone you don't know? Chances are your answer is **No**.

Most often, when we change our minds completely on such topics—or on almost any topic—it's the result of extended conversations with people we know and trust.

The writing of strangers—even of respected, experienced writers—might give us a little nudge to reconsider a position, but it will rarely change our minds completely.

When you are writing a statement of purpose, therefore, keep your purpose within reach. Don't expect to *convince my readers that gun control is bad* or *make my readers finally understand how harmful our dependence on oil is*. Instead, using verbs like the following in your statement of purpose will help you design acheivable purposes:

inform	suggest
recommend	consider
acknowledge	propose
ask	reflect
attempt	understand

FOR EXAMPLE…

Here is Riley's thesis statement:

> Microcredit should be offered to women in developing countries only accompanied by discussion support groups and classes in economics, because otherwise the women won't know how to change the community conditions that encourage poverty.

Here is her statement of purpose.

My audience is others in class—and, of course, my teacher. From talking with the others in class, I know that even if they have heard about microcredit, they don't know much about it. They've maybe heard of the man who started microcredit, Muhammad Yunus of Bangladesh, and how he won the Nobel Peace Prize in 2006. They've also only heard good things about microcredit. Unless I make my topic interesting to them, they're probably not going to have much interest.

But when they are finished reading, I'd like my readers to be informed about what microcredit is and to understand how it's way more complicated than just giving people small loans. I also want them to care about the women who need the loans, so that they can make good decisions about donating money to a microcredit organization if they want or about working with one.

I'm interested in this because I got all caught up in all the stories about microcredit when I first read about it: It was exciting to read about something that seemed so simple but that could make such huge differences in people's lives. But then as I was doing more research I realized that all the promises people were making about microcredit mostly really weren't coming true. They weren't coming true because people's lives are so much more complex than just some money can fix. It's whole communities that need "fixing."

So that's why it seems like it's so important that the loans be accompanied by support groups and classes, so that the women can really make the differences in their lives that seems possible.

I wonder if I write my paper in the way that I learned about microcredit (first, how good it seems to be and then telling about the problems and why the problems exist), then maybe my readers will get caught up in it the way I did. All those stories of all those women going from having almost nothing to having their own businesses can suck you in, I think.

If I did that, it might just move my readers from caring about the women and their stories to caring about what doesn't always work with microcredit. Then I can describe what needs to happen to make it work.

CHOICES A WRITER CAN MAKE BASED ON A STATEMENT OF PURPOSE

Choices about how and what to write aren't magic: You can use your statement of purpose to help you choose.

ETHOS

In Part 3, we discussed how ethos is the sense of a writer that readers get from a text, and how readers develop this sense from a writer's tone of voice, word choices, and so on.

Because Riley is writing to people who don't know about microcredit, and may not know why they should care about it, she may want to write with enthusiasm and curiosity, in order to carry readers along. When she writes in her statement of purpose about perhaps ordering her paper to re-create for her readers her experience of getting excited about microcredit before learning of its problems, this also suggests that she can construct an ethos of someone who is curious and who is learning right alongside the readers—which could be a friendly and inviting ethos.

WHAT LEVEL AND AMOUNT OF PATHOS TO USE

As we discussed in Part 3, pathos is a term for discussing how the aspects of a composition encourage audiences to have emotional responses to the composition.

Riley wants her readers to be informed, which sounds like a fairly emotionless position. But she also wants them to care, which means she wants to inspire warmth, concern, and, perhaps, enthusiasm. This tells her about the tone of voice she can use and that she should describe the people in her examples with compassion.

THE KINDS OF EXAMPLES AND EVIDENCE THAT WILL BE USEFUL FOR A PARTICULAR AUDIENCE

If your purpose is to show readers that you agree with them, use examples your audience will know, that are familiar, or that echo what they already know. If, on the other hand, you are trying to move your audience's focus, then you need carefully to choose examples that will start with what an audience knows but that will then move from the familiar into the new.

In Riley's case, however, she knows her readers don't know much about microcredit. Because she wants them to care about the people who receive microcredit, she should probably give examples about the women who receive microcredit, in order to bring them a little more to life for her readers.

WHICH SOURCES TO USE

In Part 3, we discussed how to tell if sources are relevant and credible. A statement of purpose can help you fine-tune your earlier choices.

Given that part of what Riley has to do is persuade her readers that there are problems with microcredit even though what they have heard before is positive, she is going to have to be careful to show that very credible sources have questioned microcredit—and that more than one source has questioned it. In fact, she will probably want to show that quite a few credible people have questioned microcredit, if she doesn't want readers to think the criticism comes from only one or two cranks.

WHETHER YOU HAVE DONE ENOUGH RESEARCH

A statement of purpose helps you see how much evidence your audience might need to be moved by your thesis.

By putting together her statement of purpose, Riley can see that she needs to define microcredit and perhaps give some history of it so that readers understand where it came from and what it is supposed to achieve. Thus she needs to have done enough research to answer those needs.

As above, her statement of purpose also helps her see that she is going to have to give compelling evidence that microcredit can have problems. She is therefore going to have to find a large number of sources—very reputable sources from different places—to demonstrate that a number of people find problems with microcredit.

(It can be frustrating to do all the research that leads to a thesis statement and then, after doing the work to put together a statement of purpose, to realize that you need to do more research. But it is much more frustrating to write a paper that no one cares to read and that is ineffective precisely because you stopped researching before you considered your audience. Composing is not a linear process, even if the form of a book can make it look linear; successful writers revisit earlier steps of the process continually, as they find places where they need more information or support, or where they need to rethink whom they are addressing with their writing, and so on.)

STARTING TO WRITE FOR AN AUDIENCE
A ROUGH DRAFT

WHAT IS A ROUGH DRAFT?

A rough draft is a testing ground. Written with the expectation that it can be strengthened through feedback from others and revision, it is an attempt to shape a coherent argument.

Successful writers write rough drafts, often many rough drafts. Such writers do not expect that any piece of writing will be finished in one sitting.

Instead, they allow themselves time to produce writing they know will be rough but that is necessary to help them figure out their final thoughts. Even though these writers have a pretty good idea of what they want to write before they sit down (by having developed a thesis statement and then a statement of purpose), they know that as they write, their ideas might shift or that they'll write something that doesn't quite do what they want it to.

TIP: FINDING WORDS WITH WHICH TO START

If you have prepared your thesis statement and statement of purpose, you should have a good idea of what your paper needs to include...but if you are stuck about how to start your writing, look at the suggestions for different kinds of introductions in Part 7.

See pages 294–295.

Pick any of the kinds of introductions that catches your fancy; the point now is to get started writing; you can always change an introduction later if the work of the draft or feedback suggests a more appropriate introduction.

ARE YOU READY TO WRITE A FULL ROUGH DRAFT?

You are not ready to write a full rough draft until you

- have a thesis statement and have gathered good evidence in support of the reasons for your thesis's claim.

- have a statement of purpose that helps you understand how to shape your thesis for your particular readers.

PREPARING TO WRITE A DRAFT

- Review any notes you have taken from your sources.

- Keep your sources (or copies of your sources) nearby so that you can check that you are summarizing, paraphrasing, or quoting properly.

- Set up your writing area so that you will have few distractions.

- Arrange your time so that you have at least an hour, but preferably two or three hours, to write at any one sitting.

- Do not expect to complete a five- to seven-page draft in one sitting. Plan for at least two or three different times that you will write.

ARRANGING THE PARTS OF A DRAFT

See pages 202–203 in Part 5, Organizing and Shaping Texts, for suggestions on how to use your thesis statement to arrange the parts of your draft.

WHILE WRITING

- Don't stop the flow of your ideas by fixating on grammar or spelling; instead, focus on writing your argument. Because this is a draft, you will have time later to revise and edit.

  → If English is not your home language, however, see the advice on page 241 for working on drafts.

- If you get stuck in your writing, you have at least three options:

  One, get up and walk away; come back to the writing later, after you've had a chance to rest, go for a walk, chat with some friends, or otherwise refresh your mind.

  Two, start rereading your writing from the beginning to see if this sparks your thinking.

  Three, review your thesis statement and statement of purpose to see if you have covered all that you know you need to cover; if you've missed anything, start writing about it.

- If you summarize, paraphrase, or quote (→ see pages 314–315) any source, be sure to include the expected in-text citation in the format you are using. Also be sure to put any such sources into a running bibliography list at the end of your draft.

  → For **MLA style**, see pages 360–405.

  → For **APA style**, see pages 426–451.

  → For **CSE style**, see pages 453–457.

  → For **CMS style**, see pages 458–462.

A ROUGH DRAFT

Riley has produced a very rough draft for an assignment that asks for a five- to seven-page paper. She is using this draft just to get her ideas onto paper, to see how they look, and to get a sense of how her ideas will work for her readers.

We've indicated some of her initial choices, as well as places she is not yet sure of her choices—and we've indicated where in this book she can look for further assistance.

As you read Riley's draft, look for how she starts to develop her argument. It's not as clear as it could be in this draft, but it is starting to take shape. Also look for how she's addressing the concerns of her readers, as she came to understand them through developing a statement of purpose.

→ Riley's polished revision of this draft is on pages 406–418.

Title

After reading the draft, return here: Do you think Riley's title accurately prepares a reader for what is to come?

Opening quotation

Will this quotation encourage readers to care for the women who receive microloans, as Riley hopes?

Introduction

Does this introductory paragraph help readers understand clearly and easily what is to follow?

→ Pages 294–295 give suggestions for introductions that meet academic expectations.

Transitions

Do you think readers will understand why Riley moves from her introductory paragraph to this sentence?

→ See pages 296–297 for information on how to write transitions that help readers follow your arguments.

A long quotation

Riley has correctly followed the standard punctuation format for quotations that take more than five lines.

→ See pages 318–319 to learn how to punctuate long quotations.

But this quotation will seem too long to practiced readers of academic texts. Riley should paraphrase and summarize at least some of this passage.

→ See pages 322–325 for information on paraphrasing and summarizing.

ROUGH DRAFT

Money Makes the World Go Round

Says Nyamba Konate, a USAID microloan beneficiary, "I can now ensure that my children go to school, and I can better support my husband by buying food and stocking it to get us through the difficult rainy season." ("Microloans and Literacy")

A Google search with "microloan" gets over 2,000,000 hits, many to organizations that offer very small loans to people who otherwise would not qualify for traditional bank loans. The websites tell stories of the changes microloans can make in the lives of poor women all over the world. But anyone who thinks microloans are always good has obviously not read enough.

Grameen Bank was the first to give microcredit.

The inspiration for Grameen Bank came to Dr. Yunus during a trip to the village of Jobra in Bangladesh during the devastating famine of 1974. He met a woman who was struggling to make ends meet as a weaver of bamboo stools. She needed to borrow to buy materials, but because she was poor and had no assets, conventional banks shunned her, and she had to turn instead to local moneylenders whose extortionate rates of interest consumed nearly all her profits.

Dr. Yunus, then a professor of rural economics at Chittagong University, gave the woman and several of her neighbors loans totalling $27 from his own pocket. To his surprise, the borrowers paid him back in full and on time. So he started traveling from village to village, offering more tiny loans and cutting out the middlemen. Dr. Yunus was determined to prove that lending to the poor was not an "impossible proposition," as he put it.

When he later formalized the loan-making arrangement as the Grameen Bank in 1983, the bank adopted its signature innovation: making borrowers take out loans in groups of five, with each borrower guaranteeing the others' debts. Thus, in place of the hold banks have on wealthier borrowers who do not pay their debts—

1

Fragment

→ See pages 490–493 for how to recognize and fix sentence fragments.

A paragraph that does too much

This paragraph covers a lot of problems with microcredit—and so is hard for readers to follow. Look at Riley's final draft on pages 406–418 to see how this paragraph is clearer when it is broken up into several smaller paragraphs, each focused on one particular point.

Logos: giving evidence

In this (too) long paragraph, Riley makes many assertions about the ways microcredit can go wrong—but she offers sources to support only two of the assertions. Each of the sentences in this paragraph makes a claim, and should have a source connected to it.

→ Riley's final draft on pages 406–418 shows how to use sources as evidence in support of claims you want to make in your writing.

A quotation without introduction or attribution

Rarely in academic writing do writers use quotations without introducing them.

→ Pages 316–321 have suggestions for how to weave quotations into your writing.

Never in academic writing do writers use quotations without an attribution.

→ See pages 319–320 for how to give the expected attributions for quotations.

Explaining terms

It seems clear by now that Riley's paper is focusing on microloans—but has she written this explicitly in any part of the paper? Has she defined *microloan*?

foreclosure and a low credit rating—Grameen depends on an incentive at least as powerful for poor villagers, the threat of being shamed before neighbors and relatives. (Giridharadas and Bradsher) Almost everyone talks about how good microloans are. As though poverty as we know it will end. Women will be liberated.

But one writer says that most studies of microcredit programs "find very small increases in income for quite large numbers of borrowers; in only a very small number of cases are there significant income increases" (Mayoux 39). It most often benefits women who are not at the lowest levels of poverty, but the poorest of the poor lose ground. Microcredit also doesn't last long because the borrowers often can't use their loans for anything but tonight's dinner or an emergency. Or maybe the women do work that doesn't make much money, like selling home-made food on the streets, cleaning the houses of others, or working at home. So women are still stuck at home or in small jobs. Meaning their communities will still be poor. "Bangladesh and Bolivia are two countries widely recognized for having the most successful microcredit programs in the world. They also remain two of the poorest countries in the world." And the loan often added to what women have to do in a day. When women use their loans to make and sell food or other stuff, they do this on top of running households and taking care of children sometimes they have to pull their children out of school to help out, in order to stay on top of the loan to pay it back (Cheston 25). And rather than learning how to use and work with the loan money themselves, a lot of women give their loans to men in their families because they live in communities where men are supposed to make money decisions. Because of this the men sometimes get mad and are both verbally and physically violent against women.

Why are women supposed to be liberated by microloans? The United Nations says

> Women's access to microfinance not only benefits women but also their families and communities, by generating:
> – Increased income, awareness, and bargaining power for women;
> – Increased resources available to the family for investment in nutrition and education;

2

Explaining terms

Do you think Riley can count on her readers knowing what FINCA is? If you are ever in doubt whether readers will understand a term you are using, explain it.

More long quotations

Academic readers will often accept one or two quotations of this length, but you can see that Riley's paper is full of them: It looks as though her writing simply strings together the words of others. Riley needs to shorten her quotations, or to paraphrase and summarize them, to show readers that she has really thought through and made her own sense of these ideas.

→ See pages 322–325 for information on paraphrasing and summarizing.

Building ethos by using the authority of others

Riley is quoting someone named Susy Cheston here; the quotation suggests that Susy Cheston knows quite a bit about women and microloans—but why should readers trust her? If Riley explains who Susy Cheston is by including Cheston's title or explaining why Cheston has authority to speak on this topic, Riley's readers are more likely to accept the authority of this quotation and so to accept that Riley has authority, too.

→ Page 320 includes information about how to give a title to or explain the authority of someone you are quoting.

Helping readers check sources

To check a source, readers usually need the name of the person(s) responsible for the words (so that they can find the source in the bibliography list at the end of the paper) and a page number. Because the name of the person who wrote these words preceded this quotation, Riley needs only to give a page number here.

→ See pages 351–359 for how to show the sources of your quotations and evidence.

– Growth in local economies through local increases in women's spending; and

– An expanded view in the larger society of social and economic norms that relate to women.

FINCA says that it lends primarily to women because

> Seventy percent of the world's poor are women, largely because of their limited access to education or to productive resources like land and credit. Another worldwide trend is an increase in woman-headed households, in which a mother provides the sole support for her children. Most victims of severe poverty are children. According to UNICEF, at least half of the 12 million children aged five or younger who die each year, die from malnutrition associated with severe poverty. The most direct way to improve childrens' survival and welfare is to strengthen their own mothers' ability to take care of them. ("Frequently Asked Questions")

Microloans are supposed to help women be confident taking care of their own money and taking part in their communities. They are expected to use any money they earn from their loans for their families. Because the families are supposed to improve, their communities are supposed to improve, too.

Research supports this, some. Susy Cheston says that:

> According to research by microfinance impact assessment specialist Suzy Salib-Bauer on Sinapi Aba Trust, an Opportunity International microfinance institution (MFI) in Ghana, 42 percent of mature clients (those in the program two years or more) had an improvement in their poverty level—either moving from "very poor" to "poor" or from "poor" to "non-poor" status, as measured by a standard household asset and income index. ASHI, an MFI in the Philippines that exclusively targets poor women, found that 77 percent of incoming clients were classified as "very poor"; after two years in the program, only 13 percent of mature clients were still "very poor." (23)

Another writer describes a program that

> had an important positive impact on a large number of women members. Over one third of the sample had been able to begin market

3

Logos: helping readers with summaries and transitions

Riley helps readers by ending this paragraph with a summary of the main point of her paragraph.

→ Pages 296–297 have suggestions for helping readers stay oriented in your writing.

Making a works cited list

For a rough draft, it is alright to start a Works Cited listing on the same page as the rest of the paper. For a final draft, however, the Works Cited listing should start on its own page in MLA format.

→ See pages 360–405 for help in constructing a Works Cited list in the MLA format.

Conclusions: a place for pathos

Riley has mostly used this last paragraph to summarize and restate her main argument, using some pathos. Academic readers expect this in essays. But what they don't expect in a conclusion is new information, such as Riley's comment about MacIsaac's report. (Riley has also not included MacIsaac in the Works Cited list.)

→ Pages 292–293 contain ideas for shaping conclusions to academic writing.

Enough sources?

There are many places in Riley's paper where she has made assertions without offering any evidence—so she should probably have more sources than she shows here. (There are two more sources listed on the next page.)

work with a loan, and the loans had enabled women to keep marginal businesses afloat in family crises without recourse to moneylenders. Access to loans was also estimated to have led to increased earnings for a quarter of all the sampled women, often through enabling them to switch jobs and trades to more lucrative ones. Some had diversified their activities, adding a second line of work or a secondary job. For other women the loan kept them out of further debilitating debt through diversion of the loan in times of major stress events such as illness, flood, death or desertion of husband and enabling them to carry out their ritual responsibilities necessary to maintaining social status. (Mayoux 39)

So no one is wrong to think that microloans can have positive effects in the lives of women.

Microloans have helped some women. But anyone who believes microloans will cure the world is way off. MacIsaac has written a report that shows how microloan programs ought to work. If we really honestly do want to end poverty, we must help women be in big business. We must help them make their own decisions. We must give them what will help them deal with the family and community stuff that stands in the way of them getting ahead.

Works Cited

Cheston, Susy. "Women and Microfinance: Opening Markets and Minds." *Economic Perspectives: An Electronic Journal of the U.S. Department of State* 9.1. Feb. 2004 <http://usinfo.state.gov/journals/ites/0204/ ijee/toc.htm>.

"Frequently Asked Questions." *FINCA* <http://www.villagebanking.org/site/ c.erKPI2PCIoE/b.2394157/k.8161/Frequently_Asked_Questions.htm>.

Giridharadas, Anand, and Keith Bradsher. "Microloan Pioneer and His Bank Win Nobel Peace Prize." *New York Times* 13 Oct. 2006 <http:// www.nytimes.com/2006/10/13/business/14nobelcnd.html?ei=5070&en= 4d992a1456a69474&ex=1187496000&adxnnl=1&adxnnlx= 1187362984-v/nuT8pwJMcXlFKKsBSiJg>.

4

Enough different kinds of sources?

Some readers will note that these sources are all websites, and will not approve—even though the websites are of different kinds: a journal article published by the U.S. Department of State, a website for a respected nonprofit organization, an article from the *New York Times*, and a United Nations report. You need to judge whether your audience will accept only webpages as sources. If an assignment does not have a clear policy about using only webpages, ask.

RECEIVING FEEDBACK TO DRAFTS

To the right is feedback Riley received from her teacher.

These comments helpfully summarize the reader's understanding of Riley's argument; now Riley can understand whether readers are hearing what she hopes they will hear.

Receiving such feedback can sometimes be hard if you've put a lot of effort into writing: You might not want to hear that you have more work to do. But it's important to know how to receive feedback, because it is what helps you strengthen your writing so that it communicates what you want.

Often it is a good idea to read feedback as soon as you get it but then to put it aside for a day or two. Read it again with a little distance, and you'll be in a better position to understand it.

Feedback is what most helps you move your words from writing-to-learn to writing-to-communicate, as we discussed on pages 18–19.

When you receive feedback, keep in mind that:

- The feedback of others is what you need to become a stronger writer. Only by hearing how others respond do you learn how words communicate what they do.

- If readers do not understand your argument, or believe it to be something other than you intended, don't blame the readers. If readers miss or misinterpret your argument, ask them why they take the understanding they do from your words. If you ask readers to go through your writing sentence by sentence, explaining out loud what they understand, you will learn the particular effects your words have—and so you will learn how to revise your words so that they do what you hope.

→ See Riley's revised paper on pages 406–418.

Mayoux, Linda. "From Vicious to Virtuous Circles? Gender and
   Micro-Enterprise Development." *United Nations Research Institute
   for Social Development.* 1995
   <http://www.unrisd.org/unrisd/website/document.nsf/0/
   5901781754E7C91580256B67005B6AF7?OpenDocument>.
"Microloans and Literacy Are Contributing to Food Security in Poor Upper
   Guinea." *USAID Africa Success Stories.* 2005 <http://
   africastories.usaid.gov/search_details.cfm?storyID=323&countryID=9&
   sectorID=0&yearID=5>.

5

Riley—

This is a fine start: I can see you are building an
argument that, even though many people believe
microloans always have positive results and that they
can make big changes in the world, microloans won't
solve poverty and don't necessarily help women.(It's
important that you acknowledge that there are good
results for microloans and don't just make them sound
all bad.)

I sometimes get a little lost in that argument, though.

Most importantly, I wonder about the order of your
paragraphs. After your introduction, you give a little
history of microloans, then describe how they are bad,
and then describe how they are good. Why do you talk
about the bad before the good?

Also, I often have trouble understanding why you move
from paragraph to paragraph; I think you could work on
providing transitions for readers.

I look forward to seeing your revisions of this. You
should take confidence from this draft so that, as you
revise, you focus on the matters I've suggested above
but also that you don't worry about telling readers
exactly what you are doing with this argument.

Please come talk if you have any questions.

Thanks! Professor Maathai

DEVELOPING A REVISION PLAN

→ See Riley's revised paper on pages 406–418.

After you receive feedback to a draft, make time to develop a revision plan for yourself. A revision plan is informal, just for you.

To the right, Riley's plan lays out how she understands the feedback she received and how she plans to respond.

Help for revising is offered in the next parts of this book:

→ For help with arranging the parts of writing, see Part 5, pages 187–236.

→ For help working with sources, see Part 8, pages 307–462.

→ For help with engaging readers more with your writing, see Part 7, pages 265–306.

→ For help with introductions, see pages 294–295.

→ For help with tone of voice, see pages 538–539.

→ For help with transitions, see pages 296–297.

REVISING, NOT EDITING

Notice that in her revision plan Riley doesn't mention anything about spelling or grammar: That's because revising is about focusing on your argument and how well readers understand those arguments.

When you revise, you need to be open to making large changes in your writing. You may have to throw out paragraphs, rearrange them, or add new ones as your writing helps you determine just what it is you want readers to take from your words.

Given Professor Maathai's feedback, I don't think I really got across the main point of my thesis statement, that microloan programs have their best chances of working when the women who receive the loans get classes in economics and business and have lots of time to talk with other women about their experiences and dealing with problems. I'm not sure I'm going to have enough space to make that argument, though. Maybe I need to revise my thesis, to argue just that people shouldn't expect microloans to solve poverty and liberate women because of all the problems with them; I could just suggest, at the end, about the classes and all that.

Given other feedback from people in class, I also need to

- Experiment with different arrangements of the parts of my paper, to see which most help people understand that microloans don't do what most people seem to think they will.
- Have more sources to support my claims about microloans.
- Figure out, still, how to get readers to care more: I still don't think I've got enough examples or am presenting stuff in ways that suck people in.
- Work out, like above, how to make my introduction more compelling.
- Experiment with my tone of voice, so that it's not so choppy and short.
- Work on the transitions between my paragraphs.

WRITING FOR DIFFERENT KINDS OF AUDIENCES

WRITING FOR ACADEMIC AUDIENCES

Over time, academic audiences have come to expect the most polished academic writing—as it appears in journals—to have the following nine features:

1 ACADEMIC WRITING IS ABOUT BUILDING KNOWLEDGE.

Academic audiences expect that you approach writing seriously because through writing you add to our understandings of the world and each other. This means that you have to take existing arguments seriously, research and gather evidence methodically and honestly, and make only the arguments that you can support with the evidence you have found.

2 ACADEMIC WRITING IS SERIOUS AND FORMAL.

Academic writers strive for a thoughtful tone of voice, and rarely tell jokes or use emotional language or colloquialisms (such as **no-brainer** or **oh, snap!**). In some disciplines, writers will use *I* and will use their own experiences as evidence or examples; reading examples of writing in a discipline will help you learn the particulars of the discipline. (For help with writing assignments in classes in disciplines that are new to you, ask your teacher.)

→ See pages 538–539 for more on creating a serious tone.

3 ACADEMIC WRITING GETS TO AND STAYS ON THE POINT.

An introduction moves quickly to stating what the paper is about. The writer ought to be able to explain how each and every sentence helps move a reader to the conclusion. There shouldn't be digressions or stories.

→ See pages 294–295 on writing introductions to academic papers.

→ See pages 280–281 on being explicit in your writing.

4 ACADEMIC WRITING IS EXPLICIT.

Academic writers say directly what their writing is about. In fiction and creative nonfiction, writers often use figurative language to pull readers in and suggest an overall point without ever stating the point; academic writing doesn't do this.

→ See pages 273–274 for more on the characteristics of explicit writing.

5 ACADEMIC WRITING ALWAYS HAS AN ELEMENT OF DOUBT.

Academic writers accept that there are very few thoughts and ideas that apply to everyone, everywhere, at all times. Instead, academic writers always consider a range of reasons and opinions.

To this end, academic writers often use phrases like *These facts suggest...* or *Given the available evidence, it would seem that....*

6 ACADEMIC WRITING IS NOT CONVERSATIONAL.

Academic writing usually uses longer words and sentences, more vocabulary, and more complex grammar than spoken language. Some of the more complex grammatical forms that academic writing uses are

→ dependent clauses, described on pages 483–485.

→ complex, compound, and complex-compound sentences, described on pages 480–489.

7 ACADEMIC WRITING TRIES TO BE OBJECTIVE AND UNBIASED.

The point of view of academic writing is rarely personal, rarely focused on the writer. Instead, the emphasis is on the argument being made and on ideas that benefit as many people as possible.

8 ACADEMIC WRITERS ARE RESPONSIBLE FOR THEIR ARGUMENTS AND TO OTHER WRITERS.

Academic writers can't just say anything; instead, they must take responsiblity for any claims they make by giving supporting evidence and by helping readers check that evidence. In addition, they are responsible for showing when the evidence they offer comes from the work or words of others.

→ Part 8 of this book is all about using the words and work of others; see pages 307–462.

9 ACADEMIC WRITING LOOKS SERIOUS.

→ See the section on Typography in Part 7, Style in Visual Texts, to see models for formatting your pages.

WRITING FOR WORKPLACE AUDIENCES

When you write for workplace audiences, keep the following five considerations in mind:

1 THE PLACES IN WHICH WE WORK DEVELOP THEIR OWN CULTURES.

Communities develop shared habits and expectations, and workplaces are no exception. Learning to write well professionally means learning the habits and expectations of a workplace: Is the workplace formal or informal, particularly focused on getting things done quickly or on group discussions aimed at consensus?

2 WRITING IN WORKPLACES NEEDS TO FIT THE CULTURE OF THE WORKPLACE.

All our earlier advice about audiences applies to workplace writing, but writing in workplaces is tied to how people in the organization solve problems, attend meetings, organize projects, manage tasks, evaluate documents and performance, use computer technologies, give presentations, run training sessions, and so on.

Connected to these activities is a range of specialized forms of communication with which you need to become familiar; each has general characteristics that you can recognize across various places of work and that also become adapted to specific workplaces. For example, workplace audiences all know the general form of a memo, but they also know the specific ways memos are written—and read—in their particular workplace.

3 BECAUSE WORKPLACES ARE ABOUT GETTING WORK DONE, PEOPLE AT WORK EXPECT WRITING TO BE EFFICIENT AND TO THE POINT.

This doesn't mean the writing is mechanical—it still needs to address its human audiences—but it needs to be very focused.

→ See pages 273–274 for suggestions on how to shape writing that is focused, quick, and to the point.

4 OFTEN IN WORKPLACES YOU WILL BE WRITING FOR TWO (OR MORE) AUDIENCES.

Earlier in this part we talked about complex audiences and about how sometimes you have a foreground and a background audience. In workplaces, where you may be writing a brochure or an instruction set to be read by potential consumers, it can be useful to keep these two audiences in mind. The foreground readers are the customers or clients; the background audience is those in the business or organization who will be looking at what you produce and making comments or suggestions along the way.

5 LARGER WORKPLACES CAN HAVE STYLE GUIDES YOU NEED TO FOLLOW WHEN YOU ARE WRITING FOR CLIENTS OR CUSTOMERS.

Companies have such style guides to be sure all the documents they produce are consistent and represent the company professionally. Style guides can include guidelines for using the company's logo, specific phrases to use in writing (for example, a hardware company could specify that writers tell customers to *click a button* rather than to *click on a button*), and formats for different kinds of documents. If you are not given a style guide, be sure to ask if one exists.

HINTS & TIPS FOR CONNECTING WITH READERS

ASK FOR FOCUSED FEEDBACK TO YOUR WRITING

Because getting feedback from readers is the main way to strengthen your writing, getting useful feedback is crucial. But giving good feedback is a learned skill, and many readers won't automatically know how to give you useful feedback.

When you are ready for feedback, tell readers what you need: For example, ask them to focus on your argument and to try to tell you what your thesis statement is. Or ask them to read the argument to see if you offer enough evidence, or if your transitions help them understand why you move from one paragraph to the next.

Choose only one or two areas for them to focus on in their reading.

BE SURE YOU UNDERSTAND FEEDBACK

If you hear something you don't understand from a reader, ask for clarification. If you don't understand feedback, it can't help you.

GET FEEDBACK FROM YOURSELF

Put your writing aside for at least several hours to get some distance from it, and then reread it. Reread it once to see if your thesis seems sufficiently developed, read it again to check your transitions, and so on.

You need to learn to be your own audience, because the paper you turn in is yours. You have the final responsibility for it.

PART 5
ORGANIZING AND SHAPING TEXTS

CONTENTS

WHERE ARE WE IN THE PROCESS FOR COMPOSING?

Understanding your project

Getting started

Asking questions

Shaping your project for others
Choosing a genre
Choosing an overall organization
Arranging paragraphs

Drafting a paper

Getting feedback

Revising

Polishing

WHAT IS ORGANIZATION?

Producing a text is like building a building: You make choices to shape your audience's experience similarly to how people experience buildings.

Think of a time you visited a new acquaintance for the first time. You went to the person's apartment or house, and from the street you got a sense of the building's age. Seeing the overall style of the building—Victorian, modern, suburban ranch, or fifties apartment block—you sensed what you would see inside. Once inside, you got a sense of the overall organization of the rooms—of the layout and floorplan—which indicated how you could move through the rooms. Then there were the individual rooms with their furnishings, which told you about how comfortable it was to live in this place and what people did there. There was also the color of the walls, and what was on the walls, and what was on the shelves or tables....

As you moved from the outside to the inside, you moved from seeing large structures to seeing smaller ones, from big shapes to small objects.

Moving through a text is the same: You first see the whole, which sets up expectations about the smaller parts. As you read, listen, or look, you see the *floorplan*—the overall structure; and then you notice the parts of the *floorplan*—the paragraphs or major divisions. Finally, you notice the details, such as tone of voice, sentence length, word choice, and so on.

In this part of the book, we focus on the major elements, the overall structure and paragraphs.

BUILDING → FLOORPLAN → ROOMS → FURNISHINGS

WHOLE TEXT → CONCEPTUAL FRAMEWORK → PARAGRAPHS → SENTENCES & WORDS

POSTER → CONCEPTUAL FRAMEWORK → MAJOR ELEMENTS → DETAILED ELEMENTS

ORGANIZATION IS ABOUT HOW YOU WORK AT EACH OF THESE LEVELS

At each level, you have many choices about how to place the relevant elements in relation to each other in order to achieve your purpose, for your audience, given your context.

In this part, we focus on the major details, the framework and paragraphs.

→ In Part 7, we focus on the details.

ORGANIZATION AND MEDIUM

When you compose, your **medium** is the physical material you use to shape your composition.

Your medium can be sound waves if you are composing a podcast, or it can be paper or the electrons that light up on a digital screen if you are composing an essay. In each case, the particular material of the medium offers possibilities and limitations for what you can do, and shapes how audiences in our time and places generally think about each medium.

The chart to the right describes some of these possibilities as they relate to how audiences *generally* think about these media. You can use this chart to help you choose a medium for a project, keeping in mind that you will have to consider the particulars of the type of text you are producing.

For example, consider whether you can use color, photographs, or illustrations, or through what sort of device your audience will encounter the text you are making, and so on.

■ ■ ■

Medium might not seem like part of organization, but if you think of organization as how composers shape a text so that an audience moves through it in particular ways (as we described on pages 186–187), then an audience's first response to a new text is to encounter the material of the text in their hands, before their eyes, or in their ears.

AUDIENCE EXPECTATIONS & ASSOCIATIONS

PAPER	DIGITAL SCREENS	SOUND
Types of texts		
books, posters, pamphlets, brochures, graphic novels, newspapers, manuals	Personal blogs, corporate websites, video and music sharing sites, e-mail, instant messaging	Conversations, interviews, speeches, podcasts, telephone conversations, music recordings
Scale		
Most paper communications are designed for handheld use, by one person; some are designed for walls—to attract individuals out of a group.	Digital screens are usually designed for one viewer at a time, to be seen on a desk-size or handheld monitor.	Sound can be produced for many people to hear at once (as with speeches), a few people, or one person at a time.
Formality		
Because of their relative permanence, print texts can seem formal and distant—although the addition of photographs, color, and illustrations can change this.	Because they can be easily changed, online texts generally have less formality than print texts. E-mail and instant messaging are very informal, like quick conversations.	When sound is the voices of others, it can seem informal because it can seem so close and direct.
Organization		
Because readers can hold print texts in their hands, they can see the whole object at once and get a sense of its size and overall organization. The binding of print texts encourages linear organizations, with obvious beginnings and endings supported by section, page, and chapter numbering.	Readers rarely know if they have seen a whole digital text because the parts are visible only when they are on-screen: There is no physical whole. In addition, the parts of a print text can be designed to be accessible in many different orders; writers have to supply visual organization hints. Screen sizes also encourage shorter paragraphs than in print.	In print and online texts, audiences can look back to check what they don't remember. Because speaking does not allow this, speakers explicitly announce the organization of presentations and use repetition to help their listeners remember the main points.

ORGANIZATION, AUDIENCE, AND GENRE

Imagine you are a clerk in a driver's license office, and there is no application form. Instead, each time someone needs a license, you say, *Please put the necessary information on a piece of paper.* How many different sizes and shapes of paper would you receive, with how many different arrangements of information? How messy would it be to try to work with all those different pieces of paper?

Think then of how the driver's license application form saves time and energy for both applicants and clerks.

Genres are categories of text that work like the application form: We say that something is a genre when it has a form that is repeated. Think of poetry, movies, journal articles, research papers, or posters. When your sister tells you she is going to write a poem, you don't picture a billboard; you probably picture a short piece of writing that has uneven lines and creative punctuation.

Genres save us time and effort because they help both composers and audiences know what to do and what to expect.

When you encounter a new rhetorical situation, you need to ask what genres your audience might expect, and how tightly you need to stay within the confines of the genre if you are to achieve your purposes.

As the chart to the right suggests, some genres have tighter and more detailed audience expectations than others, but exploring the wiggle room of genres allows you to create new ways for your text to unfold for its audiences.

WHAT IS THE WIGGLE ROOM IN VARIOUS GENRES?

SCIENTIFIC JOURNAL ARTICLES	CLASSROOM RESEARCH PAPERS	MOVIES	VIDEO GAMES
Conceptual framework			
For publication in most scientific disciplines, there is a ready-made framework of required sections.	Many conceptual frameworks for research papers fit classroom contexts.	Hollywood movies tend to have a "traditional" narrative structure, but independent films are often expected to have experimental forms.	Currently, video games tend to fall into the frameworks of action, simulation, role-playing, sports, and strategy/puzzle games.
NO WIGGLE ROOM	SOME WIGGLE ROOM	SOME WIGGLE ROOM	SOME WIGGLE ROOM
Major parts			
Paragraphs are expected to be direct and to the point, but can have many different structures. Charts, tables, and graphs are common.	Readers expect classroom research papers to have paragraphs. Charts, tables, and graphs are acceptable, if appropriate.	Scenes can have different lengths—but usually there *are* scenes. The screen can be divided into parts.	Depending on the framework, a particular video game can have a number of levels, a series of puzzles, one single world, a range of characters, a countdown, and so on.
SOME WIGGLE ROOM	SOME WIGGLE ROOM	SOME WIGGLE ROOM	SOME WIGGLE ROOM
Smaller parts			
The tone of voice is objective and passive.	As long as they are harmonious with the overall purpose, style experimentations are possible.	Hollywood movies tend to seek "realistic"-looking settings, lighting, and sound, but makers of films with different purposes can experiment.	Depending on the framework and major parts, a game can look 2- or 3-dimensional, be cartoonish or realistic, employ a range of sounds, or require a range of interactions.
NO WIGGLE ROOM	LOTS OF WIGGLE ROOM	SOME WIGGLE ROOM	LOTS OF WIGGLE ROOM

→ The organizations of smaller parts of texts—such as word choice, sentence structures, color, and so on—are addressed in Part 7, on styling your writing.

ORGANIZATION, AUDIENCE, AND GENRE

ONLINE GENRES

Although all genres are always in some flux because purposes, contexts, and audiences shift, online genres are unstable these days as the technologies for online communication change and new communication possibilities appear. You do need to pay attention to the genre expectations of people who use online communications frequently, but how you shape online communications depends less on genre than on the precise particulars of your purpose, audience, and context.

For example, friends and family expect your e-mails to be chatty and descriptive. To friends and family you can send e-mails that seem to have no purpose other than to say *Hello!* and stay in touch. In school and workplaces, however, expectations are different, and more formal arrangements at every level are expected. Only when you get to know a professor or fellow employee well can you write with any informality.

Blogs can be highly personal journals or sites for connecting formally with others interested in particular topics.

On the following pages, the guidelines we offer for online texts are for more formal situations.

▼   **Subject:** **visit on Thursday**
   From: Anne Frances Wysocki <afw@school.edu> 👤
   Date: 11:32 PM
    To: <fisher@knhp.gov> 👤

```
Dear Ms. Fisher:

I wanted to double-check that you are set for our class to visit the Keweenaw
National Historic Park Library on Thursday, the 5th. We're planning on arriving
around 4, and staying for about an hour; there will be 17 of us.

Thanks again for encouraging this visit: the people in class look forward to it.

Sincerely,
Anne Frances Wysocki
Michigan Technological University
```

E-MAIL

In formal contexts, e-mails will appear professional to their recipients if you:

- **Have a neutral-sounding e-mail address.** squirrlygrrrl@hotmail.com is fine for friends—but for formal communications, consider getting an e-mail account that uses your initials and last name. If your company or school gives you an e-mail address, use that for communicating with professors, staff, employers, and colleagues.

- **Write a subject that is descriptive but short and in a professional tone.** "Wanna meet?" is descriptive and short—but sounds like it's party time. For formal situations, "Budget meeting Tuesday 3pm?" is more appropriate.

- **Start with a salutation.** Until you have a relaxed relationship with others, the expected way for showing respect is to start a message with a formal salutation such as "Dear Professor:" or "Dear Dr. Murthy:" or "Dear Mo Folk:" (if you do not know someone's gender or title, write out the person's first and last names). Notice also that the expected punctuation following the salutation is a colon. When others end messages to you with their first names, then you can write to them using their first names. Otherwise, in any follow-up messages, address others the way they signed their e-mails.

- **State your purpose following the salutation.** Put two returns after the salutation, and then state your purpose.

- **Write the e-mail in short paragraphs separated by two returns.** Readers can rarely see whole messages at once, and e-mail software is rarely designed to support easy reading. Others can read more easily if they can see your paragraphs—so arrange your paragraphs to be short and easy to discern visually.

- **Avoid smiley faces.** They are appropriate only in informal e-mail.

- **Sign your message.** Even though your name is in the header, it is still considered polite to type your full name at the message end—until you know the person to whom you are writing well.

- **Keep in mind how easy it is for others to forward your messages.** If you do not want to risk the world knowing something, do not put it in an e-mail.

BLOGS AND OTHER SOCIAL NETWORKING WEBSITES

A blog is not a blog unless it is written in reverse chronological order with places for reader responses. Users need technological know-how to change the provided content categories of a MySpace or Facebook profile page. Beyond those constraints of arrangement that are built into the software underpinning these sites, however, blogs and other social networking sites give composers lots of wiggle room in word, color, and illustration choices.

The most important choice a composer of a social networking site profile has to make, however, ties to the overall purpose of these sites: Social networking sites exist to connect people to each other. Because connecting with people almost always involves getting personal, the largest decision composers of such profiles have to make is just how much to reveal about themselves, given the long and very very public life of information on the Web.

ARRANGING TO CONNECT

Strategies for composing a blog or profile page that brings lots of responses include:

- being an authority on the topic about which you write.
- providing useful and well-researched information on a topic of interest to others.
- writing entertainingly.
- divulging interesting or provocative personal information.

STEVENBERLINJOHNSON.COM

THE DEPARTMENT OF BLOGIOLOGY STRIKES AGAIN

We couldn't help ourselves -- it was so fun calculating America's bloggiest neighborhoods, we had to go on and do the math on America's bloggiest cities, which led to my very first role in creating a USA Today infographic.

My colleague John Geraci does an excellent job explaining the results on the outside.in blog.

Email this • Save to del.icio.us (1 save) • Digg This! • outside.in: geotag this post

August 21, 2007 in Outside.in | Permalink | Comments (0) | TrackBack (0)

LIVE SBJ

I'm doing a little long overdue maintenance on the blog and the first change you'll see in the sidebar here: a list of all my upcoming public appearances

THE BASICS

I'm a father of three boys, husband of one wife, and author of five books. In early 2007 I went and foolishly got myself a day job running the hyperlocal community site, outside.in that I co-founded the year before. We

- being famous.
- writing to ask questions of your readers so that they will want to respond.
- engaging with readers in comments.
- adding comments to others' pages.

You do not, obviously, need to have all those strategies working for you, but some combination will help you gain many readers or friends.

PERSONAL ARRANGEMENTS

Once information is posted online, it is stored on a server and can be copied and pasted elsewhere—so even if you have second thoughts about what you've posted and try to erase it, it will still be out there. Do you want what you post today to be available to people you don't know? Do you want what you post today to be available to people five or ten years in the future?

PROFESSIONAL ARRANGEMENTS

One of the pages shown below belongs to a writer seeking a professional presentation to attract book buyers; the other is designed to be understood by those who know its maker.

For a professional-looking site, audiences generally expect:

- A muted color scheme.
  → See pages 302–303.

- Lots of white space.
  → See pages 228–229.

- Writing that carefully reaches out to readers.
  → See pages 266–269.

ORGANIZATION, AUDIENCE, AND GENRE
POPULAR GENRES

Popular genres does not mean genres everyone likes; instead, popular genres are those that can be produced **by** almost anyone or that are produced **for** broad general audiences—or both.

We give examples of three quite different popular genres here. As you look at the three, consider how the writers try to achieve their purposes by meeting audience expectations: How do they organize the parts of their texts to engage readers and make happen what they desire?

TIP: GOING ONLINE

Each of the genres we present here can be produced in print or online. Here are some differences for composers to consider when using one or the other medium:

- Paragraphs and sentences are usually shorter online than in print. Generally, readers gain a stronger sense of a text's organization when they can see the text's divisions; because screen sizes are usually smaller than paper, you can help readers see a text's organization online by using smaller paragraphs.

- For the same reasons, separating paragraphs online by two returns rather than with an indent helps readers read more easily.

- Because it requires more time and effort, a letter printed on paper and sent through the mail—rather than an e-mail—will almost always show that the writer is more serious. Such letters often therefore seem more authoritative and worthy of respect.

To the Editor:

In the last five and a half weeks, five schools in the United States and Canada have suffered the invasion of gunmen: Aug. 24, Essex, Vt.; Sept. 13, Montreal; Sept. 27, Bailey, Colo; Sept. 29, Cazenovia, Wis. And now, Oct. 2, Nickel Mines, Pa.

In four of these five incidents, the gunman targeted girls and women.

At what point do a country and its news media note this lethally combustible cocktail of gender and guns?

Men and boys with guns are stalking and hunting women and girls in schools repeatedly. Until we see "the gun problem" as equally a problem of violence against women, nothing will change, and I fear that the mourning and shock will continue.

Daniel Moshenberg
Washington, Oct. 3, 2006
The writer is director of the Women's Studies Program at George Washington University.

LETTERS TO THE EDITOR

After any event—horrible events like the shootings referenced in the letter above but also happier events like fund-raising picnics for local fire departments—people want to be able to share their opinions with others. They want to join in the considerations about how we should think about what happened and how we should respond.

Letters to the editor are one existing genre of writing that allows this to happen. People who send letters to the editor reach the readers of the periodical to which the letters were sent, and so extend the reach of their ideas. These letters may seem small, but if they spark responses in readers, then their ideas start to ripple out and affect others.

Whether letters to the editor are published in print or online, audiences have similar expectations about them.

Letters to the editor are

- Short and to the point.
- Focused on one topic.
- About an issue of interest to the periodical's readers. In magazines, letters to the editor are always in response to earlier published articles; in local newspapers, they can be about current or local events.
- Begun with a statement of the issue before going on to the writer's position.
- Documents in which ethos is crucial. Unlike the example letter above, rarely in a letter to the editor are a writer's credentials given. Writers have to demonstrate why they should be heard, through giving their own credentials but also through choosing a fitting tone of voice, staying focused, and using examples and evidence.

LETTERS OF COMPLAINT

When they reach high frustration with a product or service, many people find that the following approaches bring results:

- Finding the name of the highest-level person responsible for the product or service, and writing directly to that person. (Sometimes you can find the name online; you can also call a customer service number and ask.)

- Keeping the letter short so that a busy person can read it quickly.

- Keeping it friendly and unemotional: The point is to get results with the help of someone who is on your side.

- Listing the facts: Describe the problem concisely but concretely and include any relevant dates, serial numbers, or order numbers.

- Describing a concrete—and fair—action the company can take: Make it easy for the recipient to know what to do.

- Stating a reasonable time—four to eight weeks—for hearing back.

- Including your full contact information.

Daryl Flack
Director, Customer Service
ME Consumer Appliances
7645 Industrial Way
Houston, TX 77013

February 27, 2008

Dear Mr. Flack:

On January 20, 2007, I paid $709 for an ME SpaceFit Microwave (model HEM1146) at Shrumm's Appliance Center in DeQueen, Arkansas. I have enclosed a copy of my receipt.

In the last month the paint on the inside top of the microwave started blistering, peeling, and falling into the food being microwaved.

I called the customer service numbers listed in the manual and was told that because the microwave is now out of warranty ME will only give me $75 toward the purchase of a new microwave—or will charge me $60 for a technician to come look at the problem.

I've used ME products for many years and have always praised them to others and am surprised that such an expensive product should become unusable after only 13 months. I hope you will do what you can to fix this.

To resolve this problem, I would appreciate it if you would replace this microwave at no cost to me.

I look forward to your reply and a resolution to my problem, and will wait until April 21 before seeking help from a consumer protection agency or the Better Business Bureau. Please contact me at the address or phone number below.

Sincerely,

Diana Franks

Diana Franks
357 Wasa Rd.
DeQueen, AR 71832
555-555-1234

MAGAZINE ARTICLES

Mass-market magazines focus on an area of reader interest: recent news events, knitting, NASCAR, kittens, do-it-yourself projects, or hip-hop music. The article to the right illustrates many of the considerations to which magazine article writers attend:

- Articles inform about one topic.

- Articles have succinct and often catchy titles.

- The opening is often catchy, to draw in readers.

- In spite of a magazine's focus, writers cannot assume a specialized audience and so do not use specialized vocabulary; magazine publishers want to attract a wide audience.

  For example, the article to the right comes from *Onearth* magazine, a publication of the Natural Resources Defense Council. The writer assumes that the magazine's audience—who read the magazine because of their interest in environmental issues—think global warming is a problem and know that carbon dioxide is a major contributor to global warming. Beyond that, however, the writer makes no assumptions about reader knowledge.

- Instead of specialized vocabulary, writers use common terms: **ruminant bad breath** instead of **ruminant halitosis**.

- The language is less formal than academic writing, can be humorous, and can address audiences directly, as in the first two sentences of the example to the right.

- Paragraphs and sentences are shorter than in academic writing.

- Articles are frequently accompanied by photographs and pull-quotes to entice readers. (A pull-quote is a one- or two-sentence extract from the article; the extract can either summarize the article or be a compelling introduction.)

A Nasty Gas Attack

LET'S DISPOSE OF ONE misconception right away. Cows expel methane from the mouth, not from, ahem, the other end. The average dairy cow belches or exhales between 30 and 130 gallons of methane each day as its forestomachs break down a diet of grasses heavy in tough cellulose fibers. With some 1.3 billion cows worldwide, ruminant bad breath acounts for 80 million tons of methane each year—a gas that is 20 times more efffective at trapping heat in the atmosphere than carbon dioxide.

Those alarming numbers have prompted scientists to look for alternative bovine diets that might reduce these levels of methane. Researchers at the University of Wales claim that feed containing garlic could reduce methane by as much as 50 percent. They also suggest that cultivating grasses with high sugar levels, such as white clover and birdsfoot trefoil, would reduce methane production by improving cows' digestive processes.

Would a change of diet have a negative effect on the quality of the meat? On the contrary: Improving the efficiency of the cows' digestion would mean that the energy lost with each burp would be redirected toward the creation of protein, amino acids, and fat—all the signatures of a good steak.

—BEN CARMICHAEL

ORGANIZATION, AUDIENCE, AND GENRE
ACADEMIC GENRES IN THE DISCIPLINES

Because academic work in the United States is about careful thought and analysis for creating new knowledge, certain features are valued in almost all academic writing in this country:

- Full definition of terms.
- Logical development of ideas.
- Careful and full acknowledgment of any use of the ideas of others.

Over time, different academic disciplines have developed their own conventions for how papers within the discipline are to be arranged. These various arrangements are meant to support the particular kind of analytic work performed in the discipline.

If you are asked to write papers in classes in the humanities, sciences, or social sciences, the information to the right and on the next four pages gives you a general idea of the arrangements to use. If an assignment does not specify the arrangements to use, ask your teacher what the expectations are.

WRITING IN THE HUMANITIES

Writing in the humanities can be creative, theoretic, or analytic. We focus on analytic writing, for you will be asked to produce such writing in literature, film, rhetoric, modern languages, art, philosophy, history, and gender studies classes.

When you write analytically, you focus on a text like a short story or film or on a topic as we described in Part 2. Whether you analyze a text or a topic, you analyze to understand **how** and **why** values and decisions come to be and their effects.

ANALYZING TEXTS

When you analyze a text, you can focus on one text, describing its parts and arguing how the parts create an overall effect. You might show how a poem's line lengths and soft vowel sounds evoke a reader's reflections.

You can also analyze a text by comparing it with other texts or by explaining how it (and perhaps other similar texts) embodies cultural values, events, and structures. You might compare contemporary graphic novels and short stories, to show how both use quick, pictorial description and argue that this echoes the timing of fast food or video edits.

ANALYZING TOPICS

When you analyze a topic, you do the work we described in Parts 2, 3, and 4 of this book. You look to texts—books, journals, films, interviews—to help you learn about the topic and, using what you have learned from those other texts as evidence, you develop an argument focused on some aspect of the values, ideas, or effects of the topic.

ORGANIZING ANALYTIC PAPERS

1 A title. Examples: "Counterfeit Motion: The Animated Films of Eadweard Muybridge" or "'To Protect and Serve': African American Female Literacies"

2 An introduction. In humanities papers, an introduction can begin with a relevant quotation or example to pique interest, but the introduction's purpose is to draw readers' attention to the question or problem being discussed and to make clear why the question or problem should matter to them.

3 Body. This contains the writer's analysis of the text or topic. Evidence drawn from texts supports the analysis: In the analysis of a text, the evidence is drawn from the text itself, through quotation; in the analysis of topics, evidence comes from a range of texts.

→ See pages 104–113 on the kinds of evidence used in humanities writing.

4 A conclusion. The conclusion summarizes the paper's argument while offering no new information.

5 Works Cited list. At the end of the paper, list any works by other writers that are cited in the paper. (→ See pages 351–420 to learn MLA style, most often used in the humanities.)

In addition, if the writer's purpose and the context of the writing make it appropriate, writing in the humanities can be expressive: Writers can use I, draw on their own personal experiences or those of others, and use narratives as evidence. Check with your teacher if you are considering doing any of this in a class assignment.

DEVELOPING THE CONCEPTUAL FRAMEWORK FOR WRITING IN THE HUMANITIES

You know that a paper needs an introduction, a body, and a conclusion, but what goes into those sections—and why?

If a reader cannot figure out why one paragraph or section follows another in a piece of writing, the reader will be confused—and the writing will lose its force.

But **the reader** won't be able to figure out why one paragraph or section follows another if **the writer** hasn't figured it out. Writers must be able to say why each paragraph is where it is in a composition, why one paragraph comes before or follows another. To do this, writers need a conceptual framework.

A conceptual framework (which we introduced on page 186) is like a skeleton: It is a bare-bones idea about organization, a sense of what generally needs to come first, second, and third in a piece of writing.

Having a thesis statement for a piece of writing helps writers develop a conceptual framework. A thesis statement can show the major steps a writer needs to take and in what order; a statement of purpose helps the writer begin to flesh out those steps.

USING A THESIS STATEMENT TO DETERMINE THE THREE MAIN PARTS OF YOUR WRITING

On page 103, we showed that the major components of a thesis statement are a claim, a reason, and a warrant. If you believe that a piece of writing should persuade an audience to move from where they are to a consideration of something new and debatable, then you can organize a paper in this order:

1 The warrant.

2 The reason.

3 The claim.

You will still need to choose how to compose the paragraphs and sentences of each part, and the transitions between the parts, but the three main parts work in that order because:

1 The warrant is what your audience already believes. It is common ground that you and your audience share, so if you start your writing by discussing the warrant, you start with what the audience's beliefs or values already are.

2 The reason is where you put the bulk of your argumentative attention, using your evidence; this will be the longest part of the paper. By starting with your warrant, you've got your audience part of the way toward being open to your thesis; the reason is what completes the logic.

3 If you have given your readers sufficiently persuasive evidence for your reason, then you have completed the logic that builds to your claim. You can conclude by pointing this out.

Notice that these three parts correspond to the introduction, body, and conclusion. The body of your writing will present the evidence for your reason. Combine the general purpose of an introduction with the specifics of your warrant to shape the opening paragraph or two of your writing; use the claim to shape the specifics of your conclusion.

TIP: **NOT LOGIC ALONE**

As we show on these two pages, a thesis statement can help you considerably in making some of the big choices about organizing a paper. But, because persuasion does not happen based on logic alone, remember that a statement of purpose helps you make other very important choices in your writing. (For example, Riley has to define *microcredit* and argue why her readers should care about it.)

→ See pages 160–163 for help with developing a statement of purpose.

AN EXAMPLE

Here is Riley's thesis statement (→ See pages 146–147.)

> Microcredit should be offered to women in developing countries only accompanied by discussion support groups and classes in economics, because otherwise the women won't know how to change the community conditions that encourage poverty.

Her warrant—what she believes her audience already believes—goes something like this:

> Microcredit should help change the community conditions that encourage poverty.

(Note that this warrant implies that Riley's readers will readily accept that ending poverty is good.)

Following what we've written to the left, Riley has a conceptual framework—a large-scale organization for her paper:

1 She will start by discussing how most people believe that microcredit should end poverty.

2 She will spend the major part of her writing presenting evidence showing that, when microcredit is offered to women without discussion support groups and economics classes, microcredit does not end poverty.

3 She can conclude by stating that given her evidence, microcredit should be offered only with discussion support groups and economics classes.

→ See pages 234–235 to learn how Riley fine-tuned this conceptual framework.

WRITING IN THE SCIENCES

Research reports by scientists and engineers usually follow a specific arrangement of parts and a specific style of writing. The arrangement directs readers' attention to how an experiment was performed; readers can then judge the results and perhaps replicate the experiment.

The arrangement that scientists and engineers have developed to support communications about experiments asks that any report have, in order:

1 **A title,** which describes the experiment. One example: *The Physiological Effects of Pallidal Deep Brain Stimulation in Dystonia.*

2 **An abstract,** which is a short and concise overview of the paper; abstracts allow readers to see quickly if a paper is relevant to their work.

3 **An introduction.** This states why the research was done, what was being tested, and the predicted results—the hypothesis. There might also be a review of earlier relevant research here.

4 **Methods.** Researchers describe the procedures they undertook to perform their experiments, including the materials and equipment used.

5 **Results.** Researchers describe what they learned from the experiment.

6 **Discussion.** Here, the researchers discuss their understanding of the results. Did the results support the hypothesis? Why—or why not?

7 **A conclusion.** In this section, the researchers describe possible implications of their experiment as well as possible further research.

8 **References list.** Any works by other researchers that are cited in the report—or any reports written at an earlier time by the authors—are listed at the end of the paper. (→ See pages 453–457 to learn CSE style, which is most often used in the sciences.)

In a scientific report, all the above sections are separated and are labeled by the names listed above.

In addition, scientific writing usually has the following features:

• Because experiments are supposed to be repeatable anywhere by anyone, the experiment is emphasized, not the experimenter—and so scientific writers rarely use the first person **I** or **we** in writing; instead, they often use passive voice.

→ See pages 298–299.

• Because scientific and engineering evidence is often quantifiable, writers use charts, graphs, and tables as evidence. Photographs of objects used in experiments are also used as evidence.

• Because science and engineering research is most often carried out in labs where many people work, or across labs, research reports often have multiple authors.

TIP: CLASS ASSIGNMENTS

If you are asked to write a report in a science or social sciences class, your teacher will probably expect you to include at least several of the parts described on these pages. If the organization or features are not described in the assignment, ask.

WRITING IN THE SOCIAL SCIENCES

As the term *social sciences* suggests, the disciplines that come under this name apply scientific methods to studying people as social groups and as individuals within social groups. The social sciences include anthropology, economics, education, geography, linguistics, political science, psychology, sociology, and speech communication. (At some schools, history and gender studies might be listed as social sciences, if those areas use primarily scientific approaches to support their research.)

In writing papers for the social sciences, the arrangements that have developed over time follow the overall pattern of science writing as on the opposite page, but within the steps are some differences:

1 **A title,** which describes the study being reported in the paper. One example: *What Determines Cartel Success?*

2 **An abstract** of 100–200 words that summarize the purpose of the study, its methods, and its results.

3 **An introduction.** This defines the problem that was studied, reviews previous writing on the problem, notes the gaps in the previous writing that the current study will address, and gives an overview of the methods used. Writers also tell readers why the research being described matters.

4 **Methods.** Evidence used in the social sciences is usually observational, because social scientists are making and testing claims about human behavior. The sorts of methods for gathering this evidence are surveys and questionnaires, observations, interviews, and fieldwork. (→ See pages 78–79.) In the methods section of the paper, the writer describes which of these methods was used, and the details of how the method was carried out (how many people were interviewed or surveyed, for example, and what questions were asked).

5 **Results,** a description of what can be learned from the research.

6 **Discussion.** The researchers argue how the results of the study do (or do not) help with the problem described in the introduction.

7 **A conclusion,** which summarizes the problem, the research carried out, and what was learned.

8 **References list.** Any works by other researchers that are cited in the writing are listed at the end of the paper.

> → See pages 421–452 to learn APA style, which is most often used in the social sciences.

If the social sciences paper is longer than about five pages, the above sections are labeled by the names listed.

Because the social sciences seek as much objectivity as possible, further features of social science writing echo what we have described for science writing:

• Use of passive voice.

• Use of charts, graphs, tables, and photographs as evidence.

• Multiple authors.

ORGANIZATION, AUDIENCE, AND GENRE
WORKPLACE GENRES

Communications within and between workplaces in the United States focus on getting things done quickly and with as little misunderstanding as possible. People in workplaces communicate to set meeting times, to make decisions about company actions or policies, and to communicate with customers and suppliers.

Because of the time element, workplace genres in the United States share similar qualities, which composers can use as guidelines. Most workplace communications:

- Have a single purpose.
- Are designed to highlight that one purpose—and they state the purpose clearly, usually in the beginning of the text.
- Are short, concise, and direct.
- Use a formal but courteous tone.

On the next few pages is more specific information about audience expectations for three much-used workplace genres.

→ See pages 192–193 for suggestions for writing e-mails in formal situations like workplaces.

TIP: GENRES FOR INTERNATIONAL WORKPLACES

The conventions of workplace genres are very much related to national culture. If you land a job with a company that has international offices, you may receive training in the forms of communication the company expects; if not, ask co-workers about the expected ways communication happens in the company.

If your company is in the United States but you must communicate with people in other countries, ask if the company will pay for you to take a workshop in cross-cultural communications or will hire a consultant who knows about communications expectations in the other countries.

MEMOS

Workplace memos can be delivered on paper or by e-mail. Used for brief communications—usually one page only—they make announcements, ask questions, set up meetings, make requests, or confirm agreements.

Readers have come to expect memos to have the following parts:

- A heading
- An introduction
- A body
- A closing

A heading

At the top, memos have, on separate lines:
- the date
- the recipient's name (and title if appropriate)
- your name (and title if appropriate); sometimes writers initial their names
- a subject line

An introduction

Describe—quickly—your main purpose in writing the memo.

A body

Give the background information that supports or explains your purpose. If this information breaks into two or more parts, as in this example, consider using bold headings to make these parts easier to see.

A closing

Provide a one- or two-sentence summary, with contact information (if necessary). (Unlike letters, memos do not end with a signature.)

---

4 October 2006

To: STC Arts Project Teams
From: Jason Dryja
Re: New Print Project Protocol

stcarts
enterprise

{design}
<writing>
[media]

I want to take this opportunity to congratulate you on three consecutive successful projects. You and your project team members have met all deadlines and I think we have impressed our clients.

We learned a good lesson along the way—that we need to develop additional project protocols: an in-house preflight checklist and a print check.

Preflight Checklist
When we are preparing to deliver a client's project files for printing, we need to ensure that we have labeled and included all necessary files and documentation for the printer. Each project will have its own preflight checklist depending on the printer that the client is using and the nature of the project. Every print project, however, will have basic checklist items:

- RGB conversion to CMYK
- Page layout files converted to EPS
- Trims
- Bleeds
- Linked art files
- Paper mock-up for printer review

Print Check
When using a local printer, we should either accompany the client or deliver preliminary files ourselves to ensure that the printer has all the necessary information and files that she needs to complete the print job successfully.

These new print-project protocols will become part of our new-member orientation materials, but I would like to implement them immediately, including current projects. If you have any comments, questions, or concerns about how we might implement these protocols, please feel free to contact me.

| 112 Walker. MTU. 1400 Townsend. Houghton MI. | 906.487.1197 |
| www.stcarts.org. | info@stcarts.org |

RESUMÉS

Resumés summarize the experiences and education that make you appropriate for a new job. Because a resumé (and cover letter; → see pages 210–211) is often how a potential employer first encounters an employee, it deserves time and attention. And because employers often receive hundreds of resumés, they look at them quickly. Therefore, a resumé needs to be:

- short, to the point, and easy to read.
- focused on the position for which it is being sent.
- accurate.

COMPOSING A RESUMÉ

- For entry-level positions, a resumé should be one page so that employers can scan it quickly.
- Use white or cream paper. Use good-quality paper, but don't use papers such as parchment or vellum unless they are appropriate for the position (graphic designer, for example).
- Use black ink.
- Use a typeface such as Times or Helvetica. (Times takes up less space and so fits more information on a page.)
- Use 11- or 12-point type.
- Use headings, bullets, and indents so that readers can see the parts quickly.
  → See pages 300–301 on formatting.
- Look at your first draft; for each line in the body of the resumé, ask yourself, *Does this help an employer see my suitability for this position?* If the answer is no, remove or replace the information.

- If possible, get feedback from someone who works in or supervises the sort of position for which you are applying: Do they find your resumé readable, appropriately formatted, and strong?
- Always have someone else proofread it for you. Because employers receive so many resumés, they are looking for reasons to exclude; don't give them such a simple one as a typo.
- Do not lie or pad your experiences.

THE FORMAT OF A RESUMÉ

Name

Center your name at the top. Do not use nicknames. Bold your name, and put it in a slightly larger size (14 or 16 points).

Contact information

Be sure your address will be current for several months; if you are still in school or planning to move, put a permanent address. Most companies will contact you by phone or e-mail, so include both. Be sure whoever answers your phone knows to answer professionally; have a professional answering machine or voice mail message. Your e-mail address should be your name or initials; hotdude7@hotmail.com does not suggest a reliable, focused employee. If it is appropriate to the position, include a Web or blog address—as long as they are professional in both presentation and content.

Objective

Fit this on one line only; if you are responding to an ad, use the job title as part of the objective.

Education

Don't include high school unless there is something about your high school education that is relevant to the position for which you are applying.

Employment

Put your most recent employment first. Put your title first, then the place of employment, then the duration of time you held the position.

List your main accomplishments and responsibilities underneath the job title. Use action verbs in the past tense for past positions; use present tense for ongoing positions. If you have an accomplishment an employer will value, include it (such as *Website visits increased by 125%* under *Employment*).

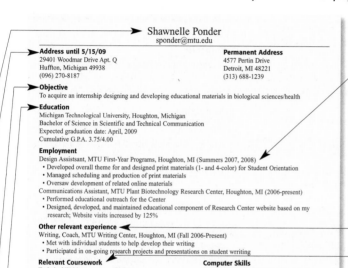

Shawnelle Ponder
sponder@mtu.edu

Address until 5/15/09
29401 Woodmar Drive Apt. Q
Huffton, Michigan 49938
(096) 270-8187

Permanent Address
4577 Pertin Drive
Detroit, MI 48221
(313) 688-1239

Objective
To acquire an internship designing and developing educational materials in biological sciences/health

Education
Michigan Technological University, Houghton, Michigan
Bachelor of Science in Scientific and Technical Communication
Expected graduation date: April, 2009
Cumulative G.P.A. 3.75/4.00

Employment
Design Assistsant, MTU First-Year Programs, Houghton, MI (Summers 2007, 2008)
 • Developed overall theme for and designed print materials (1- and 4-color) for Student Orientation
 • Managed scheduling and production of print materials
 • Oversaw development of related online materials
Communications Assistant, MTU Plant Biotechnology Research Center, Houghton, MI (2006-present)
 • Performed educational outreach for the Center
 • Designed, developed, and maintained educational component of Research Center website based on my research; Website visits increased by 125%

Other relevant experience
Writing, Coach, MTU Writing Center, Houghton, MI (Fall 2006-Present)
 • Met with individual students to help develop their writing
 • Participated in on-going research projects and presentations on student wrriting

Relevant Coursework

Technical Writing	Biology
Technical Editing	Chemistry
Information Design	Anatomy
Interactivity Design	Journalism
Usability	Graphic Design
Creative Writing	

Computer Skills
Operating Systems: Windows, Macintosh, Linux
Language: C++, Java, HTML, CSS
Software: InDesign CS3, Photoshop CS3, Illustrator CS3, Flash CS3, Dreamweaver CS Acrobat 8 Professional, WQuark Xpress, Microsoft Professional Suite

Honors
Dean's List (2006, 2007, 2008)
Susan Lewis Anthony Memorial Award (2007)
University Student Award (2006)

Extracurricular Activities
Scientific and Technical Communication, student association, president (2007-2008)
Black Student Assocaition (BSA) (2005-present)
BSA Big Brother/Big Sister Mentoring Program (2007-present)
ExSEL Peer Mentoring Program (2006-Present)

References
Available upon request

Other relevant experience

List here—in the same format as for employment—experiences for which you received no pay but from which you gained abilities relevant to the position for which you are applying. You can include hobbies—if they are relevant.

Relevant coursework

List only those classes that are directly applicable for the position.

Computer skills

List these if the position requires computer skills.

References

It is fine to say these are *Available upon request*—but do check with your references that they don't mind being contacted.

Honors

List any awards, in the order in which you received them.

Extracurricular activities

If you belong to any clubs or societies relevant to the position, list them.

COVER LETTERS

Unless a job advertisement requests only a resumé, always send a cover letter with your resumé. A resumé lists your accomplishments; in a cover letter you address an employer directly, to describe why you are a fit for the job.

GENERAL FEATURES

- Because employers receive many job letters and are always pressed for time, keep a cover letter to one page.

- Research the company by reading their website carefully or talking with people who work there; you need this knowledge for an effective letter.

- Put the cover letter on the same kind of paper as your resumé, and send originals, not copies.

- When you send a cover letter and resumé, put the cover letter on top. You can fold the two together to go into a regular-size envelope, or you can send them in a large envelope so that they remain uncreased.

- Make it perfect. Most employers will use even one typo as a reason for discarding a letter and resumé.

SPECIFIC FEATURES

Date

Name and address of recipient

A job listing should give you a name and address. If you are writing to inquire if a company has any job openings, you'll have to do some research: Call the company and ask a receptionist for the name of the person who does the hiring in the department where you would work; you can also often find this information online.

Salutation

Use **Dear** and the title of the person being addressed; if there is no title, use **Ms.** or **Mr.** Be sure to spell the name accurately.

Introduction

There are two kinds of cover letters:

- Those written in response to job advertisements.

- Those expressing interest in a company when you don't know if there is an opening.

Each kind of cover letter requires a different introduction.

For the first kind, include the name of the job—exactly as it is listed in the job ad—and any job number.

For the second kind, explain why you are writing to the particular company and how you learned about them, and describe the position you desire. If someone has recommended you to the company, say so.

March 1, 2008

Dr. Louisa Bramant
Community Education Director
Toivola Health Services
500 Campus Drive
Toivola, MI 49956

Dear Dr. Bramant:

A professor at my college whom you know, Dr. Richard Otherly, came to me to suggest that I write to you. He heard that I am looking for an internship in health education and said he thought I would be a perfect fit for your organization because of my knowledge and background. He did not know if you have any internship openings starting in early June (which is when I will be available for three to six months), but I am writing in hopes that you will keep me in mind should you have any openings.

From looking at your website, I see that your hospital provides a wide range of materials for helping people learn healthy habits or manage ongoing health issues. If you look at my resumé, which I've attached, you'll see that I have experience in both the technical and the scientific aspects of designing online educational materials for general audiences. In my position working at the Plant Biotechnology Research Center, my background education in biology and chemistry helped me communicate with the scientists whose work I translated into educational materials, and my technical knowledge and education in technical communication allowed me to suggest strategies for developing creative and effective learning materials. (When I redesigned the Center's educational website, visits to the website increased by 125%.) I know how to make interactive animations that help people see and so understand how plants uptake water, and I can imagine how useful an interactive animation about how insulin works (for example) would be on your diabetes education webpages. I also have experience developing print materials, should that be of use to you.

What my resumé doesn't show is that I am a solid and cheerful team player who gets things done on time. All my previous employers have commented on my responsibility and energy. I would be excited to be part of the good educational efforts your hospital is making, and hope that my qualifications appeal to you.

I would appreciate the opportunity to discuss an internship with you. I will contact you within the next ten days to see if you might have an opening and to see if you need any other information from me such as an application form, recommendations, or transcripts. Thank you for your time and consideration.

Sincerely,

Shawnelle Ponder

Shawnelle Ponder
29401 Woodmar Drive Apt. Q
Huffton, Michigan 49938
(096) 270-8187
sponder@mtu.udu

Body

Use your research in the company to show how your abilities fit the company's goals and values. Don't just repeat what's listed in your resumé but flesh it out: Give examples, describe achievements, and help the potential employer see how you are suitable; be positive and enthusiastic.

Sum up

Let the person know that you will be contacting the company to request an interview.

Close

Use *Sincerely* or *Cordially*.

Signature and contact information

Leave four lines after the closing for your signature, and sign in blue or black ink. Type your name and full contact information, including your phone number and e-mail address.

SHAPING PARAGRAPHS FOR AUDIENCE AND PURPOSE

In the preceding pages we've discussed the larger-scale organizational structures of different kinds of texts, and how and why to use them.

Now we discuss the next level of written organization, paragraphs.

PARAGRAPHS

Writing is not simply about conveying ideas to someone else. It also involves conveying the structure and relations of the ideas that have led writers to hold the beliefs, opinions, and values they do.

Paragraphs break reading—conceptually and visually—into units a reader can easily see. Because readers can see them, paragraphs help readers remember and so think about the structure and relations of the ideas in a text.

Readers' expectations about paragraphs have developed over several centuries. What we present on the next pages are current expectations about paragraphs in formal writing.

QUALITIES THAT READERS EXPECT IN PARAGRAPHS

- **Unity.** In the twenty-first century, readers expect a paragraph to contain sentences focused around only one idea or point.

- **Coherence.** Readers expect the sentences of a paragraph to grow out of each other.

- **Development.** Readers expect paragraphs not to repeat the same idea over and over, but instead to add to their understanding of the idea being discussed, as it relates to the writing of which the paragraph is a part.

In the next pages we go over these qualities in order.

PURPOSES OF PARAGRAPHS

There are three main categories of paragraphs:

- paragraphs that introduce readers to a piece of writing.

- paragraphs that make up the body of the writing, where the main arguments of the writing are developed.

- concluding paragraphs.

In the next pages, we focus on the paragraphs that make up the body of any piece of writing. Such paragraphs can function to

- describe.

- define.

- narrate.

- give examples.

- compare.

- classify.

- use analogies.

- divide.

Paragraphs can also mix these functions.

In the coming pages, we give examples of and discuss some of these paragraph functions. Once you understand how paragraphs perform functions like these, you can shape paragraphs to function as you need for your own purposes.

→ Pages 292–295 address introductory and concluding paragraphs.

SHAPING PARAGRAPHS FOR
AUDIENCE AND PURPOSE

UNIFIED AND COHERENT PARAGRAPHS

Whether you write for an academic journal or a music blog, readers these days expect paragraphs to be unified and coherent.

To be unified, each sentence of a paragraph is on the same topic.

To be coherent, each sentence of a paragraph will seem to a reader to follow directly from the paragraph that preceded it. Writers use strategies like these to achieve coherence:

• Repeating crucial words and phrases.

• Repeating crucial concepts by using synonyms for the concepts.

• Using pronouns to show that successive sentences refer to the same topic.

• Using parallel structures (→ see pages 286–287).

• Using words that show relations and connections among sentences (→ see pages 216–217).

• Having a consistent point of view.

• Using the same tense throughout.

When a paragraph is coherent, a reader should be able to draw connections between various parts of the paragraph, as the examples to the right show.

UNIFIED BUT INCOHERENT

It is possible to have paragraphs that are unified but not coherent:

Dolphins are highly intelligent mammals that live in the oceans. They are closely related to whales. Some people think they are gentle and cute. Dolphins are predators who can act violently. Dolphins can hear better than people. Some people think dolphins are a symbol of freedom and joy. The Dolphins are a football team in Miami.

The paragraph is unified because each sentence is on the topic of **dolphins**. The paragraph is incoherent because nothing else connects one sentence to the next. Instead, the paragraph offers random facts about dolphins—and Dolphins.

Another of the scorpion's exceptional features is the ability to glow under ultraviolet light, like a psychedelic poster.

The exoskeleton of the scorpion is made of a tough layer of tissue that feels like fingernail but is composed of another type of cuticle protein, chitin. This coat reflects the ultraviolet rays from moonlight and other light sources so brightly that even a black scorpion will be a fluorescent shade of green or pink. Fossilized scorpions from 300 million years ago still gleam brilliantly under ultraviolet light. The glow may have evolved to attract insects, which are drawn to ultraviolet light, or it may be an incidental byproduct of the chitin's chemical nature.

Whatever the reason, the unmistakable shine, visible from twenty feet away, makes it easy to spot scorpions at

UNITY
Every sentence in this paragraph is about the hard outer covering that is a scorpion's skeleton and, even more specifically, on how that covering responds to ultraviolet light.

COHERENCE
The writer keeps a scientfically descriptive tone in each sentence, and each sentence is in the present tense. Notice how the writer repeats one word, **chitin**, but uses synonyms to refer several times to the exoskeleton and its shiny nature.

■ ■ ■

...ground were the result of deep and personal individual reactions to a new environment.

The knottiest mystery of survival is how one unequipped, ill-prepared seventeen-year-old girl gets out alive and a dozen adults in similar circumstances, better equipped, do not. But the deeper I've gone into the study of survival, the more sense such outcomes make. Making fire, building shelter, finding food, signaling, navigation—none of that mattered to Juliane's survival. Although we cannot know what the others who survived the fall were thinking and deciding, it's possible that they knew they were supposed to stay put and await rescue. They were rule followers, and it killed them.

In the World Trade Center disaster, many people who were used to following the rules died because

UNITY
In this paragraph, the first sentence describes a **mystery**—and then every following sentence works to explain that mystery.

COHERENCE
In this paragraph, the writer has chosen a straightforward, emphatic tone throughout. The writer repeats **survival** often because that it is the paragraph's unifying idea. The writer refers to a young woman in two different ways. After a first reference to those who did not survive the airplane crash that the young woman did, the writer uses pronouns to refer to them.

LINKING WORDS THAT BUILD COHERENCE IN PARAGRAPHS

If you use words from the following list in a paragraph's sentences, you will help your readers understand why the sentences belong together. When you use the words below, you can repeat them to build parallel structures (→ see pages 286–287) that also show how the sentences belong together. If you do use such repetition, read your paragraph aloud to be sure you have not built a boring, singsong rhythm (unless a boring, singsong rhythm supports your purpose).

To show that information in one sentence adds to information in a preceding sentence: *additionally, also, and, besides, equally important, furthermore, in addition, moreover, too*

To emphasize the information in a sentence: *indeed, in fact, of course*

To help readers understand that you are building a sequence of events or a description of a process: *again, also, and, and then, besides, finally, first... second...third, furthermore, last, moreover, next, still, too*

To build sentences to describe events that take place over time: *after a few days, after a while, afterward, as long as, as soon as, at last, at that time, at the same time, before, during, earlier, eventually, finally, immediately, in the future, in the meantime, in the past, lately, later, meanwhile, next, now, simultaneously, since, soon, then, thereafter, today, until, when*

To help readers compare information in one sentence with that in another: *also, in the same manner, in the same way, likewise, once more, similarly*

To help readers see any important differences between your sentences: *although, but, despite, even though,* *however, in contrast, in spite of, instead, nevertheless, nonetheless, on the contrary, on the one hand...on the other hand..., otherwise, regardless, still, though, yet*

To indicate to readers that a sentence contains an example: *for example, for instance, indeed, in fact, of course, specifically, such as, to illustrate*

To help readers see cause and effect: *accordingly, as a result, because, consequently, for this purpose, hence, so, then, therefore, thus, to this end*

To make clear to readers the spatial relations among objects you are describing: *above, adjacent to, behind, below, beyond, closer to, elsewhere, far, farther on, here, in the background, near, nearby, opposite to, there, to the left, to the right*

To concede that your arguments are open to question: *although it is true that, granted that, I admit that, it may appear that, naturally, of course*

To show that sentences are summarizing or concluding: *as a result, as I have argued, as mentioned earlier, consequently, in any event, in conclusion, in other words, in short, on the whole, therefore, thus, to summarize*

USING THE LINKING WORDS AND PHRASES, AND PARALLELISM, TO BUILD COHERENCE

The paragraph below shows how each sentence connects to the next through repetition of words and phrases, as we noted on page 214. (We've highlighted **war** to help you see one repetition, and shown one pronoun use.)

But we also show how coherence is additionally built through linking words and parallelism.

You can see that only a few linking words are used; too many linking words can fragment a paragraph, so, generally, writers use only a few but combine them with the other strategies we listed on page 214 to link sentences.

parallelism

This sentence has three clauses, each of which has the same structure; the clauses are linked with semicolons. This structure shows that the three ideas have equal weight.

"in fact"

In fact precedes an explanation here and emphasizes the explanation. In this way, *in fact* indicates that the words following it amplify the words that precede it.

It is a remarkable fact about the United States that it fought a civil war without undergoing a change in its form of government. The Constitution was not abandoned during the American Civil War; elections were not suspended; there was no coup d'état. The war was fought to preserve the system of government that had been established at the nation's founding—to prove, in fact, that the system was worth preserving, that the idea of democracy had not failed. This is the meaning of the Gettysburg Address and of the great fighting cry of the north: "Union." And the system was preserved; the union did survive. But in almost every other respect, the United States became a different country. The war alone did not make America modern, but the war marks the birth of a modern America.

"this"

This refers to "that the system was worth preserving, that the idea of democracy had not failed." The pronoun carries forward those concepts into the next sentence, linking them.

"and"

And indicates to readers that the sentence it begins adds information to the sentence before it.

"but"

But signals to readers that there will be a change from what the preceding sentences were arguing.

SHAPING PARAGRAPHS FOR
AUDIENCE AND PURPOSE
PARAGRAPHS THAT DEVELOP

WHAT DOES "DEVELOPMENT" MEAN FOR PARAGRAPHS?

No matter its specific purpose, all writing is meant to move readers: It can move them from knowing nothing about a proposal in an upcoming election to understanding why some people are against the proposal, or it might move them out of daily routines into stopping to savor the pleasures of breathing.

If writing is to move readers, it has to begin with ideas familiar to them and then, from paragraph to paragraph and within paragraphs, develop those ideas in new or unexpected directions.

Effective paragraphs thus start with a sentence that grows out of the preceding paragraph—and then each following sentence develops or adds to the idea that is the focus of the first sentence.

You can shape this development from the familiar to the unfamiliar in many ways; in the next pages, we describe patterns—moving from simpler to more complex—for developing paragraphs.

The simpler kinds of paragraphs (such as description, definition, and narrative) usually appear near the beginning of a composition because they help writers lay out the ideas and terms at stake. Later, when a writer is trying to persuade readers to make particular connections among ideas, the more complex kinds of paragraphs (classification and division, comparison and contrast, cause and effect, syllogistic, and analogical) are more useful.

→ Because introductory and concluding paragraphs have very specific stylistic functions, we discuss them in Part 7 on style; see pages 292–295.

PARAGRAPHS THAT DESCRIBE

Descriptive paragraphs give details about people, places, or things, and thus they serve two functions. Because they appeal to our senses, they make what is being described more immediate and so engage readers' attention. Such paragraphs also help writers set the scene: They provide the background within which discussions, controversies, and experiments take place. Because they engage readers in and set the scene, writers often use descriptive paragraphs at the very beginning of writing. Whenever writers need to make a scene clear, however, or describe a situation that affects their arguments, they can use descriptive paragraphs.

> DARK NIGHT in the mountains and no drums beating. No flute music like birdsong from the forest above the village—the men controlled the flutes and this was women's business, secret and delicious, sweet revenge. In pity and mourning but also in eagerness the dead woman's female relatives carried her cold, naked body down to her sweet-potato garden bordered with flowers. They would not abandon her to rot in the ground. Sixty or more women with their babies and small children gathered around, gathered wood, lit cooking fires that caught the light in their eyes and shone on their greased dark skins. The dead woman's daughter and the wife of her adopted son took up knives of split bamboo, their silicate skin sharp as glass. They began to cut the body for the feast.
>
> New Guinea was the last wild place on earth. Its fierce reputation repelled explores.

■ ■ ■ This paragraph is the very first paragraph of a book about certain neurological diseases. The writer's descriptions appeal to ears as well as eyes and describe skin sensations. Attention to a range of senses helps writers make descriptions as vivid as possible.

> the Peppermill. Especially Flowers.
>
> As a rock star, he's a strange case: A crushworthy frontman and a bit of a peacock, he's given to showy, flamboyant stage performances. But in person, he's shy and sweet, a married, practicing Mormon (who enjoys the occasional beer or cigarette). When he talks about Vegas, he constantly ends up talking about his roots. "Vegas is my hometown, and it's turned into a place that's really sentimental to me," he says. "I think a lot of people can identify with that."
>
> The son of parents who hooked up in a Vegas trailer park when

■ ■ ■ This paragraph appeals to readers' expectations and emotional senses by using concrete adjectives and nouns (**crushworthy**, *flamboyant*, **shy**) and by using words spoken by the person being described.

PARAGRAPHS THAT DEFINE

If you are unsure whether your readers will understand a particular term or concept, give a definition. When you use a term or concept special to a particular discipline or field, chances are you will not be able to proceed in your argument without defining it. And if the term or concept is central to your argument, then defining it allows you and your readers to be in agreement about its meaning.

Because writers and readers have to develop a shared understanding of terms and concepts if discussion and argument are to be possible, the definition usually comes early in a text or early in a section that uses the term or concept.

Sometimes a one-sentence definition is all you will need—but if a term or concept is in any way complex or central to your purpose, then use a whole paragraph to build a detailed definition.

■ ■ ■

The paragraph to the right comes from a book arguing that food in the United States is now a petroleum product because of how crops and livestock are raised. This paragraph comes from a chapter in which the author describes Joel Salatin's farm in Virginia. The author uses this farm as an example of how crops and livestock can be raised without petroleum.

Notice how the first sentence gives a general definition of **grass farmer** (which itself includes a quick definition of **keystone species**). The following sentences add further detail and description—and use the words of an expert to support the definition being offered.

meat and milk) than anyone had ever thought possible.

Grass farmers grow animals—for meat, eggs, milk, and wool—but regard them as part of a food chain in which grass is the keystone species, the nexus between the solar energy that powers every food chain and the animals we eat. "To be even more accurate," Joel has said, "we should call ourselves sun farmers. The grass is just the way we capture the solar energy." One of the principles of modern grass farming is that to the greatest extent possible farmers should rely on the contemporary energy of the sun, as captured every day by photosynthesis, instead of the fossilized sun energy contained in petroleum.

For Allan Nation, who grew up on a cattle ranch in Mississippi, doing so is as much a matter of sound economics as environ-

---

TIP: WHEN USING DICTIONARY DEFINITIONS

Except when they are comparing definitions given by dictionaries, or want to comment on the shortcomings of a dictionary definition, few published writers quote from dictionaries when they need to define terms. Instead, they quote experts, people who know what a term means in practice. This gives the writer's words more authority.

PARAGRAPHS THAT NARRATE

Paragraphs that narrate tell stories. Stories personalize issues. When we hear the fortunes—or misfortunes—of others, we imagine ourselves in those situations. We know what feelings must be involved and might feel them ourselves. Stories can build emotional connections—positive or negative—between readers and topics.

Because stories are always about the experiences of one person or a few people, rarely can they stand alone as evidence: Readers will question attempts to generalize from limited experience to a broad claim. But stories can be useful in introductory or concluding paragraphs (to a whole essay or to a section) to engage readers emotionally with a topic or to make the topic memorable.

To write a narrative paragraph, tell what happened, in order. Include details—where the event took place, who was involved—but keep the narrative focused on your purpose. What is the main idea or feeling you want readers to remember?

(Note that stories based on real experiences are more effective than made-up stories; because they are not real, readers will not accept made-up stories as evidence.)

Death Nap

THE DANGERS OF TILTING BACK THE FRONT SEAT—DON'T DO IT!

By Emily Bazelon

Posted Friday, Sept. 7 2007, at 4.24 PM ET

A couple of weeks ago, I was sleeping in the front passenger seat of our car when it slammed into the vehicle in front of us. We were on the highway coming home from a family trip. The other three people in our car weren't hurt. But I'd reclined my seat, and my seat belt, which was riding high, left a long welt around my rib cage and along my stomach. As it turned out, I had internal bleeding from a lacerated spleen and three cracked ribs. I spent the next two days in intensive care.

I've recovered nicely, thank you. But the more I thought about my accident, the more I wondered whether I'd inadvertently done myself in by tilting my car seat back—as I do on just about every long drive. We worry a lot about car seats and

The paragraph to the left introduces an article on the dangers of sitting in a tilted-back front seat of a car. The author's own story makes the topic real—and scary. In the paragraphs that follow, the writer describes what she learned about tilted front seats through research and offers much more evidence than her own experience to argue that the dangers of riding in a reclined front car seat ought to be more well known.

PARAGRAPHS THAT GIVE EXAMPLES

If you write, *No wonder people don't watch television news—there are so many commercials!* readers might respond, *Sure, sure....* But imagine you wrote this:

> **No wonder people don't watch television news anymore—there are so many commercials! Last night, for example, I counted 12 commercials during one thirty-minute local newscast and 15 during a thirty-minute national newscast.**

Examples give readers vivid, concrete evidence, and so give them reason to consider the situation you are discussing.

→ The evidence you offer as examples can be of different kinds; see pages 112–113.

■ ■ ■

> feet of their mothers for nearly all of their first eight years of life, after which young females are socialized into the matriarchal network, while young males go off for a time into an all-male social group before coming back into the fold as mature adults.
>
> When an elephant dies, its family members engage in intense mourning and burial rituals, conducting weeklong vigils over the body, carefully covering it with earth and brush, revisiting the bones for years afterward, caressing the bones with their trunks, often taking turns rubbing their trunks along the teeth of a skull's lower jaw, the way living elephants do in greeting. If harm comes to a member of an elephant group, all the other elephants are aware of it. This sense of cohesion is further enforced by the elaborate communication system that elephants use. In close proximity they employ a range of vocalizations, from low-frequency rumbles to higher-pitched screams and trumpets, along with a variety of visual signals, from the waving of their trunks to subtle anglings of the head, body, feet and tail. When communicating over long distances—in order to pass along, for example, news about imminent threats, a sudden change of plans or, of the utmost importance to elephants, the death of a community member—they use patterns of subsonic vibrations that are felt as far as several miles away by exquisitely tuned sensors in the padding of their feet.
>
> This fabric of elephant society, Bradshaw and her colleagues concluded, had effectively been frayed by years of habitat loss and poaching, along with

This paragraph comes from a newspaper magazine article about a breakdown in the social structures of elephant groups. Elephants are performing violent acts against other animals, other elephants, and humans; young elephants suffer from what looks to researchers like post-traumatic stress syndrome. To argue that we should therefore treat elephants differently than we currently do, the writer needs readers to think of elephants as complex beings deserving of our sympathies, respect, and awe.

This paragraph lists examples of concrete elephant behaviors, shaped to encourage readers to think of elephants differently.

PARAGRAPHS THAT USE ANALOGY

If you wish explain to small children why cars need gasoline, you can talk with them about eating: The children probably understand that they need to eat because food gives them energy—so they can understand that cars need gasoline because otherwise the cars won't run. This explanation is an analogy: It uses a concept an audience already understands to explain a concept they don't.

Science writing for popular audiences uses analogies frequently, because the writing's purpose is usually to explain complex processes and concepts to people who don't have a technical background; using analogies to draw on an audience's experiences bridges their unfamiliarity.

You can use paragraphs based on analogies when you need to make a complex concept or process seem simpler. In addition, when you use an analogy, whatever associations your audience has with the more well-known concept will shape their attitudes toward the new or more complex concept. With the above analogy of food and gasoline, for example, it is likely that, because the audience probably likes food, they will think gasoline is a good thing. If you did not want the children to think in such generous ways toward cars or gasoline, the analogy could get you into trouble later.

■ ■ ■

The paragraph to the right draws on an audience's basic understanding of what computers are in order to help them understand how and why humans can be physically but not socially adept, as with conditions like autism (which, as you can see, is what the paragraph following the example is about).

individual, they later expect the individual to approach the character that helped it and to avoid the one that hurt it.

Understanding of the physical world and understanding of the social world can be seen as akin to two distinct computers in a baby brain, running separate programs and performing separate tasks. The understandings develop at different rates: the social one emerges somewhat later than the physical one. They evolved at different points in our prehistory; our physical understanding is shared by many species, whereas our social understanding is a relatively recent adaptation, and in some regards might be uniquely human.

That these two systems are distinct is especially apparent in autism, a developmental disorder whose dominant feature is a lack of

PARAGRAPHS THAT DIVIDE

Paragraphs that define can easily become or lead into paragraphs that divide: A definition establishes a criterion that names what something is (or is not). Once you have done that, you can use the criterion to categorize and divide.

Academic writing often hinges on such categorization or division because such categorization or division is analysis. Analysis allows us to name and so to sort through the components of a process or event. We do that to learn what happened or to learn what stands in our way of accomplishing what we desire.

Paragraphs that divide are often followed by paragraphs that compare and contrast—because it is possible to compare and contrast two objects, processes, or events only when we can see that the objects, processes, or events are different.

(The opposite kind of paragraph—a paragraph that unites—is also central to academic work. Just as it is important to show that what had seemed the same is really different, it helps us when we can see that what had seemed different is really the same.)

Danah Boyd, working on her PhD at Berkeley and a Fellow at the Berkman Center for Internet and Society at the Harvard Law School, researches how young people use social networking software like MySpace and Facebook. In a recent blog article she uses sociologist Nalini Kotamraju's definition of "class" to consider differences between MySpace and Facebook. Kotamraju argues that in the United States class isn't about money but rather about social connection: who you know is going to shape your life and what you can do more than how much much money you make. Based on that distinction, Boyd argues that the difference between who uses Facebook and who uses MySpace is one of class: Facebook is where the "goodie two shoes, jocks, athletes, or other 'good' kids" go, while MySpace

> is still home for Latino/Hispanic teens, immigrant teens, burnouts, alternative kids, art fags, punks, emos, goths, gangstas, queer kids, and other kids who didn't play into the dominant high school popularity paradigm.

Boyd argues that marketers and the military have figured out this distinction and are making decisions on it; Boyd hopes that teachers and social workers will figure this out, too, in order to talk with young people about how cultural structures and decisions shape individual lives.

In this example, the writer summarizes part of the argument of another writer's work. The summary shows how the original writer—Danah Boyd—starts with a definition of **class**. She then uses that definition to show a division in an area that many had thought was the same throughout: social networking websites that allow users to make personal profiles.

By using the definition to make a division in an area that had seemed the same throughout, Boyd can point to problems we might not otherwise have seen.

PARAGRAPHS THAT BLEND ORGANIZATIONS

Depending on your arguments, paragraphs can get complex: Writers need them to perform multiple functions.

(Keep in mind, though, that even when paragraphs blend several kinds of organizations together, the paragraph will still have one main function in the overall argument of which it is a part: It needs to move the argument forward one step.)

■ ■ ■

This example is part of a newspaper editorial, published on Labor Day, in which writer Mike Rose argues that we should "honor the brains as well as the brawn of American labor."

In this paragraph, Rose lists examples of the mental work that different kinds of blue-collar work require.

But this paragraph is not only examples. The examples ground Rose's argument that we need to unite rather than divide: We need to see that blue-collar and white-collar work have much in common.

Rose thus combines examples and analysis—unifying disparate elements—in this one paragraph.

beauty salons and restaurants, auto factories and welding shops. And I've been struck by the intellectual demands of what I saw.

Consider what a good waitress or waiter has to do in a busy restaurant. Remember orders and monitor them, attend to an ever-changing environment, juggle the flow of the work, make decisions on the fly. Or the carpenter: To build a cabinet, a staircase, or a pitched roof requires complex mathematical calculations, a high level of precision. The hairstylist's practice is a mix of scissors technique, knowledge of biology, aesthetic judgment, and communication skills. The mechanic, electrician, and plumber are trouble-shooters and problem-solvers. Even the routinized factory floor calls for working smart. Yet we persist in dividing labor into the work of the hand and the work of the mind.

Distinction between blue collar and white collar do exist. White-collar work, for example, often requires a large investment of time and

TIP: MANY KINDS OF PARAGRAPHS

We have described some of the most used kinds of paragraphs. But there are also paragraphs that classify, that explain processes, that show cause and effect, and that function in other ways depending on a writer's particular purposes. As you read others' writing, try to classify their paragraphs, and to determine why they used a particular kind of paragraph when they did; such observations will not only help you expand your tool kit of kinds of paragraphs but will also help you strengthen your own argumentative choices.

VISUAL ORGANIZATION

As our chart on page 187 suggests, written and visual texts share similar overall organization: They can both be analyzed for their overall conceptual framework, their major elements, and their detailed elements.

Just as with written texts, we will consider the conceptual frameworks and major elements of visual texts in these pages; in Part 7 we will consider the detailed elements of visual texts.

■ ■ ■

We'll start here by discussing the major elements of visual texts that mix words and visual pieces, and then we'll consider the organizational frameworks that are built from them.

MAJOR ELEMENTS OF TEXTS THAT MIX WORDS, PICTURES, AND OTHER VISUAL PIECES

You might have been taught about paragraphs so long ago that you don't realize you are creating major organizational elements as you write. When you work with texts that mix words and visual elements, you similarly have to create (or at least choose) the elements you will organize.

When you work with photographs, paintings, drawings, charts, and graphs, your choices shape readers' and viewers' possible responses.

→ If in your composition you use a photograph, painting, drawing, chart, diagram, graph, or table made by someone else, you need to cite the source; see pages 398–402.

PHOTOGRAPHS

Use photographs to document how a person, place, or object looks or looked (because of digital technologies, however, you might need to assure readers that photographs have not been manipulated). Use photographs to create emotional connections between readers and a topic: Seeing a person or place encourages readers to feel physically, and hence emotionally, closer than words.

When you use photographs, keep in mind that how the elements within a photograph are organized or cropped affects how readers respond. In the two photographs here, one creates a more intimate relation between viewer and photographed subject than the other.

PAINTINGS AND DRAWINGS

Kehinde Wiley composed the painting to the left. Wiley asks Black men to look at paintings of saints from the Renaissance and Baroque periods and to choose poses from the paintings; Wiley then paints them in those poses.

Paintings—and drawings—show a composer's imagination. Like photographs, paintings and drawings are arranged to direct your visual attention and shape your attitude toward the subject.

Photographs, because they come out of cameras, seem more direct and less abstract than paintings or drawings. Use paintings and drawings, then, when you need to present or illustrate abstractions.

PHOTOGRAPHS, PAINTINGS, DRAWINGS—AND WORDS

How would you respond to the family photograph above if it were titled "The Scientist as a Girl, with Her Family"? What if were titled "From the W.E.B. Du Bois albums of photographs of African Americans in Georgia exhibited at the Paris Exposition Universelle in 1900"? What would you think about the Wiley portrait if our writing didn't tell you that its pose was derived from a Renaissance painting?

When words are not attached to a photograph, painting, or drawing, viewers use their own experiences to make associations with or interpretations of the text; when words are added—as a title or explanation—the words limit how freely a viewer can interpret or make associations and instead start to shape the viewer's interpretation.

BUILDING VISUAL ORGANIZATIONS

Print texts have a clear beginning, a clear order to follow, and a clear end. Films and videos have linear organization similar to print, but one-page visual texts (posters, flyers, each page in a newsletter or brochure) do not. To build visual organizations with one-page texts, construct visual relationships among the elements.

MAKE SOME ELEMENTS STAND OUT

Arranging a visual text's organization requires making obvious which elements are most important and should be seen first, and which second and third. Elements are made to stand out—and be what is first seen—through contrast, placement, and leaving some space unemphasized.

■ ■ ■

Which movie flyer to the left would catch your eye on a campus wall? What do your eyes see in each flyer?

With the top flyer, you probably see a mass of text; no part stands out. With the second, your eyes are probably caught first by the rhinoceros and the big words at the bottom; then you notice the text at the upper right. The second flyer immediately tells you what it is about and perhaps piques your interest enough that you move close to read the details—which the flyer composer knew you would read if you were pulled in by the rhino.

Contrast

The second flyer works because the bottom words are so big compared to the words at the top right. Create contrast by giving elements **very** different sizes, colors, or styles.

Placement

Western reading patterns accustom our eyes to moving left to right and top to bottom, as well as to page centers. If you organize page elements so that the biggest element is at the top left or overlaps the center, you double its visual emphasis and so make it even more eye attracting.

Unemphasized Space (or "White Space")

White space is the design term for space on a page that only appears unused. But white space (which can be any color; **white space** comes from white paper) makes visual organization possible. Areas of a visual composition cannot be emphasized if every bit of space is full. Leaving some spaces empty allows the parts that are full to stand out.

GROUP ELEMENTS OR MAKE THEM SIMILAR

When you group visual elements or make them similar (and sometimes you do both at once), you create a page that feels unified and coherent to viewers—for all the same reasons that we gave for unified and coherent paragraphs on page 214.

Also, elements that are grouped or similar can create a background against which other elements can stand out.

Group Elements

When several elements on a page serve the same function—giving the time, date, and location information about an event, for example, or serving as the eye-catching elements—group them close to each other. A viewer's eyes see and so understand that they belong together.

You can see this in the rhinoceros movie flyer, where the rhinoceros and the big words are overlapped to make one element. The words at the top right of the flyer are also grouped: A viewer can quickly see that information about the movie is in one place.

■ ■ ■

Grouping can happen at the level of headings in a text, too. Compare the two text boxes to the right. The top box looks as though it contains seven different bits of text, because there is the same amount of space above and below the bold text.

The second box has more space above the bold text and none underneath; this groups the bold text with the words underneath. The grouping makes very obvious to a viewer that the bold text serves as heads for the words underneath.

Notice, too, how the second box looks as though it contains only four elements.

The components of color are hue, saturation, and brightness:

HUE

Hue describes what many of us just think of as color: When you name the hue of a color, you describe it as red or blue or yellow or green…

SATURATION

Saturation describes how much hue is present in a color. Vivid pink is highly saturated, while pastel pink is not.

BRIGHTNESS

Brightness describes how light or dark a color is.

The components of color are hue, saturation, and brightness:

HUE
Hue describes what many of us just think of as color: When you name the hue of a color, you describe it as red or blue or yellow or green…

SATURATION
Saturation describes how much hue is present in a color. Vivid pink is highly saturated, while pastel pink is not.

BRIGHTNESS
Brightness describes how light or dark a color is.

Repeat Elements

Any aspect of a visual composition can be related to another: a typeface, the alignment, the size of elements, a color, shapes. The idea of the title of a presentation can be repeated in a photograph used to illustrate a flyer or can be repeated in the kind of typeface used.

When composers repeat the elements of a visual layout, the resulting organization will look unified and coherent to viewers.

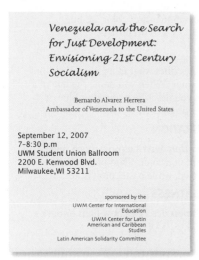

The top flyer to the left has sufficient contrast, expected placement, and appropriate grouping to enable viewers easily to see the major elements of the flyer. But the elements still do not seem as though they belong together. Each grouping is in a different typeface, and the elements seem randomly placed horizontally.

The redesign of the flyer adds a photograph to the top, to make the title even more visually engaging. But notice, too, what is now repeated in this organization:

- Only two typefaces are used: a big bold one at the top and for the speaker's name, and a more traditional serifed typeface repeated for everything else.

  → See pages 300–301 to learn about the typeface classifications of serif and sans serif.

- The typefaces are modern typefaces, repeating the concept of the twenty-first century mentioned in the talk's title.

- The left alignment is repeated for all the text elements.

- A gray square is repeated down the left side of the composition, helping separate the type groups.

- The gray of the square repeats the gray and the rectangular shapes of the buildings in the photograph.

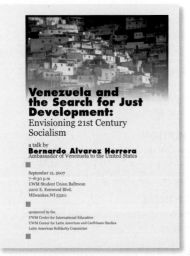

ALIGN ELEMENTS

Aligning each element of a visual composition with at least one other element will help a layout look coherent and unified. Elements are aligned when you can draw straight lines along the edges of elements:

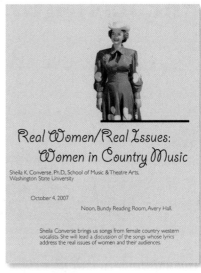

The top flyer at right has sufficient contrast, expected placement, and appropriate grouping and typefaces to enable viewers to see the major elements of the flyer; it also has a photograph appropriate to the presentation topic.

But the bottom flyer feels still more unified and coherent because the composition is now organized around two (imaginary) vertical lines, one on the left and one on the right.

Notice that the title of the presentation stretches between both the lines, as do the bottom lines of text; this reinforces the unity the alignment brings.

(Notice also that the design repeats the photograph twice, making it smaller and flipped upside down at the bottom but keeping it aligned.)

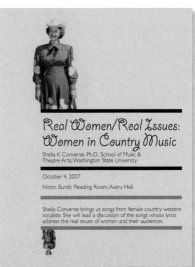

> **TIP: PHOTOGRAPHIC INTEREST**
>
> You've probably noticed in each redesigned flyer that a photograph or illustration is added. Photographs— especially of people—attract eyes. If added to a composition and placed to have contrast, eyes will be drawn to start there.

ORGANIZATION FOR ORAL PRESENTATIONS

Audiences for written presentations can look back over pages and paragraphs if they need help remembering where they are in a text; audiences for oral presentations cannot do this.

When you develop oral presentations, your biggest consideration about organization should be helping your audience hear the parts of the presentation.

THE PARTS OF AN ORAL PRESENTATION

Like written papers, oral presentations have the basic structure of introduction, body, and conclusion. But as you prepare, use strategies that make the organization audible to your audience.

- **Introduction.** Explicitly and clearly tell your listeners what your presentation is about and describe the parts that make up its structure.

  As you plan your introduction, be sure to state your purpose near the beginning. If you start with an anecdote, quotation, or another attention-getting strategy, state your goal next and then describe the main points or parts that structure your presentation. You want your audience to hear your purpose and organization several times so that they will remember them.

  Vary the sentence patterns you use to describe your purpose and organization (➜ see pages 470–471 about sentence patterns), but use the same or similar noun phrases to describe your purpose and organization so that audiences remember them well (➜ see pages 466–467 on noun phrases).

- **Body.** As you work out the body of your presentation, choose an easy-to-remember structure and plan to keep your audience aware of each movement you make from one point to the next.

  Easy-to-remember structures have few parts: In a five- to ten-minute presentation, audiences will be able to remember three to five steps in an argument. Easy-to-remember structures are

  - *Chronological.* Audiences can easily follow presentations that present events in the order in which they occurred.

  - *Logical.* Use your thesis statement (→ as we describe on pages 202–203) to organize the body into three parts: one for the warrant, one for the reason, and one for the claim.

  - *Problem-Solution.* Describe the problem and then argue for the solution you favor.

  - *Comparative.* If you are recommending one approach to a problem over another, first present the approach you least favor and then the one you want audiences to remember.

  Keeping your audience aware of your movement from one point to the next involves phrases like the following:

- **My third point is...**

- **Now that I have described the problem, let me tell you what I think the best solution is.**

- **I've described what microcredit is, so let me tell you why economists think it is so important.**

- **Finally...** or **In conclusion...**

  → All the phrases listed on pages 216–217 can help you help your audience hear your presentation's movements.

- **Conclusion.** Remind your audience of your argument and main points. If you can find one that fits well with your purposes, use an anecdote, story, or quotation to end memorably, so that your listeners hold on to your talk.

OTHER ORGANIZATIONAL FEATURES

- As our advice above and to the left suggests, repeating your purpose and main points in your introduction, as you move from paragraph to paragraph, and in your conclusion helps audiences follow your arguments. Use similar words as you repeat.

- Pare it down. These days, when we rarely receive instruction in how to listen, audiences benefit from straightforward, focused presentations.

TIP: AN ORGANIZATIONAL FUNCTION FOR VISUAL AIDS

If you use visual aids such as slides, overheads, or handouts during your presentation, include an opening screen or page that sketches or outlines the overall organization of the presentation.

As you move through the parts of your presentation, use screens that name the parts as you move into them.

FIGURING OUT WHAT TO DO WITH A PARAGRAPH THAT IS TOO LONG

Riley's draft (→ see pages 168–177) has a paragraph that is too long; it starts with this:

> But one writer says that most studies of microcredit programs "find very small increases in income for quite large numbers of borrowers; in only a very small number of cases are there significant income increases" (Mayoux 39). It most often benefits women….

To break this long paragraph into paragraphs that are of expected length, Riley needs to decide how the revised paragraphs ought to function in the overall organization of her paper. Because she has given her paper an organization that follows the basic form of her thesis (→ see pages 202–203 to see how she has done this), she has some guidelines to help her decide: She knows that she needs to start her paper by talking about her warrant—how most people believe that microcredit can end poverty—and she will conclude with her reason, that microcredit should be offered only with discussion support groups and economics classes. In the part of her paper from which the long paragraph comes, **Riley has to argue—and argue forcefully—that when microcredit is offered to women without discussion support groups and economics classes, it does not end poverty.** Her first draft shows that she has plenty of evidence to make this case— but how should she break up her long paragraph to give it an organization that will be easier for readers to read?

THE THESIS SUGGESTS AN OUTLINE FOR THE PAPER'S BODY

One way to see what the body of a paper must address is to separate out the terms used in the thesis. Riley's thesis has four main terms:

- microcredit
- women
- discussion support groups and economics classes
- poverty

Implied in Riley's thesis are these relations among the terms:

microcredit + women = poverty

microcredit + women + discussion support groups and economics classes = end of poverty

Riley needs to devote paragraphs to each of these topics and to explaining the relationships between the topics implied by the equation.

A rough outline for the body of Riley's paper could thus be:

1 **What is microcredit?**

2 **Why is microcredit focused on women?**

3 **Why does microcredit, alone, fail to bring women out of poverty?**

4 **What do discussion support groups and economics classes bring to the mix that can end poverty?**

THE OUTLINE SUGGESTS HOW TO BREAK UP THE LONG PARAGRAPH

Riley's overly long paragraph comes in the third section: *Why does microcredit, alone, fail to bring women out of poverty?*

As she revises her paper and works on the second section—why microcredit is focused on women—Riley's research shows her that people expect microcredit to help women in two ways. First, a microcredit loan is supposed to help women gain confidence and bargaining power. Second, a microcredit loan is supposed to help women make more money and spend it in their communities, and thus help their communities move out of poverty.

The long paragraph causing Riley trouble will follow the section on why microcredit is focused on women. Riley now knows that she will use a paragraph that divides (→ see page 224) to lay out why microcredit is focused on women. In the section on why microcredit alone fails to bring women out of poverty, Riley can then build on that division to make two paragraphs out of the long one:

- One paragraph will show how microcredit alone doesn't help women gain confidence or bargaining power.

- One paragraph will show how microcredit alone has not resulted in women making money or spending it in their communities.

→ Riley's final draft, using the outline and paragraphs described here, is on pages 406–418.

HINTS & TIPS FOR ORGANIZING TEXTS

BE WARY OF SETTLING ON AN ORGANIZATION TOO QUICKLY

If you want to produce writing that is smart, complex, and creative, you have to let your writing direct you. Although you have a thesis statement and a statement of purpose, and although they can help you give a rough shape to your writing before you sit down to write, it is in writing that you really test out and find the ideas you want.

All experienced writers will tell you of times that, in working out an argument in writing, they came to different or more focused conclusions than they had originally planned. Because they listened to their words, and followed the logic of their initial ideas or of new evidence, their writing had to take on new organizations.

So don't try to force an organization on your ideas; listen to your ideas and the directions they take you. You can always reorganize a paper once you have found a new or shifted argument.

CHECKING ORGANIZATION THROUGH AN AFTER-THE-FACT OUTLINE

Once you are confident in your arguments and know that your conclusion is exactly what you want (→ see pages 292–293), check back over all your other paragraphs: Does each logically follow what precedes it and lead to what comes next?

Experienced writers often make outlines for their papers **after** they have a first (or later) draft:

- Summarize each paragraph in one sentence. (If you cannot summarize a paragraph in a sentence, then you probably need to break the paragraph into two or more new paragraphs.)

- List the paragraph summaries in order.

- Does this outline step you logically from the introduction to the conclusion? If not, you may need to add, take out, or clarify paragraphs to have different summaries.

HOW OTHERS CAN HELP YOU CHECK ORGANIZATION

When you have a draft, cut it apart so that each paragraph is on its own piece of paper. Shuffle the pieces of paper and give them to someone else; ask the other person to tape the paragraphs back into a whole, leaving out any paragraphs that don't make sense or marking any places where it is impossible to tell what should come next.

Sometimes the other person will hand you back something with a clearer order, and sometimes you will learn where you need to make clarifications, additions, or subtractions.

PART 6
WRITING FOR DIVERSE AUDIENCES

CONTENTS

WHERE ARE WE IN THE PROCESS FOR COMPOSING?

Understanding your project

Getting started

Asking questions

**Shaping your
project for others**

Drafting a paper

Varieties of English
Writing for global audiences
Inclusive language uses

Getting feedback

Revising

Polishing

VARIETIES OF ENGLISH

> *I been thru a lot of struggles to get where I'm at today.*

I've struggled to accomplish what I have.

■ ■ ■

> *My brother was into skydiving and he got me hooked on this stuff.*

My brother, who is a skydiving fan, introduced me to the sport.

Some would react negatively to the top statement in each set above, saying, "That's not good English." By *good English*, they mean what is often called *Standard English*, represented by the second statement in each set above. Standard English—and its grammatical rules and patterns—is what is taught in schools and used in many formal situations.

Standard English is a historical accident: It resulted from the language practices of those who were economically and politically advantaged at the time people were thinking that grammar and English usage should be standardized.

LANGUAGE STANDARDIZATION AND LANGUAGE VARIETY

That we assign *good* or *bad* to different statements reflects two opposite tendencies in language use:

1

LANGUAGE STANDARDIZATION

Languages tend to become standardized in formal practice. In any language, one set of grammatical practices and speaking patterns will be favored more than others, as we noted on the page to the left.

Some argue that such standardization supports wider communication among speakers of different varieties of a language. Standard forms of language are thus often used in the media (think of how network television news reporters speak or of the writing in big-city newspapers) and in schooling, which is often meant to provide people from different backgrounds with a common culture and an ability to speak across their differences.

2

LANGUAGE VARIETY

Because of a language's use in different contexts for different purposes, different varieties of a language develop. In their daily use, people who fix cars will tend to use different sets of words than people who treat diseases. Different occupations can become so specialized—as law has, for example—that they have their own language patterns.

Similarly, different communities of people will shape local vocabularies and grammars. For example, the Gullah people, who live on islands off the southern states of North Carolina south to Florida, hold on to African words and speech patterns; these words and patterns have been brought into and have changed English in the area.

Depending on the influence that different groups have, and how much they interact with others, their words and language patterns can be accepted into the standard variety of a language, as the words of computer programming—*interface*, *platform*, and *input*—have become part of our day-to-day talk.

VARIETIES OF ENGLISH
ACADEMIC ENGLISH

> " ...by the time I came to the United States as a...student in foreign and second language education..., I was not competent in writing in my second language. Although I had no trouble expressing myself in English, I was not familiar with the standards of academic writing. I remember the first assignment I had in an education course....I spent hours and hours composing the essay, and yet, with great disappointment, the paper turned out to be a Chinese composition in English, although the instructor did not comment on this. "

In the words above, Chinese student Jun Liu describes his struggles to learn to write papers in academic English. What he describes is common for all writers entering a new writing context, whether or not their first language is English.

Every time you are asked to write a document you haven't written before, there is a learning curve. You have to learn the textual conventions, style preferences, and reader expectations unique to the new context. These new exigencies may seem challenging and uncomfortable at first, but you carry some basic tools with you from all your previous reading and writing instruction that can be adapted for the new context.

Following are some principles of academic writing and some strategies to help you tackle new academic writing contexts.

THE ORGANIZATION **OF ACADEMIC WRITING IN ENGLISH**

Readers of academic writing in English expect written texts to be organized around the following principles:

THESIS

❑ The main argument is usually explicitly stated in the introduction and is probably also repeated in the conclusion. Writers rarely leave readers to infer the argument.

❑ Subsequent ideas and information are related to the thesis; nothing is put into the text that doesn't support or further the thesis.

EVIDENCE IN SUPPORT OF THE ARGUMENT

❑ Evidence is given to support the main argument. Different disciplines will value different types of support and will use it in specific ways; but, in general, academic writers tend to avoid using only stories or examples to support a thesis.

→ See pages 104–113 for the types of evidence used in academic and technical writing.

→ See pages 200–205 to see the kinds of evidence valued in different disciplines.

❑ The body of the writing is composed almost exclusively of evidence.

❑ Statistics, examples, and facts are used to support any generalizations needed for the argument.

ARRANGEMENT OF IDEAS

❑ Writers state the main argument in the beginning of the paper and then provide evidence for it; they do not lead the reader to the main argument.

❑ Logic is used to build arguments.

→ Pages 202–203 explain some aspects of logic used in academic writing.

❑ Each paragraph usually picks up on and develops a point from the preceding paragraph, moving readers forward with little unnecessary repetition.

❑ Writers consolidate or group issues that are related to make their writing less repetitive. They also signal the progression of their ideas using headings, transition sentences, and connecting words.

→ Pages 300–301 discuss headings.

→ Pages 296–297 discuss transition sentences and connecting words.

CONNECTING TO THE AUDIENCE

❑ Arguments are timely and provide readers with either new information or a new perspective on a topic.

❑ Writers anticipate what their readers need to know so that the readers can enter into and follow the argument. (There is one exception: When writing for courses, student writers are often expected to display what they have learned, and thus are expected to provide more background information than their readers might need.)

UNDERSTANDING HOW WRITING IS ORGANIZED IN A NEW DISCIPLINE

When you need to write for a discipline or academic area new to you, analyze writing of the kind you need to produce. Ask teachers or those who write in the area to give you sample texts they consider effective *and* well written. Use the following strategies to understand what makes this type of writing successful.

- Look for background information. What kind and how much background information is provided before the writer launches into the argument?

- Look for supporting evidence. What kinds of supporting evidence are provided? How is this supporting information used?

- Where in the document does the main argument appear?

- How is the text organized? How does the writer signal this organization? With headings? With transitional phrases?

- Are headings standard from one document to another or are they author-created? What function do they serve? If they are standard headings, what information appears in each section of the document?

- Are ideas repeated? If so, which ideas and where does the repetition appear?

- How does the writer make important information stand out? Bullet points? Numbering? Headings? Bold text?

THE STYLE OF ACADEMIC WRITING IN ENGLISH

In addition to the features listed in the comparison chart to the right, readers of such writing expect to see:

- Language that clarifies complex ideas.

- Writing that shows familiarity with the terms and concepts of the discipline.

UNDERSTANDING WRITING STYLE IN A NEW DISCIPLINE

Analyze writing of the kind you need to produce, and then use the questions below to help you understand—and be able to reproduce—the style.

Questions to ask as you read

- What is the tone of the text? Is the vocabulary formal or informal? Does it use words that are subjective and judgmental or objective?

- Is the text simple and direct or more dense and involved? To determine this, look at the length of sentences.

- Does the writer rely more on noun phrases and technical terms or on a variety of verbs?

- When the writer uses the verb **to be**, is it followed by adjectives or complex noun phrases?

- Are there parts of the text in which the writer uses more informal language and a more personal style? If so, in what sections?

ACADEMIC WRITING

Today nearly every job requires good performances on more than one task. Employees have to deal with several simultaneous demands, and good job performance is therefore linked to good multitasking performance. This holds true for many jobs, as shown by data from the Occupational Information Network (O*NET; cf. Peterson, Mumford, Borman, Jeanneret, & Fleishman, 1999) and other job analyses (e.g., Maschke & Goeters, 1999, for airline pilots). In terms of personnel selection, therefore, it would appear to be essential to identify future employees with adequate multitasking abilities.

Bühner, M., et al. (2006). Working memory dimensions as differential predictors of the speed and error aspect of multitasking performance. *Human Performance, 19,* 253–275.

1 Uses technical terms: *good multi-tasking performance, personnel selection.*

2 Has long noun phrases: *several simultaneous demands, adequate multitasking abilities.*

3 Has long sentences.

4 Uses verbs that refer to unchanging conditions (such as mental or bodily states): is...*linked, requires.*

5 Has an element of doubt: *nearly every job, it would appear.*

6 Has a neutral tone.

7 Shows respect for the ideas and work of others by citing names and sources.

POPULAR WRITING

Recently I poked fun at those New Age marvels we call the multi-taskers. If you missed it, the salient point was this: Laboratory experiments prove that multi-tasking is, contrary to all hype, hugely inefficient.

Balzar, J. (2003, April 27). One thing at a time, please. *Los Angeles Times.*

1 Mixes popular words and expressions (*hype, marvels*) with technical terms and formal vocabulary (*salient, Laboratory experiments*).

2 Has few long noun phrases; instead, if nouns are modified, it is usually with one adjective.

3 Has shorter sentences.

4 Uses verbs that refer to actions: *poked fun, missed.*

5 Can make confident and wide-ranging claims: *multi-tasking is...hugely inefficient.*

6 Can have a playful, even sarcastic, tone.

7 Doesn't cite sources in the text.

ENGLISH AS A GLOBAL LANGUAGE

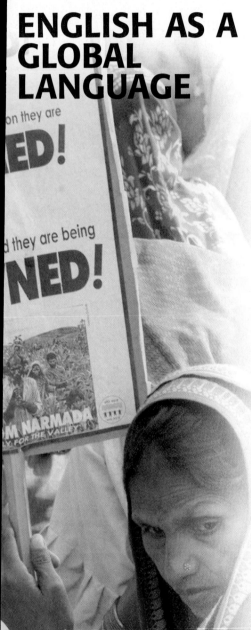

> *I became boring.*
> **I became bored.**

> *I will climb machine to the junction. I cannot trek.*
> **I will ride my motorcycle to the junction. I can't walk the short distance.**

The two examples above show English used in different countries. In the first set of sentences, Singaporean English contrasts with what some consider to be Standard English; the second set starts with Nigerian English.

As transportation and communication technologies bring once-distant communities in touch through commerce and culture, language standardization and language variation shape English.

Standardization steps in because businesses now operate worldwide and because media are on a twenty-four-hour, worldwide news cycle. Some believe the use of one language can ease this communication. English has taken on that role, in most cases being the language of business, science, and to some extent, the Internet.

English has taken on this role not because it is a superior language but simply because of accidents of history: English happened to be in the right place at the right time. And, possibly, English will be displaced by another language at some time in the future when it is no longer politically or economically advantageous.

Language variation is also at work. Because English has been adopted in so many countries, many varieties of English have emerged, such as Singaporean English, Nigerian English, Indian English, Caribbean English, Malaysian English, and so on. Language experts refer to these varieties as **world Englishes**. Each group of new English users changes the grammar and vocabulary of what we think of as **Standard English** to reflect their culture and needs—just as, starting in the sixteenth century, people in the British colonies (including what is now the United States) changed English as it was spoken and written in England.

WRITING FOR A GLOBAL AUDIENCE

Globalization in markets, science, and media has meant that texts produced for business or technical purposes—reports, advertisements, business plans—are translated between languages. Sometimes, as the following example shows, the translation process creates problems:

Original meaning: Sexual harassment is your concern.

Translation into another language: Make sexual harassment your business.

Whatever the final result, the globalization of communication is influencing the language of writing. When writers of business or technical reports produce a document, they must take into account the translation process their texts will undergo.

TO ENSURE ACCURACY AND EASE OF TRANSLATION

• Use clear (not simple) sentence structures.

For example, this sentence is difficult to translate:

The rapid level of increase in entry of women into the workforce has changed people's shopping patterns from daily shopping to weekly or monthly.

Easier to translate is this sentence:

Because more women have entered the workforce, people no longer shop daily, but weekly or monthly.

• Use straightforward vocabulary. Avoid idioms and vague word choice that might create confusion.

The *italicized words* in the following text will be difficult to translate because they are idiomatic or make cultural references that are not shared outside the United States:

Recently I *poked fun* at those *New Age marvels* we call the multi-taskers. If you missed it, the salient point was this: Laboratory experiments prove that multi-tasking is, contrary to *all hype*, hugely inefficient.

• Anticipate vocabulary that might have multiple meanings and cause translation difficulties

For example, **concern** in the sexual harassment example on the left causes difficulty because it has two potential meanings: **business concern** and **problem**.

WRITING ENGLISH WHEN ENGLISH IS NOT YOUR HOME LANGUAGE

WRITING AS A SECOND LANGUAGE

We learn to speak as we grow up in the comfort and informality of home. Without thinking about it, we imitate what we hear those around us saying, and our families teach us informally while we eat or work together.

But we learn to write through formal instruction. In the United States, the first five or six years of school focus on the basics of writing; in other countries, the amount of time given to writing instruction varies.

Given that learning to write is so formalized and separated from learning to speak, it is as though writing is a second language for everyone.

Anytime we move from one writing context to another—whether we move from texting a friend to writing a school essay or from writing in a home language to writing in English—we have to shift how we write. From any previous learning experience, we carry some knowledge of how to shape writing, but in new contexts and with a new language, we have to attend carefully to textual conventions, style preferences, and reader expectations that are unique to the new context. All of these can be learned.

> Because I had not learned to write more than a paragraph in English before, I had much to learn in the first-year composition class I took during that first semester. In the first class, the teacher told us that there are some rules in English composition we have to follow, but that if we follow the rules, anybody can write a reasonably good composition. The teacher's statement sounded like God's blessing to me, as I was already struggling with the quantity of writing requirements in other classes. The *rules* I learned in the composition class included the concepts of unity and cohesion, which have since helped my English writing a great deal.
>
> I also learned several effective patterns of paragraph development such as *cause and effect* or *comparison and contrast*. Although I later learned that not all writers of English follow such rules and patterns, these rules were truly helpful for a new writer like me.
>
> Another important thing I learned in the first-year composition class was the idea of writing as a process. I learned that a good end product can only be achieved through a long revising process. I had never learned such things either in my previous English or Japanese classes in Japan.
>
> —Miyuki Sasaki

MULTILINGUAL WRITERS WRITING IN ENGLISH

If English is your second or third language, you may feel at a disadvantage when you use English to communicate in writing—but having already mastered writing in a second or third language is an advantage to you in several ways:

- You are comfortable gathering ideas and putting them together in an extended text.
- You have experience with successfully writing for various audiences and purposes in the other languages in which you write.
- You can draw on vocabulary and language resources from two or three languages.

Especially when gathering and thinking through ideas, you might find it more comfortable to gather ideas and plan your text in your first language.

Also, writing involves turning unformed ideas into concrete words and sentences. That means all writers must translate ideas into words, a difficult process even if the language you speak in is the language in which you are most comfortable writing.

If you know a second or third language, use it to help you put your thoughts into words. Later, as you are drafting, you can find the English equivalents for those words. Doing this will make the process of composing more efficient and will lessen the frustration of **word hunting**.

USING INCLUSIVE LANGUAGE

> My name is Jane Takagi-Little. Little was my dad, a Little from Quam, Minnesota. Takagi is my mother's name. She's Japanese. Hyphenation may be a modern response to patriarchal naming practices in some cases, but not in mine. My hyphen is a thrust of pure superstition. At my christening, Ma was stricken by a profound Oriental dread at the thought of her child bearing an insignificant surname like Little through life, so at the very last minute she insisted on attaching hers. Takagi is a big name, literally, comprising the Chinese character for "tall" and the character for "tree." Ma thought the stature and eminence of her lofty ancestors would help equalize Dad's Little. They were always fighting about stuff like this.
>
> "It doesn't *mean* anything," Dad would say. "It's just a *name!*," which would cause Ma to recoil in horror. "How can you say '*justa name*'? Name is very *first* thing. Name is face to all the world."

This passage from Ruth L. Ozeki's novel *My Year of Meats* describes how the main character comes to be named and, in so doing, describes how we use words to shape our relations with those who may have grown up in cultures different from ours. Jane's mother is alert to the social weight of words, of how the words we use to describe ourselves—and others—shape how we are seen and treated by others. She insists that her daughter carry a name that gives her importance and so respect in the eyes of others.

This matter of how we are named comes up elsewhere in Ozeki's novel, as in the following exchange:

> **Then, at the pancake breakfast where we had been filming, a red-faced veteran from WWII** drew a bead on me and my crew, standing in line by the warming trays, our plates stacked high with flapjacks and American bacon.
>
> "Where are you from, anyway?" he asked, squinting his bitter blue eyes at me.
>
> "New York," I answered.
>
> He shook his head and glared and wiggled a crooked finger inches from my face. "No, I mean where were you *born?*"
>
> "Quam, Minnesota," I said.
>
> "No, no...*What* are you?" He whined with frustration.
>
> And in a voice that was low, but shivering with demented pride, I told him, "I...am...a...*fucking...* AMERICAN!"

Neither the questioning man nor Jane comes across well in Ozeki's writing, both insistent, neither willing to back off. It is precisely because our identities—the words we use to describe who we are—carry so much weight that this scene in the novel matters.

But Jane's position is the one with which Ozeki asks us to sympathize, in the end, because Jane, in spite of her expletives, is defending herself. The man wants to judge her based only on how she looks.

Instead, Jane insists on naming herself, on choosing to be seen through a word that belies the assumptions the man wants to make.

Who does not want the right to be known by a name that speaks truthfully to and respectfully of one's background and experiences?

■ ■ ■

It is important, then, that we grant each other the right to choose the names by which we are called and understood by others.

When others write or talk about us using names we believe do not reflect our backgrounds or experiences accurately or respectfully—or when they write or talk about us in ways we believe to be disrespectful—they show us either that they have made mistakes about us or that they do not see us as worthy of the same respect that they expect for themselves.

When we write about others, it would seem only right that we grant the same respect to them. If your readers feel excluded because of your word choices, because of how you refer to them, then they will either stop reading or they will read your words with a hostile, sad, or distanced attitude, thus undermining your purpose in writing.

Writing that connects with readers connects because readers feel respected by the writing. When you write, it is not about you. It is about your readers, and about giving them the same respect and courtesy you believe you deserve.

HOW DO YOU SHOW RESPECT TO YOUR READERS?

Here are general guidelines:

- **Ethnicity, gender, sexual orientation, age, religion, and mental and bodily ability are sensitive characteristics in our time. Anytime in your writing you refer to one of these areas, check that your word choice is both necessary and respectful of those to whom you are referring.** Educate yourself about why these issues are sensitive, because knowing the reasons behind these issues will help you make good decisions about how to write.

  How we refer to each other will shape how we think of and treat each other. How are the following sentences likely to affect a reader's attitude toward the people being described?

  Given how she finished the race before so many others who had two real legs, you would almost think she was a real athlete.

  A pert woman in a short leather skirt, the prime minister spoke about the financial relations between our countries.

  He has two children and a daughter adopted from China.

  Equally important, how are readers likely to think about the person who wrote these sentences?

- **Have you referred to people by the names they have chosen for identification?** If you are writing a description of a person you have interviewed, for example, ask the person what terms to use. Avoid using names that people find offensive; again, ask if you are unsure or do not know.

  As political and social changes affect our lives, the names people prefer may change; you will have to ask or do research to stay current. Members of a group may disagree about their preferred name; you can acknowledge this in your writing.

- **Do you refer to a person's characteristics only if your purpose requires it?** Imagine that the following sentences began newspaper articles about speeches given on a college campus.

  The speaker, a cute blonde, talked at length about world hunger.

  The speaker, a feisty old guy, lectured on parenting mishaps.

  From his wheelchair, the speaker argued against current tax policies.

  Do the descriptions in the sentences help you learn about the content of the speeches? Do they have anything to do with the speeches?

  The descriptions turn our attention away from the speeches and from the hard work done by the speakers, instead asking us to focus on qualities of the speakers that are incidental to their abilities as serious speakers.

- **Have you made assumptions about the lives of others based on your own experiences?** Only one team wins in a big sporting event, but different people experience that win differently: One set of fans will be jubilant and one will be frustrated. It is the same with elections, judicial cases, and world happenings: While everyone might agree on the facts of the outcome, different people, because of their different backgrounds, will respond differently.

  This is also true of reading. You might read one set of words and think they are just fine, but the person across the table from you might be annoyed, hurt, or angered by the same words.

  If you have a lot in common with others, you can make some predictions about their responses to different events, but in all cases, if you find yourself writing statements like these—

  Who could possibly believe that?

  All reasonable people will take this action.

  Only an uninformed person could respond in this way.

  —then you are making assumptions based on your own particular experiences and beliefs. You should not be surprised when some or many readers are turned off by how you characterize those who believe differently from you.

- **Have you avoided stereotyping?** Stereotyping happens when you focus on only one of a person's characteristics, with that characteristic being a negative or limited belief about a group.

  Just like a man!

  He's acting like an old lady!

  What else could you expect from a teenage girl?

- **Have you expected one person's experience to represent everyone's?** To expect one woman to be an expert about the lives of all other women can result in creating stereotypes—just as asking one African American man to speak for all African Americans, or for one teenager who is a lesbian to speak about the lives of all teenagers or all lesbians, or for one Christian to speak about the lives of all Christians.

In the following pages are guidelines for specific areas of inclusive language.

> **TIP: FOLLOWING THESE SUGGESTIONS WON'T FIX EVERYTHING**
> The word choice issues we discuss on these pages matter—but keep in mind that they work together with the tone of voice you use, the attitude you convey, and the other positions you consider in your writing to give your readers an overall sense of your fairness and integrity.

USING INCLUSIVE LANGUAGE
INCLUDING ALL ETHNICITIES

"ETHNICITY" OR "RACE"?

More and more, scientists argue that *race*—as a genetic basis for categorizing humans—does not exist. We have tended to define someone's race based on the physical appearance of the person, but people may have similar physical appearances (such as skin color) because their ancestors grew up far apart although in similar physical environments; even though two people might look alike, their genetic differences might be so considerable that they share little common heritage.

Because there is controversy over *race*, and because *race* focuses our attention on physical characteristics, we have found it generally better—when we must refer to others through such lenses—to use the term *ethnicity*.

Ethnicity refers to heritage and culture: Ethnic groups tend to come into being because of a people's common ancestry, language, or religion.

TIP: CONSIDERING "RACE"

For centuries, in this country as in many others, the idea of *race* was used to justify the unequal treatment of different peoples. We need to keep this historical fact in mind because, sadly, it is still shaping people's relationships and livelihoods. Therefore, unless you are writing about *race* as a topic, use *ethnicity* to encourage your readers to enact more thoughtful and more accurate relationships.

CHECKING YOUR WRITING

- **Have you referred to a person's ethnicity or national origin only when it is relevant to your argument?**

- **Have you used names that people from an ethnicity prefer for themselves?** As political and social changes affect people of different ethnicities, the names they prefer may change; you will have to ask or do research to find currently preferred names. Members of a group may disagree about their preferred name for different reasons; you can acknowledge this in your writing.

   Learn the names that people find offensive so that you do not inadvertently use them; these are often names that other cultures assigned or used in the past.

- **Have you assumed that your readers share the same ethnicity or experiences as you?** Unless you are writing to people who have precisely the same background as you do, be careful not to assume that your readers hold the same beliefs as you. This can be hard since much of what we believe, think, and feel is implicit; when in doubt, ask someone not of your ethnicity and who has grown up differently from you to read what you have written, to be sure that you are not inadvertently attributing to your readers qualities or beliefs that you hold because of your particular upbringing.

- **Have you been as specific as you can in naming an ethnic group?** The more specific you can be about an ethnicity, the less likely you are to slip into

stereotyping. For example, use *Ojibwa* or *Cherokee* instead of *American Indian;* use *Bahraini* or *Saudi* instead of Arab.

- **Have you used hyphens in multiword names?** In current usage, you should write (for example) *Japanese American* rather than *Japanese-American* because the hyphen implies both dual citizenship (which may not be the case) and that one is not completely American. In the nonhyphenated form, such as *Swedish American,* the first word is an adjective modifying the second word, emphasizing the second word but also holding on to the particular experiences that the first word conveys.

- **Have you avoided phrases that use ethnically tied terms?** You may have grown up with phrases that seem to you just part of language, such as *Latin lover* or *Jewish mother*—but these terms stereotype people. They imply that all people of that ethnicity share some set of broadly defined (and often derogatory) characteristics.

- **Have you capitalized the names of ethnicities?** For example, write *Polish American* or *Filipino American.*

- **Have you checked that any adjectives you put before the name of an ethnic group are appropriate?** To write that someone is (for example) *a quiet American* can imply that Americans are loud.

Because language is social and is therefore continually changing, these usages can change. Keep your ears open to stay current so that your writing is always respectful.

INCLUDING ALL AGES

AGEISM

In other cultures, people who have gray hair and many wrinkles are often respected for the knowledge and understanding that can come with many years of life. In the United States now, however, most people want to stay young as long as possible, with the result that people who are older are often stereotyped as frail, rigid, reactionary, and incompetent—or as soft, kindly, and powerless grandparents. Oddly, however, people who are young are often stereotyped as reckless, loud, selfish and self-absorbed, unambitious, sex-crazed, and lazy.

If you think about all the people you know who are younger than you and all the people you know who are older than you, however, your experiences ought to give you many counter-examples to these stereotypes. Ageism, the stereotyping of people because of how old they are, is therefore—like racism and sexism—a form of prejudice because it shapes our understanding of others in negative, limiting, and rarely true ways.

CHECKING YOUR WRITING TO AVOID AGEISM

- **Have you referred to the age of a person only when your purpose requires it?** To check the necessity of referring to age in your writing, try taking it out; if your readers can still understand your purpose, then remove the reference. If, for example, in an article about poker you have written, *Ms. Jucovy, who is 63, won the final pot,* change the sentence to *Ms. Jucovy won the final pot* and ask others to read the article. If they still understand your article as you intended, then stay with the second version.

- **Have you used ageist terms to describe others?** Terms to avoid for people who are older are the following: *geriatrics, over the hill, ancient, old-timers, matronly, well-preserved.*

  Terms to avoid for young people are the following: *punk, gangbanger, juvie.*

- **Have you used terms that patronize people because of their age?** Treat older—and younger—people with the same respect, using the same titles.

  The standard in Anglo culture in the United States, then, is not to call an old man *Grandpa* (unless he really is your grandfather) or to refer to an older woman as *Honey, Dear,* or *Auntie*: These terms imply a level of familiarity you wouldn't assume with people of other ages.

- **Don't refer to older people as "our seniors" or "our elders."** Again, this is a practice in Anglo culture in the United States. The use of *our* implies that the group of people being discussed is the writer's property or possession instead of individual humans.

- **Have you referred to older people as the vital, interesting, productive people they are?** People who are retired do not share any common characteristic other than that they are retired: Some people retire in their forties, and others retire in their seventies; some retire from one career to take up another while others take on active volunteer work. The more you learn about what a range of older people does, the more you are likely to write respectfully, fairly, and accurately about them.

USING INCLUSIVE LANGUAGE
INCLUDING ALL GENDERS

SEXISM

Language is sexist when it implies that women are not only different from men but also somehow inferior.

CHECKING YOUR WRITING TO AVOID SEXISM

- **Anytime you have described someone's gender—or used descriptive terms that are culturally gender-related—ask yourself if the description is necessary.** One way to check this is to rewrite the sentence, changing the gender. For example, if you have written, *The musician, a pretty redheaded girl, played the Bach concertos effortlessly* but would not write, *The musician, a pretty redheaded boy, played the Bach concertos effortlessly*, then change the original sentence to, simply, *The musician played the Bach concertos effortlessly.*

- **Have you used *man, men, he,* or *him* to refer to a group of people that might include women?** Some argue that these words are always inclusive of both men and women, but look at these sentences:

  On this form, everyone should add the name of his husband or wife.

  When pregnant, men ought to aim for more sleep.

  Pantyhose fit properly if a man feels a slight cling at his waist.

  Because these words are not inclusive, revise any such uses so that your words don't exclude the women in your audience.

To revise:

Substitute gender-neutral nouns for *man* or *men* or words that include them. For example, instead of *chairman*, use *chairperson*.

Make a sentence plural so that you can change *he* and *him* to the gender-neutral *they* and *them*: *Everyone should bring his own umbrella* can become *All visitors should bring their own umbrellas*.

- **Have you used unequal terms to refer to men and women in equal positions?** If, for example, you are writing about the presidents of two countries, it is incorrect to write *Mrs. Halonen and President Bush*; instead, write *Presidents Halonen and Bush*. Similarly, *man and wife* puts the woman in a subordinate position; *husband and wife* treats both with equal respect. If you write *the girls' team*, then refer to the boys' team as *the boys' team*; to call one team *the team* and the other *the girls' team* is to imply that the first team is the standard and the second is a deviation.

- **Have you avoided stereotyped uses of occupations?** The sentences *Each computer programmer has his own style of coding* and *A teacher can have a tremendous impact on her students* imply that these occupations are the domain of one gender only. Make the sentences plural to avoid the stereotypes: Write, *All computer programmers have their particular styles of coding* and *Teachers can have a tremendous impact on their students.*

- **Have you used any words that stereotype behavior according to gender?** If you are describing a group made up only of women or only of men, check that your sentences do not use words that belittle some members.

You can check this by rewriting the sentence for the other gender. For example, if you've written, *The women were gossiping about the senatorial candidate,* see if *The men were gossiping about the senatorial candidate* sounds right. If it does not, then change the original sentence to *The women were discussing the senatorial candidate.*

- **Have you used salutations that include all members of an audience?** Do not start a letter with *Dear Sirs* if you do not know your audience; you can start with *To whom it may concern* or *Dear Colleagues,* or you can leave off the salutation.

USING INCLUSIVE LANGUAGE
INCLUDING ALL ABILITIES

> *It is recommended that the word* disability *be used to refer to an attribute of a person, and* handicap *to the source of limitations. Sometimes a disability itself may handicap a person, as when a person with one arm is handicapped in playing the violin. However, when the limitation is environmental, as in the case of attitudinal, legal, and architectural barriers, the disability is not handicapping—the environmental factor is. This distinction is important because the environment is frequently overlooked as a major source of limitation, even when it is far more limiting than the disability. Thus, prejudice handicaps people by denying access to opportunities; inaccessible buildings surrounded by steps and curbs handicap people who require the use of a ramp.*

ABLEISM

The passage above comes from the American Psychological Association's guidelines on language use. The passage acknowledges implicitly what people with disabilities have been working to counteract for many years: People with disabilities are often seen as though they are defined by their disabilities. For example, the expressions a *crippled woman* or *confined to his wheelchair* focus our attentions on the disability rather than on the people and their intelligence and abilities.

This is a form of prejudice that has been named **ableism**.

CHECKING YOUR WRITING TO AVOID ABLEISM

- **Have you emphasized the person and not the disability?** This practice is known as *person-first language*, and is called for by the Americans with Disabilities Act (ADA), legislation passed in 1990. This practice asks us to use language that treats all people as possessing a complex and wide range of strengths, abilities, and skills.

  To practice person-first language, describe the person before you describe the disability. For example, write, *person who has AIDS* rather than *AIDS sufferer*, or *child who uses a wheelchair* rather than *wheelchair-bound child*.

  Also, use adjectives rather than nouns to describe someone with a disability. To call someone *a mute, a cripple*, or *an epileptic* is to imply that the person is completely swallowed up by the disability; to say, *a child who cannot speak, a doctor with an amputation*, or *a musician who has epilepsy* starts to let the person—who has many other characteristics besides the disability—come forward.

- **When you refer to someone's disability in your writing, is it necessary to your purpose?** As with sexist and ageist writing, try rewriting the passage in question without the reference; if your purpose is still clear to your readers, then omit the reference.

- **Have you avoided asking your readers to think of the person as deserving only of sympathy?** If you use emotional words to describe someone with a disability (*the poor child with the limp* or *the helpless quadriplegic*), you are asking your readers to see the person as incapable of doing anything but passively accepting our concern.

- **Have you used *disability* and *handicap* according to accepted uses?** The quotation at the top of the page to the left describes how to use these terms.

- **Does your writing emphasize that people with disabilities contribute widely and in multiple ways to their communities?**

USING INCLUSIVE LANGUAGE
INCLUDING ALL SEXUAL ORIENTATIONS

HETEROSEXISM

To write as though all readers have the same sexual orientation is to risk losing their attention and respect just as much as writing as though all readers are male, European American, or of one age risks losing their attention and respect.

CHECK YOUR WRITING TO AVOID HETEROSEXISM

- **When you refer to someone's sexual orientation in your writing, is it necessary to your purpose?** If you would not write, *The heterosexual engineer was fluent with both the aesthetic and the technical aspects of design,* then do not write, *The gay engineer was fluent with both the aesthetic and the technical aspects of design.*

  As we have similarly recommended on the previous pages, if you are unsure about the appropriateness of including references to sexual orientation in your writing, remove the references. If readers still understand your purpose, then you can omit the references from your final draft.

- **Have you used *sexual orientation* rather than *sexual preference*?** To write *sexual preference* is to imply that sexuality is the result of conscious choice, a view that neither scientific research nor the reported experiences of lesbians, gays, or heterosexuals support.

- **Have you used terms that those you are describing themselves prefer?** Currently, *gay* is the preferred term for homosexual men and *lesbian* is the preferred term for homosexual women; people whose sexual orientation includes both men and women prefer *bisexual. Transgendered* is preferred for those whose sex is not congruent with their gender identity.

Homosexual emphasizes sexuality over relationships and in the past has been associated with mental illness and criminality. It has also been used primarily to refer to male sexuality, and thus erases lesbians from the discussion. Many people thus avoid using *homosexual.*

Keep in mind that, in the twenty-first century, *lesbian* and *gay* are primarily about communities of people rather than sexual activity. This is important because some people have sex with others of the same gender but do not consider themselves *lesbian* or *gay.*

If you have any concerns about the terms you are using, ask and do research. As with all your writing, ask a range of people to read what you write, to be sure none feel pushed away by your word choices.

- **Have you avoided assuming heterosexuality?** In a manual for a large corporation, the sentence *All employees are encouraged to bring their wives to these yearly events* is a problem because it assumes that all the employees are married heterosexual males. In contrast, *all employees are encouraged to bring their partners or significant others to these yearly events* includes employees of all genders and sexual orientations as well as those who are not married.

USING INCLUSIVE LANGUAGE
INCLUDING ALL RELIGIONS

EXCLUSIONARY LANGUAGE ABOUT RELIGION

While there is no single term to define language that promotes one religion while discouraging or being derogatory toward others, the matter of religion is just as sensitive in our time as any of the other aspects of people's identities we have been discussing in Part 6.

As with the other aspects of identity, our beliefs about deities—that they exist or not—and religions—whether or not to belong to an organized religion—matter very deeply to each of us. Therefore, as with each of the other aspects of identity we have discussed in this part, the main guideline for writing when you want to build common ground with a wide audience is to respect others' beliefs as you would want yours respected.

CHECK YOUR WRITING TO AVOID DISCRIMINATING BASED ON RELIGION

- **Have you referred to someone's religion only when it is central to your purpose?** Whenever you include a reference to someone's religion in your writing, try taking it out and having others read your writing. If your readers still understand your purpose, then leave the reference out from your final draft. We recommend this not because we believe that religion should be excluded from all writing but rather because, given the weight of religious beliefs in people's lives, particular care is warranted.

- **When you write about religious beliefs and practices in general, have you used terms that reflect a range of religions?** For example, if you are writing about how varying communities construct special buildings for religious observances, you should not write, *All over the world, members of communities build churches for practicing their religions;* instead, write, *All over the world, people build mosques, temples, churches, and other specially named buildings used specifically for religious practices.*

  Similarly, be alert to the names religions use for their members and leaders. *Rabbi, priest, reverend, imam,* and *bishop* are only some of the possibilities. This is another case where doing a little research can help you show your respect for your readers.

- **Have you avoided assuming that your readers hold the same religious beliefs as you?** Many people who believe in a deity do not belong to an established church, and many people do not believe in a deity. Also, the names of deities in different religions are different. If you are trying to reach a broad audience—whether on a national or international level—be careful that any references you include about your own faith and religion do not imply that everyone else does or should believe just as you do.

- **Have you used the terms the people you are describing use for their beliefs?** When you want your writing to be read by a wide audience, be careful about your use of terms like *cult* instead of *religion* or *myth* instead of *religious belief.*

  If you need to describe religious practices and beliefs, do research. Have a range of others read your writing to be sure it is respectful.

- **Have you acknowledged the broad beliefs that people in the same religion might hold?** When you write about a religion, do not assume that its members hold the same beliefs or act the same. Catholics, for example, hold a range of views on abortion, the death penalty, birth control, and the status of women. The same is true of Muslims, Jews, Baptists, and the members of any other religion you can name, on any topic.

USING AN ESL DICTIONARY

There are English-English dictionaries specifically designed to support learning English as a new language. Such dictionaries have special features to help you learn the subtleties of the language; below is a sample excerpt from such a dictionary:

entry word

This dictionary color-codes each entry word. Not only does this help you see the words being defined, but in this dictionary, pink tells you a word is a noun; blue tells you it is a verb.

frequency information

These codes tell you that the word "card" is one of the top 1,000 words used in spoken English and one of the top 2,000 words used in written English; you can look through the dictionary to learn the most commonly used words.

pronunciation

This phonetic transcription tells you how the word is pronounced.

part of speech

n: noun
v: verb
adj: adjective
adv: adverb
prep: preposition

usage categories

The highlighted words tell you that the use of this word shifts in different categories.

definitions

ESL dictionaries provide definitions in easier-to-understand language than other dictionaries do.

sample sentences

Sample sentences can be more useful to you than definitions because they show a word in use and help you remember usage patterns.

frequency use of definition

The numbers before the categories indicate that the definitions are listed by frequency of use.

card¹ S1 W2 / kɑːd $ kɑːrd / *n*

1 INFORMATION [C] a small piece of plastic or paper containing information about a person or showing, for example, that they belong to a particular organization, club etc: *Employees must show their **identity cards** at the gate.* | *I haven't got my **membership card** yet.*
2 MONEY [C] a small piece of plastic, especially one that you get from a bank or shop, which you use to pay for goods or get money: *Lost or stolen cards must be reported immediately.* | *a £10 phone card* | *Every time you use your store card, you get air miles.* → CHARGE CARD, CHEQUE CARD, CREDIT CARD, DEBIT CARD
3 GREETINGS [C] a piece of folded thick stiff paper with a picture on the front, that you send to people on special occasions: **birthday/Christmas/greetings etc card** *a Mother's Day card*
4 HOLIDAY [C] a card with a photograph or picture on one side, that you send to someone when you are on holiday; ▤ **postcard**: *I sent you a card from Madrid.*
5 STIFF PAPER [U] *BrE* thick stiff paper; → **card-board**: *Cut a piece of white card 12 x 10cm.*
6 FOR WRITING INFORMATION [C] a small piece of thick stiff paper that information can be written or printed on: *a set of recipe cards* | *a score card*

count and noncount nouns

C: count noun
U: noncount noun

→ See pages 511–512 to learn about this important distinction between kinds of nouns.

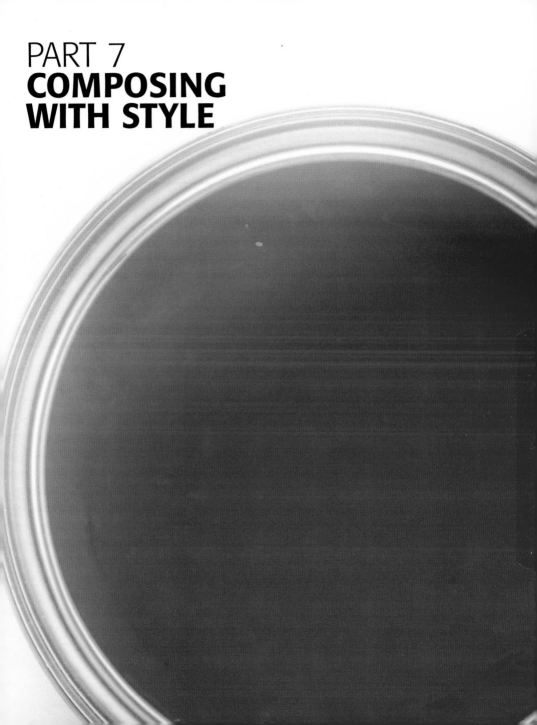

PART 7
COMPOSING WITH STYLE

CONTENTS

WHERE ARE WE IN THE PROCESS FOR COMPOSING?

Understanding your project

Getting started

Asking questions

Shaping your project for others

Drafting a paper

Getting feedback

Revising   Paying attention to style

Polishing

STYLE AND AUDIENCE

ALL COMMUNICATIONS HAVE STYLE

This paragraph comes from a book about the senses:

One scent can be unexpected, momentary, and fleeting, yet conjure up a childhood summer beside a lake in the Poconos, when wild blueberry bushes teemed with succulent fruit and the opposite sex was as mysterious as space travel; another, hours of passion on a moonlit beach in Florida, while the night-blooming cereus drenched the air with thick curds of perfume and huge sphinx moths visited the cereus in a loud purr of wings; a third, a family dinner of pot roast, noodle pudding, and sweet potatoes, during a myrtle-mad August in a midwestern town, when both of one's parents were alive.

This paragraph comes from a webpage describing the work of two scientists:

In 1991 Axel and Buck discovered a family of roughly 1,000 genes that encode the odorant receptors of the olfactory epithelium, a patch of cells on the wall of the nasal cavity. The olfactory epithelium contains neurons that send messages directly to the olfactory bulb of the brain. When an odor excites a neuron, the signal travels along the nerve cell's axon and is transferred to the neurons in the olfactory bulb.

Both paragraphs describe the sense of smell. The differences between the paragraphs result because the writing is aimed at two different audiences:

- The first paragraph is for an audience of general readers, who have no particular scientific background. The paragraph is the opening of a chapter; it leads into passages that contain somewhat technical information. The style of the paragraph suggests to the readers that even though what the chapter covers is somewhat technical, readers will still enjoy it because the information will be detailed, sensual, and concrete.

- The second paragraph, as you could probably tell, was written by scientists for scientists. Individual words are not defined, because the writer assumes the reader knows them. The sentences are much shorter than in the first example, and they focus on describing processes as directly as possible, with few adjectives.

Although the second paragraph may not seem to have much style, many choices went into it, choices about individual words, the length of sentences, and the grammatical construction of the sentences.

OVERALL STYLE—AND FINELY DETAILED STYLE

The two example paragraphs probably suggest to you what the larger pieces from which each comes are like: The first paragraph comes from a book that is full of fine and luscious descriptions; the second comes from a short, to-the-point, descriptive piece of writing.

Notice, then, that style is about:

- **The overall feel a piece has for a reader.** Does the piece feel lush and detailed, or quick and precise? In what contexts and for what purposes will audiences expect writing like the first example paragraph or like the second?

- **The feel of words, sentences, and paragraphs.** The overall style of a piece is built from the choices you make at the level of words and sentences. We've already pointed out the differences in sentence length and word choice between the two examples; what other differences can you see between the two?

Style is not about being fancy;
it is about the detailed choices you make
to design your ideas for your audience.

STYLE IN WRITING

STYLING FOR CLARITY, CONCISION, COHERENCE, EMPHASIS, AND ENGAGEMENT

If you construct your writing to be clear, concise, coherent, emphatic, and engaging, you will have writing that works for present-day readers in most contexts. Your readers may not be able to name those five values, but in the United States we are in a culture that desires information to come quickly and easily as well as with some pleasure. (Or, to look at it in another way, no one likes having to work hard for boring information.)

If you are to construct writing that has these values, you need to know your purposes in writing. To decide how to style a sentence or paragraph, you need to ask how your choices will help your readers understand your purposes.

CLARITY

Clarity comes from a Latin word that means **clear**, as when the air is clear on a bright day. When you strive for clarity in writing, you shape sentences to help your readers see what is most important, quickly and easily.

CONCISION

Being concise means getting to the point. To be concise in writing, use as few words as possible. Concision supports clarity.

COHERENCE

When writing is coherent, it feels as though all its parts belong together. Readers see connections between the parts of a writing, and can easily grasp the overall purpose of the writing.

EMPHASIS

To persuade others to listen to your concerns, you need to make your purposes clear and you need to offer reasons. Some reasons will be more persuasive to your audience than others, and so the following pages offer strategies for emphasizing the parts of writing that you want your audience most to notice and remember.

Keep in mind, when you want to emphasize specific parts of your writing, that you cannot emphasize every single word or phrase. That would be like yelling continually at your audience—and, as you know, when someone yells at you continually, you stop listening. Instead, emphasis is when someone has been talking in a regular tone for a while and only now and then raises (or lowers) her voice.

ENGAGEMENT

Humans are lively, energetic, social beings. We like to tell jokes. We like to hear about odd events in the lives of others. We need to learn the practical details of living well and healthily. We need to learn how others live with the sorrows of death and pain.

We learn best from each other when our minds are active and engaged.

Writing that helps readers feel and understand someone else's delight or sorrow will be more effective than writing that doesn't. Writing that helps readers understand concretely and comfortably how to put together a stereo system will be more effective than writing that doesn't. Writing that helps readers understand the consequences of a melted polar ice cap is much more likely to bring readers to action than writing that just lists sterile facts.

■ ■ ■

The following pages discuss strategies you can use—with your own choices of individual words and your own constructions of sentences and paragraphs—to shape your writing to include all these values.

Because style is present in all levels of writing, we divide the following pages into the following order:

WORDS

SENTENCES

PARAGRAPHS

STYLING WORDS

All writing takes shape from the particular words you choose. On the next pages we offer you specific strategies for choosing words that will help you achieve your specific purposes in writing.

Compare these two sentences:

What did the first settlers of Easter Island eat when they were not eating the local equivalent of maple syrup?

What did the first settlers of Easter Island eat when they were not glutting themselves on the local equivalent of maple syrup?

Which sentence gives you a clearer and sharper sense of action? Why? When might you use one sentence rather than the other?

Compare these sentences:

The Canadian Rangers protect the Canadian Arctic, an area of Precambrian earth covered with 1,000-year-old Inuit settlements and ice.

The Canadian Rangers protect the Canadian Arctic, an old hunk of Precambrian earth, ice carpeted and spotted with Inuit settlements dating back 1,000 years.

The differences are subtle—but the second sentence (we think) asks you to think about the Canadian Arctic as a familiar, almost living, piece of the earth.

In what writing contexts would the second sentence be appropriate for shaping an audience's relations to the topic?

The dictionary defines cancer as "A malignant growth of cells caused by their abnormal and uncontrolled division." Chances are, however, that you cannot read *cancer* without some fear; it's possible you read the word with memories of someone close to you who has had cancer.

The definition of *cancer* is what we call the **denotation** of the word. The denotation of any word is simply its analytic definition, what we can count on most anyone else knowing.

Connotation, on the other hand, is what individuals bring to a word because of their personal or cultural background. Connotation describes the ideas or mental pictures that come to people's minds—unbidden from their memories and experiences—when they hear a word.

As you choose words, consider what associations—the ideas and mental pictures—your readers are likely to have. Do you want your readers to have positive or negative associations?

Most importantly—and especially if you are writing for an audience you do not know very well—you want to avoid using words that will have associations opposite to those that will help you achieve your purposes.

DICTIONARY DEFINITIONS & ASSOCIATIONS WITH WORDS

What is on this page will help you style your writing for:

- ☑ CLARITY
- ☐ CONCISION
- ☐ COHERENCE
- ☐ EMPHASIS
- ☑ ENGAGEMENT

TIP: FIND A READER

To be sure your word choices do not encourage readers to think of connotations that will undermine your purpose, have people from your audience read drafts of your writing.

STYLING WORDS
THE NAMES WE USE

If the problem were called *Atmosphere cancer* or *Pollution death*, the entire conversation would be framed differently.

The writer of the above sentence is discussing **global warming**, and argues that we might, as individuals and as a culture, be less sanguine about global warming if the concept had been named more compellingly.

The words used to name a condition, a syndrome, or a place carry considerable weight through their connotations (→ discussed on page 271). Consider how the following terms ask readers to think about the person or position named:

pro-choice	pro-abortion
right-wing	conservative
heterosexual	straight
gun rights	gun control
affirmative action	racial preferences
illegal alien	undocumented immigrant

Readers respond to the names you use based on how they interpret the names. Someone in favor of affirmative action, for example, will likely be less amenable to writing that uses **racial preferences**.

What is on this page will help you style your writing for:

- ☑ CLARITY
- ☐ CONCISION
- ☐ COHERENCE
- ☐ EMPHASIS
- ☑ ENGAGEMENT

TIP: KNOW YOUR AUDIENCE
Ask people from your audience about any terms you are considering so that you can learn how they respond. This will help you decide which terms help you make the arguments you desire.

Jump. Giggle. Estimate. Play. Clarify. Balance. Sing. Compare. Interpret.

These are action verbs: They name actions readers can imagine themselves taking. (This is connotation at work again.) Because action verbs encourage readers to imagine doing what a sentence describes, action verbs help readers connect with writing.

Action verbs describe concrete actions and so clarify what is going on:

He is enjoying performing.

He revels in performing.

The second sentence uses an action verb instead of **is**. **Revels** carries associations of energetic delight, and so will likely convey that emotion to readers.

Here are other examples:

The wasp put her stinger through the roach's exoskeleton and directly into its brain.

The wasp slipped her stinger through the roach's exoskeleton and directly into its brain.

The second sentence helps a reader understand more precisely what the wasp did—and makes the wasp's action scarier and more compelling.

STYLING WORDS
ACTION VERBS

What is on this page will help you style your writing for:

☑ CLARITY

☐ CONCISION

☐ COHERENCE

☑ EMPHASIS

☑ ENGAGEMENT

TIP: REPLACING "IS"

When you want your writing to connect with readers, underline every use of **is** (including its variations, such as **are** and **was** and **will be**) in your writing, and if you see more than a few, replace those words with action verbs.

STYLING WORDS
CONCRETE NOUNS

What is on this page will help you style your writing for:

- ☑ CLARITY
- ☐ CONCISION
- ☐ COHERENCE
- ☐ EMPHASIS
- ☑ ENGAGEMENT

When you hear the word **it**, what picture comes into your head? Any?

In the sentence *After he ordered his lunch he had to wait 30 minutes for it to be delivered,* **it** clearly refers to **his lunch**—and readers can make concrete connections with the word. But when you read the sentence below, what associations can you make with the **It** at the beginning?

It is wasteful of their energies if full-grown orangutans move randomly through trees looking for food.

It in the sentence above refers to nothing. Here is a revised sentence:

Full-grown orangutans can't afford to lumber along randomly through the trees, hoping to blunder upon food.

The replacement of **is *wasteful*** with ***can't afford to*** and the movement of ***full-grown orangutans*** to the front of the sentence make this sentence concretely descriptive and thus clearer and more engaging.

When you want readers to have concrete (and hence compelling) pictures in their heads about what you are writing, start your sentences with words that refer to specific people, animals, or objects.

TIP: REPLACING "IT IS"
Sometimes you need to use **it is** (or ***there are***). But when you want your writing to connect with readers, underline every use of **is**, **it is**, and ***there are***, and if you see more than a few, replace those phrases with concrete nouns and verbs.

Playing with fire. No place like home. Have a field day. From bad to worse. Bad hair day. Like a breath of fresh air.

Clichés are phrases that once stood out because they were—at one time—new and funny or compelling. Because they were new and stood out, however, people used them, and used them…and used them until they stopped being new and compelling.

Because clichés have been used so much, they have become just part of language—and so they come to mind easily when you are writing. Readers will notice them, however, and because they've seen them before, the writing will seem tired and boring.

CLICHÉS

What is on this page will help you style your writing for:

- ☑ CLARITY
- ☐ CONCISION
- ☐ COHERENCE
- ☑ EMPHASIS
- ☑ ENGAGEMENT

TIP: TO CATCH AND FIX CLICHÉS

To catch clichés, read your writing aloud; you can often hear clichés.

To fix clichés, be clear about your purpose: You need to explore wording that carries the meaning and emotion of your purpose. For example, instead of *His proposal was dead as a doornail*, you could write *His proposal received no response* or, more emotively, *Given how little attention others gave his proposal, he might as well never have spoken.*

TIP: NEW LANGUAGE CLICHÉS

If you are not writing in your home language, clichés can be hard to hear because you are not familiar enough with them in the new language. Ask someone who grew up with your new language to read your writing and identify—and explain—clichés.

STYLING WORDS
JARGON

What is on this page will help you style your writing for:

- ☑ CLARITY
- ☑ CONCISION
- ☐ COHERENCE
- ☐ EMPHASIS
- ☑ ENGAGEMENT

Jargon can describe the specialized language of an organization or a profession; it can also describe fancy-sounding words someone else uses that you don't understand. Jargon, then, is useful when you are writing to those inside your profession and need to be precise; it is bad to use outside the profession because readers can't follow your writing.

To a reader immersed in computer culture, this probably makes sense:

In architecting our software, build systems, and engineering processes, we have given considerable thought to how our code will be able to evolve alongside the Mozilla code, without forking it.

Most readers know **architect** and **fork** as nouns, not verbs, and probably do not know what a **build system** or **Mozilla** is. A general audience is more likely to understand:

In developing our software and engineering processes, we have considered how our code will be able to evolve alongside the existing code with which it must work—without messing up that existing code.

TIP: KNOW YOUR AUDIENCE

If you are writing for people who share a vocabulary, use that vocabulary to be precise. If you do not know your audience, err on the side of caution: Use only words almost anyone would understand. Check this by having someone else read your writing.

As far as we can see, it is a fact that there are a whole lot of ways you can end up with way too many words in your sentences and, as a result of the too many words, make your readers bored or make it too hard for them to figure out your purpose.

When we see sentences like the above, it is usually a sign that the writer isn't sure what to say and is fumbling for a way to say it; sometimes people write like that when they aren't confident.

The sentence above is characterized by both empty words (words that add nothing to the purpose of the sentence) and redundant words (words that repeat uselessly what has already been said).

If we modify the sentence, we can end up with this, which is more concise and hence clearer for readers:

There are many ways to have too many words in a sentence, boring your readers, and getting in the way of their understanding.

To compose focused sentences, ask yourself, *What is it exactly that I want readers to take from this sentence?*

What is on this page will help you style your writing for:

- ☑ CLARITY
- ☑ CONCISION
- ☐ COHERENCE
- ☐ EMPHASIS
- ☑ ENGAGEMENT

TIP: REREAD

Put your writing aside for a while, and then reread it: Looking at your writing anew will help you see where you have used more words than you need. You can also ask others to read it, to help you find the sentences that need tightening to clarify your points.

STYLING SENTENCES

Style is all about how you connect with audiences in order to achieve your purposes.

On the next pages, we consider sentence style from two angles:

1 How do you construct sentences with the grammatical structures that readers expect in a formal, academic style of writing?

2 How do you construct sentences that readers want to read and that help you make your points?

Perhaps you think these two angles are really the same. After all, if sentences have the structures audiences expect, doesn't that mean readers will want to read them? Doesn't that mean the sentences will help writers make their points?

Consider this paragraph:

I must be real. Hear what I'm saying. We ain't going nowhere, as the boys in the hood be saying. Nowhere. If you promote all the surviving Afghans to the status of honorary Americans, Mr. President, where exactly on the bus does that leave me. When do I get paid. When can I expect my invitation to the ranch. I hear Mr. Putin's wearing jingle-jangle silver spurs around his dacha. Heard you fixed him up with an eight-figure advance on his memoirs. Is it true he's iced up to be the Marlboro man after he retires from Russia. Anything left under the table for me. And mine.

That paragraph breaks just about every rule one can imagine for formal writing. The writer uses periods instead of question marks. There are sentence fragments. The writer uses what some would call **colloquial phrasing**.

The paragraph's writer is John Edgar Wideman, who has won many prestigious awards for his writing and has taught writing at the university level. The paragraph comes from an essay, "Whose War," that appeared in the highly respected collection *The Best Essays of 2003*.

Given what he understood about his purposes—questioning the U. S. government's use of resources in the opening years of the twenty-first century—Wideman chose to write as he did. He chose to go against expectations of formal writing so that his essay would stand out, so that his essay would convey anger and frustration, so that his essay would read as though it were being spoken, passionately.

■ ■ ■

Wideman chose to break expectations because he was in a position to do so. He was in a position to do so both because he is a practiced writer who knows and can use the expectations and standards of formal writing when he wants, and also because he is a well-known writer. Because he is a well-known writer, others know that he usually does write in more expected formats, and that he must therefore have had his reasons for writing differently.

As you are styling your sentences, then, keep in mind the expectations of your readers, in regard to your words and to you. Will your readers expect a formal piece? Do your readers know you well enough to know that, if you break expectations, it is because you chose to do so? If you break expectations, how do you let readers know that you did so for a reason?

■ ■ ■

On the next pages, we offer angles for learning the expectations readers have for formal, academic writing.

Learn these well so that you can use them but also so that you can modify them as your purposes demand.

ACADEMIC SENTENCES

All academic writing will have the stylistic features listed below:

What is on this page will help you style your writing for:

- ☑ CLARITY
- ☑ CONCISION
- ☑ COHERENCE
- ☐ EMPHASIS
- ☐ ENGAGEMENT

CHECKLIST FOR FORMAL, ACADEMIC SENTENCES

❏ Your sentences have positive structures.

> → See page 281 to learn about sentences without double negatives.

> → See page 281 to learn about sentences that are positive rather than negative.

❏ Each sentence fits one of the four sentence patterns.

> → See pages 470–471.

❏ You use no sentence fragments— except, rarely, for emphasis.

> → See pages 490–493.

❏ Your sentences do not shift among grammatical forms.

> → See page 537 to learn about shifts in person and number.

> → See pages 522–523 to learn about shifts in verb tense.

> → See pages 538–539 to learn about shifts in voice.

> → See page 536 to learn about shifts in direct and indirect discourse.

> → See page 539 to learn about shifts in levels of formality.

❏ Your sentences are easy to read.

> → See pages 282–283.

SENTENCES DO NOT USE DOUBLE NEGATIVES

In formal writing, convention requires using only one negative in a sentence.

NEGATIVES: *barely hardly neither no not never none nothing scarcely*

Sometimes there will be more than one way to fix a double negative:

INCORRECT Bob did not have no solution for the problem.
          NEGATIVE   NEGATIVE

CORRECT **Bob had no solution for the problem.**
                  NEGATIVE

CORRECT **Bob did not have a solution for the problem.**
                  NEGATIVE

Sometimes only one solution will be obvious:

INCORRECT Nobody said nothing about how to make quotations in a paper.
          NEGATIVE   NEGATIVE

CORRECT **Nobody said anything about how to make quotations in a paper.**
          NEGATIVE

SENTENCES ARE POSITIVE, NOT NEGATIVE

The following two sentences are both grammatically correct—but the second sentence is easier to read and understand because it presents its information in a straightforward, positive manner.

Classic gangster films were not without a message, showing audiences that if a gangster's life had no order, it was because society had no order.

Classic gangster films had a message, showing audiences that the chaos of a gangster's life mirrored the chaos of society.

TIP: READ!

Formal, academic writing—even in scientific disciplines—leaves considerable room for working with style. Reading widely respected writers in a discipline is the best way to learn the leeway you have.

TIP: WHERE TO FOCUS?

You are probably already in good control of several of these features of academic sentences. Ask someone who is familiar with your writing—a teacher or someone in your Writing Center—which of these features needs your attention, and then focus your attention just on those.

STYLING SENTENCES
SENTENCES THAT ARE EASY TO READ

What is on this page will help you style your writing for:

- ☑ CLARITY
- ☑ CONCISION
- ☑ COHERENCE
- ☐ EMPHASIS
- ☑ ENGAGEMENT

Easy-to-read sentences have the following six qualities:

SENTENCES ARE NOT WORDY

Due to the matter of the final report, which was turned in after the due date, I did not acquire the grade I hoped for in class and now therefore I appeal for a second chance to succeed.

Because of a late final report, I failed the class; I hope to retake the class.

Wanting to sound formal or legal, writers stretch for long phrases and a complex vocabulary; the resulting sentences are often stilted and hard to read.

Those who study writing know that writers' language gets wordy and awkward precisely when writers are trying hard, perhaps because of a challenging or emotionally touchy project (like a grade appeal). If you have taken on a project that makes you nervous, or if you are worried about wordiness, ask a reader to look over your writing.

SENTENCES AVOID EXPLETIVES

An expletive can be a swear word, but it can also be a phrase that adds length but no meaning to a sentence, such as *There is…*, *There are…*, or *It is necessary….*

Using one or two such phrases in several pages of writing is not a disaster, but learn to be on the lookout for expletives and replace them:

If we are to end global warming, one thing that is necessary is that people get out of their cars and walk.

To end global warming, people need to get out of their cars and walk.

SENTENCES USE FEW PREPOSITIONAL PHRASES

One argument of the parents from the neighborhood was that all parks in the city should be child-friendly.
Neighborhood parents argued that all city parks should be child-friendly.

Too many prepositions block readers from seeing your ideas.

When you can, convert prepositional phrases into adjectives (which you then place before the noun being modified):

the girl with red hair
the red-haired girl

the ambition of the senator
the senator's ambition

SENTENCES USE FEW RELATIVE PRONOUNS

The relative pronouns *who*, *which*, *whom*, *whose*, and *that* can slow readers:

Childhood is the audience sector that is most exposed to media seduction.
Childhood is the audience sector most exposed to media seduction.

Children who are breast-fed usually have stronger immune systems.
Breast-fed children usually have stronger immune systems.

If you can remove a relative pronoun without upsetting your sentence, do so, or try changing a relative clause (*who are breast-fed*) into an adjective.

SENTENCES FOCUS ON ACTION

A carefully chosen active verb can make sentences come alive for readers:

The never-ending war brought on a reduction in the morale of citizens.
The never-ending war demoralized citizens.

New parking regulations caused great confusion among the commuters.
New parking regulations befuddled the commuters.

SENTENCES AVOID NOMINALIZATIONS

When you change a verb or adjective into a noun, you nominalize the verb or adjective:

difficult → difficulty

destroy → destruction

investigate → investigation

analyze → analysis

Nominalizations shift a sentence's focus from verbs and adjectives to abstract nouns—and thus deaden sentences.

Change nominalizations back to verbs or adjectives to enliven sentences:

In this paper I give an analysis of the difficulty of the task of the crash investigation of the space shuttle.
In this paper I analyze the difficult task of those who investigated the space shuttle crash.

My observation was of the locals' table in a busy local restaurant.
I observed the locals' table in a busy local restaurant.

STYLING SENTENCES
USING COORDINATION AND SUBORDINATION

What is on this page will help you style your writing for:

☑ CLARITY

☐ CONCISION

☑ COHERENCE

☑ EMPHASIS

☐ ENGAGEMENT

When you have two ideas to express to readers, do you want the ideas to have equal weight in their minds, or is one idea less important than the other?

When the ideas are equal, they are coordinate.

When one idea is less important than another, it is subordinate.

As you build sentences with independent clauses, you relate the clauses through coordination or subordination.

Both coordination and subordination are signs of formal, academic writing.

TO COORDINATE OR TO SUBORDINATE?

It's up to you: What understanding do you want readers to have of a sentence?

For example, if you want readers to consider knitting's traditional role to be equal to its more recent role, use **coordination**:

Knitting has traditionally been a domestic activity for women, but in the last decades it has been turned into a fine art.

Knitting has traditionally been a domestic activity for women; however, in the last decades it has been turned into a fine art.

If, however, you want to emphasize the recently growing importance of knitting over its past role, use **subordination**:

Although knitting has traditionally been a domestic activity for women, in the last decades it has been turned into a fine art.

→ To learn more about independent and dependent clauses, see pages 483–487.
→ To learn more about conjunctions, see pages 532–535.

COORDINATION

There are two patterns for building a sentence that uses coordination:

1 independent clause + **,** + coordinating conjunction + independent clause + **.**

COORDINATING CONJUNCTIONS: *and but for nor or so yet*

Stone is bad insulating material, but it makes a tight wall that radiates stored heat for hours.

2 independent clause + **;** + conjunctive adverb + independent clause + **.**

CONJUNCTIVE ADVERBS: *consequently furthermore however moreover otherwise therefore thus nevertheless*

With normal communication channels cut down during the war in Bosnia, the only news came by word of mouth; consequently posters became a cheap and easy way to spread information.

SUBORDINATION

There is one pattern for building a sentence that uses subordination, but you can reverse its order:

independent clause + **,** + subordinating conjunction + dependent clause + **.**

OR

subordinating conjunction + dependent clause + **,** + independent clause **.**

SUBORDINATING CONJUNCTIONS: *after although as because before if since that though unless until when where whether which while who whom whose*

After she placed a doily on top of a cupcake, my grandmother would sift sugar on top to make a lacy pattern.

My grandmother would sift sugar on top of a cupcake to make a lacy pattern, after she had placed a doily on top of the cupcake.

STYLING SENTENCES
PARALLELISM

What is on this page will help you style your writing for:

☐ CLARITY

☐ CONCISION

☑ COHERENCE

☑ EMPHASIS

☑ ENGAGEMENT

If you want readers to see similarities between two or more ideas, use sentence structure: Parallel grammatical form makes the ideas look and sound similar. Readers will take that similarity away with them.

Would you prefer to go swimming, biking, or kayaking?

First we heard whispers, then giggles, then screams of laughter.

Under the eclipse's brief, false night, birds will cease their singing, cows will head for the barn, and people will get weak in the knees.

Parallelism can set up a rhythm that engages readers: As they read, they fall into the rhythm and thus into the movement of your ideas.

CERTAIN KINDS OF WORDS AND PHRASES HELP IN BUILDING PARALLELISM

You use **coordinating conjunctions** (*and*, *but*, *or*, *nor*, *for*, *so*, and *yet*) to join words or phrases that have equal importance—and you can use them to build parallel structures:

I may still have a young man's body, but now I have an old man's heart.

Correlative conjunctions (*both…and*, *either…or*, *neither…nor*, *not only…but also*, and *whether…or*) function similarly, so also be sure the words or phrases following each part of these conjunctions have parallel structures:

The town council will decide whether to grant the zoning variance or to sue the owner over the structure.

→ See page 532 to learn about coordinating conjunctions and page 533 to learn about correlative conjunctions.

Build parallelism by repeating the same grammatical structure in a list of words, prepositional phrases, sentences, or any other grammatical unit.

She finished the work by not eating, drinking, or sleeping.
PARTICIPLE   PARTICIPLE   PARTICIPLE

My sister liked to eat chocolate and to avoid broccoli.
PREPOSITION + VERB + NOUN   PREPOSITION + VERB + NOUN

Empty stores are signs of a fading past; empty schools are a sign of a fading future.
"Empty"+ NOUN = "are a sign of a fading"+ NOUN   "empty"+ NOUN = "are a sign of a fading"+ NOUN

One way to check that you are building parallelism is to stack the parts on top of each other, to see that they follow the same grammatical structure:

For your final draft, pay close attention to proofreading your words,
                       being sure you've cited all sources,
                   and formatting your works cited list.

TIP: AVOIDING FAULTY PARALLELISM

Faulty parallelism, a common writing error, occurs when a writer builds a list that does not have parallel grammatical structures:

If you have trouble sleeping, try cutting out coffee after lunch, getting rid of the TV in your room, and to fall asleep at the same time every night.

Fix this by making all the parts of the list have the same grammatical structure:

If you have trouble sleeping, try cutting out coffee after lunch, getting rid of the TV in your room, and falling asleep at the same time every night.

STYLING SENTENCES
FIGURATIVE LANGUAGE

What is on this page will help you style your writing for:

☐ CLARITY

☐ CONCISION

☐ COHERENCE

☑ EMPHASIS

☑ ENGAGEMENT

When you want readers to understand or remember a crucial concept, use figurative language. *Figurative language* refers to a range of strategies that make concepts stand out.

FIGURATIVE COMPARISONS

As we said when we discussed analogy in Part 3 (→ see page 106), you can help readers understand new or complex ideas by describing the ideas in terms readers already know. Similarly, you can make ideas more vivid—and so more memorable—with unexpected comparisons.

COMPARISONS TO MAKE NEW IDEAS FAMILIAR

This passage uses concepts of building blocks and atoms to explain mathematical concepts:

Prime numbers, such as 17 and 23, are those that can be divided only by themselves and 1. They are the most important objects in mathematics because, as the ancient Greeks discovered, they are the building blocks of all numbers—any of which can be broken down into a product of primes. (For example, 105 = 3 x 5 x 7.) They are the hydrogen and oxygen of the world of mathematics, the atoms of arithmetic.

COMPARISONS TO MAKE IDEAS MEMORABLE

Microsoft is a middle-aged company struggling to figure out how to dance with the teenagers, and its body simply can't keep up with its intentions, no matter how correct they may be.

The passage could instead read, *Microsoft is having trouble attracting young audiences*—but would that have created such a funny picture in your head?

Michael Ondaatje's *The English Patient* is a novel whose nervous system connects books, visual art, and war.

By giving the novel it discusses a *nervous system*, the example above compares the novel to a living being, giving it a vibrancy it wouldn't otherwise have.

"Goya's Last Works," at the Frick, isn't large, but neither are grenades.

The one little word *grenades*—emphasized by its placement as the last word of the sentence—suggests that the exhibit of paintings being described is explosive and even somehow dangerous.

"I think of her as the human embodiment of Wal-Mart," said Kevvy Schlaucher, a 25-year-old engineer from Calgary, Canada, who used to watch the show with his mother. "The Oprah Empire is everywhere. She makes sure you don't get out of the system."

Saying that Oprah Winfrey's empire is a big business is not as memorable as making you hold her and Wal-Mart in your head at the same time.

TIP: HOW MUCH?
Like spice, figurative language works best in small quantities. Because figurative language can heighten readers' attention to important points in your writing, using it a lot would diffuse its effects.

FIGURATIVE PATTERNS

Experiments with familiar language patterns can make memorable sentences:

On Monday, engineers repaired the ruptured 17th Street Canal levee in New Orleans and floodwaters receded a bit as some suburban residents, carrying suitcases and heavy hearts, briefly returned to their homes and sifted through the sodden debris.

When you read *carrying suitcases and…*, you might expect the next words to be *backpacks* or *boxes*. *Heavy hearts* can slow your reading, making palpable the residents' emotions.

Experiment with any language pattern, such as those of conjunctions:

All day I keep the Shabbos. This means I do not turn on a light or tear paper or write or bathe or cook or sew or do any of the hundred kinds of work involved in building the Holy Temple.

The *or*'s stretch out the list of actions to emphasize the number of items.

Just as you can multiply conjunctions, you can also take them away:

I smiled. We smoked. We looked up at the stars. We shook from cold.

Grammatical disconnection and emotional disconnection between people are shown by a lack of conjunctions.

TIP: NEED INSPIRATION?
Listen to country-western music. Figurative language abounds there, sometimes funny, sometimes not, as when Julie Roberts sings, "Men and mascara always run."

STYLING PARAGRAPHS

What is on this page will help you style your writing for:

☐ CLARITY

☐ CONCISION

☐ COHERENCE

☑ EMPHASIS

☑ ENGAGEMENT

In Part 5 we discussed the expectations readers have about paragraph organization; we also discussed the different functions paragraphs can perform. (→ See pages 212–225.)

In the next pages, we consider smaller-scale decisions you can make about paragraphs: How do you keep readers engaged and at the same time help them follow your argument?

■ ■ ■

Here are some strategies for composing engaging paragraphs:

VARY SENTENCE LENGTH

If every sentence in a paragraph is the same length, readers might fall into a lulling rhythm and stop paying attention. The paragraph below shows—with the last sentence a contrast to all that precedes—one possible strategy for keeping such rhythms from developing:

In the Web 2.0 model, we have thousands of services scrutinizing each new piece of information online, grabbing interesting bits, remixing them in new ways, and passing them along to other services. Each new addition to the mix can be exploited in countless new ways, both by human bloggers and by the software programs that track changes in the overall state of the Web. Information in this new model is analyzed, repackaged, digested, and passed on down to the next link in the chain. It flows.

VARY SENTENCE PATTERNS

In Part 9 we describe the four patterns of sentences. (➡ See pages 470–471.) Varying a paragraph's sentence patterns can keep readers engaged:

In the thirties, Harold Gray's comic strip *Little Orphan Annie* had 47 million readers. Then it languished until the 1970s when Martin Charnin thought it would make a good stage musical. It did. For the film, fresh songs and scenes were added, and 8,000 girls auditioned for the part of Annie. Director John Huston wanted "a girl who can sing, dance and act, with tons of personality, so that for two hours audiences won't take their eyes off her." Aileen Quinn's high spirits in the role have caused children to say, after seeing the film, that they too want to be orphans.

You don't have to use all four patterns in every paragraph you write; just be aware that, if a paragraph's sentences are sounding repetitive to you, varying the patterns is one solution.

VARY SENTENCE ORDER

In English, readers expect sentences to have the order of subject-verb-object. (➡ See pages 476–477.) Because this expectation is so widespread, you can create emphasis in a paragraph by reversing the word order of a sentence. Just be careful to do this infrequently, only when you want to create special emphasis. The following paragraph would be less strong if the first sentence were *Potential homebuyers should check basements first.*

Basements are where potential home-buyers should go first. The most expensive home repairs come up from weak and shaky foundations, and after you buy a house you do not want the surprise of thousands of dollars in bills for digging out and replacing the stone or cement block that is supposed to support your house. Only a detailed inspection by a foundation specialist can tell you whether a crack results from simple settling or the foundation breaking in two.

VARY PARAGRAPH LENGTH

Audiences expect different paragraph lengths, depending on medium and genre. For example, because many people are still becoming accustomed to reading online, paragraphs in online genres such as newspapers are often much shorter than paragraphs in print, only two or three sentences each. Paragraphs in academic genres, on the other hand, can extend over a page or two in a twenty-page paper. (In a paper shorter than ten pages, readers expect paragraphs to be shorter than a whole page.)

In general, all the paragraphs in any text will be of similar length, just long enough to develop and make clear the concept the writer needs to make at that point in the composition. But when you want to emphasize one point, you can use a paragraph that is much shorter than the others. Readers will see visually and through a change in reading rhythm that what the short paragraph discusses is important.

STYLING PARAGRAPHS
CONCLUDING PARAGRAPHS

What is on this page will help you style your writing for:

 CLARITY

☐ CONCISION

 COHERENCE

 EMPHASIS

 ENGAGEMENT

Why talk about concluding paragraphs before introductory paragraphs?

Because you cannot have a shining, strong introductory paragraph until you know the exact end toward which that paragraph points readers.

FUNCTIONS OF CONCLUDING PARAGRAPHS FOR READERS

- Concluding paragraphs sum up the arguments of the paper.
- Concluding paragraphs give readers a take-away memory of the writing.

STRATEGIES FOR CONCLUDING

As you write, you cannot separate the two functions of concluding paragraphs. As you read the following examples, look for how they mix functions, but also try to imagine what preceded the conclusion; a strong conclusion should enable that.

RESTATING OR SUMMARIZING YOUR ARGUMENT

Provide a crisp summary, not a rote repetition. You can include a question, quotation, or recommended action:

In sum, the globalization of English does not mean that if we who speak only English just sit back and wait, we'll soon be able to exchange ideas with anyone who has anything to say. We can't count on having much more around the world than a very basic ability to communicate. Outside of certain professional fields, if English-speaking Americans hope to exchange ideas with people in a nuanced way, we may be well advised to do as people elsewhere are doing: become bilingual.

RECOMMENDING ACTION

The following conclusion recommends specific actions its audience can take:

The problem at hand is so huge it requires a response like our national mobilization to fight—and win—World War II. To move our nation off of fossil fuels, we need inspired, Churchillian leadership and sweeping statutes à la the Big War or the Civil Rights Movement. So, frankly, I feel a twinge of nausea each time I see that predictable "10 Things You Can Do" sidebar in a well-meaning magazine or newspaper article. In truth, the only list that actually matters is the one we should all be sending to Congress *post haste*, full of 10 muscular clean-energy statutes that would finally do what we say we want: rescue our life-giving Earth from climate catastrophe.

(Note: In the examples of introductory paragraphs on page 294 is the introduction that leads to this conclusion.)

SUGGESTING MORE QUESTIONS FOR RESEARCH

Such suggestions about the conduct of technical writing courses, however, must remain suggestions and not firm recommendations, until we know more about the composing processes of engineers. Additional research on composing might reveal how Nelson, his firm, and his subdiscipline are and are not typical. It might show how his composing habits are more efficient or less efficient than those of his colleagues. It might suggest that some tasks call for very different composing habits and skills than others, or it might imply that technical writers should develop several composing styles that they can call upon in different composing situations. One thing seems certain, however: Only when more research is completed will teachers know how to better prepare students for the kinds of writing they will do at work.

REFLECTING ON HOW YOUR WRITING OR RESEARCH HAS AFFECTED YOU

Using your own voice pulls readers closer, making your observations more compelling.

In the interviews I conducted for this paper, I learned that men and women learn to be men and women through experiencing all the photographs, movies, magazine covers, and popular songs that portray what men and women are supposed to be and do. I've also learned how the simplest of tossed-off sentences in different situations can shape someone's sense of what's proper behavior. I heard how a teacher's comments are remembered for a long time. As an education major, it's that last observation I will carry with me, to help me think about the responsibilities I'll be taking on.

> **TIP: FUNCTIONS OF CONCLUDING PARAGRAPHS FOR WRITERS**
> Once they are drafted, concluding paragraphs provide surprisingly useful suggestions to writers about revising.
> → See page 306.

INTRODUCTORY PARAGRAPHS

What is on this page will help you style your writing for:

- ☑ CLARITY
- ☐ CONCISION
- ☐ COHERENCE
- ☑ EMPHASIS
- ☑ ENGAGEMENT

Introductory paragraphs function to:

- Engage readers with the topic.
- Focus readers' attention on the particular aspects of the topic that matter to you.

STRATEGIES FOR INTRODUCING

You can explictly state why readers should care about a topic, or you can engage them indirectly, through how you talk about a topic. You can also state your thesis directly or imply it.

BE DIRECT AND EXPLICIT

In the following pages I will argue that, even though many people consider microcredit capable of ending poverty, it instead can exacerbate poverty, especially for women and for the most poor.

USE A QUESTION

Millionaire Steve Fossett has been missing since last Monday, when he took off from a Nevada airstrip on a short flight. Rescue crews have yet to find the famous adventurer or his plane, but according to news reports, they've discovered at least six *uncharted wrecks* **across a 17,000-square-mile swath of the Sierra Nevada—or nearly one a day since the search began. Why are there so many undocumented crash sites around the Sierra Nevada?**

MAKE A SUPRISING CLAIM

Strange but true: Energy-efficient light bulbs and hybrid cars are hurting our nation's budding efforts to fight global warming.

MAKE A COMPELLING CLAIM

The rate of bipolar disorder diagnoses in children and adolescents seen as outpatients by physicians shot up dramatically between 1994 and 2003, raising new concerns about possible overdiagnosis of this severe mood disorder among young people.

USE A QUOTATION

In the 1820s, Fanny Trollope, that perceptive, sharp-tongued traveller, described North America as "a vast continent, by far the greater part of which is still in the state nature left it, and a busy, bustling, industrious population, hacking and hewing their way through it." That hewing, hacking, and shooting was to cause a lot of environmental damage.

PAINT A VISUAL PICTURE

Lady, an Australian shepherd mix who had been lounging in a sunny window seat at the Bothell Regional Library, pricked up her ears and wagged her tail when she saw 10-year-old Nicholas Goodman. When he sat down next to her with the book *Down in the Subway* and started to read aloud, she leaned against him, eyes closed, and appeared to listen intently. Her expression never changed, not even when Nicholas stumbled over tricky words like "guava."

That's the whole idea behind "Reading with Rover," a summer program for children at the Bothell and Kenmore branches of the King County Regional Library System.

WHAT TO AVOID

- **Introductions that are broad and vague.** *From the beginning of time, humans have…* or *Life is amazing.* If you see similar phrases in your introduction, state as explicitly as you can what matters to you in this writing.

- **Starting with a dictionary definition.** Readers will think you are not confident enough about your own arguments to put them in your own words.

- **Excuses.** Don't make excuses about not being an expert. Readers don't expect experts to be writing college papers; they expect well-researched arguments that acknowledge other possible positions.

TIP: WHAT'S YOUR DISCIPLINE?

Writers in the humanities frequently do not explicitly state their thesis; instead, they develop it over the writing. Writers in the sciences and social sciences are expected to be explicit about their thesis and to announce the structure of their papers.

If you have any questions about what is appropriate for an assignment, ask your teacher.

TIP: HOW LONG?

In five- to ten-page papers, an introduction, like a conclusion, should rarely take up more than two-thirds of a page. A longer introduction will have readers wondering, midway through, when the paper starts; a longer conclusion will have readers wondering if a new paper or argument is starting.

TRANSITIONS BETWEEN PARAGRAPHS

What is on this page will help you style your writing for:

 CLARITY

CONCISION

 COHERENCE

 EMPHASIS

 ENGAGEMENT

In Part 5, we discussed creating coherence within paragraphs; here we discuss creating coherence **between** paragraphs.

Most writers need to learn how to provide transitions between paragraphs, but learning how to do this will help your writing be confident and effective. When you use the strategies we discuss here, you tell readers why one paragraph follows another; you enable readers to follow and so better understand your arguments.

STRATEGIES FOR BUILDING TRANSITIONS

- Repeat crucial words, phrases, or concepts from one paragraph to the next.
- Repeat crucial concepts by using synonyms.
- Use the linking words listed on page 216 to show relationships between the paragraphs.

LINK THE LAST SENTENCE OF ONE PARAGRAPH TO THE FIRST SENTENCE OF THE NEXT

In constructing transitions from one paragraph to the next, choose the most important words, phrases, or concepts of the last sentence of a paragraph; and then weave those words, phrases, or concepts into the the first sentence of the next paragraph.

The paragraphs to the right use the strategies above to build transitions.

ozone in Mexico City have exceeded the country's air-quality standards 284 days per year, on average. Geography doesn't help: Mexico City lies on a broad basin ringed by tall mountains that can block the movement of air masses that might clear out pollution.

Furthermore, the city's rapid spread in recent decades has aggravated its pollution problems. Mexico City now covers about 1,500 square kilometers—about 10 times as much as it occupied just 50 years ago.

In this example, the writer uses the first paragraph to discuss connections between pollution in Mexico City and the city's geography; in the second paragraph, he turns to discussing how the city's size contributes to its pollution problems. **Furthermore** tells readers that additional information is being added, and **city** and **pollution** carry the topic from one paragraph to the next.

■ ■ ■

still-unawakened self, a collective psyche dangerously out of balance, and this awareness united many of the poets in an effort to support and produce a poetry of protest whose fundamental aim was not to destroy the establishment but to rethink it, heal it, render it more flexible and self-aware.

The work of Allen Ginsberg paved the way for this sensibility by claiming the right of the self to be what it has to be and write the poetry it has to write; but Ginsberg also went a step further "to insist" as James E. Mersmann points out in his

In this example's first paragraph, the writer generally describes poets' desires in the mid-twentieth century; in the second paragraph, he turns to discussing how one poet helped shape those desires. Note how **this sensibility** summarizes and repeats the description of the poets' desires, thus linking the two paragraphs.

■ ■ ■

the same thing he does, you do it using plain words without instruments. Words are like music. Well-reasoned thoughts, conveyed with well-chosen words, can touch us deeply as a moving symphony or a driving drum beat.

But Maggie Simpson doesn't possess language and doesn't speak. In the twentieth century, philosophers concerned with humanity's place in the universe have turned to the relationship between words and thoughts. How do we think if

In this example, the writer argues first that words matter in communication; in the second paragraph, the discussion shifts to focus on a character who doesn't use words. **But** signals this shift to readers. The two paragraphs are still strongly connected by the repetition of concepts concerning words and language.

PASSIVE VOICE

What is on this page will help you style your writing for:

- ☐ CLARITY
- ☐ CONCISION
- ☐ COHERENCE
- ☑ EMPHASIS
- ☑ ENGAGEMENT

Passive voice is a feature of individual sentences, and we define it in Part 9 (→ see page 515).

Even though passive voice is a feature of sentences, we discuss it here because it is in paragraphs that passive voice has its largest effects. Readers will rarely notice the use of passive voice in one or two sentences within several paragraphs or sections; when a whole paragraph is in passive voice, however, what readers take from the paragraph will be affected because the whole sense of the paragraph is affected.

In addition, as we point out to the right, writing some sentences in passive voice can constrain your other sentences.

PASSIVE VOICE IN SCIENTIFIC AND TECHNICAL WRITING

By using passive voice, writers can shift readers' focus away from who performs an action to the object acted upon. Because science writing is meant to be objective—that is, to imply that the actions (experiments, surveys, observations) being described could be performed by anyone—scientific writing often uses passive voice:

The behavior of fiber reinforced polymer (FRP) strengthened reinforced concrete beams subjected to torsional loads has not been well understood, compared to other loads. Interaction of different components of concrete, steel, and FRP in addition to the complex compatibility issues associated with torsional deformations have made it difficult to provide an accurate analytical solution. In this paper an analytical method is introduced for evaluation of the torsional capacity of FRP-strengthened RC beams. In this method, the interaction of different components is allowed by fulfilling equilibrium and compatibility conditions throughout the loading regime while the ultimate torque of the beam is calculated similarly to the well-known compression field theory. It is shown that the method is capable of predicting the ultimate torque of FRP-strengthened RC beams reasonably accurately.

PASSIVE VOICE—OR NOT?—IN WRITING FOR NONSCIENTIFIC AUDIENCES

Compare this paragraph—

During the last couple weeks, American snouts have increased dramatically in my garden and the surrounding area. But that is nothing like the masses that were recorded farther south in Texas a few weeks ago. An estimated 7.5 million snouts were reported in the Alamo area of the Lower Rio Grande Valley on September 5. And there is a chance that our numbers will continue to build over the next few weeks, at least until the really cold weather sets in.

—with this one:

In the last few weeks, I thought American snouts had taken over my garden. On September 5, however, observers farther south in Texas recorded numbers that make my garden seem empty: They saw almost 7.5 million snouts in the Alamo area of the Lower Rio Grande Valley. And until the cold weather sets in, these small butterflies might very well overwhelm us with their numbers.

When they wish to sound scientific—which requires longer and less direct grammatical constructions—writers often carry the patterns of passive voice into their other sentences, making all of them longer and more complex than they need to be.

If an occasional passive voice sentence supports your purposes, be alert to keeping your other sentences in the active voice.

STYLE IN VISUAL TEXTS

TYPOGRAPHY

SERIF AND SANS SERIF TYPEFACES

Knowing this major distinction between kinds of typefaces will help you choose typefaces to fit your purposes.

serif   sans serif

Serif is a French word meaning **tail**, and it describes typefaces that have little swashes (circled above) added to the ends of letters. *Sans* is French for **without**; thus **sans serif** typefaces have no serifs.

Serifed typefaces generally look more classical or old-fashioned than sans serif typefaces. Audiences in the United States are accustomed to seeing serifed typefaces in long sections of text that are meant to be readable.

DECORATIVE TYPEFACES

Typefaces that look like this are called "**DECORATIVE.**" They are not easy to read in anything but short phrases and so they are most often used for short pieces of text like titles and headers. OCCASIONALLY A PARTICULAR PURPOSE JUSTIFIES USING THEM FOR BLOCKS OF TEXT YOU WANT PEOPLE TO READ, BUT ONLY OCCASIONALLY.

SOME NOTES ON USING TYPEFACES

Since the invention of the printing press in the fifteenth century, conventions for the use of type in different genres have developed.

- Academic and other texts that are meant to be serious or formal almost always use one size of a single, serifed typeface throughout. For example, teachers might expect you to use the typeface Times in 12-point type for papers; at most, then, you would use the plain, italic, and bold versions of the Times typeface.

  Occasionally, writers will use a second typeface in such writings: A plain, sans serifed typeface such as Helvetica or Arial, in its bold version, can provide sufficient contrast for headings, as described to the right.

- Visual unity, a value of many genres, underlies the number of typefaces experienced visual designers use. Even in genres that have considerable wiggle room in choice of type—genres such as posters or brochures— designers most often use only two or three typefaces: one for the title or main head, another for the information or body text, and perhaps a third if there is another text function that needs to be visually differentiated.

HEADINGS

When you chunk a text by inserting headings, you allow readers to better see the sections of your text. This can help readers both comprehend and remember your arguments.

- Headings should be short, taking up only one line, so that readers can see them at a glance.

- Headings should have space before them so that readers see a heading as part of the text that follows it.

- The typeface of a heading should be different (in size, thickness, or style) from the typeface used in the body of the text, again so that readers can see and read the heading easily.

To create a conservative look in a heading
Use a bold version of the typeface you use for the body of text.

To create a more modern look in a heading
Use a sans serif typeface heading with a serifed typeface for the body of the text. Usually, you will have to use a bold version of the sans serif typeface to create an easy-to-see contrast between the heading and the body.

NOTE: Unless a heading is very short, use upper- and lowercase letters. Using only uppercase letters is hard to read for more than just a few words.

COLOR

COLOR TERMINOLOGY

To use color in support of your purposes, you need to know why you are choosing one color over another—and to do that, you need to know color terminology.

HUE

Hue describes what many of us think of as color. When you name the hue of a color, you say whether it is red or blue or yellow or....

Hue, saturation, and brightness are present in all colors. In the examples above, the leftmost color is red-hued, with as much saturation and brightness as possible. The middle color is not very bright, but is still a fairly saturated red hue. The color on the right has a hue of blue, is fairly bright, but is not very saturated.

COLOR CONNOTATIONS

Colors and color combinations have connotations just as words do (→ see page 271). For example, we often associate bright red, blue, and yellow with childhood, while combinations of highly saturated red and green or orange and blue will remind some of concert posters from the 1960s.

BRIGHTNESS

Brightness (sometimes also referred to as **value**) describes how light or dark a color is. In the bar above, the color at the extreme left has no brightness; the color at the extreme right is as bright as it can be.

When you choose colors to use in composing, keep in mind that the connotations we have with certain colors will be affected by the shape of the color and what is around it. For example, blue can suggest cold when used with **ice** or **winter**, but warmth and relaxation when used with **Caribbean summer afternoon**.

SATURATION

Saturation describes how much of a hue is present in a color. In the bar above, the colors at the far left are unsaturated; they have no blue in them. As you move to the right in the bar above, the color becomes more saturated: It has more blue.

USING COLOR

CHOOSING HARMONIOUS COLORS

- Choose colors close to each other on the color wheel:

Colors next to each other—or one step apart—will be harmonious.

- Choose one color that supports your purpose, and then increase or decrease its saturation or brightness to create a set of harmonious colors to use:

- Choose a range of different hues, but give each the same brightness and saturation:

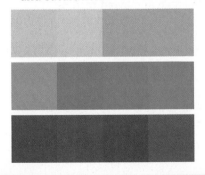

COLOR AND TYPE

Type is easiest to read when there is as much contrast as possible between the color of the type and the color of the background. The contrast between the colors can be a contrast in hue, saturation, or brightness.

> **STRONG CONTRAST**
> WEAK CONTRAST

> **STRONG CONTRAST**
> WEAK CONTRAST

> **STRONG CONTRAST**
> WEAK CONTRAST

> **STRONG CONTRAST**
> WEAK CONTRAST

Sometimes, however, you can create a very strong contrast in hue, but if the colors are very saturated and very bright, they can hurt our eyes rather than be easy to read:

> **STRONG CONTRAST**
> **BUT HARD TO READ.**

> **STRONG CONTRAST**
> **BUT HARD TO READ.**

STYLE IN ORAL PRESENTATIONS

In oral presentations, the main component of style is you: Your voice and gestures will be your main strategies for creating emphasis and engagement.

CONNECTING WITH AN AUDIENCE

Public speaking might make you anxious. In addition to remembering to breathe deeply before and during a talk, making eye contact with people in your audience and even addressing them directly can help you relax. These actions are also style decisions.

As you prepare, decide how to connect with your audience. Few presentation contexts and purposes require formality. Rather, in almost all circumstances, you can engage your audience—and thus encourage their generosity toward your arguments—by asking them questions, speaking directly to them while looking into their faces, or smiling.

SPEAKING STYLES

Your voice—its volume, speed, and tone—gives you a wonderful range of style choices while you speak. To take advantage of your voice, have your presentation organized in time so you can practice often: Seek a conversational style and avoid reading.

Identify the presentation parts (words or sentences) you wish to emphasize. Then experiment with different ways of saying those parts. Exaggerate volume and tone, playfully, and make yourself laugh. This will help you relax—but will also help you find what works best for the real presentation.

BODY LANGUAGE

For most presentations, you need to use your body language—expressions and gestures—to put your audience at ease and to emphasize the major points of your presentation.

Look over what you have written for your presentation, and decide what facial expressions, and where, support your arguments. In the past, audiences expected almost theatrical gestures and expressions; now, simple smiles, frowns, nods, or occasional head shakes are enough.

Similarly, current audiences do not expect grand hand gestures. You will make audiences uncomfortable if you nervously wring your hands, but you can instead keep your hands clasped in front of or behind you, placed on the lectern, or holding your notes.

Do check over your words, seeing where a gesture will emphasize what needs emphasizing. And then practice.

Practicing your presentation over and over will help you make your body language relaxed and friendly.

USING VISUAL SUPPORTS

Visual supports can be slide presentations (using software like PowerPoint or Keynote), overheads, handouts, or physical objects.

Use visual supports to help your audience see the main points of your presentation.

Use objects that help you demonstrate procedures you are discussing or that illustrate your main points: A stretched-out plastic bag holding the amount of trash an average American throws out in one day will make the point about

American's resource use much more strongly than a spoken statistic.

Whatever your visual aids, practice with them. You need to be able to use them comfortably so that your audience focuses on the points you are making rather than on your trying to use a projector. Also, using visual aids slows down a presentation; if you have a time limit, practicing with your visuals will help you stay within that time limit.

PARALLELISM IN ORAL PRESENTATIONS

Apply to the paragraphs you will speak the same guidelines for building parallelism in sentences that we described on page 286. Paragraphs that use parallelism create rhythmic and emotionally compelling paragraphs, as in this Convocation Address by Nikki Giovanni:

We are Virginia Tech.

The Hokie Nation embraces our own and reaches out with open hearts and hands to those who offer their hearts and minds. We are strong, and brave, and innocent, and unafraid. We are better than we think and not quite what we want to be. We are alive to the imaginations and the possibilities. We will continue to invent the future through our blood and tears and through all our sadness.

We are the Hokies.

We will prevail.

We will prevail.

We will prevail.

We are Virginia Tech.

HINTS & TIPS FOR CONCLUDING PARAGRAPHS

USING CONCLUDING PARAGRAPHS TO HELP YOU REVISE

You are writing your first draft. You type the last period for the last sentence, and breathe deeply: You are done.

But, no, wait, sorry: You are not done, not if you want the strongest possible writing. Definitely take a deep breath and leave your paper for a while—but come back several hours or a day later.

For writers, the first draft of a conclusion provides crucial information:

- Often, a conclusion is when you realize what your argument really is. Experienced writers know that a first draft is only a beginning, and that often they don't know what they really want to argue until that first attempt at a conclusion. Sometimes writers use the concluding paragraph of a first draft—because it is often a succinct and passionate statement of an argument—as the first paragraph of the next draft.

- If you do feel that the concluding paragraph is an accurate and strong statement of your argument, go back through the rest of the paper to ask yourself: Do all the other paragraphs lead up to and support the conclusion?

- Because most writers intuitively know that concluding paragraphs should include a little passion, they include passion—but often there is no passion in the rest of the writing, and so the conclusion will seem unsuitable to readers. When you finish a conclusion, check that its emotional tone is supported by the rest of the writing, just as you check to make sure its logical claims are likewise supported.

- Use the concluding paragraph to help you make your introductory paragraph as strong and engaging as possible. Knowing the end point where you want to take readers, what might be the most effective starting point?

PART 8
DOCUMENTING

useful pressure to ack...
activity of composing [...].
the material. It makes writing, li
musical, graphic, handicraft, engin
literally fashions the world. (697)

perhaps more than George and Tri

he language of design ("Available

ell with our view of social life and

societies" (20). What this chang

h again the New L

CONTENTS

WHERE ARE WE IN THE PROCESS FOR COMPOSING?

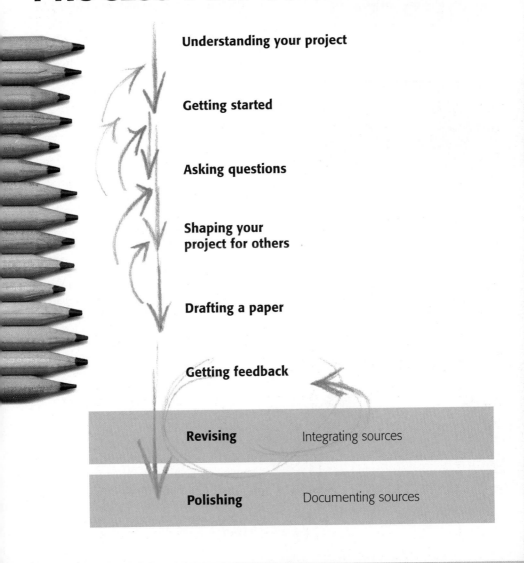

Understanding your project

Getting started

Asking questions

Shaping your project for others

Drafting a paper

Getting feedback

Revising   Integrating sources

Polishing   Documenting sources

WHY CITE AND DOCUMENT SOURCES?

CONSIDERING PLAGIARISM—AND HOW TO AVOID IT

Do you want to live and work in communities—school districts, neighborhoods, cities, countries—where people respect each other and each other's ideas, and where people try to persuade you and each other based on the best possible evidence?

If you do, some of your part in shaping such communities is knowing cultural expectations for showing respect in spoken or written deliberations—even when you disagree. Your part is understanding how to determine and use the best possible evidence and letting others know where that evidence comes from, so that they can judge and check it.

To *cite* is to name the people from whom you drew your ideas; **to document** is to record where—print or online books, journals, or newspapers—you found the ideas.

Many people think that using, citing, and documenting sources is only for academic writing. There are certainly academic conventions for doing such work—and helping you learn those conventions is a large part of the following pages. But these conventions exist because people who write academic papers, no matter what discipline, want to be sure that they are using the best possible evidence and that they are making that evidence available to others to check.

Citing and documenting sources shows that you want to take part in ongoing deliberations while being respectful of the research and thinking others have done before you. It shows that you want others to understand where your good reasons and thinking come from.

WHAT IS PLAGIARISM?

Plagiarism is using the ideas or words of others without acknowledgment, as though they were your own.

Plagiarism can happen inadvertently: While doing research, you might take notes or copy some text from a webpage and in the rush to finish a paper, lose track of where the words came from and put them straight into your paper. Plagiarism can also happen when you don't have enough confidence in your own ideas or the quality of your research to take your own positions; you let the words of others stand in for your words.

Whether plagiarism is inadvertent, purposeful, or the result of not enough confidence, it is considered wrong in the United States. It can cause you to have to redo an assignment, to fail an assignment or a class, or to be expelled from school. It stops you from learning how to have confidence in presenting your ideas in ways others will respect; it also stops you from developing your own ideas and learning.

PLAGIARISM—OR MISUSE OF SOURCES?

Sometimes students and other novice writers are accused of plagiarism because they did not cite all their sources or did not cite their sources conventionally. This can happen when writers are inexperienced with or simply do not know the conventions.

To avoid this happening to you, here are steps you can take:

- If you receive an assignment that asks you to use sources, be sure you know what citation style your teacher wants you to use. If an assignment does not specify a style, ask.

- Ask your teacher or someone in a Writing or Learning Center to look at a draft of your writing: Are you using citation styles as conventions ask?

- Pay close attention to the conventions as they are presented in this handbook. The conventions are detailed, and can seem tedious to learn, but the conventions are detailed precisely because it is a cultural practice in the United States to be very careful with the words and ideas of others.

CULTURAL ATTITUDES TOWARD THE WORDS AND IDEAS OF OTHERS

In some cultures, using the words of respected authorities and knowing when others are using them, without mentioning the source, are signs of being educated. In some cultures, students use the words of their teachers and other authorities as their own to indicate that they have learned what they were supposed to. In the United States, however, concern for the value of property—and a belief that words and ideas can be individual property—lead to a valuing of and the development of conventions for acknowledging uses of others' words or ideas.

WHAT WORDS AND IDEAS DON'T NEED TO BE CITED

You don't need to cite sources when the ideas you are using are

- *Common and shared knowledge.* Most people will accept without question that there are seven days in a week or that the capital of Maryland is Annapolis. To be sure whether you need to give a source, ask yourself if everyone in your audience will know. If the answer is **yes**, then you can write without citing a source. If you're unsure if what you are writing is common knowledge, find and cite a source for it.

- *Facts that are available in a wide range of sources.* If every encyclopedia or newspaper article you check states that Joan of Arc died in 1431 or that somewhere between 22 and 26 inches of snow fell in upstate New York on Monday, then you can include these facts in your writing without citing any source for the facts.

- *The results of your own field research.*

WHAT WORDS AND IDEAS ALWAYS NEED TO BE CITED

Cite the origins of ideas and words you use in writing or oral presentations if the words and ideas are

- *Someone else's exact words* that you copied from a book, website, or interview.

- *Your paraphrase or summary of someone else's words or ideas.* (→ See pages 322–325 on paraphrasing and summarizing.)

- *Facts not known or accepted by everyone in your audience.* While global climate change is accepted by almost all scientists, many nonscientific audiences are still unsure about the details. If you are writing to a nonscientific audience, you should provide sources for any evidence you offer that the climate is changing.

- *Photographs, charts, graphs, or illustrations.* Give the source—and permissions, if necessary—for any visual object you place into writing or a webpage. Do this even if you made the object, to calm any concerns readers might have.

HOW TEACHERS TRY TO PREVENT OR RECOGNIZE PLAGIARISM

Teachers have developed ways both to avoid and to detect plagiarism. Teachers help you avoid plagiarism by asking you to develop research projects through notes, drafts, and revisions so that they can see and encourage the progress of your ideas. (Teachers who ask you to do this will therefore be curious if you abandon a topic at the last moment and turn in a final paper on a new topic.) Some software programs can check papers online against existing writing to recognize if writers have used words from others; this software is controversial because it is not always accurate and can impinge on students' privacy and intellectual property rights.

TIPS FOR AVOIDING PLAGIARISM

The best way to avoid plagiarism is to have integrity toward your sources and toward yourself as a researcher: Respect the words and ideas of others as you would like your own words and ideas respected.

Your work habits can help you: If you take notes carefully and record your research, you will know when you are using the words and ideas of others.

• Keep a working bibliography of all sources you might use. This will help you have at hand the information you need when you need it so that you can cite sources as others expect.

→ To learn about working bibliographies, see pages 82–83.

• If you record someone else's words because you might use them later, mark that they are someone else's words; this will help keep you from inadvertently using those words as though they were yours.

If you copy words from a webpage into your notes, color-code the notes or put quotation marks around them; always record the information you need for citing the words.

→ See pages 342–347 for the information you need to record to cite webpages.

If you record words from print sources, put quotation marks around them immediately and record the source information.

→ See pages 326–341 for the information to record to cite print texts.

• If you work online, take advantage of websites like furl.com or citeulike.com to track your sources. Similarly, make copies of print sources you might use so that you can check—after you've finished your writing—that you have cited with integrity.

• Understand how to quote, summarize, and paraphrase.

→ See pages 314–325.

• Understand how to cite the words of others in your text.

→ For MLA in-text citations, see pages 350–359; for APA, see pages 421–425; for CSE, see pages 452–457; for CMS, see pages 458–459.

• Understand how to build an appropriate and accurate Works Cited page.

→ For sample sets of MLA Works Cited pages, see pages 404–405 and 416–418; for a sample APA References list, see pages 450–451.

TIP: HOW TO CHECK THAT YOU HAVE CITED ALL YOUR SOURCES

When your writing is very close to finished, give it to a friend (one who is a careful reader) with two different colored highlighters. Ask the friend to mark your paper, highlighting your ideas in one color and the ideas of everyone else in the other color. If your friend highlights the ideas correctly, then your paper should be good to go. If not, you need to add citations and other indications—as we show later in these pages—so that it is clear when the ideas and words in your paper are not your own.

There are four facets to
CITING AND DOCUMENTING

1

USING OTHERS' WORDS IN YOUR WRITING BY QUOTING, SUMMARIZING, OR PARAPHRASING

Quoting is using others' exact words; summarizing is reporting the main idea of someone else's words, without details; paraphrasing is putting others' ideas into your own words.

QUOTING

"We started making videos to send home that showed what our life here was like," says Wright in an e-mail from his Antarctic base.

SUMMARIZING

Pollan's book tells us about the origins of four meals from widely different sources, asking us to question how our eating habits embed us in social, economic, political, and ecological webs.

PARAPHRASING

Sabido describes how he wants his *telenovelas* to reach his audience's limbic brain, which governs emotions.

→ Go to pages 314–325.

2

COLLECTING THE CITATION INFORMATION YOU NEED FOR ANY SOURCE YOU USE

Anytime you quote, summarize, paraphrase, or otherwise use any kind of source (including photographs, drawings, charts, and graphs) in your writing, you need to give readers information about the source.

For different sources you need to collect different information.

→ To learn the information to collect, see pages 326–349.

→ To determine the kinds of sources you have, see pages 44–59.

→ For help figuring out if the kinds of sources you are using are right for your arguments, see pages 42–43.

THE STYLES OF CITATIONS

There are four styles for citing sources: MLA, APA, CMS, and CSE. Each style is used by a different set of disciplines. As we note on the opposite page, we devote separate pages of this book to each of these styles; see the section on a style to learn who uses it.

3

CREATING IN-TEXT CITATIONS FOR YOUR SOURCES

When you use the words or ideas of someone else, provide information to help readers find those words themselves. Each style provides ways for you to give this information.

MLA STYLE

Monroe reminds us that there is no generic access to computers: Access at home is not the same as access at work or school (19–20, 26–27).

APA STYLE

Whalen (1995) analyzed how the talk of operators responding to emergency 911 calls was organized in part by the task of filling in required information on a computer screen with a specific visual organization.

4

CREATING WORKS CITED, REFERENCES LISTS, AND BIBLIOGRAPHIES

Each style has its own name for the list of sources at the end of a piece of writing, but all of them require writers to list all the sources used in their writing.

APA STYLE

Panofsky, E. (1970). *Meaning in the visual arts.* Harmondsworth, England: Penguin.

CSE STYLE

20. Latchman DS. From genetics to gene therapy: the molecular pathology of human disease. London: Bios Scientific Publishers; 1994. 362 p. (UCL molecular pathology series).

Because each style for in-text citations and works cited lists is different, we provide separate sections for each style.

→ The **MLA style** for in-text citations is described on pages 350–359; the style for the list of works cited at the end of a paper is described on pages 360–405.

→ The **APA style** for in-text citations is described on pages 421–425; the style for the list of works cited at the end of a paper is described on pages 426–451.

→ The **CSE style** for in-text citations is described on page 453; the style for the list of works cited at the end of a paper is described on pages 454–457.

→ The **CMS style** for in-text citations is described on pages 458–459; the style for the list of works cited at the end of a paper is described on pages 460–462.

QUOTING, SUMMARIZING, AND PARAPHRASING

DECIDING WHETHER TO QUOTE, SUMMARIZE, OR PARAPHRASE

Whenever you quote, summarize, or paraphrase others' words, you show readers that you are engaging with the ideas of others; you show readers that you are working to make sense of and build on available ideas and information. This is a hallmark of academic writing, as well as of any deliberative writing, writing that is about considering with others the choices we might make as citizens and community members.

The chart below can help you decide when to use one method rather than another for incorporating the words and ideas of others into your writing.

QUOTING

- emphasizes the exact words being used, which helps you emphasize ideas you want to highlight because they support your arguments or provide important counter-positions.

- carries the authority of the person being quoted into your writing.

- can bring vibrant and memorable language into your writing.

SUMMARIZING

- focuses readers on the main points of an argument you are using to support your own purposes.

- shows that you are considering extended arguments made by others.

PARAPHRASING

- allows you to modify language your readers might not understand (technical language, for example) into language they will.

- allows you to bring in the opinions of others if their ideas are not presented succinctly or in memorable ways.

→ When you quote, paraphrase, and summarize, you have to show the sources for the words and ideas you are using. Each citation style handles this differently. For the MLA style, see pages 360–420; for the APA style, see pages 426–451; for the CSE style, see pages 453–457; for the CMS style, see pages 458–462.

EXAMPLE PASSAGE

So that we can best explain how to follow the conventions of quoting, paraphrasing, and summarizing, here is a passage to which we will refer on the following pages. The passage is from the article "You're not studying, you're just...," written by Ravi Purushotma and published in the journal *Language Learning & Technology* in January 2005. (Note that **L2** means ***second language***.)

Perhaps the most successful innovation in game designs is the development of modern massively multiplayer online games—MMOGs. In these games, rather than playing within a pre-programmed environment, players exist as characters in a virtual world formed through their interactions with other live players on the Internet. The unparalleled success of these games should be of interest to anyone trying to understand adolescent motivation and attention. In stark contrast to the high school language teacher sometimes struggling to receive 30 minutes worth of homework from students, the alarming success of MMOGs has prompted the establishment of government organizations to control their use and psychological addiction (Yee, 2002) after a set of players neglecting to break for food collapsed following up to 84 hours straight at their keyboards (Farrell, 2002; Gluck, 2002). Makers of the popular online game *Everquest* (commonly referred to as "Evercrack" for its addictive properties) found the average player spends over 20 hours a week playing the game (Everquest or Evercrack?, 2002).

While it might be nice to get teens to spend 20 hours a week solely on their Spanish homework, we should consider the educational potential for leveraging the phenomenal ability of MMOGs to capture the attention of adolescent audiences and bring them into a manipulatable world with players from all over the planet. Some studies have reported success at integrating MOOs, the historical predecessor to modern MMOGs, into the language classroom (Von der Emde, Schneider, & Kötter, 2001), although the educational potential for MMOGs is only just beginning to be examined (Coleman, 2004; Squire & Jenkins, in press). Simply by having such an international population together in a virtual community based on communicative interaction, motivated players have access to countless native L2 speakers and tasks to discuss with them—though much could be done to extend this possibility to encourage shy learners to find and interact with players speaking their L2. For example, in a game like *The Sims Online*—the MMOG version of *The Sims*—players begin by choosing a city to live in, finding a house, then chatting with and getting to know their roommates. Besides merging international editions to form bilingual versions, another almost effortless modification game designers could make to interest language learners would be to create incentives and ways in which players could find and partner with native speakers of their L2 trying to learn their L1. This would not only provide the above-mentioned benefits of playing a bilingual game, but also provide learners with an L2 native from whom to learn about culture and language while performing a series of entertaining tasks requiring communicative exchanges. Alternatively, teachers could collaborate with classes in other countries and assign their students L2 speaking roommates.

→ This long journal quotation uses the APA style for in-text citations; see pages 421–425.

QUOTING, SUMMARIZING, AND PARAPHRASING
QUOTING THE WORDS OF OTHERS

Here is one way to use the words of the journal excerpt on page 315:

Because of the "addictive qualities" of massively multiplayer online games (MMOGs), a researcher of uses of digital technologies for language learning, Ravi Purushotma, argues that teachers ought to use such games "to capture the attention of adolescent audiences and bring them into a manipulatable world with players from all over the planet" (86).

When you quote the words of others, it is as though you invite the words to speak for you: You bring both the sense of speaking and the authority of the speaker into your writing.

Because of this, use the exact words of others in your writing when those words add something to your argument that you cannot provide with your own words.

- Use words from those whom your readers are likely to recognize either by name, work, or affiliation. This will give readers more reason to accept your points.

- Quote words that will be funny, poignant, striking, or otherwise memorable for your readers. This will help readers better remember your points.

- When in your writing you are considering the positions of people with whom you disagree, it can be useful to quote their words. This shows your audience that you are being fair by letting others speak for themselves.

THE PARTS OF QUOTING WELL

Here is the example of quoting the journal article excerpt on page 315. We repeat the example—with color coding—to show the many conventions that readers of more formal texts have come to expect:

Because of the " addictive qualities " of massively multiplayer online games (MMOGs), a researcher of uses of digital technologies for language learning, Ravi Purushotma, argues that teachers ought to use such games " to capture the attention of adolescent audiences and bring them into a manipulatable world with players from all over the planet " (86).

The points to the right can be a checklist for when you quoting another's words, to be sure you follow the conventions.

It is a convention that all direct quotations are indicated by quotation marks.
→ See page 318 for details on using quotation marks.

The words you are quoting should be the exact words, with no changes.
→ Sometimes, however, you will need to modify the words you are quoting—perhaps to shorten the quotation, to give an explanation readers might need, or to correct spelling—see page 319.

Using a title or affiliation of the person you are quoting, or the source of the quote, can help your audience understand why they should pay attention to this person.
→ See page 319 for ways to do this.

It is a fairly consistent convention to give the name of the person(s) responsible for the words you are quoting.
→ See page 320 for ways to do this.

Signal to your readers that you are quoting the words of others with the verb you choose to introduce the quoted words; use these verbs to weave the quotation into your writing.
→ See pages 320–321 for a list of signal words and for hints on weaving others' words into your own writing.

Each citation style specifies how to reference the page or paragraph of a citation's source. Readers can then find the exact place from which you drew your cite.
→ For MLA style, see pages 350–359.
→ For APA style, see pages 421–425.
→ For CSE style, see page 453.
→ For CMS style, see pages 458–459.

USING QUOTATION MARKS

Quotation marks are an immediately visible indicator to readers that you are using someone else's exact words—and there are many conventions regarding their use.

→ See pages 597–599 for the specific details of using quotation marks. *Pay particular attention to using quotation marks with other punctuation; this is an area where many people lose track of the details.*

WHEN WORDS YOU QUOTE CONTAIN THEIR OWN QUOTATION MARKS

Suppose you want to quote these words, from marketing author and blogger Seth Godin, on how the name *Global Warming* shapes how we talk about environmental change:

If the problem were called "Atmosphere cancer" or "Pollution death" the entire conversation would be framed in a different way.

The U.S. convention for quoting words that are already within quotation marks is to change the double quotation marks to single quotes:

As marketing author Seth Godin suggests, the general public might be more alarmed about global warming if "the problem were called 'Atmosphere cancer' or 'Pollution death.'"

Notice how this use of quotations means that the passage ends with a single quotation mark followed immediately by a double quotation mark.

WHEN **NOT** TO USE QUOTATION MARKS

If your quotation will take up more than four lines in your paper, make it into a **block quotation**. Introduce the quotation as you would any other, but:

• Make the quotation its own paragraph.

• Indent the paragraph from the left margin of your writing (but don't additionally indent the first line).

• Put the parenthetical information at the end of the quotation, following the style you have been asked to use.

• Put the parenthetical information outside the punctuation mark that ends the quotation.

• Follow a long quotation with words of your own.

Marie Vassiltchikov, a Russian refugee, worked in Berlin during World War II with a group that tried to kill Hitler. Her diaries give the only eyewitness account. In her diaries she also describes the night bombings of Berlin; after one such bombing, a friend of hers stopped by:

> During the night's raid (which I had described as "nothing serious") his driver had been killed and he himself had been buried in the cellar of his house, which had caved in; he had only managed to crawl out in the morning. He announced—and this is typical for our times!—that he had just bought one hundred oysters. (121)

Another time she tries on a new hat while buildings burn around her. Her diaries give a sense of how people try to hold on to what's normal.

WHEN AND HOW TO MODIFY THE WORDS YOU ARE QUOTING

Occasionally, for the sake of clarity, you need to make some modifications, as we discuss here.

IF YOU NEED TO REMOVE WORDS FROM A QUOTATION

If you need to remove words to emphasize the main information, use square brackets and an ellipsis punctuation mark:

In a recent article on tapeworms, science writer Carl Zimmer describes how some tapeworms called monogeans that live inside fish "give birth to offspring without releasing them from their bodies. Their offspring mature inside them and give birth as well [...]. A monogenean may contain twenty generations of descendents inside its body!"

→ See page 589 for more on using ellipses in this way.

IF YOU NEED TO ADD AN EXPLANATORY COMMENT TO A QUOTATION

Put the explanation in square brackets:

Leslie Collins (1976: 620) notes that "over 1000 women leaders were killed in China in 1927 by [members of a center-right political party opposed to the Communists]; many of [the women] were not Communists but simply active participants in the women's movement."

→ See page 583 for more on using brackets.

WHEN THERE IS AN OBSOLETE SPELLING OR A MISSPELLING IN THE WORDS YOU ARE QUOTING

If you are quoting an old text in which the spelling differs from what current readers expect, use the original spelling; including the words' date or providing an explanatory preface will help readers understand:

"Terrour," reasoned Thomas Churchyard in 1579, "made short warres."

USING TITLES, AFFILIATIONS, OR SOURCES

If you know that your readers know the person you are quoting, then you probably do not need to explain who the person is. But if you think your readers won't know why it is worth quoting a particular person, introduce the person with a title, affiliation, or other relevant information such as the source of the quotation so that readers understand the authority behind the person's words.

As Professor George argues...

In her article in *Neurological Studies of the Eye*, Doctor Binti Musa has explained...

USING THE NAME OF THE PERSON BEING QUOTED

Giving the full name of the person or persons you are citing—and referring to them formally by last name or appropriate pronoun in following sentences—is a convention in formal writing. It is a way of acknowledging that ideas are always connected to thinkers.

The sports historian James Riordan suggests that after the revolutionary stirrings of 1905, factory owners introduced soccer to their workers "as an attempt to encourage a form of civil loyalty and to divert their employees from revolutionary and other disruptive actions."

SIGNALLING THAT YOU ARE QUOTING: CHOOSING AN INTRODUCTORY VERB AND WEAVING IN THE WORDS OF OTHERS

It is a convention to introduce others' words with phrases that

• signal to readers that you are about to quote.

• weave the quoted words into your writing so that they fit the structure of your own words.

CHOOSING SIGNALLING VERBS

You can choose among many verbs to signal to readers that they are about to read the words of others; we list many of them to the right.

Note, however, that the verb you choose not only signals that you are about to quote the words of someone; your verb choice can also signal to

readers your position about the words you are quoting. Consider these examples, looking at how they ask you to think about what Paulk says.

In his article about interior design in the computer game *The Sims*, Charles Paulk says that the Sims are "hard-wired social climbers" (n.p.).

In his article about interior design in the computer game *The Sims*, Charles Paulk charges that the Sims are "hard-wired social climbers" (n.p.).

In his article about interior design in the computer game *The Sims*, Charles Paulk complains that the Sims are "hard-wired social climbers" (n.p.).

Signalling verbs

acknowledges	*adds*	*admits*
advises	*agrees*	*analyzes*
answers	*argues*	*asks*
asserts	*believes*	*charges*
claims	*comments*	*complains*
concedes	*concludes*	*concurs*
condemns	*confirms*	*considers*
contends	*criticizes*	*declares*
denies	*describes*	*disagrees*
disputes	*emphasizes*	*explains*
expresses	*finds*	*holds*
illustrates	*implies*	*insists*
interprets	*lists*	*maintains*
notes	*objects*	*observes*
offers	*opposes*	*points out*
predicts	*proposes*	*refutes*
rejects	*remarks*	*replies*
reports	*responds*	*reveals*
says	*shows*	*speculates*
states	*suggests*	*thinks*

WEAVING QUOTED WORDS INTO YOUR WRITING

Anytime you quote, watch that:

- Your own words weave together with the quoted words to make a sentence that is **logical**.

"Poverty is more than a problem of economics," Farah claims, because it is also a public health problem.

The words that follow the quotation do not explain why Farah thinks poverty is a public health problem. Here is a fix:

"Poverty is more than a problem of economics," Farah claims, because it can adversely affect how the brain functions and so effect what people are capable of doing.

- Your own words weave together with the quoted words to make a sentence that is **grammatical**.

If poverty can "literally damage our brains," as Farah asserts, then it "directly affecting the biological substrate of who we are and what we can become."

Because the verb forms used above are inconsistent, the sentence is ungrammatical. Here is a fix:

If poverty can "damage our brains," as Farah asserts, then it damages also "the biological substrate of who we are and what we can become."

QUOTING, SUMMARIZING, AND PARAPHRASING

SUMMARIZING THE WORDS OF OTHERS

A summary condenses the main points of someone else's words and ideas. When you summarize, you leave out illustrations, examples, and details not necessary for your arguments: Go for the main points.

Here is a summary of the journal article excerpted on page 315:

In an article in *Language Learning & Technology*, Ravi Purushotma argues that the addictive qualities of massively multiplayer online computer games make them highly appropriate for engaging adolescents in learning a second language.

Notice that this summary:

• Is much shorter than the original.

• Tells whose ideas are being summarized.

• Indicates where this information was found.

• Focuses on the excerpt's main point, drawing on information from throughout the excerpt.

Notice what this summary **does not** do:

• The summary's words do not repeat the exact words used in the excerpt (although it is fine to use a short quotation in a summary).

• The summary does not include any statistics, facts, or commentary from the article (although you might include such information in following sentences or paragraphs if it were necessary to support your own developing arguments).

AVOIDING PLAGIARISM IN SUMMARIES

This summary—

To appeal to the motivation of adolescents, Ravi Purushotma argues, language teachers should take advantage of the phenomenal ability of computer games to capture adolescent attention (86).

—takes most of its words and phrases directly from the original article; even though the author of the article is named and a page number is given, this is still plagiarism. Here is a revision, another possible summary, that does not plagiarize:

To appeal to adolescents, Ravi Purushotma argues, language teachers can draw on "the phenomenal ability" of computer games to appeal to such audiences (86).

Notice that the words taken directly from the excerpt have quotation marks around them and the page number is cited. Synonyms have been used in place of the original authors' words, to avoid any possibility of accidentally plagiarizing their words.

→ See pages 350–359 for how to cite pages in MLA style, pages 421–425 for APA style, page 453 for CSE style, and pages 458–459 for CMS style.

TIP: HOW TO SUMMARIZE TO AVOID PLAGIARISM

- Read several times the piece you want to summarize, jotting down the ideas and points that stick out for you—using your own words. (Use a thesaurus to look up synonyms for important terms.)
- Without looking at the piece, try to say out loud what you think the main point of the piece is. (This is easier to do if you can say it out loud to someone else.)
- Write down what you said, and check it against the piece to be sure you are accurate.

TIP: SUMMARIZING WELL

- A summary should always be considerably shorter than the original.
- Weave summaries into your writing using the same sorts of introductory phrases and strategies you use with quotations. (→ See pages 320–321.)
- Use the same sorts of strategies for alerting readers to the authority of the authors of the piece you are summarizing as you use for quotations. (→ See pages 319–320.)
- A summary should be truthful to the ideas of the piece being summarized and focus on main points instead of details, facts, and examples.

PARAPHRASING THE WORDS OF OTHERS

A paraphrase is about as long as the original passage, but it is a restatement of the original in your own words. You paraphrase when you do not want to quote someone else's words, perhaps because you already have used many quotations or because the original words are not memorable or need modification so that your audience will understand them.

Here is a passage from the journal article excerpted on page 315:

Besides merging international editions to form bilingual versions, another almost effortless modification game designers could make to interest language learners would be to create incentives and ways in which players could find and partner with native speakers of their L2 trying to learn their L1. This would not only provide the above-mentioned benefits of playing a bilingual game, but also provide learners with an L2 native from whom to learn about culture and language while performing a series of entertaining tasks requiring communicative exchanges.

Here is a paraphrase of the passage:

Purushotma suggests that if game designers want to make their software more useful to adolescent language learners, they could design games that encourage the language learners to play alongside and talk with native speakers of the language being learned; in the process of solving game tasks together, the language learners would also learn about culture from a native.

Notice that this paraphrase:

- Retells in new words all the points of the passage's sentences.
- Makes the passage more accessible to a nonspecialist audience, often a reason for paraphrasing.
- Is more detailed than a summary would be: Summaries tend to be about whole arguments; paraphrases are usually of parts of arguments.

AVOIDING PLAGIARISM IN PARAPHRASES

This summary—

Purushotma argues that the extreme success of some massively multiplayer online games should interest anyone trying to get the attention of adolescents: In contrast to high school language teachers trying to get their students to do half an hour of homework, computer games have been so successful at attracting teenagers for long periods of time that some governments are trying to control their use.

—is plagiarism because:

- It repeats, overall, the grammatical and sentence structures of the original; it also repeats the order of the sentences.
- It simply removes a few words from the original, rearranges a few others, and replaces some words with synonyms.

TIP: HOW TO PARAPHRASE TO AVOID PLAGIARISM

- Read several times the passage you want to paraphrase.
- On a piece of paper, break the passage up into its parts: What are the main points of the passage?
- Without looking at the passage or your notes, write down what you understand the passage to be communicating.
- Check your writing against the original to be sure you have the main ideas and have not inadvertently used the same words and structures in the original.

TIP: PARAPHRASING WELL

- A paraphrase is usually shorter than the original.
- Weave paraphrases into your writing using the same sorts of introductory phrases and strategies you use with quotations. (→ See pages 320–321.)
- Use the same sorts of strategies for alerting readers to the authority of the authors of the piece you are paraphrasing as you use for quotations. (→ See pages 319–320.)
- The point of a paraphrase is to present the ideas of another as you think that writer wants others to understand them—so don't offer your interpretation or any comments until after you have finished a full and honest paraphrase.

There are five kinds of
SOURCES and each requires different citation information.

1

PRINTED BOOKS

For the purposes of academic documentation, the category of printed books includes the following:

- edited collections and anthologies
- novels
- graphic novels
- computer documentation and software instructions bound like books
- conference proceedings
- textbooks and handbooks

→ See pages 328–331 to learn what you need to find for documenting books.

2

PARTS OF PRINTED BOOKS

If you are summarizing, paraphrasing, or quoting from any of the following—

- an essay in a book that contains essays written by different authors (and this could include one story in a collection of graphic stories, for example)
- a single chapter in a book that is written by the same author as the book
- an article in a reference collection
- one poem in a collection of one author's poems
- one poem in a collection of many authors' poems
- the preface, introduction, foreword, or afterword in a book

—then you need to find the same information you would find for the book in which you found the part you are citing, as well as additional information.

→ See pages 332–335 to learn what additional information to find to cite a part of a book.

3

PRINT PERIODICALS

Periodicals are printed regularly: every day, every week, every month, four times a year, or on some other schedule. Every issue of a periodical has the same name and similar formatting.

If you are summarizing, paraphrasing, or quoting from any of the following print materials—

- a newspaper or newsletter
- a letter to the editor
- an editorial
- a popular journal, such as a magazine published once a month or even weekly
- an academic journal
- an article on microfilm
- a government booklet, pamphlet, or brochure
- a comic book that is published in a series

—then you are working with a periodical.

→ See pages 336–341 to learn what information to find in order to cite print periodicals.

4

WEBPAGES

If you are documenting an article in an online database,

→ See pages 346–347 to learn what information to find to create a citation.

For documenting any other kind of webpage,

→ See pages 342–345 to learn what information to find to create a citation.

→ To determine the kind of webpage you are using, see pages 50–59.

5

EVERYTHING ELSE...

If you wish to cite a source other than the four kinds listed here,

→ See pages 348–349.

COLLECTING CITATION INFORMATION FROM PRINTED BOOKS

Most often, you find a book's citation information in two places:

- On the Title page, which is usually the second or third page of a book and has the title, the author's name, and the name and location of the publisher.

- On the Copyright page, which usually is the back of the Title page. (In some books, this information is on the very last page.)

No matter what citation style you use, record the five pieces of information described on the next page, some of which you will use for in-text citations and all of which you will use for the works cited section of your paper. All the styles require this same information; they just use it differently.

YOU MIGHT ALSO NEED...

→ See pages 395–397 for the additional information you need for dissertations, translations, multiple-volume series, and second (or later) editions.

→ See pages 332–335 for the additional information you need if the book you are using is a collection of essays or articles written by different authors; a chapter in a reference work; a poem in an anthology.

Girls Make Media

Mary Celeste Kearney

Routledge
Taylor & Francis Group
New York · London

Routledge is an imprint of
Taylor & Francis Group, an informa business

Title page

Published in 2006 by
Routledge
Taylor & Francis Group
270 Madison Avenue
New York, NY 10016

Published in Great Britain by
Routledge
Taylor & Francis Group
2 Park Square
Milton Park, Abingdon
Oxton OX14 4RN

© 2006 by Taylor & Francis Group, LLC
Routledge is an imprint of Taylor & Francis Group

Printed in the United States of America on acid-free paper
10 9 8 7 6 5 4 3 2 1

International Standard Book Number-10: 0-415-97278-7 (Softcover)
International Standard Book Number- 13: 978-0-415-97278-9 (Softcover)
Library of Congress Card Number 2005029586

No Part of this book may be reprinted, reproduced, transmitted, or utilized in any form
by electronic, mechanical, or other means, now known or hereafter invented, including
photocopying, microfilming, and recording, or in any information storage or retrieval
system, without written permission from the publishers.

Trademark Notice: Product or corporate names may be trademarks or registered
trademarks, and are used only for identification without intent to infringe.

Library of Congress Cataloging-in-Publication Data

Copyright page (detail)

BOOK'S TITLE

Record the book's title exactly as it appears on the Title page of the book, including punctuation (also record the subtitle if there is one). If the book's title is not in English, copy it exactly, including any punctuation.

AUTHOR'S NAME

Record the author's name exactly as it appears on the Title page of the book.

→ See pages 330–331 for what to record in cases of no or multiple authors, if a company or organization is listed, or if the author is described as an editor.

PUBLISHER'S NAME

Record the publisher's name exactly as it appears on either the Title or the Copyright page. (For the sample to the left, you would record *Routledge*; the other corporate information is not used in citations.)

PLACE OF PUBLICATION

Record the city and state, or the city and country if the book was not published in the United States. If you cannot find a place of publication, make a note of this. If more than one place is listed, use the first.

DATE OF PUBLICATION

Record the year listed on the Copyright page (sometimes it is also on the Title page). If no year is listed, record that there is no date. Record the latest date if more than one is listed.

COLLECTING CITATION
INFORMATION FROM PRINTED
BOOKS

WHAT TO DO WHEN THERE IS NO SINGLE PERSON LISTED AS AUTHOR

❏ **If you cannot find an author's name,** make a note of this.

❏ **If there is not a person's name but instead the name of a government organization,** record the information exactly as it appears.

❏ **If there are two or three author names listed,** record them all exactly as they appear, in the order they appear. For the example below, you would record, *Bowker, Geoffrey C., and Susan Leigh Star*.

> *Sorting Things Out*
> *Classification and Its Consequences*
>
>
> Geoffrey C. Bowker
> Susan Leigh Star

❏ **If there are more than three authors**

→ See pages 375–376 to record this information in the MLA format.

→ See pages 433–434 to record this information in the APA format.

→ See page 456 to record this information in the CSE format.

→ See page 461 to record this information in the CMS format.

Images of an Era: the American Poster 1945-75

National Collection of Fine Arts   Smithsonian Institution   Washington, D.C. 1975
Distrubuted by The MIT Press   Cambridge, Massachusetts   London, England

☐ **If no person's name is listed but there is instead the name of an organization or business,** you have what is called a **corporate author.** Record the name exactly as it appears on the Title page. For example, for the book above, you would record and cite "National Collection of Fine Arts."

Aesthetic Computing

edited by Paul Fishwick

☐ **If the person listed on the Title page is described as an editor** (as on the left), record the person's name and that the person is the editor. (If more than one person is listed, record the names just as you would record multiple authors' names, as described on page 330.)

THE ELEMENTS OF STYLE

by
WILLIAM STRUNK, JR.

With Revisions, an Introduction, and a New Chapter on Writing

by E. B. WHITE

☐ **If the book has an author listed as well as the name of someone who revised that person's work** (as to the left), record the name of the author as well as the name of the person who revised the book, indicating that the second person did a revision.

COLLECTING CITATION INFORMATION WHEN YOU ARE CITING PART OF A PRINTED BOOK

When you are citing a part of a book—

- a poem in an anthology
- one essay or article from an edited collection of essays or articles
- a chapter in a reference work
- the preface, foreword, introduction, or afterword to a book

—collect the same information you would for a book, as shown on pages 328–331, as well as the following:

❑ The name of the person(s) who wrote it

❑ Its title

❑ Its page number(s)

On the following pages we show you where to find this information.

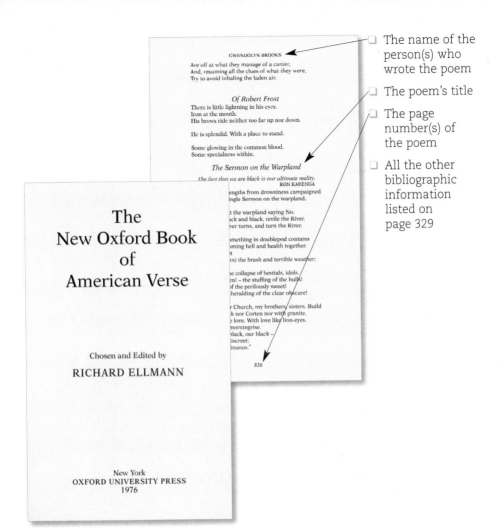

The name of the person(s) who wrote the poem

The poem's title

The page number(s) of the poem

All the other bibliographic information listed on page 329

GWENDOLYN BROOKS

Are off at what they manage of a canter,
And, resuming all the clues of what they were,
Try to avoid inhaling the laden air.

Of Robert Frost

There is little lightning in his eyes.
Iron at the mouth.
His brows ride neither too far up nor down.

He is splendid. With a place to stand.

Some glowing in the common blood.
Some specialness within.

The Sermon on the Warpland

The fact that we are black is our ultimate reality.
RON KARENGA

engths from drowsiness campaigned
ingle Sermon on the warpland.

t the warpland saying No.
ack and black, revile the River.
ver turns, and turn the River.

omething in doublepod contains
oming hell and health together.
t
rs) the brash and terrible weather;

e collapse of bestials, idols.
en! – the stuffing of the hulk!
f the perilously sweet!
heralding of the clear obscure!

r Church, my brothers/sisters. Build
k nor Corten nor with granite.
e love. With love like lion-eyes.
morningrise.
black, our black –
iscreet:
inuous."

826

The
New Oxford Book
of
American Verse

Chosen and Edited by

RICHARD ELLMANN

New York
OXFORD UNIVERSITY PRESS
1976

A POEM IN AN ANTHOLOGY

For the poem on the page above, you would record:

Brooks, Gwendolyn. "The Sermon on the Warpland." *The New Oxford Book of American Verse*. Edited by Richard Ellmann. New York: Oxford UP, 1976. p. 826

(Note that this is not the final format for a works cited page.)

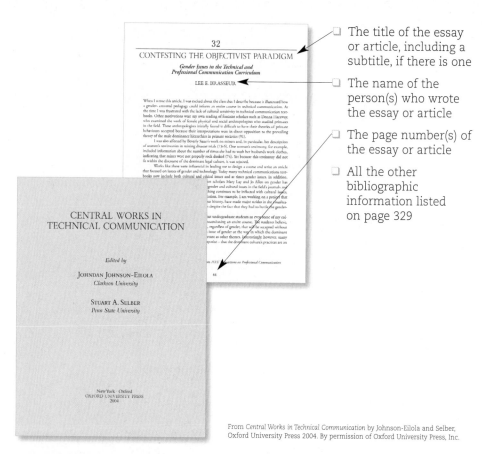

The title of the essay or article, including a subtitle, if there is one

The name of the person(s) who wrote the essay or article

The page number(s) of the essay or article

All the other bibliographic information listed on page 329

From *Central Works in Technical Communication* by Johnson-Eilola and Selber, Oxford University Press 2004. By permission of Oxford University Press, Inc.

ONE ESSAY OR ARTICLE IN AN EDITED COLLECTION OF ESSAYS OR ARTICLES

For the Introduction shown above you would record:

Brasseur, Lee E. "Contesting the Objectivist Paradigm: Gender Issues in the Technical and Professional Communication Curriculum." *Central Works in Technical Communication*. Editors Johndan Johnson-Eilola and Stuart A. Selber. New York: Oxford UP, 2004. pp. 64-x.

(Note that we had to find some of this information on other pages in this book, and that this is not the final format for a works cited page.)

Literacy

In common usage, *literacy* and rhetoric... illuminates the ways that individual acts of writing are connected to larger cultural, historical, social, and political systems. Serving this broadened perspective, interest in literacy has grown as part of a general focus on the social contexts and social ideologies of written language use. Neighbouring fields that research literacy, particularly anthropology, psychology, history, and critical education, have helped to enrich writing research, both theoretically and empirically.

By the time Modern Language Association sponsored the first Right to Literacy Conference at Ohio State University in 1988, literacy studies had become an appealing rubric for a wide range of concerns and interests in the field of composition and rhetoric. The term is useful for conceptualizing underlying language abilities that may be common to both reading and writing. It is also useful for identifying pedagogical interests that may be common to teachers of both composition and literature (as well as English teachers in all settings).

Relationships between the oral and the written and their implications for cultural and cognitive development organize many of the key debates among scholars of literacy in anthropology and psychology. In 1968 anthropologist Jack Goody and literary scholar Ian Watt published the influential essay "The Consequences of Literacy." The essay argues that when the Greeks invented a phonetic alphabet, they underwent a transformation from mythical to logical thinking. According to Goody and Watt, thinking in oral societies is concrete, associative, formulaic, synthetic, and conformist, tied always to the present tense. But because the technology of writing allows language and thought to be represented and preserved separately from lived experience, literate thinking can become conceptual, objective, analytical, sceptical, logical, and idiosyncratic, capable of representing both past and future. In Goody's and Watt's view, the epitome of literate thinking is the syllogism, an impersonal mode of thinking not tied to common sense or ordinary experience. Goody and Watt go on to argue that the technology of literacy enabled a host of other social and intellectual innovations, including even democracy.

Walter Ong argues a similar case for the dramatic cognitive and social consequences of literacy. Ong's works are concerned with how writing and...

(main body columns continue — reproduced encyclopedia pages, partially legible)

Deborah Brandt
University of Wisconsin, Madison

392 LITERACY

LITERACY 393

Encyclopedia of Rhetoric and Composition

Communication form Ancient Times to the Information Age

Edited by
Theresa Enos

GARLAND PUBLISHING, INC.
New York & London
1996

❑ The title of the chapter, including a subtitle if there is one

❑ The name of the person(s) who wrote the essay or article. Note that, as in this example, the name of the author in reference works can come at the end of the chapter; sometimes you will find only the initials of the person at the end of the chapter and will have to find the full name listed elsewhere in the book (usually at the very front or back).

❑ The starting and ending page number(s) of the chapter

❑ All the other bibliographic information listed on page 329

A CHAPTER IN A REFERENCE WORK

For the reference work entry shown here, you would record:

Brandt, Deborah. "Literacy."
<u>Encyclopedia of Rhetoric and Composition</u>. Editor Theresa Enos. New York: Garland Publishing, 1996. pp. 392–393.

(Note that this is not the final format for a works cited page.)

COLLECTING CITATION INFORMATION WHEN YOU ARE CITING PRINTED PERIODICALS

The six pieces of information listed to the right are used by every citation style, with some minor shifts.

IF YOU ARE WORKING WITH THE FOLLOWING…

you will need to record some additional or different information:

❑ if you are citing a letter to the editor, an editorial, a published interview, a review (of a book, movie, CD, performance, or anything else), or a microfilm, **record the kind of publication** (that is, along with all the other information listed to the right, record *letter to the editor* or *review*).

❑ a daily newspaper; see page 338.

❑ a periodical that is published every week or every other week; see page 339.

❑ a periodical that is published every month or once a season; see page 340.

❑ an article whose pages are numbered by volume, not by issue; see page 341.

❑ an article that does not have sequential page numbering; see page 341.

→ See pages 48–49 for descriptions of different kinds of periodicals and how they can be useful for different projects.

→ What do *volume*, *issue*, and *number* mean? See page 341.

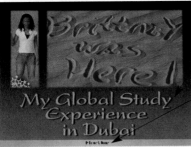

TITLE OF ARTICLE
Record the title exactly as appears. If the title is not in English, copy it exactly, including the punctuation.

AUTHOR'S NAME
Record this exactly as it appears. In some periodicals, the author's name is at the end of the writing.

PERIODICAL NAME
Record the name exactly as it appears on the periodical's Table of Contents or in the header or footer.

PAGE NUMBERS
Record the page numbers for all the pages, even if the article is not on sequential pages. The example to the left is on pages 62–63, but you might have an article that goes from pages 72–75 and from 120–123; record all the pages.

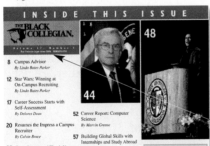

DATE OF PUBLICATION
Record the exact date: It may be a month and year, two months, or a specific day. The date can appear in a page header or footer, but it is always on the Table of Contents. In this example, the date is *2006*.

VOLUME AND ISSUE NUMBER
Record the volume and issue number from the Table of Contents. Sometimes this information is at the top of the page, but it might be at the bottom or on a second page. Look carefully—but know that some periodicals do not include this information. Record what you can find.

A DAILY NEWSPAPER

Daily newspapers do not have volume and issue numbers; instead, they have dates. They also often have sections labeled by letters of the alphabet, so that page numbers might be **A12** or **J3** instead of simply **12** or **3**.

When you record citation information for a daily newspaper, record the same information as for any other periodical article (as shown on page 337), but record the full date (day, month, and year) listed and the section letter for the pages.

In addition, if what you are citing is a letter to the editor or an editorial, record that information.

For the letter to the editor shown below, here is what you would record:

Vocke, Timothy L. "Sheboygan Judge Did
    the Right Thing." Letter to the Editor.
    <u>Milwaukee Journal Sentinel</u>. 23
    September 2007. page 5J.

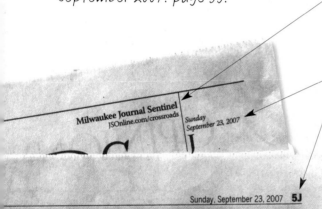

❑ Newspaper name; if a local (not national) newspaper does not include the city name in its title, record the city name as well.

❑ Date (day, month, and year)

❑ Page number(s), including any letters that designate the section of the newspaper. If the article is on multiple pages, record all of its pages, even if they are not sequential.

A PERIODICAL THAT IS PUBLISHED EVERY WEEK OR EVERY OTHER WEEK

Different citation styles require different information for periodicals that are published every week or every other week. To be sure that you will have the information you need, record every item listed for periodical articles (as shown on page 337) when you are citing a periodical that is published every week or every other week. When you create your citations, you may or may not need what you have recorded, but you will be prepared if you have recorded everything.

For the article shown below, here is what you would record:

Barry, Patrick. "Curry Powder: An Age-Old Seasoning Could Help Combat Alzheimer's." <u>Science News</u>. Volume 172, Number 11, 15 September 2007. pages 167–168.

❑ Date (day, month, and year)

❑ Volume and issue numbers

❑ Page number(s). If the article is on multiple pages, record all of its pages, even if they are not sequential.

SEPTEMBER 15, 2007   PAGES 161-176   VOL. 172, NO. 11

the stem of consciousness

...ing antimatter

SCIENCE NEWS

THE WEEKLY NEWSMAGAZINE OF S...

CURRY POWER

An age-old seasoning could help combat A...

BY PATRICK BARRY

magine that you're living 3,000 years ago in a village in what's now southern India. When you get sick or injured, you visit the healer, who most likely is a practitioner of the herbal medicine called ayurveda. For whatever ails you, you'll probably get a treatment that includes a bit of bright, yellow-orange powder, the spice turmeric.

If you have a scrape, the healer will put turmeric on it. Indigestion? Turmeric. Jaundice? Turmeric. "Nervous weakness"? That's right—turmeric.

Alzheimer's disease involves in the brain, leading to dement ease arises when a small protein called plaques. In this scenario by triggering inflammation, a activity that can damage the b duce free radicals, which caus

"We looked at [curcumin] thing which is anti-inflamm curcumin was also a better said, 'This thing has got all t test it,'" against Alzheimer's

Those experiments and have shown that, in additio

A PERIODICAL THAT IS PUBLISHED EVERY MONTH OR ONCE A SEASON

Different citation styles use different citation information for periodicals that are published every month or seasonally, so to be safe, record every item listed for periodical articles (as shown on page 337).

For the book review shown below, here is what you would record:

Kunkel, Benjamin. "Last Things: The Sinister Charm of Frederick Seidel." A review of Seidel's book <u>Ooga-Booga</u>. <u>Harper's</u>. Volume 315, Number 1888, September 2007. pages 92–96, 98.

❑ Date (month and year)

❑ Volume and issue numbers

❑ Page number(s). If the article is on multiple pages, record all of its pages, even if they are not sequential.

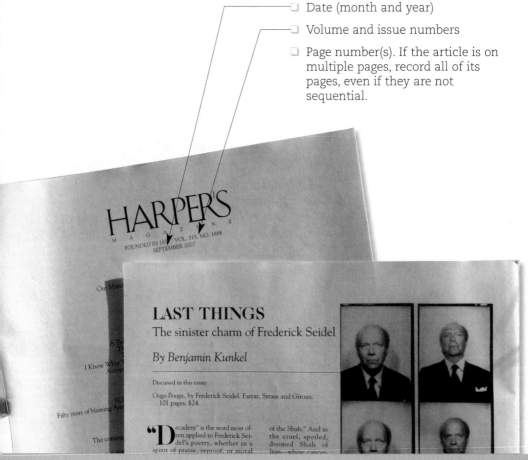

AN ARTICLE WHOSE PAGES ARE NUMBERED BY VOLUME INSTEAD OF ISSUE

Some journals start each new issue with a page numbered **1**. Some start the volume that way and do not change the page numbering throughout the whole volume: For example, if volume 25, issue 1, starts at page 1, and issue 1 has 176 pages, issue 2 will start on page 177.

When you are citing an article whose pages are numbered by volume, you need to record only the volume number, the date, and the page numbers of the article you are citing; you do **not** need to record the issue number. Readers will be able to find the article based simply on the volume number, date, and page numbering.

AN ARTICLE THAT DOES NOT HAVE SEQUENTIAL PAGE NUMBERING

In many magazines and newspapers, articles will start on one page of the periodical and then be interrupted by another article; the original article will start up again after several pages or in the back of the periodical.

Different citation styles record nonsequential page numbering differently. To be well prepared for composing your bibliography, record all the pages on which the article appears.

For example, in a newspaper you might record:

B3, B5

In a magazine, you might record:

32–35, 62–65.

WHAT DO "VOLUME," "ISSUE," AND "NUMBER" MEAN?

An **issue** is probably what comes to your mind when you hear **magazine** or **journal**: It is the paper-bound collection of articles that comes out once a week, once a month, or seasonally.

Often, after a year, an organization that publishes magazines or journals will bind together all the issues published in that year. The bound-together set of issues is the **volume**.

When you look at the Table of Contents page of a magazine or journal and see Volume 25, Issue 8, what that means is that the periodical has been published for 25 years, and that you are looking at the eighth issue published in that year.

Sometimes, instead of **issue**, you'll see **number**: This is just another way of referring to **issue**.

COLLECTING CITATION INFORMATION WHEN YOU ARE CITING WEBPAGES

For the purposes of citation, there are two kinds of websites:

• Databases of journals

• All others

We start with **all others** because it requires collecting less information than when you cite an article you found through an online database.

→ To determine the kind of webpage you are using, see pages 50–59.

ALL WEBPAGES EXCEPT THOSE FROM DATABASES

To the right we list the seven pieces of information you should try to collect for most webpages you cite. Because webpages can be so different, on the two following pages we show some examples of what to do when you can't find all seven pieces of information.

For the website shown to the right, here is a way to record the information you would collect; what we show is not the final format for a citation, but will help you keep track of a website in a running list.

Zinn, Lennard. "Tech Talk: Real Bikes for Real People." VeloNews. 3 Oct. 2006. Inside Communications. 5 June 2007. <http://www.velonews.com/tech/report/articles/10960.0.html>.

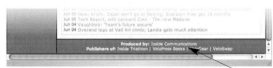

URL
Record the whole URL.

WEBSITE NAME
If there is a name for the overall webpage or web-site, record it exactly.

TITLE OF ARTICLE YOU ARE CITING/ TITLE OF WEBPAGE
Record the title exactly as it appears on the webpage, with its punctuation.

AUTHOR'S NAME
Record this exactly.

PUBLICATION DATE
This can be near the author's name, at the end of the text you are citing, or at the bottom of the page. If you find only a year, record that. If you find nothing, note that, too.

SPONSORING ORGANIZATION
If there is a company or organization that spon-sors the information on the page, copy the name exactly. If this informa-tion is not obvious at the top of the page, look at the bottom of the page.

DATE ACCESSED
Record the date on which you visited the webpage. If readers visit later, they can then see if the infor-mation has changed.

TIP: LOOK EVERYWHERE!
The information listed to the right could be anywhere on a webpage. If some of this information is not included on a webpage, leave it out of your final citation.

INDIVIDUAL'S WEBSITE OR BLOG

Sometimes a personal website or blog will have a sponsoring organization, but often it won't, as with the website above. Note that the website does have a name, different from the entry, and that you can find the writer's name (at both top and side) and that the date is given in European format, with the day of the week coming before the month. Here is what you would record:

Rettberg, Jill Walker. "The Swedish Minister for Foreign Affairs Blogs Differently to U.S. Politicians." jill/txt. 5 May 2007. 27 May 2007 <http://jilltxt.net/?p=2026>.

GOVERNMENT WEBSITE

This website gives no date; in such cases, it is a good idea to note that the date you record for accessing the site is the access date, as shown below.

"How do I register as a candidate for federal office?" U.S. Federal Election Commission. Accessed 10 Nov. 2007. <http://www.fec.gov/ans/answers_candidate.shtml#register>.

NONPROFIT ORGANIZATION

This webpage does not give an individual writer for the article being cited, and the sponsoring organization is the same as the website name, so record the following:

"Automakers Summer Prescription for American Drivers." Union of Concerned Scientists. 24 May 2007. 26 June 2007. <http:// www.ucsusa.org/news/ press_release/automakers- summer-0034.html>.

ONLINE PERIODICAL

Here is what you record for an article like the above, where the website and the sponsoring organization are the same:

Miller, Laura. "Panic in the Pages." Rev. of The Ten-Cent Plague, by David Hajdu. Salon.com. 25 Mar. 2008. 15 May 2008 <http:// www.salon.com/books/ review/2008/03/24/hajdu/>.

CITATION INFORMATION FOR DATABASES OF JOURNALS

Because it is often easier and more convenient to find relevant and credible journal articles through online databases than through print searches, more and more researchers are having to learn how to cite these sources.

When you cite an article that you found through an online database, you need to collect the same information you would for a print article—but you also need to collect information about the database, as we show on the next page.

→ See pages 64–71 to learn how to use online databases.

First, collect the same information as you would for a print article; this will usually be in one place on the page, as in the example to the right.

- ❏ **THE NAME(S) OF THE AUTHOR(S)**
- ❏ **THE TITLE OF THE ARTICLE**
- ❏ **THE NAME OF THE PERIODICAL**
- ❏ **THE PUBLICATION DATE**
- ❏ **THE VOLUME AND ISSUE NUMBERS**
- ❏ **THE ARTICLE'S PAGE NUMBERS**

—but note that some databases will give you the article as a pdf and some will not. *When the article is a pdf,* the page numbers will be the same anywhere, and so you can copy the page numbers exactly as they are given. *When the article is **not** a pdf,* like the example to the right, copy only the first page number, however it is presented. (The *p50(16)* in the information to the right means that the article starts on page 50 in the journal, and is 16 pages long.)

For the article shown on the right, you would record what is shown below.

Schultz, Ulrike, Asia Maccawi, and Tayseer El-Fatih. "The credit helps me to improve my business: The experiences of two microcredit programs in greater Khartoum." Ahfad Journal 23.1 (June 2006): 50. subscription service: Thomson Gale. database: InfoTrac OneFile. Michigan Technological University. 5 June 2007.

Then, collect information about the database and your use of it:

☐ **THE NAME OF THE SUBSCRIPTION SERVICE**
This is the name of the service you used to search for the database. The name will usually be on the webpage you click to access the full-text article, but if not, you need to keep track of which service you used. (It is a good idea to record which is the subscription service and which is the database name so that you can keep them straight.)

☐ **THE NAME OF THE DATABASE**
This is usually at the top left of the webpage.

☐ **LIBRARY NAME**
This is the name of the library where you accessed the database.

☐ **THE URL OF THE DATABASE**
Record the URL for the database, not the URL for the article you are citing.

COLLECTING CITATION INFORMATION FOR OTHER KINDS OF SOURCES

Any time you hear or see someone else's ideas and those ideas can support an argument you are making, you can use those ideas as a source—but you have to cite the source.

Because there are so many possible places you can find the ideas of others, it is impossible to list every possible kind of citation. Instead, collect as much information as you can as that listed in the pattern below.

THE PATTERN

Collect as much of the following information as you can:

- ❏ **NAME(S) OF AUTHOR(S) OR COMPOSER(S)**

- ❏ **THE NAME OF THE SOURCE YOU ARE CITING**

- ❏ **THE KIND OF SOURCE**

- ❏ **WHO IS RESPONSIBLE FOR THE PUBLICATION**
  If there is a company or organization that supported the publication, record this.

- ❏ **THE PLACE WHERE THE SOURCE WAS PUBLISHED OR PERFORMED**
  Record the city and state—or the URL.

- ❏ **THE DATE THE SOURCE WAS PUBLISHED OR PERFORMED**

- ❏ **PAGE NUMBERS, IF THEY EXIST**

SPECIFIC INFORMATION YOU NEED FOR PARTICULAR KINDS OF TEXTS

For the following kinds of sources, record what is listed in addition to what is in the pattern shown on the left.

FILM OR VIDEO

Record the title; the names of the director, the main actors, or the narrator; the name of the distributor; and the year of release. If it is an online film or video, record the name of the website on which you see the piece, as well as the URL and the date you see the piece.

INTERVIEW YOU CONDUCT

Record the name of the person you interview and the date.

LECTURE

Record the name(s) of the speaker(s), the title of the lecture, and the organization sponsoring the lecture, as well as the location and date. If you see the lecture online, record the name of the website on which you see it, as well as the URL and date you see it.

LEGAL DOCUMENTS

Record the name of the document, its Public Law number, the date it was enacted, and its Statutes at large number.

LIVE PERFORMANCE

Record the title of the work being performed and the name of the artist, author, or composer. Also get as much information as you can about the director, the choreographer, the conductor, and the major performers. If there is a group or company doing the performance, record this as well. Record the name of the theater.

MUSICAL SOUND RECORDING

Record the name of the recording company and the date.

PERSONAL LETTER

Record the name of the person who wrote the letter and the letter's date.

RADIO OR TELEVISION INTERVIEW

Record the name of the person being interviewed and the name of the person doing the interview, as well as the information listed below for a radio or television program.

RADIO OR TELEVISION PROGRAM

Record the name of the particular episode, if there is one, as well as the series title. If there is a host or a writer, get the name. Record the network name, the local station (if there is one), and the date of the broadcast.

■ ■ ■

→ For MLA citation formats for a range of such texts, see pages 398–403.

→ For APA citation formats, see pages 448–449.

→ For CSE citation formats, see pages 455–457.

→ For CMS citation formats, see page 462.

HINTS & TIPS FOR COLLECTING CITATION INFORMATION

COLLECT IT NOW!

If there is any possibility that you might use a source, record its citation information immediately.

Nothing will vex you more than having to try to find a source at the last minute, as you are putting the finishing touches on a paper.

KEEP ALL YOUR SOURCE INFORMATION IN ONE PLACE

Get in the habit of having a notebook or folder or single online document in which you keep track of all your sources.

You want to be able to put together your final, formal list of works cited all at once, and you want to be able to check your in-text citations all at once.

DO COLLECT INFORMATION ABOUT ONLINE SOURCES

Even though you can bookmark webpages and go back to them later, two problems will confront you if you do not collect citation information immediately:

• You have to wade through all your other bookmarks to find the ones you want.

• The information on the page might have changed from when you first visited it.

If you are publishing your paper online, you might think that you do not need to provide a works cited list because you can provide links directly to the webpages you cite. But many readers will still want to see the full list, in one place, of all your citations—and, because websites can change (or disappear), a citation will reference when you saw the site.

IF YOU KNOW THE STYLE EXPECTED FOR YOUR FINAL PAPER, PUT YOUR SOURCES INTO THAT FORMAT RIGHT AWAY

This will save you time when you are finishing your paper.

→ For MLA style, see pages 360–405.

→ For APA style, see pages 426–451.

→ For CSE style, see pages 454–457.

→ For CMS style, see pages 460–462.

KEEP IN MIND THAT YOU MIGHT NOT USE ALL THE SOURCES YOU COLLECT

Until you have the absolute, final version of a paper, you will not know exactly which sources you will need. Sometimes you can become attached to a source, or to all your sources, because of the time and energy you put into researching—but this doesn't mean you will need the source.

Remember that you cite only the sources that you quote, paraphrase, summarize, or otherwise reference in your writing.

MLA DOCUMEN- TATION FOR IN-TEXT CITATIONS

nderstandings between

ple dichotomous opposition. For example

onoclasm—rejection of images—in Marx

argues that images contain more than

by those he labels iconoclasts; instead, he

having a dialectical nature, containing

—as object in the world, as representation

figure—most of all as a Janus-faced emb

tory, and a window beyond it" (*Iconology*

ticular dichotomies Mitchell lists are

The MLA style comes from the Modern Language Association, which is an organization of scholars and teachers of languages and literature. *The MLA Handbook for Writers of Research Papers* is now in its sixth edition, published in 2003. The MLA style is used primarily in English studies, comparative literature, foreign-language, literary criticism, and humanities fields.

PURPOSES OF IN-TEXT CITATIONS

The overall purpose of an in-text citation is to help readers see your cited sources for themselves. People who value the free exchange of ideas—who want to think for themselves—want to trace the sources of your ideas.

In-text citations also help give your writing authority: When readers see that your sources are respected and well established, they are more likely to take your writing seriously.

Stemming from these overall purposes, in-text citations in the MLA style have two more focused purposes:

1 In-text citations are guides to the Works Cited page: By giving authors' names or the title of a reference, they help readers learn from the Works Cited list where you found the words and ideas that you quote, paraphrase, or summarize.

2 By giving a page number, in-text citations also tell readers exactly where in a source to find the words or ideas being referenced.

natural to today's student cohort, there's nothing innate about knowing
how to apply their skills to the processes of democracy.

Although there is nothing innate about such knowledge, David Buckingham ◄——— the quoted
argues that this knowledge is necessary for young people because 'to   person's name
become an active participant in public life necessarily involves making use of
modern media" (5) and eng

technologies provides a "bas
media production in the fut   WORKS CITED
amplification of global econ   Barry, Lynda. "Common Scents." In *One Hundred Demons*. Seattle:
     Sasquatch, 2002.

page number of   Berger, John. *The Success and Failure of Picasso*. London: Penguin, 1965.
the quoted piece

     Buckingham, David. *Media Education: Literacy, Learning, and Contemporary
full information of the ——➤   Culture*. Cambridge, UK: Polity, 2004.
source's publication

     Clark, T. J. *The Painting of Modern Life: Paris in the Art of Manet and His
     Followers*. Rev. ed. Princeton: Princeton UP, 1999.

HOW IN-TEXT CITATIONS FUNCTION

In an in-text citation in the MLA style, as shown above, the writer gives—at a minimum—the name of the person being quoted and the page number from which the quotation comes.

- A reader can use the quoted person's name to find full information about the source's publication in the Works Cited list at the end of the paper.

- The reader can then use the page number from the body of the paper to find the exact passage being cited.

THE BACK-AND-FORTH OF CREATING IN-TEXT CITATIONS

In composing a research paper, you move back and forth between creating in-text citations and a Works Cited list. Here is one way to create these essential parts of a research paper:

- Whenever you weave a citation into your paper, put the basic information for the citation into the body of your writing. → See pages 352–359.

- As soon as you weave a citation into your paper, add the source to the Works Cited list. → See pages 360–420 to learn about MLA Works Cited lists.

- Because you may have to make some adjustments to your in-text citations after your Works Cited page is complete, always leave time to double-check your citations against your Works Cited. You will need to make such adjustments if, for example, you use two or more sources from the same author or use sources by authors who have the same last name. → See pages 404–405 to learn what to do about these conditions.

IN-TEXT CITATIONS IN THE MLA STYLE

Whether you are citing books or electronic sources, in-text citations in the MLA style generally contain:

1

The **name of the author** of the words or ideas being quoted, summarized, or paraphrased.

The author's name can appear within the sentence containing the quoted words, or it can appear within parentheses at the end of the sentence.

2

The **page number(s)** of or some other reference to the words or ideas being cited.

The number of the page from which quoted words come goes at the end of the sentence, in parentheses.

In her article on two nineteenth-century women preachers, Patricia Bizzell argues that "a conjunction between the female sex and moral activism is traditional in Methodism" (379).

One writer on nineteenth-century women preachers argues that "a conjunction between the female sex and moral activism is traditional in Methodism" (Bizzell 379).

PUNCTUATION IN MLA IN-TEXT CITATIONS

- The parentheses that contain page numbers go at the end of the sentence, followed by the punctuation that ends the sentence.
- When you put an author's name in the parentheses with the page number, put a single space between the name and the page number.
- If the words you are quoting run across several pages, cite them like this: (23-25).
- If the words you are quoting are from several nonsequential pages, cite them like this: (45, 76).

VARIATIONS ON THE PATTERN

What if you run into one of the following cases?

→ No author is named for the source. See page 354.

→ There is no page number (for example, you are citing a brochure or a webpage). See page 354.

→ Your Works Cited contains two or more sources by the same author. See page 355.

→ Your Works Cited contains sources by two authors with the same last name. See page 355.

→ The work you are citing has two or three authors. See page 356.

→ The work you are citing has four or more authors. See page 356.

→ The work you are citing has a corporate author or is a government document. See page 357.

　　→ See page 331 for what *corporate author* means.

→ You are quoting words that another writer quoted. See page 357.

→ You are citing part of an edited collection or anthology. See page 357.

→ You are citing an encyclopedia or dictionary. See page 357.

→ Your sentence references a whole source (such as a whole book or webpage). See page 358.

→ Your sentence references two or more sources. See page 358.

→ You are citing a novel. See page 358.

→ You are citing a short story. See page 359.

→ You are citing a sacred text, such as the Bible or Koran. See page 359.

→ You are citing lines from a play. See page 359.

→ You are citing lines from a poem that is divided into parts or that has line numbers. See page 359.

VARIATIONS ON THE PATTERN

NO AUTHOR IS NAMED

If you cannot find a named author, use the title of the work instead:

To "watch the rejects crash and burn" is why we watch American Idol, according to <u>Rolling Stone</u> magazine ("Idol Worship").

→ See page 375 for the corresponding Works Cited listing.

→ If you find the name of a company or government organization as author, see pages 376–377.

THERE IS NO PAGE NUMBER

If you cite a source that has no page number, give a paragraph or part number if there is one; otherwise, give just the name of the author.

The World Health Organization identifies obstetric fistulas as a global problem, estimating that over two million women suffer from them, with 50–100 thousand new cases occurring each year (64).

For the example above, readers will look in the Works Cited for a listing under *World Health Organization.*

→ See page 405 for the corresponding Works Cited listing.

The pamphlet printed to accompany the Museum of Modern Art's exhibit, "The Changing of the Avant-Garde," argues that architecture following World War II was influenced by "Pop culture, the first stirrings of the information age, and the radical politics of the 1960s."

The words preceding the citation make clear that the source is a pamphlet; readers won't expect a page number, and will look in the Works Cited for an entry under *Museum of Modern Art*.

→ See page 376 for the corresponding Works Cited listing.

YOUR WORKS CITED CONTAINS TWO OR MORE SOURCES BY THE SAME AUTHOR

When you use two or more works by the same author, indicate which work you are referencing at any one time, to help your readers. You can do this by giving the name of the work in your sentence or in the in-text citation.

If you give the name in the in-text citation, do not use the complete name of the work cited, to save space; instead, use the title's first main noun. These are citations for the first work cited from one author:

That meat from grass-fed cows is more nutritious than that from corn-fed cows is one of Pollan's arguments in The Omnivore's Dilemma (68).

That meat from cows fed on grass is more nutritious than that from corn-fed cows is just one of the many arguments Pollan makes (Omnivore 68).

Here is how a second work is cited:

By the end of The Botany of Desire, Pollan knows how commercial potatoes are raised and cannot bring himself to eat one given to him as a gift (235).

Because his research shows just what chemicals go into a commercial potato, Pollan cannot bring himself to eat one given to him as a gift (Botany 235).

→ See page 405 for how these two citations appear in the Works Cited listing.

When you put an author's name, the work's title, and a page number into the citation, there is a comma between the author's name and the title, and a space between the title and the page number.

YOUR WORKS CITED CONTAINS SOURCES BY TWO AUTHORS WITH THE SAME LAST NAME

So that readers can find the right citation in your Works Cited list, either use authors' full names in your sentences or use each author's first initial and full last name in the parenthetical citation. (If both authors have the same first initial, use their full first names instead.)

Here are examples from the same paper using authors' full names:

Richard Rorty argues that our under-standing of what knowledge is has changed over two hundred years: We ought no longer to think of our minds as "mirrors" that directly and only reflect what is already in the world.

Amélie Oksenberg Rorty shows how Aristotle's Rhetoric brings together understandings of situations in which people communicate, the psychology of audiences, the character of communicators, the structures of communication, and politics.

Here are examples that avoid ambiguity through their parenthetical citations:

Some philosophers argue that our understanding of what knowledge is has changed over the last two hundred years: We ought no longer to think of our minds as "mirrors" that directly and only reflect what is already in the world (R. Rorty).

Aristotle's <u>Rhetoric</u> brings together understandings of situations in which people communicate, the psychology of audiences, the character of communicators, the structures of communication, and politics (A. Rorty).

→ See page 405 for how these two citations appear in the Works Cited listing.

THE WORK YOU ARE CITING HAS TWO OR THREE AUTHORS

List the names in the same order as they are given in the source.

For two names, use *and* between the names, whether you use the names in your sentence or in parentheses at the end of a sentence:

As "much an activist as an analytical method" is how Moeller and Moberly, in an online review, describe McAllister's approach to computer games.

As "much an activist as an analytical method" is how two online reviewers describe McAllister's approach to computer games (Moeller and Moberly).

→ See page 375 for the corresponding Works Cited listing.

With three names, put commas between the names:

DeVoss, Cushman, and Grabill draw our attention to "the institutional and political arrangements" that make new media compositions possible (16).

A recent article draws our attention to "the institutional and political arrangements" that make new media compositions possible (DeVoss, Cushman, and Grabill 16).

→ See page 375 for the corresponding Works Cited listing.

THE WORK YOU ARE CITING HAS FOUR OR MORE AUTHORS

If the work you cite has four or more authors, you can list each author's name (following the same guidelines as for two or three authors). You can also use only the first author's name, followed by the expression *et al. Et al.* is Latin for *and others*. When you use *et al.*, put a period after *al*.

What happens when a ninth-grade World Literatures class is offered at the high honors level for all students, without tracking? Fine, Anand, Jordan, and Sherman offer a two-year study of such a class in "Before the Bleach Gets Us All."

What happens when a ninth-grade World Literatures class is offered at the high honors level for all students, without tracking? Fine et al. offer a two-year study of such a class in "Before the Bleach Gets Us All."

When a ninth-grade World Literatures class is offered at the high honors level for everyone, without tracking, students "who never expected to be seen as smart" come to see themselves as capable and sharp, and "questions of power are engaged" (Fine et al. 174, 175).

→ See page 376 for the corresponding Works Cited listing.

THE WORK YOU ARE CITING HAS A CORPORATE AUTHOR OR IS A GOVERNMENT DOCUMENT

Use the name of the corporation or government office in full, unless there is a common shortened form of it. (If the name is long, including it in the sentence will read less awkwardly than including it within the parentheses.)

In a pamphlet published by the U.S. Dept. of the Interior, the Keweenaw National Historic Park is described as giving a "view of the birth of an industrialized society" in the United States.

Because the writer explains that the quotation comes from a pamphlet, readers will not expect a page number; they will look in the Works Cited for a listing under *United States. Dept. of the Interior.*

→ See page 377 for the corresponding Works Cited listing.

YOU ARE QUOTING WORDS THAT ANOTHER WRITER QUOTED

Use the expression *qtd. in* (for *quoted in*) before the source reference to show where you found the quoted words.

Elizabeth Durack, a blogger, argues that *Star Wars* "and other popular media creations take the place in modern America that culture myths like those of the Greeks or Native Americans did for earlier peoples" (qtd. in Jenkins 153).

Readers will look for the corresponding Works Cited listing under *Jenkins.*

YOU ARE CITING PART OF AN EDITED COLLECTION OR ANTHOLOGY

Use the name of the author who wrote the words you quote, not the name of the collection's editor. For example, if you are citing an article on soap operas by Tania Modleski in a collection on visual culture edited by Amelia Jones, use Modleski in your in-text citations:

Tania Modleski's article "The Search for Tomorrow in Today's Soap Operas" examines the different pleasures women find in soap opera narratives.

One researcher has argued that women find many different pleasures in soap opera narratives (Modleski).

→ See page 375 for the corresponding Works Cited listing.

YOU ARE CITING AN ENCYCLOPEDIA OR DICTIONARY

If you cite a section of a reference work that has a named author, then set up your citation and Works Cited entry just as you would for a part of a book, starting with the author's name.

If you cite a section of a reference work that does not list an author, put the section into your Works Cited list alphabetically, by the title. Because such sections are usually arranged in alphabetical order, you do not need to give a page number; readers can easily find what you are referencing without the page number.

Mad cow disease, the popular name given to bovine spongiform encephalopathy (a fatal neurological disorder of cattle), appears to be transferable to humans, in whom it is called Creutzfeldt-Jacob disease; mad cow disease is spread when cows are fed processed remains of other cattle who have the disease ("Bovine Spongiform Encephalopathy").

→ See page 380 for the corresponding Works Cited listing.

YOUR SENTENCE REFERENCES A WHOLE SOURCE

Sometimes you will want to refer to a whole source in your writing, not just part of it. In such cases, do not reference page numbers; instead, you can include the author's name and the name of the work in your writing, or just reference the source in the parentheses at the end of the sentence.

Oliver Sacks's Seeing Voices is an argument that sign languages are indeed real languages, so that when people who are deaf learn to sign, they gain the same neurological benefits as people who can hear gain when they learn to speak.

An increase in childhood sports injuries seems related to increased competition (Gorman).

→ See page 393 for the corresponding Works Cited listing.

YOUR SENTENCE REFERENCES TWO OR MORE SOURCES

There are two ways you can include more than one source.

First, if your sentence refers to the different sources in different parts of the sentence, put a citation after each reference:

While some research finds a link between violent games and aggressive behavior in children (Provenzo 12), many recent studies challenge the idea of a direct connection between gaming and real-world behaviors (Jones 144).

Second, if multiple sources support your point, put them all into the parentheses, separated by semicolons:

Although there is agreement that hundreds of languages were spoken in the Americas before Europeans arrived, there is disagreement over the number of linguistic families into which all those languages fit (Crystal 403-08; Wade 113-18).

CITING LITERARY WORKS

Because literary works—novels, poems, plays—come in many editions, someone who wishes to find the original words in the source may look in a different edition—so giving only page numbers will not help.

NOVELS

In addition to the page number, give the chapter or part number:

At the end of The Yacoubian Building, it is hard to tell whether Al Aswany wants us to see hope or futility for Egypt in Busayna and Zaki's marriage, when old Zaki starts dancing with the young woman, "raising his arms aloft amid the joyful laughter" (246, part 2).

SHORT STORIES

Because short stories *are* short, you can give just the page number:

In Lahiri's story "Interpreter of Maladies," the Indian family that lives in the United States need guidebooks to visit their old country—but even so it is lost to them, so that it is "no longer possible to enter the temple, for it had filled with rubble years ago" (57).

YOU ARE CITING A SACRED TEXT, SUCH AS THE BIBLE OR KORAN

Give the chapter and verse of the words you quote, separated by periods. You can use common abbreviations for chapters in the Bible.

The sermon took as its starting point the theme of love: "Love is patient and kind; love is not jealous or boastful; it is not arrogant or rude" (New Jerusalem Bible, 1 Cor. 13.4-5).

When you include a sacred text in your Works Cited list, include the name of the edition you are using.

YOU ARE CITING LINES FROM A PLAY

Instead of page numbers, include the act, scene, and line numbers of the lines, separated by periods.

Claudius recognizes that his prayers are in vain when he concludes that "words without thoughts never to heaven go" (Hamlet 3.3.98).

Readers should know from the context that *Hamlet*'s author is Shakespeare.

→ See page 405 for the corresponding Works Cited listing.

YOU ARE CITING LINES FROM A POEM THAT IS DIVIDED INTO PARTS OR THAT HAS LINE NUMBERS

Give the part and line numbers (and most often you will have to count the line numbers):

In the middle of his long poem "Sphere," about how life is in the movement from big to small and back again, A. R. Ammons gives this small metaphor: "crush a bug and the universe goes hollow / with hereafter" (80.1-2).

If the poem is not divided into parts, give only the line numbers. The first time you reference a poem, include "lines" in the parentheses; afterward, just include the line numbers. For example, this sentence starts a short essay on a poem:

Like the poet Barbara Ras, I too would like "to write myself out of grief, dig out / to a place washed by heaven-haunted light" (lines 1-2).

This sentence would come later:

Ras's poem shows, however, that writing is a momentary distraction and perhaps no comfort; she ends the poem with "I am left / writing into emphatic wet matter and the singular pain / of missing my mother" (22-24).

→ See page 381 for the corresponding Works Cited listing.

MLA DOCUMENTA- TION FOR WORKS CITED

The following pages show you how to format the individual entries of the Works Cited listing at the end of any research project.

This is the basic format for all texts you list in the Works Cited section of an MLA-style paper:

Author's Name. <u>Title of Text</u>. Where and When the Text Was Published.

For example, here is a citation for a book:

Treichler, Paula. <u>How to Have Theory in an Epidemic: Cultural Chronicles of AIDS</u>. Durham, NC: Duke UP, 1999.

(Note the indenting: This is standard when formatting your list of Works Cited, as we describe on pages 404–405.)

Most often your sources will be books, periodicals, webpages, or online databases, so we focus on those formats. But because there are so many other kinds of texts you can also cite, we include those as well.

Note that when you cite a book, periodical, or webpage, the format of the citation—the punctuation of the title of a book, the inclusion of a periodical's issue number, or the listing of a URL—tells a reader what kind of text you are citing. When you cite a text that isn't a book, periodical, or webpage, you may also need to indicate what kind of text you are citing.

TO MAKE WORKS CITED LISTS

FIRST, MAKE AN INDIVIDUAL LISTING FOR EACH WORK YOU ARE CITING

You should have determined the kind of source you have and collected the kinds of information listed for the source, as described on pages 328–329.

Then go to the page for the kind of source you have.

BOOK
Go to page 362.

PART OF A BOOK
Go to page 364.

ARTICLE FROM A PERIODICAL
Go to page 366.

WEBPAGE
Go to page 368.

TEXTS FROM ONLINE DATABASES
Go to page 370.

OTHER KINDS OF TEXTS
Go to page 372.

Each page shows the pattern for the Works Cited listing for that kind of source.

- Follow the pattern to construct your listing part by part, starting with the author, moving on to the title, and so on.
- If your citation varies from the pattern, follow the page references to see the format for the variation.

THEN CONSTRUCT YOUR WORKS CITED PAGE

When you have all your individual citations, put them together into the Works Cited page.

→ See page 404 for how to format the Works Cited page.

FOR BOOKS

Here is a citation for a book, in the MLA format:

Berger, John. <u>About Looking</u>. New York: Vintage, 1992.

THE PATTERN

Here is the MLA citation pattern with its parts labeled and with information about how to modify the citation depending on a book's particularities.

Author's Name. <u>Title of the Book</u>.

The pattern for an author's name is on page 374.

WHAT TO DO WHEN YOU HAVE:

- no author named: page 375
- one author: page 375
- two or three authors: page 375
- four or more authors: page 376
- a book revised by a second author: page 376
- an edited collection: page 376
- a corporate author: page 376
- a government author: page 377
- a pamphlet without an author: page 377
- a pseudonym in place of an author's name: page 377
- the preface, introduction, foreword, or afterword to a book: page 377

The pattern for the title is on page 378.

WHAT TO DO WHEN YOU HAVE:

- a book: page 380
- a title that is in a language other than English: page 381
- a religious text: page 381
- a title of another text mentioned within the main title: page 382

Where do you look in a book to find all this information?
How do you know when you have all the information you need to cite a book?

➜ See pages 329–331 for help.

Place of Publication: Publisher, Year.

The pattern for the place of publication is on page 388.

WHAT TO DO WHEN:

- the state is not listed: page 389
- the book was published in another country: page 389
- publication information is missing: page 389

From the publisher's full name, you can leave off information such as *Press* or *Company*. Instead of *University Press* put *UP*: for example, *Oxford UP*.

If you find more than one copyright date for a book, list the most recent.

WHAT TO DO WHEN YOU HAVE:

- a book that has been republished: page 391
- a book published before 1900: page 391
- a book with no publication date: page 391

YOU MAY NEED TO INCLUDE ADDITIONAL INFORMATION HERE...

- if the book is translated from another language: page 396
- if the book is a published or unpublished dissertation: page 396
- if the book is part of a multivolume series: page 397
- if the book is a second (or later) edition: page 397

FOR PARTS OF BOOKS

When you are citing an essay from an edited collection; a poem from an anthology; an article from a reference book; or the preface, introduction, foreword, or afterword to a book, here is how the citation will look in the MLA format:

Smitherman, Geneva. "Toward a National Public Policy on Language." <u>The Skin that We Speak</u>. Ed. Lisa Delpit and Joanne Kilgour Dowdy. New York: New P, 2002. 166-78.

THE PATTERN

Here is the MLA citation pattern with its parts labeled and with information about how to modify the citation depending on a book's particularities.

Author's Name. "Article Title." <u>Title of the Book</u>.

The pattern for an author's name is the same as for the books shown on page 374.

WHAT TO DO WHEN YOU HAVE:

• no author named: page 375

• one author: page 375

• two or three authors: page 375

• four or more authors: page 376

• a corporate author: page 376

• a government author: page 377

The pattern for titles of parts of books is on page 379.

WHAT TO DO WHEN YOU HAVE:

• an essay or a chapter in a book: page 380

• an article from a reference book: page 380

• a poem or short story in a book: page 381

• the preface, introduction, foreword, or afterword to a book: page 382

The pattern for the book's title is the same as when you cite a whole book, shown on page 378.

WHAT TO DO WHEN YOU HAVE:

• a book: page 380

• a title that is in a language other than English: page 381

• a religious text: page 381

• a title of another text mentioned within the main title: page 382

Where do you look in a book to find all this information?
→ See pages 333–335 for help.

Editor's Name. Place of Publication: Publisher, Year. Pages

Put *Ed.* (even if you have multiple editors) after the title of the book.

Then put the full names of the editor or editors exactly as they are printed on the Title page of the book.

The pattern for the place of publication is on page 388.

WHAT TO DO WHEN:

- the state is not listed: page 389
- the book was published in another country: page 389
- publication information is missing: page 389

From the publisher's full name, you can leave off information such as *Press* or *Company*. Instead of *University Press* put *UP*: for example, *Oxford UP*.

If you find more than one copyright date for a book, list the most recent.

WHAT TO DO WHEN YOU HAVE:

- a book that has been republished: page 391
- a book published before 1900: page 391
- a book with no publication date: page 391

Put the number of the article or essay's first page, then a hyphen, and then the number of the article or essay's last page. If there is only one page, put only that number. Add a period after the numbers.

FOR ARTICLES FROM PERIODICALS
(JOURNALS, MAGAZINES, OR NEWSPAPERS)

Here is a citation for an article from an academic journal in the MLA format:

> Omoniyi, Tope. "Hip-hop through the World Englishes Lens: A Response to Globalization." <u>World Englishes</u> 25.2 (2006): 195-208.

THE PATTERN

Here is the MLA citation pattern with its parts labeled and with information about how to modify the citation depending on a periodical's particularities.

Author's Name. "Title of Article."

The pattern for an author's name is on page 374.

WHAT TO DO WHEN YOU HAVE:

- no author named: page 375
- one author: page 375
- two or three authors: page 375
- four or more authors: page 376
- a corporate author: page 376
- a government author: page 377

The pattern for the article name is on page 379.

WHAT TO DO WHEN YOU HAVE:

- a title in a language other than English: page 381
- a letter to the editor: page 382
- an editorial: page 383
- a published interview: page 383
- a review: page 383
- a government document: page 383

Where do you look in a periodical to find all this information?
How do you know you have all the information you need for a periodical?
→ See pages 337–341 for help.

Periodical Volume.Issue (Date): Pages.

If the journal name begins with A or *The*, you can leave out those words.

Italicize the journal name (or underline it if you are not working on a computer).

If you are citing a local (not national) newspaper, see the example on page 382.

The pattern for the volume and issue numbers and date is on page 392.

WHAT TO DO WHEN YOU HAVE:

• no issue number: page 393

• only a date: page 393

• a daily newspaper: page 393

• a weekly or biweekly journal or magazine: page 393

• a monthly or seasonal journal or magazine: page 393

The pattern for page numbers is on page 394.

WHAT TO DO WHEN YOU HAVE:

• an article in a journal that is paginated by volume: page 394

• an article that does not have sequential page numbering: page 394

MLA WORKS CITED
FOR WEBPAGES
OTHER THAN DATABASES

Here is a citation for an article from an online journal in the MLA format:

Lloyd, David. "Mobile Figures." <u>Vectors</u> 2005. 21 Feb. 2006.
    <http://vectors.iml.annenberg.edu/ index.php?page=7|1&projectId=54>.

THE PATTERN

Here is the MLA citation pattern with its parts labeled and with information about how to modify the citation depending on a webpage's particularities:

Author's Name. "Title." <u>Website</u>. Publication Date.

The pattern for an author's name is on page 374.

WHAT TO DO WHEN YOU HAVE:

• no author named: page 375

• one author: page 375

• two or three authors: page 375

• four or more authors: page 376

• a corporate author: page 376

• a government author: page 377

The pattern for presenting the titles of webpages is the same as for titling articles; see page 379.

For help determining the title of either a webpage or a website, see pages 342–345 and 384–386.

WHAT TO DO WHEN YOU HAVE:

• no date of publication: page 391

• a date for the last time the page was revised: page 385

The pattern for giving the title of a website is on page 384.

WHAT TO DO WHEN YOU HAVE:

• a personal website: page 385

• a blog: page 385

• an online scholarly journal: page 385

• an online newspaper: page 386

• a popular magazine, online: page 386

• an article from a database: page 393

• a webpage with no apparent affiliation: page 386

Where do you look on webpages to find all this information?
How do you know you have all the information you need for a webpage?

→ See pages 342–345 for help.

Sponsoring Organization. Date accessed <URL>.

If there is a company or organization associated with the website, give its name exactly as it appears on the webpage, using the same capitalization and including *The* if it is used in the title.

If you cannot find any sponsoring organization listed in the webpages you are citing, just omit this information from the citation.

If you have already listed the sponsoring organization as the author or as the website name, do not repeat the information; instead, just omit it from this place in the citation.

Put the day first, then the month (abbreviated as shown), then the year:

5 Jan. 2006

27 Feb. 2008

19 Mar. 2007

1 Apr. 2006

1 May 2006

11 June 2008

22 July 2009

17 Aug. 2006

22 Sept. 2007

31 Oct. 2006

10 Nov. 2006

3 Dec. 2008

If there is no date on the webpage, put *Accessed*: before the date you accessed the website, so that readers won't mistake this date for the publication date.

WHAT TO DO WHEN YOU HAVE:

• a very long URL: page 387

MLA WORKS CITED
FOR TEXTS FROM ONLINE DATABASES

Here is a citation for a full-text article retrieved from an online database in the MLA format:

Forman, Richard T. T., and Lauren E. Alexander. "Roads and Their Major Ecological Effects." <u>Annual Review of Ecology and Systematics</u> 29 (1998): 207-31. <u>JSTOR</u>. J. Robert Van Pelt Lib., Houghton, MI. 8 Aug. 2006 <http:www.jstor.org>.

THE PATTERN

Notice how the above citation consists of two major parts: There is information about the article that is given exactly as though the article were in print, following the pattern on pages 366–367; then there is the information about the database itself.

Citation of article as on pp. 366–367. <u>Name of Database</u>.

Cite the article exactly as you would cite a print article, following the pattern given on pages 366–367, except:

- If the article is not a pdf, give the page number of the first page as it is listed on the database entry, followed by a hyphen, a space, and a period (for example, "97- .").

- If the article is a pdf, give the page numbers as they appear in the pdf, because these pages numbers reflect the print article's page numbers.

Give the name of the database exactly as it appears on the webpage, using the same capitalization and including *The* if it is used in the name.

Where do you look on database webpages to find all this information?
How do you know when you have all the information you need to cite a database?

→ See pages 346–347 for help.

Subscription Service. Library. Date accessed <URL>.

The subscription service is the company that provided the search engine you used to find the database (for example, InfoTrac or LexisNexis). Enter the name exactly as it appears on the webpage, using the same capitalization and including *The* if it is used in the name.

Give the name of the library where you accessed the article and the library's city and state (with the state name abbreviated):

Van Pelt Lib., Houghton, MI

Annapolis Public Lib., Annapolis, MD

Put the day first, then the month (abbreviated as shown), then the year:

5 Jan. 2006

19 Mar. 2007

1 May 2006

11 June 2008

22 July 2009

22 Sept. 2007

31 Oct. 2006

10 Nov. 2006

You can leave out the URL, but if you include it, give the URL for the subscription service, not the article you are citing.

WHAT TO DO WHEN YOU HAVE:

• a very long URL: page 387

FOR OTHER KINDS OF TEXTS

In addition to books, periodicals, and webpages, there are many other kinds of texts you can use to support your writing. The list on these pages does not include all the possibilities—but it comes close. If you find a source you want to use that is not listed in these pages, follow the basic pattern of all the citations by listing as much information as you can about an author, the title of the piece, and where and when it was published. You may also need to specify the kind of text it is. Look at the samples for these kinds of texts to see the pattern.

SOUND RECORDING
page 399

SOFTWARE
page 399

MAP, GRAPH, CHART
(print or online)
page 399

CD-ROMS
page 398

A PUBLIC TALK
(a presentation at a professional conference or a speech, debate, or lecture)
page 399

ADVERTISEMENTS
(print or online)
page 398

FILM OR VIDEO
(print or online)
page 400

MLA WORKS CITED
AUTHOR'S NAME

Note how the patterns for author names are consistent across citations for all kinds of texts in all kinds of media.

→ On these pages, we show how authors' names appear in individual citations for a range of sources; on pages 404–405 we show you how to bring together individual citations like these to create a full Works Cited section that goes at the end of any MLA-style research paper.

The first author listed is always written with the last name first, then a comma, and then the first name.

Last Name, First Name.

Singh, Amardeep.

If the writer you are citing uses a middle name or initials, those follow the first name. Sometimes a writer will use only initials.

Phelps, Louise Wetherbee.

Mitchell, W. J. T.

If what you are citing has more than one author, the additional names should be listed after the initial author, with the first name first and the last name last. List the authors in the order in which they are listed in the book.

Phelps, Louise Wetherbee, and Janet Emig.

Fine, Michelle, Lois Weis, Linda Powell Pruitt, and April Burns.

Note that, in a citation, there is a period after the author's name or the list of authors' names.

NO AUTHOR NAMED

If you cannot find an author's name, start the citation with the name of the book or article.

TEXT AND IMAGE ARCHIVE, ONLINE

The Cinderella Project. Ed. Michael N. Salda. Vers. 1.1. Dec. 1997. De Grummond Children's Lit. Research Collection, U of Southern Mississippi. 9 Mar. 2003. <http://www.usm.edu/english/fairytales/cinderella/cinderella.html>.

MAGAZINE ARTICLE, NO AUTHOR LISTED

"Idol Worship." Rolling Stone 8 Feb. 2007: 7.

REFERENCE WORK

Ultimate Visual Dictionary. Rev. ed. New York: Dorling Kindersley, 2002.

ONE AUTHOR

BOOK

Brodkey, Linda. Writing Permitted in Designated Areas Only. Minneapolis: U Minnesota P, 1996.

BLOG

Jerz, Dennis G. "Citing a Weblog in MLA Style." Weblog entry. Jerz's Literacy Weblog. 11 Dec. 2003. Seton Hill U. 9 Sept. 2006. <http://jerz.setonhill.edu/weblog/permalink.jsp?id=2000>.

CHAPTER, IN EDITED BOOK

Modleski, Tania. "The Search for Tomorrow in Today's Soap Operas." The Feminism and Visual Culture Reader. Ed. Amelia Jones. London: Routledge, 2003. 294-302.

TWO OR THREE AUTHORS

In these citations, the first author appears with last name first; all following authors' names are listed starting with their first names.

TWO AUTHORS

BOOK

Flint, Julie, and Alex de Waal. Darfur: A Short History of a Long War. London: Zed Books, 2006.

REVIEW, ONLINE
REVIEW, OF BOOK

Moeller, Ryan M., and Kevin Moberly. Rev. of Game Work: Language, Power, and Computer Game Culture, by Ken S. McAllister. Kairos 10.2 (2006). 23 Feb. 2006. <http://english.ttu.edu/kairos/10.2/binder.html?reviews/moeller_moberley/index.html>.

THREE AUTHORS

ARTICLE, IN ACADEMIC JOURNAL

DeVoss, Dànielle Nicole, Ellen Cushman, and Jeffrey T. Grabill. "Infrastructure and Composing: The When of New-Media Writing." CCC 57 (2005): 14-44.

BOOK

Joyce, Justin A., Dwight A. McBride, and Melvin Dixon. A Melvin Dixon Critical Reader. Jackson: Mississippi UP, 2006.

REVIEW, ONLINE
REVIEW, OF CONFERENCE

Wittig, Rob, Scott Rettberg, and William Gillespie. "&Now Conference Review." Electronic Book Review. 26 July 2005. 29 Feb. 2006. <http://www.electronicbookreview.com/thread/wuc/festivarian>.

FOUR OR MORE AUTHORS

You can write out the names of all the authors, following the pattern described earlier for multiple authors—or you can give only the name of the first author listed. All the other authors are then represented by *et al.*, which is a Latin abbreviation meaning *and others*.

CHAPTER, IN EDITED BOOK

Fine, Michelle, Bernadette Anand, Carlton Jordan, and Dana Sherman. "Before the Bleach Gets Us All." <u>Construction Sites</u>. Ed. Lois Weiss and Michelle Fine. New York: Teachers College P, 2000. 161-79.

ARTICLE, IN ONLINE ACADEMIC JOURNAL

Imus, Anna, et al. "Technology: A Boom or a Bust? An Understanding of Students' Perceptions of Technology Use in the Classroom." <u>Inventio</u> 6.1 (2004). 1 Mar. 2006 <http://www.doit.gmu.edu/inventio/past/display_past.asp?pID=spring04&sID=imus>.

BOOK

Shema, Mike, et al. <u>Anti-Hacker Tool Kit</u>. 3rd ed. Emeryville, CA: McGraw-Hill/Osborne Media, 2006.

A BOOK REVISED BY A SECOND AUTHOR

The second author is considered to be an editor:

BOOK

Strunk, William. <u>Elements of Style</u>. Ed. E. B. White. 4th ed. Boston: Allyn, 2000.

→ On page 331 you can see the Title page of a book revised by a second author.

AN EDITED COLLECTION

Put *ed.* (or *eds.*, for multiple editors) after the names that begin the citation.

ONE EDITOR

BOOK, EDITED

Le Faye, Deirdre, ed. <u>Jane Austen's Letters</u>. 3rd ed. Oxford: Oxford UP, 1995.

TWO EDITORS

If the book has more than two editors, follow the pattern for a book with multiple authors.

BOOK, EDITED

Hocks, Mary, and Michelle Kendrick, eds. <u>Eloquent Images: Word and Image in the Age of New Media</u>. Cambridge, MA: MIT UP, 2003.

> **NOTE!**
> If you are citing only a piece from an edited collection and not the whole collection, create the citation following the pattern shown on pages 364–365.

A CORPORATE AUTHOR

Start the citation with the name of the corporate author exactly as it is listed in the source (but omit *A*, *An*, or *The*):

BOOK

Museum of Modern Art. <u>The Changing of the Avant-Garde: Visionary Architectural Drawings from the Howard Gilman Collection</u>. New York: Museum of Modern Art, 2002.

A GOVERNMENT AUTHOR

Start the citation with the country name, then give the name of the government organization responsible for the publication, exactly as it appears in the publication:

BROCHURE

United States. Dept. of the Interior. Keweenaw. Washington: GPO, 2002.

(GPO stands for **Government Printing Office** and is a standard abbreviation you can use.)

REPORT

United Nations. Development Program. Beyond Scarcity: Power, Poverty, and the Global Water Crisis. New York: United Nations, 2006.

(Documents from the United Nations start with **United Nations**.)

A PAMPHLET WITHOUT AN AUTHOR

PAMPHLET

Renoir Lithographs. New York: Dover, 1994.

A PSEUDONYM IN PLACE OF AN AUTHOR'S NAME

Start the citation with the pseudonym, then put the author's real name in brackets:

BOOK

LeCarre, John [David Cornwell]. The Russia House. New York: Knopf, 1989.

THE PREFACE, INTRODUCTION, FOREWORD, OR AFTERWORD TO A BOOK

Put the name of the person who wrote the preface, introduction, foreword, or afterword in the author name position.

After that person's name, put **Preface**, **Introduction**, **Foreword**, or **Afterword**.

Then put the title of the book, followed by the name of the person responsible for the book (preceded by **By** if the person is the author or **Ed.** if the person is the editor).

At the end of the citation, give the page numbers of the cited part.

AFTERWORD, BOOK
AFTERWORD, TRANSLATED

Zizek, Slavoj. Afterword. The Politics of Aesthetics. By Jacques Rancière. Trans. Gabriel Rockhill. London: Continuum, 2004. 67-79.

NOTE!

In the examples on these pages, we show the citations with what is called **hanging indentation**: The first line of a citation sticks farther into the left margin than the other lines. This is the standard form of indenting for MLA citations; your teacher might also ask you to double-space the citations.

If you are working on a computer, italicize the titles of books or other texts that you underline on a typewriter.

If you are working online, always italicize the titles; if you underline, the titles look like links to other webpages.

MLA WORKS CITED
TITLES

Note how the patterns for titles are consistent across citations for all kinds of texts in all kinds of media.

→ Many full citation examples follow, on pages 380–386.

→ On these pages, we demonstrate how to include titles for individual citations for a range of sources; on pages 404–405 we show you how to bring together individual citations like these to create a full Works Cited section that goes at the end of any MLA-style research paper.

→ Many full citation examples follow, on pages 380–386.

→ On these pages, we demonstrate how to include titles for individual citations for a range of sources; on pages 404–405 we show you how to bring together individual citations like these to create a full Works Cited section that goes at the end of any MLA-style research paper.

THE PATTERN

BOOK TITLES

Follow these steps to build the pattern:

1 Capitalize all the words of the title except for

articles (*a, an, the*)

short prepositions (*to, at, by, for, from, in, of, with*)

conjunctions (*and, but, for, or*)

the word **to** when it is part of an infinitive (as in **to read** or **to write**)

2 Capitalize the first word and the last word even if the words are one of the exceptions above.

3 Underline the whole title.

4 Put a period after the title. (If the title ends with a question mark or exclamation point, use that instead.)

The Title of the Book.

Crow Lake.

The Diving Bell and the Butterfly.

If the book has a subtitle, put the subtitle after a colon and capitalize it as you would the title:

Scribbling the Cat: Travels with an African Soldier.

The Quick and the Dead: Artists and Anatomy.

A Country Doctor's Casebook: Tales from the North Woods.

TITLES OF PARTS OF BOOKS, PERIODICAL ARTICLES, AND WEBPAGES

Follow these steps to build the pattern:

1 Capitalize the title, following the same guidelines for a book title.

2 Put quotation marks around the title.

3 Put a period after the last word of the title but inside the final quotation mark. (If the title ends with a question mark or exclamation point, use that.)

4 Follow the pattern below for finishing the title depending on the source.

PARTS OF BOOKS

Put the title of the whole book after the title of the part of the book you are citing. (If you are using a computer, italicize the book's title.)

"The Title of the Part of the Book." <u>The Title of the Book</u>.

"The New Dionysianism." <u>The Sticky Sublime</u>.

"Meno." <u>The Collected Dialogues of Plato</u>.

"Pointers for Pets." <u>Living with the Animals</u>.

JOURNAL ARTICLES

Put the name of the journal after the article name. (If you are using a computer, italicize the journal's title.)

"The Article." <u>Journal Name</u>

"Will the Next Election Be Hacked?" <u>Rolling Stone</u>

"What if It's (Sort of) a Boy and (Sort of) a Girl?" <u>New York Times</u>

"A Bookling Monument." <u>Kairos</u>

WEBPAGES

Put the name of the website after the name of the webpage. (If you are using a computer, italicize the webpage's title.)

"The Article." <u>Website Name</u>.

"Project Description." <u>The Nora Project</u>.

"My Favorite Mozart." <u>Marginal Revolution</u>.

"Pictures Without Bias: How to Avoid Discrimination in Visual Media." <u>Center for Media Literacy</u>.

A BOOK

BOOK

Lawson, Mary. <u>Crow Lake</u>. New York: Delta Trade, 2002.

BOOK

Petherbridge, Deanna, and Ludmilla Jordanova. <u>The Quick and the Dead: Artists and Anatomy</u>. Berkeley: U of California P, 1997.

BOOK, ONLINE

Sharp, Lesley A. <u>The Possessed and the Dispossessed: Spirits, Identity, and Power in a Madagascar Migrant Town</u>. Berkeley: U of California P, 1993. *eScholarship Editions*. 22 Sept. 2004 <http://ark.cdlib.org/ark:/13030/ft6t1nb4hz/>.

AN ESSAY OR CHAPTER IN A BOOK

ESSAY, IN ONLINE BOOK

Makhan, Jha. "Island Ecology and Cultural Perceptions: A Case Study of Lakshdweep." <u>Lifestyle and Ecology</u>. Ed. Baidyanath Saraswati. New Delhi: Indira Gandhi National Centre for the Arts, 1998. 30 June 2006 <http:// www.ignca.nic.in/ cd_08012.htm>.

ESSAY, IN EDITED BOOK

Plato. "Meno." <u>The Collected Dialogues of Plato</u>. Ed. Edith Hamilton and Huntington Cairns. Trans. W. K. C. Guthrie. Princeton: Princeton UP, 1961. 353-85.

ESSAY, IN EDITED BOOK

van Proyen, Mark. "The New Dionysianism." <u>The Sticky Sublime</u>. Ed. Bill Beckley. New York: Allworth, 2001. 165-75.

AN ESSAY IN AN ONLINE COLLECTION

ESSAY, IN ONLINE COLLECTION

Badger, Meredith. "Visual Blogs." <u>Into the Blogosphere: Rhetoric, Community, and Culture of Weblogs</u>. Ed. Laura J. Gurak, Smiljana Antonijevic, Laurie Johnson, Clancy Ratliff, and Jessica Reyman. June 2004. 23 Sept. 2006 <http://blog.lib.umn.edu/ blogosphere/visual_blogs.html>.

AN ARTICLE FROM A REFERENCE BOOK

Reference works rarely give the name of the person who wrote the article. Put the article's title in quotation marks at the beginning of the entry, leaving off *A* or *The*.

ARTICLE, IN REFERENCE BOOK

"Islam." <u>The New York Public Library Desk Reference</u>. 1989.

ARTICLE, IN ONLINE REFERENCE BOOK

"Bovine Spongiform Encephalopathy." *Encyclopædia Britannica*. 2007. <u>Encyclopædia Britannica Online</u>. 25 Feb. 2007 <http:// www.search.eb.com/eb/ article-9002739>.

A POEM OR SHORT STORY IN A BOOK

POEM, IN BOOK BY ONE AUTHOR

Ras, Barbara. "Where I Go When I'm Out of My Mind." <u>One Hidden Stuff</u>. New York: Penguin, 2006. 19-20.

SHORT STORY, IN EDITED BOOK
SHORT STORY, TRANSLATED

Mina, Hanna. "On the Sacks." <u>Literature from the "Axis of Evil."</u> Trans. Hanadi Al-Samman. New York: New P, 2006. 179-206.

POEM, IN EDITED COLLECTION

Mông-Lan. "Trail." <u>The Best American Poetry 2002</u>. Ed. Robert Creeley. New York: Scribner, 2002. 108-17.

In the following example, note that the date of the book's original publication follows the book's title; if you can find it, put the date of the book's digitization (when it was placed online) after the name of the website.

SHORT STORY, IN ONLINE BOOK

Woolf, Virginia. "Monday or Tuesday." <u>A Haunted House</u>. 1921. <u>Bartleby.com: Great Books Online</u>. 1999. 17 Feb. 2001 <http://bartleby.com/85/3.html>.

A TITLE THAT IS IN A LANGUAGE OTHER THAN ENGLISH

BOOK OF POETRY, TITLE IN LANGUAGE OTHER THAN ENGLISH

Baudelaire, Charles. <u>Les Fleurs du mal</u>. Paris: Pocket, 2000.

BLOG ENTRY, TITLE IN LANGUAGE OTHER THAN ENGLISH

Doreau, Delphine. "Merci à tous ceux qui ont fait coucou hier." Weblog entry. <u>Non Dairy Diary</u>. 10 Aug. 2007. 10 Aug. 2007 <http://del4yo.blogs.com/non_dairy_diary/2007/08/merci-a-tous-ce.html>.

ARTICLE, IN ACADEMIC JOURNAL
ARTICLE, TITLE IN LANGUAGE OTHER THAN ENGLISH

Tapia, Rosa. "'Mia o de Naiden.' La Reescritura de la Violencia en 'Pasion de Historia' de Ana Lydia Vega." <u>Hispanic Review</u> 75.1 (Winter 2007): 47-60.

Note that the citation follows the capitalization conventions of the original language.

A RELIGIOUS TEXT

If you are not citing a particular edition of a religious text such as the Bible or the Koran, you do not need to include it in the Works Cited listing at the end of your paper.

A TITLE OF ANOTHER TEXT MENTIONED WITHIN THE MAIN TITLE

If you are citing the title of a book that contains the title of another book, the embedded title should not be italicized or underlined.

BOOK

Kummings, Donald D. Approaches to Teaching Whitman's Leaves of Grass. New York: MLA, 1991.

■■■

If you are citing a journal article, and the title contains the title of a book, underline the book title:

ARTICLE, IN ACADEMIC JOURNAL

Froula, Christine. "Out of the Chrysalis: Female Initiation and Female Authority in Virginia Woolf's The Voyage Out," Tulsa Studies in Women's Literature 5.1 (1986): 63-90.

■■■

If you are citing a part of a book, and the title contains the title of still another work, put the embedded title within single quotation marks:

CHAPTER, IN EDITED BOOK

Gruber, Sibylle. "'I, a Mestiza, Continually Walk Out of One Culture and into Another': Alba's Story." Feminist Cyberscapes: Mapping Gendered Academic Spaces. Ed. Kristine Blair and Pamela Takayoshi. Stamford, CT: Ablex. 1999. 105-32.

THE PREFACE, INTRODUCTION, FOREWORD, OR AFTERWORD TO A BOOK

Put the name of the person who wrote the preface, introduction, foreword, or afterword as the name of the author.

After that person's name, put the appropriate word (without the quotation marks): *Preface*, *Introduction*, *Foreword*, or *Afterword*.

Then put the title of the book, followed by the name of the person responsible for the book (preceded by **By** if the person is the author or by **Ed.** if the person is the editor).

At the end of the citation, give the page numbers for the cited part.

AFTERWORD, IN BOOK
AFTERWORD, TRANSLATED

Zizek, Slavoj. Afterword. The Politics of Aesthetics. By Jacques Rancière. Trans. Gabriel Rockhill. London: Continuum, 2004. 67-79.

A LETTER TO THE EDITOR

Put **Letter.** after the title of the letter.

LETTER TO THE EDITOR

McDonald, Mary. "Pandemic Prep." Letter. Scientific American March 2006: 14.

LETTER TO THE EDITOR, ONLINE

Coté, Cynthia. "Hancock is OK." Letter. Daily Mining Gazette: MiningGazette.com. [Houghton, MI] 18 Aug. 2007. 19 Aug. 2007 <http://www.mininggazette.com/stories/articles.asp?articleID=8250>.

A city name follows the local newspaper name because the name does not identify the city.

AN EDITORIAL

Put *Editorial.* after the title of the letter.

EDITORIAL, UNTITLED

Schulte, Margaret F. Editorial. <u>Frontiers of Health Services Management</u> 24 (Fall 2007): 1.

EDITORIAL, TITLED

Nasibu, Charles. "Africa's Weapons of Mass Destruction." Editorial. <u>The Independent</u>. 16 Aug. 2007: 1.

EDITORIAL, ONLINE
EDITORIAL, NO AUTHOR NAMED

"Failure Is Not an Option." Editorial. <u>Milwaukee Journal-Sentinel: JSOnline</u>. 16 Sept. 2007. 31 May 2008. <http:// www.jsonline.com/ story/index.aspx?id=662244>.

A PUBLISHED INTERVIEW

An interview is considered published when it is presented in words on a page or screen. Start the citation with the name of the person who was interviewed. If you have the name of the person who conducted the interview, follow the pattern established by the entry for Satrapi, below.

INTERVIEW, PUBLISHED
INTERVIEW, UNTITLED

Robbins, Trina. Interview with Michelle Garcia. <u>Bitch</u> 18 (Fall 2002): 60+.

INTERVIEW, ONLINE

Satrapi, Marjane. Interview with David Welsh. "Marjane Satrapi Returns." <u>Powells.com</u>. 17 Sept. 2004. 21 Apr. 2008 <http://www.powells.com/ authors/satrapi.html>.

A REVIEW

REVIEW, OF MOVIE

Davies, Sam. Rev. of <u>Electroma</u>, dir. Thomas Bangalter, Guy-Manuel de Homam-Christo. <u>Sight & Sound</u> 17.8 (Aug. 2007): 62.

REVIEW, ONLINE
REVIEW, OF MOVIE

Stephens, Dana. "The Metaphysics of David Cronenberg's <u>Violence</u>." Rev. of <u>Eastern Promises</u>, dir. David Cronenberg. <u>Slate</u>. 13 Sept. 2007. 14 Sept. 2008 <http://www.slate.com/ id/2173900/fr/flyout>.

A GOVERNMENT DOCUMENT

GOVERNMENT DOCUMENT, STATE
GOVERNMENT DOCUMENT, REVISED EDITION

Montana. Fish, Wildlife, and Parks. "2007 Montana Fishing Regulations." Helena, MT: State of Montana, 2007.

GOVERNMENT DOCUMENT, FEDERAL
GOVERNMENT DOCUMENT, ONLINE

United States. Federal Trade Commission. "The Truth about Cellphones and the National Do Not Call Registry." 15 Apr. 2005. 27 Nov. 2006 <http://www.ftc.gov/opa/ 2005/04/ dnc.shtm>.

GOVERNMENT DOCUMENT, FEDERAL
GOVERNMENT DOCUMENT, REVISED EDITION

United States. National Institutes of Health. "Marijuana: Facts for Teens." Rev. ed. Washington: GPO, 2004.

MLA WORKS CITED
WEBSITE TITLES

Webpages are almost always part of larger websites. When you cite a webpage, you must also cite the website of which it is a part—just as when you cite an article or essay, you also cite the book in which you find the article or essay.

In their capitalization, website titles function just like the titles of books.

In their placement, website titles are like book titles when you are citing part of the book: You place the website title after the title of the webpage being cited.

■ ■ ■

Because of the similarities we've just listed, we could have included information on website titles on the preceding pages. But because citing websites is still new to many, and because there are so many possible variations in websites, we are focusing on them here.

→ On these pages, we demonstrate how to include titles for individual citations for a range of sources; on pages 404–405 we show you how to bring together individual citations like these to create a full Works Cited section that goes at the end of any MLA-style research paper.

WEBSITE TITLES
Take the title exactly as you find it on the website, and follow these steps to build the pattern:

1 Capitalize all the words of the title except for

articles (*a, an, the*)

short prepositions (*to, at, by, for, from, in, of, with*)

conjunctions (*and, but, for, or*)

the word **to** when it is part of an infinitive (as in **to read** or **to write**)

2 Capitalize the first word and the last word even if the words are one of the exceptions above.

3 Underline the whole title. If you are using a computer, italicize the title.

4 Put a period after the title. (If the title ends with a question mark or exclamation point, use that instead.)

<u>The Title of the Website</u>.

<u>Electronic Book Review</u>.

<u>Google</u>.

<u>ScientificAmerican.com</u>.

<u>The Institute for the Future of the Book</u>.

<u>We Make Art, Not Money</u>.

<u>PeaceWomen Across the Globe</u>.

A PERSONAL WEBSITE

After the website author's name (or after the website title, if it has one), put *Home page*.

Sometimes people name their websites:

PERSONAL WEBSITE

Najib M. El-Sayed. "The El-Sayed Laboratory." Home page. 2006. 23 June 2007 <http://www.najibelsayed.org/>.

If a personal website does not have a title, cite the website this way:

PERSONAL WEBSITE

Mullis, Kary. Home page. 2004. 1 Jan. 2009 <http://www.karymullis.com/>.

A BLOG

The general pattern for a blog entry is

Author's Name. "Title of blog entry." Weblog entry. Name of Weblog. Sponsoring organization, if any. Date posted. Date accessed <URL>.

When you give the URL for a blog entry, look for the **permalink** for the particular entry you are citing; do not give the URL for the blog itself because then a reader who wants to find the particular entry you cite will have to scroll to find the entry in its chronological order.

BLOG BY ONE PERSON

Mueller, Derek. "Miscellaneous Notes." Weblog entry. Earth Wide Moth. 23 May 2007. 23 May 2007 <http://www.earthwidemoth.com/mt/archives/001553.html>.

GROUP BLOG

Overton, Spencer. "Reflections on 'Advice for New Law Students of Color.'" Weblog entry. Blackprof.com. 14 Sept. 2007. 17 Sept. 2007 <http://www.blackprof.com/archives/2007/09/reflections_on_advice_for_new_1.html>.

AN ONLINE SCHOLARLY JOURNAL

When you cite an article from an online scholarly journal, the citation looks just like a citation for an article in a print journal—except that where the page reference would go, you put the date you accessed the website and its URL.

ARTICLE, IN ONLINE ACADEMIC JOURNAL

Sorapure, Madeleine. "Between Modes: Assessing Student New Media Compositions." Kairos 10.2 (Spring 2006). 25 June 2006 <http://english.ttu.edu/kairos/10.2/binder2.html?coverweb/sorapure/index.html>.

INTERVIEW, IN ONLINE ACADEMIC JOURNAL

Metinides, Enrique. Interview with Daniel Hernandez. The Journal of Aesthetics and Protest 5. 5 Aug. 2007. <http://www.joaap.org/5/articles/hernandez/hernandez.htm>.

AN ONLINE NEWSPAPER

NEWSPAPER ARTICLE, ONLINE

Benjamin, Mark. "Want a Water Study? Dig Deep." The Fresno Bee 17 Sept. 2007. 17 Sept. 2007 <http://www.fresnobee.com/263/story/140717.html>.

NEWSPAPER ARTICLE, ONLINE

Sukma, Rizal. "Managing Disasters Should Be Government's Top Priority." The JakartaPost.com 18 Sept. 2007. 18 Sept. 2007 <http://www.thejakartapost.com/detailheadlines.asp?fileid=20070917.B06&irec=5>.

A POPULAR MAGAZINE, ONLINE

ARTICLE, IN POPULAR MAGAZINE, ONLINE

Shepherd, Julianne. "The Making of Keyshia Cole's 'Let It Go.'" Vibe 25 June 2007. 1 July 2007 <http://www.vibe.com/news/online_exclusives/2007/06/keyshia_let_go_vid/>.

ARTICLE, IN POPULAR MAGAZINE, ONLINE
ARTICLE, IN POPULAR MAGAZINE, NO AUTHOR

"Man Dies from Three-Day Gaming Binge." Time 17 Sept. 2007 <http://www.time.com/time/world/article/0,8599,1662526,00.html>.

A WEBPAGE WITH NO APPARENT AFFILIATION

You might find yourself needing to cite a webpage that is not a personal home page and that provides no information about itself other than its URL.

The following website is an art project.

WEBSITE

"jodi.org." n.d. 15 Mar. 2005 <http://404.jodi.org/index.html>.

TIP: LINE BREAKS AND URLS

To assist readers in correctly retyping a URL when they want to find a source you've cited, be sure that URLs break only after slashes when you enter them in your Works Cited list.

Do this:

http://www.jsonline.com/story/index.aspx?id=662796

Not this:

http://www.jsonline.com/story/index.aspx?id=662796

A VERY LONG URL

Use the approach below that works best for your situation.

GIVE THE URL OF THE WEBSITE'S SEARCH PAGE

Someone using your citation to find the cited webpage can find the page by entering its name into the site's search page.

BOOK, ONLINE

Pratt, Harry T. "Selected writings and addresses." Baltimore, MD: H.S. Patterson, 1899. The Library of Congress American Memory. 5 Oct. 2005 <http://memory.loc.gov/ammem/murraybibquery.html>.

GIVE THE URL OF THE SUBSCRIPTION SERVICE'S HOME PAGE FOR AN ARTICLE IN A DATABASE

Someone using your citation to find the cited article can find it by going to the database home page and using the search tools linked there.

ARTICLE, IN ACADEMIC JOURNAL IN DATABASE

Tamony, Peter. "More on Supercalifrag-ilisticexpialidocious." American Speech 4.3/4 (Autumn, 1972): 307-08. JSTOR. University of Wisconsin–Milwaukee Lib. Milwaukee, WI. 30 July 2007 <http://www.jstor.org>.

GIVE THE URL OF THE SEARCH PAGE FOR THE WEBSITE

Someone using your citation to find the cited webpage can find the cited page by entering its name into the search page.

LETTER, ONLINE

Jefferson, Thomas. Letter to Angelica Schuyler Church. 11 Jan. 1798. University of Virginia Library. Electronic Text Center. Jefferson Digital Library. 15 Mar. 2007 <http://etext.virginia.edu/jefferson/texts/>.

You can also give the keyword assigned by the service. If you follow this strategy, put **Keyword** into the citation.

GIVE A SHORTER URL THAT GETS TO THE WEBSITE AND PROVIDE THE PATH TO THE CITED PAGE

If you do this, put **Path** before the list of links that describe the path.

Example: To avoid using the twelve-line URL that would otherwise be required, you can use the shortened URL shown in the citation below, with the path afterward that shows what to click if you go to the website referenced in the shorter URL.

ORGANIZATION TOOL, ONLINE

"Google Notebook." Google. 2007. 18 Sept. 2007 <http://www.google.com/intl/en/options/>. Path: Notebook.

PLACE OF PUBLICATION

Note how the pattern for listing the place of publication for a text is consistent across citations for all kinds of texts in all kinds of media.

→ On these pages, we show how the place of publication appears in individual citations for a range of sources; on pages 404–405 we show you how to bring together individual citations like these to create a full Works Cited section that goes at the end of any MLA-style research paper.

THE PATTERN

Put the place of publication after the title of the book, followed by a colon.

Place of Publication:

Boston:

Cambridge:

Santa Monica, CA:

Calumet, MI:

If more than one place of publication is listed, use the first one.

EXAMPLE

Jackson, Leslie. <u>Twentieth-Century Pattern Design: Textile and Wallpaper Pioneers</u>. Princeton: Princeton Architectural P, 2002.

Merrell, Floyd. <u>Unthinking Thinking: Jorge Luis Borges, Mathematics, and the New Physics</u>. West Lafayette, IN: Purdue UP, 1991.

Wardlow, Gayle Dean. <u>Chasin' That Devil Music: Searching for the Blues</u>. San Francisco: Miller Freeman, 1998.

WHEN TO MENTION THE STATE

A majority of books are published in major cities whose states most readers already know: Boston, Chicago, New York, San Francisco, and so on.

But if you are concerned that the name of a state will not come immediately to the mind of your readers, you should add the state. (The convention for adding the state is to use the two-letter abbreviation that the U.S. Postal Service uses.)

BOOK

Eisner, Will. <u>Graphic Storytelling and Visual Narrative</u>. Tamarac, FL: Poorhouse, 1996.

BOOK

Hargittai, István, and Magdolna Hargittai. <u>Symmetry: A Unifying Concept</u>. Bolinas, CA: Shelter Publications, 1994.

BOOK

Harris, Stephen L. <u>Agents of Chaos: Earthquakes, Volcanoes, and Other Natural Disasters</u>. Missoula, MT: Mountain, 1990.

WHEN THE BOOK WAS PUBLISHED IN ANOTHER COUNTRY

If the country ought to be obvious to readers because the city is well known, use the same citation pattern for books published in the United States:

BOOK

Yanagi, Soetsu. <u>The Unknown Craftsman: A Japanese Insight into Beauty</u>. Tokyo: Kodansha, 1989.

■ ■ ■

If you think your readers might not be familiar with the city, add the country or province, abbreviated (if it has a common abbreviation).

BOOK

Bourriaud, Nicolas. <u>Relational Aesthetics</u>. Dijon-Quetigny, France: Les Presses du Réel, 2004.

A BOOK WITHOUT PUBLICATION INFORMATION

If you find a book that does not include complete information about the place of publication, use the abbreviation *n.p.* (an abbreviation for *no publication information*).

YEAR OF PUBLICATION

Note how the pattern for listing the year of publication for a text is consistent across citations for many kinds of texts in many kinds of media.

→ On these pages, we show how the publication dates of books appear in individual citations for a range of sources; on pages 404–405 we show you how to bring together individual citations like these to create a full Works Cited section that goes at the end of any MLA-style research paper.

Put a comma after the publisher's name, then put the year of publication, followed by a period.

, Year of Publication.

, 2002.

, 1996.

, 2012.

If you find more than one copyright date for a book, use the most recent date.

EXAMPLES

Davis, Neil. <u>The Aurora Watcher's Handbook</u>. Fairbanks: U of Alaska P, 1992.

González-Crussi, F. <u>On Seeing: Things Seen, Unseen, and Obscene</u>. New York: Overlook Duckworth, 2006.

WHAT TO DO WITH A BOOK THAT HAS BEEN REPUBLISHED

A republished book has been previously published by a different publisher or published in a different form (for example, a hardback book is republished as a mass-market paperback edition).

For such books, use the standard pattern for book entries, but insert the original publication date after the book's title; put the date of the republished edition at the end.

BOOK, REPUBLISHED WITH THE SAME TITLE

Johnson, Steven. <u>Emergence: The Connected Lives of Ants, Brains, Cities, and Software</u>. 2001. New York: Touchstone-Simon, 2002.

If the republication adds material such as an introduction, this needs to be added to the citation: Put it after the original publication information.

▪ ▪ ▪

If the republished book has a different title from the original, put the new title and publication date, then put **Rpt. of** (for **reprint of**) and the original title and publication information.

BOOK, REPUBLISHED WITH DIFFERENT TITLE

Isherwood, Christopher. <u>The Last of Mr. Norris</u>. New York: New Directions, 1945. Rpt. of <u>Mr. Norris Changes Trains</u>. London: Hogarth, 1935.

WHAT TO DO WITH A BOOK PUBLISHED BEFORE 1900

You do not need to list a publisher's name when you cite a book published before 1900.

BOOK, PUBLISHED BEFORE 1900

Whitman, Walt. <u>Leaves of Grass</u>. Brooklyn, 1855.

BOOK, PUBLISHED BEFORE 1900
BOOK, ONLINE

Nightingale, Florence. <u>Notes on Nursing: What It Is, What It Is Not</u>. 1860. <u>Internet Archive</u>. 16 Feb. 2005. 21 Nov. 2006 <http://www.archive.org/details/nightingalenotes00york>.

WHAT TO DO WITH A BOOK THAT HAS NO PUBLICATION DATE

If a book does not list a date of publication on its Copyright page, put the abbreviation **n.d.** (for **no date**) where the year of publication usually goes in a citation.

BOOK, NO PUBLICATION DATE

Baudrillard, Jean. <u>Simulations</u>. New York: Semiotext(e), n.d.

PERIODICAL VOLUME, ISSUE, NUMBER, AND DATE

When periodicals were first printed, publishers would bind a sequential set of issues into one volume; eventually the pattern developed of binding a full year's set into one volume. This made finding and referring to any particular issue easy: One could find the volume first, and then the article in the volume by its issue number or date.

→ On these pages, we show how periodical volume numbers and dates appear in individual citations for a range of sources; on pages 404–405 we show you how to bring together individual citations like these to create a full Works Cited section that goes at the end of any MLA-style research paper.

THE PATTERN

VOLUME AND ISSUE NUMBER, AND DATE

The volume number goes directly after the name of the periodical; there is a space but no punctuation between the two. If there is an issue number, put a period after the volume number and then the issue number.

The date follows, in parentheses.

Volume Number.Issue Number (Date)

5.2 (Summer 2004)

27.11 (Nov. 1976)

EXAMPLES

French, R. M. "Using guitars to teach vibrations and acoustics." <u>Experimental Techniques</u> 29.2 (Mar./Apr. 2005): 47-48.

Watts, Steven. "Walt Disney: Art and Politics in the American Century." <u>The Journal of American History</u> 82.1 (June 1995): 84-110.

WHEN THERE IS NO ISSUE NUMBER

The volume number and date still give readers enough information for finding the source.

REVIEW, OF SOUND RECORDING, IN JOURNAL
REVIEW, IN JOURNAL

Ostrow, Saul. Rev. of Sharp? Monk? Sharp! Monk! Bomb 100 (Summer 2007): 15.

WHEN THERE IS ONLY A DATE

Many popular magazines do not list volume numbers, just a date.

ARTICLE, IN POPULAR MAGAZINE

Birnbaum, Charles A. "Cultivating Appreciation." Dwell Sept. 2007: 196+.

A DAILY NEWSPAPER

Because daily newspapers don't have volumes and issues, they are cited only with the date—which does not have parentheses around it.

EDITORIAL, NO AUTHOR NAMED

"Rethinking Abstinence." Editorial. Bangor Daily News. 17 Sept. 2007: 8.

NEWSPAPER ARTICLE

Rozek, Dan. "Girls' Squabble Over iPod Over: And in the End, Neither Will Get Music Player." Chicago Sun-Times 10 Nov. 2006: 3.

A WEEKLY OR BIWEEKLY JOURNAL OR MAGAZINE

Do not give the volume and issue numbers even if they are listed. Do not put parentheses around the date.

ARTICLE, IN WEEKLY JOURNAL, RETRIEVED FROM ONLINE DATABASE

Gorman, Christine. "To an Athlete, Aching Young." Time 18 Sept. 2006: 60. Expanded Academic ASAP. Thomson Gale. Michigan Technological University. 25 Feb. 2007.

REVIEW, OF BOOK, IN WEEKLY JOURNAL

Schlei, Rebecca. "Faithful Comrade: A Monumental Affair." Rev. of Loving Frank, by Nancy Horan. Shepherd Express. 6 Sept. 2007: 48.

A MONTHLY OR SEASONAL JOURNAL OR MAGAZINE

Do not give the volume and issue numbers even if they are listed. Do not put parentheses around the date.

REVIEW, OF BOOK, IN WEEKLY JOURNAL

Fallows, James. "Macau's Big Gamble." Atlantic Sept. 2007: 96-105.

PAGE NUMBERS FOR ARTICLES FROM PERIODICALS

AN ARTICLE IN A JOURNAL THAT IS PAGINATED BY VOLUME

Some journals start each new issue with page 1. Some start a volume that way but do not change the page numbering for a new issue: If volume 25, issue 1, starts at page 1, and issue 1 has 176 pages, issue 2 will start on page 177.

In such cases, leave out the issue:

ARTICLE, IN ACADEMIC JOURNAL
ARTICLE, IN JOURNAL PAGINATED BY VOLUME

Bizzell, Patricia. "Frances Willard, Phoebe Palmer, and the Ethos of the Methodist Woman Preacher." Rhetoric Society Quarterly 36 (Dec. 2006): 377-98.

AN ARTICLE THAT DOES NOT HAVE SEQUENTIAL PAGE NUMBERING

In newspapers and magazines, articles are often broken across nonsequential pages. In such cases, give the number of the first page, followed by +.

ARTICLE, IN POPULAR MAGAZINE

Lenzer, Jean. "Citizen, Heal Thyself." Discover Sept. 2007: 54+.

THE PATTERN

PAGE NUMBERS FOR ARTICLES FROM PERIODICALS

Place a colon after the date of the periodical and then put the page number or numbers. End the citation with a period.

Even if you refer to only a small portion of an article, give the page numbers for the entire article.

: xx-xx.

: 52.   :721-86.   :237-58.

: B5.   :21-28.   :237-358.

(Note that if the ending page is above 100, you cite only the last two digits of the page number unless more are necessary for clarity.)

EXAMPLES

French, R. M. "Using Guitars to Teach Vibrations and Acoustics." Experimental Techniques 29.2 (Mar./Apr. 2005): 47-48.

Watts, Steven. "Walt Disney: Art and Politics in the American Century." The Journal of American History 82.1 (June 1995): 84-110.

MLA WORKS CITED

ADDITIONAL INFORMATION

Books are published under varying circumstances. On these pages, we show how to handle citations for several circumstances that occur frequently.

→ On pages 404–405 we show you how to bring together individual citations like these to create a full Works Cited section that goes at the end of any MLA-style research paper.

IF YOU ARE CITING AN ARTICLE, ESSAY, OR POEM FROM AN EDITED COLLECTION

In this case, in addition to all the information listed on pages 364–365, you also need to include

- the title of the text
- the title of the collection
- the name of the editor or editors (preceded by **Ed.** to help readers distinguish between the author and the editor)
- the page numbers of the article

Note the punctuation in this pattern:

Author's Name. "Title of Text." <u>Title of Collection</u>. Ed. Editor's Name. Place of Publication: Publisher, Year of Publication. Page numbers of the article.

SHORT STORY, IN EDITED BOOK

Lebowitz, Fran. "Pointers for Pets." <u>Living with the Animals</u>. Ed. Gary Indiana. Boston: Faber, 1994. 61-64.

CHAPTER, IN EDITED BOOK

van Proyen, Mark. "The New Dionysianism." <u>The Sticky Sublime</u>. Ed. Bill Beckley. New York: Allworth, 2001. 165-75.

IF THE BOOK OR ARTICLE IS TRANSLATED FROM ANOTHER LANGUAGE

In this case, in addition to all the information listed on pages 362–363, you need also to include

- the name of the translator or translators, preceded by **Trans.** to help readers distinguish between the author and the *translator*.

- the page numbers of the article (if you are citing an article).

The translator's name comes after the title of the book or after the names of any editors:

Author's Name. Title of Book. Trans. Translator's Name. Place of Publication: Publisher, Year of Publication.

BOOK, TRANSLATED

Bauby, Jean-Dominique. The Diving Bell and the Butterfly. Trans. Jeremy Leggatt. New York: Knopf, 1997.

BOOK, TRANSLATED

Grossman, David. See Under: Love. Trans. Betsy Rosenberg. New York: Washington Square P, 1989.

ESSAY, IN EDITED BOOK
ESSAY, TRANSLATED

Plato. "Meno." The Collected Dialogues of Plato. Ed. Edith Hamilton and Huntington Cairns. Trans. W. K. C. Guthrie. Princeton: Princeton UP, 1961. 353-85.

IF THE BOOK IS A PUBLISHED OR UNPUBLISHED DISSERTATION

If you are citing a published dissertation, follow the pattern for a book but add the abbreviation **Diss.** to make clear that the source is a *dissertation*. Include the name of the university that granted the degree as well as the date the degree was granted in addition to the publication date.

DISSERTATION, PUBLISHED

Arola, Kristin L. Invitational Listening: Exploring Design in Online Spaces. Diss. Michigan Technological U, 2006. Ann Arbor: UMI, 2006. AAT 323176.

(If the dissertation has been published by University Microfilms International [UMI], you can include the order number, which is preceded by **AAT**.)

■ ■ ■

If the dissertation is unpublished, put its title in quotation marks instead of underlining it.

DISSERTATION, UNPUBLISHED

Babior, S. L. "Women of a Tokyo Shelter: Domestic Violence and Sexual Exploitation in Japan." Diss. UCLA, 1993.

IF THE BOOK IS PART OF A MULTIVOLUME SERIES

In some cases, you will use and cite only one part of a multivolume set. In such cases, list only the volume to which you are referring.

BOOK, PART OF MULTIVOLUME SERIES, A PART

Rothenberg, Jerome, and Pierre Joris, eds. <u>Poems for the Millennium: The University of California Book of Modern & Postmodern Poetry</u>. Vol. 1. Berkeley: U of California P, 1995.

■ ■ ■

In cases when you need to refer to two or more parts of a multivolume set, give the total number of volumes in the work (**2 vols.**) following the title of the work.

BOOK, PART OF MULTIVOLUME SERIES, COMPLETE

Rothenberg, Jerome, and Pierre Joris, eds. <u>Poems for the Millennium: The University of California Book of Modern & Postmodern Poetry</u>. 2 vols. Berkeley: U of California P, 1995-98.

Since the two volumes in this example were published over a period of years, the complete date range is included in the publication information.

IF THE BOOK IS A SECOND (OR LATER) EDITION

Put the number of the edition, followed by *ed.* after the title of the book.

BOOK, SECOND OR LATER EDITION

Lynch, Patrick J., and Sarah Horton. <u>Web Style Guide: Basic Principles for Creating Web Sites</u>. 2nd ed. New Haven: Yale UP, 2001.

MLA WORKS CITED
FOR OTHER KINDS OF TEXTS

You can use almost any kind of published or online text as support or evidence for your arguments—and you need to cite any text you use as support or evidence.

→ On pages 404–405 we show you how to bring together individual citations like these to create a full Works Cited section that goes at the end of any MLA-style research paper.

CD-ROMS

Because they are usually published only once, like books, the citation format of CD-ROMs follows that of books, except that the medium is noted:

CD-ROM, THREE OR MORE AUTHORS

Blue, Carroll Parrott, Kristy H. A. Kong, and the Labyrinth Project. The Dawn at My Back: Memoir of a Black Texas Upbringing. CD-ROM. Los Angeles: Annenberg Center for Communication, 2003.

If instead of an author, you find an editor or compiler, cite that information instead, with the appropriate abbreviation (ed. or comp.). If you cannot any of this information, cite what you do find:

CD-ROM, NO AUTHOR

Three Winters in the Sun: Einstein in California. CD-ROM. Los Angeles: Annenberg Center for Communication, 2005.

ADVERTISEMENTS

Give the name of the product or company advertised, followed by *Advertisement*. End with the publication information for the source where you found the advertisement.

ADVERTISEMENT, IN JOURNAL OR MAGAZINE

Goin' Home: A Tribute to Fats Domino CD Set by Vanguard Records. Advertisement. The Nation 285.9 (1 Oct. 2007): 40.

ADVERTISEMENT, ON TELEVISION

PETA. Advertisement. KTRK [Houston]. 18 Sept. 2007.

SOUND RECORDINGS

When you cite commercial recordings, start with the name of the person(s) you reference in your writing: the performer or band, the composer, or the conductor. Then give the title of the recording, the artist (if not mentioned at the beginning of the citation), the manufacturer, and the date.

SOUND RECORDING, ENTIRE ALBUM

Bach, J. S. The Goldberg Variations. Perf. Simone Dinnerstein. Telarc, 2007.

SOUND RECORDING, ENTIRE ALBUM

Black Francis. Bluefinger. Cooking Vinyl, 2007.

To cite only one song, put it (within quotation marks) after the artist name.

SOUND RECORDING, ONE SONG

Simone, Nina. "Please Don't Let Me Be Misunderstood." The Lady Has the Blues. Tomato Records, 2003.

SOFTWARE

Cite software as you would a book without a named author (→ see page 375)—but include *Computer Software.*, after the title. If there is a publisher, include the name and date of publication; for software you have downloaded, give the date of the download and the URL.

SOFTWARE

Encyclopedia Britannica 2008 Ultimate. Computer Software. Encyclopedia Britannica, 2008.

SOFTWARE, DOWNLOADED

Firefox. Version 2.0.0.7. Computer Software. 22 Sept. 2007. <http://en.www.mozilla.com/en/>.

MAP, GRAPH, CHART

Cite a map, graph, or chart as you would a book without a named author (→ see page 375)—but include *Map.*, *Graph.*, or *Chart.* after the title.

CHART, ONLINE

Choose Your Weapon: The Global Arms Trade. Chart. International Networks Archive. 12 Apr. 2007 <http://www.princeton.edu/~ina/infographics/weapons.html>.

MAP

Milwaukee By Bike. Map. Milwaukee: Bicycle Federation of Wisconsin, 2005.

A PUBLIC TALK

For presentations at professional conferences or speeches, debates, or lectures, give the speaker's name, the title of the presentation (in quotation marks), the sponsoring organization (if there is one), the place, and the date. (If there is no title, give a descriptive label.)

PRESENTATION AT A PROFESSIONAL CONFERENCE

Cooper, Marilyn. "The Animal Who Writes." Penn State Conference on Rhetoric and Composition. State College, PA. 10 July 2007.

LECTURE

Trimble, Virginia. "Astrophysics Meets the Millennium." LIGO Public Lectures. Richland, WA. 11 Nov. 2003.

FILM OR VIDEO

Begin the citation with the name of the film or video, and then list the director(s), the distributor, and the year of release. If your purpose in citing the film or video suggests it, include the names of any writers, performers, or producers before the distributor.

FILM

The Longest Day. Dir. Ken Annakin, Andrew Marton, Bernhard Wicki, and Darryl F. Zanuck. Twentieth Century-Fox, 1962.

VIDEO, ONLINE

Fantoche (two times). Animatorblu. BLU/blog. 15 Sept. 2007. 10 Nov. 2007 <http://www.blublu.org/blog>.

You do not need to include whether you saw the film or video in a theater or on television. If you saw it on a DVD, however, include that information:

FILM, ON DVD
FILM, FOREIGN

Pan's Labyrinth [El Laberinto del fauno]. Dir. Guillermo del Toro. DVD. New Line, 2006.

(Notice, too, that you include—after the English title—the original title of a film that was made in another country.)

If, in the writing where you cite the film or video, you are commenting on the part played by a particular person, start the citation with that person's name. (*Perf.* abbreviates *performer*.)

FILM, FOCUS ON ACTOR OR DIRECTOR

Newman, Paul, perf. The Price of Sugar. Dir. Bill Haney. Uncommon Productions, 2007.

CARTOON OR COMIC STRIP

If you have only an author's name or a title, start with what you have; otherwise, give both the name and then the title. Follow that with **Cartoon.** or **Comic Strip.** End with the full publication information for the source where you found the cartoon or comic strip. (If the source's date matters to your argument, put it after the title.)

CARTOON, IN NEWSPAPER

Carlson, Stuart. Cartoon. Milwaukee Journal Sentinel 23 Sept. 2007: 2J.

CARTOON, ONLINE
CARTOON, NO KNOWN AUTHOR

The Last Rail Split by 'Honest Old Abe.' 1816. Cartoon. 17 May 2006 <http://elections.harpweek.com/ 1860/cartoon-1860-Medium. asp?UniqueID=19&Year=1860>.

COMIC STRIP, IN BOOK
COMIC STRIP, REPRINTED

Chapman Hank, story. Kida, Fred, art. The Last Tattoo! Comic strip. 1952. Arf Museum. Ed. Craig Yoe. Seattle: Fantagraphic Books, 2007. 60-64.

COMIC STRIP, ONLINE
COMIC STRIP, TWO AUTHORS

Home, Emily, and Joey Comeau. A Softer World. Comic strip. 15 Sept. 2007 <http://www.asofterworld.com/ index.php?id=235>.

> **TIP: FINDING INFORMATION ABOUT FILMS**
>
> The *Internet Movie Database* (<http://www.imdb.com>) gives you access to all the information you need in citing films.

MUSICAL COMPOSITION

Begin with the composer's name, followed by the title of the work. (If you cite a composition that is identified by a number, do not underline it or put quotation marks around it.)

MUSICAL COMPOSITION

Price, Florence. <u>Mississippi River Suite</u>.

MUSICAL COMPOSITION

Sibelius, Jean. Symphony no. 7 in C major.

TELEVISION OR RADIO PROGRAM

Start with the name of the particular episode you are citing, then give the name of the title of the program. List the writer (using **By**), the director (**Dir.**), or the Host; also list the performers (**perf.**) if appropriate for your use of the source. Give the name of the network and then the call letters of the station (if the station is local, give the city name) on which you saw or heard the broadcast. End with the show's broadcast date.

TELEVISION PROGRAM

"Homer's Phobia." <u>The Simpsons</u>. By Ron Hauge. Dir. Mike B. Anderson. Fox. WITI, Milwaukee. 16 Feb. 1997.

RADIO PROGRAM

"<u>Babysitting</u>." <u>This American Life</u>. Host Ira Glass. Public Radio International. WNMU, Marquette, MI. 1 June 2001.

RADIO PROGRAM, ONLINE

"The Melody of Murder." <u>The Avenger</u>. 3 Aug. 1945. RadioLovers. 4 June 2007 <http://www.radiocrazy.com/shows/A/avenger/AVENGER450803e0932-22-m28m51sTheMelodyOfMurder.mp3>.

BROADCAST INTERVIEW

For interviews you see on television or hear on the Internet or on the radio, follow the same pattern as for print interviews (➜ see page 383).

INTERVIEW, ONLINE VIDEO

Salzmann, Marc. Interview with Jonathan Mann. <u>Awaiting "Halo 3."</u> CNN.com. 24 Sept. 2007. 24 Sept. 2007 <http://www.cnn.com/video/>.

INTERVIEW, ONLINE RECORDING

Harper, Ben. Interview with David Dye. <u>Transcending Genre</u>. npr.org. 7 Sept. 2007. 12 Sept. 2007 <http://www.npr.org/templates/story/story.php?storyId=14251932>.

AN INTERVIEW YOU CONDUCT

Give the name of the person interviewed, the kind of interview (**Personal interview.**, **Telephone interview.**, or **E-mail interview.**), and the date.

INTERVIEW, CONDUCTED BY YOU

Bok, Hillary. E-mail Interview. 24 Feb. 2005.

PAINTING, DRAWING, SCULPTURE, OR PHOTOGRAPH

Put the artist's name first, then the title of the work. If you are citing artwork from a museum, give the museum's name and place. If you are citing artwork you found in a publication, give the full publication information. If you wish to include the date of the artwork, put it after the title.

PAINTING, IN MUSEUM

Bastien-Lepage, Jules. <u>Joan of Arc</u>. 1879. Metropolitan Museum of Art, New York.

PAINTING, ONLINE

Bruegel, Pieter, the Elder. <u>The Triumph of Death</u>. c. 1562. Prado, Madrid. 3 Dec. 2007 <http://museoprado.mcu.es/imuerte.html>.

PHOTOGRAPH, ONLINE
PHOTOGRAPH, PHOTOGRAPHER UNKNOWN

<u>Clown</u>. Nelson-Atkins Museum of Art, Kansas City. 2007. 12 Jan. 2008 <http://www.nelson-atkins.org/art/Exhibitions/DevGreat/CollectionDatabase_ImageView.cfm?id=47176&theme=exhibition>.

PHOTOGRAPH, IN MAGAZINE

Todd, Mark. <u>Man in the Moon</u>. <u>Raygun</u> (Nov. 1994): n.p.

For a personal photograph that has not been published or shown, give a descriptive title, tell who took the photograph, and give its date.

PHOTOGRAPH, PERSONAL

Big Snowfall, Upper Peninsula. Personal photograph by Dennis Lynch. 18 Oct. 1992.

PERFORMANCE

To cite a musical, dramatic, dance, poetic, or other artistic performance, start with the title—unless you can name the performer(s). Give information about participants (as with films: → *see page 400). End with the location of the performance and its date.*

PERFORMANCE, THEATRICAL

<u>King Lear</u>. By William Shakespeare. Dir. Trevor Nunn. Perf. Ian McKellen. Guthrie Theater, Minneapolis. 14 Oct. 2007.

PERFORMANCE, MUSICAL

<u>Of Montreal</u>. Ogden Theater, Denver. 12 Nov. 2007.

ONLINE SOURCES OTHER THAN THOSE WE'VE ALREADY MENTIONED

To cite e-mail, give the writer's name and the subject line. Then put **E-mail to** followed by the recipient's name. End with the message's date.

E-MAIL

Taylor, Sarah. "Arkansas Attorney Firing." E-mail to Kyle Sampson. 16 Feb. 2007.

To cite a posting to a listserv, give the writer's name and the subject line. Then put **Online posting** followed by the date of the posting and the list's name. End with the message's date, the date you accessed it, and a URL or the list's e-mail address.

LISTSERV POSTING

Spinuzzi, Clay. "Re: Google, Tech Comm, and Professionalism." Online posting. 10 Sept. 2007. Association of Teachers of Technical Writing. 12 Sept. 2007 <attw-l@lyris.ttu.edu>.

To cite an online synchronous discussion (such as a MOO, MUD, chat, or IM), you can decide to cite the whole discussion or only one contribution.

To cite the whole discussion, give the title of the event, a description of the event and its date, the forum in which the discussion took place, the date you accessed the discussion, and the URL.

ONLINE SYNCHRONOUS DISCUSSION, WHOLE DISCUSSION

"MOO: The Second Decade." Online discussion. <u>Computers and Writing Conference Online 2005</u>. 8 June 2005. 12 July 2006 <http://www.accd.edu/ sac/english/lirvin/encore/CW2005/ TranscriptC&W2005.htm>.

To cite one person's contribution, follow the same format as above, but put the name of the person first. (Although the MLA has not yet caught up with some of the indexing possibilities of online texts, you can help your readers in cases like this by going beyond what the MLA format asks: You can help them find a listing in a discussion by giving its time as well as date, as we show below.)

ONLINE SYNCHRONOUS DISCUSSION, SINGLE ENTRY

MaxoidLittleL. "Chat Transcript." Online discussion. <u>The Sims2 Community</u>. 16 Aug. 2007 5:00:57 PM. 1 Jan. 2008 <http://thesims2.ea.com/ community/chat_08_16_07.php>.

A WORKS CITED PAGE IN MLA FORMAT

To format an MLA Works Cited listing:

❑ Put the listing at the very end of the paper.

❑ Use the same margin measurements as the rest of the paper (➔ see page 407).

❑ The Works Cited starts on its own page.

❑ Number each Works Cited page at the top right of the page (as you do each page in the MLA format; ➔ see page 407). The number on the first page follows the number of the last page of the paper. For example, if the last page of the paper is 8, the first page of the Works Cited will be 9.

❑ **Works Cited** is centered at the top of the page.

❑ The listings are arranged alphabetically by the author's last name. (If a listing starts with the title of a source, place it into the whole list alphabetically, using the first letter of the title. If the title begins with **A**, **An**, or **The**, alphabetize by the second word of the title.)

❑ If you list two or more sources by the same author, alphabetize them by the source titles. List the author only once; start all subsequent entries with three hyphens and a period.

❑ If you have two authors with the same last name, alphabetize by the first name.

❑ Double-space the entries.

Works Cited

Bauby, Jean-Dominique. <u>The Diving Bell and the Butterfly</u>. Trans. Jeremy Leggatt. New York: Knopf, 1997.

<u>King Lear</u>. By William Shakespeare. Dir. Trevor Nunn. Perf. Ian McKellen. Guthrie Theater, Minneapolis. 14 Oct. 2007.

"The Melody of Murder." <u>The Avenger</u>. 3 Aug. 1945. <u>RadioLovers</u>. 4 June 2007 <http://www.radiocrazy.com/shows/A/avenger/ AVENGER450803e0932-22-m28m51sTheMelodyOfMurder. mp3>.

Pollan, Michael. <u>Botany of Desire: A Plant's Eye-View of the World</u>. New York: Random House, 2001.

---. <u>The Omnivore's Dilemma: A Natural History of Four Meals</u>. New York: Penguin, 2006.

Rorty, Amélie Oksenberg. "Structuring Rhetoric." <u>Essays on Aristotle's Rhetoric</u>. ed. Amélie Oksenberg Rorty. Berkeley: U of California P, 1996. 1-33.

Rorty, Richard. <u>Philosophy and the Mirror of Nature</u>. Princeton: Princeton UP, 1979.

Shakespeare, William. <u>Hamlet</u>. Ed. A. R. Braunmuller. New York: Penguin Classics, 2001.

World Health Organization. <u>The World Health Report 2005: Make Every Mother and Child Count</u>. Geneva, Switzerland: World Health Organization, 2005. 13 Mar. 2006 <http://www.who.int/whr/2005 /whr2005_en.pdf>.

Use hanging indentation

So that readers can scan the alphabetic list easily and quickly, indent by 1/2 inch all lines underneath the first.

SAMPLE PAPER IN MLA FORMAT

To the right is the final draft of Riley's paper, which we've shown developing from Part 2 through Part 5 of this book.

→ Pages 84–85 in Part 2 show Riley's initial research on the topic of microcredit.

→ Pages 146–147 in Part 3 show how Riley developed a thesis statement.

→ Throughout Part 4, you can see how Riley developed a statement of purpose for her paper by analyzing her audience.

→ Pages 168–179 show Riley's first draft and revision plan. Look for differences between the two drafts to learn choices you can make to strengthen your writing.

→ Pages 202–203 in Part 5 show how Riley used her thesis statement to figure out the arrangement of her paper and what to include in her paragraphs.

FORMATTING

We have indicated margins in blue to the right. Other features that characterize the MLA style of formatting papers are:

- The paper is double-spaced throughout.
- Every page is topped with the writer's name at top right, as the pages to the right show.
- The title is centered above the body of the paper.
- The paper is presented in a traditional serifed typeface like Times in a readable size, such as 12 point.

Opening quotations

Riley has added more quotations than she had in her original draft, to help readers understand why microloans matter.

Defining terms

Notice that Riley has defined *microloan*—and how quickly she is able to do this.

Providing signposts to readers

Riley gives readers a sense of what is to come. Such paragraphs are like road maps: They help readers understand how a paper's parts fit together. Because readers don't have to figure this out, such paragraphs help readers focus on and understand the paper's argument.

Riley M. Savage
Professor Lynch
UN2001
17 Dec. 2007

Do Microloans Cure Women's Poverty?

In Afghanistan, under the Taliban regime, Estorai ran her home-based beauty parlor in secret, fearing reprisals for violating the ban against cosmetics. Today, with FINCA loans, her business is flourishing and Estorai is determined her daughter will receive the education she needs to succeed in the new Afghanistan. ("Change for the Better in Afghanistan")

Says Nyamba Konate, a microloan beneficiary, "I can now ensure that my children go to school, and I can better support my husband by buying food and stocking it to get us through the difficult rainy season." ("Microloans and Literacy")

"Miriam began operating her own taxi business a few years ago with the help of microloans […]. Miriam and her husband were able to build a home, and now put the profits towards their children's education and saving for the future. Miriam even purchased a computer for her daughter, which helps with her university studies and also allows her to offer desktop publishing services to other students and community members." ("Improving Lives")

Google "microloan" and you'll get over two million results. Many results link to organizations that offer very small loans—called "microloans"—to people who do not qualify for traditional bank loans. The websites tell stories like the ones above, about the positive changes microloans make in poor women's lives worldwide, including the United States.

In this paper, I question what microloans are capable of doing. After giving a brief history and explaining how microloans work, and then describing the claims many make for microloans, I show how different critics question the purposes and potentials of microloans for women. I consider how microcredit could be offered to poor women

Summarizing

This paragraph was a long quotation in Riley's first draft. By summarizing the quotation, Riley keeps her readers focused on the points important to her argument—and also then has more room to make her arguments.

Transitions between paragraphs

By repeating concepts and words from the end of one paragraph at the beginning of the next, Riley helps readers see how her ideas connect from one paragraph to the next.

→ See pages 296–297 about transitions between paragraphs.

Asking questions

Riley focuses the purpose of her paper further by asking whether the microloan system works for borrowers. Questions also challenge readers to answer them, and so can increase their engagement. (Asking questions can be overdone, however; in a paper of this length, two to three questions will seem reasonable to readers.)

Using the words of others to make your point

Riley wants to show that many people expect microloans to end poverty and change the status of women. Because she makes this point using the words of the Nobel Peace Prize Committee—a group that should have considerable authority with readers—her readers are likely to accept her point about people's expectations about microcredit.

so that their communities really are enriched and the women join the global economy in ways that make sense to them and not just to the people who make the loans.

Microcredit originated in Bangladesh. In the 1970s, Muhammad Yunus, an economics professor at a Bangaldeshi university, started making very small loans to villagers so they could buy supplies for their small businesses; Yunus had learned that traditional banks would not give loans to the villagers. Eventually, out of Yunus's loan-making came the Grameen Bank. The Bank makes loans to groups of five villagers, who are responsible for each other's debts. Because of the groups, villagers have repayment incentive: "the threat of being shamed before neighbors and relatives" (Giridharadas and Bradsher).

The successes of Grameen Bank led to many other organizations following the same pattern: Loans are made to a small group, each member of which is responsible that all repay their loans. In addition, Grameen started another pattern, of loan recipients meeting regularly to learn community-building habits. For the loanmakers, this system seems to work: The repayment rate on microloans through microenterprise organizations is at least 95% ("Microenterprise Quick Facts"). But does the system work for borrowers?

The "microloan" Google search described at the beginning of this paper brings up, in addition to microloan organization websites, many newspaper and magazine articles. Almost all the writing celebrates the microloan movement's successes, describing—as in my opening quotations—how women in poor communities turn small loans into small businesses, have enough money to send their children to school, and sometimes even start providing jobs for others. These writings also often show the same expectations about microloans as the Nobel Peace Prize committee did when they gave the 2006 prize to Yunus and the Grameen Bank: The Committee wrote that "Lasting peace can not be achieved unless large population groups find ways in which to break out of poverty" and that "Microcredit has proved to be an important liberating force in societies where women in particular have to struggle against repressive social and economic

Supporting your claims

By quickly citing all these sources in addition to the Nobel Peace Prize Committee, Riley has probably provided enough support for her claim that many people expect microloans to end poverty and change the status of women.

Notice that, because she is referring to an overall argument made by each of these sources, she does not need to refer to page numbers of specific parts of the sources.

Summarizing and paraphrasing

This is another paragraph that, in the rough draft, was composed of long quotations. Compare this draft and the rough draft (→ see page 171) to see how Riley used summary and paraphrase to make the argument hers.

Spelling things out

In her original draft, Riley didn't explain what what *FINCA* meant (→ see page 173). Notice here how she gives the full name of the organization and then puts the abbreviation in parentheses. (Notice too that throughout this draft she explains the background of the people she cites, to give readers reason to take their words seriously.)

Being careful with your claims

Riley is not arguing that microloans are always and everywhere bad; instead, she acknowledges that they often do benefit women and their families. Academic writing is characterized by such attempts at being careful in arguments and taking into account evidence that shows issues to be gray rather than starkly black or white.

conditions" ("Nobel Peace Prize"). Again and again in writings about microcredit those two themes emerge: Microcredit will help poor populations break out of poverty and it will be women who do this by using microloans to help themselves and their families. From the Nobel Peace Prize Committee to New York Times opinion pieces (Bajaj; Freid; Kristof; Temes), from bills passed in the U.S. Congress (Smith) to articles in environmental magazines (Kelly), those two claims are repeated over and over.

Why are women so important as beneficiaries of microloans? In its early years, the Grameen Bank loaned money almost equally to men and to women—but more recently its loans go overwhelmingly to women (Rahman, slide 9). Another well-known microfinance organization, the Foundation for International Community Assistance (FINCA), says that it lends primarily to women because

> Most victims of severe poverty are children. According to UNICEF, at least half of the 12 million children aged five or younger who die each year die from malnutrition associated with severe poverty. The most direct way to improve childrens' survival and welfare is to strengthen their own mothers' ability to take care of them. ("Frequently Asked Questions")

The United Nations has put out a "Guide for Best Practices" in microcredit, which argues that women's "access to microfinance not only benefits women but also their families and communities" because it not only improves women's economic lives but also improves women's places in society (Burjorjee, Deshpande, and Weidemann 7). Microloans are supposed to help women gain confidence in taking part in local economies and asserting themselves in their communities, and any income they get from the loans is expected to be applied to their families and so to the betterment of their communities.

The anecdotes that begin this paper, like the others that appear in almost every source I've mentioned so far, suggest that, to some extent, microloans do help women make their—and their children's—lives better. There has been some research to support these claims. For example, Susy Cheston, an official with the aid organization

2" for indented quotations

A transition paragraph

Riley uses words she quoted earlier to return to her main questions and keep her readers aware of how and why she is moving from one paragraph to the next.

Focused paragraphs

In her first draft, this paragraph and the next were all one (→ see page 173). By turning back to her thesis statement (→ see page 163), Riley was able to break the original paragraph into two. Each of the paragraphs now focuses on one specific point about how microloans work.

When you quote words that you found in a quotation

Riley found the words about Bangladesh and Bolivia quoted in a journal article. She decided to use the exact words, so she has to show that she found them in that article. Putting *qtd. in* before the in-text citation to the source indicates that she is doing this.

Opportunity International, provides evidence that, in one program in the Philippines, "77 percent of incoming clients were classified as 'very poor'; after two years in the program, only 13 percent of mature clients were still 'very poor'" (23). Another writer, in a paper written for the United Nations Research Institute for Social Development, describes how women in India use loans to start work in local markets and keep their families and small businesses going in hard times (Mayoux 39). So no one is wrong to think that microloans can have positive effects in the lives of women.

But can those effects really "liberate women" and help "large population groups.... break out of poverty" as the Nobel Prize committee suggested? Many do not think so, given the evidence.

For example, in terms of poverty, the writer of the paper for the United Nations Research Institute for Social Development, quoted above, says, immediately after the passage I summarized, that most studies of microcredit programs "find very small increases in income for quite large numbers of borrowers; in only a very small number of cases are there significant income increases" (Mayoux 39). In addition, studies also find that microcredit benefits women who are not at the lowest levels of poverty; the poorest of the poor may, in fact, get poorer trying to repay (MacIsaac 11-12; Mayoux 40-44). The benefits from microcredit also don't last long because borrowers often can't use loans for anything but immediate need (MacIsaac 15; Mayoux 41) or the borrowers take up work where they make only a little bit of money and where they gain no economic clout (Feiner and Barker; Roy). Under such conditions, women's positions within the overall economy do not change, meaning that their communities are unlikely to "break out of poverty." Even though microcredit has been in existence for over twenty years, Robert Pollin, co-director of the Political Economy Research Institute at the University of Massachusetts, pointed out in 2006 that "Bangladesh and Bolivia are two countries widely recognized for having the most successful microcredit programs in the world. They also remain two of the poorest countries in the world" (qtd. in Cockburn 9).

Using and referring to multiple sources

From her original audience analysis (→ see page 163), Riley knew she needed to give lots of evidence that microloans have problems. In this paragraph she shows that she has done her research and that she has lots of support for her claims. Notice that she doesn't have to quote the words of the people she cites; instead, she summarizes their points, and uses the parenthetical documentation at the end of the sentences to list the sources. (When you do this, put semicolons between the names of the different sources.)

Getting to the claim

Compare these last two paragraphs to the last paragraph of Riley's original draft (→ see page 175). By having used her thesis statement to help her organize her writing (→ see page 203), Riley can now address her thesis statement's claim in this next-to-last paragraph. Prior to this, she has offered much evidence that microloans are problematic when money is just given to women; here, then, she can make her claim explicit. If her prior evidence has been sufficient, readers should be prepared to accept Riley's claims; do you think Riley has offered enough prior evidence?

Concluding

Compare this last paragraph to the last paragraph of Riley's original draft (→ see page 175). Riley no longer brings in new evidence but instead summarizes her claim and ends with a pathos appeal to future possibility.

And what of women being liberated by microcredit? Using the loan often adds to, rather than changes, women's daily work: When women use their loans to make and sell food or other items, it is on top of running their households and taking care of their children, and sometimes they have to pull their children out of school to work in order to repay loans (Cheston 25; MacIsaac 13). And rather than learning about money use themselves, a significant number of women give their loans to male relatives because in their communities, men are supposed make economic decisions (Cowen; MacIsaac 13; Mayoux 25). For the same reasons, when women do use their loans, it can lead to both verbal and physical violence against them from their families (MacIsaac 22; Mayoux 24; Rahman, slides 23-24).

There is no question that microloans have helped some women, as all the anecdotes on all the organizational websites and in many writings show—but the evidence does not support the grand hopes for microloans that many hold. There are studies indicating what approaches to microcredit seem to work best for helping women take advantage of the potentials of microloans (Burjorjee, Deshpande, and Weidemann; MacIsaac). These studies acknowledge the problems I've noted about microloans, and, in response, acknowledge that women have to be given support in addition to loans. When women take part in regular support groups where they talk about how to use money and make economic decisions—and where they can talk about family and social circumstances—they gain both knowledge and confidence; they learn they have support for making decisions about money. In addition, when they are given information about economics and building businesses, and when they are provided mentoring, they are in better position to understand possibilities for and consequences of their decisions.

As I have described, there has been much good that has come from microcredit. But if we truly do want to end poverty, we cannot just give loans to women. We must also help women learn how to operate within the larger economy, help them make their own decisions, and give them resources for dealing with the familial and community structures that stand in the way of their confidence and abilities.

Works Cited

Bajaj, Vikas. "Out to Maximize Social Gains, Not Profit." <u>New York Times</u> 9 Dec. 2006.

    22 Nov. 2007 <http://www.nytimes.com/2006/12/09/business/worldbusiness/

    09yunus.html>.

Burjorjee, Deena M., Rani Deshpande, and C. Jean Weidemann. "Supporting Women's

    Livelihoods: Microfinance that Works for the Majority. A Guide to Best Practices."

    <u>United Nations Capital Development Fund</u>. Jan. 2002.

"Change for the Better in Afghanistan." FINCA International. July 2007. 20 Nov. 2007

    <http://www.villagebanking.org/site/c.erKPI2PCIoE/b.2607027/k.5050/

    Newsbriefs_FINCA_eNews.htm>.

Cheston, Suzy. "Women and Microfinance: Opening Markets and Minds."

    <u>Economic Perspectives: An Electronic Journal of the U.S. Department of State</u>

    9.1 (Feb. 2004). 19 Nov. 2007 <http://usinfo.state.gov/journals/ites/0204/

    ijee/toc.htm>.

Cockburn, Alexander. "The Myth of Microloans." <u>The Nation</u> 6 Nov. 2006: 9.

Cowen, Tyler. "Microloans May Work, but There Is Dispute in India Over Who Will

    Make Them." <u>New York Times</u> 10 Aug. 2006. 19 Nov. 2007 <http://

    www.nytimes.com/2006/08/10/business/10scene.html>.

Feiner, Susan F., and Drucilla K. Barker. "Microcredit and Women's Poverty." <u>Dollars</u>

    <u>and Sense</u> Nov./Dec. 2006: 10-11.

Freid, Joseph P. "From a Small Loan, a Jewelry Business Grows." <u>New York Times</u> 12

    Nov. 2006. 19 Nov. 2007 <http://www.nytimes.com /2006/11/12/jobs/

    12homefront.html?ex=1187236800&en=98c5c088749b383b&ei=5070>.

"Frequently Asked Questions." FINCA. 20 Nov. 2007

    <http://www.villagebanking.org/site/c.erKPI2PCIoE/b.2394157/k.8161/

    Frequently_Asked_Questions.htm>.

Giridharadas, Anand, and Keith Bradsher. "Microloan Pioneer and His Bank Win Nobel
    Peace Prize." New York Times 13 Oct. 2006. 19 Nov. 2007 <http://
    www.nytimes.com/2006/10/13/business/
    14nobelcnd.html?ei=5070&en=4d992a1456a69474&ex=1187496000&adxnnl=
    1&adxnnlx=1187362984-v/nuT8pwJMcXlFKKsBSiJg>.

"Improving Lives: Miriam Carolina Mejía, Juticalpa, Honduras." Global Partnerships.
    2007. 21 Nov. 2007 <http://www.globalpartnerships.org/sections/impact/
    impact_miriam.htm>.

Kelly, Sean. "Banking on Women: Microcredit in Northern Ghana." Natural Life
    May/June 2007. 34-35.

Kristof, Nicholas D. "You, Too, Can Be a Banker to the Poor." New York Times 27 Mar.
    2007. 21 Nov. 2007 <http://select.nytimes.com/2007/03/27/opinion /27kristof.html>.

MacIsaac, Norman. "The Role of Microcredit in Poverty Reduction and Promoting
    Gender Equity: A Discussion Paper." Canadian International Development Agency.
    Gatineau, Quebec. 1997. 18 Nov. 2007 <http://www.acdi-cida.gc.ca/
    INET/IMAGES.NSF/vLUImages/Policy/ $file/microe.pdf>.

Mayoux, Linda. "From Vicious to Virtuous Circles? Gender and Micro-Enterprise
    Development." United Nations Research Institute for Social Development. 1995.
    18 Nov. 2007 <http://www.unrisd.org/unrisd/website/document.nsf/
    0/5901781754E7C91580256B67005B6AF7?OpenDocument>.

"Microenterpise Quick Facts." Economic Perspectives: An Electronic Journal of the U.S.
    Department of State 9.1 (Feb. 2004). 16 Nov. 2007 <http://usinfo.state.gov/
    journals/ites/0204/ijee/quick.htm>.

"Microloans and Literacy Are Contributing to Food Security in Poor Upper Guinea."
    USAID Africa Success Stories. 2005. 24 Nov. 2007 <http://africastories.usaid.gov/
    search_details.cfm?storyID=323&countryID=9&sectorID=0&yearID=5>.

"Nobel Peace Prize for 2006." Press release. <u>The Norwegian Nobel Committee</u>. Oslo. 13
    Oct. 2006. 22 Nov. 2007 <http://nobelprize.org/nobel_prizes /peace/
    laureates/2006/press.html>.

Rahman, Aminur. "Microfinance and Gender-Based Violence: Experience from the
    Grameen Bank Lending." Canadian International Development Agency. Slide
    program. 9 Nov. 2004. 8 Nov. 2007 <http://siteresources.worldbank.org/
    INTGENDER/Resources/AminurPresentationtext.pdf>.

Roy, Ananya. "Against the Feminization of Policy." Woodrow Wilson International
    Center for Scholars. Nov. 2002. 23 Nov. 2007 <http://www.wilsoncenter.org/
    topics/pubs/urbanbrief01.pdf>.

Smith, Christopher H. "Microcredit Loans are Critical Tools for Helping the World's
    Poor." <u>Economic Perspectives: An Electronic Journal of the U.S. Department of
    State</u> 9.1 (Feb. 2004). 17 Nov. 2007 <http://usinfo.state.gov/journals/ites/
    0204/ijee/toc.htm>.

Temes, Peter. "Bridgeport v. Bangladesh." <u>New York Times</u> 1 July 2007. 20 Nov. 2007
    <http://www.nytimes.com/2007/07/01/opinion/nyregionopinions/01CTtemes.html>.

GUIDE TO MLA DOCUMENTATION MODELS

WORKS CITED SAMPLES

WEBSITES AND OTHER ONLINE SOURCES

OTHER TYPES OF SOURCES

APA DOCUMENTATION FOR IN-TEXT CITATIONS

The American Psychological Association (APA) publishes the *Publication Manual of the American Psychological Association*, which is now in its fifth edition, published in 2001.

This style's title might suggest that only psychologists use this style, but APA style is also used in other disciplines such as business, education, sociology, nursing, social work, and criminology. APA style was developed for researchers to report research results, and—in line with twentieth-century beliefs about how scientific research is supposed to be objective—this style encourages writing in the third person or passive voice; it also encourages the straightforward presentation of data, tables, charts, and graphs.

THE PURPOSES OF IN-TEXT CITATIONS IN APA STYLE

Although (as you will see) APA style uses a slightly different format for in-text citations than the MLA style uses, the reasons for using in-text citations are the same.

→ See page 351 to learn the purposes of in-text citations.

IN-TEXT CITATIONS IN APA STYLE

Whether you are citing books, periodicals, or electronic sources, in-text citations in the APA style generally contain these three elements:

1

The **name of the author** of the words or ideas being quoted, summarized, or paraphrased. The name can appear within a sentence containing quoted words, or it can appear in parentheses at the sentence's end.

2

The **date** when the source being cited was published.

3

The **page number(s)** of or some other reference to the cited words or ideas. The number of the page from which quoted words come goes at the end of the sentence, in parentheses. Note that **p.** goes before the page number.

These three elements can be arranged in one of two different ways to create an in-text citation in the APA style:

In her article on two nineteenth-century women preachers, Bizzell (2006) argues that "a conjunction between the female sex and moral activism is traditional in Methodism" (p. 379).

One writer on nineteenth-century women preachers argues that "a conjunction between the female sex and moral activism is traditional in Methodism" (Bizzell, 2006, p. 379).

→ Pages 422–425 list variations on this pattern for APA in-text citations.

PUNCTUATION IN APA IN-TEXT CITATIONS

- The parentheses that contain page numbers go at the end of the sentence, followed by the punctuation that ends the sentence.
- When you include an author's name in the parentheses with the year and page number, put a comma between each element.
- If the words you are quoting run across several pages, cite them like this: **(pp. 23–25)** (**pp.** stands for **pages**).
- If the words you are quoting are from several nonconsecutive pages, cite them like this: **(pp. 45, 76)**.

VARIATIONS IN THE APA PATTERN OF IN-TEXT CITATIONS

→ No author is named for the source. See page 422.

→ There is no page number (for example, you are citing a brochure or a webpage). See page 422.

→ Your Reference list contains two or more sources by the same author. See page 423.

→ Your Reference list contains sources by two authors with the same last name. See page 423.

→ The work has two authors. See page 423.

→ The work has three, four, or five authors. See page 424.

→ The work has six or more authors. See page 424.

→ The work has a group or corporate author or is a government document. See page 424.

   → See page 331 for what "corporate author" means.

→ You are citing two or more sources in one sentence. See page 424.

→ You are citing a classical work, sacred text, or other work with no date listed. See page 425.

→ You are citing an electronic source such as a webpage or e-mail. See page 425.

APA PATTERN FOR IN-TEXT CITATIONS

VARIATIONS ON THE PATTERN

NO AUTHOR IS NAMED

If you cannot find a named author, use the title of the work instead:

To "watch the rejects crash and burn" is why we watch *American Idol*, according to *Rolling Stone* magazine ("Idol Worship," 2007).

→ See page 433 for the corresponding References list entry.

→ If you find that a government or corporate organization is the author, see page 424.

THERE IS NO PAGE NUMBER

If you cite a source that has no page number, give a paragraph or part number if there is one; otherwise, give only the name of the author.

The World Health Organization identifies obstetric fistulas as a global problem, estimating that over two million women suffer from them, with 50 to 100 thousand new cases occurring each year (2006, para. 64).

For the example above, readers will look in the References for a listing under *World Health Organization*.

→ See page 451 for the corresponding References list entry.

YOUR REFERENCES LIST CONTAINS TWO OR MORE SOURCES BY THE SAME AUTHOR

When you use two or more works by the same author, indicate which work you are referencing at any one time, to help your readers. You can do this by giving the date of the work in your sentence or in the in-text citation.

Here is a citation for the first work cited from one author:

That meat from cows fed on grass is more nutritious than that from corn-fed cows is just one of the many arguments Pollan makes (2006, p. 211).

Here is how a second work by the same author is cited:

Because his research shows just what chemicals go into a commercial potato, Pollan cannot bring himself to eat one given to him as a gift (2001, p. 98).

→ See page 451 for how these two citations appear in the References list.

YOUR REFERENCES LIST CONTAINS SOURCES BY TWO AUTHORS WITH THE SAME LAST NAME

In such a case, include the authors' initials in your citations so that readers know which citation to check in the References list. Here are examples from the same paper, using the authors' initials:

R. M. Rorty (1979) argues that we ought no longer to think of our minds as "mirrors" that directly and only reflect what is already in the world.

A. O. Rorty (1996) shows how Aristotle's *Rhetoric* brings together understandings of situations in which people communicate, the psychology of audiences, the character of communicators, the structures of communication, and politics.

Here are examples that avoid ambiguity in their parenthetical citations:

Some philosophers argue that our understanding of what knowledge is has changed over the last two hundred years: We ought no longer to think of our minds as "mirrors" that directly and only reflect what is already in the world (R. M. Rorty, 1979).

Aristotle's *Rhetoric* brings together understandings of situations in which people communicate, the psychology of audiences, the character of communicators, the structures of communication, and politics (A. O. Rorty, 1996).

→ See page 451 for how these two citations appear in the References list.

THE WORK HAS TWO AUTHORS

List the names in the same order as they are given in the source. Use *and* between the names in the body of your paper, but use an ampersand (&) in parenthetical references:

As "much an activist as an analytical method" is how Moeller and Moberly (2006) describe McAllister's approach to computer games.

As "much an activist as an analytical method" is how two online reviewers describe McAllister's approach to computer games (Moeller & Moberly, 2006).

→ See page 433 for the corresponding References list entry.

THE WORK HAS THREE, FOUR, OR FIVE AUTHORS

The first time you cite the work, list each author's name. After that, list only the first author's name followed by the expression *et al.* (*Et al.* is Latin for *and others*.) When you use *et al.*, put a period after *al*.

What happens when a ninth-grade World Literatures class is offered at the high honors level for all students, without tracking? Fine, Anand, Jordan, and Sherman (2000) offer a two-year study of such a class.

Later in the same paper:

As a result of their study, Fine et al. (2000) argue that students "who never expected to be seen as smart" come to see themselves as capable and sharp, and "questions of power are engaged" (pp. 174, 175).

→ See page 433 for the corresponding References list entry.

THE WORK HAS SIX OR MORE AUTHORS

Include only the first author's name, followed by the expression *et al*. *Et al.* is Latin for *and others*. When you use *et al.*, put a period after *al*.

Statistical data can be useful but is "easily misinterpreted" (Walpole et al., 2006, p. 217).

Walpole et al. (2006, p. 217) argue that statistical data is useful but "easily misinterpreted."

→ See page 434 for a Reference list entry for a source with six or more authors.

THE WORK HAS A GROUP OR CORPORATE AUTHOR OR IS A GOVERNMENT DOCUMENT

If you need to cite a work by a group author (an association, government agency, or corporation), write out the name of the group author in your citation.

When organizing catalogs, librarians typically follow a set of guidelines established by the American Library Association (2004).

When organizing catalogs, librarians typically follow established guidelines (American Library Association, 2004).

→ See page 435 for the corresponding References list entry.

YOUR ARE CITING TWO OR MORE SOURCES IN ONE SENTENCE

If you need to cite two or more sources in a single reference, list the sources in alphabetical order by each author's last name and separate the entries by a semicolon.

The language used to describe issues of race and ethnicity often shapes the way people respond to calls for diversity or social justice (Adams, 2000; Fletcher, 2007).

Adams (2000) and Fletcher (2007) argue that language plays a vital role in shaping the way people respond to calls for diversity and social justice.

→ See pages 433 and 434 for the corresponding References list entries.

YOU ARE CITING A CLASSICAL WORK, SACRED TEXT, OR OTHER WORK WITH NO DATE LISTED

Use the author's name followed by a comma and **n.d.** for **no date**.

Early in its history, rhetoric was defined as the use of the available means of persuasion (Aristotle, n.d.).

You can also use the date of translation, if known, preceded by **trans.**

Early in its history, rhetoric was defined as the use of the available means of persuasion (Aristotle, trans. 1954).

If you are citing passages from a sacred text like the Bible or the Koran, you do not need to provide a References list entry. The first time you cite the work, identify the version you are using.

John 11:7 (Revised Standard Version)

YOU ARE CITING AN ELECTRONIC SOURCE SUCH AS A WEBPAGE OR E-MAIL

Many electronic sources do not have page numbers. If your source includes paragraph numbers, use that number, preceded by **para**.

Some researchers have suggested the concept of "virtual wives" to describe the new role of technology in personal life (Clark-Flory, 2007, para. 12).

If your source does not number paragraphs, you can cite the nearest main heading and number the paragraph following it to refer to a specific passage.

Some researchers have suggested the concept of "virtual wives" to describe the new role of technology in personal life (Clark-Flory, 2007, Introduction section, para. 1).

→ See page 446 for the corresponding References list entries.

Because personal e-mails cannot be retrieved by your readers, do not include them in your References list. You should cite them in your text only.

Austin's famous Congress Avenue bats first appeared in 1980 (E. C. Lupfer, personal communication, March 17, 2003).

APA DOCUMENTATION FOR REFERENCES LIST ENTRIES

The following pages show you how to format entries in the References list that goes at the end of any APA-style paper.

This is the basic format for all texts in the References list of an APA-style paper:

Author's Last Name, Initials. (Year the work was published). *Title of work.* **Location: Publisher.**

For example, here is a book citation:

Treichler, P. A. (1999). *How to have theory in an epidemic: Cultural chronicles of AIDS.* **Durham, NC: Duke University Press.**

(Note the indenting: This is standard when formatting your References list, as we describe on pages 450–451.)

In distinguishing among the kinds of sources to be cited, the APA distinguishes between periodicals and nonperiodicals. (Nonperiodicals are books and any other kind of source not printed on a regular schedule.) We follow the same distinction in the pages that follow.

Note that when you cite a book, periodical, or webpage, the format of the citation—the capitalization of the title of a book, the inclusion of a periodical's issue number, or the listing of a URL—tells a reader what kind of text you are citing. When you cite a text that isn't a book, periodical, or webpage, you may also need to indicate what kind of text it is.

TO MAKE APA REFERENCES LISTS

FIRST, MAKE AN INDIVIDUAL LISTING FOR EACH WORK YOU ARE CITING

You should have determined the kind of source you have and collected the kinds of information needed to cite the source, as described on pages 326–350.

Then go to the page for the kind of source you have.

PERIODICALS
Go to
page 428.

NON-PERIODICALS
Go to
page 430.

Each page gives a pattern for the References list entry for that kind of source.

• Follow the pattern to construct your listing part by part, starting with the author, moving on to the year of publication, and so on.

• If your citation varies from the pattern, follow the page references to see the format for the variation.

THEN CONSTRUCT YOUR REFERENCES LIST

When you have all your individual citations, put them together into the References list.

→ See page 450 for how to format the References list.

FOR PERIODICAL SOURCES

Here is a citation for a periodical in the APA format:

> Atkinson, M. (2006). Straightedge bodies and civilizing processes. *Body and Society, 12*(1), 69–95.

THE PATTERN

Here is the APA citation pattern with its parts labeled and with information about how to modify the citation depending on a periodical's particularities.

Author's Name. (Date). Title of article.

The pattern for an author's name is on page 432.

WHAT TO DO WHEN YOU HAVE:

- no author named: page 433
- one author: page 433
- two to six authors: page 433
- more than six authors: page 434
- two or more works published by the same author in the same year: page 434
- a government author: page 434
- a corporate author: page 435
- a work signed *Anonymous* author: page 435

The pattern for the article title is on page 439.

WHAT TO DO WHEN YOU HAVE:

- a letter to the editor: page 441
- a review: page 441

The pattern for year of publication is on page 436.

WHAT TO DO WHEN YOU HAVE:

- a monthly magazine article: page 437
- a daily newspaper article: page 437

Where do you look in a periodical to find all this information?
How do you know you have all the information you need to cite a periodical?

→ See pages 337–341 for help.

WHAT COUNTS AS A PERIODICAL?

A periodical is a publication that is published at regular intervals: every week, every month, every season. Journal, magazine, or newspaper articles, *including when they are published online,* are periodicals.

Periodical Name, Volume(Issue), Pages.

If the periodical name begins with **A** or **The**, you can leave off those words.

Italicize the journal name.

The pattern for the volume and issue numbers is on page 444.

WHAT TO DO WHEN YOU HAVE:

• no issue number: page 445

• only a date: page 445

• a daily newspaper: page 445

• a weekly or biweekly journal or magazine: page 445

IF YOUR SOURCE IS ONLINE:

The pattern for online sources is on pages 446–447.

Give the inclusive page numbers: **37–52** or **121-145**.

If you cite a newspaper article, put **p.** (for single page articles) or **pp.** (for multipage articles) before the page numbers: **p. J3** or **pp. C2-C5**. If the pages are discontinuous, put a comma between the numbers: **pp. B1, B4**.

FOR NONPERIODICAL SOURCES

Here is a citation for a nonperiodical in the APA format:

Berger, J. (1992). *About looking*. New York: Vintage.

THE PATTERN

Here is the APA citation pattern with its parts labeled and with information about how to modify the citation depending on a book's particularities.

Author's Name. (Year). *Title*.

The pattern for an author's name is on page 432.

WHAT TO DO WHEN YOU HAVE:

- no author named: page 433
- one author: page 433
- two to six authors: page 433
- more than six authors: page 434
- an edited collection: page 434
- a government author: page 434
- a corporate author: page 435
- a work signed *Anonymous*: page 435

The pattern for titles is on pages 438–439.

WHAT TO DO WHEN YOU HAVE:

- an essay or chapter in a book: page 440
- an essay in an online collection: page 440
- an article from a reference book: page 440

Put the year in parentheses, followed by a period. If you have no publication date, put **n.d.** (for **no date**) inside the parentheses, without quotation marks.

Where do you look to find all this information? How do you know when you have all the information you need to cite a nonperiodical?

➔ See pages 328–335 and 342–349 for help.

WHAT COUNTS AS A NONPERIODICAL?

The category of nonperiodical includes books, parts of books (like essays and chapters in books), films, videos, CDs, audio recordings, and reports—*including when they are published online.*

Place of Publication: Publisher.

The pattern for the place of publication is on page 442.

WHAT TO DO WHEN:

• the state is not listed: page 443

• the book was published in another country: page 443

IF YOUR SOURCE IS ONLINE:

The pattern for online sources is on pages 446–447.

From the publisher's full name, you can leave off words such as **Press** or **Company**.

Note that a colon precedes the publisher's name and that a period follows it.

YOU MAY NEED TO INCLUDE ADDITIONAL INFORMATION IN YOUR CITATION IF...

• you are citing a report from the Educatioal Resources Information Center (ERIC): page 441

• the work is translated: page 441

• a book is a second (or later) edition: page 441

• the work is in more than one volume: page 441

• the work is a review: page 441

• you are citing software, visual sources like charts or photographs, film and television shows, interviews, conference papers, or sound recordings: pages 449–450

APA PATTERN FOR REFERENCES

AUTHOR'S NAME

Note how the patterns for author names are consistent across citations for all kinds of texts in all kinds of media.

→ On these pages, we show you how authors' names appear in individual citations for a range of sources; on pages 450–451 we show you how to bring together individual citations like these to create a full References list that goes at the end of any APA-style research paper.

The first author listed is always written with the last name first, then a comma, and then the initials.

Last Name, Initials.

Singh, A. R.

If an author's first name includes a hyphen, include that hyphen with the initials.

Chen, K.-H.

If a work you are citing has more than one author, the additional names should be listed in the order in which they are given in the source. All authors are cited last name first. Use an ampersand (&) before the last author's name.

Phelps, L. W., & Emig, J.

Fine, M. T., Weis, L., Pruitt, L. P., & Burns, A.

Note that, in a References list entry, there is a period after the author's name or the list of authors' names.

NO AUTHOR NAMED

If you cannot find an author's name, start the entry with the title of the book or article.

MAGAZINE ARTICLE

Idol worship. (2007, February 8). *Rolling Stone, 1016*, 7.

REFERENCE WORK

Ultimate visual dictionary (Rev. ed.). (2002). New York: Dorling Kindersley.

ONE AUTHOR

BOOK

Pollan, M. (2006). *The omnivore's dilemma: A natural history of four meals*. New York: Penguin.

BLOG POSTING

Xavier, J. (2007, June 11). Timo Veikkola (Nokia): A vision for the future. Message posted to http://julianax.blogspot.com/2007/06/timo-veikkola-nokia-vision-of-future.html

ESSAY, IN EDITED BOOK

Fletcher, M. A. (2007). At the corner of progress and peril. In K. Merida (Ed.), *Being a black man: At the corner of progress and peril*. New York: Public Affairs.

TWO TO SIX AUTHORS

In References list entries, include the names of up to six authors. Separate names and initials with commas and use an ampersand (&) before the last author.

BOOK

Levitt, S. D., & Dubner, S. J. (2006). *Freakonomics: A rogue economist explores the hidden side of everything*. New York: HarperCollins.

REVIEW, ONLINE
REVIEW, OF BOOK

Moeller, R. M., & Moberly, K. (2006). [Review of the book *Game work: Language, power, and computer game culture*]. *Kairos, 10*, 2. Retrieved from http://english.ttu.edu/kairos/10.2/binder.html?reviews/moeller_moberley/index.html

ARTICLE, IN ACADEMIC JOURNAL

DeVoss, D. N., Cushman, E., & Grabill, J. T. (2005). Infrastructure and composing: The when of new-media writing. *CCC, 57*, 14–44.

CHAPTER, IN EDITED BOOK

Fine, M., Anand, B., Jordan, C., & Sherman, D. (2000). Before the bleach gets us all. In L. Weiss & M. Fine (Eds.), *Construction Sites* (pp. 161–79). New York: Teachers College Press.

MORE THAN SIX AUTHORS

If you need to cite a source by seven or more authors, list only the first six names and abbreviate the rest as *et al.* *Et al.* is not italicized and always includes a period after *al.* (*Et al.* is Latin for *and others*.)

BOOK, MORE THAN SIX AUTHORS

Nash, G. B., Jeffrey, J. R., Howe, J. R., Frederick, P. J., Davis, A. F., Winkler, A. M., et al. (2006). *The American people: Creating a nation and society* (7th ed.). New York: Longman.

TWO OR MORE WORKS PUBLISHED BY THE SAME AUTHOR IN THE SAME YEAR

If you need to cite two or more works by the same author that have the same year of publication, list the works in alphabetical order by title, and use lowercase letters (*a*, *b*, *c*, etc.) following the year to distinguish the works.

Helfand, G., & Walker, C. J. (Eds.) (2001a). *Mastering APA style: Instructor's resource guide.* Washington, DC: American Psychological Association.

Helfand, G., & Walker, C. J. (Eds.) (2001b). *Mastering APA style: Student's workbook and training guide.* Washington, DC: American Psychological Association.

Note that your in-text citations would also need to include the lowercase letters so that readers know which source you are referring to.

AN EDITED COLLECTION

BOOK, EDITED

Adams, M. (Ed.). (2000). *Readings for diversity and social justice: An anthology on racism, sexism, anti-semitism, heterosexism, classism, and ableism.* New York: Routledge.

NOTE!

If you are citing only a piece from an edited collection and not the whole collection, create the citation following the pattern *An Essay or Chapter in a Book* shown on page 440.

A GOVERNMENT AUTHOR

REPORT

National Center for Educational Statistics. (2005). *Comparative indicators of education in the United States and other G8 countries: 2004.* Washington, DC: U.S. Department of Education Center for Educational Studies.

ARTICLE FROM GOVERNMENT WEBSITE

United States Department of Health and Human Services. (2002). *Mental health aspects of terrorism.* Retrieved from http://mentalhealth.samhsa. gov/publications/allpubs /KEN-01-0095/default.asp

A CORPORATE AUTHOR

A corporate author is an organization, corporation, association, or government agency. Start your citation with the name of the corporate author exactly as it is listed in the source (but omit **A**, **An**, or **The**):

BOOK

American Library Association. (2004). *Anglo-American cataloguing rules* (2nd ed.). Chicago: Author.

BROCHURE

American Counseling Association. (2007). *Basic facts about clinical depression* [Brochure]. Alexandria, VA: Author.

REPORT FROM A PRIVATE ORGANIZATION

Employee Benefit Research Institute. (2007). *How are retirees doing financially in retirement?* (Issue Brief No. 302). Washington, DC: Author.

WORK BY ANONYMOUS AUTHOR

If the work is signed **Anonymous**, use **Anonymous** as the author's name. If no author is named, list the source by its title.

WIKI POSTING

Anonymous. (2007). How to be an anarchist. Retrieved from *WikiHow:* http://www.wikihow.com /Be-an-Anarchist

NOTE!

In the examples on these pages, we show the citations with what is called **hanging indentation**: The first line of a citation sticks farther into the left margin than the other lines. This is the standard form of indenting for APA citations; your teacher might also ask you to double-space the citations.

If you do not have access to a computer, underline the titles of books and periodicals instead of italicizing them.

If the paper on which you are working will be read online, always italicize the titles; if you underline them, the titles will look like links to other webpages.

See pages 450–451 for specific instructions on how to format individual citations in your References list.

APA PATTERN FOR REFERENCES

DATE OF PUBLICATION

Note how the pattern for listing the year of publication for a text is consistent across citations for many kinds of texts in many kinds of media.

→ On these pages, we show you how the publication dates appear in individual citations for a range of sources; on pages 450–451 we show you how to bring together individual citations like these to create a references list that goes at the end of any APA-style research paper.

THE PATTERN

Place the copyright date or year of publication in parentheses, followed by a period.

(Year of Publication).

(2007).

If you find more than one copyright date for a book, use the most recent one.

For monthly magazines, newspapers, and newsletters, give the year followed by the month.

(2006, July).

Include the day for periodicals published daily, like newspapers.

(2007, August 23).

WHAT TO DO WITH A BOOK THAT HAS BEEN REPUBLISHED

A republished book is one that has been previously published by a different publisher or published in a different form (for example, a hardback book being republished as a mass-market paperback edition).

For such books, use the standard pattern for book entries, and insert the original publication date at the end.

BOOK, REPUBLISHED

Johnson, S. (2002). *Emergence: The connected lives of ants, brains, cities, and software.* New York: Touchstone-Simon. (Original work published 2001)

WHAT TO DO WITH A BOOK THAT HAS NO PUBLICATION DATE

If a book does not list a date of publication on its copyright page, put the abbreviation *n.d.* (for *no date*) where the year of publication usually goes in a citation.

BOOK, NO PUBLICATION DATE

Baudrillard, J. (n.d.). *Simulations.* New York: Semiotext(e).

MAGAZINE ARTICLE

For magazines and other monthly periodicals, include the month of publication following the year.

ARTICLE, MAGAZINE

Ehrenreich, B. (2000, April). Maid to order: The politics of other women's work. *Harper's,* 59–70.

NEWSPAPER ARTICLE

For newspapers and other daily periodicals, include the month and day of publication following the year.

ARTICLE, NEWSPAPER

Lipton, E. (2007, September 2). Product safety commission bears heavy scrutiny. *Austin American Statesman,* p. A11.

APA PATTERN FOR REFERENCES
TITLES

Note how the patterns for titles are consistent across citations for all kinds of texts in all kinds of media.

→ Sample References list entries follow, on page 440.

→ On these pages, we demonstrate how to include titles for individual citations for a range of sources; on pages 450–451 we show you how to bring together individual citations like these to create a References list that goes at the end of any APA-style research paper.

BOOK TITLES
Follow these steps to build the pattern:

1 Capitalize only the first word of the title and the first word of the subtitle.

2 Capitalize any proper nouns within a title.

3 Italicize the whole title. If you are not using a computer, underline the title.

4 Put a period after the title. (If the title ends with a question mark or exclamation point, use that instead.)

The title of the book.

Crow Lake.

The diving bell and the butterfly.

If the book has a subtitle, put the subtitle after a colon and capitalize its first word.

Scribbling the cat: Travels with an African soldier.

The quick and the dead: Artists and anatomy.

A country doctor's casebook: Tales from the north woods.

TITLES OF PARTS OF BOOKS, PERIODICAL ARTICLES, AND WEBPAGES
Follow these steps to build the pattern:

1 Capitalize only the first word of the title and the subtitle.

2 Do not italicize or put quotation marks around the title.

3 Put a period after the last word of the title. (If the title ends with a question mark or exclamation point, use that instead.)

4 Follow the pattern below for finishing the title depending on the source.

PARTS OF BOOKS
For a chapter in an edited book, list the title of the chapter first, followed by the word **In** and the editor's name, followed by the title of the book.

The title of the chapter. In Editor's name (Ed.), *The title of the book.*

At the corner of progress and peril. In K. Merida (Ed.), *Being a black man: At the corner of progress and peril.*

JOURNAL ARTICLES
Put the name of the journal—in italics—after the article name. (If you are not using a computer, underline the journal's title.)

The article. *Journal Name*

Will the next election be hacked? *Rolling Stone*

Animal magnetism and curriculum history. *Inquiry*

WEBPAGES
Put the name of the website—in italics—after the name of the webpage. (If you are not using a computer, underline the webpage's title.)

The article. *Website name.*

Project description. *The Nora Project.*

Pictures without bias: How to avoid discrimination in visual media. *Center for Media Literacy.*

A BOOK

BOOK

Lawson, M. (2002). *Crow Lake*. New York: Delta Trade.

BOOK

Petherbridge, D., & Jordanova, L. (1997). *The quick and the dead: Artists and anatomy*. Berkeley: University of California Press.

A WEBSITE

WEBSITE, ENTIRE SITE

Austin City Connection: The Official Web Site of the City of Austin. (n.d). *Childhood Lead Poisoning Prevention Program*. Retrieved from http://www.ci.austin.tx.us /health/education.htm

AN ESSAY OR CHAPTER IN A BOOK

ESSAY, IN ONLINE BOOK

Makhan, J. (1998). Island ecology and cultural perceptions: A case study of Lakshdweep. In B. Saraswatie (Ed.), *Lifestyle and ecology*. New Delhi: Indira Gandhi National Centre for the Arts. Retrieved from http://www.ignca.nic.in /cd_08012.htm

ESSAY, IN EDITED BOOK
ESSAY, TRANSLATED

Plato. (1961). Meno (W. K. C. Guthrie, Trans.). In E. Hamilton & H. Cairns (Eds.), *The collected dialogues of Plato* (pp. 353–385). Princeton: Princeton University Press.

ESSAY, IN EDITED BOOK

Van Proyen, M. (2001). The new Dionysianism. In B. Beckley (Ed.), *The sticky sublime* (pp. 165–175). New York: Allworth.

AN ESSAY IN AN ONLINE COLLECTION

ESSAY, IN ONLINE COLLECTION

Badger, M. (2004, June). Visual blogs. In L. J. Gurak, S. Antonijevic, L. Johnson, & J. Reyman (Eds.), *Into the blogosphere: Rhetoric, community, and culture of weblogs*. Retrieved from http://blog.lib.umn.edu /blogosphere/visual_blogs.html

AN ARTICLE FROM A REFERENCE BOOK

Reference works rarely give the names of the people who wrote the articles. Put the title in place of the author in these cases.

ARTICLE, IN REFERENCE BOOK

Islam. (1989). In *The New York public library desk reference*.

ARTICLE, IN ONLINE REFERENCE BOOK

Bovine spongiform encephalopathy. (2007). In *Encyclopedia Britannica*. Retrieved from Encyclopedia Britannica Online: http:// www.search.eb.com/eb /article-9002739

ADDITIONAL INFORMATION

Sources are published—and cited—under varying circumstances. On these pages, we show you patterns for how to handle citations for several circumstances that occur frequently.

⟶ On these pages, we show you how to create individual citations for a range of sources; on pages 450–451 we show you how to bring together individual citations like these to create a References list that goes at the end of any APA-style research paper.

REPORT FROM THE EDUCATIONAL RESOURCES INFORMATION CENTER (ERIC)

If you are doing research in the field of education, you are likely to find and use reports available through ERIC. These sources are usually numbered; provide this ERIC number in parentheses at the end of the reference entry.

REPORT, FROM ERIC

Polette, N. (2007). *Teaching thinking skills with picture books, K-3.* Portsmouth, NH: Teacher Ideas Press. (ERIC Document Reproduction Service No. ED497152)

A WORK WITH A TRANSLATOR

BOOK, TRANSLATED

Burgat, F. (2008). *Islamism in the age of al-Qaeda* (P. Hutchinson, Trans.). Austin: University of Texas Press.

A BOOK IN A SECOND OR LATER EDITION

BOOK, IN A SECOND OR LATER EDITION

Rubenstein, J. M. (2004). *The cultural landscape: An introduction to human geography* (8th ed.). Upper Saddle River, NJ: Prentice Hall.

WORK IN MORE THAN ONE VOLUME

BOOK, MULTIVOLUME

Goldman, B. A., & Mitchell, D. F. (2007). *Directory of unpublished experimental mental measures* (Vol. 9). Washington, DC: American Psychological Association.

A BOOK REVIEW

REVIEW, OF BOOK

Julius, A. (2007, September 2). A people and a nation [Review of the book *Jews and power*]. *New York Times Book Review*, p. 27.

AN ABSTRACT

ABSTRACT, JOURNAL ARTICLE

Lacy, E., & Leslie, S. (2007). Library outreach near and far: Programs to staff and patients of the piedmont healthcare system. *Medical Reference Services Quarterly.* Abstract obtained from Library, Information Science & Technology Abstracts database.

LETTER TO THE EDITOR

LETTER TO THE EDITOR

Delaney, J. (2007, August 28). Helping the world's sexually abused children [Letter to the editor]. *Washington Post*, p. A12.

APA PATTERN FOR REFERENCES

PLACE OF PUBLICATION

Note how the pattern for listing the place of publication for a text is consistent across citations for all kinds of texts in all kinds of media.

→ On these pages, we show you how the place of publication appears in individual citations for a range of sources; on pages 450–451 we show you how to bring together individual citations like these to create a Reference list that goes at the end of any APA-style research paper.

Put the place of publication after the title of the book, followed by a colon.

Place of Publication:

Boston:

Cambridge:

Santa Monica, CA:

Calumet, MI:

If more than one place of publication is listed, use the first one.

EXAMPLE

Jackson, L. (2002). *Twentieth-century pattern design: Textile and wallpaper pioneers.* Princeton: Princeton Architectural Press.

Merrell, F. (1991). *Unthinking thinking: Jorge Luis Borges, mathematics, and the new physics.* West Lafayette, IN: Purdue University Press.

Wardlow, G. D. (1998). *Chasin' that devil music: Searching for the blues.* San Francisco: Miller Freeman.

WHEN TO MENTION THE STATE

A majority of books are published in major cities whose states most readers already know: Boston, Chicago, New York, San Francisco, and so on.

But if you are concerned that the name of a state will not come immediately to the mind of your readers, you should add the state. (The convention for adding the state is to use the two-letter abbreviation that the U.S. Postal Service uses.)

BOOK

Eisner, W. (1996). *Graphic storytelling and visual narrative.* Tamarac, FL: Poorhouse.

BOOK

Hargittai, I., & Hargittai, M. (1994). *Symmetry: A unifying concept.* Bolinas, CA: Shelter Publications.

BOOK

Harris, S. L. (1990). *Agents of chaos: Earthquakes, volcanoes, and other natural disasters.* Missoula, MT: Mountain Press.

WHEN THE BOOK WAS PUBLISHED IN ANOTHER COUNTRY

If the country ought to be obvious to readers because the city is well known, use the same citation pattern for books published in the United States:

BOOK

Yanagi, S. (1989). *The unknown craftsman: A Japanese insight into beauty.* Tokyo: Kodansha.

■ ■ ■

If you think your readers might not be familiar with the city, add the country or province, abbreviated (if it has a common abbreviation).

BOOK

Bourriaud, N. (2004). *Relational aesthetics.* Dijon-Quetigny, France: Les Presses du Réel.

APA PATTERN FOR REFERENCES
PERIODICAL VOLUME AND ISSUE

When periodicals were first printed, publishers would bind a sequential set of issues into one volume; eventually the pattern developed of binding a full year's set into one volume. This makes finding and referring to any particular issue easy: One can find the volume first, and then the article in the volume by its issue number or date.

→ On these pages, we show you how periodical volume and issue numbers appear in individual citations for a range of sources; on pages 450–451 we show you how to bring together individual citations like these to create a full References list that goes at the end of any APA-style research paper.

THE PATTERN

VOLUME AND ISSUE NUMBER
The volume number, italicized, follows the name of the periodical; there is a comma between the two. If there is an issue number, put it in parentheses immediately after the volume number. Issue numbers are not italicized.

Volume(Issue)

5(2)

27(11)

EXAMPLES
French, R. M. (2005, March/April). Using guitars to teach vibrations and acoustics. *Experimental Techniques, 29*(2), 47–48

Watts, S. (1995, June). Walt Disney: Art and politics in the American century. *The Journal of American History, 82*(1), 84–110.

WHEN THERE IS A VOLUME AND AN ISSUE NUMBER

If a journal you are citing paginates each issue separately, include the issue number in your References list entry.

ARTICLE IN A JOURNAL PAGINATED BY ISSUE

Baker, B. (2007). Animal magnetism and curriculum history. *Inquiry, 37*(2), 123–158.

WHEN THERE IS NO ISSUE NUMBER

The volume number and date still give readers enough information for finding the source.

ARTICLE IN A JOURNAL PAGINATED BY VOLUME

Lawrence, R. (2000). Equivalent mass of a coil spring. *Physics Teacher, 38,* 140–141.

WHEN THERE IS ONLY A DATE

Many popular magazines do not list volume numbers, just a date.

ARTICLE, IN POPULAR MAGAZINE

Birnbaum, C. A. (2007, September). Cultivating appreciation. *Dwell,* 196+.

A DAILY NEWSPAPER

Because daily newspapers don't have volumes and issues, they are cited only by the date.

EDITORIAL, NO AUTHOR
NEWSPAPER ARTICLE, NO AUTHOR

Rethinking abstinence. (2007, September 17). [Editorial]. *Bangor Daily News,* p. 8.

NEWSPAPER ARTICLE

Rozek, D. (2006, November 10). Girls' squabble over iPod over: And in the end, neither will get music player. *Chicago Sun-Times,* p. 3.

A WEEKLY OR BIWEEKLY JOURNAL OR MAGAZINE

ARTICLE, IN WEEKLY JOURNAL, RETRIEVED FROM ONLINE DATABASE

Gorman, C. (2006, September 18). To an athlete, aching young. *Time, 168*(12), 60. Retrieved from Expanded Academic ASAP database.

If a weekly or biweekly journal or magazine doesn't have volume and issue numbers, cite only the date.

REVIEW, OF BOOK, IN WEEKLY JOURNAL

Schlei, R. (2007, September 6). Faithful comrade: A monumental affair [Review of the book *Loving Frank*]. *Shepherd Express,* 48.

FOR ONLINE TEXTS

APA references to Internet sources and other online works need to include a title or description of the document, a date, and a Web address (URL). If you can identify the authors, include their names as well.

In 2007, APA published the *APA Style Guide to Electronic References,* which updates APA style for online sources. Sample references shown here conform to the updated APA guidelines. Some scholarly publications are now being identified using a Digital Object Identifier (DOI), a unique number intended to be more permanent than a URL. If you are citing a source with a DOI, include the DOI in place of the URL.

Berke, J. H., & Schneider, S. (2007). Nothingness and narcissism. *Mental Health, Religion, and Culture,* 10(4), 335-351. doi:10.1080/13694670600722452

You do not need to list a database name or URL in a reference if you provide the DOI for your source.

→ On these pages, we show you how to create individual citations for a range of sources; on pages 450–451 we show you how to bring together individual citations like these to create a References list that goes at the end of any APA-style research paper.

CITING AN ENTIRE WEBSITE

WEBSITE

Austin City Connection: The Official Web Site of the City of Austin. (n.d.). *Childhood Lead Poisoning Prevention Program.* Retrieved from http://www.ci.austin.tx.us/health/education.htm

CITING ONLINE ARTICLES

ARTICLE, ONLINE VERSION OF PRINT SOURCE

Lieberman, J. E. (2005, November/December). Coming clean [Electronic version]. *Psychology Today,* 38(6), 8.

ARTICLE, ONLINE ONLY

Clark-Flory, T. (2007, August 10). Roundup: Virtual wives, non-ironic feminism and more. Salon.com. 1-1. Retrieved from http://www.salon.com/mwt/broadsheet/2007/08/10/roundup

ARTICLE, FROM DATABASE

Smith, S. K. (2007). Bioarchaeology: The contextual study of human remains. *Anthropology,* 133, 1171. Retrieved August 31, 2007, from Academic Search Complete database.

NEWSPAPER ARTICLE, ONLINE

Rockwell, L. (2004, January 21). UT task force releases report on race relations. *The Daily Texan.* Retrieved from http://www.dailytexanonline.com

CITING PART OF AN ONLINE DOCUMENT

ONLINE DOCUMENT, PART

Sales, L. (2005). Part II. In *Hurricane Katrina: Reporter's diary*. Retrieved from http://www.abc.net.au/news /newsitems/200509/s1460732

CITING E-MAIL

Because personal e-mail cannot be retrieved or viewed by your readers, the APA says that you should not include it in your references list (→ see page 425 on in-text citations for e-mail).

For retrievable online postings, like discussion groups or mailing lists, use the following format:

DISCUSSION GROUP OR MAILING LIST POST

McLaughlin, B. (2007, September 4). Webinar for enviromental bench-marking survey. Message posted to AAUP-L mailing list, archived at http://ucp.uchicago.edu/mailman /listinfo/aaup-l

CITING BLOGS AND WIKIS

BLOG POSTING

Xavier, J. (2007, June 11). Timo Veikkola (Nokia): A vision for the future. Message posted to http:// julianax.blogspot.com/2007/06 /timo-veikkola-nokia-vision-of-future.html

WIKI POSTING

Wiki. (2007, 25 October). Retrieved October 28, 2007, from Wikipedia: http://en.wikipedia.org/wiki/Wiki

APA PATTERN FOR REFERENCES

FOR OTHER KINDS OF SOURCES

You may need to create references for other types of sources, including visual and multimedia sources. In APA style, a note or identifying description usually helps clarify the type of source you are citing.

→ On these pages, we show you how to create individual citations for a range of sources; on pages 450–451 we show you how to bring together individual citations like these to create a References list that goes at the end of any APA-style research paper.

SOFTWARE

Cite software as you would a book without a named author (→ see page 433)—but include *Computer software* in brackets after the title. If there is a publisher, include the name and date of publication; for software you have downloaded, give the date of the download and the URL.

SOFTWARE

PsychMate (Version 2.0) [Computer software]. (2007). Philadelphia: Psychology Software Tools.

VISUAL SOURCES

CHART, ONLINE

Fruitrich, C., & Ward, S. (2007). Groups' Goodwill helps [Chart]. USATODAY.com. Retrieved from http://www.usatoday.com/news /snapshots/25anniversary /goodwill.htm

PHOTOGRAPH, ONLINE

Cubitt, C. (2006). *Church*. Katrina: A gallery of images. Retrieved from http://www.claytoncubitt.com /publish/katrina

PHOTOGRAPH

Adams, A. (ca. 1930). *Factory Building, San Francisco*. Santa Fe, NM: Museum of Fine Arts.

FILM AND TELEVISION

FILM, VIDEOTAPE, OR DVD

Gibney, A. (Director). (2005). *Enron: The smartest guys in the room* [Motion picture]. United States: Magnolia.

TELEVISION SHOW OR SERIES

Hanson, H. (Writer), & Yaltanes, G. (Director). (2005, September 13). Pilot [Television series episode]. In B. Josephson & H. Hanson (Producers), *Bones*. New York: Fox Broadcasting.

AN INTERVIEW YOU CONDUCT

Because it does not consider an unpublished interview to be data that someone can check, the APA says not to include such an interview in the References list. You may, however, give an in-text citation for the interview:

> Some music composers believe digital technologies slow down their composing processes because they offer so many options (M. Boracz, personal communication, October 18, 2007).

CONFERENCE PAPER PRESENTATION

Use this format if you need to cite a conference presentation or similar lecture or speech that has not been published.

PRESENTATION OR LECTURE

Kleinberg, S. L. (2005, June). *The changing face of Texas in the twenty-first century: Perspectives on the new immigration.* Paper presented at Gateway on the Gulf, a Humanities Texas Institute for Texas Teachers.

SOUND RECORDING

MUSIC OR AUDIO RECORDING

Arcade Fire. (2004). Neighborhood (Tunnels). On *Funeral* [CD]. Durham, NC: Merge Records.

TIP: FINDING INFORMATION ABOUT FILMS

The *Internet Movie Database* (http://www.imdb.com) gives you access to all the information you need for citing films.

A REFERENCES PAGE IN APA FORMAT

FORMATTING PAGES FOR THE APA STYLE

For a paper in APA style:

- ❏ Use one inch margins at the top, left, right, and bottom of each page.
- ❏ Double-space each page.
- ❏ Use one of the two typefaces recommended by the APA *Publication Manual*: 12 pt. Times Roman or 12 pt. Courier.
- ❏ Number each page at top right. (The numbers should appear one inch in from the right margin, and approximately 1/2 inch from the top of the page.)
- ❏ Start the paper with a title page, with the paper's title, and your name centered on it.
- ❏ If you are asked to include an abstract, include that immediately after the title page, in its own page.

To format an APA References listing:

- ❏ Put the listing at the very end of the paper.
- ❏ The References list starts on its own page.
- ❏ Number each References page at the top right of the page. The number on the first page follows the number of the last page of the paper. For example, if the last page of the paper is 8, the first page of the References will be 9.
- ❏ "References" is centered at the top of the page.
- ❏ The listings are arranged alphabetically by the author's last name. (If a listing starts with the title of a source, place it alphabetically in the list by the first letter of the title. If the title begins with **A**, **An**, or **The**, alphabetize by the second word of the title.)
- ❏ If you list two or more sources by the same author, arrange them by the year of publication, earliest first. If the sources are published in the same year, arrange them alphabetically by title.
- ❏ If you have two authors with the same last name, alphabetize by the first name.
- ❏ Double-space the entries.

References

Anonymous. (2007). How to be an anarchist. Retrieved January 29, 2008, from
WikiHow: http://www.wikihow.com/Be-an-Anarchist

Idol worship. (2007, February 8). *RollingStone, 1016*, 7.

Moeller, R. M., & Moberly, K. (2006). [Review of the book *Game work: Language,
power, and computer game culture*]. *Kairos, 10*(2). Retrieved from
http://english.ttu.edu/kairos/10.2/binder.html?reviews
/moeller_moberley/index.html

Pollan, M. (2001). *The botany of desire: A plant's-eye view of the world*. New York:
Random House.

Pollan, M. (2006). *The omnivore's dilemma: A natural history of four meals*. New York:
Penguin.

Rorty, A. O. (1996). Structuring Rhetoric. In A. O. Rorty (Ed.), *Essays on Aristotle's
rhetoric* (pp. 1–33). Berkeley: University of California Press.

Rorty, R. M. (1979). *Philosophy and the mirror of nature*. Princeton: Princeton
University Press.

United States Department of Health and Human Services. (2002). *Mental health
aspects of terrorism*. Retrieved from http://mentalhealth.samhsa.gov
/publications/allpubs/KEN-01-0095/default.asp

World Health Organization. (2005). *The world health report 2005: Make every mother
and child count*. Retreived from http://www.who.int/whr/2005
/whr2005_en.pdf

1/2"

Use hanging indentation

So that readers can scan the alphabetical list easily and
quickly, indent by 1/2 inch all lines underneath the first.

GUIDE TO APA DOCUMENTATION MODELS

REFERENCE LIST SAMPLES

PART 8
CSE AND CMS DOCUMENTATION

CSE DOCUMEN-TATION

[2] J. Allan: Automatic hy...

[4] R. Hammwöhner / R. Kuhlen...
Information Science, 20(3), 175-18...

[5] R. Hammwöhner / M. Rit...
Management, 33(2), 243-254. 1997

[6] Z. Zhang: Experiemnteller Auth...
Hypertext-System (KHS). Master Th...
Feb.,1995.

[7] M. Agosti / J. Allan: Introducti...
construction of hypertext. Information P...

[8] R. Aßfalg: Integration eines offenen...
Web. Hartung-Gorre Verlag: Konstanz. 19...

[9] R. Furuta / C. Plaistant / B. Scheinerma...
(2), 179-195, 1989.

0] M.H. Chignell et al.: The HEFTI mod...
91.

P. Thistlewaite: Automatic construction ...
magement, 33(2), 161-174. 1997

This style used to be called CBE, after the Council of Biology Editors, which developed it. But because this style has become so widespread in the sciences, the CBE changed its name in 2000 to the Council of Science Editors (CSE).

In 2006, the CSE published a new seventh edition of their style guide, *Scientific Style and Format*. CSE documentation style is used by authors in the life sciences, physical sciences, and mathematics.

The citation system advocated by the seventh edition of the CSE manual is known as **the citation-name system**. In this system, writers must create their list of references before they can insert their in-text citations— and so to the right we discuss the reference list before we discuss the in-text citation format.

CSE REFERENCES

In the citation-name system, writers complete the list of references and then create the in-text citations. The reference list (called **References**, **Cited References**, **Literature Cited**, or **Bibliography**) is arranged alphabetically by author and then numbered:

References

1. Amann RI, Ludwig W, and Schleifer KH. Phylogenetic identification and in situ detection of individual microbial cells without cultivation. Microhi01 Rev. 1995;59:143-169.

2. Barns SM, Fundyga RE, Jeffries MW, and Pace NR. Remarkable arched diversity detected in a Yellowstone National Park hot spring environment. Proc Natl Acad Sci USA. 1994;91:1609-1613.

3. Dojka, MA, Harris JK, and Pace NR. Expanding the known diversity and environmental distribution of an uncultured phylogenetic division of bacteria. Appi Environ Microbiol. 2000;66:1617-1621.

→ See pages 454–457 for information on how to format CSE style references.

CSE IN-TEXT CITATIONS

The numbers alphabetically assigned to these end references are then used for in-text references, regardless of the sequence in which the works appear in the text:

Early studies [2] used molecular methods to reveal remarkable microbial diversity in the sediment of Yellowstone hot springs.

or:

Early studies (2) used molecular methods to reveal remarkable microbial diversity in the sediment of Yellowstone hot springs.

In order to avoid ambiguity, citation numbers appear immediately after the relevant word, title, or phrase rather than at the end of a sentence. Usually, the citation number appears as superscript, but it can also be set in parentheses. Set the citation number with one space both before and after, except when followed by a punctuation mark. This spacing makes the citation number easier to see.

When there are several in-text citations occurring at the same point in the text, put them in numerical order so that a reader can find them easily in the list of references. Separate the numbers by commas; if the numbers are consecutive, they can be joined by a hyphen.

Researchers have studied brucellosis for the better part of a century [3,5,16-18,43], finding that ...

CSE REFERENCES

FOR BOOKS

Number. Author's Name. Title of the book. City of Publication (State): Publisher; Year.

19. Stewart J. Calculus. Boston (MA): Brooks/Cole; 2002.

FOR ARTICLES FROM PERIODICALS

Number. Author's Name. Article title. Periodical. Date;Volume(Issue):Pages.

17. Richie DJ, Lappos VJ, Palmer PL. Sizing/optimization of a small satellite energy storage and attitude control system. JOSR. 2007 Jul-Aug;87(52):940-952.

FOR ONLINE SOURCES AND ELECTRONIC MEDIA

Number. Title of source [Kind of electronic medium]. Edition. Place of Publication: Publisher; date of publication [date updated; date cited]. Notes.

44. WebElements: chemistry nexus [Internet]. Sheffield (UK): University of Sheffield; c1993-2007 [cited 2007 Jun 18]. Available from: http://www.webelements.com/nexus/

When you cite a book, periodical, or webpage, the format of the citation—the punctuation of the title of a book, the inclusion of a periodical's issue number, or the listing of a URL—tells a reader what kind of text you are citing. When you cite a text that isn't a book, periodical, or webpage, indicate what kind of text you are citing, in brackets after the title (as in the pattern for online sources).

→ See pages 456–457 for more sample CSE references.

DETAILS OF THE PATTERNS

AUTHOR'S NAME

An author's name is listed last name first, with initials for first and middle names. If there are two initials, they are not separated by space or periods. A period separates the author's name from the title.

TITLES OF BOOKS AND PARTS OF BOOKS

1. Capitalize only the first word and any proper nouns.

2. Do not italicize or underline book titles.

3. Put a period after the title.

JOURNAL TITLES

Journal titles in CSE are always abbreviated according to ISO (International Organization for Standardization). For example, the full title of the journal in the example numbered 17 to the left is the *Journal of Spacecraft and Rockets*.

The CSE manual has guidelines for abbreviations. Your school's library will have this manual.

DATES

If a date is not given in any of the usual places (copyright page, etc.) but it can be discerned from other information in the publication, set the date in brackets [2002]. If only a copyright date is available, use that with a **c** for **copyright** (c1962). If there is a publication date and a copyright date, and there is more than three years between them, give both dates (2007, c1962). If there is no date of publication, use the words *date unknown* in brackets: [date unknown].

With a website, the copyright or publication date will be a span of years. In this case, use a hyphen (c1993-2007). For multiple years of publication, separate the years by a hyphen (2004-2005).

ONLINE SOURCES AND ELECTRONIC MEDIA

References for Internet sources and electronic media do not differ significantly from what is required for print sources. There is still an author or organization who is responsible for the content, a title, a place of publication, and a date of publication. Additional information will be the URL and access date, and with some media, technical information.

Always put the medium (Internet; CD-ROM; DVD) in brackets.

CSE also notes dates of updates (which are most applicable to websites) and dates accessed for Internet sources. In some cases, a date of update will not be provided, but you should always note the date of access, especially for materials that change frequently, such as a blog or wiki.

In a CSE citation, notes include URLs as well as technical information. See the examples for audio and video recordings and CD-ROM for examples of technical notes.

CSE SAMPLE REFERENCES

NO AUTHOR NAMED

Start the citation with the work's title.

8. Handbook of geriatric drug therapy. Springhouse (PA): Springhouse; c2000.

MORE THAN ONE AUTHOR

17. Sebastini AM, Fishbeck DW. Mammalian anatomy: the cat. 2nd ed. Burlington (NC): Carolina Biological; 2005.

A CORPORATION OR ORGANIZATION AS AUTHOR

Start with the abbreviated name of the corporate author as it appears in the source.

3. [CCPS] Center for Chemical Process Safety. Guidelines for safe and reliable instrumented protective systems. Indianapolis (IN): Wiley Publishing, Inc.; 2007.

AN EDITED BOOK

Put *editor* or *editors* after the name(s) that begin(s) the citation.

2. Brockman J, editor. What we believe but cannot prove: today's leading thinkers on science in the age of certainty. New York (NY): HarperCollins; 2006.

A GOVERNMENT AUTHOR

6. [GPO] US Government Printing Office. Style manual. Washington (DC): The Office; 2000.

GPO stands for *Government Printing Office*.

AN ESSAY OR CHAPTER IN A BOOK

8. Feynman RP. The making of a scientist. In: Leighton R, editor. Classic Feynman: All the adventures of a curious character. New York (NY): Norton; 2006. p. 13-19.

A REVISED OR LATER EDITION OF A BOOK

Add the edition after the title.

22. Tufte ER. The visual display of quantitative information. 2nd ed. Cheshire (CT): Graphics Press; 2001.

AN ONLINE BOOK

7. Ebert D. Ecology, epidemiology, and evolution of Parasitism in Daphnia [Internet]. Bethesda (MD): National Library of Medicine (US), National Center for Biotechnology Information; 2005 [cited 2007 Sep 4]. Available from: http://www.ncbi.nlm.nih.gov/entrez/query.fcgi?db=Books

A VOLUME IN A SERIES

Place the series information in parentheses after the date of publication.

9. Honjo T, Melchers F, editors. Gut-associated lymphoid tissues. Berlin (Germany): Springer-Verlag; 2006. (Current Topics in Microbiology and Immunology; vol. 308).

A TECHNICAL REPORT

Include the performing and/or sponsoring organization. (The following example shows the performing organization [the group that performed the research], the University of Washington Department of Statistics; the sponsoring group funded the research.) Often, the very end of the citation acknowledges the funding; for example: *(Sponsored by the Nuclear Regulatory Commission)*. The report number goes at the end of the citation (before the URL if there is one). If there is a contract number, include it.

14. Krivitsky P, Handcock M, Raftery AE, Hoff P. Representing degree distributions, clustering, and homophily in social networks with latent cluster random effects models. Seattle (WA): University of Washington Department of Statistics; 2007. No. 517. Available from: http://www.stat.washington.edu/www/research/reports/

A CONFERENCE PRESENTATION
Include the location and dates.

2. Braun F, Noterdaeme JM, Colas L. Simulations of different Faraday screen configurations for the ITER ICRH Antenna. In: Ryan PM, Rassmussen D, editors. Radio frequency power in plasmas: 17th topical conference on radio frequency power in plasmas; 2007 May 7-9; Clearwater (FL). Melville (NY): [AIP] American Institute of Physics; 2007. p. 175-178.

A JOURNAL PAGINATED BY VOLUME

8. Gradstein FM, Og JG. Geologic time scale 2004—why, how, and where near! Lethaia. 2004;(37):175-181.

AN ARTICLE IN A DAILY NEWSPAPER

24. Revkin AC. Cooking up a fable of life on melting ice. New York Times. 2007 Jul 22;Sect. 2:11.

AN ONLINE ARTICLE

24. Spiesel S. Can a rollercoaster really scare you to death? And more. Slate [Internet]. Aug 28 [cited 2007 Sep 3]. Available from: http://www.slate.com/id/2172960/fr/flyout

A WEBPAGE

5. DNA Interactive [Internet]. Cold Spring Harbor (NY): Cold Spring Harbor Lab; c2003 [cited 2007 Aug 12]. Available from: http://www.dnai.org/

AN ONLINE DATABASE

3. Catalysts and catalysed reactions [Internet]. London (UK): RSC Publishing. 2002 [updated 2007 Aug; cited 2007 Sep 5]. Available from: http://pubs.rsc.org/Publishing/CurrentAwareness/CCR/CCRSearchPage.cfm

A BLOG POSTING

4. Diganta [screen name]. Pushing the limits of speciesism. In: Desicritics.org [Web log]. [posted 2007 Jun 18; cited 2007 Sep 2].

A WIKI ENTRY

20. Quantum gates. In: Quantiki [Internet]. Available from: http://www.quantiki.org/wiki/index.php/Quantum_gates. [accessed 4:00 pm CST, Sep 5, 2007].

A CD-ROM

11. Hagen EH, Walker PL. Human evolution: a multimedia guide to the fossil record [CD-ROM]. 4th ed. New York (NY): Norton; 2003. 1 CD-ROM: color, 4 3/4 in.

AN AUDIO OR VIDEO RECORDING

1. Arledge B, director. NOVA-Cracking the code of life [DVD]. Boston (MA): WGBH Boston; 2001. 1 DVD: sound, color, 4 3/4 in.

CHICAGO MANUAL OF STYLE DOCUMEN-TATION AND IN-TEXT CITATIONS

The **Chicago Manual of Style** (CMS) is now in its fifteenth edition (published in 2003). It is used by writers in the arts and humanities, especially history.

Rather than using the author and date in-text citation format of MLA and APA, most CMS advocates prefer the footnote or endnote style of citation. In this style, a superscript number is placed after any quotation, paraphrase, or summary. These numbers are consecutive throughout the text, and correspond either to a footnote set at the bottom of the page or to endnotes that come at the end of the text.

Because CMS notes provide full bibliographic information for the sources cited, writers do not need to provide a **Works Cited** or **References** listing—although they can.

[12] Wang, 84. On the increas the Qing, see the articles by E to ban *Western Chamber*, see Change and Dissemination,"

[13] Jin's claim is echoed by kenkyu," 107. Wang Ji-si, howe a convenient discussion of the Hargett in the *Indiana Comp* H. Nienhauser (Bloomington:

CMS IN-TEXT CITATIONS AND FOOTNOTES

Here is a sample sentence containing a quotation as it would appear in the body of a paper with a superscript number at its end, and the footnote to that sentence, linked by the number. (This sample is numbered 12 because there are eleven source references before it.)

> In *Marriage, a History*, Stephanie Coontz states that, "whether it is valued or not, love is rarely seen as the main ingredient for marital success."[12]
>
> 12. Stephanie Coontz, *Marriage, a History: From Obedience to Intimacy or How Love Conquered Marriage* (New York: Viking, 2005), 18.

SUBSEQUENT NOTE ENTRIES

After the first reference to a book or other source, CMS conventions say that writers should put into a footnote the following:

- the author's last name
- the title of the work (or a shortened version if the title is long)
- a page number.

Some writers, however, use only the author's name and the page number if there will be no ambiguity as to which source is being cited. The footnote could thus read

10. Coontz, *Marriage*, 99.

Or

10. Coontz, 99.

If a reference is to the same work as in the preceding note, you can use the abbreviation **Ibid.** (**Ibid.** is a shortened form of the Latin word **ibidem**, which means **in the same place**.)

11. Ibid., 103.

BIBLIOGRAPHY

If the writer of these sample citations were to include a bibliography listing at the paper's end, the citation would be:

Coontz, Stephanie. *Marriage, a History: From Obedience to Intimacy or How Love Conquered Marriage*. New York: Viking, 2005.

(Notice, in this case, that the listing has the same formatting as MLA style.)

→ See pages 460–462 for more sample CMS footnotes.

CMS SAMPLE REFERENCES

BOOKS

For a footnote:

16. J. H. Plumb, *The Italian Renaissance* (New York: Mariner Books, 2001), 86.

In the bibliography:

Plumb, J. H. *The Italian Renaissance.* New York: Mariner Books, 2001.

AN ESSAY OR CHAPTER IN A BOOK

For a footnote:

8. F. J. Byrne, "Early Irish Society (1st–9th Century)," in *The Course of Irish History*, eds. T. W. Moody and F. X. Martin (Lanham, MD: Roberts Rinehart, 2002), 55.

In the bibliography:

Byrne, F. J. "Early Irish Society (1st–9th Century)." In *The Course of Irish History*, eds. T. W. Moody and F. X. Martin, 43–60. Lanham, MD: Roberts Rinehart, 2002.

ARTICLES FROM PERIODICALS (JOURNALS, MAGAZINES, OR NEWSPAPERS)

For a footnote:

13. Valerie A. Kivelson, "On Words, Sources, and Historical Method: Which Truth About Muscovy?" *Kritika: Explorations in Russian and Eurasian History* 3, no. 3 (2002): 490.

In the bibliography:

Kivelson, Valerie A. "On Words, Sources, and Historical Method: Which Truth About Muscovy?" *Kritika: Explorations in Russian and Eurasian History* 3, no. 3 (2002): 487–99.

A JOURNAL ARTICLE RETRIEVED FROM ELECTRONIC DATABASE

The citation should follow the same form for a journal, but the URL for the article is included.

For a footnote:

23. Bryon MacWilliams, "Yale U. Press Strikes Deal with Russian Archive to Open Stalin's Papers to Scholars," *Chronicle of Higher Education* 53, no. 44 (July 2007), http://web.ebscohost.com.ezproxy.lib.utexas.edu/ehost.

In the bibliography:

MacWilliams, Bryon. "Yale U. Press Strikes Deal with Russian Archive to Open Stalin's Papers to Scholars." *Chronicle of Higher Education* 53, no. 44 (July 2007), http://web.ebscohost.com.ezproxy.lib.utexas.edu/ehost.

ONLINE SOURCES (OTHER THAN DATABASES)

For a footnote:

4. Chris Johnson, "Statement from Human Rights Campaign President Joe Solmonese on Recent ENDA Developments," Human Rights Campaign, September 28, 2007, http://www.hrcbackstory.org/2007/09/statement-from-.html.

In the bibliography:

Johnson, Chris. "Statement from Human Rights Campaign President Joe Solmonese on Recent ENDA Developments." Human Rights Campaign, September 28, 2007, http://www.hrcbackstory.org/2007/09/statement-from-.html.

NO AUTHOR NAMED

Start the citation with the work's title.
For a footnote:

4. *Broad Stripes and Bright Stars* (Kansas City, MO: Andrews McMeel, 2002), 15.

In the bibliography:

Broad Stripes and Bright Stars. Kansas City, MO: Andrews McMeel, 2002.

TWO OR THREE AUTHORS

In a footnote, put all of the authors' full names. For subsequent references, give the authors' last names only. In the bibliography, give full names.
For a footnote:

2. Larry J. Reynolds and Gordon Hutner, eds., *National Imaginaries, American Identities: The Cultural Work of American Iconography* (Princeton, NJ: Princeton University Press, 2000), 56.

In the bibliography:

Reynolds, Larry J., and Gordon Hutner, eds. *National Imaginaries, American Identities: The Cultural Work of American Iconography*. Princeton, NJ: Princeton University Press, 2000.

FOUR OR MORE AUTHORS

In a footnote, give the name of the first author listed, followed by *and others*. List all the authors in the bibliography.
For a footnote:

3. James Drake and others, *James Drake* (Austin, TX: UT Press, 2008), 40.

In the bibliography:

Drake, James, Bruce Ferguson, Steven Henry Madoff, and Jimmy Santiago Baca. *James Drake*. Austin, TX: UT Press, 2008.

A CORPORATE AUTHOR

Start with the name of the corporate author as it appears in the source.
For a footnote:

5. Texas State Historical Association, *The Portable Handbook of Texas* (Austin, TX: Texas State Historical Association, 2000).

In the bibliography:

Texas State Historical Association. *The Portable Handbook of Texas*. Austin, TX: Texas State Historical Association, 2000.

A GOVERNMENT AUTHOR

List the full agency or department name as author.
For a footnote:

11. Central Intelligence Agency, *The World Fact Book 2007* (Washington, DC: Potomac Books, Inc., 2007), 136.

In the bibliography:

Central Intelligence Agency. *The World Fact Book 2007*. Washington, DC: Potomac Books, Inc., 2007.

AN EDITED BOOK

Put *ed.* (or *eds.* for multiple editors) after the names that begin the citation.
For a footnote:

14. J. Peter Burkholder and Claude V. Palisca, eds., *Norton Anthology of Western Music*, Vol. 1, *Ancient to Baroque* (New York: Norton, 2005), 550.

In the bibliography:

Burkholder, J. Peter, and Claude V. Palisca, eds. *Norton Anthology of Western Music*. Vol. 1, *Ancient to Baroque*. New York: Norton, 2005.

continued on the next page

CMS SAMPLE REFERENCES, continued

AN ARTICLE FROM A REFERENCE BOOK

Well-known reference materials are not usually listed in a CMS bibliography, so you need to know only the footnote format. Start with the name of the reference work, and then list its edition. Put **s.v.** (**sub verba**, Latin for **under the word**) and then put the title of the entry you are citing in quotation marks:

9. *Riverside Dictionary of Biography,* 2004 ed., s.v. "Aaron, Hank (Henry Lewis)."

AN ARTICLE FROM AN ONLINE REFERENCE

The access date should be included in the citation only for sources that are frequently updated, such as Wikis. (And, as with reference works in print, there should be no listing in the bibliography.)

26. Wikipedia, s.v. "Deadwood, South Dakota," http://en.wikipedia.org/wiki/Deadwood%2C_South_Dakota (accessed September 4, 2007).

A RELIGIOUS TEXT

Citations for religious texts appear in the notes, but not in the bibliography.

12. Qur'an 18:16–20.

A WEBPAGE

For a footnote:

19. New York Historical Society, "Galleries," New York Divided: Slavery and the Civil War, http://www.slaveryinnewyork.org/tour_galleries.htm (accessed September 2, 2007).

In the bibliography:

New York Historical Society. "Galleries." New York Divided: Slavery and the Civil War. http://www.slaveryinnewyork.org/tour_galleries.htm (accessed September 2, 2007).

AN E-MAIL

If you reference e-mails in the text of your paper, you do not need to provide a note. E-mails are not listed in a CMS bibliography.

In an e-mail message to the author on November 6, 2006, Jason Craft noted....

If you do need to include a footnote:

24. Jason Craft, e-mail message to author, November 6, 2006.

A BLOG POSTING

When you give the URL for a blog entry, give the **permalink** to the entry rather than the URL of that blog so a reader can go directly to the entry without having to scroll through the entire blog.

For a footnote:

8. Pink Lady [Screen name], "Howard's End," In the Pink Texas Blog, comment posted June 29, 2007, http://www.inthepinktexas.com/2007/06/29/howards-end-3/ (accessed August 3, 2007).

In the bibliography:

In the Pink Texas Blog. "Howard's End." http:// www.inthepinktexas.com/2007/06/29/howards-end-3/.

PART 9
EDITING AND PROOFREADING YOUR WORK

CONTENTS

WHERE ARE WE IN THE PROCESS FOR COMPOSING?

Understanding your project

Getting started

Asking questions

Shaping your
project for others

Drafting a paper

Getting feedback

Revising

Polishing   Editing and proofreading

EDITING AND PROOFREADING

EDITING

To edit your own writing, try reading it aloud to yourself (which will help you really hear how your words are working) or to someone else (which will really make you aware of how others respond to your words).

Whether you read aloud or work with hardcopy, keep an ear and eye out for the following:

- Are your verbs active? Are your nouns concrete?
  → See pages 273–274.

- Have you avoided jargon?
  → See page 276.

- Will your readers know easily why one sentence or paragraph follows another?
  → See pages 296–297 on transitions.

- Do your sentences have all the qualities that make them easy to read?
  → See pages 282–283.

- Are your introductory and concluding paragraphs engaging and strong?
  → See pages 292–295.

- Have you used inclusive language?
  → See pages 248–263.

PROOFREADING

For both editing and proofreading, keep the following in mind:

- If you have been writing exclusively on a computer screen, **print a hard copy** for editing and proofreading: Seeing the text differently will help you see changes you can and ought to make to help your audience read the text easily.

- Almost all word processing software comes with **grammar checkers**. Use them, but use them carefully: They simply are not as sophisticated as humans. They often miss or misidentify sentence fragments, recommend that you shorten sentences that are just fine, and suggest grammatical changes that are just plain wrong. At this time, there is no better grammar checker than another human.

- Like grammar checkers, **spell checkers** are imperfect. They cannot tell whether you are using **they're**, **there**, or **their** correctly, and they will sometimes recommend replacement words for words they do not have in their reference lists; for example, one spell checker has recommended **salmon's** to replace **someone's**. Spell checkers do not recognize many names. So use spell checkers, but use them carefully: If you are unsure whether a change they recommend is correct, check a dictionary or ask someone whose knowledge you trust.

→ To learn more about using spell checkers, see page 609.

IF ENGLISH IS NOT YOUR HOME LANGUAGE

- Proofread and edit little by little. Don't wait until the paper is finished to edit and proofread. Instead, once you have a thesis, a statement of purpose, and a completed draft, spend a little time editing. If you leave all the language work until the end of the process, you may not have enough time or you may find it too overwhelming and discouraging.

- Determine the aspects of style, punctuation, or grammar that give you trouble. Focus on those aspects when you proofread.

- Proofread your text more than once. Look for a different style, punctuation, or grammar point each time.

- Be an active proofreader. Use strategies that allow you to focus on the mechanics and language of what you have written. In addition to the strategies we have described to the left, try:
  - Underlining or highlighting the aspects of style, punctuation, or grammar on which you are focusing.
  - Moving a pencil along each sentence as you proofread to focus your attention on your words and punctuation.
  - Reading sentence by sentence, covering the rest of the text with a blank sheet of paper.
  - Putting slash marks (//) between each sentence. This will help you focus on the grammar, punctuation, and vocabulary choices you have made in each sentence.

GRAMMAR

WHAT IS GRAMMAR?

The grammars that appear in handbooks and textbooks attempt to capture language patterns that develop as humans talk and write. Not only do grammars change as times change but they shift from group to group.

The grammar we present in the next pages is **the grammar of academic American English writing**. You may have grown up into this pattern if you grew up where people write and read a lot. You may have grown up where other patterns—other grammars—of English are used. You may have grown up in another language.

No matter what your language background, studying the current patterns in academic American English writing can help you move between different grammar communities and help you decide how you want to shape the words you use to reach others.

■ ■ ■

The illustration to the right shows the basic parts—and how they build—of English sentences.

Like any illustration, it is not perfect, but it is accurate enough for you to see how sentences are broken down into clauses, subjects and predicates, noun and verb phrases, and then the parts of speech.

You can also move from the bottom up, to see how words—the parts of speech—come together to form phrases and then subjects and predicates and then clauses and finally sentences.

The nineteenth-century Society for the Diffusion of Really Useful Knowledge published and widely distributed *The Penny Magazine* and *The Penny Cyclopedia*, because its members were worried about the reading practices of its working-class audience.

SENTENCES
are made of…

The nineteenth-century Society for the Diffusion of Really Useful Knowledge published and widely distributed *The Penny Magazine* and *The Penny Cyclopedia*

because its members were worried about the reading practices of its working-class audience.

CLAUSES, of which there are two kinds, both of which are made of…

The nineteenth-century Society for the Diffusion of Really Useful Knowledge

its members

SUBJECTS,
which are made of…

published and widely distributed *The Penny Magazine* and *The Penny Cyclopedia*

were worried about the reading practices of its working-class audience.

PREDICATES,
which are made of…

The nineteenth-century Society for the Diffusion of Really Useful Knowledge

The Penny Magazine and *The Penny Cyclopedia*

its members

the reading practices of its working-class audience

NOUN PHRASES,
which can be made of…

published and widely distributed

were worried

VERB PHRASES,
which can be made of…

NOUNS: Society, Diffusion, Knowledge, members, *Magazine, Cyclopedia,* practices, audience
PRONOUNS: its
ARTICLES: the
ADJECTIVES: nineteenth-century, Useful, working-class
ADVERBS: Really
CONJUNCTIONS: and
PREPOSITIONS: of

VERBS: published, distributed, worried
HELPING VERBS: were
ADVERBS: widely
CONJUNCTIONS: and

Nouns, pronouns, articles, adjectives, adverbs, conjunctions, prepositions, and verbs, taken all together, are referred to as

THE PARTS OF SPEECH.

THERE ARE 4 SENTENCE FUNCTIONS.

With sentences, we can…

1

MAKE STATEMENTS

These kind of sentences are called **DECLARATIVE SENTENCES**, and they are the main kind of sentence you will see in all writing, including academic.

Lyle sits hunched over on the tailgate.

In the fifth and sixth centuries, Ireland was the center of high culture in Europe.

In the last years of his life, Ray began to manifest a strange relationship with snow.

Between the end of the Civil War and the turn of the century, the controversy in American life about who women were and ought to be played itself out in popular self-improvement manuals that offered condensed versions of academic and practical subjects including the principles of elocution, oratory, and composition.

2

ASK QUESTIONS

These are **INTERROGATIVE SENTENCES**, and they matter in all writing. In academic writing, authors often use questions to set up the problems they want to address.

What should we do now?

How can an experiment be "wrong"?

How lethal was the flu of 1918?

Will all broadband infrastructures be privately owned?

What is it like to live in a cell in one of the most notorious prisons in the country?

Why is it that people have such strange attitudes toward images, objects, and media? Why do they behave as though pictures were alive, as if works of art had minds of their own, as if images had a power to influence human beings, demanding things from us, persuading, seducing, and leading us astray?

3

COMMAND

These are **IMPERATIVE SENTENCES.** They tell someone to do something. You also find them in instruction sets and manuals.

Go home.

Put down the weapon and raise your hands.

Watch out that the temperature of the beaker's contents does not rise about 275°.

In a large saucepan over low heat, warm the oil until hot but not smoking. Add the curry paste. It should just sizzle; if it spits and pops wildly, remove the pan from the heat for a moment.

(Note that imperative sentences have an implied subject: It is as though every imperative sentence begins with the implied word **You**.)

4

BE EMOTIONAL

These are **EXCLAMATORY SENTENCES.** Exclamations are expressions of strong feeling. Writers often use exclamatory sentences when they are describing the speech of others. These sentences end with exclamation points.

Anthrax!

When we were little, how we loved to be scared silly!

If the electrons are not seen, we have interference!

THERE ARE 4 SENTENCE PATTERNS.

It is out of these four patterns that all American English sentences are built.

1

SIMPLE SENTENCES

are used in all writing:

Dogs bark.

Jumping dogs bark loudly.

She and I were going to the park.

An autumn wind gusts up to thirty miles an hour.

He pointed to a pile of smooth bricks.

They giggle and laugh.

Simple sentences are the building blocks of the other kinds of sentences, so it is important that you have a good understanding of them because the other kinds of sentences are much used in academic and formal writing. (Notice, too, that simple sentences are neither necessarily short nor uninformative even though they are called **simple**.)

→ GO TO PAGE 472.

2

COMPOUND SENTENCES

join two simple sentences:

Dogs bark and cats meow.

She and I were going to the park while everyone else was swimming.

An autumn wind gusts up to thirty miles an hour; a winter wind can gust up to fifty miles an hour.

I am not worried about getting lost in the woods; besides, the point of wilderness is to lose yourself in it.

Compound sentences are important in academic and other kinds of formal writing because they help you express a range of relationships among the elements of your sentences.

→ GO TO PAGE 480.

→ The parts out of which sentences are built are words, which we discuss in the Parts of Speech pages beginning on page 496.

3

COMPLEX SENTENCES

allow you to express complicated relations among the elements you are describing. These sentences are also very important in academic and other kinds of formal writing.

Those who want to learn more should come to the Friday-evening classes.

In this chapter I examine the development of Piaget's thought, which has three main features.

Although his mother remarried after his father died, she was soon abandoned by her second husband.

I argue that James's use of metaphor is not so straightforward when one considers it in light of his family background.

→ GO TO PAGE 483.

4

COMPOUND-COMPLEX SENTENCES

As their name suggests, compound-complex sentences result when you combine a compound sentence with a complex sentence. These sentences tend to be long, and are used almost exclusively in academic writing.

Georgette de Montenay, who came from a noble family in southwest France, lived at the court of the Queen of Navarre and wrote the first religious emblem book.

Chinese mathematical thought was always profoundly algebraic instead of geometrical, and in the Sung and Yuan dynasties of the twelfth to fourteenth centuries A.D., the Chinese school led the world in the solution of equations; thus the triangle we now call Pascal's was already old in China in 1300 A.D.

→ GO TO PAGE 488.

SIMPLE SENTENCES 1

The simplest sentences are most often composed of two words. The first word names a person, place, thing, or idea; the second word describes what that person, place, thing, or idea is, was, or will be doing.

THE PATTERN

person, place, thing, or idea + **action** = **simplest sentence**

NOUN	VERB
Sylvia	walks.
Men	swam.
Chairs	rock.
Lakes	glisten.
Air	moves.
Dogs	barked.
You	smile.
I	sleep.
Happiness	is.
SUBJECT	**PREDICATE**

INDEPENDENT CLAUSE

→ When we wish to speak of persons, places, objects, and ideas as a grammatical category, we call them nouns (pages 498–501).

→ As a grammatical category, actions are called verbs (pages 514–527).

→ The part of a sentence that names who or what acts is the subject (pages 475–478); the part that names the action is the predicate (pages 474–478).

→ A subject and predicate together are a clause (page 483); when they can stand alone as a sentence, they are independent clauses (pages 484–487).

GRAMMAR: SIMPLE SENTENCES

SIMPLE SENTENCES 2

To the simplest sentences you can add descriptions to help readers understand more about the nouns and verbs in them.

THE PATTERN

noun and description + **verb and description** = **sentence**

NOUN PHRASE	VERB PHRASE
The woman	walks quickly.
A man	swam slowly.
Rocking chairs	swayed jauntily.
Blue lakes	glisten lightly.
Cool air	moves quietly.
A dog	barked loudly.
You	smile widely.
I, tired,	sleep contentedly.
Our happiness	stays still.
SUBJECT	**PREDICATE**
INDEPENDENT CLAUSE	

→ The words that help us say descriptive things about nouns are called adjectives (pages 508–509). Articles are the words *a, an,* and *the,* and are a special kind of adjective (pages 510–513).

→ The words that help us say descriptive things about verbs are called adverbs (pages 528–529).

→ When nouns and verbs have descriptive words added to them, as above, they are called (respectively) noun phrases (page 474) and verb phrases (page 474).

SIMPLE SENTENCES 3

There are sentence patterns that help us describe how a person, place, object, or idea performs an action on another person, place, object, or idea.

THE PATTERN

NOUN PHRASE + **VERB PHRASE** + **OBJECT (NOUN PHRASE)** = **SENTENCE**

The woman quickly walks her barking dog.

An irritated man slapped a whiny mosquito.

The chair legs dented the floor.

The wind easily moves the lake water.

She shifted her weight.

You warily watch the changing weather.

I make the bed.

Our happiness fills me.

SUBJECT PREDICATE

INDEPENDENT CLAUSE

Notice that objects are always nouns or noun phrases.

→ To learn more about objects, see pages 476–477.

Notice also that, when you compose sentences that contain objects, the predicates of the sentences include the objects, even though the objects are nouns or noun phrases. This is because the predicate tells a reader about an action, including the object of the action.

→ To learn more about predicates, see pages 475–478.

SUBJECTS & PREDICATES

To move from writing simple sentences to writing compound, complex, and compound-complex sentences, writers need to understand about subjects and predicates.

SUBJECTS

Subjects are the word or words in a sentence that name who or what is performing some action. Subjects can be composed of one word (in which case it is always a noun) or multiple words (in which case they are some combination of nouns and articles, conjunctions, and/or adjectives).

<u>Yang</u> smiles.

<u>Michael and the new student</u> went to lunch together.

<u>Their sad songs</u> filled the valley and echoed in the air.

SUBJECT

→ To learn more about the kinds of words that make up subjects, see pages 498–501 for nouns, pages 510–513 for articles, pages 508–509 for adjectives, and pages 532–535 for conjunctions.

PREDICATES

Predicates are the word or words in a sentence that describe the action taken by the subject. Predicates can be made of one word (in which case it is always a verb) or multiple words (in which case they are some combination of verbs and adverbs, conjunctions, or noun phrases that are objects).

Yang <u>smiles</u>.

Michael and the new student <u>went to lunch together.</u>

Their sad songs <u>filled the valley and echoed in the air.</u>

PREDICATE

→ To learn more about the kinds of words that make up predicates, see pages 514–527 for verbs, pages 528–529 for adverbs, pages 476–477 for objects, page 474 for noun phrases, and pages 532–538 for conjunctions.

MORE ON PREDICATES

As we described on the preceding page, a predicate always contains a verb (see pages 514–527 to learn more about verbs). The verb in a predicate can be one of three kinds:

- a verb that takes objects
- a verb that does not take objects
- a linking verb

VERBS THAT TAKE OBJECTS

Objects can be parts of predicates. Objects are the nouns or nouns phrases that describe the person, place, thing, or idea affected by the verb's action. Verbs that take objects are called *transitive verbs*.

She **smelled the roses**.

Jamieson **interviewed a variety of experts**.

Neanderthals **were cooking shellfish** in Italy about 110,000 years ago.

There are two kinds of objects: **direct object** and **indirect objects**.The examples above all show direct objects.

Indirect objects only appear in sentences that have direct objects. Indirect objects answer the questions *For whom was this action carried out?* or *To whom was the object given?*

	indirect objects	direct objects
He gave	me	water.
Mark read	his son	a story.
The carpenter will build	us	new bookshelves.

An indirect object usually comes between the verb and the direct object.

Indirect objects do not follow prepositions (➜ see pages 530–531). Sentences with indirect objects can be rewritten with prepositions—

He gave water to me.

Mark read a story to his son.

The carpenter will build new bookshelves for us.

—but then the indirect object becomes the object of the preposition before it and is no longer an indirect object.

VERBS THAT DON'T TAKE OBJECTS

Verbs that don't take objects or subject complements (see below) are called *intransitive verbs.*

Meredith left. • Margarete complained. • The train arrived.

Intransitive sentences can have adverbs (see pages 528–529) or adverbial phrases (see page 486) following the verb, but these modify the verb; they are not objects:

Meredith left sadly. • Margarete complained about her haircut.

The train arrived two hours late.

LINKING VERBS

Linking verbs "link" a noun to a fuller description.

Luisa is happy.

Communication overload may be sapping your productivity.

The words following a linking verb are a **subject complement**: the subject complement fills out (or **complements**) what readers know about the noun. The subject complement in a sentence can be a noun, noun phrase, or pronoun—

"Why Did I Get Married" is the big screen adaptation of Tyler Perry's stage play.

—or it can be an adjective—

The process was difficult for everyone involved.

Linking verbs are usually a form of the verb *be* (see page 519) but can also be verbs such as *appear, become, feel, look, make, seem, smell, sound,* or *taste*:

The cheese smelled stinky but delicious.

TIP: DOES A VERB TAKE A DIRECT OBJECT, NO OBJECT, OR A SUBJECT COMPLEMENT?
A dictionary entry will tell you.

TIP: SOME VERBS CAN BE BOTH TRANSITIVE AND INTRANSITIVE

She moved the furniture to her new house.

Molecules and ions moved through the cell membrane.

In the first sentence above, **moved** functions as a transitive verb, with **the furniture** as its direct object. In the second sentence, **moved** functions as an intransitive verb; **through the cell membrane** is an adverbial phrase. A dictionary entry can help you learn about such verbs and how to use them.

COMPOUND SUBJECTS & PREDICATES

You can use the patterns on the preceding pages to build more detailed sentences. One way to do this is to use a kind of word called a conjunction to build:

SUBJECTS THAT DESCRIBE MORE THAN ONE PERSON, PLACE, THING, OR IDEA

You can substitute any of the following subjects for any of the noun phrases in the simple sentence patterns on the preceding pages (as long as you make the verb agree):

Sylvia and Luisa walk.

Neither the air nor my heart moved.

Dogs or coyotes barked.

Paul, Tonio, and I make the bed.

SUBJECT PREDICATE

The subjects above are called **compound subjects** because they are compounded out of multiple nouns.

→ Note that the form of verbs sometimes has to change when you change the subject of a sentence; see pages 524–526.

PREDICATES THAT DESCRIBE MORE THAN ONE ACTION

You can substitute any of the following predicates for any of the verb phrases in the simple sentence patterns on the preceding pages (as long as the subject and predicate agree in number):

Sylvia walks or runs.

My heart jumped and stilled.

The dogs both barked and snored loudly.

Paul makes the bed and sweeps the floor.

SUBJECT PREDICATE

The predicates above are called **compound predicates** because they are made of multiple predicates.

→ To learn more about conjunctions, see pages 532–535.

PREPOSITIONAL PHRASES

Prepositions are kinds of words that allow you to say more precisely where a noun is in space or time or where the action of a verb takes place. Prepositions do this by being the first word of **prepositional phrases**, which show where one noun is in relation to another or where the action of a verb takes place relative to some noun. Prepositional phrases thus allow you to make subjects and predicates that can be very descriptive.

MORE DESCRIPTIVE SUBJECTS

As parts of subjects, prepositional phrases function like adjectives, telling your readers more about the nouns you are using:

The dog on the sidewalk was barking.

The air in the tent shimmered.

Paul, on the telephone, sounds less serious.

Children at school tend to be quieter.

SUBJECT PREDICATE

MORE DESCRIPTIVE PREDICATES

As parts of predicates, prepositional phrases function like adverbs, telling your readers more about the action being described by the verb, such as where or when the action takes or took place:

Sylvia walks into the store.

My heart jumped at the sound of your voice.

The dogs hid underneath the table.

Paul makes the bed over the course of the day.

SUBJECT PREDICATE

→ To learn more about prepositions, see pages 530–531.

→ To learn more about adverbs, see pages 528–529.

COMPOUND SENTENCES

Compound sentences are made up of two or more simple sentences joined by punctuation or conjunctions—or both punctuation and conjunctions.

THE FUNCTION OF COMPOUND SENTENCES

When you write with compound sentences, your sentences can show readers more complex relations among events than simple sentences allow. Compound sentences show up frequently in academic writing.

Because compound sentences are made up of two independent clauses joined together, they show that the writer wants to give equal emphasis to both clauses.

THE PATTERN

MAKING COMPOUND SENTENCES USING PUNCTUATION

INDEPENDENT CLAUSE **;** INDEPENDENT CLAUSE **=** COMPOUND SENTENCE

Cecelia walks; Martha bikes.

I was sleeping; you were reading.

Dogs bark; coyotes howl.

The cell was large; it could attach to the molecule.

You jump; he leaps; we all dance.

This pattern implies that the events described in the joined independent clauses happened at the same time and are of equal importance.

→ To learn more about using semicolons as punctuation to join two independent clauses, see pages 565–567.

MAKING COMPOUND SENTENCES USING CONJUNCTIONS

INDEPENDENT CLAUSE + CONJUNCTION + INDEPENDENT CLAUSE = COMPOUND SENTENCE

Cecelia walks and Martha bikes.

I was sleeping while you were reading.

Dogs bark but coyotes howl.

The cell was large but it could attach to the molecule.

This pattern—which uses *coordinating conjunctions*—allows you to show various kinds of relations between the events of the independent clauses.

→ To learn more about coordinating conjunctions and the relations they can help you build between independent clauses, see page 532.

MAKING COMPOUND SENTENCES USING PUNCTUATION AND CONJUNCTIONS

Some kinds of conjunctions take the following pattern for joining independent clauses (note the comma after the conjunction):

INDEPENDENT CLAUSE ; CONJUNCTION , INDEPENDENT CLAUSE
= COMPOUND SENTENCE

Cecelia walks; meanwhile, Martha bikes.

I slept; instead, you read.

It rained while we were there; moreover, it was cold.

She was found innocent; accordingly, she will go free.

This pattern uses the kind of conjunction named **conjunctive adverbs**. Depending on the conjunction you use, this pattern allows you to show readers that the events of one independent clause happened at a different time than another event, or are less important, or that one event caused another. You can build subtle relations between the different independent clauses.

→ To learn more about conjunctive adverbs, see page 535.

COMPLEX SENTENCES: WORKING WITH INDEPENDENT AND DEPENDENT CLAUSES

To move to complex sentences, we need to explain the difference between independent and dependent clauses.

It will help you understand the difference if you think of what the words *independent* and *dependent* mean: Something that is independent can stand alone; something that is dependent cannot.

Independent clauses can be sentences, and dependent clauses cannot.

THE PATTERN

AN INDEPENDENT CLAUSE CAN STAND ALONE AS A SIMPLE SENTENCE

SUBJECT + PREDICATE = INDEPENDENT CLAUSE

Martha bikes.

Dogs and coyotes bark in the lonely night.

The cell was large and unevenly shaped.

The fast growth of cities causes trouble for mapmakers.

When an independent clause stands by itself, it is a simple sentence. When it is combined with dependent clauses (as we show on the next pages), you build complex sentences.

THE FUNCTION OF COMPLEX SENTENCES

Because complex sentences combine one independent clause with one dependent clause, the sentences are made of unequal partners. In writing such sentences, then, the writer gives the information in the independent clause more weight than the information in the dependent clause.

A COMPLEX SENTENCE COMBINES AN INDEPENDENT CLAUSE WITH ONE OR MORE DEPENDENT CLAUSES

There are two kinds of dependent clauses: *adjective clauses* and *adverb clauses*. In formal written English, dependent clauses cannot stand alone as sentences.

THE PATTERN

COMPLEX SENTENCES WITH ADJECTIVE CLAUSES

RELATIVE PRONOUN **+** PREDICATE **=** ADJECTIVE CLAUSE

who was biking

which was in the street

that hid under the bushes

whose shape kept changing

Adjective clauses allow you to give additional information about subjects, and so they help you write expressive sentences. Adjective clauses are inserted into independent clauses to make **THE FIRST KIND OF COMPLEX SENTENCE:**

The woman who was biking is my sister.

The bicycle, which was in the street, is missing.

The cell whose shape kept changing has been identified.

→ To learn more about relative pronouns, see page 504.

→ *Whom* is also a relative pronoun, and it can cause writers lots of trouble; see page 507 to learn about the standard ways of using *whom*.

→ To learn more about the punctuation of adjective clauses when you weave them into independent clauses, see pages 558–562. Pay close attention to this; punctuating adjective phrases can cause writers trouble.

Adjective clauses can look like independent clauses because they have a similar structure to sentences: There is a word and then there is a predicate. But, in formal English, relative pronouns cannot take the place of nouns—and so adjective clauses cannot stand alone as sentences.

NOT SENTENCES

who was biking

which was in the street

that hid under the bushes

whose shape kept changing

→ The phrases above are fragments of sentences that can be turned into sentences. To learn more about sentence fragments, see pages 490–493.

SENTENCES

If, in the adjective clauses above, you were to replace the relative pronouns with subjects, you would have sentences:

Mary was biking.

The bicycle was in the street.

The woodchuck hid under the bushes.

The cell's shape kept changing.

SENTENCES

Sometimes, if you put a question mark on the end of an adjective clause—and you capitalize the first letter of the relative pronoun—you can make interrogatory sentences out of adjective clauses:

Who was biking?

Whose shape kept changing?

When you do this, you are changing the function of the pronoun, and so you are changing the type of the pronoun, from a relative pronoun to an interrogative pronoun.

→ To learn more about interrogative pronouns, see page 503.

COMPLEX SENTENCES WITH ADVERB CLAUSES

SUBORDINATING CONJUNCTION + **SUBJECT** + **PREDICATE** = **ADVERB CLAUSE**

after it rains

although she was biking

before it was in the street

when it hid under the bushes

while the cell's shape changed

Adverb clauses help writers express complex ideas—and so they are important in academic writing. You can combine adverb clauses with independent clauses to make sentences that express subtle relationships, as in the examples below. Add adverb clauses to independent clauses to make **THE SECOND KIND OF COMPLEX SENTENCE:**

After it rains, we will go for a bike ride.

Although she was biking, she wore her high-heel shoes.

The bicycle was in the garage before it was in the street.

The woodchuck was safe when it hid under the bushes.

While the cell's shape changed it could not be identified.

→ To learn more about subordinating conjunctions, see page 534. Try to recognize the pattern and don't worry about names: If the word at the beginning of a clause isn't a noun or pronoun, it is likely a subordinating conjunction or correlative adverb—and the clause is therefore a dependent clause.

→ Notice that adverb clauses can come at the beginning or the end—and even in the middle—of sentences. Sometimes the conventions of written English require commas around the clauses. To learn more about the punctuation of adverb clauses when you weave them together with independent clauses, see pages 558–562. Pay close attention to this; punctuating adverb phrases can cause writers trouble.

Adverb clauses are not independent clauses, so they cannot stand alone as sentences.

NOT SENTENCES

after it rains

although she was biking

before it was in the street

when the woodchuck hid under the bushes

while the cell's shape changed

→ The phrases above are fragments of sentences that can be turned into sentences. To learn more about sentence fragments, see pages 490–493.

SENTENCES

If you remove the subordinating conjunctions or correlative adverbs, you have sentences:

It rains.

She was biking.

It was in the street.

The woodchuck hid under the bushes.

The cell's shape kept changing.

COMPOUND-COMPLEX SENTENCES

Compound-complex sentences are a sure sign of academic writing. Writers who know how to compose and mix compound and complex sentences into compound-complex sentences are writers who can build sentences for the widest range of contexts and purposes.

THE PATTERN

Compound-complex sentences have at least two independent clauses and one dependent clause, in any order.

INDEPENDENT CLAUSE + **INDEPENDENT CLAUSE** + **DEPENDENT CLAUSE** = **COMPOUND-COMPLEX SENTENCE**

The clauses can be joined together in any of the ways we have described for compound and complex sentences. Look back over the preceding pages for compound and complex patterns to see how they add up in the examples below.

Because compound-complex sentences are made up of many parts, they tend to be long. Because they characterize academic writing, we have taken our examples from essays in various academic disciplines.

> In his essay, Tolman proposed that rats who were able to find food in a maze weren't simply reacting to a conditioned behavioral stimulus but the rats had generated a cognitive map of the overall environment.

The compound-complex sentence above consists of:

- A compound sentence that has a dependent clause (an adjective clause).
- The conjunction **but**.
- A simple sentence.

Below is a compound-complex sentence made of:
- A simple sentence.
- The conjunction *and*.
- A compound sentence that has a dependent clause (an adverb clause).

> **The American colonies were initially as jealous of their autonomy as the Cherokee chiefdoms, and their first attempt at amalgamation under the Articles of Confederation in 1781 proved unworkable because it reserved too much autonomy for the ex-colonies.**

Can you see the parts making up this compound-complex sentence?

> **We readily recognize people's distinctive handwriting when they put addresses on envelopes, and our signatures remain a key way in which we can identify ourselves during a variety of transactions.**

GRAMMAR
AVOIDING SENTENCE FRAGMENTS

A sentence fragment is an incomplete sentence.

And hid under the steps.

Because Vered said so.

When.

A capital letter and appropriate punctuation do not turn a string of words into a sentence. A sentence, grammatically, is an independent clause, which we describe on page 483.

Your brother hid under the steps.

Vered said so.

When is Collin fixing us lunch?

STEPS FOR DETERMINING IF YOU HAVE A SENTENCE—OR A FRAGMENT

You have to apply each of the three steps below to a sentence to be sure it is not a fragment.

	example 1	example 2	example 3	example 4
1 Is there a subject? ⇨ See pages 475–479.	**Danced in the streets.**	**The computer on the desk.**	**Unless there is old wiring in the house.**	**Nevertheless, they plotted.**
	NO. This is a fragment.	YES. Keep going.	YES. Keep going.	YES. Keep going.
2 Is there a predicate? ➡ See pages 474–478.		NO. This is a fragment.	YES. Keep going.	YES. Keep going.
3 Do the words make up a dependent clause without an attached independent clause? ➡ See pages 483–487.			YES. This is a fragment.	NO. THIS IS A SENTENCE.

➡ To fix fragments that lack subjects, see page 492.

➡ To fix fragments that lack predicates, see page 492.

➡ To fix fragments that are dependent clauses, see page 493.

FIXING FRAGMENTS THAT LACK SUBJECTS

Fix fragments that lack subjects by one of the following two approaches:

1 Add a subject

2 Join the fragment to a sentence

ADDING A SUBJECT TO A FRAGMENT

These phrases are fragments because they lack subjects:

Danced in the street.

Sensing their delight in winning.

To add a subject, ask, *Who is doing the action described in the sentence?*—and then give that information:

Mary and Elaine danced in the street.

Christa was sensing their delight in winning. [OR] Christa sensed their delight in winning.

As with the second example, note that you may have to modify the verb when you add a subject.

JOINING A FRAGMENT TO A SENTENCE

Often people inadvertently write fragments in longer descriptions:

Mary and Elaine won the guitar contest last June. They were so happy they threw a party. Danced in the street.

The *danced in the street* fragment can be joined to the sentence before it with a coordinating conjunction:

Mary and Elaine won the guitar contest last June. They were so happy they threw a party and danced in the street.

→ We discuss coordinating conjunctions on page 532 and pages 556–557.

FIXING FRAGMENTS THAT LACK PREDICATES

Fix fragments that lack predicates by one of the following two approaches:

1 Add a predicate

2 Join the fragment to a sentence

ADDING A PREDICATE TO A FRAGMENT

These phrases are fragments because they lack predicates:

The computer on the desk.

Only the lonely.

To add a predicate, ask *What is happening to the objects named the fragment?*—and then give that information:

The computer on the desk was broken.

Only the lonely know how I feel tonight.

JOINING A FRAGMENT TO A SENTENCE

Just as with fragments that lack subjects, fragments without predicates often occur when people write descriptions:

Nobody was out walking after midnight. Only the lonely.

The *only the lonely* fragment can be joined to the sentence before it by making it into the subject:

Only the lonely were out walking after midnight.

Or you can use a conjunction to join the fragment to the end of the sentence:

Nobody was out walking after midnight, except for the lonely.

→ We discuss conjunctions on pages 532–535.

FIXING FRAGMENTS THAT ARE SUBORDINATE CLAUSES WITHOUT ATTACHED INDEPENDENT CLAUSES

This fragment type is a common problem for those learning to write formal prose.

THE PATTERN

To recognize these fragments, you need to be able to recognize dependent clauses. Dependent clauses begin in two ways:

- with one of the *subordinating conjunctions*, which we list on page 534.

  Rather than build a road.

  Although we lived under the Nazi regime for only one year.

  When the people of this part of Peru were building their cities.

- with one of the *relative pronouns*, which we describe on page 504.

  Who regularly sat in hot tubs.   *Whom* he had met in high school.

Anytime you see a phrase that begins with a subordinating conjunction or a relative pronoun, it cannot stand on its own; each gray text above is a fragment.

■ ■ ■

To fix these fragments:

JOIN SUBORDINATE CLAUSE FRAGMENTS TO INDEPENDENT CLAUSES

Rather than build a road, they installed a tram over the trees.

Although my family lived under the Nazi regime for only one year, I will never forget the fear and humiliation I experienced that year in Vienna.

When the people of this part of Peru were building their cities, there was only one other urban complex on earth.

REMOVE THE SUBORDINATING CONJUNCTION TO MAKE A SENTENCE

Note that this gives you two sentences, separated by a period:

We lived under the Nazi regime for only one year. I will never forget the fear and humiliation I experienced that year in Vienna.

INSERT A CLAUSE BEGINNING WITH A RELATIVE PRONOUN INTO AN INDEPENDENT CLAUSE

All the men who regularly sit in hot tubs showed signs of infertility.

Talib Kweli began recording with Mos Def, whom he had met in high school.

AVOIDING RUN-ON SENTENCES

Run-on sentences result when you put two independent clauses together with unconventional or no punctuation.

→ See pages 483–487 to learn about independent clauses.

Run-on sentences have two varieties:

FUSED SENTENCES
A fused sentence has no punctuation between its two independent clauses:

> Flower was one of the meerkats on the Animal Planet documentary series *Meerkat Manor* she died after being bitten by a cobra.

COMMA SPLICES
A comma splice puts a comma between its two independent clauses:

> Flower was one of the meerkats on the Animal Planet documentary series *Meerkat Manor* , she died after being bitten by a cobra.

ONE WAY COMMA SPLICES HAPPEN
Conjunctive adverbs (see page 535) imply a logical relation between the two independent clauses they join. When writers use conjunctive adverbs, they can hear the logic—but miss that they are working with two independent clauses that can't be joined with a comma.

> Corporations expect their employees to move in response to the corporations' needs , consequently, employees tend not to live where they grew up.

GIVING RUN-ON SENTENCES CONVENTIONAL PUNCTUATION

Five strategies help you convert run-on sentences into the forms expected in academic writing.

1 MAKE THE TWO INDEPENDENT CLAUSES INTO TWO SENTENCES

Flower was one of the meerkats on the Animal Planet documentary series *Meerkat Manor*. She died after being bitten by a cobra in South Africa.

This is the easiest strategy: Put a period between the two independent clauses. (Be sure to capitalize the first letter of the second sentence.)

2 JOIN THE INDEPENDENT CLAUSES WITH A SEMICOLON OR COLON

Flower was one of the meerkats on the Animal Planet documentary series *Meerkat Manor*; she died after being bitten by a cobra.

Corporations expect their employees to move in response to the corporations' needs; consequently, employees tend not to live where they grew up.

In less formal writing, you can also join independent clauses with a dash.

→ See page 567 to learn about joining independent clauses with semicolons.

→ See page 573 to learn about joining independent clauses with colons.

3 JOIN THE INDEPENDENT CLAUSES WITH A COMMA AND A COORDINATING CONJUNCTION

Flower was one of the meerkats on the Animal Planet documentary series *Meerkat Manor*, but she died after being bitten by a cobra.

The coordinating conjunctions are *and*, *but*, *or*, *nor*, *for*, *so*, and *yet*; we describe coordinating conjunctions on pages 532 and 556–557.

4 MAKE ONE OF THE INDEPENDENT CLAUSES INTO A DEPENDENT CLAUSE

Flower, who was a meerkat on the Animal Planet documentary series *Meerkat Manor*, died after being bitten by a cobra.

→ Pages 483–487 discuss dependent clauses.

5 RESTRUCTURE THE TWO INDEPENDENT CLAUSES INTO ONE INDEPENDENT CLAUSE

Flower, one of the meerkats on the Animal Planet documentary series *Meerkat Manor*, died after being bitten by a cobra in South Africa.

You might be able to turn one of the independent clauses into a phrase that you can then place next to the word it modifies.

GRAMMAR
PARTS OF SPEECH

The parts of speech are the most basic units of sentences: The parts of speech are the individual words of sentences, named according to the functions they serve in sentences.

The illustration to the right gives a quick introduction to the parts of speech; on the following pages, we go into the parts of speech in more detail.

■ ■ ■

Keep in mind that identifying a word as a particular part of speech depends on how the word is used in a sentence. In the following sentences—

I fish for my dinner.

There aren't many fish in this lake.

I do not like to bait fish hooks.

—the word *fish* serves first as a verb, then as a noun, and then as an adjective.

■ ■ ■

There is one part of speech that we do not mention in the illustration because it does not show up much in academic writing. This kind of word usually stands alone as a sentence:

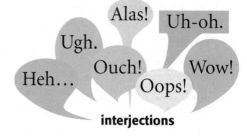

interjections

Words that describe the person, place, thing, or idea being discussed are **NOUNS.**

Words that describe what the person, place, thing, or idea is doing are **VERBS.**

Alice walks.

She walks.

A certain kind of noun that refers back to an earlier mentioned noun is a **PRONOUN.**

Words that give more details about nouns are **ARTICLES** and **ADJECTIVES.**

Words that give more detail about how an action is done (where, when, or in what manner) are **ADVERBS.**

The smiling woman walked happily yesterday.

Words that allow us to talk about more than one noun or action at a time are **CONJUNCTIONS.**

Alice and Shereen walk and talk.

Words that allow us to describe how the actors and actions in a sentence are placed in space or time are **PREPOSITIONS.**

After saying good-bye, Alice walked into the store.

Prepositions are always the first words of phrases; those phrases can tell us more about nouns (in what shape was Alice?), in which case they are **ADJECTIVAL PREPOSITIONAL PHRASES...**

Out of breath, Alice leaned against the wall .

... or those phrases can tell us more about verbs (where did Alice lean?), in which case they are **ADVERBIAL PREPOSITIONAL PHRASES.**

NOUNS

Nouns are the parts of speech we use to name people, animals, places, things, and ideas or concepts.

Most nouns are **common nouns**; when a noun names a particular person or place, then it is called a **proper noun** and is capitalized.

	PEOPLE		ANIMALS

common noun	person	woman	dog
proper noun	Philip Andrews	Doctor Lincoln	Champion Frida

Singular nouns name one person, object, or idea (as in all the examples above).
Plural nouns name more than one. Most nouns become plural when you add **-s** to the end, but some nouns have irregular plural forms, as in the examples to the right.

common noun plural	people	women	dogs

→ See page 500 to learn more about making nouns plural.

PLACES	THINGS	IDEAS OR CONCEPTS	
building	leaf	religion	emotion
City Hall	*Ficus repens*	Buddism	

buildings	leaves	religions	emotions

IF YOU GREW UP SPEAKING A LANGUAGE OTHER THAN ENGLISH...

→ English differentiates between two kinds of nouns—count and noncount nouns—that challenge many writers. See pages 511–513.

MAKING NOUNS PLURAL

In English, a noun's ending usually indicates whether it is singular or plural.

THE PATTERNS

PLURAL ENDINGS

If you have any questions about a noun's plural form, a dictionary will show you the plural form.

SINGULAR	PLURAL	
-s		
a boy	the boys	
the site	many sites	If a noun ends in an -o preceded by a **vowel**, it usually takes an -s to make it plural.
freedom	seven freedoms	
my radio	their radios	
father-in-law	fathers-in-law	With compound hyphenated words, add -s to the main noun, even if that noun is not at the end of the word.
-es		
a box	six boxes	Nouns that end in -s, -sh, -ch, and -x add -es to become plural.
my church	our churches	
one potato	two potatoes	If a noun ends in an -o preceded by a *consonant*, it usually takes an -es to make a plural.
-ies		
the summary	several summaries	Nouns that end in -y lose the -y and add -ies to become plural.
a boundary	the boundaries	
-ves		
my life	our lives	Nouns that end in -f or -fe replace the -f or -fe with -ves to become plural.
a calf	six calves	
other endings		
one medium	the media	Sometimes the plurals of words that derive from other languages take their plural form from the original language.
the analysis	the analyses	
one criterion	three criteria	
his child	his children	
changed form		
one man	many men	Words that have been in use since the beginning of language often change their forms to make plurals.
a mouse	three mice	
no change		
one moose	two moose	Many names for large animals keep the same form in both singular and plural.
one deer	many deer	

MAKING NOUNS POSSESSIVE

A possessive noun comes before another noun, and its possessive form indicates possession of or other close association with the noun it precedes.

POSSESSIVES USING SINGULAR NOUNS

Add -'s to the end of the noun even if the noun ends in -s:

a cell's wall   **Magnolia's cupcakes**   **my life's story**

Luis's award   **the grass's height**   **a potato's texture**

With nouns ending in -s, you can leave off the -'s and simply use an apostrophe if pronouncing the words would be awkward:

Jesus's sayings   **Jesus' sayings**

Aesops's stories   **Aesops' stories**

POSSESSIVES USING PLURAL NOUNS

If the plural noun does not end in -s, add -'s.

the children's choir   **the media's analysis**   **the deer's diseases**

If the plural noun *does* end in -s, add only an apostrophe.

a bakers' dozen   **the Kennedys' compound**   **the grasses' heights**

the boxes' interiors   **many potatoes' textures**   **our lives' stories**

POSSESSIVES USING COMPOUND NOUNS

The last word in a compound noun becomes possessive, following the above guidelines:

a NASCAR driver's car   **the school nurse's office**

the fathers-in-law's meeting   **some swimming pools' depths**

POSSESSIVES USING TWO OR MORE NOUNS

If the object in question is owned jointly by the nouns, make the last noun possessive:

Abbott and Costello's "Who's on first?" routine was developed in the 1930s.

If each of the two nouns has possession, make both possesive:

Abbott's and Costello's lives had very different endings.

> **TIP: LEARN THE DIFFERENCE BETWEEN PLURALS AND POSSESSIVES**
> Both plurals and possessives usually add an -s at the end of a noun. The difference is that possessives always have an apostrophe; plurals do not.

PRONOUNS

Pronouns can take the place of nouns in many different ways, as the examples below show.

Pronouns allow us to take sentences like these—

Tara put Tara's hat on the shelf. The hat had been given to Tara by Tara's sister. Tara sat down and poured a cup of coffee for Tara. Tara is usually a very patient person. Tara burned Tara's tongue on the coffee because Tara was too tired to wait for the coffee to cool.

—and make them much simpler and less awkward:

Tara put her hat, which her sister had given her, on the shelf. She sat down and poured herself a cup of coffee. Tara, who is usually a very patient person, burned her tongue on the coffee because she was too tired to wait for it to cool.

PERSONAL PRONOUNS   I, me, he, him, she, her, it   we, our, they, their

Personal pronouns refer to specific people or things. In writing, you must first name the person or thing; then you can refer to the person or thing later with a pronoun:

Jasper finished work and then he walked to the store. (*he* and *him* are masculine.)

Jenna came prepared: She brought her briefcase. (*she* and *her* are feminine.)

The dog wasn't gray; it was brown and black.

Sara and Lia played on the beach and then they ate lunch.

Jamshed and I worked for a while, and then we ate lunch.

The person or thing to which the pronoun refers is called the pronoun's **antecedent**. (Notice that *I* does not have an antecedent in writing; a reader will always understand the person to whom it refers.)

POSSESSIVE PRONOUNS my, mine, his, her, its   our, their

Possessive pronouns indicate close relationship or ownership. As with personal pronouns, you need to make clear to readers the person or thing for which the pronoun is standing in. (Again, as with **I**, the antecedent of **my** is understood.) Possessive pronouns are like adjectives, telling us about the noun they precede: They tell us to whom the noun belongs (and so the pronouns are **possessive**).

Eva lost her backpack. • The dog leaned into my hand—its nose was cold!

Jonathan and Mack got on the same train even though their destinations varied.

The buildings should withstand the winters well because of their thick walls.

My opinion is unsettled.

INDEFINITE PRONOUNS one, each, every, another, anybody, none, no one, neither, either, both, few, some, many, most, all

Indefinite pronouns exist to help us communicate about occasions when we do not want to or cannot be specific about people or things. Indefinite pronouns function as adjectives, telling readers something about the noun they precede: They give readers a rough (that is, indefinite) idea about the noun, not specifiying, for example, exactly which person or how many people did something.

One person climbed the stairs. • Each woman brought a book.

Few people complained. • Some dogs like to swim. • Most homes here are old.

INTERROGATIVE PRONOUNS who, which, what

We use interrogative pronouns to ask questions about people, places, things, or ideas. When we build such questions, there is a noun implied by the question

Who climbed the stairs? (That is, someone climbed the stairs. Who was that someone?)

Which man spoke to you? • Which people were there?

Who ate the pies? • What animals are most popular as pets in the United States?

RELATIVE PRONOUNS   who, whoever, whom, which, that, what, whatever

Relative pronouns allow us to combine sentences that are about the same person, place, thing, or idea. By using them, we can help readers see the connections that exist between two sentences:

The man was tired. The man climbed all the stairs.

The man who climbed all the stairs was tired.

(The single sentence implies more strongly than the two separate sentences that the man was probably tired because he climbed the stairs. Note that *who* replaces *The man*.)

The dogs like the beach. The beach has many sticks.

The dogs like the beach that has many sticks.

(The single sentence implies more strongly than the two separate sentences that the dogs like the beach because of the sticks. Note that *that* replaces *The beach*.)

The buildings burned. The buildings were old.

The buildings that burned were old.

(The single sentence implies more strongly than the two separate sentences that the buildings burned because they were old. Note that *that* replaces *The buildings*.)

■ ■ ■

Relative pronouns function as the first words of clauses (page 483) that give additional information about a noun. Clauses made with relative pronouns are called dependent clauses (pages 484–487) because they are not sentences by themselves; to make a sentence with such a dependent clause, join it to an independent clause (page 483):

DEPENDENT CLAUSE: who climbed all the stairs

INDEPENDENT CLAUSE: The man was tired.

SENTENCE: The man who climbed all the stairs was tired.

→ For more on using relative pronouns, see pages 484–485, 493, and 507.

DEMONSTRATIVE PRONOUNS   this, that   these, those

These pronouns help us be specific about a person or object we want to discuss.

This woman is my friend. • **That** dog belongs to Mavis.

These people went to the museum. • **Those** buildings are on Washington Street.

In the examples above, the demonstrative pronouns function like adjectives, telling readers or listeners exactly what person or thing is meant. In the examples below, the pronouns function like nouns:

This is the most important issue of our time: Are we running out of oil?

That is my best pen. • **Those** who care for others will themselves be cared for.

REFLEXIVE PRONOUNS   myself, oneself, himself,   ourselves, themselves
                          herself, itself

Reflexive pronouns refer back to the person or thing performing an action, to emphasize who did the action.

Mark cut **himself**. • Luisa made **herself** dinner. • The dog licked **itself**.

The men took **themselves** out of the race.

The buildings were **themselves** victims of time.

RECIPROCAL PRONOUNS   each other, one another

Use reciprocal pronouns when you want to show people or objects acting on each other.

The survivors helped **one another**. • The dogs chased **each other**.

IF YOU GREW UP SPEAKING A LANGUAGE OTHER THAN ENGLISH...

→ See page 506 to make sure you have chosen the correct pronoun for the noun to which you are referring.

→ See page 507 for help with using **who** and **whom**.

CHOOSING THE EXPECTED PERSONAL PRONOUN

Personal pronouns can function as subjects, objects, or possessives in sentences. (Those three uses—subjective, objective, possessive—are referred to as **the cases** of pronouns.) Choose a personal pronoun based on its function in a sentence.

SUBJECTIVE CASE PERSONAL PRONOUNS: I, he, she, it, we, they

When you replace a subject with a pronoun, use a subjective case pronoun.

Lisa called John. → **She** called John.

Simone and Jack visited Teresa. → **She** and Jack visited Teresa.
Simone and Jack visited Teresa. → Simone and **he** visited Teresa.
Simone and Jack visited Teresa. → **They** visited Teresa.

Subject complements follow linking verbs, and they complete the subject. Subject complements take subjective case pronouns:

Going on vacation are Pedro and Marji. → Going on vacation are Pedro and **she**.

Going on vacation are Pedro and Marji. → Going on vacation are **we**.

OBJECTIVE CASE PERSONAL PRONOUNS: me, him, her, it, us, their

When you replace a direct object, indirect object, or the object of a preposition with a pronoun, use an objective case pronoun.

Simone and Jack visited Teresa. → Simone and Jack visited **her**.

Vada put the car in the garage. → Vada put **it** in the garage.

Amrit gave the spices to Jon. → Amrit gave the spices to **him**.

POSSESSIVE CASE PERSONAL PRONOUNS: my, mine, his, her, its, our, their

When you replace a possessive noun with a pronoun, use a possesive case pronoun.

Lisa's dog is named Yaz. → **Her** dog is named Yaz.

The book's cover is torn. → **Its** cover is torn.

The car that I own is old. → **My** car is old.

PRONOUN REFERENCE

Check your writing for sentences in which a pronoun could have two antecedents. Revise the sentences to remove the ambiguity.

Marisa told Gretel that she had passed the class after all.

Marisa told Gretel, "I passed the class after all."

After Mabel put the book in her bag, she couldn't find it.

After Mabel put it in her bag, she couldn't find the book.

	NUMBER	singular	plural
PERSON	first person	I, me	we, us
	second person	you	you
	third person	it, one, she (f), he (m), her (f), him (m)	they, them

PRONOUN AGREEMENT

Pronouns agree with their antecedents. (An antecedent is the person or thing to which the pronoun refers.)

Pronouns must agree in person, number, and (in singular number) gender.

Karen quickly wrote **her** paper.
third person, singular, feminine
third person, singular, feminine

Max and Aiko brought **their** new kitten.
third person, plural
third person, plural

Stefan picked up **his** mail.
third person, singular, masculine
third person, singular, masculine

Statistics has **its** pleasures.
third person, singular, neuter
third person, singular, neuter

WHO OR WHOM?

Who is the subjective case of the relative pronoun; **whom** is the objective case. Which relative pronoun—**who** or **whom**—should go in the blanks in the subordinate clauses below?

My sister,   **I visited in November, just graduated.**

Paul Holc,   **had a heart transplant when he was just three hours old, is now twenty.**

1 Write the subordinate clause as though it were an independent clause. You might need to rephrase the clause:

I visited her in November.
————— *her* is the object of *visited*, so replace it with *whom*.

He had a heart transplant when he was just three hours old.
—— *He* is the subject of this sentence, so replace it with *who*.

2 If the noun you are replacing is the object of the sentence; replace it with **whom** to build a dependent clause:

My sister, whom I visited in November, just graduated.

If the noun is the subject, replace it with **who**:

Paul Holc, who had a heart transplant when he was just three hours old, is now twenty.

ADJECTIVES

Adjectives help us make writing precise by allowing us to describe the particular qualities of people, places, objects, and ideas.

WHICH ONE? WHAT KIND?

Adjectives allow us to specify exactly which people, places, objects, or ideas we are discussing.

He wore his green shoes. • Could you bring me the red shoes, please?

HOW MANY?

Adjectives help us say how many people, places, objects, or ideas are at stake.

Four potatoes make enough mashed potatoes for three people.

HOW DO THEY COMPARE?

Adjectives help us specify which people, places, objects, or ideas we mean by allowing us to make comparisons.

He asked for the smallest book. I would like the largest book. She asked for a book that was smaller than mine.

PLACEMENT OF ADJECTIVES

1 Adjectives usually come before the nouns they modify:

Use only the sharpest tools to prune your bushes.

A brilliant green aurora shimmers in the dark night.

There is no biological reason for this condition.

The jubilant procession advanced through the narrow streets.

2 Adjectives come after the verbs *appear*, *be*, *feel*, *look*, *seem*, *smell*, *sound*, and *taste*:

She was not at her sharpest.

The frog looked a brilliant green in the sun.

The reason is purely biological.

The team sounded jubilant after their win.

The bay appeared narrow after we had been out on the lake.

IF YOU GREW UP SPEAKING A LANGUAGE OTHER THAN ENGLISH…

→ Pages 552–553 give you more help with placing adjectives correctly and ordering multiple adjectives.

ARTICLES

Articles are a special kind of adjective.

There are three articles: *a*, *an*, and *the*.

indefinite articles: *a, an*

a and *an* have the same function: They are used when a noun is not referring to a known or specific person, animal, place, thing, or idea.

■ ■ ■

Use indefinite articles before nouns when you are making general statements:

A computer is useful for homework. • A birthday happens only once a year.

Also use indefinite articles before nouns when you are not writing about a particular person or thing of its kind:

An hour passes quickly when you are focused on your work. (It could be any hour of the day.)

■ ■ ■

Use *a* before nouns (or adjectives placed before nouns) that begin with a consonant sound; use *an* before nouns (or adjectives placed before nouns) that begin with a vowel sound.

A knife is useful on a camping trip. • An octopus is an unusual pet.

Note that *h* and *u* can sometimes sound like vowels and sometimes like consonants at the beginning of words. Use the sound of the word following the article to determine whether to use *a* or *an*:

An honest person returned my wallet. • A history book was on the table.

the definite article: *the*

the is used when your reader or listener will know or be able to figure out exactly which person, animal, place, thing, or idea you are describing.

■ ■ ■

To decide whether to use the definite or indefinite article, consider the context in which you are writing or speaking. If you know for sure that your readers or listeners will know the exact person or thing to which you refer, use *the*:

The rosebush needs water. (If you are standing in your yard speaking with neighbors, and there is only one rosebush, everyone will know exactly which rosebush you mean.)

ARTICLES AND NOUNS
COUNT AND NONCOUNT NOUNS
Knowing this distinction between kinds of nouns can help you decide which article (if any) to use with a noun.

Count nouns refer to objects that exist distinctly as countable units: dogs, chairs, words, toes, plates, books, glances. Count nouns refer to what you can perceive with your senses.

| **COUNT NOUN singular** | a woman | the dog | his emotion |

| **COUNT NOUN plural** | women | dogs | emotions |

Noncount nouns cannot be counted. Noncount nouns name what can't be cut into parts: They can name abstractions (justice, anger, education, weather) and can name collections of objects (furniture, silverware, rice, coffee).

| **NONCOUNT NOUN** | justice | weather | anger |

COUNT AND NONCOUNT NOUNS AND ARTICLES

Singular count nouns *always* need an article or another adjective (**this**, **that**, **my**, **each**) in front of them. The five sentences below use singular count nouns; notice how every single one has an article or other adjective before it.

ARTICLE OR OTHER ADJECTIVE	SINGULAR COUNT NOUN

A snowstorm hit our town this week.

That dog ate a toy.

The teacher gave an apple to each child.

His emotion showed on his face.

Does a monkey see itself in a mirror?

Plural count nouns do not need articles—but can have other adjectives.

PLURAL COUNT NOUN

or

ADJECTIVE	PLURAL COUNT NOUN

Dogs don't eat toys often, do they?

How did we come to associate teachers with apples?

Emotions show on bodies and faces.

Our winters have big snowstorms.

Do nonhuman animals such as monkeys, dolphins, crows, or ants experience subjective feelings?

Noncount nouns are the only kind of noun that can stand alone without an article. Because they cannot be counted, they cannot be used with quantifiers (*one*, *two*, *many*) or made plural. Use **much** (not *many*), **little** (not *few*), **amount of** (not *number of*) in front of these nouns.

NONCOUNT NOUN

Privacy is under attack online.

You can study emotion in psychology.

Do you prefer rice, bread, or pasta?

The amount of homework is killing me!

PROOFREADING FOR ARTICLES

Here are two common mistakes in writing and advice for proofreading for them.

MISSING "a" OR "an"

Underline all singular nouns that appear in your writing without an article or adjective. Decide whether the noun is countable or uncountable. (Many nouns can be either, depending on their contexts.)

☐ If what you've underlined is a non-count noun, it does not need *a*, *an*, or an adjective in front of it.

☐ If what you've underlined is a count noun, it must be marked in some way:

If it refers to an indefinite or unspecified person, place, or thing, add *a* or *an*:

When I was young, I used an abacus instead of a calculator in math class.

If a noun is used as a representative of a class of nouns rather than of a particular individual member of that class, add *a* or *an*:

An abacus is a Chinese counting device.

If the noun refers to *all* members of the group or is general, make the noun plural and use no articles.

For some math problems, abacuses work as well as calculators.

MISSING "the"

As we mentioned on page 510, we use *the* when we know readers will understand exactly what object is meant by a noun we use. To be sure you have used *the* when you should, underline all singular nouns that appear without an article or adjective. If the noun fits one of the three categories described below, it is "specific," so put *the* before it.

1 *Shared knowledge.* For example, because two people who live together can be expected to know that they have children, one could send this e-mail to the other:

Can you pick up the kids from school on your way home?

(*Can you pick up kids* would mean *Pick up some kids, any kids…!*)

2 *Second mention.* When a singular count noun is used more than once, readers will know what is meant by the second reference—and so *the* goes before its later uses:

Depo-Provera, a contraceptive, first mention **may cause serious side effects. Some drug companies, however, have promoted the contraceptive** second mention **outside the U.S. with no warnings about its side effects.**

3 If a noun is followed by a relative clause or a prepositional phrase that modifies it, and *if there is a count noun in the clause or phrase*, put *the* before the count noun:

He described the ways in which the sound of music calms him. ◄

prepositional phrase

→ See pages 479 and 530–531 to learn more about prepositional phrases.

VERBS

Verbs describe what the nouns of a sentence do in time. Verbs are about actions (whether of body or of mind) or about states of being in the present, past, or future.

AT THE PRESENT TIME: **The man runs.** • **The man is running.**

IN THE PAST: **The man ran.** • **The man was running.**

IN THE FUTURE: **The man will run.**

AT THE PRESENT TIME: **The woman thinks.** • **The woman is thinking.**

IN THE PAST: **The woman thought.** • **The woman was thinking.**

IN THE FUTURE: **The woman will think.**

AT THE PRESENT TIME: **The dog plays.** • **The dog is playing.**

IN THE PAST: **The dog played.** • **The dog was playing.**

IN THE FUTURE: **The dog will play.**

IN ENGLISH, VERBS CHANGE THEIR FORMS TO INDICATE:

TIME (OR TENSE).

Some tenses are shown on the preceding page.

→ For more on the tenses of English verbs, see pages 516–521.

WHO IS DOING THE ACTION (OR BEING ACTED ON).

This is called the person of the verb.

first person: I run.   I was thinking.   We will play.

second person: You run. You were thinking. You will play.

third person: She runs.   He was thinking.   It will play.

→ The person of the verb has to agree with the verb form; see pages 524–526.

HOW MANY PEOPLE ARE DOING THE ACTION.

This is called the number of the verb.

singular: I am thinking.   You, Kris, forgot.   She has run.

plural: We are thinking.   You three forgot.   They have run.

→ The number of the verb has to agree with the verb form; see pages 524–526.

VOICE.

There are two voices:

active: The person, animal, place, object, or idea named by the noun is performing the action described by the verb:

You run. • She will play.

passive: The person, animal, place, object, or idea named by the noun has the action described by the verb performed on it:

The record was played. • The store was run by two sisters.

→ For more on the voice of English verbs, see pages 298–299 and 538.

MOOD.

There are three moods:

indicative: The indicative mood states facts, opinions, and questions.

The song plays for twenty minutes.

imperative: The imperative mood is for commands and requests.

Run! • Please think. • Play!

subjunctive: The subjunctive mood is for wishes and hypothetical situations.

I wish we could play. • Were he to think, he might pass the class.

→ For more on the subjunctive mood of English verbs, see page 527.

THE TENSES OF ENGLISH VERBS

The examples below show the tense forms for the first person singular forms of the regular verb **talk** and the irregular verbs **begin** and **be**.

THE PATTERNS

SIMPLE TENSES

In the present, the simple tense describes actions taking place at the time a sentence is written or spoken, or for actions that occur regularly. The simple past describes actions that were completed in the past. The simple future describes actions that have not yet begun.

PRESENT	I talk.	I begin.	I am.
PAST	I talked.	I began.	I was.
FUTURE	I will talk.	I will begin.	I will be.

PROGRESSIVE TENSES

The progressive tenses describe actions that continue—or will continue—over time.

PRESENT	I am talking.	I am beginning.	I am being.
PAST	I was talking.	I was beginning.	I was being.
FUTURE	I will be talking.	I will be beginning.	I will be being.

PERFECT TENSES

The perfect tenses describe actions that have been (or will have been) completed.

PRESENT	I have talked.	I have begun.	I have been.
PAST	I had talked.	I had begun.	I had been.
FUTURE	I will have talked.	I will have begun.	I will have been.

PERFECT PROGRESSIVE TENSES

The present perfect progressive tense describes an action that began in the past, continues in the present, and may continue into the future. The past perfect progressive tense describes a stretched-out action that was completed before some other past action; this tense usually appears in sentences that describe the other past action (→ see pages 520–521). The future perfect progressive tense describes a stretched-out action that will occur before some specified future time.

PRESENT	I have been talking.	I have been beginning.	I have been being.
PAST	I had been talking.	I had been beginning.	I had been being.
FUTURE	I will have been talking.	I will have been beginning.	I will have been being.

→ To learn more about these tenses and how they are used in academic English writing, see pages 520–521.

FORMING THE TENSES OF ENGLISH VERBS, PART 1

Except for the verb **be**, all English verbs have five forms.

	BASE FORM	–S FORM	PRESENT PARTICIPLE	PAST FORM	PAST PARTICIPLE
REGULAR VERB	walk	walks	walking	walked	walked
IRREGULAR VERB	sing	sings	singing	sang	sung
IRREGULAR VERB	ride	rides	riding	rode	ridden

THE BASE FORM

The base form is how you find a verb in a dictionary, and it is the form from which all the verb's tenses are built. If you place **to** in front of the base form, you make what is called **the infinitive**.

THE -s FORM

This form is the third person singular present tense of any verb.

THE PRESENT PARTICIPLE

The present participle, made by adding **-ing** to the base form, is used with a helping verb to construct the progressive tenses of any verb. (Note that if a verb's base form ends in **-e**, the **-e** is dropped before the **-ing** is added.)

The present participle can also be used as an adjective: **Let sleeping dogs lie**.

THE PAST FORM

The past form is used for the simple past tense. Because English has been formed from so many other languages, many frequently used verbs have irregular past forms. A dictionary will show you the past form of any verb.

THE PAST PARTICIPLE

With a helping verb, the past particple is used to construct the perfect tenses of any verb. For regular verbs, the past participle is the same as the past form; for irregular verbs, you will need to check a dictionary to learn the past participle.

MAIN VERBS AND HELPING VERBS

In the patterns to the left, note that—except for the simple present and simple past—verb tenses are constructed from a main verb and a helping verb, as shown on page 518.

The main verb is one of the five forms of a verb described above; a helping verb is one of the forms of the irregular verbs **be**, **have**, and **do**.

→ In addition to the helping verbs **be, have**, and **do**, there is another kind of helping verb. To learn about these modal auxiliary verbs, see page 519.

FORMING THE TENSES OF ENGLISH VERBS, PART 2

The pattern chart to the right shows all the verb forms for the tenses shown for one regular verb. (Look in the dictionary for the past form and participle forms of irregular verbs.)

VERB FORMS WITH SUBJECTS

	singular	plural

SIMPLE PRESENT

Only the third person singular changes to the –s form.

first	I ask.	We ask.
second	You ask.	You ask.
third	She/He/It asks.	They ask.

SIMPLE PAST

All persons and numbers use the past form of the verb.

I/We/You/You/He/She/It/They asked.

SIMPLE FUTURE

All persons and numbers use *will* + the simple form of the verb.

I/We/You/You/He/She/It/They will ask.

PRESENT PROGRESSIVE

Use the appropriate simple present form of *be* + the present participle.

first	I am asking.	We are asking.
second	You are asking.	You are asking.
third	She/He/It is asking.	They are asking.

PAST PROGRESSIVE

Use the appropriate simple past form of *be* + the present participle.

first	I was asking.	We were asking.
second	You were asking.	You were asking.
third	She/He/It was asking.	They were asking.

FUTURE PROGRESSIVE

All persons and numbers use *will be* + the present participle.

I/We/You/You/He/She/It/They will be asking.

PRESENT PERFECT

Use the appropriate simple present form of *have* + the past participle.

first	I have asked.	We have asked.
second	You have asked.	You have asked.
third	She/He/It has asked.	They have asked.

PAST PERFECT

All persons and numbers use *had* + the past participle.

I/We/You/You/He/She/It/They had asked.

FUTURE PERFECT

All persons and numbers use *will have* + the past participle.

I/We/You/You/He/She/It/They will have asked.

PRESENT PERFECT PROGRESSIVE

All persons and numbers use *have been* + the present participle.

I/We/You/You/He/She/It/They have been asking.

PAST PERFECT PROGRESSIVE

All persons and numbers use *had been* + the present participle.

I/We/You/You/He/She/It/They had been asking.

FUTURE PERFECT PROGRESSIVE

All persons and numbers use *will have been* + the present participle.

I/We/You/You/He/She/It/They will have been asking.

THE FORMS OF HELPING VERBS

BASE FORM	PRESENT SINGULAR	PLURAL	PARTICIPLE	PAST SINGULAR	PLURAL	PARTICIPLE
be	I am You are He/She/It is	We are You are They are	being	I was You were He/She/It was	We were You were They were	been
have	I have You have He/She/It has	We have You have They have	having	I had You had He/She/It had	We had You had They had	had
do	I do You do He/She/It does	We do You do They do	doing	I did You did He/She/It did	We did You did They did	done

MODAL HELPING VERBS

Helping verbs also include the verbs called modals, whose form never changes: *can*, *could*, *may*, *might*, *must*, *ought to*, *shall*, *should*, *will*, *would*. Modals help us express abilities, possibilities, necessity, intentions, requests, or obligation.

ABILITY, POSSIBILITY, REQUEST: You could have gone running with us last night.
• Can you play with our band this weekend?

POSSIBILITY, REQUEST: May I think a little longer about it? • Conrad might run in the race.

OBLIGATION: You must think about a vacation. • The senator really ought to run harder in this election.

INTENTIONS: I shall play over the weekend. • You should run over to school. • Jamshed will practice his violin every day.

USING THE TENSES OF ENGLISH VERBS IN ACADEMIC WRITING

Because verb tenses convey so much information, writers use them to show relationships among the events about which they write. In turn, readers understand verb tenses as signals that help them understand the relationships and order of events.

The descriptions below focus on verb tenses in academic writing. Look at different types of writing—lab reports, summaries and responses to literature, research proposals—to learn what verb tenses tend to be used in each type of writing.

THE SIMPLE PRESENT
is used to...

- describe the present situation
  Conservationists at the Masai Mara work hard to protect the wildebeest from poachers.

- generalize
  Studies show that chronic stress contributes to heart attacks and other diseases.

- describe the contents of a book, movie, or other text
  In his thesis, "Intimate Relationships with Artificial Partners," Levy conjectures that robots will become so human-like that people will fall in love with them.

THE PRESENT
PROGRESSIVE
is used to...

- describe actions in progress at the moment of speaking
  Women are dying from complicated pregnancies and childbirth at almost the same rate they were in 1990.

- compare two present actions. One action is described in simple present, the other in present progressive.
  Children with strict parents follow rules when under supervision, but often engage in reckless actions when their parents are not watching.

THE PRESENT PERFECT
is used to...

- describe actions begun in the past but not completed
  The once vanished gray wolf has made a comeback in the Northern Rockies.

- describe actions begun at an unspecified past time
  Over half of adolescents have tried alcohol and drugs at least once.

- introduce a topic
  Once a disease of the Western world, breast cancer has become a global concern.

THE SIMPLE PAST is used to...	• describe completed events or states **Charles M. Schulz drew "Peanuts" for nearly half a century.**
	• report past research or events, summarize lab or research results, and to give narrative examples **Steven C. Amstrup of the United States Geological Survey led a recent exhaustive study of polar bears.**
THE PAST PERFECT is used to...	• compare two past events. The past perfect signals the event that happened first. **The protesters were demanding the freedom and democracy for which their parents had fought.**
THE SIMPLE FUTURE is used to describe...	• intentions and promises **In this paper I will explore the relations between media portrayals of men and men's body images.**
	• predictions **American employers will hire 270,000 fewer IT workers this year than they did in 2003.**

TIP: EDITING WRITING FOR VERB TENSES

1 Underline or highlight each sentence's main verb. The main verb has a subject.

2 Each sentence should contain a complete verb phrase: **Main verb** or **Helping verb + Main verb**.

3 For each sentence, ask if your verb tenses signal your desired meaning.

SHIFTING VERB TENSES

Every time you write a new verb, you must decide if the verb will be the same tense as any verbs that preceded it.

Because you want to create cohesion in your writing, using the same verb tense consistently is usually a safe choice.

But because writing also often involves describing relations among events that might have occurred at different times, you will sometimes need to change tenses.

A new study offers some relief to parents who worry that their children will never eat anything but chocolate milk, Gummi vitamins, and the occasional grape. Researchers examined the eating habits of 5,390 pairs of twins between eight and eleven years old and found children's aversions to trying new foods are mostly inherited.

Present tense
The present tense verbs describe how a study can ease parental worries now.

Past tense
The past tense verbs describe the actions that had to have taken place before the study could be useful now, in the present.

Future tense
The future tense describes parents' fears about their children's future actions.

SIGNALING TENSE SHIFTS BY WORD CHOICE

In the following paragraph tenses shift from present to past, but the writer signals each shift. The highlighted nouns—which name events and objects that belong to different time periods—signal to readers that the time period being discussed is changing, and so the verb tense must also change.

Authors of American history textbooks seem to prefer writing about distant historical events rather than more recent events like the Persian Gulf War or the Vietnam War. By definition, the recent past is controversial because readers bring to it their own knowledge and understanding. But this practice of slighting recent history in favor of discussing distant historical events is perverse. Comparing textbook coverage of the Vietnam War and the War of 1812 illuminates this perversion.

The War of 1812 took place almost two centuries ago and killed maybe two thousand Americans. Nevertheless, high school history books devote the same number of pages—nine—to the War of 1812 and the Vietnam War, even though almost sixty thousand Americans died in Vietnam.

USING PRESENT PERFECT AND PAST PERFECT TO INDICATE TIME DIFFERENCES

Writers can show relationships between actions or states by shifting from simple or progressive present tense to present perfect; they can also shift from simple or progressive past tense to past perfect. The perfect tenses signal that the action or state they describe occurred before the action or state in the other tense.

Present perfect maintains a present focus; past perfect maintains a past focus.

Switching Tenses When the Time Focus Is the Present

The homeless can be roughly divided into two groups: those who have had homelessness forced upon them and want nothing more than to escape it, and those who have chosen it for themselves and now accept it, or in some cases, embrace it.

Present tense   **Present perfect tense**

This sentence focuses on a distinction that can be made in the present; for that distinction to be possible, however, the people being described had to have become homeless before the distinction could be made.

Switching Tenses When the Time Focus Is the Past

In 1965, a new drug was introduced that is responsible for much of the homeless problem we see today. The drug is Thorazine. Before it was introduced, people diagnosed with mental illness, particularly schizophrenia, had been considered incurable and had been confined to mental institutions.

Past progressive tense

Past perfect tense

This sentence focuses on a distinction that occured in the past. The writer uses the past progressive tense to describe how a drug was introduced in the past; the writer then uses the past perfect tense to show conditions that happened even further in the past than the drug.

TIP: EDITING FOR SHIFTS IN VERB TENSES

1 Using different color pens, highlight each verb tense in a different color. Pay particular attention to shifts in tense from present to past or past to present tense.

2 When you have switched verb tenses, ask whether readers will understand why the tense shifts.

3 If needed, do one of the following:
- Add words or time expressions that signal a tense shift.
- Change the verb to present or past perfect to indicate that an action or state occurred prior to another.
- Change the tense of the verb to maintain a consistent time focus.

SUBJECT-VERB AGREEMENT

THE PATTERN

To build sentences that fit with academic expectations, the form of the verb must agree with the subject in both person and number, as shown in the pattern on page 518.

PERSON

- First person means *I* or *we*.
- Second person means *you* (singular) or *you* (plural).
- Third person means *he*, *she*, *it*, or *they*. All singular or plural nouns are also third person: *woman*, *dog*, *plants*, *The President of the United States*, *furniture*, or *justice*.

NUMBER

A verb form can be singular or plural in number.

■ ■ ■

Some third person subjects cause writers trouble in making agreement:

THIRD PERSON SINGULAR SUBJECT	THIRD PERSON SINGULAR VERB
Everybody	**spoke** in our class.
Macaroni and cheese	**is** my favorite dinner.
The woman with green glasses	**was** in my class.

THIRD PERSON PLURAL SUBJECT	THIRD PERSON PLURAL VERB
All students	**will speak** in this class.
José and I	**designed** a small robot.
The men on the field	**are** there every Thursday.

■ ■ ■

To check subject-verb agreement:

1 Identify a sentence's subject.

2 Determine whether the subject of a sentence is singular or plural.

3 Use the information on pages 518–519 to create the appropriate singular or plural verb.

1 IDENTIFYING A SENTENCE'S SUBJECT

The information on page 475 can help you identify the subject of a sentence.
Sentences that contain prepositional phrases, however, can confuse writers trying to identify the subject because they add nouns to the sentence in addition to the subject. The following steps will help you identify the subject.

1 Underline any prepositional phrases (→ see pages 530–531) or other descriptive phrases that come before the verb.

The boy <u>with the gloves</u> dances particularly well.
The record <u>that he set for driving across country</u> is thirty-one hours.

2 Rewrite the sentence **without** the phrases you underlined. This should put the subject next to the verb.

The boy dances particularly well.
The record is thirty-one hours.

2 DETERMINING WHETHER THE SUBJECT IS SINGULAR OR PLURAL

Use the information about the plurals of nouns on pages 511–512 to help you determine the number of the subject. Keep an eye out, however, for the following kinds of subjects, whose number might not be immediately obvious.

Compound subjects joined by *and*
Compound subjects joined by **and** are usually plural:
Leela and Joe worked on their homework together.

There are exceptions:

- If the compound subject names what we consider to be one object or activity— as with **peanut butter and jelly** or **drinking and driving**—it is singular. (Company names using **and** are also singular, as with a law firm named **Black and Bland**.)

- If the compound subject refers to the same person or thing, then it is singular:

  My best friend and advisor is my father.

- If the compound subject is preceded by **each** or **every**, then it is singular:

  Each dog, cat, and pet ferret is to be registered.
  Every girl and boy deserves health insurance.

WATCH OUT FOR THIS!

Phrases like **along with**, **in addition to**, and **together with** can sound as though they build compound nouns—but they do not.

Hasan, together with Kim, is driving to Appleton. The subject of this sentence is *Hasan; together with Kim* is an adjectival phrase.

continued on the next page

Compound subjects joined by *or, nor, either... or,* or *neither... nor*

The number of the subject is determined by the noun closest to the verb:

A dog or crows get into our garbage every week. Because *crows* is closest to the verb and is plural, the subject of this sentence is plural.

Crows or a dog gets into our garbage every week. Because *a dog* is closest to the verb and is singular, the subject of this sentence is singular.

Subjects that use indefinite pronouns

The indefinite pronouns (➤ see page 503) *anybody, anyone, anything, each, everybody, everyone, everything, nobody, no one, someone, somebody,* and *something* are singular:

Everyone in my class is late with homework! • Everything has gone wrong.

The indefinite pronouns *both* and *many* are plural:
Both motorcycles were broken. • Many have visited our town.

The indefinite pronouns *all, any, none,* and *some* can be singular or plural, depending on the noun or pronoun to which they refer:

SINGULAR **All my money goes to rent.**   **Some of his dinner was overcooked.**

PLURAL **All my nieces go fishing.**   **Some of his books were lost.**

Collective nouns

Nouns that refer to collections of people—*audience, class, committee, crowd, family, group, public, team*—are usually singular because the collection is usually described as acting as one.

The audience was delighted by the performance.

When such a nouns refers to its members acting individually, however, it is plural:

The audience were looking at each other.

Clauses and phrases

When a sentence's subject is a clause or a phrase, the subject is singular:

What frustrates me is my math homework.

Going to the dentist makes me nervous.

If the verb is a form of **be** and the subject complement (➤ see page 477) is plural, then the verb is plural even if the subject is singular:

What frustrates me are inconsiderate drivers.

THE SUBJUNCTIVE MOOD OF ENGLISH VERBS

In the subjunctive mood, verbs express what isn't factual or what the speaker would like to come into being. The subjunctive is therefore used to express doubts, wishes, suggestions, recommendations, requests, demands, or statements that are contrary to fact.

In the present subjunctive mood, verbs stay in their base form; they do not change to indicate the subject's number or person.

In 1974 laws were passed requiring that automobiles be made smaller and more fuel efficient.

In the past subjunctive mood, verbs stay in simple past form. If you use **be**, use **were** for all persons and numbers of the subject.

If only she drove a stick shift, she could borrow my car.

He wishes he were able to help.

RECOMMENDATIONS, SUGGESTIONS, REQUESTS, AND DEMANDS, WITH *that*

Recommendations, suggestions, requests, and demands express a speaker's or writer's desire for a current situation to change, which is why they are put into the subjunctive mode. Words that express such desires—*ask*, *demand*, *insist*, *recommend*, *request*, and *suggest*—are followed by *that*; put the verb in the *that* clause into the subjunctive.

Doctors recommend that a person get 50-55% of total daily energy intake from carbohydrates.

Professor Ball suggested that the experiment be expanded to a new population.

CONTRARY-TO-FACT STATEMENTS, WITH *if*

If-clauses describing conditions that do not exist are put into the subjunctive.

If I were on the jury, I could not vote for the death penalty.

ADVERBS

Adverbs are most often used to show when, how, or where the action of a verb takes place. Adverbs can also modify adjectives or other adverbs.

ADVERBS OF TIME

Adverbs of time describe when something happened; they can also describe for how long and how often something happens.

She expects breakfast now.

He slept all winter.

She plays sometimes.

ADVERBS OF MANNER

Adverbs of manner describe how something happened. Adverbs of manner are usually formed by adding **–ly** to the end of an adjective.

He shook wildly.

He rolls the ball happily.

She rested lazily on the floor.

She waited patiently.

ADVERBS OF PLACE

Adverbs of time describe where or the direction in which something happened.

He walked forward.

She worked uphill.

She sat down on the grass.

He jumped high.

PLACEMENT OF ADVERBS

Adverbs generally follow the verb or the object.

She drives carefully. • She drives the car carefully.

The older children stayed behind.

The number of scholarships has dropped slightly.

ADVERBS OF MANNER AND EMPHASIS

To add emphasis, you can place adverbs of manner before the verb.

The lion carefully approached the elephants.

The man repeatedly claimed his innocent.

For even more emphasis, you can start a sentence with an adverb of manner.

Proudly he accepted his diploma.

Belatedly the soldiers received their new protective bodywear.

ADVERBS OF TIME

Adverbs of time that express how often something happens are usually placed before the verb. (If there is a helping verb with the main verb, the adverb goes between the two.)

Small refinements in energy production are rarely considered newsworthy.

An issue decided in the past can always be discussed again.

Physicians often change their decisions about management of cancer patients based on results of PET scans.

When an adverb tells the exact number of times something happens, it usually goes at a sentence's end.

The city's alternative newspaper is published weekly.

A new drug for preventing hip fractures in older people is taken once a year.

PREPOSITIONS

Prepositions help us express a relationship in time or space between (usually) two nouns in a sentence.

Prepositions start prepositional phrases:

on the Web   in Asia and Europe

at almost the speed of light   to the first year of parenthood

Prepositional phrases serve as adjectives or adverbs within sentences:

Would you put your health records on the Web? In this sentence, *on the Web* is an adverbial prepositional phrase.

My cellphone works in Asia and Europe. In this sentence, *in Asia and Europe* is an adverbial prepositional phrase.

Einstein's special theory of relativity describes the motion of particles at almost the speed of light. In this sentence, *at almost the speed of light* is an adjectival prepositional phrase.

Anna and Otto wrote a guide to the first year of parenthood. In this sentence, *to the first year* is an adjectival prepositional phrase—and so is *of parenthood*.

Prepositions functioning like adverbs can go anywhere in a sentence, depending on the emphasis you want to put. Prepositions that function like adjectives generally go right after the noun they modify.

TIP: PREPOSITIONS ARE IDIOMATIC

Certain verbs are followed by certain prepositions: *He was listening to music. We rely on each other.* Checking a verb in the dictionary will tell you which prepositions follow it.

Similarly, certain nouns and adjectives are followed by certain prepositions: *He has an interest in anthropology. She puts emphasis on the importance of rules.* Again, checking nouns and adjectives in the dictionary will tell you which prepositions follow them.

PREPOSITIONS DESCRIBING RELATIONSHIPS IN TIME

The prepositions *at*, *on*, and *in* are conventionally used for certain time relations:

TIME WITH at

- exact time: at 3 P.M., at midnight
- meal times: at dinner, at breakfast
- parts of the day, when no article is used for the part of the day: at night, at daybreak, at noon (*compare*: in the morning, in the evening)
- age: At 21 you are legally considered a full adult.

TIME WITH on

- days of the week: on Monday, on Tuesdays
- parts of the day, when the day is named: on Friday evening, on Saturday morning
- dates: on July 28th, on September 22nd

TIME WITH in

- seasons: in spring, in summer
- months: in April, in November, in the third month
- years: in 2056, in 1956
- durations: in ten minutes, in four days, in a month

PREPOSITIONS DESCRIBING RELATIONSHIPS IN SPACE

at, by, in, on show an object's settled position or position after it has moved	I arrived at the Baghdad airport. An old power plant sat unused by the school. In this town most people work at the call center. They carry their children on their backs.
to, onto, into show the direction of movement toward a point, surface, or area	They brought their babies to the clinic. She placed the crown onto his head. Walking into his office is like walking into a zoo.
by, along, through show the direction of movement next to or past a point, surface, or area	We drove by the ocean. From their castles along the Rhein River, German princes could regulate river traffic. Omero Catan, a salesperson from New York, drove the first car through the Lincoln Tunnel after waiting in line for 30 hours.
from, out of show the direction of movement away from a point, surface, or area	The *joropo* is a waltzy musical form from Venezuela. After the airplane crashed, she had to walk out of the jungle.

CONJUNCTIONS

Conjunctions connect words or groups of words. There are four kinds of conjunctions, each of which helps you express different kinds of relations between the words you are connecting.

THE PATTERN

COORDINATING CONJUNCTIONS

Coordinating conjunctions can connect nouns (including pronouns), adjectives, adverbs, prepositions, clauses, and sentences.

Use a coordinating conjunction when you want a reader to see that the words you are connecting have equal—coordinate—emphasis. The coordinating conjunctions, together with the relations they show, are

and	addition	Jacob and Ali went to the store. Loretta cooked and ate dinner.
for	cause	The dog is wet, for she swam. I am hungry, for I forgot to eat.
but, yet	contrast	Jacob went to the store, but Ali stayed home. Loretta cooked dinner, yet she did not eat right away.
or	choice	Jacob or Ali can go. • Loretta can cook dinner or eat out.
so	effect	I am hungry, so I will eat. The dog is wet from the rain, so I will dry her.
nor	exclusion	José doesn't swim, nor do I.

To connect individual words—such as nouns (including pronouns), adjectives, adverbs, and prepositions—**or phrases** use this pattern:

To connect sentences, use this pattern:

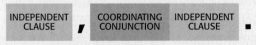

CORRELATIVE CONJUNCTIONS

Correlative conjunctions are like coordinating conjunctions in that they help you give equal emphasis to the words you are connecting—but correlative conjunctions come in two parts, and readers always expect to see both parts:

both...and, not only...but also addition	Both Miguel and Rav are on vacation. She did both her English and her math work.
either...or, whether...or choice	I could hire either Paul or Shawna. I want either to go out for dinner or to sleep. Either you will eat at home, or you will go out.
just as...so equality	Just as the smell of the air brought back memories, so too did the taste of the bread bring back memories.
neither...nor exclusion	Neither this car nor that is running. Neither will Omi go out, nor will she stay in!

To connect individual words—such as nouns (including pronouns), adjectives, adverbs, and prepositions—**or phrases**, use this pattern:

CORRELATIVE CONJUNCTION, PART 1	WORD OR PHRASE	CORRELATIVE CONJUNCTION, PART 2	WORD OR PHRASE

To connect sentences, use this pattern:

CORRELATIVE CONJUNCTION, PART 1	INDEPENDENT CLAUSE	CORRELATIVE CONJUNCTION, PART 2	INDEPENDENT CLAUSE

, ■

SUBORDINATING CONJUNCTIONS

These conjunctions join two sentences. The sentence following the conjunction is subordinate to—less emphasized than—the other sentence.

as, because, since
cause or reason

I am angry because she told lies.
Since you left, our group has no women.

so that
effect or result

He packs a lunch so that he can save money.
So that you can travel, you must get a passport.

if, even if, provided that, unless
condition

You couldn't get in even if you wanted.
If you want, he can bake the cake.

although, even though, though
contrast

He took the test even though he had not studied.
Although she was tired, she went out.

where, wherever
location

Nan sings where there is karaoke.
Wherever Heather goes, laughter follows.

after, before, once, since, until, when, whenever, while
time

She went to the movies after she had dinner.
While it rains, the city cannot fix the road.

Putting a subordinating conjunction in front of a sentence turns the sentence into a dependent clause.

When you put the dependent clause at the beginning of a sentence, put a comma after it:

| SUBORDINATING CONJUNCTION | INDEPENDENT CLAUSE | **,** | INDEPENDENT CLAUSE | **.** |

When you join two sentences by putting a subordinating conjunction between them, you need no comma:

| INDEPENDENT CLAUSE | SUBORDINATING CONJUNCTION | INDEPENDENT CLAUSE | **.** |

CONJUNCTIVE ADVERBS

Independent clauses can be joined with a semicolon and conjunctive adverb to show the relationships listed here:

also, besides, furthermore, moreover	addition	We don't need a car; **besides,** we can't afford one. The city repaved our street; **moreover,** they put up a new sign.
however, instead, likewise, nevertheless, nonetheless, otherwise, similarly, still	comparison and contrast	We could eat; **otherwise,** we should go home. Their team went into the game with a three point advantage; **nonetheless,** they lost.
accordingly, consequently, hence, then, therefore, thus	result or summary	The jury found her not guilty; **thus,** she was freed. She went home with a migraine; **consequently,** she missed the lecture.
finally, meanwhile, next, now, then	time	The first expedition set out; **meanwhile,** the second expedition gathered its equipment.

When you use conjunctive adverbs, start with an independent clause followed by a semicolon; then, put the conjunction (followed by a comma) and then put the second independent clause.

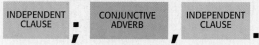

AVOIDING SHIFTS IN GRAMMATICAL FORMS

Shifts occur when a sentence begins with one grammatical form but ends with another. The conventions of formal, academic writing call for none of the five kinds of shifts we describe on these four pages.

SHIFTS BETWEEN DIRECT AND INDIRECT DISCOURSE

When you quote someone's words directly, you are using **direct discourse**:

"Are you going to the store without me?" Harriet's sister wanted to know.

In **indirect discourse**, you report what someone else said:

Harriet's sister wanted to know if we were going to the store without her.

A convention of formal written English is not to shift from one of these forms to another in a sentence:

Harriet's sister wanted to know are we going to the store without her.

SHIFTS IN PERSON AND NUMBER

To understand what it means to make a shift in person and number in a sentence or across sentences, keep in mind the chart to the right.

Whenever you mention the same noun twice, or use a noun and a pronoun, check that both have the same person and number. The pattern below shows you what to look for:

NUMBER	singular	plural
PERSON		
first person	I, me	we, us
second person	you	you
third person	it, one, she, he, her, him	they, them

THE PATTERN

USING PERSON CONSISTENTLY

correct **You can write. All you have to do is pick up a pen.**
second person, singular   second person, singular

incorrect **Anyone** can write. All **you** have to do is pick up a pen.
third person, singular   second person, singular

USING NUMBER CONSISTENTLY

correct **We all have to be careful about our effects on the**
first person, plural

environment. To help, each of us should drive less,
first person, plural

recycle more, and talk to our political representatives.
first person, plural

incorrect **We all have to be careful about our effects on the**
first person, plural

environment. To help, I should drive less, recycle
first person, singular

more, and talk to my political representatives.
first person, singular

→ For more information about using pronouns, see pages 502–507.

SHIFTS IN VOICE

| **THE PATTERN** | Is the subject of a sentence performing an action or being acted upon? When the subject is performing an action, the sentence is in active voice; when the subject is being acted upon, the sentence is in passive voice. |

ACTIVE VOICE

Jade fed the macaw.
subject

We caught and ate some of the mice that came into our camp.
subject

PASSIVE VOICE

The macaw was fed by Jade.
subject

Who ate the mice? The sentence doesn't say…

Some of the mice that came into our camp were caught and eaten.
subject

Active voice uses active verbs, which convey movement and energy (→ see page 273). Passive voice uses forms of **be**, and can also need a preposition before the noun that explains who performed the action—and so passive sentences tend to be wordy and slower to read.

The passive voice is useful, however, when a writer wants to avoid naming who performed an action—as in the sentence about the mice. Scientific and technical writing often uses passive voice because it can seem fact-based and objective. Writers present their research and conclusions without attribution, so the writing appears to be unshaped by individual bias.

→ For more on uses of active and passive voices, see pages 298–299.

MIXED VOICE

When writers mix active and passive voice together, the resulting sentences are often wordy and awkward.

Jade fed the macaw even though it had been been fed earlier by David.

When we had no food that winter, some of the mice that came into our camp were caught and eaten.

CONSISTENT VOICE

Sentences with consistent voice are both easier to understand and have more direct movement than the mixed voice sentences. In formal written English, readers expect consistent voice:

Jade fed the macaw even though David had fed it earlier.

When we had no food that winter, we caught and ate the mice that came into our camp.

SHIFTS IN VERB TENSE

If you shift tenses in a sentence, you shift from one sense of time to another. Readers can be confused by shifts in verb tense because they will not know if the actions of a sentence happened in the past, present, or future.

Here is one example:

Jenna sent me a letter about her trip to Botswana; she says many big companies are coming in to start the uranium mining.

Jenna sent me a letter about her trip to Botswana; she said many big companies are coming in to start the uranium mining.

This example involves writing about a literary text:

In Colette's novels *Cheri* and *The Last of Cheri*, the character Léa worked hard to seem young at the start but by the end she is gray-haired and stout.

The sentence above is wrong because it starts with the past tense (**worked**) but then shifts to the present tense (**is**). In addition, the sentence doesn't follow an academic convention of writing about fiction: When you are summarizing the plot or describing the actions of fiction, write as though the events are happening in an eternal present, and put all descriptions in present tense.

In Colette's novels *Cheri* and *The Last of Cheri*, the character Léa works hard to seem young at the start but by the end she is gray-haired and stout.

→ For more information on verb tenses, see pages 517–523.

SHIFTS IN LEVELS OF FORMALITY

Even in academic writing, there are levels of formality. Convention says to choose one level and stay with it.

FORMAL WRITING
Coltrane's saxophone playing is tender, but there is a searching quality to it, and this searching is perhaps the most salient characteristic of both his work and his life.

LESS FORMAL WRITING
Saxophones can whisper or shriek, breathe warmth or spit fire, and a quick listen to John Coltrane's 1965 album, *Transition*, will disabuse anyone of the misimpression that the saxophone is limited to that canned sound you heard during the credits of *L.A. Law*.

MIXED LEVELS
Coltrane's saxophone playing is tender, but there is a searching quality to it and sometimes his changes can really bug a listener.

TIP: **PURPOSEFUL SHIFTS**
Sometimes shifts are required if you are to make the meaning you want in a sentence. To be sure that you use shifts only when necessary, follow this rule: **When you are checking your writing and find any of the shifts we have described on these pages, remove the shift unless you can give a solid reason why the shift is necessary.**

GRAMMAR
AVOIDING MISPLACED AND DANGLING MODIFIERS

Modifier is the collective name for adjectives, adjectival phrases, adverbs, and adverbial phrases.

Modifiers make writing concrete and engaging—if readers can tell what words are being modified. Unfortunately, writers can easily put modifiers in odd places, which is why we offer the following suggestions.

PUT MODIFIERS CLOSE TO THE WORDS THEY MODIFY

In this sentence—

Covered in chocolate icing, my friends will love this cake.

—the friends sound like people we should approach with spoons in hand. When the adjectival phrase *covered in chocolate icing* is moved closer to the noun it is meant to modify, the result—

My friends will love this cake covered in chocolate icing.

—is clearer about the icing's location.

You are most likely to produce such slips when you write sentences with several modifiers. The following sentence has two modifiers (*all over Europe* and *passing close to earth*) placed to make it sound as though Europe passed close to earth in 1577:

The Great Comet of 1577 was viewed by people all over Europe passing close to earth.

When *passing close to earth* is moved closer to the noun phrase it should modify, the sentence is clearer:

Passing close to earth, the Great Comet of 1577 was viewed by people all over Europe.

TIP: CHECKING YOUR MODIFIERS

Modification slips are easy to produce as you write—and easy to fix. Fixing them requires finding them, however, and finding them takes time and careful reading.

To check your modifiers:

1 Underline every modifier in your writing and then draw a line from each to the word it modifies.

2 Move modifiers that are far from the words they modify closer to those words.

3 If the underlined word is a limiting modifier (→ see page 541), is it placed so that the sentence means what you desire it to?

4 If you cannot find a noun to which the modifier refers, you have a dangling modifier. Choose one of the options on page 541 to fix the dangling modifier.

PAY PARTICULAR ATTENTION TO LIMITING MODIFIERS

Limiting modifiers are words such as *almost*, *even*, *hardly*, *just*, *nearly*, *not*, *only*, and *simply*. They can be placed almost anywhere in a sentence, which makes them dangerous: Their placement can change a sentence's meaning.

For example, this sentence says that Luther thought about donating his collection, but didn't:

Luther almost donated his entire collection of LPs to the auction.

This sentence says that Luther **did** donate a large part of his collection:

Luther donated almost his entire collection of LPs to the auction.

Check each instance of limiting modifiers in your writing to be sure your sentences say what you want.

MOVE DISRUPTIVE MODIFIERS

Modifiers are disruptive when they disrupt a sentence's grammatical elements. In the first sentence below, a long phrase creates a distracting pause for readers between the sentence's subject and predicate:

Palenquero, although its grammar is so different that Spanish speakers cannot understand it, is thought to be the only Spanish-based Creole language in Latin America.

Moving the phrase makes the sentence easier to read:

Although its grammar is so different that Spanish speakers cannot understand it, Palenquero is thought to be the only Spanish-based Creole language in Latin America.

FIX DANGLING MODIFIERS

A modifier **dangles** when it cannot logically modify anything in its sentence. For example, unless the writer of this sentence has an unusual dog—

Reading a book, my dog rested her head on my knee.

—the sentence describes an impossible situation because the position of the modifier **reading a book** implies that the dog can read.

In addition, the person we assume is reading is not made explicit as a noun in this sentence. Because there is no such noun, the sentence cannot be fixed by moving the modifier closer to the nonexistent noun.

Because dangling modifiers cannot be fixed by being moved, there are two other options for fixing them:

1 Revise the dangling modifier to make explicit the noun that is to be modified:

   As I was reading a book, my dog rested her head on my knee.

2 Revise the rest of the sentence so that the noun appears elsewhere:

   Reading a book, I was warmed when my dog rested her head on my knee.

PUNCTUATION

Before writing, there was no punctuation: People simply spoke, not thinking of what they said as being words, much less as being divided up by punctuation. People simply put sounds together in different orders, and they understood each other.

After the invention of writing, it was still many centuries before punctuation (or even spaces between words) was invented. What seems to have given rise to punctuation was the need for speakers to read printed words aloud to listeners, as in churches. Imagine reading this passage aloud if you hadn't had time to figure out the passage beforehand:

most punctuation marks are composed to be seen but not heard these subtle often understated devices are quite important however for they are the meter that determines the measure within the silent voice of typography punctuation directs tempo pitch volume and the separation of words periods signify full stops commas slow the reader down question marks change pitch quotation marks indicate references

Punctuation is thus an important part of writing to communicate: It shows readers how you are shaping your ideas, where you are putting emphasis, and when you are using others' words.

There is considerable room for you to choose how to punctuate in order to reach the audiences for whom you write—but the information in the following pages will help you make informed decisions.

THERE ARE TWO MAIN DIVISIONS OF PUNCTUATION MARKS:

PUNCTUATION THAT GOES WITHIN SENTENCES

- commas
- semicolons
- colons
- parentheses
- dashes
- brackets
- hyphens
- slashes
- quotation marks
- apostrophes

PUNCTUATION THAT GOES AT THE END OF SENTENCES

- periods
- exclamation points
- question marks

AND...

There is another form of punctuation that is not really a mark and that you might not think of as punctuation, but—like all punctuation—it is very important for helping readers understand where sentences begin and end:

CAPITALIZATION

Punctuation, then, is a matter of care. Care for words, yes, but also, and more important, for what the words imply. Only a lover notices the small things: the way the afternoon light catches the nape of a neck, or how a strand of hair slips out from behind an ear, or the way a finger curls around a cup. And no one scans a letter so closely as a lover, searching for its small print, straining to hear its nuances, its gasps, its sighs and hesitations, poring over the secret messages that lie in every cadence. The difference between "Jane (whom I adore)" and "Jane, whom I adore," and the difference between them both and "Jane—whom I adore—" marks all the distance between ecstasy and heartache.

PICO IYER,
"In Praise of the Humble Comma"

COMMAS

have four main uses.

1

USING COMMAS TO MAKE NUMBERS, PLACE-NAMES, AND DATES CLEAR

To learn how and when to use commas in sentences like the following—

Virginia's population was 1,000,000 in 1830. It took eighty more years for it to reach its second million (2,061,612 in 1910).

If you visit Emily Dickinson's house in Amherst, Massachusetts, you won't see anything that truly belonged to Emily Dickinson.

Abraham Lincoln was shot the night of April 14, 1865, and died the following morning.

→ GO TO PAGE 546.

2

USING COMMAS TO HELP INDICATE WHEN YOU ARE QUOTING (EXACTLY) THE WORDS OF SOMEONE ELSE

To learn how and when to use commas in sentences like the following—

"Hello," she said, "can I help you with that?"

"The real problem with having a robot to dinner," argues Ellen Ullman, "is pleasure."

—or to learn about the following kinds of sentences (in which you aren't quoting someone else's words directly)—

She asked if she could help me.

Ellen Ullman has argued that pleasure (or the lack of it) is why people don't have robots to dinner.

→ GO TO PAGE 548.

3

USING COMMAS TO SEPARATE WORDS THAT ARE PARTS OF LISTS IN SENTENCES

To learn how and when to use commas in sentences like the following—

At lunch I ate potato chips, a peanut butter and jelly sandwich, a banana, two cupcakes, and some barbecued eel.

The stinking, reeking water roiled down the street.

She caught a cab, her breath, and then the flu.

He was livid, he was angry, and he was mad.

→ GO TO PAGE 550.

4

USING COMMAS TO BUILD SENTENCES THAT CONTAIN MULTIPLE PARTS

To learn how and when to use commas in sentences like the following—

To hear him tell it, the bananas were not exactly conducive to a happy stomach.

Her father, who was born in Saudi Arabia, always longed for the hottest days in August.

Can you bring me the ladder, which is in the backyard?

You'd think it would be enough that she earned A's in all her classes, but my roommate, a biomechanical engineering major, also wanted to have the highest GPA on campus.

He looked up at me, and he burst into tears.

→ GO TO PAGE 554.

WHEN SHOULDN'T YOU USE COMMAS? → GO TO PAGE 563.

COMMA USE 1

USING COMMAS TO MAKE NUMBERS, PLACE-NAMES, AND DATES CLEAR

NUMBERS

When you are writing numbers, use commas to separate the digits in numbers higher than 999.

1,000 (but 999)

2,304,504

$87,000,000,000

Note that the commas separate the long numbers into groups of three, *moving from the right to the left.*

Here are examples of commas in numbers in sentences:

How had 9,125 relatively uneventful days passed so quickly, and how might I slow the days ahead?

In 1889 more than 3,000,000 acres in the Indian Territory, now Oklahoma, were opened to non-Indian homesteaders, so that a territory that had held virtually no non-Indians in 1880 had 730,000 in 1900.

Here is comma use with large numbers when money is at issue:

On the $65,000,000 bond sale, Morgan and Belmont made a perfectly legal profit somewhere between $1,500,000 and $16,000,000; no one outside the banks knew exactly how much.

BUT!

In the examples above, notice that there are no commas in numbers that represent years. It is also conventional not to use commas in street addresses:

20419 West Second Street

PLACE-NAMES

When you mention a location and the larger place of which it is a part—such as a neighborhood in a city, a city in a state, a state or province in a country—separate the two place-names with commas:

Neighborhood, city: **Algiers, New Orleans**

City, state: **Houghton, Michigan**

State, country: **Oregon, United States**

Province, country: **Tangier, Morocco**

In sentences:

In 1948, Adrian Piper, an artist and philosopher, was born in Harlem, New York City.

Fela Kuti was born in Abeokuta, Nigeria, to a middle-class family.

To finish his Ph.D. at the University of California, Davis, he had to figure out how to put a rattlesnake on a leash.

■ ■ ■

To put a multiline address—

**Habitat for Humanity/Metro Jackson
P.O. Box 55634
Jackson, MS 39296-5634**

—onto one line in your writing, put commas between the sections:

Please send your donations to Habitat for Humanity/Metro Jackson, P.O. Box 55634, Jackson, MS 39296-5634.

Note that there is no comma between the state and the zip code.

DATES

There are three common formats for written dates in the United States, only one of which requires a comma:

1
February 17, 1951

When you include a full date in this order—month, day, year—put a comma after the day:

On January 26, 1950, the Constitution of India was adopted and gave many powers to the individual states.

2
17 Feb. 1951

This format is for citing webpages in the MLA style:

Hayden, Teresa Nielsen. "Yo, Wocky Jivvy, Wergle Flomp." Weblog entry. <u>Making Light</u>. 29 June 2005. 18 Feb. 2006 <http://nielsenhayden.com/makinglight/archives/006498.html>.

→ See pages 369 and 371 for more information on this use of dates.

3
February 1951

If you are writing only the month and year, you do not need a comma between them:

In February 1912 La Follette delivered an angry, rambling, and—according to some—drunken speech at an important dinner for newspaper publishers, extinguishing whatever slender chances he had had for gaining the Republican nomination.

COMMA USE 2

USING COMMAS TO HELP INDICATE WHEN YOU ARE QUOTING (EXACTLY) THE WORDS OF SOMEONE ELSE

When you embed someone else's spoken or written words into your own, use commas to separate the words you are quoting from the phrases that signal you are quoting:

"I've got to sing," he said, hoarsely.

WHEN YOU **DON'T** BREAK UP THE SENTENCES YOU ARE QUOTING

You can put quoted words at the beginning or at the end of a sentence.

"Keep the hard hat on," she said to me when we parked.

As the poet W. H. Auden put it, "The chances are that, in the course of his lifetime, the major poet will write more bad poems than the minor."

In the first case, notice that the comma goes *inside* the quotation mark and *before* the *she said* phrase. In the second case, the comma goes *after* the (equivalent of the) *she said* phrase, *before* and *outside* the quotation mark.

WHEN YOU **DO** BREAK UP THE SENTENCES YOU ARE QUOTING

You can break up the words of others for effect:

"Why," asks Jonathan Burt, "should the rat be such an apt figure for horror and the target of so much hatred and loathing?"

Note that the first comma goes *inside* the quotation marks and *before* the (equivalent of the) *he said* phrase; the second comma goes *after* the (equivalent of the) *he said* phrase, *before* and *outside* the quotation mark.

WHEN YOU DON'T QUOTE A WHOLE SENTENCE

These examples use no comma before the quoted words because the quoted words are not sentences.

In describing his cityscapes of Paris, Fox Talbot says that photography "chronicles whatever it sees," noting the complex and jumbled array of chimney pots and lightning rods.

She finally cobbled together some mumbo jumbo about a "man from the West" who would "walk on water" to the "East."

WHEN YOU QUOTE SEVERAL SENTENCES

The following example starts in the usual way, with a comma following *observed*—but notice that there are two complete sentences being quoted, separated by a period.

The cop observed, "In the older generations we didn't even drink a beer. If your mom and dad smelled a beer on you, oh my God, you might have to stay in for a year."

In the next example, because the *he said* words break up the sentences being quoted, the *he said* has a comma before it:

"It was the sociological nadir of the American spirit," a Pepsi executive recalled. "Protests. Woodstock. Drugs. A surly and sullen generation occupying the dean's office, burning it down—whatever it was. It was all that sixties stuff."

WHEN YOU DON'T QUOTE WORDS EXACTLY

When you refer to something that someone else said but don't use the person's exact words, you are using indirect quotation. In indirect quotation, you do not use quotation marks or commas. Very often, **that** introduces the words that are being indirectly quoted.

INDIRECT QUOTATION:
Mr. Quiring has told me that essays and stories generally come, organically, to a preordained ending that is quite out of a writer's control.

DIRECT QUOTATION:
In class, Mr. Quiring said, "Essays and stories come to a preordained ending organically—completely out of a writer's control!"

→ See pages 314–325 for help in thinking about how and why to incorporate the words of others in your academic writing.

→ See pages 597–599 for more information on using quotation marks to punctuate quotations.

COMMA USE 3

USING COMMAS TO SEPARATE WORDS
THAT ARE PARTS OF LISTS IN
SENTENCES

In official grammar-speak, a list of
words—such as **dogs**, **tables**, **justice**, **snow**,
and **imagination**—is referred to as a series.

THE PATTERN

1

If you are listing only two nouns, verbs, adjectives, phrases, or clauses in a
sentence, here is the pattern to follow:

 and

For example:

She ran and dove into the water.

or

The audience sing-along was flaccid and unenthusiastic.

2

If you are combining **three or more** nouns, verbs, adjectives, phrases, or
clauses, here is the pattern to follow:

 , ▓ **, and** ▓

For example:

She grinned, ran, and dove into the water.

or

The audience sing-along was short, flaccid, and unenthusiastic.

This pattern can be expanded to include any number of items:

In the past week we had rain, hail, snow, and a desire for springtime.

USING COMMAS IN LISTS OF INDIVIDUAL NOUNS

When you list only two nouns in a sentence, no comma is necessary:

A hat and gloves are necessary for winter.

We find ourselves entering a realm of fantasy and paradox.

When you make a list of **three or more** nouns, put a comma after each item in the list—except the last:

A hat, gloves, and boots are necessary for winter.

After spending the bulk of the afternoon talking with patients who had no idea what year, month, or day it is, I myself felt rather disoriented.

Mr. Armstrong pleased most of the audience; he has timing, charisma, and plenty of eyeliner—and he's not afraid to sweat.

The player is then set loose in a huge, colorful fantasy world with cities, plains, oceans, mountains, forests, rivers, jungles, deserts, and (of course) dungeons.

Other writers who scholars have argued had temporal lobe epilepsy include Tennyson, Lear, Poe, Swinburne, Byron, de Maupassant, Molière, Pascal, Petrarch, Dante, Teresa of Avila, and Saint Paul.

USING COMMAS IN LISTS OF INDIVIDUAL VERBS

When you list only two verbs in a sentence, no comma is necessary:

The infant burped and grinned.

I learned to shovel coal and haul clinkers at an early age.

When you make a list of **three or more** verbs, put a comma after each item in the list—except the last:

On that rooftop, she sees, imagines, and remembers.

Lawrence North High School basketball center Greg Oden passes, blocks, shoots, scores, rebounds, and smiles.

→ The ability to use commas as we describe on these pages is important in building parallelism, which is a form of list building. See pages 286–287 to learn about parallelism.

COMMA USE 3 continued

USING COMMAS IN LISTS OF PHRASES AND CLAUSES

As with nouns and verbs, when you list **three or more** phrases or clauses, use a comma between each.

Furious, Buffmeier walked through the front door, exited to the back, crossed the parking lot, and went into his shack.

Gilligan's work emphasizes relationships over rules, connection over isolation, caring over violence, and a web of relationships over hierarchy.

The Egyptians mummified their dead in a complex process that involved pulling the brain through the nostrils with an iron hook, washing the body with incense, and, in later dynasties, covering it with bitumen and linen.

BUT!

Use semicolons—and not commas—between a series of phrases that themselves contain commas:

The four common principles that ran through much of this thought through the end of the Cold War were a concern with democracy, human rights, and, more generally, the internal politics of states; a belief that American power can be used for moral purposes; a skepticism about the ability of international law and institutions to solve serious security problems; and, finally, a view that ambitious social engineering often leads to unexpected consequences and thereby undermines its own ends.

USING COMMAS IN LISTS OF INDIVIDUAL ADJECTIVES

When you put together **two or more adjectives**, you have to decide two things:

1

whether or not to use a comma between them

AND

2

whether to use **and** between them.

WHEN TO USE A COMMA OR "AND" IN LISTS OF ADJECTIVES

*Use a comma or **and*** to separate two adjectives if you can change their order without changing the meaning of the sentence. For example, the meaning of

He was a thin, dapper fellow who preferred a suit and vest to ordinary clothes.

isn't changed when it is written as

He was a dapper, thin fellow who preferred a suit and vest to ordinary clothes.

or as

He was a thin and dapper fellow who preferred a suit and vest to ordinary clothes.

In these examples, *thin* and *dapper* are called **coordinate adjectives**, the name for adjectives whose order can be changed without the meaning of the sentence changing.

WHEN TO USE NEITHER A COMMA NOR "AND" IN LISTS OF ADJECTIVES

If you cannot rearrange the adjectives in a sentence without changing the meaning of the sentence, do not put a comma between them, *no matter how many adjectives you are using*:

The prize for my banana costume was a radio designed to look like a box of frozen niblets corn.

This sentence doesn't have a comma between *frozen* and *niblets* because, in the United States, we would not say *niblets frozen corn* or *niblets and frozen corn*.

Here is another example:

Three huge gray whales swam by.

Because *three* is describing how many *huge gray whales* this writer saw, *three* goes before the other adjectives.

Adjectives that cannot be rearranged are called **noncoordinate adjectives**, and they do not have commas between them.

WHEN TO USE A COMMA AND "AND" IN LISTS OF ADJECTIVES

When you have three adjectives whose order can be changed without changing the meaning of the sentence, use the same pattern as with lists of nouns, verbs, phrases, and clauses. Put a comma after each of the adjectives except the last:

Reappropriate.com is a political, current-events, and personal blog written from the perspective of a loud and proud Asian-American woman.

We have come to know zero intimately in its mathematical, physical, and psychological embodiments.

WHEN SHOULDN'T YOU USE COMMAS IN A LIST OF WORDS?

Sometimes writers want to emphasize the length of time that goes into a series of actions, so they link the words or phrases of a series with *and* or *or*:

Instead, we arrange the platters of food and remove bread from the oven and fill cups with grape juice and wine.

The example at the left is correct, as is the example below (which creates a quicker sense of the time involved in all the actions):

Instead, we arrange the platters of food, remove bread from the oven, and fill cups with grape juice and wine.

COMMA USE 4

USING COMMAS TO BUILD
SENTENCES THAT CONTAIN
MULTIPLE PARTS

Here is a paragraph of simple
sentences:

**There was a racist bombing of a
church in Alabama. This happened in
1963. *ID* magazine published an
article about race in industrial design.
The article discussed only one female
African American designer. Her name
is Madeleine Ward.**

Here are those sentences joined into
one:

**In 1963, in response to a racist
bombing of a church in Alabama, *ID*
magazine published an article about
race in industrial design, but they
discussed only one female African
American designer, Madeleine Ward.**

The ideas are more tightly woven
together in the single sentence, and
(some would argue) they suggest more
strongly than the individual sentences
that something is wrong with the
magazine article if it discusses only one
female African American designer.

   If you decide that the audience and
purpose motivating your writing
require using sentences like the single-
sentence example, then your sentences
will need commas. When you write
such sentences, which complicate the
basic subject-verb-object structure,
commas set off the sentence's parts
and help readers see and better
understand how the sentence's parts
relate to each other.

There are two patterns for building such sentences:

1

USING COMMAS TO ADD ONE SENTENCE ONTO THE END OF ANOTHER

To learn how and when to use commas in sentences like the following—

Her body seems distracted, but her mind is not.

Every limb was broken, and he ended up a triple amputee.

Music has got to be useful for survival, or we would have gotten rid of it years ago.

Will I get a second chance, or am I supposed to remain a suspect for the rest of my life?

One woman in each tent started dinner, and the other finished securing the tent and sleds for the night.

St. Sebastian was condemned to be shot by arrows, but a tradition says that he survived this torment only to be stoned to death.

→ GO TO PAGE 556 TO SEE THIS PATTERN.

2

USING COMMAS TO ADD ADDITIONAL INFORMATION TO THE MAIN IDEA OF A SENTENCE

To learn how and when to use commas in sentences like the following—

A parrot that cannot talk or sing is, we feel, an incomplete parrot.

Kudos are due to Dwyane Wade, who pretty much single-handedly won the NBA Finals.

Without raising his voice above a murmur, this artist-thinker gives the condition of exile an existential, universalist weight.

The freshwater vertebrates, originally found in the slow waters of East India, are fast replacing the lab rat as a prime model for studies in genetics and development.

→ GO TO PAGE 558 TO SEE THIS PATTERN.

→ The kinds of sentences we discuss here are part of the style of most academic and other nonfiction writing; see pages 480–489 to learn about other aspects of these kinds of writing.

PATTERN 1

USING COMMAS TO ADD ONE SENTENCE ONTO THE END OF ANOTHER

When you combine two sentences, the convention of written English is to put a comma and then a coordinating conjunction between the two:

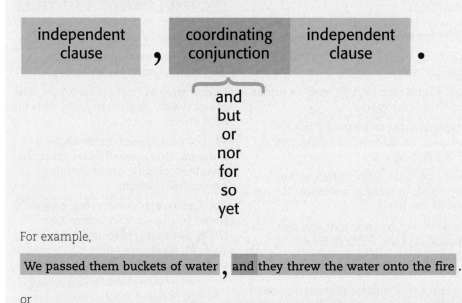

For example,

We passed them buckets of water **,** and they threw the water onto the fire .

or

He swung his arms wildly **,** but the mosquitoes still swarmed around him .

or

The molecules attach to this material **,** for they have proper affinity with it .

When you combine sentences in this way, be sure to put a comma before the coordinating conjunction.

Here are more examples. Note how each follows this pattern:

independent clause + **,** + coordinating conjunction + independent clause •

I tried to draw him out, but it saddens Hugh to discuss his childhood monkey.

The sweaters I've made aren't impressive specimens, but they've taught me a lot.

Part of Goldstein's work was concerned with the effects of brain damage, and he found that, whenever there was extensive damage, there tended to be an impairment of abstract-categorical capacity.

Twenty years later there were 3,000 factory hands at Baldwin, and by 1900 there were more than 8,000.

Several selective pressures may act similarly and simultaneously on trees, so it is difficult to tease apart the contributions those pressures make to tree evolution.

It sounds like something you'd read on a movie poster, but sometimes the sins you haven't committed are all you have to hold on to.

Like most Kenyans, I was not taught about my culture or about the things my parents learned from their parents in school, yet I was taught about the American Revolution, Niagara Falls, and the Second World War.

BE CAREFUL...
If you were to take these sentences—

In this section I focus on fluorescent biological samples.

The techniques may be applied to material science.

—and combine them without using a coordinating conjunction—

In this section I focus on fluorescent biological samples, the techniques may be applied to material science.

—you would have *a comma splice*. Writing teachers notice comma splices—so if you have been making this error without knowing it, now is the time to learn how to keep your writing teacher smiling at you.

Here is the version that will make a writing teacher put away the red pen:

In this section I focus on fluorescent biological samples, but the techniques may be applied to material science.

You can avoid comma splices by following the pattern shown on these two pages, joining two sentences with a comma and a coordinating conjunction.

→ There are other strategies for mending comma splices; see pages 494–495.

→ For more on coordinating conjunctions, see page 532.

PATTERN 2

USING COMMAS TO ADD ADDITIONAL INFORMATION TO THE MAIN IDEA OF A SENTENCE

You can add additional information to a sentence at the beginning, middle, or end.

In my dreams,   , on occasion,

I play the drums.

, who have no musical sense,

, to the delight of my neighbor downstairs

You can add the suggested insertions (some of which are adjective phrases, some adverb phrases) to the sentence above to build the following:

In my dreams, I play the drums.

I, who have no musical sense, play the drums, to the delight of my neighbor downstairs.

I play, on occasion, the drums.

Notice the pattern of comma use around the inserted information;

- When you add information at the **beginning of a sentence**, put a single comma after what you add.
- When you add information in the **middle of a sentence**, put a comma before and a comma after what you add.
- When you add information at the **end of a sentence**, put a comma before what you add.

WHAT DO WE MEAN BY ADDITIONAL (OR "NONESSENTIAL") INFORMATION?

Each of the additions to the sentence *I play the drums* to the left brings something new to the sentence, but if you took away all the additions, you would still understand the basic idea of the sentence.

If you can remove information from a sentence without harming a reader's ability to understand the main point, then the information is additional.

In the following pages, we will refer to such additional information as *nonessential*, because that is the **official** grammatical term.

If you can remove a phrase from a sentence without changing the basic meaning of the sentence, separate the phrase from the rest of the sentence with commas.

NONESSENTIAL INFORMATION AT THE BEGINNING OF A SENTENCE

These examples show ways you can start a sentence with a nonessential phrase. Notice the comma in each:

Unlike many other producers who step to the mic, Kanye is also an extremely talented emcee who flexes a relaxed but focused flow that's never short on clever lyrics.

At the time of her husband's assassination, Mary Todd Lincoln had already buried two young sons.

Because data are always ambiguous, it can be years before physicists feel confident enough to publish potentially controversial results.

As unions waxed stronger after 1886, the number of strikes to enforce union rules grew steadily.

Once upon a time, I was one of those nerds who hung around Radio Shack and played with LEDs, resistors, and capacitors.

Even in the harsh penal environment of early America, some colonies had laws against feeding lobsters to inmates because it was thought to be cruel and unusual, like making people eat rats.

If you use only one or two introductory words, you can omit the comma:

On Wednesday we conduct the experiment.

NONESSENTIAL INFORMATION IN THE MIDDLE OF A SENTENCE

Short interjections of words can add a conversational tone to writing; these interjections remind readers that a person wrote the words, so interjections can help writers build relations with their readers. Put a comma before and after such interjections:

Dirt, it seems, is an important ingredient in particle physics experiments.

Some sequels, as we all know, are better than the originals.

Let me clarify two points that will, I hope, make clear our disagreement.

■ ■ ■

When you use explanatory words and phrases such as *though* and *for example*, they should be set off by commas:

Once I'm awake, though, I tend to lie there wondering if I've made a terrible mistake.

Among Plains tribes, for example, certain forms of design knowledge, such as quill embroidery and beadwork, are sacred.

BUT!

Do not put a comma after *though* if the word introduces a phrase:

Though she had already been executed, Joan of Arc was acquitted on July 7, 1456.

■ ■ ■

The following sentences have phrases that come after nouns (very often names) and that explain what the noun is; put a comma before and after all such phrases:

Aunty Lau, an accomplished weaver, teaches Hawaiian culture in the schools.

My son, who is eleven, has a memory like wet cement.

Lascelles Brown, an athletic Jamaican butcher who had briefly dabbled in boxing, first got interested in bobsledding after seeing the 1993 Disney film *Cool Running,* based on Jamaica's 1988 Olympic team.

Scissors, a mundane object to which we are introduced in kindergarten, are a sophisticated tool requiring opposable thumbs and some dexterity.

The Space Shuttle, on track and on schedule, came into view just after 5:53 Pacific time.

Nature, when abused, may react eventually like a tiger whose tail has been pulled.

We know from research that dogs, even kennel-raised puppies, do much better than generally more brilliant wolves or human-like chimpanzees in responding to human cues in a food-finding test.

STEPS FOR DECIDING IF INFORMATION IS ESSENTIAL OR NOT

1

For a sentence about which you are unsure, describe to yourself exactly what is most important to you in the sentence: *What exactly is it that you want your readers to take away from your sentence?*

Example 1
Your sentence emphasizes some events that took place in New York City.

Example 2
Your sentence focuses your readers' attention on society's responses to the women who died in Vietnam.

2

Identify in the sentence the information that may or may not be essential.

All of this took place in New York City, <u>which is cruelly, insanely expensive</u>.

This website is dedicated to women <u>who died in the Vietnam War</u>.

3

Remove the information you identified in step 2.

All of this took place in New York City.

This website is dedicated to women.

4

Ask yourself this question about the shortened sentence: Does it give your readers exactly what you want them to take from the sentence?

If you are writing this sentence to emphasize that the events you are describing took place in New York City and not to emphasize the cost of being in New York City, the answer is **yes**.

If you are writing this sentence to focus your readers' attention on society's responses to the women who died in Vietnam and not on all women, the answer is **no**.

5

If the answer is **yes**, then the information you identified in step 2 is nonessential, and should be separated from the rest of the sentence with commas.

If the answer is **no**, then the information you identified in step 2 is essential and should not be separated with commas.

All of this took place in New York City, which is cruelly, insanely expensive.

This website is dedicated to women who died in the Vietnam War.

NONESSENTIAL INFORMATION AT THE END OF A SENTENCE

These examples show some of the many ways you can end a sentence with a nonessential phrase. Notice where the comma is in these examples:

I used to play that song over and over in the dark when I was nine, the year I really became aware of my own existence.

Ray has exceptionally large glasses, like an underwater mask, as if he never knows when he'll have to do some welding or shield himself from a solar eclipse.

Shani Davis stood out as a rare African American in a mostly white sport, supported by a single mother who helped bulldoze any barriers she sensed were in front of him.

Knitting is a skill that has come in handy throughout my life, mostly because I am so afflicted with the Protestant work ethic that I can't bear to watch television unless I am doing something productive with my hands.

Dogs are said to be the first domestic animals, displacing pigs for primal honors.

TIP: IF YOU ARE NOT SURE WHETHER INFORMATION IS ESSENTIAL OR NONESSENTIAL, REVISE THE SENTENCE TO SAVE YOURSELF ANY WORRY

In this sentence, is the phrase *seeing how quickly glaciers are melting* essential or nonessential?

Scientists seeing how quickly glaciers are melting say we cannot ignore global warming.

You could make arguments in either direction for the phrase, meaning that the sentence will be ambiguous for its readers and hence potentially confusing.

Moving and rewording the phrase in question can remove the ambiguity:

When they see how quickly glaciers are melting, scientists say we cannot ignore global warming.

Sometimes, rewording the sentence can help you create the sense you want your readers to understand:

Those scientists who see how quickly glaciers are melting are the most emphatic that global warming is occurring now.

WHEN NOT TO USE COMMAS

We list here kinds of sentences in which people are often tempted to use commas—but for which the conventions of formal writing say not to.

BEFORE INFORMATION ESSENTIAL TO A SENTENCE

delete

I am writing about the woman, who was nominated for president by the Republican Party in 1964.

I am writing about the woman who was nominated for president by the Republican Party in 1964.

Read the sentence without the part following the comma; if the sentence loses the meaning you want it to have, then you **do not** need the comma.

→ For more information on making this decision, see page 561.

BETWEEN TWO CLAUSES THAT ARE NOT INDEPENDENT CLAUSES

delete

Some people look at war, and see nothing but violence and chaos.

Some people look at war and see nothing but violence and chaos.

→ If you need help determining whether you are writing independent clauses, see pages 483–487.

BEFORE "THAN"

Some scientists argue that there is no *delete* clearer indication of global warming, than Greenland's melting glaciers.

Some scientists argue that there is no clearer indication of global warming than Greenland's melting glaciers.

BETWEEN A SENTENCE'S VERB AND ITS SUBJECT OR OBJECT

delete

Everything good, is bad for you.

Everything good is bad for you.

delete

One of the dominant themes in American science policy this past year was, how we can maintain a competitive edge in a global economy.

One of the dominant themes in American science policy this past year was how we can maintain a competitive edge in a global economy.

If you include more than one word in a subject, it can be tempting to put a comma after it because you might read the sentence out loud with a pause after the subject—which can suggest that a comma should go there. The same temptation can happen with long objects: If you were reading it out loud, you would probably pause before the object. But in writing, the convention is not to put commas in these places.

BEFORE OR AFTER PARENTHESES

delete

A political career, (or a legal one) is the surest ticket to a historical legacy.

A political career (or a legal one) is the surest ticket to a historical legacy.

or

A political career, or a legal one, is the surest ticket to a historical legacy.

The convention is to use parentheses or commas around parenthetical comments, but not both.

AFTER A SUBORDINATING CONJUNCTION

delete

Although, scientists no longer consider Pluto to be a planet, many still seek that little celestial body in their telescopes.

Although scientists no longer consider Pluto to be a planet, many still seek that little celestial body in their telescopes.

→ Page 534 lists and explains subordinating conjunctions.

BEFORE THE FIRST ITEM IN A LIST, OR AFTER THE LAST ITEM

delete

E-mail spammers endure, legal harassment, exclusion from polite society, and the disgust of nearly every computer user.

E-mail spammers endure legal harassment, exclusion from polite society, and the disgust of nearly every computer user.

delete

Many accidents of geography, history, and biology, created our lopsided world.

Many accidents of geography, history, and biology created our lopsided world.

→ See pages 550–553 for the conventional uses of commas with lists.

SEMICOLONS
have two main uses.

1

USING SEMICOLONS TO SEPARATE THE ITEMS IN A LIST WHEN THE ITEMS ARE COMPLEX.

To learn how and when to use semicolons in a sentence like the following—

Arbus's subjects included a child in the park, holding a toy grenade; a woman, cozily ensconced in her kitchen, holding a chimpanzee; and the fire-eater of a Maryland circus.

→ GO TO PAGE 566.

2

USING SEMICOLONS TO JOIN TWO SENTENCES

To learn how and when to use commas in sentences like the following—

Some writers write many drafts of a piece; some write one draft, at the pace of snail after a night on the town.

I'm not arguing that the postmodern shift erases traditional texts or narratives; instead, I'm trying to make clear that our traditional texts are changing.

→ GO TO PAGE 567.

SEMICOLON USE 1

USING SEMICOLONS TO SEPARATE THE ITEMS IN A LIST WHEN THE ITEMS ARE COMPLEX

USING SEMICOLONS TO JOIN ELEMENTS THAT CONTAIN THEIR OWN PUNCTUATION

Usually, we use commas to build lists of items—

A hat, gloves, and boots are necessary for winter.

—but in a complex sentence, commas might not be of help to readers:

Istanbul's steep hills and harbor views remind you of San Francisco, its overcrowded streets recall Bombay, its transportation facilities evoke Venice, for you can go many places by boats, which are continually making stops.

Instead, with semicolons separating the items, it is easier to see the separate items:

Istanbul's steep hills and harbor views remind you of San Francisco; its overcrowded streets recall Bombay; its transportation facilities evoke Venice, for you can go many places by boats, which are continually making stops.

If you are building a list using items that contain their own punctuation, use semicolons to separate the items:

As the leech began to suck, it released several other substances into his ear: a powerful anticoagulant, which prevented his blood from clotting; a vasodilator, which opened his vessels, helping to increase blood flow; and a spreading factor, which moved these chemicals quickly into tissue farthest from the bite, liquefying any hardening blood.

SEMICOLON USE 2

USING SEMICOLONS TO JOIN TWO
SENTENCES

JOINING SENTENCES

Be sure you have two complete
sentences (that is, independent
clauses), and then join them with a
semicolon. The first letter of the word
following the semicolon is not
capitalized, unless it is a proper noun.

**The father didn't move out; he just
moved to a different bedroom.**

**The ceiling, freshly painted, was
luminous as the sky; I almost thought
I could smell the paint.**

**My fears were powerful and troubling
and annoyingly vague; I couldn't
establish exactly what it was that
frightened me.**

**The highway went for miles between
high mud walls and canebrakes; the
black tracery of date palms rose above
them, against the brilliant night sky.**

You can use semicolons to join
multiple sentences:

**Work made people useful in a world of
economic scarcity; it staved off the
doubts and temptations that preyed on
idleness; it opened the way to deserved
wealth and status; it allowed one to
put the impress of mind and skill on
the material world.**

→ To be sure you are joining complete
sentences, read about independent and
dependent clauses, pages 483–487.

COLONS
have three main uses. 1

USING COLONS IN CERTAIN CONVENTIONAL PATTERNS.

To learn how and when to use colons in writing situations like the following—

Dear Senator Gonzaga:

The experiment took place at 3:22 P.M.

Her article is titled "Concrete: A Hard History."

New York: Longman, 2008.

→ GO TO PAGE 570.

2

USING COLONS TO PREPARE READERS FOR INFORMATION AT THE END OF A SENTENCE.

To learn how and when to use colons in sentences like the following—

He brought along his equipment: some collecting jars, a microscope, and his lunch.

The shops gave the street a strange air: They all looked alike from the outside.

→ GO TO PAGE 572.

3

USING COLONS TO LINK TWO SENTENCES.

To learn how and when to use colons in sentences like the following—

In April, Stefano and his team completed preliminary research on the medicinal leech: They found morphine in its head region, which contains the leech's salivary glands.

→ GO TO PAGE 573.

TIP: CHOOSING HOW MUCH EMPHASIS YOU WANT TO GIVE

The next three punctuation marks—colons, parentheses, and dashes—have some overlaps in their uses: Each of these punctuation marks can be used to emphasize parts of a sentence.

For you to decide which punctuation mark to use in your writing, you have to decide how much emphasis you want to give. Look at the examples here and on the following pages, where words are set off by colons, parentheses, or dashes, in order to determine the level of emphasis you want your words to have.

COLON USE 1
USING COLONS IN CERTAIN CONVENTIONAL PATTERNS

SALUTATIONS

In formal or business letters, colons are used after the greeting at the beginning of the letter:

Dear Sir or Madam:

Dear Dr. Lucchesi:

Dear Ms. Poole:

BUT!

In the past, it was acceptable to start any business letter with *Dear Sirs:*—but now, with more women than ever before in workplaces, you cannot know the gender of the person opening a letter you send. It is better to write, "Dear Sir or Madam:"

MEMO HEADINGS

In workplaces, memos (less formal than letters) are often used to inform others of the progress of a project, or of meetings or other events. The top of a memo will usually look like this:

To: The members of the Research Committee

From: Ralph Bunker

Re: Next Steps

(**Re:** means *regarding*; think of it as being like the subject heading of an e-mail.)

TIME

When you are writing the time of day, use a colon between the hour, the minutes, and the seconds (if you include them):

12:32 P.M.   4:50:32 P.M.

I awoke just before the alarm went off, at 5:59:59 A.M.

Similarly, when you are recording the duration of an event, such as a race or experiment, use colons between the hour, minutes, and seconds:

She ran her first mile in 4:35 and her second in 4:50.

Sometimes, however, you need to spell out the time:

The cells separated after 2 hours and 35 seconds.

Otherwise, it might be unclear to readers whether you are describing the time of day or the duration you are recording:

The cells separated after 2:35.

BETWEEN TITLE AND SUBTITLE

When you are writing the title of any communication—book, article, movie, television show—that has a subtitle, put the title, then a colon, then the subtitle:

Katherine Dunham: Dancing Queen

Wind: How the Flow of Air Has Shaped Life, Myth, and the Land

Fibroids: Women Seek Answers, Treatment

MLA WORKS CITED LISTINGS

When you are putting together a listing of the works you have cited in a paper, put a colon after the name of the city where the book was published, and then put the name of the publisher:

Le Faye, Deirdre, ed. *Jane Austen's Letters*. 3rd ed. Oxford: Oxford UP, 1995.

Mông-Lan. "Trail." *The Best American Poetry 2002*. Ed. Robert Creeley. New York: Scribner, 2002. 108–17.

Monroe, Barbara. *Crossing the Digital Divide; Race, Writing, and Technology in the Classroom*. New York: Teachers College Press, 2004.

→ For fuller explanation of how to punctuate MLA citations, see pages 360–403.

BIBLE VERSES

If you cite verses from the Bible, put a colon between the chapter and the verse:

Matthew 6:5

Deuteronomy 5:17

Psalm 46:9

COLON USE 2

USING COLONS TO PREPARE
READERS FOR INFORMATION AT
THE END OF A SENTENCE

Use a colon at the end of a sentence to
introduce an explanation:

If the three prongs of the suburban
American dream are family, job, and
house, there is a ghostly, under-
discussed consequence: yardwork.

In a year full of big blockbusters and
heavy message films, *Wallace &
Gromit: The Curse of the Were-Rabbit*
offered audiences something
altogether different: pure fun.

The networked information economy
holds out the possibility of reversing
two trends in cultural production
central to the project of control:
concentration and commercialization.

Use a colon to introduce an example:

Writers ought to consider how the
defense- and commercially tied
history of computers has shaped the
thinking encouraged by the design of
the software we use for writing: How
many word processing or webpage
composing software packages do you
know that encourage scribbling,
doodling, or writing outside the
margins?

Use a colon to introduce a list:

I improvised with my equipment:
fashioning together a hook and a line,
making my own harpoons, or
gathering up cast-off pieces of net
from the fishermen.

→ When you put a list at the end of a sentence, punctuate it just as you would any
other list; see pages 550–553.

COLON USE 3
USING COLONS TO LINK TWO
SENTENCES

→ Use colons to link sentences only when the sentences meet the criteria to the right; for other cases, join sentences using the punctuation described on pages 532–535 and 567.

WHEN THE SECOND SENTENCE EXPLAINS OR SUMMARIZES THE FIRST

If you are joining two sentences where you could lead into the second sentence with *for example* or *that is*, use a colon between the two:

Her illness confined her to a sofa, and so she did the one thing she could think to do on a sofa: She started writing.

There's a reason that freedom of the press was enumerated in the First Amendment: It's more fundamental to our liberty than even guns.

The late nineteenth century witnessed a dramatic increase of women doctors in the United States: Their numbers rose from 200 or fewer in 1860 to 2,423 in 1880 to more than 7,000 by 1900.

It is the style of some journals—and the preference of some teachers—that the sentence following the colon start with a capital letter.

WHEN THE SECOND SENTENCE IS A QUOTATION

If you use a sentence to introduce a quotation, use a colon between them:

In order to write today's novel, movie, or song, I need to use and rework existing cultural forms, such as story lines and twists. This characteristic is known to economists as the "on the shoulders of giants" effect, recalling a statement attributed to Isaac Newton: "If I have seen farther it is because I stand on the shoulders of giants."

PARENTHESES
have four main uses.

1

USING PARENTHESES TO EXPLAIN ABBREVIATIONS

To learn how to use parentheses in a sentence like the following—

Technobabe Times (TBT) produces our campus's feminist newspaper.

Burning Man participants who wish to bring motorized art cars or mutant vehicles must submit their designs in advance to the event's own "Department of Mutant Vehicles" (DMV) for approval.

Nevertheless, the NRA (National Restaurant Association) has vehemently opposed any rise in the minimum wage.

→ GO TO PAGE 576.

2

USING PARENTHESES FOR NUMBERS IN LISTS

To learn how to use parentheses in a sentence like the following—

The steps are (1) punctuate, (2) capitalize, (3) proofread.

Writer John Hodgman's steps for winning a fight are (1) always make eye contact, (2) go ahead and use henchmen, (3) run lots of attack ads.

If you want to get over your fear of clowns, (1) make a list of why you are afraid of clowns, (2) sort items on the list into rational and irrational fears, (3) work your way down the list until all your fears are in the irrational category, (4) stop being afraid.

→ GO TO PAGE 577.

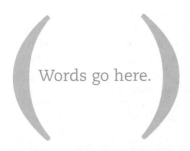
Words go here.

3

USING PARENTHESES FOR IN-TEXT CITATIONS

To learn how to use parentheses to refer to a source in your writing—

Bronson (1950) notes that since their muscles are so flexible, cats seem to bounce when they fall rather than break any bones (p. 32).

"Whatever is profound loves masks; what is most profound even hates image and parable" (Nietzsche 50).

→ GO TO PAGE 578.

4

USING PARENTHESES TO ADD INFORMATION

To learn how to use parentheses in a sentence like the following—

According to Clara Pinto-Correia, some tombs were even outfitted with toilet facilities for the *ka* (soul).

Anything that you include in your paper that is not from you (or from the piece of literature with which you are working) is considered *a secondary source.*

Fundamentally, a *ragú* is an equation involving a solid (meat) and a liquid (broth or wine), plus a slow heat, until you reach a result that is neither solid nor liquid.

→ GO TO PAGE 579.

PARENTHESES USE 1

USING PARENTHESES TO EXPLAIN ABBREVIATIONS

Through use, long titles—of organizations, laws, and objects—often get abbreviated into acronyms. Acronyms are usually composed of the first letters of the title's main words, as *United States of America* is abbreviated USA.

If you are writing about something that has an acronym, don't assume that all your readers will know the acronym. The first time you mention the organization, law, or object, put the acronym in parentheses following the full name. After that, use the acronym:

The builders closely followed the Americans with Disabilites Act (ADA) when they constructed the entry to the building; the ADA requires that all buildings be accessible to people with a range of abilities.

Depending on the species of plant and the level of volatile organic compounds (VOC) present in your house, a plant for every ten square feet should provide adequate air filtration. Plants such as English ivy and philodendrons do an excellent job of absorbing VOCs.

San Francisco's Museum of the African Diaspora (MoAD) has a different goal than many other museums: The staff of MoAD work to put together exhibitions that represent the global impact of Africans—in South America, Central America, Europe, and Asia.

Technobabe Times (TBT) is our campus feminist newspaper. Some people are bothered by the "babe" in our title, but we who work with TBT understand it as a way to take back good words that have been given unfortunate meanings.

TIP: INTRODUCING ACRONYMS

There are other acceptable punctuation strategies for introducing acronyms:

The basic genre that World of Warcraft belongs to is called the massively multiplayer online game, or M.M.O.

The habits of the U.S. Postal Service support this new style of abbreviation: The USPS requests that we abbreviate state names with only two letters and no period.

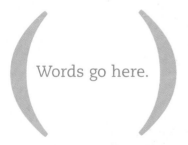

Words go here.

PARENTHESES USE 2

USING PARENTHESES FOR NUMBERS IN LISTS

If you are including a numbered list in your writing, use parentheses to indicate the steps:

The steps for checking writing that you think is done are (1) edit for readability, (2) check spelling, (3) check grammar, (4) proofread.

The networked information economy improves the practical capacities of individuals along three dimensions: (1) It improves their capacity to do more for and by themselves; (2) it enhances their capacity to do more in loose commonality with others, without being constrained to organize their relationship through a price system or in traditional hierarchical models of social and economic organization; and (3) it improves the capacity of individuals to do more in formal organizations that operate outside the market sphere.

Note the punctuation above: If the steps are short, put a comma before each number; otherwise, put a semicolon.

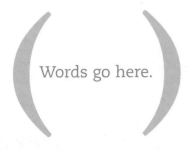

Words go here.

PARENTHESES USE 3

USING PARENTHESES FOR IN-TEXT CITATIONS

Readers of academic research writing expect—whenever a writer quotes another's words—that the writer will give readers the information they need to find those words in the original source. One part of providing this information is to give the name of the author being quoted as well as the number of the page from which the quoted words come (readers can then look to the list of works cited at the end of the essay to find the biblio-graphic information that will help them find the cited work):

In Carruther's argument, a sacred book is given a bejeweled cover to signify to readers that one's memory, growing out of the book, was "a storehouse, a treasure-chest, a vessel, into which the jewels, coins, fruits, and flowers of text are placed" (246). But, by the twelfth century, for those who could not afford treasure chests, the same books could also appear in "cheap and decorative binding" (Foot 118).

Notice that, if the author's name is included as part of a sentence, it is not noted in the parentheses; if the author's name is not included, then it is put in the parentheses along with the page number.

To be an academic writer yourself, you need to learn these conventions.

→ The example above is for the MLA cita-tion style, about which there is more on pages 360–403. For the APA style, see pages 426–452.

Words go here.

PARENTHESES USE 4

USING PARENTHESES TO ADD INFORMATION

You can use parentheses to insert comments or additional information into a sentence. When you do this, you are adding **parenthetical remarks** to the sentence. Many writers use this strategy to add humor to a sentence:

Sometimes in the morning Mrs. Murrow asks me if I heard the cobras singing during the night. I have never been able to answer in the affirmative, because in spite of her description ("like a silver coin falling against a rock"), I have no clear idea of what to listen for.

This afternoon, Johnny Depp is wearing a white undershirt tucked into gray tweed slacks hiked a tad too high (in the style of certain retirement-aged Italian gentlemen).

You can also use parenthetical information to add dates, definitions, a URL, or anything else you think will help readers understand:

Katherine Dunham's dance piece "Southland" (1951), which was a protest against lynching and depicted a lynching on stage, created a lot of controversy in America.

Traditionally, a hysterectomy (removal of the uterus) was the primary way to treat fibroids, and it remains the only permanent cure.

"I'm not an ice cream guy," says Jim Baxter, the technologist behind the design of the MooBella vending machine (www.moobella.com), which churns out a 4.5-ounce cup of ice cream in 45 seconds.

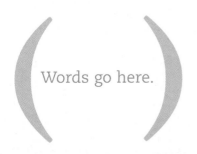

Words go here.

DASHES
have four main uses.

1

USING A DASH TO EMPHASIZE INFORMATION AT THE END OF A SENTENCE

Sometimes writers want to put particular emphasis on a word or phrase. Should you choose to do this, using a dash to set off a word or phrase at the end of a sentence helps to emphasize that word or phrase:

I stood in my empty room. In place of the bed was—shame?

She danced a bit by herself in the corner to a wailing Brenda Lee record, but it was obvious she couldn't dance—she had the white girl's embarrassing habit of brandishing an invisible tambourine.

One woman whispered something to her friend, who responded to the whisper by twisting around in her chair to peer at me—the pair were so unsubtle that I tossed them a decidedly impertinent wave.

2

USING DASHES TO INDICATE A RESTATEMENT OR A CHANGE IN TONE

To make writing sound conversational, and to add particular emphasis to phrases that might otherwise sound out of place because of the explanation or emotion they provide, writers will use dashes:

The wall-to-wall carpet—roughly the color of brains—was frayed and worn.

Sisters in black habits and a doctor in white—no, there were two doctors—hurried among those who waited.

It dawned on him that he knew plenty of Americans—he was one himself—who held apparently contradictory beliefs, such as faith in both medicine and prayer.

"The Making of Americans" was a work that Stein evidently had to get out of her system—almost like a person having to vomit—before she could become Gertrude Stein as we know her.

3

USING DASHES TO SET OFF EXPLANATORY INFORMATION

Sometimes writers use dashes to put more emphasis on infomation, which could also be set off by commas:

A jay can store up to five acorns—depending on their size and his—in his throat.

When the explanatory information itself contains commas, writers use dashes instead of commas to set off the information so that readers will have no confusion:

Markets full of live animals—rabbits, chickens, lambs, and cows—were part of our lives.

Here is the sentence with commas instead of dashes; notice that you have to tease apart the commas to decide what is explanatory and what is not:

Markets full of live animals, rabbits, chickens, lambs, and cows, were part of our lives.

4

USING DASHES TO SHOW HESITATION IN SPEECH

When writers are transcribing speech or are trying to emulate speech for readers, they use dashes to show where a speaker has hesitated or changed direction in mid-sentence:

On the witness stand, Michael Eisner responded to a lawyer's question by saying, "I think you're getting into an area that—that—I just want to say that this is ill-advised...."

TIPS: **THE FINE POINT OF DASHES**

- You can use dashes to give a slowed-down, conversational tone to your writing, but they can also make writing seem very informal. If you use dashes frequently, they can break up the flow of writing so much that readers have trouble following.

- Keep in mind these differences between hyphens and dashes: hyphens are shorter than dashes, and hyphens are used in between words and parts of words; dashes are used between phrases and sentences.

[BRACKETS]
have two main uses.

1

USING BRACKETS INSIDE PARENTHETICAL COMMENTS

Sometimes writers need to put parenthetical information inside other parenthetical information. When this is the case, the convention is to put the embedded information inside brackets instead of inside another set of parentheses:

(For further discussion, see Abdo [2000] and Burgat [2003].)

Khubz marquq (also called *lavash tannour* [mountain bread]) is a flat bread with a slightly tangy taste.

2

USING BRACKETS TO INSERT INFORMATION INTO A QUOTATION

Anytime writers use the words of someone else, the words are removed from their full context; sometimes, then, writers have to fill in some information or change a few words so that readers can understand the quotation.

If writers need to do this in the middle of a quotation, the convention is to put the changed or added information inside brackets so that readers can see where the original has been changed. For example, here are words as they were originally spoken by Anthony B. Pinn, a professor of Humanities and Religion at Rice University in Houston:

What you get with mega-churches is a kind of caricature of the social gospel thrust. In terms of the hard issue of social justice, such churches tend to be theology-lite.

Here is how a magazine article quoted those words, in order to fit them to its needs:

What you get with mega-churches is a...caricature of the social gospel thrust. In terms of...social justice, [they] tend to be theology-lite.

→ If you need to leave words out of quotations, use ellipses, a punctuation mark explained on pages 588–589, to show the omissions.

■ ■ ■

To figure out whether you need to add or modify the information in a quotation, ask yourself if your readers will understand a quotation exactly as it is written. If not, modify the quotation in the smallest way you can while still helping your readers.

For example, imagine that the words in brackets below contained someone's name (which was in the original quotation); would the quotation make sense?

In Field's most recent novel, *The Lawyer's Tale*, Harry Cain asks his private eye to dig up dirt on an opponent. Harry "didn't want to commit extortion if he could avoid it," Fields writes. "But he had to get a message to [the opponent] that would change his mind."

Here is a quotation in which the bracketed words are used to explain a term that comes from the British educational system:

Miss Lee reports that "the other day a child in the reception class [kindergarten] in Myatt Gardens told me a story about September 11."

Without the bracketed information, would you have known what a *reception class* is?

With quotations, then, notice how you can use brackets to replace a term that readers might not know with familiar information or to add explanatory information.

HY▨▨▨ PHENS have three main uses.

1

USING HYPHENS TO BREAK WORDS AT THE END OF LINES

If you are using a typewriter, you need to know about hyphens in order to fit part of a word at the end of a line when you run out of space for the whole word. Watch the lines as you type them, and—if you need to break a word—break if after a syllable and put a hyphen at the end of the line. (If you are unsure, check a dictionary to learn where the syllables break in a word.)

Clarkston High School now has students from more than 50 countries.

Poets use hyphens to create wordplay:

when sunsnap
sheet-
back-
boys-
slip
pinned
to shade

If you are writing with a word processing program on a computer, the computer will automatically break words at syllables and insert hyphens at the end of lines.

2

USING HYPHENS FOR CLARITY

A precise reader sees considerable difference between these two sentences:

He was a big city man.

He was a big-city man.

The first is about a man from the city who is big; the second is about a man from a big city. When using two words as an adjective, put a hyphen between them if you wonder whether others will read your words as you intend.

■ ■ ■

When you use the prefixes *re-*, *anti-*, and *pre-* with verbs, use a hyphen between the prefix and the verb if, without the hyphen, a different meaning is made.

I resent her letter.

I re-sent her letter.

■ ■ ■

Use hyphens if the first word of a compound word you are making begins with the same letter as the second:

doll-like   **non-native**

3

USING HYPHENS IN COMPOUND WORDS

Compound words are made when writers put together any two (or more) other words to make one new word:

Operating on an off-the-shelf Linux-based computer, MooBella's fresh-on-the-spot system changes the blueprint of traditional ice-cream vending machines, which spit out months-old bars.

In the above sentence, the compound words are *off-the-shelf*, *Linux-based*, *fresh-on-the-spot*, *blueprint*, *ice-cream*, and *months-old*.

The longer a compound word has been in use, the more likely it won't have a hyphen in it (think of *bathtub*, *earthquake*, *bookshelf*, or *website*); conversely, the newest compound words will most likely have hyphens in them. (Some writers who want to sound cool make up compound words; you'll find new compound words in blogs and science fiction writing.)

■ ■ ■

Some compound words, however, do conventionally keep their hyphens:

In Rochester, Dr. Bonnez's solution was to approach veterinarians treating dairy cows, which grow grapefruit-sized warts loaded with virus. He still has a block of 20-year-old cow warts in his freezer.

When compound words are used as adjectives before nouns—such as **20-year-old** and **grapefruit-sized** above or in the term **nineteenth-century art**—they tend to be hyphenated.

To be safest, check a dictionary: Because our uses of compound words are time-sensitive, it is wise to check whether a compound word is in the dictionary. If you cannot find the word in a dictionary, put hyphens in it.

■ ■ ■

When you write out numbers between 21 and 99, a hyphen is conventional:

twenty-three

one hundred twenty-three

one thousand two hundred and ninety-four

> **TIP: U.S. HYPHENS**
> In the United States, it is customary **not** to put spaces around hyphens or dashes: write **nineteenth-century**, *not* **nineteenth - century**.

SLASH / SLASHES
have three main uses.

1

USING SLASHES IN PAIRED TERMS

There are some terms in English that are hard to separate:

on/off switch	and/or
a pass/fail class	yes/no
an either/or situation	

It is the preferred convention for writing in Humanities disciplines **not** to use such terms, but sometimes a slash is the only way to give readers the sense you intend:

If we consider all writing as a form of quotation—as blogs invariably include a mix of "original" text and text copied from other weblogs or sites—students (and teachers) learn to question the "original"/"copied" dichotomy.

If you need to use a slash to indicate two terms that are inseparably bound together, do not put spaces on either side of the slash.

■ ■ ■

A sentence like the following—

Each person brought his own tent and sleeping bag.

—implies there were only male campers present. Many writers have recognized that such sexist choices in writing affect women readers negatively—but English does not have a singular pronoun that includes both women and men. How then should you work with such a sentence?

The conventions that have emerged say not to use **he/she** or **he or she** because these are awkward solutions:

Each person brought his/her own tent and sleeping bag.

Each person brought her or his own tent and sleeping bag.

Instead, you can make the subject of the sentence plural (and then adjust the verb and objects) or modify the sentence to do away with the problem:

The campers brought their own tents and sleeping bags.

Each camper was responsible for bringing a tent and a sleeping bag for personal use.

→ See pages 256–257 for more on avoiding sexist writing.

2

USING SLASHES TO INDICATE LINE BREAKS IN POEMS YOU ARE QUOTING

Poets consider carefully where to stop one line of a poem and start another: Their choices shape how readers respond. Because these line breaks matter, be careful to reproduce line breaks when you quote poems.

In the MLA style, this is easy to do if you are quoting four or more lines of the poem: Reproduce the lines exactly as they appear on the page.

→ See pages 318 and 411 for quoting four or more lines in MLA style.

If, however, you need to quote three or fewer lines, the following example shows the convention. Here are lines from a poem by Charles Simic:

**Like the sound of eyebrows
Raised by a villain
In a silent movie.**

Here is a quotation using those lines:

Simic can create striking metaphors, as in these lines from "The Wooden Toy," where the toy is quiet, "Like the sound of eyebrows / Raised by a villain / In a silent movie."

Note that there is a space on either side of each slash.

3

USING SLASHES WITH DATES AND FRACTIONS

DATES

In informal and business writing in the United States, the convention is to write dates with slashes, giving the month, day, and year:

11/10/56   10/31/2009

Note that there are no spaces around the slashes, and that you can use two or four digits for the year. In Europe, the day comes before the year, which can lead to confusion in cross-continent communication; if you are corresponding with someone from a European country, you can avoid confusion if you use the form for dates expected in academic and other formal writing:

November 10, 1956

October 31, 2009

FRACTIONS

Put a slash between the two numbers of a fraction:

1/2   2/3   15/16

There are no spaces between the numbers and the slash.

ELLIPSES…
have two main uses.

1

USING ELLIPSES TO SHOW A PAUSE OR AN INTERRUPTION IN SPEECH THAT YOU ARE QUOTING

Because readers cannot hear words that you quote but can only see your transcription of them on a page, use ellipses to signal, visually, where someone you are quoting paused:

In an interview with Powells.com's Dave Weich, chef and writer Anthony Bourdain said: "I knew already that the best meal in the world, the perfect meal, is very rarely the most sophisticated or expensive one.... Context and memory play powerful roles in all the truly great meals in one's life."

In contexts less formal than the academic one, writers sometimes use ellipses to show hesitation or surprise; the following sentence, for example, comes from a science magazine for general audiences:

In the grand tradition of linking raunchy music with irresponsible sexual activity comes a new study touting a link between sexual risk taking and listening to...gospel music.

→ You can also use dashes to show hesitation in speech that you are quoting; see page 581.

2

USING ELLIPSES TO SHOW THAT YOU HAVE OMITTED WORDS FROM A QUOTATION

IN A PROSE QUOTATION

If you need to drop words from a sentence you are quoting, use ellipses.

Here are George Lucas's original words from an interview:

> When I was younger, I had a collection of history books that I was addicted to, a whole series about famous people in history from Ancient Greece and Alexander the Great, up to the Civil War—the Monitor and the Merrimac. I think they were called "Landmark" books, and I collected a whole library of them. I used to love to read those books. It started me on a lifelong love of history.

Here is one way to quote those words:

> When I was younger, I had a collection of history books that I was addicted to, a whole series about famous people in history from Ancient Greece and Alexander the Great, up to the Civil War [...]. I collected a whole library of them. I used to love to read those books. It started me on a lifelong love of history.

By putting the ellipsis inside brackets, you show that you have removed words; an ellipsis alone would indicate that the speaker or writer had paused in the original. (You do not need to use an ellipsis if you are taking words from the beginning or end of someone's words.)

IN A QUOTATION OF POETRY

Sometimes when you are quoting poetry, you need to emphasize several lines while omitting others. If you ever need to quote a passage from which you must drop one or more lines, use a whole line of ellipses to show where you have dropped the lines.

In "Elegy for Thelonius," Yusef Komunyakaa brings Thelonius Monk back to life:

> damn the alley cat
> wailing a muted dirge
> off Lenox Ave.
> Thelonious is dead.
> ....
>
> Let's go to Minton's
> & play "modern malice"
> till daybreak. Lord,
> there's Thelonious
> wearing that old funky hat
> pulled down over his eyes.

QUOTATION MARKS
have six main uses.

1

USING QUOTATION MARKS FOR TITLES OF SHORT WORKS

For sentences like the following—

The radio is playing The Romantics' "That's What I Like About You."

→ GO TO PAGE 592.

2

USING QUOTATION MARKS TO INDICATE YOU ARE USING A WORD AS A WORD

For sentences like the following—

And by "malignant" and "addictive" I do not mean evil or hypnotizing.

→ GO TO PAGE 593.

5

USING QUOTATION MARKS TO INDICATE DIRECT QUOTATION

For sentences like the following—

David Foster Wallace believes that "fiction writers as a species tend to be oglers" (21).

→ GO TO PAGE 596.

6

USING QUOTATION MARKS TO INDICATE SPEECH

For sentences like the following—

**The woman at Macy's asked me, "Would you be interested in full-time elf or evening and weekend elf?"
I said, "Full-time elf."**

→ GO TO PAGE 597.

Words go here.

3

USING QUOTATION MARKS TO INDICATE TECHNICAL TERMS AND WORDS FROM OTHER LANGUAGES

For sentences like the following—

"Malar" means relating to the cheek.

The pub's advertisement promised "ceol agus craic," which, as we happily found out, means "music and good times."

→ GO TO PAGE 594.

4

USING QUOTATION MARKS TO SHOW IRONY

For sentences like the following—

To quantify the "benefit" side of the equation, a dollar amount is assigned to each saved human's life.

Barbies are marked as "ethnic," or foreign, only to the extent that they differ from the original doll.

→ GO TO PAGE 595.

QUOTATION MARKS USE 1

USING QUOTATION MARKS FOR
TITLES OF SHORT WORKS

Use quotation marks to indicate the name of a show or exhibition—

"Goya's Last Works," at the Frick, isn't large, but neither are grenades.

—the titles of poems and musical pieces—

I had to study why Van Halen moved (certain) people as much as the Beatles, but, folks, they did, in the same way Whitman did. "Hot For Teacher" is "Song of Myself" with crappier words but much better lead guitar.

—and the titles of essays—

"The Making of Americans" was a work that Stein evidently had to get out of her system—almost like a person having to vomit—before she could become Gertrude Stein as we know her.

—or the titles of almost any work that is not book length.

→ Information on how to indicate the titles of book-length works is on page 607.

Words go here.

QUOTATION MARKS USE 2

USING QUOTATION MARKS TO
INDICATE YOU ARE USING A WORD
AS A WORD

Sometimes, writers need to refer to a word as a word. If ever you need to do this, put quotation marks around the word:

"Doctor" comes from the Latin word *docere*, "to teach."

The term "preservation" usually comes up in reference to buildings, not to the graffiti that covers them.

His student asked him how to use "until" according to English conventions.

Franziska often spews repetitive insults using the word "fool."

→ The use of quotation marks for this function goes back to the days of typewriters. With computers, italics can replace quotation marks; see page 607 on using italics.

→ Because quotation marks are almost always woven with other punctuation, it is tricky to use them as academic readers and readers of published work expect. On pages 598–599 we go over the little but important details of using quotation marks in expected ways.

Words go here.

QUOTATION MARKS USE 3

USING QUOTATION MARKS TO INDICATE TECHNICAL TERMS AND WORDS FROM OTHER LANGUAGES

Use quotation marks to indicate technical terms and words from other languages:

Ringed seals, ivory gulls, and other birds and mammals whose lives are ice-oriented are called "pagophylic."

During the thirteenth century, the Dutch instituted a "wind brief," a tax paid to the lord or king over whose fields the wind blew before reaching a mill.

Consider, for example, a form of creativity that seems strange to many Americans but that is inescapable within Japanese culture: "manga," or comics.

As I explain in the pages that follow, we come from a tradition of "free culture"—not "free" as in "free beer" (to borrow a phrase from the founder of the free software movement), but "free" as in "free speech," "free markets," "free trade," "free enterprise," "free will," and "free elections."

→ The use of quotation marks for this function goes back to the days of typewriters. With computers, italics can replace quotation marks; see page 607 on using italics.

→ Because quotation marks are almost always woven with other punctuation, it is tricky to use them as academic readers and readers of published work expect. On pages 598–599 we go over the little but important details of using quotation marks in expected ways.

" Words go here. "

QUOTATION MARKS USE 4

USING QUOTATION MARKS TO SHOW IRONY

Writers sometimes want to distance themselves from words: They need to use particular words, as in the examples below, but want to show that they don't agree with the word choice. In such cases, writers can put quotation marks around the words.

Look, for example, at how novelist Janet Frame, in her autobiography, uses quotation marks to let readers know how she feels about the sincerity of the women who visited her mother after her sister's death:

They sat patting and arranging their "permanent" waves.

Here are sentences from scientists commenting on how others have characterized scientific practice:

How can an experiment be "wrong"?

The problem I am posing here is not one of individual morality, of individual scientists doing "dirty" work or "clean" work; rather, the problem is institutional.

In each case, the quotation marks let readers know that the writers question the characterizations of experiments and other scientific work contained in the punctuated words.

→ Because quotation marks are almost always woven with other punctuation, it is tricky to use them as academic readers and readers of published work expect. On pages 598–599 we go over the little but important details of using quotation marks in expected ways.

Words go here.

QUOTATION MARKS USE 5

USING QUOTATION MARKS TO INDICATE DIRECT QUOTATION

Over the centuries, conventions have developed in different languages for indicating to readers that writers are quoting the words of others. In English, quotation marks—placed on either side of the words being quoted—have become the expected way of doing this, even if a writer is quoting only one word from someone else:

Fukasawa's approach to designing electronic gadgets, based on over 25 years' experience, has been called "anti-technical" because it dispenses with unnecessary buttons, displays, and other high-tech signifiers.

A comparison to make a point is Sarah Vowell's claim that "Going to Ford's Theatre to watch the play is like going to Hooter's for the food."

At the time the Wright brothers invented the airplane, American law held that a property owner owned not just the surface of his land, but all the land below, down to the center of the earth, and all the space above, to "an indefinite extent, upwards."

→ Because quotation marks are almost always woven with other punctuation, it is tricky to use them as academic readers expect. On pages 598–599 we go over the details of using quotation marks in expected ways.

" Words go here. "

QUOTATION MARKS USE 6
USING QUOTATION MARKS TO INDICATE SPEECH

When you wish to suggest to your readers that the words you are writing were spoken out loud by someone else, quotation marks are the customary strategy in English:

"He was going to write the definitive book on leeches," she says. "It was his primary ambition in life."

"Reading ability is a proxy for intelligence in American culture," said Dr. Sally E. Shaywitz of Yale University School of Medicine, a pediatrician who is an expert on dyslexia.

"You have to listen to music before you go out on a mission and get real hyped," says Sgt. Junelle Daniels, a twenty-five-year-old generator mechanic from Miami who is gearing up for a second deployment to Iraq. "If not, you start thinking, 'What if? What if this happens? What if that happens?' You start to get the fear."

Note that indicating speech is sometimes the same as indicating a direct quotation.

→ Because quotation marks are almost always woven with other punctuation, it is tricky to use them as academic readers and readers of published work expect. On pages 598–599 we go over the little but important details of using quotation marks in expected ways.

→ In academic writing, any time you quote someone else, the expectation is that you will give a source of the quotation; see pages 308–350 for how to do this.

Words go here.

USING QUOTATION MARKS AND OTHER PUNCTUATION IN EXPECTED WAYS TO INCLUDE OTHERS' WORDS IN YOUR WRITING

To quote others' words in the patterns that readers of academic and other formal texts expect, pay close attention to these details in the examples below:

- The use of a comma or period at the end of the quotation. (And note that, whether a comma or period is used, it is included inside the quotation mark.)
- The capitalization of the words at the beginning of the quotation

THE PATTERN	QUOTING A COMPLETE SENTENCE
AT THE BEGINNING OF YOUR WRITING	"Most of what we teach is wrong," said Johndan Johnson-Eilola.
IN THE MIDDLE OF YOUR WRITING	Johndan Johnson-Eilola said, "Most of what we teach is wrong," while speaking at a recent conference.
AT THE END OF YOUR WRITING	Johndan Johnson-Eilola said, "Most of what we teach is wrong."
WITH IN-TEXT CITATION (MLA STYLE)	Johndan Johnson-Eilola said, "Most of what we teach is wrong" (77).

→ For more on in-text citations, see pages 350–359 for MLA style; pages 420–425 for APA style; page 453 for CSE style; page 459 for CMS style.

→ If your quotation will take up more than four lines in your paper, use different conventions for embedding it in an academic paper; see page 318.

→ See page 320 for help with choosing the words to use to introduce or explain the words you are quoting.

QUOTING PARTS OF A SENTENCE

"A natural sense of geometry" is innate in babies, argues cognitive psychologist Elizabeth Spelke.

All babies have "a natural sense of geometry," argues cognitive psychologist Elizabeth Spelke.

Cognitive psychologist Elizabeth Spelke argues that all babies have "a natural sense of geometry."

All babies have "a natural sense of geometry," argues cognitive psychologist Elizabeth Spelke (qtd. in Talbot 92).

If you are quoting only part of a sentence, don't capitalize the first word, unless the quoted words start your sentence.

Note also that the quoted words in these examples do not have commas before them.

QUOTING A SENTENCE ENDING WITH A QUESTION MARK OR EXCLAMATION POINT

"Why did wealth and power become distributed as they are now, rather than in some other way?" Jared Diamond asks at the beginning of his book.

Jared Diamond asks, "Why did wealth and power become distributed as they are now, rather than in some other way?" at the beginning of his book.

At the beginning of his book, Jared Diamond asks, "Why did wealth and power become distributed as they are now, rather than in some other way?"

"Why did wealth and power become distributed as they are now, rather than in some other way?" Jared Diamond asks at the beginning of his book (15).

NOTE: If you are quoting a sentence that ends with an exclamation point, the punctuation pattern is the same as when the sentence ends with a question mark.

APOSTROPHES
have three main uses.

1

USING APOSTROPHES TO MAKE PLURALS OF CERTAIN KINDS OF WORDS

Use an apostrophe to make plurals of lowercase letters; if you do not use an apostrophe, readers might confuse the plural with a word or think you have made a mistake:

Is it "cross your is and dot your ts," or is it the other way around?

Is it "cross your i's and dot your t's," or is it the other way around?

Use an apostrophe to make plurals of uppercase letters if the addition of an **-s** without an apostrophe would make a word:

She earned As throughout school but could never rise above an entry-level position.

She earned A's throughout school but could never rise above an entry-level position.

Otherwise:

He never earned higher than Cs or Ds in school, yet he's a well-known newscaster.

2

USING APOSTROPHES TO MAKE CONTRACTIONS

Use apostrophes to show where letters have been taken out of a contraction:

I am	=	I'm
I would	=	I'd
you are	=	you're
she is	=	she's
he is	=	he's
it is	=	it's
we are	=	we're
we have	=	we've
they are	=	they're
do not	=	don't
did not	=	didn't
cannot	=	can't

One odd pattern to learn:

will not	=	won't

I'm sure that we didn't leave the window open, but shouldn't we go back and check?

We've got time; he won't expect us to arrive until late.

3

USING APOSTROPHES TO MAKE POSSESSIVES

When readers see a word ending with an apostrophe and the letter **s**, they will usually assume that the word is in the possessive case.

This blog's underlying message is "Stop Buying Crap."

Discovery Channel's new reality television show is *Last One Standing*.

The New Mexico Spaceport Authority's design for Spaceport America—the world's first public launching and landing site for space vehicles—includes a passenger terminal and a hangar big enough for seven craft.

→ To learn more about the possessive case, see page 501.

TIP: LEARN THE DIFFERENCE BETWEEN *it's* AND *its*

it's = it is
its = the possessive form of the pronoun it

It's going to rain. (It is going to rain.)

Democracy can be said to be its own biggest threat. (*its* is a stand-in for *democracy's*)

PERIODS
have two main uses.

1

USING PERIODS WITH SOME ABBREVIATIONS

Abbreviations are shortenings of words:

Mon.	Mr.	Jr.	Co.
etc.	Inc.	Dr.	St.

are shortenings of

Monday, Mister, Junior, Company,

etcetera, Incorporated, Doctor, Street

These abbreviations are made of the first letter of the word and the last letter, or are truncated versions of the words (*Mon.* for *Monday* or *Co.* for *Company*). When an abbreviation is made this way, it will most likely have a period after it.

■ ■ ■

When you abbreviate a name—

John Fitzgerald Kennedy

Mary Francis Kennedy Fisher

—the custom is to use a period:

John F. Kennedy

M. F. K. Fisher

■ ■ ■

Some abbreviations—

a.m.   r.s.v.p.   U.N.I.C.E.F.

—are the first letters of word series:

ante meridiem (Latin for *before noon*)

respondez, s'il vous plait (French for *Please respond*)

United Nations International Children's Emergency Fund

When an abbreviation is made this way, it is becoming common not to use periods:

am   rsvp   UNICEF

The U.S. Postal Service supports this; the USPS requests that we abbreviate state names this way:

MI   CA   RI   AK

If you have any hesitations about whether to use periods in an abbreviation, check your dictionary.

■ ■ ■

If an abbreviation is of names—

W. J. T. Mitchell

—put a space after each period. If an abbreviation is of other words, do not put spaces after the periods.

2

USING PERIODS TO END SENTENCES THAT MAKE STATEMENTS OR COMMANDS

There are four kinds of sentences (➜ pages 468–469); two of them, declarative and imperative sentences, conventionally are indicated by ending with periods.

These are declarative sentences, which make statements:

Water buffalo do not exist in Africa.

Smaller species of exploding ants are more likely to combust than larger ones.

Neil Burger's movie *The Illusionist*, based on a short story by Steven Millhauser, is a delicate film, almost a fairy tale.

Though armed with a sharp, venom-coated barb on their tail, stingrays use the weapon only defensively, and attacks on humans are extremely rare.

These are imperative sentences, which make commands:

Mix the sliced pears and walnuts together.

Fasten your seat belt by sliding the metal notch into the buckle.

Use a period after most abbreviations.

TIP: **THE FINE POINTS OF USING PERIODS**

• If a sentence ends with an abbreviation, do not put another period at the end of the sentence; let the abbreviation's period end the sentence:

The basic genre that World of Warcraft belongs to is called the massively multiplayer online game, or M.M.O.

• If you put a complete sentence inside parentheses, end the sentence with a period *inside* the parentheses.

She told me to walk as far as the corner. (At least, I think that's what she said.)

Do not put such parenthetical comments within other sentences; the example below is not customary usage in formal writing:

She told me (At least, I think that's what she said.) to walk as far as the corner.

If parentheses contain less than a complete sentence, do not give them any end punctuation:

The toxins are mostly made up of 5-nucleotidase and phospho-diesterase, which are cytotoxins (which kill cells and tissue) and result in local necrosis (tissue death).

➜ Using periods with quotation marks requires careful attention. See pages 598–599.

QUESTION MARKS ?
have two main uses.

1

USING QUESTION MARKS TO END SENTENCES THAT ARE QUESTIONS

Of the four functions that sentences can have (→ pages 468–469), asking questions is one; sentences that ask questions are called interrogatory sentences:

What is education?

Have you ever browsed a sperm bank catalog?

You bought the CD or DVD, and that means you own it, right?

If prisons are meant to make troubled men and women into citizens, he wondered, might there be a social cost to bad prison design?

BUT!

The examples above are *direct questions*; there are also *indirect questions*, in which a writer describes someone else asking a question, without direct quotation. *These end with a period, not a question mark:*

I heard her ask whether the mail had arrived.

He asked how the test had gone.

2

USING QUESTION MARKS TO SHOW DOUBT ABOUT DATES AND NUMBERS

Ir you have doubts about a date or quantity, or if your sources describe doubt about a date or quantity, put *(?)* after the date or quantity.

In this photograph, Reynolds is seen with his mother in 1928 (?).

Witness reports put the number of people trapped in the building at 180 (?).

→ Using question marks with quotation marks requires careful attention. See pages 598–599.

EXCLAMATION POINTS !
have one main use.

1

USING EXCLAMATION POINTS TO INDICATE TO READERS THAT A SENTENCE CARRIES EMOTIONAL WEIGHT

It is customary in written American English to put a single exclamation point after a sentence when the sentence is an exclamation—

Yikes! Oh no!

—a strong command—

Help!

Don't touch that burner!

Don't go beyond the perimeter!

—or is meant by its writer to encourage a strong emotional response in a reader—

Each treehouse is built in two main pieces: the playhouse and the log. The log is a real, old, fallen tree that we hollow out using a chainsaw!

Age is absolutely no barrier in today's world. In fact, some 30 percent of students today are "non-traditional," meaning us, of course! Your age is not an issue unless you choose to make it one; don't!

In academic writing, exclamation points are almost nonexistent because academic writing is meant to appeal primarily to reason. In most other kinds of writing, the exclamation point is also rare, because people who grow up into American English tend to think that exclamation points are a sign of youth or silliness—especially when several sentences in a row have them or when a single sentence ends in many of them.

There are exceptions: In blogs, for example, writers sometimes use them excessively, as a self-conscious indication that they know exclamation points are dangerous but still potent:

It's not that we know we aren't writing well—and so tack on some exclamations!!!—it's that we know what we're saying doesn't deserve to be written at all.

→ Using exclamation points with quotation marks requires careful attention. See pages 598–599.

→ Many interjections use exclamation points. See page 496.

MECHANICS

In academic writing, convention determines spelling, capitalization, italicizing and underlining, and abbreviations and numbers. When you attend to these details of writing (which you should do as the last step of writing), you make few decisions; instead, you follow the conventions of English writing that have developed over time.

In the next pages, we discuss the following aspects of mechanics:

- using italics and underlining
- spelling
- capitalizing
- abbreviating
- using numbers

USING ITALICS AND UNDERLINING

Italic type

Italic type was developed during the Italian Renaissance, and over time, those who used printing presses developed specific uses for it.

Until computers were developed, those who didn't have access to printing presses but who instead used typewriters—like most college students—could not use italic type. A convention developed to use underlining wherever a printer would use italics.

If you cannot use italics as we discuss below, use underlining.

FOR THE TITLES OF BOOKS AND OTHER LONG PUBLICATIONS

Use italics for the titles of books, magazines, journals, newspapers, websites, feature films, radio and television shows, book-length poems, comic strips, plays, operas and other musical performances, ballets and other dance performances, paintings, sculptures, pamphlets, and bulletins.

Marilyn's book will be titled *The Animal Who Writes*.

***Little Nemo* was a popular comic strip of the early twentieth century.**

(Quotation marks are used for shorter publications; see page 592.)

FOR FOREIGN TERMS

The environmental studies professor, who is from Pakistan, was first educated in a *madrassah*, or Muslim school.

China is shifting resources away from state-directed scientific research into initiatives designed to stimulate *zizhi chuangxin* (indigenous innovation).

You do not need to italicize commonly used foreign expressions and abbreviations:

cum laude, e.g., et al., ex officio, i.e., in vitro, vice versa, vis-à-vis

FOR SCIENTIFIC NAMES IN LATIN

It is conventional to put the Latin names of organisms in italics.

Foot-and-mouth disease (*Aphtae epizooticae*) is a highly contagious and sometimes fatal viral disease of cattle and pigs.

The Bengal Tiger is *Panthera tigris tigris* and the Siberian Tiger is *Panthera tigris altaica*.

FOR REFERRING TO WORDS AS WORDS

When you need to discuss a word in its functions as a word, you can italicize it. (In this case, if you cannot italicize, use quotation marks.)

The English articles are *a, an,* and *the*.

FOR EMPHASIS

Do this sparingly. This kind of visual emphasis works only when it can stand out against large passages that receive no visual emphasis.

Sacks said, "I didn't just care for these patients. I *lived* with these patients."

MECHANICS
SPELLING

In Shakespeare's time, spelling was not standardized: **Been** was spelled **beene**, **bene**, or **bin**—and **Shakespeare** was spelled **Shakspere**, **Shaksper**, **Shakespere**, and **Shackspeare**. As governments grew and required standardized documents—and as printing presses replaced scribes for reproducing documents—people came to expect that a word would be spelled the same way every time it appeared on a page.

In our time, then, it is an expected sign of formal documents that the words are all spelled according to conventions that have developed over time and that are recorded in dictionaries.

SPELLING RULES? CHECK A DICTIONARY!

Spelling is the attempt to put spoken language into consistent patterns on the page, using just the twenty-six characters of the English alphabet. Because English developed out of many different languages, the spelling of a word often results from an attempt in the past to use the English alphabet to translate sounds made in other languages.

English spelling can therefore be vexing, even if your home language is English. There are some spelling rules for English, but all have considerable exceptions and variations, and many people find them confusing.

The best advice we can give you when you are trying to spell a word is to use a dictionary.

USING SPELL CHECKERS

Spell checkers only check spelling; they cannot tell if you are using the wrong word or have made other mistakes.

To use spell checkers well, follow these steps:

1 Use a spell checker after you have a complete draft to catch obvious spelling errors.

2 Use the items listed below under *What spell checkers miss* to find specific kinds of mistakes.

3 Proofread the whole text at least one more time, using any of the strategies we describe on page 465.

WHAT SPELL CHECKERS MISS

- **Incorrect words that are spelled correctly.** In the sentence "He might loose his job," all the words are spelled correctly, but **loose** should be **lose**. The Glossary shows many words that are commonly confused.

- **Homonyms.** *Peace* and *piece* are homonyms: They are words that are spelled differently but sound the same. When writing quickly, it is easy to use a homonym in place of the word you want. The Glossary on pages 616–623 contains some common homonyms.

- **Possessives used as plurals—and vice versa.** If you are writing about more than one dress, it is easy to write **dress's** instead of **dresses**.

→ See page 501 to learn about possessives.

→ See page 500 to learn about plurals.

- **Pronouns that don't match their antecedents.** For example, *If a person wants to write well, you have to write a lot* should be *If you want to write well, you have to write a lot*.

→ See pages 502 and 506 to learn about pronouns and antecedents.

- **Words that are missing.** A spell checker will not catch when you have left a word out of a sentence. Reading your work out loud, slowly, will help you hear if you have left out any words.

- **Misspelling someone's name.** Spell checkers rarely check for proper nouns because there are so many of them. Misspelling the name of an author or major figure about whom you are writing is not only embarrassing, but readers can also interpret this as a sign you were not paying close and careful attention while you were writing. Anytime you use a proper noun, check its spelling by looking up the name in a newspaper, magazine, or biographical dictionary.

CAPITALIZING WORDS

Conventionally, capital letters are used for:

THE FIRST WORDS OF SENTENCES

We must become spies on behalf of justice.

A combination of ego and gin stood between me and my ability to learn from my mistakes.

THE FIRST WORD IN A DIRECT QUOTATION

She said, simply, "No."

Roddy Doyle wrote, "One thing about my life, it has a great soundtrack."

Chris Magnus, Chief of Police in Richmond, California, has said, "There's a mentality among some people that they're living some really violent video game."

DAYS, MONTHS, AND PUBLIC HOLIDAYS

On Tuesday, we'll be home late.

Is spring break in February or March?

My family could celebrate Hanukkah, Christmas, and Kwanzaa.

NAMES OF PEOPLE

Capitalize first and last names, whether you use one or both.

Heidi worked until the early morning.

Li Templeton was my roommate.

Thomas Pynchon begins his novel *Gravity's Rainbow* with the sentence, "A screaming comes across the sky."

NAMES OF CITIES, STATES, AND COUNTRIES

Capitalize these names when they are nouns and when they are adjectives.

My cousins were visiting from San Salvador, El Salvador.

Seattle has changed since I was born there.

Have you ever been to Arkansas?

The Waifs are an Australian band.

NAMES OF ORGANIZATIONS

My brother belonged to Habitat for Humanity.

On the twenty-fifth of May 2007, the Social Democratic Party walked out of Croatian Parliament after being accused of posting videos on YouTube.

"Doctors Without Borders" is the English name for the organization started in France, *Médecins Sans Frontières*.

PROFESSIONAL TITLES

Whether they are spelled out or abbreviated, capitalize all professional titles.

It was Colonel Peacock in the kitchen with the knife.

Dr. Jack operated on my mother.

Professor Yunus won the Nobel Prize.

Surgeon General Joycelyn Elders said, "When hope dies, moral decay can't be far behind."

TITLES OF ARTWORKS

The artworks can be paintings, sculptures, photographs, musical compositions, and songs.

Art historians do not know who posed for *The Mona Lisa*.

I wish I knew all the words to that Mose Allison song "Your Mind Is on Vacation, But Your Mouth Works Overtime."

Many people think Dali's painting *The Persistence of Memory* should be titled *The Limp Watches*.

TITLES OF BOOKS AND OTHER WRITINGS

Arundhati Roy's book, *The God of Small Things*, won the Booker Prize.

"The Moral Equivalent of War" is an essay by William James.

→ See page 592 to learn when to use quotation marks around titles; see page 607 to learn when to italicize titles.

ABBREVIATIONS

TITLES

Dr. and **St.** (**Saint**) are abbreviated before a name but not after.

...said Dr. Robert Cantu.

...said Robert Cantu, a doctor specializing in neurosurgery.

Prof., Sen., Gen., Capt., and other titles can be abbreviated when placed before a full name (i.e., first and last names, or initials and last name) but not before the last name when it is given alone:

Sen. Hattie Wyatt Caraway
Sen. H. W. Caraway
Senator Caraway

Put academic and professional titles— **Sr., Jr., J.D., Ph.D., M.F.A., R.N., C.P.A.—** after names. (The periods are often left out of abbreviated titles.)

Ralph Simmons, Ph.D., will speak.

PLACE-NAMES

Spell out the names of continents, rivers, countries, states, cities, streets, and so on, except in these three cases:

1 Use **D.C.** when referring to Washington, D.C.
   Citizens of Washington, D.C., have no voting representation in Congress.

2 Use U.S. as an adjective, not as a noun:
   U.S. soldiers
   soldiers from the United States

3 To put a full address in a sentence, write it as you would on an envelope, using the state's postal abbreviation.
   Please send your applications to Habitat for Humanity International, 121 Habitat St., Americus, GA 31709.

TIP: MAKING ABBREVIATIONS PLURAL AND POSSESSIVE

To make an abbreviation plural, put **-s** after it.

Analysts estimate that more than 6,000 PCs become obsolete in California every day.

To make an abbreviation possessive, put **'s** after it.

IBM's earning forecast was grim.

TIP: ABBREVIATIONS IN DIFFERENT DISCIPLINES

Different disciplines—mathematics, social sciences—use abbreviations differently. The advice we offer on these pages is general, so if you are writing for a specific discipline, ask someone familiar with the field (or a reference librarian) for help in learning the field's conventions.

Otherwise, spell out the state name: **Habitat for Humanity International's head office is in Americus, Georgia.**

COMPANY NAMES

If a company name contains an abbreviation, write the name as the company does:

Charlie and the Chocolate Factory, **distributed by Warner Bros. Studios, is based on a novel by Roald Dahl.**

MEASUREMENTS

In the body of a paper, spell out units of measurement—such as *foot, percent, meter*—but abbreviate them in charts, tables, and graphs.

HMS *Titanic* was 883.75 feet long and 92.5 feet wide.

DATES

Spell out months and days of the week.

"Statistically, you are more likely to have an accident on Monday, November 27, than any other day of the year," the insurance official said.

For dates, the following abbreviations are customary:

399 B.C.	399 B.C.E.
1215 C.E.	A.D. 1215

B.C. (*Before Christ*), B.C.E. (*Before the Common Era*), and C.E. (*Common Era*) are placed after the year. A.D. (*Anno Domini, Year of Our Lord*) goes before the year. B.C.E. and C.E. are currently the most favored abbreviations.

TIMES

The conventional abbreviations for time of day are A.M. or a.m. for before noon and P.M. or p.m. for afternoon.

ACRONYMS

An acronym is a word formed by the initial letters of a phrase or title.

PC	*personal computer*
NPM	*National Poetry Month*
BBC	*British Broadcasting Corporation*

If you use an acronym that readers might not know, spell it out first, put the acronym in parentheses, and then use the acronym for all later references.

Folding At Home (FAH) is Stanford University's distributed computing project to study and understand protein folding, protein aggregation, and related diseases. So far, almost 500,000 users have donated processing time to FAH's projects.

LATIN EXPRESSIONS

Some Latin expressions, commonly used in academic writing, appear only as abbreviations:

cf.	*compare*	**e.g.**	*for example*
et al.	*and others*	**etc.**	*and so forth*
i.e.	*that is*	**n.b.**	*note well*

IN DOCUMENTING SOURCES

Different documentation styles use different abbreviations for words like *anonymous, editor,* or *no date.* Check the style manual you are using for any abbreviations you need to use.

→ See page 602 for how to use periods with abbreviations.

NUMBERS

WRITING NUMBERS

Spell out numbers that can be expressed in one or two words (and note the hyphen). Give the numerals for longer numbers.

seven	178
sixty-one	1,347
forty-one dollars	$77.17
twenty-two years	250 years
ninety people	2,200 people
ten miles	352 miles

Spell out any number that precedes another number expressed in numerals; otherwise readers might have trouble understanding the numbers. (For example, in the first sentence below, it is possible to see the two numbers as 10,250.)

The game is run from 10 250 gigabyte servers.

The game is run from ten 250 gigabyte servers.

WRITE OUT NUMBERS THAT BEGIN SENTENCES

19% of survey respondents knew when the U.S. Constitution was written.

Nineteen percent of survey respondents knew when the U.S. Constitution was written.

Except: Sentences can begin with a year:

1787 is the year the U.S. Constitution was written.

TIP: NUMBERS IN DIFFERENT DISCIPLINES

Different disciplines—mathematics, social sciences—use numbers differently. The advice we offer on these pages is general, so if you are writing for a specific discipline, ask someone familiar with the field (or a reference librarian) for help in learning the field's conventions.

USE NUMBERS CONSISTENTLY IN WRITING

If you spell numbers out or use numerals in a series, do so consistently.

Walsh notes that on average there are between 10,000 and fifteen thousand avatars in Second Life at any given time.

Walsh notes that on average there are between 10,000 and 15,000 avatars in Second Life at any given time.

DATES AND TIMES

Use numerals for dates and times.

On July 22, 1929, Alvin Macauley, president of Packard Motor Company, was on the cover of *Time* magazine.

President John F. Kennedy was shot and killed on November 22, 1963, at 12:30 P.M.

ADDRESSES AND PHONE NUMBERS

Use numerals for addresses and phone numbers.

Grauman's Chinese Theatre is located at 6801 Hollywood Boulevard in Hollywood. For showtimes, call (323) 464-8111.

DECIMALS AND PERCENTAGES

Use numerals for percentages and use the percentage sign (%).

By one estimate, 26% of all electric-cable breaks and 18% of all phone-cable disruptions are caused by rats.

(If the percentages come at the beginning of a sentence, however, spell out both the number and the percentage sign, as shown in the U.S. Constitution example on the preceding page.)

SCORES AND STATISTICS

Use numerals for scores and statistics.

The average age of the most frequent game buyer is 38 years old. In 2007, 92% of computer game buyers and 80% of console game buyers were over the age of 18.

The home run hit by New York Giants outfielder Bobby Thomson to win the National League pennant at 3:58 P.M. on October 3, 1951, is called the "Shot Heard 'Round the World." The Giants won the game 5 to 4, defeating the Dodgers in their pennant playoff series, two games to one.

PAGES AND OTHER PARTS OF BOOKS

Use numerals for pages, chapters, and other book divisions.

In his book *The Uses of Disorder*, Richard Sennett defines adulthood as the time when people "learn to tolerate painful ambiguity and uncertainty" (108).

Chapter 3 of John Stuart Mill's *On Liberty* is titled, "On Individuality, as one of the elements of well-being."

GLOSSARY OF GRAMMATICAL TERMS AND USAGE

In this glossary, we provide definitions of grammatical terms (shown in **blue**) and guidelines for usage. We also list homonyms (words that are spelled differently but sound the same) and other words that writers can easily confuse.

As you use this glossary, just as you use this handbook, keep in mind that the guidelines for usage are not strict rules but are, rather, academic and professional conventions developed over time. When you follow these conventions, your writing is more likely to be perceived by readers as academic and professional.

One further note: In academic and professional writing, words considered colloquial, nonstandard, or informal (as we label them below) are usually avoided by writers.

a/an   **A** and **an** are indefinite articles because they indicate general objects (*a book, an apple*) rather than specific objects (*the president*). **A** is used when the following word begins with a consonant (*a tire*); **an** is used when the following word begins with a vowel sound (*an hour, an orange*).

a lot/alot   **A lot** and **alot** are often used in informal writing to mean *many* or *much*. It is better to use *many* or *much* instead of **a lot** in academic writing. **Alot** is nonstandard.

accept/except/expect   **Accept** is a verb meaning "to receive." **Except** is usually used as a conjunction or preposition meaning "other than," but it can also be used as a verb meaning "leave out." **Expect** is a verb, meaning "to regard something as likely."

active voice   In a sentence or clause in active voice, the subject of the clause or sentence performs the action. See **passive voice** also. (See pp. 298–299 and p. 538.) *We installed a new operating system on the computer.*

ad/add   **Ad** is a shortened form of *advertisement*; **add** is a verb meaning "to join or combine."

adjective   An adjective is a word that modifies a noun or pronoun. (See pp. 508–513.) *I like salty snacks.*

adjective clause   An adjective clause is a subordinate clause that modifies a noun or pronoun. Adjective clauses are also called relative clauses because they begin with a relative pronoun. (See pp. 484–485.) *The park allows only dogs that are on leashes.*

adverb   An adverb is a word that modifies a verb (*talk quietly*), another modifier (*very inexpensive*), or a whole clause or sentence (*Fortunately, we had an umbrella*). (See pp. 528–529.)

adverb clause   An adverb clause is a subordinate clause that modifies a verb, another modifier, or a whole clause or sentence. (See pp. 486–487.) *We did not leave until all of the trash had been picked up.*

advice/advise   **Advice** is a noun meaning "an opinion." **Advise** is a verb meaning "to give opinion or advice."

affect/effect   **Affect** is usually used as a verb meaning "to influence," and **effect** is a noun meaning "a result." Sometimes **affect** is used as a noun meaning "an emotional state or feeling" and sometimes **effect** is used as a verb meaning "to bring about."

agreement Agreement refers to the correspondence of one word to another in gender, number, or person. For example, a verb should agree with its subject (*The <u>mechanic knows</u> how to fix the engine*) and a pronoun must agree with its antecedent (*The <u>factory workers</u> are on strike for <u>their</u> benefits*). (See pp. 524–526 on subject-verb agreement.)

all ready/already **All ready** is an adjective phrase meaning "ready to go." **Already** is an adverb that means "before" or "previously."

all right/alright **All right** means "acceptable" and is all right to use in academic writing. **Alright** is considered nonstandard.

all together/altogether **All together** means "in one place" or "in unison." **Altogether** means "entirely."

allude/elude **Allude** means "to refer to." **Elude** means "to escape."

allusion/illusion An **allusion** is an indirect reference to something. An **illusion** is a false or misleading impression.

among/between Use **between** when referring to two objects; use **among** when referring to three or more objects.

amount/number **Amount** is used for quantities of things that can be measured but not counted, such as *energy*. **Number** is used for quantities of things that can be counted, such as *bananas*.

an See **a/an**.

antecedent An antecedent is the noun or pronoun referred to by a pronoun. (See p. 502.) In the following sentence, "Betty" is the antecedent of "her." *<u>Betty</u> was on <u>her</u> way to pick up <u>her</u> grandchildren.*

any more/anymore **Any more** means "no more." **Anymore** means "now." Both are used in negative constructions. (*I don't want to hear any more lies; I don't believe you anymore.*)

anybody/any body/anyone/any one **Anybody** and **anyone** are indefinite pronouns that have the same meaning. **Any body** and **any one** are usually followed by the noun each modifies (*any body of water, any one incident*).

anyway/anyways **Anyway** is used to support a point that was just made and is the correct form, but the nonstandard **anyways** is often used in informal writing and conversation.

apt/liable/likely **Apt** and **likely** are interchangeable, but apt specifically means "having a tendency to." *He is apt to make mistakes like that.* **Liable** means "in danger of" and is best used only in contexts describing a dire situation. *You are liable to start a fire if you light a match near a gas tank.*

article Articles are always followed by a noun. *A, an,* and *the* are articles. (See pp. 510–513.)

as/like Use **as** instead of **like** before dependent clauses, which contain a noun and a verb (*He ran as if his life depended on it*). Use **like** before a noun or pronoun (*He ran like a cheetah*).

assure/ensure/insure **Assure** means "promise," **ensure** means "make certain," and **insure** means to "arrange for compensation in case of damage." These words are often used incorrectly in place of each other.

at/where Using **at** after **where** is unnecessary and makes writing seem wordy. *We are right at where we started.*

auxiliary verb See **helping verb**.

awful/awfully **Awful** is an adjective that means "awe inspiring" but it is more commonly used to mean "really bad." **Awful** and the adverb form **awfully** should not be used interchangeably, and they do not require intensifiers such as "very" or "extremely." *We heard an awful sound and were frightened awfully.*

awhile/a while **Awhile** is an adverb and **a while** is a pairing of an article and noun. Consequently, **awhile** cannot be used as the object of a preposition (**a while**, however, can), and **a while** cannot be used to modify a verb. *We waited <u>awhile</u> because Mario said he would be back in <u>a while</u>.*

bad/badly **Bad** should be used only as an adjective; **badly** is the adverb. *I sing badly.*

being as/being that Both **being as** and **being that** are colloquial and should not be used in academic writing.

beside/besides **Beside** means "next to." **Besides** means "except." *No one, besides Mary, would sit beside Archie.*

between See **among/between**.

bring/take **Bring** describes movement from a more distant location to nearby. **Take** describes movement away from. *Bring me that box so I can take it with me to work.*

but/however/yet   But, **however**, and **yet** can all be used to indicate a contrast. Using them together in the same sentence will make it wordy.

can/may   In academic writing, **can** indicates the ability to do something, while **may** indicates permission to do something. Informally, these words are often used interchangeably.

capital/capitol   A **capital** is the main governmental city of a state or country. *Annapolis is the capital of Maryland.* A **capitol** is the building in which government bodies meet. *The senator gave a press conference on the steps of the capitol.*

case   Case is the form of a noun or pronoun that indicates its function. Nouns change case only to show possession. (See p. 501.) *I wrote a letter outlining my concerns* (subject). *He wrote a letter to me outlining his concerns* (object of preposition). *The letter's purpose was clear* (possessive noun).

censor/censure   To **censor** is to ban or silence. To **censure** is to reprimand publicly.

cite/sight/site   **Cite** is a verb meaning to "reference specifically." **Sight** is used as a verb meaning "to view" and as a noun meaning "vision." **Site** is usually used as a noun to mean "location," but it can also be used as a verb to mean "to locate."

clause   A clause is a group of words containing a subject and a verb. A **main** or **independent clause** can stand alone as a sentence (see p. 483), but a **subordinate** or **dependent clause** acts as a part of speech and cannot stand alone (see pp. 484–487).

comma splice   A comma splice occurs when two independent clauses are joined incorrectly by a comma. (See pp. 494–495.) *Jose did not approve of our choice, he wanted to hire the other candidate* (incorrect). *Jose did not approve of our choice; he wanted to hire the other candidate* (correct).

common noun   A common noun names a general person, place, or thing. Common nouns are not capitalized unless they are the first word of a sentence. (See pp. 498–499.) *Did Johnny Depp portray a pirate in that movie?*

complement/compliment   To **complement** something is to complete it. To **compliment** is to flatter. Because they are spelled so similarly, they are often confused.

complex sentence   A complex sentence is a sentence that contains at least one subordinate clause attached to an independent clause. (See pp. 483–487.) *Despite the heat, we had a really good time at the festival.*

compound sentence   A compound sentence contains at least two main clauses. (See pp. 480–482.) *We ate dinner and then we went for a walk.*

compound-complex sentence   A compound-complex sentence contains at least two independent clauses and a subordinate clause. (See pp. 488–489.) *Even though my parents are both Italian, I have not visited Italy and I do not speak the language.*

conjunction   A conjunction is a word that links and relates parts of a sentence. (See pp. 532–535.) *Eric arrived late, but the movie had not started yet.* See **coordinating conjunction**, **correlative conjunction**, and **subordinating conjunction**.

conjunctive adverb   A conjunctive adverb is an adverb (such as *however, besides, consequently*, or *therefore*) that relates two main or independent clauses. (See p. 535.) *Our car is broken; consequently, we had to carpool with the neighbors.*

conscience/conscious   **Conscience** is a noun meaning "a sense of right or wrong." **Conscious** is an adjective meaning "awake."

continual/continuous   **Continual** is an adjective meaning "recurring." **Continuous** is an adjective meaning "constant." *That continual noise is a continuous bother.*

coordinating conjunction   A coordinating conjunction is a word (such as *and, but, or, for, nor, yet,* and *so*) that links two grammatically equal parts of a sentence. (See p. 532 and pp. 556–557.) *I brushed my teeth and went to bed.*

correlative conjunction   Correlative conjunctions are two or more words (*neither…nor, either…or, not only…but also*) that work together to link parts of a sentence. (See p. 533.) *Not only were we excited, but we were also a little bit afraid.*

could of   **Could of** is often used in informal writing, but *could have* is more appropriate.

count noun   A count noun names things that can be counted. (See pp. 511–513.) *goats, shoes, computers*

criteria/criterion   A **criterion** is a singular noun that means "a measure" or "a condition." **Criteria** is the plural form of **criterion**.

dangling modifier   A dangling modifier does not have a clear connection to the word it modifies. (See pp. 540–541.) *Spicier than expected*, *she spat out the soup.*

data/datum   Datum is a singular noun that refers to a piece of information or a fact. **Data** is the plural of **datum**, and although it is often used as a singular noun, it should be treated as a plural noun and take a plural verb.

declarative   A declarative sentence is a statement. (See p. 468.) *The measurements were incorrect.*

dependent clause   See **subordinate clause**.

differ from/differ with   To **differ from** means "to be unlike." To **differ with** means "to disagree with."

different from/different than   **Different from** is preferred in academic writing to **different than** except in situations where **different from** would be wordy.

direct object   A direct object is the noun, pronoun, or noun clause naming the person or thing that takes the action of a transitive verb. (See pp. 476–472.) *The chef threw the meatloaf in the trash.*

discreet/discrete   **Discreet** is an adjective meaning "careful" or "prudent." **Discrete** is an adjective meaning "separate."

disinterested/uninterested   **Disinterested** is an adjective that means "impartial." It is often used incorrectly in place of **uninterested**.

double negative   A double negative is the use of two negatives to convey one negative idea. It should be avoided in academic writing. (See p. 281.) *I don't have no time to go with you.*

due to the fact that   **Due to the fact that** is a wordy substitute for **because**.

each other/one another   **Each other** should be used for two things; **one another** should be used for more than two things.

effect   See **affect/effect**.

elicit/illicit   **Elicit** is a verb that means "to bring out." **Illicit** is an adjective that means "unlawful." These words are often incorrectly used in place of each other.

emigrate from/immigrate to   **Emigrate** is a verb meaning "to leave one's country." **Immigrate** is a verb that means "to settle in another country."

ensure   See **assure/ensure/insure**.

etc.   **Etc.** is an abbreviation for the Latin *et cetera* and is used to shorten a list of items. **Etc.** is mostly used in informal writing.

every body/everybody/every one/everyone   **Everybody** and **everyone** are both collective nouns referring to all parties under discussion. **Every body** and **every one** are both adjective-noun combinations that refer to individuals within the larger group.

except   See **accept/except/expect**.

except for the fact that   **Except for the fact that** is a wordy substitute for *except that*.

expect   See **accept/except/expect**.

expletive   *There* and *it* are expletives, or "dummy subjects" that are used to fill a grammatical slot in a sentence. (See p. 282.) *It is very clear.*

farther/further   **Farther** refers to distance, while **further** refers to time or another abstract concept.

fewer/less   **Fewer** is used for things that can be counted, while **less** is used for things that cannot be counted.

fragment   A fragment is a group of words that is capitalized and punctuated like a sentence but lacks a subject and predicate. Fragments are used in some forms of writing, such as fiction and advertising copy, but they are usually not acceptable in academic writing. (See pp. 490–493.) *A representative who cares.*

further   See **farther/further**.

gender   Gender is the classification of nouns or pronouns as masculine and feminine. (See p. 507.)

good/well   **Good** can be used only as an adjective, while **well** can be used as both an adjective and an adverb. *His last album was good. He sings well. Is your mother well?*

hanged/hung   **Hanged** is a verb that specifically refers to an execution. **Hung** is used in all other instances. *In the past, criminals were often hanged. The noose hung from the gallows.*

have/of   **Have**, rather than **of**, should be used after auxiliary or helping verbs such as *could, should, would, might*, and so on.

he/she; s/he   Academic audiences prefer writing that is gender inclusive (unless a distinction of gender is necessary). (See pp. 256–257.)

helping verb Helping verbs are also known as auxiliary verbs. These verbs (forms of *be*, *do*, and *have*) join with other verbs to indicate tense and mood. Modal verbs can also be used as helping verbs. (See p. 517 and p. 519.) *By Friday, she had collected enough signatures to be listed on the ballot.*

herself/himself/myself/yourself These –*self* pronouns refer to or intensify nouns or other pronouns. They are often used colloquially in place of personal pronouns, but not usually in academic writing.

hopefully **Hopefully** is an adverb that is often used to modify a sentence, but it is considered nonstandard.

if/whether **Whether** is clearer than **if** when you are posing an alternative. *Whether your vote matters depends on the integrity of the electoral process.*

illusion See **allusion/illusion**.

immigrate See **emigrate from/immigrate to**.

impact **Impact** is used as a noun referring to a violent collision and, less commonly, as a verb meaning "to collide violently." The use of **impact** as a noun to mean "an effect" or as a verb to mean "to have an effect on" is prevalent, but it is considered nonstandard.

imperative An imperative sentence expresses a command. The subject of an imperative sentence is often implied. (See p. 469.) *Be quiet!*

implicit See **explicit/implicit**.

imply/infer **Imply** is a verb meaning "to suggest." **Infer** is a verb meaning "to conclude."

in regards to **In regards to** is a wordy substitute for *regarding*.

incredible/incredulous **Incredible** is an adjective that means "unbelievable." **Incredulous** is an adjective used to mean "not believing." *Our incredulous minds could not fathom the incredible sight before us.*

independent clause An independent—or main—clause is a group of words with a subject and predicate that can stand alone as a sentence. (See p. 483.)

indirect object An indirect object is a noun, pronoun, or noun phrase that names the person or thing that is affected by the action of a transitive verb. (See pp. 476–477.) *The waiter served us fresh coffee.*

interjection An interjection is a word that expresses strong emotion. (See p. 496.) *Ouch! That hurt!*

interrogative An interrogative sentence asks a question. (See p. 468.) *What did you do this weekend?*

intransitive verb An intransitive verb does not take an object. (See pp. 476–477.) *I just wanted to participate.*

irregardless/regardless **Irregardless** is often used as a substitute for **regardless**, but using **irregardless** in that way is considered nonstandard.

irregular verb An irregular verb does not take –*ed* or –*d* to form its past tense or past participle. (See pp. 517–519.) *slept, swam*

it is my opinion that **It is my opinion that** is a wordy substitute for *I believe that*.

its/it's **Its** is the possessive form of **it** and does not take an apostrophe. **It's** is the contraction of *it is*. *As the fish swam, its fins undulated. It's a sad day when the Cubs lose.*

-ize/-wise The suffix **-ize** turns a noun or an adjective into a verb (*motorize*). The suffix **–wise** turns a noun or an adjective into an adverb (*clockwise*).

kind of/sort of/type of These three constructions are used to classify things. Informally or colloquially they are used to mean *somewhat* or *rather*. *That kind of soup makes me rather queasy.*

knew/new **Knew**, a verb, is the past tense of "to know." **New** is an adjective meaning "fresh, not seen before."

lay/lie **Lay** is a verb that means "to place," and it takes a direct object. **Lie** means "to recline" or "to position" and does not take a direct object.

leave/let **Leave** and **let** are interchangeable only when followed by "alone." **Leave** means "go" and **let** means "allow."

less See **fewer/less**.

lie See **lay/lie**.

linking verb A linking verb connects a subject to a complement. (See p. 477.)

literally **Literally** means "actually" or "just as the words say." It is often used colloquially to intensify a word.

loan/lone A **loan** is money that is borrowed; **lone** is an adjective meaning "single, isolated."

loose/lose **Loose** is an adjective meaning "not tight." *His pants were so loose he couldn't walk.* **Lose** is a verb meaning "to misplace" or "to be defeated." *Don't lose your homework.*

lots/lots of **Lots** and **lots of** are often used as substitutes for *many*, but they are considered nonstandard.

main clause See **independent clause**.

may/can See **can/may**.

may be/maybe **May be** is a verb phrase. **Maybe** is an adverb.

media/medium **Medium** is a singular noun referring to a means of conveying information. **Media** is the plural of **medium** and takes a plural verb. *The media portray…*

might of See **have/of**.

modifier A modifier is a word, phrase, or clause that describes another word. Modifiers are adjectives (see pp. 508–513), adverbs (see pp. 528–529), adjective clauses (see pp. 484–485), and adverb clauses (see pp. 486–487).

must of See **have/of**.

noncount noun A noncount noun names things that cannot be counted. (See pp. 511–513.) *electricity, history, peace*

nonrestrictive modifier A nonrestrictive modifier is not essential to the meaning of the word, phrase, or clause it modifies and should be set off by commas or other punctuation. (See pp. 559–562.) *My uncle, Misha, used to work on Wall Street.*

noun A noun names a person, place, or thing. (See pp. 498–501.)

number See **amount/number**.

object An object is the receiver of an action within a sentence, clause, or phrase. (See pp. 474–477.)

OK/O.K./okay **OK**, **O.K.**, and **okay** are all okay for informal writing but are less okay in academic writing.

owing to the fact that **Owing to the fact that** is a wordy substitute for *because*.

parallelism Parallelism is the practice of putting similar elements in a sentence in a similar grammatical pattern. (See pp. 286–287.) *His resume stated that he had trained and supervised employees, analyzed and evaluated software, and organized and maintained records.*

parts of speech There are eight parts of speech, or groups of words classified by their grammatical functions and meanings: nouns, pronouns, verbs, adjectives, adverbs, prepositions, conjunctions, and interjections. (See pp. 496–541.)

passed/past **Passed**, a verb, is the past tense of "to pass." **Past** is a noun or adjective, describing something that happened prior to the present moment.

passive voice Passive voice is indicated by a clause with a transitive verb that is acting upon the subject. (See pp. 298–299 and p. 538.) *The issue was called to our attention by the maintenance crew.*

peace/piece **Peace** is a state of harmony. A **piece** is a part of something.

people/persons Use **people** to refer to a general group, unless it is necessary to emphasize individuals within the group. In that case, use **persons**.

per The Latin word **per** means "for each." It is best used in familiar phrases such as *miles per gallon*.

phenomena/phenomenon **Phenomenon** is a singular noun meaning "observable fact" or "unusual event." The plural form of **phenomenon** is **phenomena**, which takes a plural verb. *Among the phenomena that were discussed were alien abductions and reincarnation.*

phrase A phrase is a group of words that does not contain both a subject and a predicate. (See pp. 473–479.) *A lovely day*

plenty **Plenty** is often used as a colloquial substitute for *very*.

plus **Plus** is often used incorrectly to join clauses or sentences. It is better to use *and, also, moreover, furthermore*, or another conjunctive adjective instead.

possessive case The possessive case indicates ownership. (See p. 501.) *my lunch, his shoes, Tran's car*

precede/proceed **Precede** and **proceed** are both verbs, but precede means "come before" and proceed means "continue."

predicate   The predicate is the part of a clause that expresses the action or tells something about the subject. The predicate includes the verb and its complements, objects, and modifiers. (See pp. 474–478.)

prejudice/prejudiced   **Prejudice** is a noun meaning "bias." **Prejudiced** is an adjective meaning "biased" or "intolerant."

preposition   A preposition is a part of speech that shows relationships or qualities. (See pp. 530–531.)

prepositional phrase   A prepositional phrase is a phrase formed by a preposition and its object. A prepositional phrase includes the modifiers of the object. (See p. 479.)

pretty   **Pretty** is often used as a colloquial substitute for *very*. Avoid using **pretty** to mean *very* in academic writing.

principal/principle   **Principal** can be a noun, meaning "the head of a school" or it can be an adjective, meaning "the most important element." **Principle** is a noun meaning "a rule or standard."

pronoun   A pronoun is a part of speech that stands for other nouns or pronouns. Classes of pronouns include: **possessive pronouns**, **personal pronouns**, **demonstrative pronouns**, **indefinite pronouns**, **relative pronouns**, **interrogative pronouns**, **reflexive pronouns**, and **reciprocal pronouns**. (See pp. 502–507.)

pronoun case   Pronouns that act as the subject of a sentence are in the **subjective case** (*I, you, he, she, it, we, they*). Pronouns that act as direct or indirect objects are in the **objective case** (*me, you, him, her, it, us, them*). Pronouns that indicate ownership are in the **possessive case** (*my, your, his, her, its, our, their*). (See pp. 502–507.)

proper noun   A proper noun is a noun that names a particular person, place, thing, or group. Proper nouns are capitalized. (See pp. 498–499.) *Anthony Bourdain, Dublin, Yom Kippur*

question as to whether/question of whether   These phrases are both wordy substitutes for *whether*.

raise/rise   The verb **raise** means "lift up" and takes a direct object. The verb **rise** means "get up." It does not take a direct object.

real/really   **Real** is an adjective, while **really** is an adverb. These words are often used incorrectly in place of each other.

reason is because   **Reason is because** is often used to explain causality. *Reason is* and *is because* are less wordy.

reason why   **Reason why** is a redundant construction that should be avoided in academic writing. Instead of *The reason why he went to Malaysia is for work*, you can write *He went to Malaysia for work.*

relative pronoun   A relative pronoun initiates clauses. *That, which, what, who, whom,* and *whose* are relative pronouns. (See p. 504.) *The woman who makes those funny, furry purses will have a booth at the fair.*

restrictive modifier   A restrictive modifier is essential to the meaning of the word, phrase, or clause it modifies. Unlike a nonrestrictive modifier, it is not set off by punctuation. (See pp. 559–562.) *My uncle who lives in Canada is visiting next week.*

rise/raise   See **raise/rise**.

run-on sentence   A run-on sentence occurs when two main clauses are fused together without punctuation or a conjunction. (See pp. 494–495.) *I don't like Wednesdays they are too far away from the weekend.*

sentence   A sentence is a grammatically independent group of words that contains at least one independent clause. (See pp. 468–495.)

set/sit   The verb **set** means "to put" and it takes a direct object. **Sit** means "to be seated" and does not take a direct object.

shall/will   **Shall** is very formal, and is most often used in first person questions, while **will** can be used in the future tense with all persons.

should of   See **have/of**.

simple/simplistic   Although it is often used as such, **simplistic** is not a synonym of *simple*. **Simplistic** means "crude" or "unsophisticated," while **simple** means "easy."

since   **Since** most commonly refers to time, but it can also be used as a synonym of *because*. Keep in mind, though, that some readers prefer that **since** not be used as a synonym of *because*.

sit/set   See **set/sit**.

some time/sometime/sometimes   **Some time** refers to a period of time, while **sometime** refers to an unspecified time. **Sometimes** means "occasionally."

somebody/some body; someone/some one **Somebody** and **someone** are indefinite pronouns that mean the same thing. **Some body** and **some one** are adjective-noun combinations.

sort of See **kind of/sort of/type of.**

subject A subject is a noun, pronoun, or noun phrase that identifies what the clause is about and is connected to the predicate. (See p. 475.)

subject-verb agreement See **agreement.**

subjunctive mood The subjunctive mood expresses a wish, a condition contrary to fact, a recommendation, or a request. (See p. 527.)

subordinate A subordinate relationship is a relationship of unequal importance, in either grammar or meaning. (See pp. 284–285.)

subordinate clause A subordinate clause, also called a dependent clause, is a clause that cannot stand alone but must be attached to a main clause. (See pp. 483–487 and p. 493.)

subordinating conjunction A subordinating conjunction is a word that introduces a subordinate clause. Some subordinating conjunctions are *after, although, as, because, before, if, since, that, unless, until, when, where,* and *while.* (See p. 534.)

such **Such** means "of the previous kind" (*such behavior, such praise*), but it is often used informally as a synonym for *very.*

sure **Sure** is often used as an adverb to mean *certainly,* but it is more properly used as an adjective.

sure and/sure to; try and/try to **Sure to** and **try to** are correct; do not add *and* after *sure* or *try.*

take See **bring/take.**

than/then **Than** is a conjunction expressing difference. *I would rather watch a movie than go out tonight.* **Then** is an adverb expressing time. *First we went to church, then we went shopping.*

that/which **That** introduces a restrictive or essential clause, while **which** is usually used to introduce nonrestrictive or nonessential clauses.

their/there/they're **Their** is a possessive pronoun (see p. 503); **there** is most commonly used as an

expletive (see p. 282); and **they're** is a contraction of *they are* (see p. 503).

to/too/two **To** is a preposition, while **too** is an adverb. **Two** is a number.

transition A transition is a word or phrase that notes movement from one unit of writing to another. (See pp. 296–297.)

transitive verb A transitive verb is a verb that takes a direct object. (See pp. 476–477.)

try and/try to See **sure and/sure to.**

unique If something is **unique,** it is one of a kind and can't be compared to anything else. Consequently, it is not necessary to use words such as *most* to modify **unique.**

usage/use/utilize **Utilize** and **usage** are often used in informal writing as synonyms for **use.**

verb A verb is a word that shows action or characterizes a subject in some way. (See pp. 514–527.)

well/good See **good/well.**

weather/whether **Weather** is a noun, describing whether it is sunny, raining, hot, or cold outside. **Whether** is a conjunction that can mean "if" or can introduce a set of opinions.

which/that See **that/which.**

who/whom **Who** is the subject pronoun, while **whom** is the object pronoun. *Who is that in the yard? With whom did you dance?*

who's/whose **Who's** is a contraction of *who is,* while **whose** is a possessive. *Who's there? Whose shoes are those?*

will/shall See **shall/will.**

-wise/-ize See **-ize/-wise.**

would of See **have/of.**

you **You** is primarily used to directly address the reader, but it is often used informally to refer to people in general.

your/you're **Your** and **you're** are not interchangeable. **Your** is the possessive form of *you. Your conscience will rest easier after you vote.* **You're** is the contraction of *you are. You're a citizen, and so you are expected to vote.* (See p. 503 on possessives; see p. 601 on contractions.)

CREDITS

PHOTOS

All photos not credited below are courtesy of the author.

Part 1: Opener: Masterfile RF; 2 Stone/Allstock/Getty Images; 4 RF fotosearch; 6 Stockbyte/Getty Images; 7 top left, Image Bank/Getty Images; 7 top center, Stone/Allstock/Getty Images; 7 top right, Esbin Anderson/Omni Photo Communications, Inc.; 7 center left, ImageState/International Stock Photography, Ltd.; 7 center right, Stockbyte; 7 bottom, AP/Wide World Photos; 8 top, Vicky Kasala; 8 bottom, Stone/Allstock/Getty Images.

Part 2: Opener: Taxi/Getty Images; 18 Stockbyte/Getty Images; 19 top, Stone/Allstock/Getty Images; 19 bottom left, The Stock Connection; 19 bottom right, Jeff Greenberg/PhotoEdit, Inc.; 20 Michael Newman/PhotoEdit, Inc.; 24 Stockbyte/Getty Images; 26 Photo Disc/Getty Images; 28 David Young-Wolff/PhotoEdit, Inc,; 29 Peter Arnold, Inc.; 34 Getty Images/Photodisc; 38 Taxi/Getty Images; 46 top, Dennis MacDonald/PhotoEdit, Inc.; 46 bottom, Dorling Kindersley Media Library; 47 top, Stockbyte/Getty Images; 47 middle, Pearson Education/PH College; 47 bottom, Jonathan Nourok/PhotoEdit, Inc.; 48 top, Stockbyte/Getty Images; 48 bottom right, ©Time Magazine/Getty Images; 60 Stone/Allstock/Getty Images; 80 Colin Young/Wolff/PhotoEdit, Inc.; 82 Michelle Bridwell/PhotoEdit, Inc.; 84 Taxi/Getty Images.

Part 3: Opener: photolibrary.com.; 88 Will and Demi McIntyre/Photo Researchers, Inc.; 93 right, ©2002 Donna Tartt. Cover courtesy Alfred A. Knopf, Random House, Inc. All rights reserved; 95 right ©2002 Donna Tartt. Cover courtesy Alfred A. Knopf, Random House, Inc. All rights reserved; 97 right, ©2002 Donna Tartt. Cover courtesy Alfred A. Knopf, Random House, Inc. All rights reserved; 107 National Archives; 129 The Mayor's Office to Combat Domestic Violence, New York City; 130 Taxi/Getty Images; 144 Arresting Images; 146 Stockbyte/Getty Images.

Part 4: Opener: Photolibrary.com; 150 Skjold Photographs; 157 left, Getty/Photodisc; 157 middle, Getty Images/Stockbyte; 157 right, Getty Images/Stockbyte; 160 Getty Images/Taxi; 180 Charles Gupton/Corbis.

Part 5: Opener: photolibrary.com; 186 Six-Cats Research, Inc.; 187 top left, Jeff Greenberg; 187 left center, Sean Ellis; 187 bottom left, David McLain/Aurora; 187 top right, and bottom right, Friedrich Stark/Das Fotoarchiv; 188 Getty Images/Photodisc; 212 Lebrecht Music & Arts Photo Library; 226 Image Bank/Getty Images; 227 top, Library of Congress. Prints and Photographs Division; 227 center, Library of Congress. Prints and Photographs Division; 227 bottom, Passing/Posing/Female Prophet Ann, Who Observes the Presentation of Jesus on the Temple, oil on canvas, 2003 © Kehinde Wiley; 230 photo of Caracas, Venezuela by Rob Crandall; 231 right, Photo of Dale Evans from Hulton Archive/Getty Images; 232 PhotoEdit Inc.; 234 Getty/Taxi.

Part 6: Opener: Idris Ahmed/Dorling Kindersley Media; 238 PhotoEdit, Inc.; 244 Corbis/Reuters; 246 Creative Eye/Mira.com; 248 Allstock/Getty Images.

Part 7: Opener: Dorling Kindersley Media Library; 266 AFP/Getty Images; 268 Lonely Planet Images/Photo 20/20; 270 AP/Wide World Photos; 290 National Geographic Image Collection; 300 PhotoDisc/Getty Images; 304 AP/Wide World Photos.

Part 8: Opener: Jonathan Nourok/PhotoEdit, Inc.; 308 Stockbyte/Getty Images; 314 Kayte Deioma/PhotoEdit, Inc.; 362 RF Bloomimage/Corbis;

364 RF Bloomimage/Corbis; 372 top left, Dorling Kindersley Media Library; 372 bottom left, Lake Country Museum/Corbis; 372 top right, Dorling Kindersley Media Library; 372 center, ©Ed Young/Corbis; 372 bottom center right, Dorling Kindersley Media Library; 372 bottom right, ©Kristy-Anne Glubish/Design Pics/RF Corbis; 373 top left, Terry Sirrell/ RF@images.com/Corbis; 373 left top center, Dorling Kindersley Media Library; 373 left center, ©Bettmann/Corbis; 373 left center bottom, Pablo Corral/Corbis; 373 left bottom, ©Gideon Mendel/Corbis; 373 top right, Free Agents Limited/Corbis; 373 right center, RF Corbis; 373 bottom right, Dorling Kindersley Media Library.

Part 9: Opener: The Stock Connection; 464 Photo Disc/Getty Images; 464 Image Bank/Getty Images; 466 The Granger Collection; 498 top center, Frank Siteman/Omni Photo Communications, Inc.; 498 bottom center, Photo Researchers, Inc.; 499 top right center, Dorling Kindersley Media Library; 499 top right, David Young-Wolff/PhotoEdit, Inc.; 499 bottom center right, The Image Works; 499 bottom right, Superstock RF; 511 bottom left, Corbis–Comstock Images RF; 511 bottom center, The Image Works; 514 top, George Eastman House; 514 middle, Oscar Burrill/Photo Researchers, Inc.; 528 top left, Getty Images, Inc./Taxi; 528 top left center, Tom Stillo/Omni Photo Communications, Inc.; 528 top right center, David Parket/Omni Photo Communications, Inc.; 528 top right, David Parket/Omni Photo Communications, Inc.; 528 middle left, William Mullins/Photo Researchers, Inc.; 528 middle left center, Frederick Ayer III/Photo Researchers, Inc.; 528 middle right center, David Parket/Omni Photo Communications, Inc.; 528 middle right, Terry Wittaker/Photo Researchers, Inc.; 528 bottom left, Phil Mislinski/Omni Photo Communications, Inc.; 528 bottom left center, Ardea, London, Ltd.; 528 bottom right center, Jeanne White/Photo Researchers, Inc.; 528 bottom right, Richard Hutchings/Photo Researchers, Inc.; 542 Stone/Allstock/Getty Images; 606 Getty Images–Stockbyte.

TEXT

Part 2: 48 Copyright © 2005 Rolling Stone; 49 Cover, *African Journal on Conflict Resolution*, © The African Centre for the Constructive Resolution of Disputes (1991–2008); 49 Cover, *Peabody Journal of Education*, Routledge, Taylor & Francis Group; 49 Cover, *Social Neuroscience*, 1.1, March 2006, Routledge, Taylor & Francis Group; 51 See Jane Compute screenshot, seejanecompute.blogspot.com. Used with permission; 51 Screen shot, Neil Gaiman blog/website, http://www.neilgaiman.com. Used by permission of Neil Gaiman; 52 Boingboing screenshot, boingboing.net; 52 Crooked Timber screenshot, crooked timber.org. Used with permission; 53 Screenshot from GORE website, www.gore.com. Courtesy of W.L. Gore & Associates; 53 Google™ screenshot. GOOGLE is a trademark of Google, Inc. By permission; 54 Pew Internet & American Life Project, accessed Sept 2007, www.pewinternet.org. Used with permission; 54 Doctors Without Borders/Medecins Sans Frontieres (MSF). Used with permission; 55 State of Michigan Website screenshot, www.michigan.gov. Used by permission of The State of Michigan; 56 From *The New York Times*, 1/22/2007. © 2007 The New York Times. All rights reserved. Used by permission and protected by the Copyright Laws of the United States. The printing, copying, redistribution, or retransmission of the material without express written permission is prohibited. www.nytimes.com; 56 Reproduced with permission. Copyright © 2007 by Scientific American, Inc. All rights reserved; 56 Reprinted with the permission of Kairos: A Journal of Rhetoric, Technology, and Pedagogy http://kairos.technorhetoric.net/; 57 ENGnetBASE screenshot, www.engnetbase.com. Used by permission of Taylor and Francis; 57 ProQuest.com is produced by ProQuest LLC. Inquiries may be made to ProQuest LLC, 789 Eisenhower Parkway, Ann Arbor, MI 48108 USA. Telephone (734) 761-4700, E-mail: info@proquest.com; Web-page: www.proquest.com; 58 Reprinted with permission from Encyclopædia Britannica Online, © 2007 by Encyclopædia Britannica, Inc; 58 Bartleby screenshot, www.bartleby.com. Used with permission of Bartleby.com, Inc; 63 University of Louisiana Library, Advanced Search screenshot. Powered by SirsiDynix. Used by permission of SirsiDynix; 66 Michigan Tech, Van Pelt Library Database search screenshot, http://www.lib.mtu.edu/eresources/eresearch/eresearch.aspx. Used by permission; 67 Michigan Tech, Van Pelt Library Database search results screenshot. Used by permission; 68 Copyright 2007 LexisNexis, a division of Reed Elsevier Inc. All Rights Reserved. LexisNexis and the Knowledge Burst logo are registered trademarks of Reed Elsevier Properties Inc. and are used with the permission of LexisNexis; 69 CSA Illumina is produced by Pro Quest LLC. Inquiries may be made to: ProQuest, LLC, 7200 Wisconsin Avenue, Suite 601, Bethesda, MD 20814 USA. Telephone (301) 961-6700; E-mail: in1fo@csa.com; Web-page: www.csa.com; 70 From Gale. Screen shot from *Power Search Database*. © Gale, a part of Cengage Learning, Inc. Reproduced by permission. www.cengage.com/permissions; 71 From OCLC's WorldCat ® database. Information is used with permission of OCLC. WorldCat® is a registered trademark of OCLC Online Computer Library Center, Inc.

Part 3: 90 Used by permission of Hachette Book Group USA, Inc; 93 Used by permission of Hachette Book Group USA, Inc; 93, 95 Cover, *The Little Friend* by Donna Tartt. New York: Knopf, 2002; 95 Used by permission of Hachette Book Group USA, Inc; 101 "Food ad blitz," *The San Francisco Chronicle*, Editorial, March 29, 2007, B8. Copyright 2007 by San Francisco Chronicle. Reproduced by permission of San Francisco Chronicle in the format print and other book via Copyright Clearance Center; 112 Screenshot "Bacteria Salad" from Persuasive Games. Used by permission of Persuasive Games; 117 Malcolm Gladwell, "No Mercy." Copyright © 2006 Conde Nast Publications. All rights reserved. Originally published in *The New Yorker*. Reprinted by permission; 135 Screenshot from Wired News, July 14, 2005. Copyright © 2005 Condé Net, a division of Condé Nast Publications. All rights reserved. Reprinted by permission; 135, 139 Fishman, Jay A. "SARS. Xenotransplantation and Bioterrorism: Preventing the Next Epidemic." *American Journal of Transplantation*. 3 (2003). Used by permission of Blackwell Publishing; 139 Title page, "The Avian Flu: How Scared Should We Be," *Time*, October 17, 2005.

Part 5: 194 Home page from Steve Berlin Johnson's blog page, www.stevenberlinjohnson.com. Used by permission; 195 Courtesy A. Reindeer; 197 "Letter to the editor" written by Daniel Moshenberg, George Washington University, *The New York Times*, Oct 5, 2006. By permission of the author; 199 Copyright 2007 by Ben Carmichael. First published in *OnEarth*, (www.onearth.org) Fall 2007. Reprinted by permission; 207 Memo to STC Arts Projects Teams written by Jason Dryja, 2006. Used by permission of Jason Dryja; 215 Laurence Gonzales, *Deep Survival; Who Lives, Who Dies, and Why*. New York: W. W. Norton & Company, 2003; 219 Richard Rhodes, *Deadly Feasts: The "Prion" Controversy and the Public's Health*. New York: Simon & Schuster, 1997; 219 Christian Hoard, "The Boys Are Back in Town," *Rolling Stone*, October 5, 2006; 220 Michael Pollan, *The Omnivore's Dilemma*. New York: Penguin Press, 2006; 222 Charles Siebert, "An Elephant Crack Up?" *New York Times Magazine*, October 8, 2006; 223 Paul Bloom, "Is God an Accident?" *The Atlantic Monthly*, December 2005; 225 Mike Rose "Extol Brains As Well As Brawn of the Blue Collar," *Los Angeles Times*, September 6, 2004.

Part 6: Quote from student Jun Liu, *Reflections on Multiliterate Lives*, ed. Diane Dewhurst Belcher and Ulla Connor, Multilingual Matters Limited, 2001. Used by permission of Multilingual Matters, Ltd; 243 Bühner, M. et al. (2006). "Working memory dimensions as differential predictors of the speed and error aspect of multitasking performance," *Human Performance*, 19, 253–275; 243 J. Balzar, "One Thing at a Time, Please," *Los Angeles Times*, April 27, 2003; 247 Quote from student Miyuki Sasaki, *Reflections on Multiliterate Lives*, ed. Diane Dewhurst Belcher and Ulla Connor, Multilingual Matters Limited, 2001. Used by permission of Multilingual Matters Ltd; 248, 249 From *My Year of Meats* by Ruth L. Ozeki, copyright © 1998 by Ruth Ozeki Lounsbury. Used by permission of Viking Penguin, a division of Penguin Group (USA) Inc; 258 American Psychological Association, APA Online, apastyle.apa.org/disabilities.html; 264 *Longman Dictionary of American English*. London: Pearson Education, 2008.

Part 7: 278 John Edgar Wideman, "Whose War," *Harper's Magazine*, March 1, 2002.

Part 8: 315 Ravi Purushotma, "You're not studying, you're just . . ." *Language Learning & Technology*, Jan 2005. Used by permission of Ravi Purushotma. See updated version at www.lingualgamers.com/thesis/; 330 Title page, *Sorting Things Out* by Geoffrey C Bowker and Susan Leigh Star, Published 1999, MIT Press. Used by permission of MIT Press; 331 Title page, *Images of an Era: The American Poster, 1945–1975*, MIT Press. Used by permission of MIT Press; 331 Title page, *Aesthetic Computing* by Paul Fishwick, MIT Press 2006. Used by permission of MIT Press; 331 *The Elements of Style* by William Strunk, Jr, Longman Publishers. Used by permission. of Pearson Education, Inc; 333 "The Lovers of the Poor" by Gwendolyn Brooks. Reprinted by consent of Brooks Permissions; 333 "Of Robert Frost" by Gwendolyn Brooks. Reprinted by consent of Brooks Permissions; 333 "Sermon on the Warpland" by Gwendolyn Brooks. Reprinted by consent of Brooks Permissions; 334 "Contesting the Objectivist Paradigm" by Lee Brasseur, *IEEE Transactions on Professional Communication* 36.3 (1993):114–123. Used by permission of IEEE and the author; 335 Title page and "Literacy" by Deborah Brandt , *Encyclopedia of Rhetoric and Composition: Communication from Ancient Times to the Information Age*. Copyright 1996 by Taylor & Francis Group LLC-Books. Reproduced with permission of Taylor & Francis Group LLC-Books in the format textbook and other book via Copyright Clearance Center; 337 Screenshot, Brittany Huntley, "My Global Study Experience in Dubai," *The Black Collegian*, First September Super Issue 2006, p. 62. By permission of The Black Collegian; 337 Screenshot, "Inside This Issue," *The Black Collegian*, First September Super Issue, 2006. By permission of The Black Collegian; 338 *Milwaukee Journal Sentinel*, September 23, 2007; 339 Screenshots of cover and article "Curry Powder" by Patrick Barry from *Science News*, September 15, 2007. Reprinted with permission from Science News, copyright 2007; 340 Copyright © Harper's Magazine. All rights reserved. Reproduced from the September issue by special permission; 343 Velo News screenshot, VeloNews.com. Used by permission of Velo News. Inside Communications, Inc; 344 Screenshot jill/txt. Used by permission of Jill Walker Rettberg; 345 Used by permission of the Union of Concerned Scientists; 345 Screen shot from http://www.salon.com, featuring excerpt from Laura Miller, "Panic in the Pages," Salon.com, March 24, 2008. Reprinted by permission; 347 From Gale. Screen shot from *Power Search Database*. © Gale, a part of Cengage Learning, Inc. Reproduced by permission. www.cengage.com/permissions.

Part 9: 543 Pico Iyer, "In Praise of the Humble Comma," *Time*, June 13, 1988.

INDEX

A

X

Y

REVISION SYMBOLS

Boldface numbers refer to pages in the handbook

ab	abbreviation	**612**
agr	agreement	**524**
awk	awkward diction or construction	**274, 282**
cap	capitalization	**610**
coh	coherence	**214**
coord	coordination	**284**
cs	comma splice	**557**
d	diction, word choice	**270**
dev	development needed	**36, 218**
dm	dangling modifier	**540**
doc	check documentation	**308**
frag	sentence fragment	**490**
fs	fused sentence	**494**
hyph	hyphen	**584**
ital	italics	**607**
lc	lowercase letter	**610**
log	logic	**96, 100**
mm	misplaced modifier	**540**
no ¶	no paragraph needed	**290**
num	number	**614**
¶	paragraph	**290**
¶ dev	paragraph development needed	**218**
ref	unclear pronoun reference	**506**
search	check research or citation	**38, 60, 308**

sp	spelling error	**608**
shift	shift in voice or number	**536**
sub	sentence subordination	**284**
t	verb tense error	**516**
trans	transition needed	**296**
var	sentence variety	**278**
vb	verb form error	**515**
w	wordy	**277**
ww/wc	wrong word; word choice	**270**
//	faulty parallelism	**286**
. ? !	end punctuation	**602, 604, 605**
:	colon	**568**
⸴	appostrophe	**600**
—	dash	**580**
( )	parentheses	**574**
[ ]	brackets	**582**
…	ellipses	**588**
/	slash	**586**
;	semicolon	**565**
" "	quotation marks	**590**
⸴	comma	**544**
⌒	close up	
^	insert a missing element	
ℓ	delete	
∿	transpose order	

DETAILED CONTENTS